Firm Dominance in EU Competition Law

International Competition Law Series

VOLUME 83

Editor

In its series editor, Alastair Sutton, Kluwer is fortunate to engage and benefit from the experience and expertise of one of the world's outstanding authorities on European Union and international economic law.

Introduction

In their efforts to regulate competition in an increasingly complex business environment, competition authorities face a daunting task. The European Commission and Courts, as well as national courts and legislatures, policymakers, and regulators, are constantly proposing, enacting, reviewing, and enforcing new legal measures, often addressing novel situations. Every industry and service is affected.

Contents/Subjects

With many titles currently available and new ones appearing regularly, the series' coverage includes detailed analyses of relevant legislation and case law in major global trading jurisdictions, defences used in cases involving the digital network economy, state aid cases, enforcement methodologies and a great deal more.

Objective & Readership

The purpose of Kluwer's International Competition Law Series is to follow the ever-changing contours of this dynamic area of the law, keeping the practice in sharp focus so that practising lawyers (including in-house counsel) and academics can be assured of the most up-to-date guidance and sources, in the widest possible range of applications.

The titles published in this series are listed at the end of this volume.

Firm Dominance in EU Competition Law

The Competitive Process and the Origins of Market Power

Jorge Marcos Ramos

Wolters Kluwer

Published by:
Kluwer Law International B.V.
PO Box 316
2400 AH Alphen aan den Rijn
The Netherlands
E-mail: international-sales@wolterskluwer.com
Website: lrus.wolterskluwer.com

Sold and distributed in North, Central and South America by:
Wolters Kluwer Legal & Regulatory U.S.
7201 McKinney Circle
Frederick, MD 21704
United States of America
Email: customer.service@wolterskluwer.com

Sold and distributed in all other countries by:
Air Business Subscriptions
Rockwood House
Haywards Heath
West Sussex
RH16 3DH
United Kingdom
Email: international-customerservice@wolterskluwer.com

ISBN 978-94-035-2030-8

e-Book: ISBN 978-94-035-2000-1
web-PDF: ISBN 978-94-035-2013-1

Table of Contents

Acknowledgments xi

General Introduction 1
[A] Snapshots and Stories: A Timeline of Competitive Process 2
[B] Little Interest for a Dynamic Appraisal of Firm Dominance 4
[C] In a Nutshell 6

CHAPTER 1
The Process Paradox and Seven Conventional Origins of Firm Dominance 7
§1.01 Introduction 7
§1.02 Competition Is a Process 9
[A] The Paradox of Competition as a Process in the Case Law 9
[1] Express Considerations 9
[2] Competitive Process Through Proxies 11
[B] Competition as a Process in the Economic Literature 13
[C] The Origins of Dominance as Part of the Process of Competition 15
§1.03 Why Do the Origins of Dominance Matter? 19
[A] A Metaphor 19
[B] Diagnoses 20
[C] Remedies 22
§1.04 Seven Conventional Origins of Dominance 23
[A] Review of the Literature 23
[1] Economic Literature 24
[2] Strategic Management Literature 26
[3] Legal Scholarship 28
[B] The Seven Conventional Origins of Dominance 30
[1] Statutory Dominance 30
[2] Historical Operators 30
[3] Natural Monopolies 31
[4] Investments 31

[5] Intangible Resources 31
[6] Accident and Luck 31
[7] Anticompetitive Behavior on the Road to Dominance 32
§1.05 Limits of the Inquiry 32
[A] Merger Control 32
[B] Categorical Approach 32

CHAPTER 2
Statutory Dominance: The State at the Origin of Market Power 35
§2.01 Introduction 35
§2.02 A Conceptual Note 37
§2.03 Statutory Dominance: The State and the Market 39
§2.04 The Independent but Undifferentiated Application of Article 102 TFEU to Statutory Dominant Firms 43
[A] The Independent Application of Article 102 TFEU 44
[1] Article 106(1) TFEU and Article 102 TFEU 44
[2] State Aid Law 47
[B] The Undifferentiated Application of Article 102 TFEU 47
[1] A Judicial Choice 48
[2] The Enforcement Paradox 51
[3] A Policy Paradox 53
[C] Summation 54
§2.05 Opening the Black Box: Statutory Dominance Matters 55
[A] An Initial Perspective 56
[B] The Prospective Process 58
[C] *Quid* of Article 345 TFEU? 60
[D] Summation 61
§2.06 The *Post Danmark* Saga: An Incomplete Game Changer? 61
[A] The *Post Danmark* Saga: A Turning Point and a Word of Caution 62
[1] A Turning Point 62
[2] A Word of Caution 64
[B] Transposing the Principle of Equality of Opportunity as a *Guiding Principle* 65
[1] The Common Place of Equality of Opportunity in the Case Law 65
[2] Equality of Opportunity as a Guiding Principle in Case of Statutory Dominance 66
[C] How to Incorporate the Statutory Origins of Firm Dominance in the Analysis of Abusive Conduct 68
[1] Leveraging Statutory Advantages: A Cost Benchmark 69
[2] A Proactive Approach Toward Facilitating Entry 71
[3] Non-contestable Markets and Less Efficient Competitors 73
[4] Reducing the Range of Objective Justifications 74
§2.07 The Application of Article 102 TFEU to Foreign Statutory Dominance 76

[A] Geoeconomics and Global Competition 77
[B] Abuse of Foreign Statutory Dominance 79
§2.08 Conclusion 81

CHAPTER 3
Historical Operators: The Legacy of the State 83
§3.01 Introduction 83
§3.02 Unifying Terminology 85
§3.03 The *Post Danmark* Obiter Dictum: A Reminder 86
§3.04 Historical Operators Before *Post Danmark I* 87
[A] Describing Historical Operators 87
[B] The Absence of Competition *for* the Market and State Resources 89
[1] The Absence of Competition for (and in) the Market 89
[2] State Funding 92
[C] Historical Advantages and Equality of Opportunity 93
[1] Equality of Opportunity in Article 102 TFEU 93
[2] Equality of Opportunity and the Process of Competition 95
[D] First-Movers and Adjacent Markets 98
[1] What Is the Story? 98
[2] A Unidirectional Analysis: What About Pioneering Disadvantages? 100
[3] Standing up for Recoupment 101
[E] Incentives to Invest and Innovate 104
[1] Telefónica and Beyond 104
[2] Ex ante Incentives: Analysis for Historical Operators 107
[F] Competition Between Historical Operators and Effect on Trade 110
§3.05 Historical Operators after *Post Danmark I* 112
[A] *Orange Polska* 112
[B] *Slovak Telekom* 114
§3.06 The Transient Historical Position and Incentives to Behave Anticompetitively 115
[A] Sustainability 115
[B] Incentives to Behave Anticompetitively 116
§3.07 Conclusion 118

CHAPTER 4
The Natural Monopolist 121
§4.01 Introduction 121
§4.02 The Economic Theory of Natural Monopoly 122
[A] What a Natural Monopoly Is *Not* 122
[B] Natural Monopoly Is Found in Nature 123
[C] Natural Monopoly in Contemporary IO Terms 125
[D] Summation 128
§4.03 The Market Reality of Natural Monopolies 129
[A] Natural Monopolies and Industrial History 129

[1] Telecommunications 130
[2] Railroads 134
[3] Summation 138
[B] Natural Monopoly and the Competitive Process 139
§4.04 Whither Natural Monopolist? A Legal Analysis 141
[A] Natural Monopolies in the Case Law 141
[1] Natural Monopolies 142
[2] Are "De Facto Monopolies" Natural Monopolies? 144
[3] Efficiency and Natural Monopolies 146
[B] Natural Monopolies and Article 102 TFEU Enforcement 148
[1] Natural Monopoly Defense 148
[2] The "More Efficient" Firm Framework 150
§4.05 Conclusion 151

CHAPTER 5
The Investor Dominant Firm 153
§5.01 Introduction 153
§5.02 The Place of Investment Efforts in Article 102 TFEU 155
[A] A General Look into the Place of Investments in Article 102 TFEU Case Law 155
[1] United Brands and the Forgotten Paragraph 155
[2] Commercial Solvents and the Protection of a Rival's Investments 156
[3] Microsoft and the Echoes of United Brands and Commercial Solvents 157
[4] Intel, Moore's "Law" and Endogenous Change 159
[5] Google Shopping and Investments as an Entry Barrier 160
[B] Doctrinal Constructs and Investment Myopia 161
[1] The Existence and Exercise Dichotomy 162
[2] The Unwarranted Asymmetry Between Intellectual and Physical Property in Refusal to Deal Cases 163
§5.03 Investments, Market Uncertainty and the Competitive Process 168
§5.04 A Process-Oriented Approach to Article 102 TFEU and Investor Dominant Firms 173
[A] Depropertization and the Competitive Process 173
[B] The Misleading Non-contestable Share of the Demand 179
[1] The "Old" Leveraging Theory 180
[2] The "More-Economic" Leveraging Theory 181
[3] Incumbency Advantages: A Process Perspective 184
[4] A Simple Process Comparative and a Pragmatic Approach 190
[C] Incumbency Disadvantages: *Google Shopping* and Beyond 192
§5.05 Conclusion 197

CHAPTER 6
The Intangible Dominant Firm 199
§6.01 Introduction 199
§6.02 Why Are Some Firms More Successful than Others? A Strategic Management Perspective 200
[A] Intangible Resources 200
[B] The Inimitability of Intangible Resources 203
[C] Intangible Dominance and the Cumulative Characteristic of the Competitive Process 206
[1] Path Dependence and Reputation 207
[2] Time Compression and Experience 210
[D] Summation 212
§6.03 Intangible Resources and Unilateral Firm Behavior 213
[A] *Competitive* Asymmetries 213
[B] The Expansion of Intangible Dominance and *Google Shopping* 215
[C] The Limits of Centralized Knowledge: *Michelin I* and *Intel* 218
[1] *Michelin I* 219
[2] *Intel* 220
§6.04 Conclusion 221

CHAPTER 7
The Lucky Monopolist 223
§7.01 Introduction 223
§7.02 The Passive Acquisition of Dominance 224
[A] Who Is the Lucky Monopolist? 224
[B] The Relevance of Luck for Dominance 225
[C] Discovering the Lucky Monopolist 229
§7.03 The Lucky Monopolist under Antitrust Scrutiny 232
[A] A Window for Opportunistic Behavior 232
[B] Luck and Article 102 TFEU Case Law 235
[1] Unforeseen Events 235
[2] Wrongly Granted Monopolies 237
[3] The Luck Defenses 239
[C] Price Gouging (Regulation) 241
§7.04 Conclusion 244

CHAPTER 8
The Anticompetitive Road to Dominance 245
§8.01 Introduction 245
§8.02 Section 2 SA and Article 102 TFEU on the Road to Monopoly 247
[A] A Threshold Misjudgment 247
[B] The Paradoxical Irrelevance of Market Power in Article 102 TFEU 249
[C] Market Power at the Center of Monopolization Offenses in US Antitrust Laws 250

§8.03 The Anticompetitive Acquisition of Monopoly Power and Exercise of That Power 253
[A] The Road to and Exercise of SMP 254
[B] Deception in a Standard-Setting Process 259
[1] In re. Dell: Stiglerian and Bainian Market Power 260
[2] Rambus and the Anticompetitive Road to Monopoly on Both Sides of the Atlantic 261
[3] Broadcom: Outcomes or Processes? 270
[C] Anticompetitive Behavior *for* Dominance 271
[D] Summation 273
§8.04 Fixing the Enforcement Gap in Article 102 TFEU 274
[A] Differences Between Processes and Outcomes 274
[B] How to Bridge the Gap? 276
[C] Causation and Abuse 279
[D] Causation and Remedial Action 280
§8.05 Conclusion 282

General Conclusion 283

Bibliography 289

Table of Cases, Opinions and Decisions 321

Table of Legislation 329

Index 333

Acknowledgments

This book is the result of my PhD research, completed in September 2018. The following pages thus owe much debt to my supervisor Prof. Nicolas Petit and co-supervisor Prof. Axel Gautier. They entrusted me with the discovery process of doing a PhD at the Liege Competition and Innovation Institute (LCII). They were then, and still are, a source of great inspiration, advice, and encouragement. Thank you!

My thanks also go to my supervisory committee: Prof. Pierre Larouche, Prof. Pablo Ibáñez Colomo and Jean-François Bellis. I also thank Prof. Dr. Alexandre De Streel and Prof. Pieter Van Cleynenbreugel for being part of the examination committee. These pages contain much of their insightful and thorough commentary.

I am grateful to my former colleagues at the LCII. To Norman Neyrinck, for being always there, even if that meant eating "boulettes liégeoises" at 11:30 am; to Dr. Sébastien Broos, for teaching me that not all economics need to be conventional to be good economics; to Dr. Dirk Auer, for being a great sparring partner, always up for an insightful discussion and for another cup of coffee; to Daniel Muheme, for reading numerous drafts of this book, and for preferring to discuss his suggestions over "just one beer"; and to Caroline Langevin, who always solved any administrative issues that came my way.

Some chapters here were written while I was a visiting scholar at Georgetown University, in Washington DC. My research stay was made possible thanks to the generosity of the American Bar Association Section of Antitrust Law, that granted me a scholarship. Among the many people I met there, I would like to express my gratitude to Prof. Andrew I. Gavil (who warmly welcomed me in DC), Judge Douglas H. Ginsburg, Prof. Douglas Melamed and Prof. Robert H. Lande, for taking the time to meet and discuss my research at length.

Special thanks go to my family and, in particular, to my wife Margot. This book would not have been completed without her amazing support.

General Introduction

Modern competition law focuses on significant market power (SMP, dominance or monopoly) and conventionally discovers its existence through using proxies. The most prominent of these proxies is market shares, but others, like barriers to entry, have been incorporated into competition law analysis since the adoption of a "more-economic approach." What it is important, however, is that these proxies are fundamentally *static*, and at best provide a "snapshot" description of relevant antitrust markets. They leave little room for the consideration of dynamic or evolutionary processes. It takes for granted the conditions under which competition takes place and disregards the process leading to those conditions. This is all the most remarkable given EU competition law is designed to protect the competitive *process*.[1]

The description above is nothing new to those acquainted with EU competition law. But it serves to reveal a missing point in the context of firm dominance. Positive law is barely concerned with the origins of dominant firms, i.e., the reasons why dominant firms exist in the first place.[2] Dominance is thus taken as a given, generally as an impediment to effective competition, and—the originating process is outside of the picture. Indeed, origins of firm dominance, such as luck,[3] nature[4] or the state,[5] have been virtually overlooked by the EU Courts (Court of Justice (CJEU) and General Court (GC)) and the EU enforcement authority (European Commission).

1. GC, Case T-228/97, *Irish Sugar plc v. Commission*, ECLI:EU:T:1999:246, §186.
2. The terms origin, cause, and sources are used interchangeably.
3. Judge Learned Hand called into question the applicability of §2 of the Sherman Act to companies that would have "passively" acquired their dominant positions. *See United States v. Aluminum Co. of America* ("*Alcoa*"), 148 F.2d 416 (2d *Cir.* 1945), §430. *See also* Williamson, Oliver E. "Dominant Firms and the Monopoly Problem: Market Failure Considerations." *Harvard Law Review* 85.8 (1972): 1512-1531; The Sherman Antitrust Act of 1890 (SA, 26 Stat 209, 15 U.S.C. §§1-7).
4. Posner, Richard A. "Natural Monopoly and Its Regulation." *Stanford Law Review* 21.3 (1969): 548-643.
5. Communication from the Commission—Guidance on the Commission's Enforcement Priorities in Applying Article 82 of the EC Treaty to abusive exclusionary conduct by dominant undertakings, *OJ* C/45/7, 24.2.2009, p. 7-20 ("Guidance Paper"), §82.

That the origins of dominance are outside competition policy's zone of interest seems to be *a priori* a reason for unease. If competition policy is fundamentally concerned with anticompetitive behavior by dominant firms, then it appears necessary to understand *why* a firm has a dominant position in the first place. To inquire into the origins of firm dominance is a crucial element in the analysis of anticompetitive effects. This is not just a fanciful inquiry but, as Ronald Coase put it, it "gives us a clue as the direction in which to look in order to uncover what determines what the firm does."[6]

In other words, the legal consequences that derive from holding a dominant position cannot be disassociated from its causes. Such disassociation could lead to ill-conceived assumptions where dominance is seen as illicitly interfering with some type of idealistic market structures, or as the most efficient market structure.[7] To avoid this, it is necessary to inquire about the reasons why a firm dominates a market.

However, the EU Courts and the European Commission have not renounced to routinely deriving negative consequences about the impact of dominance in the competitive process. It is thus not a surprise that Article 102 TFEU case law is plagued with the ubiquitous and uncorroborated finding that "in consequence of the presence of an undertaking occupying a dominant position the degree of competition has already been weakened."[8] Even if we ignore *why* the dominant firm exists in the first place, the EU Courts are confident about concluding that competition has not delivered the right degree of competition. Competition has been weakened by the dominant firm's mere existence.

[A] SNAPSHOTS AND STORIES: A TIMELINE OF COMPETITIVE PROCESS

But if competition law's rationale is based on the premise that competitive markets increase efficiency, if its enforcement rests on the assumption that competition is a *process*[9] and that this process should develop in a competitive manner (no anticompetitive behavior or state interference[10] obscures the process), then one must entertain the possibility that current firm dominance, that we denote as: *t*, is the outcome of an *ex ante* competitive process, that we denote as: *t*–1.

Indeed, dominance (*t*) is not the end of the story, which is something that escapes competition enforcement appraisals.[11] Point *t* is just a snapshot of the process, and a

6. Coase, Ronald H. "Industrial Organization: A Proposal for Research" *in* Victor Fuchs (ed.) *Economic Research: Retrospect and Prospect, Volume 3, Policy Issues and Research Opportunities in Industrial Organization*. NBER, 1972: 59-73, 63.
7. Williamson, Oliver E. *The Economic Institutions of Capitalism. Firms, Markets Relational Contracting*. New York: The Free Press, 1985, at p. 366.
8. GC, Case T-286/09, *Intel v. Commission*, ECLI:EU:T:2014:547, §139.
9. GC, Case T-201/04, *Microsoft v. Commission*, ECLI:EU:T:2007:289, §1088; and Case T-228/97, *Irish Sugar plc v. Commission*, ECLI:EU:T:1999:246, §186.
10. GC, Case T-168/01, *GlaxoSmithKline Services Unlimited (GSK) v. Commission*, ECLI:EU:T:2006:265, §§125 and 140; and CJEU, Joined Cases 40/73 to 48/73, 50/73, 54/73 to 56/73, 111/73, 113/73 and 114/73 *Suiker Unie and Others v. Commission*, EU:C:1975:174, §71.
11. In the framework of the liberalization of the telecommunications, much of the discussion focused on the concept of SMP. In particular, the Commission had proposed the concept of

simple snapshot cannot be a good starting point of analysis of the competitive process. A dynamic understanding of point t = *dominance* requires looking both forwards $t+1$ and backwards $t–1$ (*see* Figure 1).

Figure 1 Dominance in a Timeline

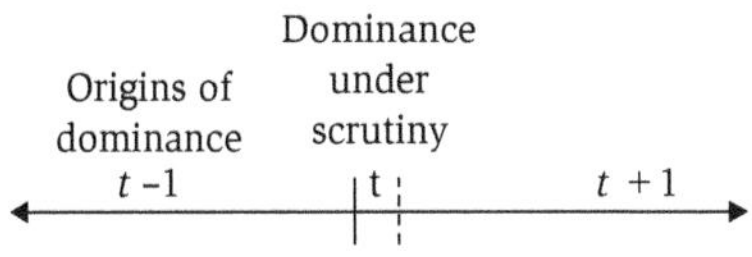

It is at $t–1$, i.e., looking at the origins of a dominant position, where the competitive process seems to have little interest for competition enforcement.[12] This approach is unjustified and risks placing on all dominant companies the same degree of antitrust liability. The following example briefly illustrates this point.

If a firm has achieved dominance thanks to anticompetitive behavior, it is a legitimate concern to claim that the degree of competition has been weakened by the very presence of that dominant firm. The current degree of competition would prove that the competitive process has not developed as it should have. This requires a counterfactual analysis: absent the anticompetitive behavior either the other firm or firms would have been selected or the dominant firm would have had a different ability to exercise its market power. This requires an inquiry into the origins of market dominance to uncover the causal link between dominance and the negative view of a weakened degree of competition. In this anticompetitively acquired dominance scenario, the market would indeed not be working as efficiently as *in fact* it could, only if the (undistorted) competitive process always supplies a more efficient outcome (assumption).[13]

---

dominance as established in competition law as the most appropriate benchmark for National Regulatory Agencies (NRAs) to dictate the implementation of specific sector obligations. More importantly, in the course of the discussions, the Commission viewed it as indispensable that "an economic market analysis and *identification of the real sources of an operator's power in a given market or market segment*" (emphasis added). Furthermore, the Commission viewed in the dominant undertaking's history an essential element for NRAs to assess significant SMP. "NRAs would designate undertakings as having SMP where: the *undertaking has financed infrastructure partly or wholly on the basis of special or exclusive rights which have been abolished,* and there are legal, technical or economic barriers to market entry, in particular for construction of network infrastructure; ... " (emphasis added). *See* Communication from the Commission—The results of the public consultation on the 1999 communications review and orientations for the new regulatory framework, COM des(2000) 239, 26 April 2000, §3.3. Some stakeholders strongly rejected the idea of historicity and the sources of SMP: "Appropriate regulation does not depend on the history of the market; it depends on the current situation." *See* EU Review of Communications Regulation—Independent Regulators Group (IRG) Common Position on Commission Working Documents (Apr. 27, 2000), at 22, n. 7. Despite the Commission's initial intentions, the body of directives stemming from these discussions ended by putting aside the sources of market dominance as a relevant factor.

12. Looking into $t+1$ is common to merger control, i.e., to answer the question: will a given concentration significantly impede competition in the future?
13. Commission Decision, Case COMP/38.636, *Rambus*.

That a firm has acquired dominance because the state has protected this firm for many years likewise tells a very different story than that of a firm that has acquired dominance due to a mix of investment efforts in R&D, or that scenario where dominance has been acquired through pure dumb luck.

In each of these, nonexhaustive, stories, the competitive process has developed in a different manner. And the way in which competition took place in the past affects the way in which competition takes place today. Put differently, differences in previous stages of the competitive process (causes) entail differences in the outcome of market competition (consequences).

Admittedly, whether or not a firm achieves a position of dominance is in some sense a matter of "luck" or entrepreneurial acumen at the "birth" of the market. In this sense, information about market opportunities is seldom transparent, let alone symmetrically known by all potential firms. That is why the dominance-generating process rests on a continuous discovery of these profit opportunities.

But this entrepreneurial acumen as a cause of dominance can also be incentivized or even contracted with the State. In this way, intellectual property rights (IPR) enabling the appropriability of the invention or the concession of a set of exclusive exploitation rights for the provision of services of general economic interest can also be conducive to dominance. The ubiquitous existence of luck or entrepreneurial acumen should not prevent an inquiry into causes and consequences of firm dominance.

[B] LITTLE INTEREST FOR A DYNAMIC APPRAISAL OF FIRM DOMINANCE

The origin of firm dominance is a subject that is little explored in legal competition scholarship. Perhaps the most relevant texts in this area are, at least in an explicit way,[14] the discussions and papers presented in Florence that gave birth to the *2003 European Competition Law Annual* book.[15] In this work, competition law scholars and practitioners debated about the relevance of the origins of firm dominance in the enforcement of Article 102 TFEU. However, the many conflicting ideas that the book compiles are dispersed and not developed at length or with any consistency.[16] This book seeks to fill this gap.

---

14. *See, e.g.*, Temple Lang, John. "Defining Legitimate Competition: Companies' Duties to Supply Competitors and Access to Essential Facilities." *Fordham International Law Journal* 18.2 (1994): 437-524, at 483 disputing the value of liberalization processes when incumbents maintain their privileged positions.
15. Ehlermann, Claus-Dieter and Isabela Atanasiu (eds.) *European Competition Law Annual 2003: What Is an Abuse of a Dominant Position?* Bloomsbury Publishing, 2006.
16. *Id. see*, among other contributors, Mario Monti claiming that the origins of dominance are only relevant in as much as they serve to mitigate the presumption that dominance is always achieved through efficiency (at p. 13), Paul Seabright arguing that history matters in the assessment of anticompetitive behavior by a dominant firm (at p. 45), John Fingleton, advocating for an incorporation of the origins of dominance (at p. 49), or Robert O'Donoghue stating that a differentiated treatment of dominance would be to open "Pandora's box" (at p. 43).

On the contrary, economic industrial scholarship has been more interested in the origins of firm dominance.[17] Research in the early 1980s by Paul Geroski and Alexis Jacquemin[18] or Richard Schmalensee[19] already speculated about the origins of dominance, its sustainability and its repercussions on industrial policy. Strategic management scholars like Margaret Peeteraf,[20] Jay Barney[21] and David Teece[22] have also taken keen interest in the study of competitive advantage sustainability and dominance. However, many of their ideas have not much caught traction in antitrust circles.

Occasionally, the EU Courts have paid attention to the origins of firm dominance. In *Post Danmark I*, the Court of Justice ruled that the legal origins of a dominant firm must be taken into account.[23] In *Post Danmark II*[24] and *KPN Telecom*[25] Advocate Generals (AGs) Kokott and Poiares Maduro argued that the origins of dominance are essential to correctly determining both the likelihood and extent of any anticompetitive *exclusionary* effect. Even if these cases are a minor exception,[26] they provide partial support for our proposition and a reason to further explore it.

The origins of dominance have had an important position on the other side of the Atlantic. In fact, the origins of dominance can be traced back to as far ago as *Alcoa*. Learned Hand's opinion contrasted firms acquiring a monopoly through illegal behavior and firms having superior skill where the monopoly is "thrust upon" them through the operation of market forces. In the latter case, the "successful competitor having been urged to compete, must not be turned upon when he wins."[27] Although this book does not directly deal with US antitrust law its closeness to EU competition law serves as a source for comparison and discussion.

In fact, why the origins of dominance have been both little researched and discussed in EU competition law, as compared to US antitrust law, is that the dominance provision of the TFEU is not a "domination" statue. The provisions of the

17. There was a long-standing tradition in economics that saw the State as the only source and necessary support of monopoly power. *See* Stigler, George J. "The Economists and the Problem of Monopoly." *University of Chicago Law Occasional Paper* No. 19 (1983): 3-22.
18. Geroski, Paul A. and Alexis Jacquemin. "Dominant Firms and Their Alleged Decline." *International Journal of Industrial Organization* 2.1 (1984): 1-27.
19. Schmalensee, Richard. "Standards for Dominant Firm Conduct: What Can Economics Contribute?" *Working Paper* (Sloan School of Management) 1723-85 (1985):1-50, 12-17.
20. Peteraf, Margaret A. "The Cornerstones of Competitive Advantage: A Resource-Based View." *Strategic Management Journal* 14.3 (1993): 179-191.
21. Barney, Jay B. "Firm Resources and Sustained Competitive Advantage." *Journal of Management* 17.1 (1991): 99-120.
22. Teece, David J. and Mary Coleman. "The Meaning of Monopoly: Antitrust Analysis in High-Technology Industries." *Antitrust Bulletin* 43 (1998): 801-858.
23. CJEU, Case C-209/10, *Post Danmark A/S v. Konkurrencerådet*, ECLI:EU:C:2012:172, §23 ("*Post Danmark I*"). *See also* GC, Case T-851/14, *Slovak Telekom v. Commission*, ECLI:EU:T:2018:929.
24. Opinion of AG Kokott in Case C-23/14, *Post Danmark A/S v. Konkurrencerådet*, ECLI: EU:C:2015:343, §42 ("*Post Danmark II*").
25. Opinion of AG Poiares Maduro in Case C-109/03, *KPN Telecom BV v. Onafhankelijke Post en Telecommunicatie Autoriteit (OPTA)* ("*KPN*"), ECLI:EU:C:2004:437, §41 (§55 of the English translation).
26. Also, for the noncompetitive origins of dominance, *see* the Opinion of AG Jacobs in Case C-7/97 *Oscar Bronner GmbH & Co. KG v. Mediaprint Zeitungs- und Zeitschriftenverlag GmbH & Co. KG and Others*, ECLI:EU:C:1998:264, §§62 and 66 ("*Bronner*").
27. *United States v. Aluminum Co. of America* ("*Alcoa*"), 148 F.2d 416 (2d Cir. 1945), at 430.

TFEU are not designed to catch anticompetitive conduct leading to monopoly as Section 2 of the Sherman Act (SA) is.[28] This has allowed, if not forced, the US courts and agencies (Federal Trade Commission (FTC) and Department of Justice (DoJ)) consider the origins of monopoly.

[C] IN A NUTSHELL

This book goes beyond measuring some degree of dominance.

The somehow predictive nature, $t+1$, of antitrust and economic analysis should not prevent seeking explanations of the past. In fact, as problematic and limited as the nature of predictive analysis can be,[29] the inquiry about dominance origins should be seen as a crucial complement to having a full understanding of the competitive process, from $t-1$ to $t+1$.

Whether the origins of dominance are one or a mix of many factors, we *first* seek to expose their positive role (if any) in the enforcement of Article 102 TFEU, and *second*, to explain that dominant firms are not created equal, nor should the effects of their conduct be equally assessed under Article 102 TFEU.

28. Markham, Jesse Jr. "Lessons for Competition Law from the Economic Crisis: The Prospect for Antitrust Responses to the 'Too-Big-to-Fail' Phenomenon." *Fordham Journal of Corporate and Financial Law* 16.2 (2011): 261-322, 295 citing *Spectrum Sports, Inc. v. McQuillan*, 506 U.S. 447 (1993) at 455.

29. The Commission has explicitly acknowledged the limitations of such an approach, even in "bricks and mortar" industries like the transportation industry and in the context of a merger analysis. *See* Commission Decision, Case COMP/M.6570, *UPS/ TNT Express*, at §1223: "the Commission is unable to predict what market share FedEx is likely to achieve in the near future."

CHAPTER 1

The Process Paradox and Seven Conventional Origins of Firm Dominance

§1.01 INTRODUCTION

Article 102 TFEU's wording, together with the EU Courts' case law suggests that dominant firms have a negative impact on the competitive process. As the EU Courts have consistently held, the mere presence of a dominant position weakens the competitive structure.[1] Commercial practices that would be irreproachable if carried out by a nondominant firm are deemed anticompetitive under Article 102 TFEU.[2] It follows from this logic that dominant firms have an obligation akin to preserving competition. The case law threshold for finding anticompetitive foreclosure is set at a minimum: when access to the market is made "more difficult."[3]

At the same time, every competition case decided by the EU Courts insists that competition is a process. As is well known, statements like "the normal competitive

1. Among others, *see* CJEU, Case 85/76, *Hoffmann-La Roche v. Commission*, ECLI:EU:C:1979:36, §§107 and 123; Case C-202/07 P, *France Télécom v. Commission*, EU:C:2009:214, §107; Case C-170/13, *Huawei Technologies Co. Ltd v. ZTE Corp. and ZTE Deutschland GmbH*, ECLI: EU:C:2015:477, §45; *and* Case C-23/14, *Post Danmark II*, ECLI:EU:C:2015:651, §§26, 70 and 71.
2. GC, Case T-340/03, *France Télécom v. Commission*, ECLI:EU:T:2007:22, §186; GC, Case T-111/96 *ITT Promedia v. Commission*, ECLI:EU:T:1998:183, §139. A clear example of this is Article 102(a) TFEU and the case law stemming from it that condemns unfair or excessive pricing. *See, e.g.*, CJEU, Case 27/76 *United Brands v. Commission*, ECLI:EU:C:1978:22. On the contrary, the US Supreme Court in *Trinko* held that the prospects of charging monopoly prices is what drives competition and cannot therefore constitute an unlawful act of monopolization under Section 2 of the SA. *See Verizon Communications v. Law Offices of Curtis V. Trinko, LLP*, 540 U.S. 398 (2004).
3. CJEU, Case C-52/09 *Konkurrensverket v. TeliaSonera Sverige AB* ("*TeliaSonera*"), ECLI: EU:C:2011:83, §63 and Case C-322/81 *Nederlandsche Banden-Industrie-Michelin v. Commission* ("*Michelin I*"), ECLI:EU:C:1983:313, §85. *See also* GC, Case T-286/09, *Intel v. Commission*, ECLI:EU:T:2014:547, §88.

process,"[4] "impact on competition"[5] or "competition as such"[6] populate the case law. A commonality that those concepts have is to underscore that both competition and process are two sides of the same coin. Furthermore, the EU Courts have asserted that the objective of EU competition rules is to protect the competitive process so that its "natural" course is preserved.[7] At the same time, the EU Courts' case law holds its preservation at risk when a firm with SMP dominates the process. This is irrespective of the origins that brought such dominance into existence in the first place. As a result, there is something suspicious about dominance. In the eyes of the EU Courts, any dominant firm, without further distinction, is an impediment to the competitive process.

But, while SMP unequivocally is a central concept of competition law,[8] it cannot be taken for granted. The question, "where do dominant firms come from?," provides a fundamental point of departure for understanding and protecting the competitive process.[9] In other words, questioning why a dominant firm exist in the first place tells us *when* dominance is a negative impediment to the competitive process that competition enforcement must correct, or rather is an efficient milestone of the competitive process that competition enforcement must not impair.

If one takes the EU Courts at their word that competition is a process, then a number of the principles that inform applied antitrust against dominant firms need to be reconsidered. Those two sets of considerations—i.e., the view of competition as a process and the view that dominance harms such a process—are in tension with one another. We call this, the "process paradox."

Captive in this paradox, the EU Courts seek the protection of the process of competition but make no major attempt to understand the causes responsible for the current state of a market dominated by a firm. The EU Courts say *process matters but focus their analysis on outcomes*. We seek to confirm or dismiss this process paradox by looking into the relevance of the origins of dominant firms in the Article 102 TFEU case law of the EU Courts and European Commission decisions.

---

4. CJEU, Case C-457/10 P, *AstraZeneca v. Commission*, ECLI:EU:C:2012:770, at §129. *See also* GC, Case T-201/04, *Microsoft v. Commission*, ECLI:EU:T:2007:289, §1088 and Case T-228/97, *Irish Sugar plc v. Commission*, ECLI:EU:T:1999:246, at §186. The Commission also shares the view that competition is a process that deserves to be protected. *See* Guidance Paper, at §6: "the Commission is mindful that what really matters is protecting an effective competitive process and not simply protecting competitors"; *and* Communication from the Commission—Guidelines on the application of Article 81(3) of the Treaty, *OJ* C 101, 27.4.2004, p. 97-118, §105 "the ultimate aim of Article 81 is to protect the competitive process."
5. CJEU, Case C-280/08 P, Deuts*che Telekom AG v. Commission*, ECLI:EU:C:2010:603, §176; and Case C-52/09, *TeliaSonera*, ECLI:EU:C:2011:83, §24.
6. CJEU, Case C-286/13 P, *Dole Food Company, Inc and Dole Fresh Fruit Europe v. Commission*, ECLI:EU:C:2015:184, and Joined Cases, C-501/06 P, C-513/06 P and C-519/06 P, *GSK v. Commission*, ECLI:EU:C:2009:610, §63; Case C-8/08, *T-Mobile Netherlands*, EU:C:2009:343, §38.
7. CJEU, Joined Cases C-280/99 P, C-281/99 P and C-282/99 P, *Moccia Irme SpA, Ferriera Lamifer SpA and Ferriera Acciaieria Casilina SpA v. Commission*, ECLI:EU:C:2001:348, §30.
8. Ortiz Blanco, Luis. *Market Power in EU Antitrust Law*. Bloomsbury Publishing, 2011.
9. Kirzner, Israel M. "Hayek, the Nobel, and the Revival of Austrian Economics." *The Review of Austrian Economics* 28.3 (2015): 225-236, explaining that undertakings' activities, knowledge, expectations and creative ideas are the drivers and inherent features of the economic process.

§1.02 COMPETITION IS A PROCESS

In the literature, a debate exists about whether the EU Courts should focus on protecting competitive *outcomes*,[10] the *process* of competition where the firms interact,[11] or both.[12] This discussion is far from settled. However, there is unanimous agreement that EU Courts and the Commission as well as economists understand that competition is a process. The question that clearly follows is how the courts look into this process where a dominant firm is present.

[A] The Paradox of Competition as a Process in the Case Law

In abuse of dominance cases, the EU Courts have repeatedly stated the idea that competition is a process. Whether influenced at its origins by ordoliberalism[13] or experiencing a shift in enforcement toward a more-economic approach,[14] the EU Courts have consistently viewed competition as a process. In truth, the various Treaty provisions on competition law as well as the Merger Control Regulation seem to be the legal embodiment of the different stages in the competitive process that the Treaty and Courts have sought to protect. Article 101 TFEU prohibits agreements that, in the absence of any efficiency justifications, could lead to a *cooperative* enforcement of market power, such as raising prices or limiting output. Article 102 TFEU prohibits the abuse of *unilateral* market power, for example, providing exclusivity rebates. Merger control *prospectively* protects the competitive process by impeding concentrations that would substantially lessen competition by, for example, creating a position of dominance.

[1] Express Considerations

The EU Courts have in several instances explicitly acknowledged that competition is a process. In *Irish Sugar*, the GC partially annulled the Commission's decision finding that Irish Sugar had selectively targeted its competitors' customers through a variety of

10. An outcome-based view would find a practice anticompetitive if it leads to a loss in surplus depicted as inefficiencies or consumer harm.
11. Classical economists were more interested in the process itself rather than in its particular outcomes. *See* Machovec, Frank. *Perfect Competition and the Transformation of Economics*. Routledge, 2002.
12. Edlin, Aaron and Joseph Farrell. "Freedom to Trade and the Competitive Process." *National Bureau of Economic Research* No. w16818 (2011); and Akman, Pinar. *The Concept of Abuse in EU Competition Law: Law and Economic Approaches*. Bloomsbury Publishing, 2012, at pp. 45-48.
13. Gerber, David J. *Law and Competition in Twentieth Century Europe. Protecting Prometheus*. Oxford, 1998, at p. 251, explaining that the ordoliberal conception of competition law would prohibit monopolies "because its very existence distorted the competitive process." *See also* Akman, Pinar. "Searching for the Long-Lost Soul of Article 82 EC." *Oxford Journal of Legal Studies* 29.2 (2009): 267-303, reviewing the "travaux préparatoires" of the Treaty, Akman concludes that Article 102 TFEU was fundamentally concerned with efficiency; the same however might not be said of its enforcement by the EU Courts and the Commission.
14. *See* Guidance Paper, bringing a more economic approach to the enforcement of Article 102 TFEU.

mechanisms.[15] In its assessment of border rebates—rebates that Irish Sugar to certain retailers located along the frontier with Northern Ireland to reduce imports of sugar packets from there into Ireland—the GC held that: "The circumstances in which an undertaking in a dominant position may be led to react to the limited competition ... form part of the competitive process which Article [102] is precisely designed to protect."[16]

In *Intel*, the GC highlighted that competition is a dynamic process. In this case, the Commission found that Intel, a chip manufacturer, had granted abusive rebates to original equipment manufacturers (OEMs) in the market for central processing unit (CPU) x86 chips. The GC, upholding the Commission's decision, considered that the "highly dynamic" nature of markets showed that this process undergoes continuous and significant change that obliges those firms in the market to reconsider their strategies.[17]

The CJEU, as the higher EU Court, has also explicitly recognized that competition is a process. In *AstraZeneca*, the CJEU had to rule whether AstraZeneca, a pharmaceutical company, had abused its dominant position by withdrawing marketing authorizations and misleading the patent authorities to prevent the erosion in sales of its blockbuster drug Losec. The CJEU, upholding the Commission decision, concluded that the withdrawal of the marketing authorization, without objective justification, would run counter to the "normal competitive process."[18]

The Advocate Generals of the CJEU have similarly emphasized the idea of competition as a process. In *TeliaSonera Finland Oyj*, AG Ruiz Jarabo Colomer drew a distinction between competition and regulation rules by underscoring that, unlike regulation, competition rules are intended to protect the "*the competitive process of the markets*" (emphasis added).[19] In a similar way, AG Jacobs in *C.I.F.* explained that even national provisions requiring undertakings to allocate production among themselves still leave space for "the competitive process" to play out, and thus the application of the competition rules cannot be excluded.[20]

Lastly, at an agency level, the adoption by the Commission of the Guidance Paper clearly shows that competition is a process. In particular, it is stated that "competition is a dynamic process," and thus the assessment of market power cannot be solely based on the existing market situation.[21]

15. GC, Case T-228/97, *Irish Sugar plc v. Commission*, ECLI:EU:T:1999:246, §105. (Namely: selective low pricing, price discrimination, border rebates, fidelity rebates and target rebates).
16. *Id.* §186.
17. GC, Case T-228/97, *Irish Sugar plc v. Commission*, ECLI:EU:T:1999:246, §551.
18. CJEU, Case C-457/10 P, *AstraZeneca v. Commission*, ECLI:EU:C:2012:770, §§129-130.
19. Opinion of AG Ruiz Jarabo Colomer in Case C-192/08, *TeliaSonera Finland Oyj*, ECLI: EU:C:2009:309, §45.
20. Opinion of AG Jacobs in Case C-198/01, *C.I.F. Consorzio Industrie Fiammiferi v. Autorità Garante della Concorrenza e del Mercato*, ECLI:EU:C:2003:58, §§68-69.
21. Guidance Paper, §16.

[2] Competitive Process Through Proxies

Since *Hoffmann-La Roche*, the EU Courts have maintained that the application of Article 102 TFEU covers not only abuses that harm consumers but also any abuse that impairs the competitive structure of the market.[22]

The importance that the EU Courts place in the protection of the competitive structure or "competition as such"[23] is often considered to be the corollary of the right to participate in the competitive process.[24] As Giorgio Monti has stated, "competition is a process whereby market actors participate in the economy without overwhelming constraints from private and public power."[25]

The preoccupation for the fragility of competition seems particularly acute in cases where the dominant firm enjoys a quasi-monopolistic position. The case of *Compagnie Maritime Belge* shows this concern. CEWAL—a shipping liner conference—had abused its 90% market share position by selectively using low pricing against its G&C's customers, its main competitor. Despite the low prices being presumably above costs, the CJEU held that CEWAL had abused its dominant position because G&C was its *one and only* competitor. This fundamental fact made the analysis of any price-cost relationship unnecessary.[26]

Nevertheless, more recent case law like *Post Danmark I* recognizes that competition is a process where less efficient firms are replaced by more efficient ones. In this case, there was a request for a preliminary reference, in which the Danish national court asked the CJEU whether Post Danmark, the historical Danish postal operator, had abused its dominant position by charging prices lower than its average total costs (ATC) but higher than average incremental costs (AIC). The CJEU answered the national court that such behavior might not be abusive. In particular, the *Post Danmark*

---

22. CJEU, Case 85/76, *Hoffmann-La Roche v. Commission*, ECLI:EU:C:1979:36, at §125: "Article 86 therefore covers not only abuse which may directly prejudice consumers but also abuse which indirectly prejudices them by impairing the effective competitive structure as envisaged by Article 3 (f) of the Treaty." *See also, e.g.*, CJEU, Case C-209/10, *Post Danmark I*, ECLI: EU:C:2012:172, §20; C-280/08 P, Deuts*che Telekom AG v. Commission*, ECLI:EU:C:2010:603, §176; *and* C-52/09, *TeliaSonera*, ECLI:EU:C:2011:83, §24.
23. CJEU, Joined Cases, C-501/06 P, C-513/06 P and C-519/06 P, *GSK*, ECLI:EU:C:2009:610, §63.
24. Ehlermann, Claus-Dieter and Mel Marquis (eds.) *European Competition Law Annual 2007: A Reformed Approach to Article 82 EC*. Bloomsbury Publishing, 2008, at 155 and 173. *See also* the explanation given by Legal Service official Banks, Karen. "Mergers and Partial Mergers under EEC Law." *Fordham International Law Journal* 11.2 (1987): 255-309, 260 explaining that "restrictions on competition, entailing as they do a diminution of entrepreneurial freedom of action, are seen as damaging the competitive *process*, which works properly only when each market operator remains free to pursue its own commercial interests." The right to compete, to free enterprise, should not be conflated with the right to succeed in that competition.
25. Monti, Giorgio. "Article 81 EC and Public Policy." *Common Market Law Review*, 39.5 (2002): 1057-1099, 1059.
26. CJEU, Joined Cases C-395/96 P and C-396/96 P, *Compagnie Maritime Belge Transports SA, Compagnie Maritime Belge SA and Dafra-Lines A/S v. Commission* ("*Compagnie Maritime Belge*"), ECLI:EU:C:2000:132 and Opinion of AG Fennelly in *Compagnie Maritime Belge*, ECLI:EU:C:1998:518, §137: "the mere fact that such prices are not pitched at a level that is actually (or can be shown to be) below total average (or long-run marginal) costs does not, to my mind, render legitimate the application of such a pricing policy."

I court held that competition entails that less efficient competitors will exit the market. This is just a natural fact of a competitive market.[27]

In merger control, the refinement of economic assessments envisaged by the EU Courts in *Airtours* and *Tetra Laval* also supports the view of competition as a process. In *Airtours*, the GC annulled the Commission's decision prohibiting a concentration between two tour-operating firms that would result in a highly concentrated industry. According to the GC, the Commission had not met the requisite legal standard proving that the acquisition would give rise to a collective dominant position that would facilitate tacit collusion.[28] Referring to the process of competition, the GC held that prospective analyses require both static and dynamic assessments. A dynamic assessment demands an analysis "over time" of the sustainability of any parallel anticompetitive conduct.[29] And in *Tetra Laval*, the CJEU reminded that prospective merger analyses "must be carried out with great care"[30] as the creation of a dominant position might not be the result of the acquisition but rather be caused by *future* conduct.[31]

These cases show that, whether by explicit or referenced proxies, the EU Courts view competition as an actual ongoing process. They show that the positive description of competition as a process is maintained over time and irrespective of the analysis done. The more ancient and forms-based approach, as in *Hoffmann-La Roche*, and the more recent and effects-based approach, as in *Post Danmark I*, reveal that the EU Courts viewed and continue to view competition as a process.

Yet, despite the EU Courts being abundantly clear on the point that competition is a process that the law seeks to protect, it is still a subject of vivid debate as to why the law should safeguard it. Perhaps it is because, as Friedrich Hayek brilliantly wrote:

> the reason why we use competition is that, in those cases in which it is interesting, the validity of the theory can never be tested empirically. We can test it on conceptual models, and we might conceivably test it in artificially created real situations, where the facts which competition is intended to discover are already known to the observer. But in such cases, it is of no practical value, so that to carry out the experiment would hardly be worth the expense. If we do not know the facts we hope to discover by means of competition, we can never ascertain how effective it has been in discovering those facts that might be discovered. All we can hope to find out is that, on the whole, societies which rely for this purpose on

27. CJEU, Case C-209/10, *Post Danmark I*, ECLI:EU:C:2012:172, §21.
28. The Court ruled that the requirements to establish that a collective position of dominance would increase the probability of tacit collusion are both structural and behavioral: market transparency, the ability of the players to detect any deviation, and punishment. For a comprehensive discussion, *see* Petit, Nicolas. *Oligopoles, Collusion Tacite et Droit Communautaire de la Concurrence*. Bruylant, Bruxelles, 2008.
29. T-342/99, *Airtours v. Commission* ("*Airtours*"), ECLI:EU:T:2002:146, §193. *Also*, CJEU, Joined Cases C-68/94 and C-30/95 *France and Société Commerciale des Potasses et de l'Azote (SCPA) and Entreprise Minière et Chimique (EMC) v. Commission* ("*Kali & Salz*"), ECLI:EU:C:1998:148, §221: "In the case of an alleged collective dominant position, the Commission is therefore obliged to assess, using a prospective analysis of the reference market."
30. CJEU, Case C-12/03, *Tetra Laval v. Commission*, ECLI:EU:C:2005:87, §42.
31. GC, Case T-5/02, *Tetra Laval v. Commission*, ECLI:EU:T:2002:264, §154. The CJEU has captured the essence of dominance as the ability of any given firm "to determine, at least to have an appreciable influence on the conditions under which that competition will develop." *See* CJEU, Case 85/76, *Hoffmann-La Roche v. Commission*, ECLI:EU:C:1979:36, §39.

> competition have achieved their aims more successfully than others. This is a conclusion which the history of civilisation seems eminently to have confirmed.[32]

[B] Competition as a Process in the Economic Literature

Competition as a process is not an exclusive idea of the EU Courts, and numerous economists also adhere to this understanding. However, unlike the EU Courts, economists have highlighted that stability, equilibrium or firm homogeneity are only distorted lenses through which one can look into the competitive process. This is shown clearly from the following review of the literature.

Schumpeter's view of the competitive process was of the economic system as an ever-evolving process in which the functions of entrepreneurship are its essential feature.[33] Development, he wrote, is "spontaneous and discontinuous,"[34] and as such, a stationary economy would not only be unachievable but would also not allow for development or growth.[35] "Our economic system is not a pure one but in full transition toward something else, and, therefore, not always ascribable in terms of a logically consistent model."[36]

Close to the Schumpeterian tradition, Friedrich A. Hayek's view of competition as a process is clearly described in the title of his essay *Competition as a Discovery Procedure*. Hayek considered that the process of competition is valuable in as much as it allows us to discover and use new data.[37] It is in fact the nature of the process that

---

32. Hayek, Friedrich A. "Competition as a Discovery Procedure." *The Quarterly Journal of Austrian Economics* 5.3 ([1968] 2002): 9-23.
33. Schumpeter, Joseph A. *Business Cycles: A Theoretical, Historical and Statistical Analysis of the Capitalist Process*. New York, Toronto and London: McGraw-Hill Book Company, 1939, at pp. 100 et seq. In the same line, *see* Walras, Léon. *Elements of Pure Economics, or The Theory of Social Wealth.* Routledge, [1874] 2003, at p. 225: "Assuming equilibrium, we may even go so far as to abstract from entrepreneurs ... " and at p. 380: "in order to come still more closely to reality we must drop the hypothesis of an annual market period and adopt in its place the hypothesis of a continuous market. Thus we pass from the static to the dynamic state ... Such is the continuous market which is *perpetually* tending towards equilibrium without ever actually attaining it, because the market has no other way of approaching equilibrium except by groping, [which, as Walras writes, "is precisely the process employed by the mechanism of free competition"] and, before the goal is reached, it has to renew its efforts and start over again, all the basic data of the problem, e.g. the initial quantities possessed, the utilities of goods and services, the technical coefficients, the excess of income over consumption, the working capital requirements, etc., having changed in the meantime."
34. Schumpeter, Joseph A. *The Theory of Economic Development*. Routledge, [1911] 2017, at pp. 62-65.
35. Schumpeter, Joseph A. *Business Cycles: A Theoretical, Historical and Statistical Analysis of the Capitalist Process*. New York, Toronto and London: McGraw-Hill Book Company, 1939, at p. 41. Schumpeter also acknowledges that the tendency toward equilibrium cannot be negated.
36. *Id.* at p. 19.
37. Hayek, Friedrich A. "Competition as a Discovery Procedure." *The Quarterly Journal of Austrian Economics* 5.3 ([1968] 2002): 9-23. The Austrian tradition has been characterized by its emphasis on the idea of process and its early reluctance to use models of perfect competition or to depict any kind of equilibrium. The fear was that the static idea of equilibrium perpetuating an outcome equilibrium like a permanent snapshot of a market state is not interested with the processes that lead those curves to intersect. This has been the case ever since Carl Menger, to whom the origins of an Austrian tradition are traced back. Menger viewed the market as a

adjusts those new facts that requires an explanation.[38] Frank Knight comes also very close to Hayek's idea of competition as a process and its value to deliver unthought-of outcomes.[39] John Clark, who first developed the idea of "workable competition," writes: "the importance of this shift from the search for levels to the study of processes can hardly be overemphasized." Its importance resides in describing the *reality* of markets, and not abstract conditions of equilibrium.[40]

With a particular focus on innovation, mainstream economists like William Baumol describe innovation as the driving force of the competitive process in free market economies.[41] Plus Metcalfe, a learned academic in the field of evolutionary economics, claims that competition is a process in which innovation acts as the major countervailing force offsetting the natural tendency of markets to concentrate.[42]

In short, the economic literature shows that the idea of competition as a process implies motion. The competitive process is nothing like *theoretical* models such as that of perfect competition, the outcome of which is that firms sell homogenous products at the level of marginal costs where a departure from this equilibrium is neither possible nor desirable.[43]

On the contrary, viewing competition as a process allows us to better grasp how markets function. Markets are where firms discover and seize opportunities, dare to be the first ones or patiently wait to fast-follow the one that dared first, invest, mange, act and react, accumulate and deploy expertise, adjust prices, differentiate products, and also where sometimes luck plays in their favor or an accident turns against them. It

continuously changing environment: "*The foundations for economic exchanges are constantly changing*, and we therefore observe the phenomenon of a perpetual succession of exchange transactions. But even in this chain of transactions we can, by observing closely, *find points of rest at particular times, for particular persons, and with particular kinds of goods*. At these points of rest, no exchange of goods takes place because an economic limit to exchange has already been reached." (emphasis added) *See* Menger, Carl. *Principles of Economics*, Ludwig von Mises Institute, [1871] 2007, at p. 188.

38. Hayek, Friedrich A. "The Meaning of Competition" *in Individualism and Economic Order*, University of Chicago Press, 1948, at 92-106.
39. Knight, Frank. *The Ethics of Competition and Other Essays*. New York: Harper Bros, 1935.
40. Clark, John M. "The Relation Between Statics and Dynamics" *in* Jacob H. Hollander (ed.) *Economic Essays Contributed in Honor of John Bates Clark*, The Macmillan Company, 1927: 46-70, at 51. *See also* Clark, John M. *Competition as a Dynamic Process*. Washington: The Brookings Institution, 1961.
41. Baumol, William J. *The Free-Market Innovation Machine: Analyzing the Growth Miracle of Capitalism*. Princeton University Press, 2002, at p. viii.
42. Metcalfe, John Stanley. *Evolutionary Economics and Creative Destruction*. Vol. 1. Psychology Press, 1998, at p. 114. *See also* Metcalfe, John Stanley and Ronald Ramlogan. "Competition and the Regulation of Economic Development." *The Quarterly Review of Economics and Finance* 45.2-3 (2005): 215-235.
43. Knight, Frank H. *The Ethics of Competition and Other Essays*. 1935, at pp. 155 et seq. Schumpeter explains that Walras "heroically" simplified his mathematical theory of the economic process. Walras hypothesized "that the quantities of productive services that enter into the unit of every product (coefficients of production) are constant technological data; that there is no such thing as fixed cost; that all the firms in an industry produce the same kind of product, by the same method, in equal quantities; *that the productive process takes no time*; that problems of location may be neglected." (emphasis added) *See* Schumpeter, Joseph A. *History of Economic Analysis*. Routledge, [1954] 2006, at 940.

implies considering that markets change quickly or slowly, inevitably and continuously moving in search of an ephemeral equilibrium that never arrives.[44] That is why we cheer competition, but at the same time we are weary of its uncertainty.[45]

If competition is a process, there must be a sequence of discovered events that unravel to become a distinct competitive state of affairs that we can observe as it continues to change.[46] But the EU Courts and the Commission, that heap praise upon the protection of the competitive *process*, seek nevertheless to pass judgment on the functioning of this process by hermetically assessing a particular point in time (t). Although they accept forecasting the future and accept the speculative nature of such a prospective endeavor ($t+1$), they overlook the sequence of events that serve as an explanation of a single competitive state of affairs ($t–1$).

That sequence of events, or the reason why markets and dominant firms exist in the first place, seems to be taken for granted. These "creation functions," which are the essence and the *raison d'être* of the competitive process, have been disregarded by the EU Courts or have been given a minor role. In short, the EU Courts want to correct markets and firm behavior without understanding what brought the market and the firms into existence in the first place.[47]

[C] The Origins of Dominance as Part of the Process of Competition

Discovering the origins that led to a particular state of affairs is not alien to academic research. Charles Darwin advanced our understanding of biology and evolution by inquiring into the origins of species[48] and Adam Smith gave birth to modern economics

44. Kirzner, Israel. *How Markets Work: Disequilibrium, Entrepreneurship and Discovery*. London: Institute of Economic Affairs, 1997, at p. 39: "Mainstream theory left entrepreneurship out of its picture because entrepreneurship seems chaotic and unpredictable. Boldness, impulse, hunch are the raw materials of entrepreneurial success (and failure); they seem to render the possibility of systematic, determinate chains of events unlikely. In order to perceive regularities amidst the apparently chaotic vagaries of real-world market volatility, it may seem methodologically sound to imagine a world with no scope for entrepreneurship. Yet, paradoxically, exactly the opposite is the case. It is only when entrepreneurship is introduced that we begin to appreciate how and why markets work."
45. Foster, John. "Competitive Selection, Self-Organisation and Joseph A. Schumpeter." *Journal of Evolutionary Economics* 10.3 (2000): 311-328, 325: "Typically, the fear of competition is itself a stimulus to innovation, thus the tendency towards a stationary state affects the stationary state itself and we have a non-equilibrium process."
46. Falcon, Andrea. "Aristotle on Causality" *in* Edward N. Zalta (ed.) *The Stanford Encyclopedia of Philosophy*. Spring 2015 Edition, available at http://plato.stanford.edu/archives/spr2015/entries/aristotle-causality/.
47. Hazlett, Thomas W., David Teece and Leonard Waverman. "Walled Garden Rivalry: The Creation of Mobile Network Ecosystems." *George Mason Law & Economics Research Paper* No. 11-50 (2011).
48. Darwin, Charles. *The Origins of Species by Means of Natural Selection*. 1859. A caveat is in place, with regard to Darwin's theory. In our view, to frame the inquiry into the origins of dominance in a purely biological/Darwinian framework would be incomplete. After all, Darwin's discussion regarding natural selection and how species might have come about was mainly concerned with equilibrium outcomes stemming from exogenous shocks, and thus disregarded any change

by inquiring into the causes of the wealth of nations.[49] This notwithstanding, the complexity of the social sciences makes the discovery of the origins of dominance perhaps more arduous than in the case of pure sciences.[50]

While the EU Courts have been reluctant to explicitly inquire backwards into the competitive process in abuse of dominance cases, some economists have ventured to describe it along the lines of Darwin's theory of evolution.[51] Of particular interest is the report of the European Commission Economic Advisory Group on Competition Policy (EAGCP) that defines competition as a process that "acts as a selection mechanism, with more efficient firms replacing less efficient ones." This is a standpoint that has gained traction at the CJEU after ruling in *Post Danmark I* that: "Competition on the merits may, by definition, lead to the departure from the market or the marginalisation of competitors that are less efficient and so less attractive to consumers ... ."[52]

As the process of competition moves on, the idea of market selection mechanisms can be read in terms of path dependence.[53] This would mean, in accordance with the economic literature, that competitive history, past firm decisions and previous market characteristics affect today's market's state of affairs.[54] "A path-dependent sequence of economic changes is one of which important influences upon the eventual outcome can be exerted by temporally remote events, including happenings dominated by chance elements rather than systematic forces."[55]

Path dependence is neither efficient nor inefficient in and of itself. It simply is an inevitable and fundamental characteristic of market processes.[56] However, as in the case of the allegedly inefficient QWERTY keyboard arrangement[57] or the purported superiority of BETAMAX over the winning VHS recording technology,[58] EU competition case law seems to exclusively draw inspiration from an inefficient view of path dependency.[59] A particular approach that views path dependence as an inefficient

brought about by endogenous action. In this line, *see* Foster, John. "Competitive Selection, Self-Organisation and Joseph A. Schumpeter." *Journal of Evolutionary Economics* 10.3 (2000): 311-328.

49. Smith, Adam. *An Inquiry into the Nature and Causes of the Wealth of Nations*. Econlib [1776] 2009, *available at* http://www.econlib.org/library/Smith/smWN.html.
50. As Hayek sets out in his Nobel Prize Lecture, we should be careful to consider that we know all the circumstances that determine the outcome of complex social processes. *See* Hayek, Friedrich A. "The Pretence of Knowledge." *The American Economic Review*, 79. 6 (1989): 3-7.
51. For a full account, *see* Vromen, Jack J. "*Economic Evolution.*" *An Enquiry into the Foundations of New Institutional Economics*. New York: Routledge, 1995.
52. CJEU, Case C-209/10, *Post Danmark I*, ECLI:EU:C:2012:172, §22.
53. Liebowitz, Stan J. and Stephen E. Margolis. "The Troubled Path of the Lock-in Movement." *Journal of Competition Law and Economics* 9.1 (2012): 125-152.
54. Mueller, Dennis C. "First-Mover Advantages and Path Dependence." *International Journal of Industrial Organization* 15.6 (1997): 827-850, 843.
55. David, Paul A. "Clio and the Economics of QWERTY." *The American Economic Review* 75.2 (1985): 332-337, 332.
56. *See* Chapter 6 for a discussion.
57. David, Paul A. "Clio and the Economics of QWERTY." *The American Economic Review* 75.2 (1985): 332-337. *See* Chapter 6 for an extended discussion.
58. Arthur, W. Brian. "Positive Feedbacks in the Economy." *Scientific American* 262.2 (1990): 92-99.
59. In *IMS Health* the Commission considered that the "relationship of dependency" created by the users of the 1,860 brick structure, by their participation in the development of the product, made

characteristic of markets seems installed in the jurisprudence. In short, this means that dominant firms are generally seen as undesirable or inefficient market outcomes. Indeed, the EU Courts have held, their mere presence weakens the competitive process. Thus, in such a position, it is necessary to correct the situation by placing a particular behavioral burden on the dominant firm that can go as far as preventing behavior that is irreproachable unless carried out by a nondominant firm.

The QWERTY case, which is often used in the literature as an example of inefficient path dependence, finds its counterpart in the GC's *Microsoft* judgment. If the QWERTY case study "decentralized decision making" allegedly locking-in consumers "in the wrong system,"[60] the GC found in *Microsoft* that the integration of Windows Media Player in Windows by unilaterally setting a de facto standard could not be the efficient result of the competitive process.[61]

This treatment of firm dominance foregoes in the first place the side of efficient path dependence. That is, firm dominance as a procompetitive state of affairs in the competitive process.[62] If this approach were adopted, the EU Courts would see firm dominance as the efficient and natural outcome given the particular decisions and environment that shaped the competitive process in *t*-1.

A view that dominance is a sort of path-dependent inefficiency pays no heed to the natural constraints imposed by market uncertainty. In a real market where knowledge is limited, the efficiency (or even desirability) of the surviving firm cannot only be judged *ex post* with new information that was unavailable at the time firms competed *for* the market. On the contrary, such an assessment would require, in any event, an *ex ante* approach that enquires about why the firm ended up being dominant in those past set of circumstances.[63]

The automatic presumption that dominance is, in all circumstances, an impediment to competition is further shown by the EU Courts' lack of interest in the origins of such dominance. As the Court of Justice ruled in *Continental Can*: "the strengthening of the position of an undertaking may be an abuse and prohibited under Article [102] of the Treaty *regardless of the means and procedure by which it is achieved, and even irrespective of any fault*"[64] (emphasis added).[65] Indeed, even before the Court of Justice

it an indispensable input that warranted that NDC Health have compulsory access to it. The Court of Justice agreed on this point but left the assessment of such dependency to the national court. *See* CJEU, Case C-418/01, *IMS Health GmbH & Co. OHG v. NDC Health GmbH & Co. KG* ("*IMS Health*"), ECLI:EU:C:2004:257, §§27 and 29.

60. David, Paul A. "Clio and the Economics of QWERTY." *The American Economic Review* 75.2 (1985): 332-337, at 336.
61. GC, Case T-201/04, *Microsoft*, §§1116, 1130 and 1152.
62. Demsetz, Harold. "Industry Structure, Market Rivalry, and Public Policy." *The Journal of Law & Economics* 16.1 (1973): 1-9, arguing that competitive behavior can yield monopoly power.
63. Liebowitz, Stan J. and Stephen E. Margolis. "Path Dependence, Lock-in, and History." *Journal of Law, Economics, & Organization* 11.1 (1995): 205-226. *See*, in particular, Chapter 5 for a discussion on market uncertainty.
64. CJEU, Case C-6/72, *Europemballage Corporation and Continental Can Company v. Commission* ("*Continental Can*"), ECLI:EU:C:1973:22, §27.
65. This line of thinking is reminiscent of certain ordoliberal thinkers. As David Gerber explains, ordoliberals agreed that monopoly power should be eliminated where possible irrespective of its origins as in cases of natural monopolies or markets won by a single firm in the competitive

rendered *Continental Can*, René Jolliet had already highlighted that "how dominant power has been originally acquired is a matter of complete indifference to EEC 'antitrust' law."[66]

The case law thus seems to suggest that the persistent influence of the competitive process in which firms vie to outcompete others can eventually lead to a market failure in the form of some degree of market dominance that is detrimental to the competitive structure. As the EU Courts have constantly held from *Hoffmann-La Roche* up to *Intel*,[67] that the existence of a dominant firm is an undesirable market reality because it weakens competition.

However, this view de facto dismisses the changing nature of markets and finds itself in a paradoxical contradiction with the competitive process that the EU Courts themselves seek to protect. It is a standpoint that further relinquishes the dynamic characteristic of the competitive process that can manifest itself as competition *for* the market in a Schumpeterian fashion where a series of dominant firms replace each other over a continuum and efficient process.[68]

This inefficient view of path dependence finds also some exceptions in the most recent Article 102 TFEU case law. As mentioned above, the *Post Danmark I* ruling showed an interest in the former legal origins of dominance[69] and indicated that *acquiring* a dominant position on its merits is different than through other means: "It is in no way the purpose of Article [102 TFEU] to prevent an undertaking *from acquiring, on its own merits*, the dominant position on a market"[70] (emphasis added).

The latter statement is a welcome admission of the relevance of the "merited origins" of dominant firms in the competitive process. However, the fact that the *Post Danmark I* court cited to the *TeliaSonera* precedent to include the "merited origins" of firm dominance is rather confusing. While *Post Danmark I* embraces the idea that competition might entail the departure from the market of less efficient competitors, *TeliaSonera* referred to the unproven but pervasive dogma that the mere presence of the dominant firm weakens the *structure* of competition.[71] This shows that the EU Courts remain somewhat anchored to a static and structuralist (mis)understanding of the process of competition.

These conclusions regarding market structures and firm dominance have "nothing to do with how markets function."[72] As such they impede the advancement of a

---

process. *See* Gerber, David J. *Law and Competition in Twentieth Century Europe: Protecting Prometheus*. Oxford, 1998, at pp. 251-252.

66. Jolliet, René. *Monopolization and Abuse of Dominant Position*. Collection Scientifique de la Faculté de Droit de l'Université de Liège 1970, at p. 247.
67. The CJEU's judgment reversing the General Court's judgment does not mention for once this repeated mantra. *See* CJEU, Case C-413/14 P, *Intel v. Commission*, ECLI:EU:C:2017:632.
68. Chadwick, Edwin. "Results of Different Principles of Legislation and Administration in Europe; of Competition for the Field, as Compared with Competition within the field, of Service." *Journal of the Statistical Society of London* 22.3 (1859): 381-420.
69. CJEU, Case C-209/10, *Post Danmark I*, ECLI:EU:C:2012:172, §23.
70. CJEU, Case C-209/10, *Post Danmark I*, ECLI:EU:C:2012:172, §25.
71. CJEU, Case C-52/09, *TeliaSonera*, ECLI:EU:C:2011:83, §§24 and 27.
72. Coase, Ronald H. "Industrial Organization: A Proposal for Research" *in* Victor Fuchs (ed.) *Economic Research: Retrospect and Prospect, Volume 3, Policy Issues and Research Opportunities in Industrial Organization*. NBER, 1972: 59-73, 62.

truly process-oriented approach in competition law enforcement. As John Metcalfe and Ronald Ramlogan have aptly written, undertakings "can certainly distort competition either in terms of market selection processes or the generation of future innovation but the appropriate question to ask is their effects on the process not their effects on market structure."[73]

In this regard, the EU Courts' case law showcases a fictitious—paradoxical—process approach in the enforcement of Article 102 TFEU that solely focuses on isolated outcomes. At the operational level, the "process" of competition is not taken seriously and is in need of redefinition. The prevailing static view of dominance, in which any further restriction will have an anticompetitive impact in the competitive structure, is at odds with the process of competition.

In particular, we submit that the process of competition cannot be fully protected without a thorough look into dominance. Dominance thus should not just be a threshold that triggers (potential) antitrust liability under Article 102 TFEU, as in: "a company is dominant, let us then assess whether its conduct is abusive." Rather, dominance and its origins and prospects should inform in a cohesive manner our understanding of the anticompetitive and procompetitive effects of any unilateral behavior. Competition enforcement should aim to do so in an idiosyncratic, articulated and transparent way; analyzing dominant firm by dominant firm.

§1.03 WHY DO THE ORIGINS OF DOMINANCE MATTER?

As the reader advances through the pages of this book, it is hoped that the importance of the origins of dominance in understanding the competitive process will become more apparent. For now, this intuition is advanced in the form of a metaphor, and it is then followed by a preliminary explanation as to why the origins of dominance matter both at the stages of competitive analysis and remedy design.

[A] A Metaphor

The field of medicine can serve to illustrate the intuition that a systematic study of the origins of dominance seems warranted, with due regard to the limits that metaphors have.

If a doctor were to examine his patient in the same fashion as the EU Courts currently deal with abuse of dominance cases, this doctor would check the patient's heartbeat, temperature, most probably also his blood pressure, and would try to come up with a diagnosis followed by a remedy (state of affairs). An imaginary antitrust doctor would, regrettably, not ask the patient about his clinical and physical history, whether the patient has felt sick before or it is the first time, whether the patient exercises and eats properly or if the patient's family have ever had particular illnesses.

73. Metcalfe, John Stanley and Ronald Ramlogan. "Competition and the Regulation of Economic Development." *The Quarterly Review of Economics and Finance* 45.2-3 (2005): 215-235, 232.

This doctor might as well not ask whether the patient has any allergies, undergone recent surgery or is taking other medicines (causes).

Fortunately, this doctor is just a metaphor, and under current medical practice a doctor would also look at the patient's clinical history. In fact, the fundamental importance of clinical history has been constantly highlighted by numerous regulatory agencies, accrediting bodies and pathologists.[74] Thus, a doctor must inquire into the origins of the symptoms that the patient shows: patient's age and gender,[75] the history of other medical diseases or illness,[76] family history of inheritable diseases, are just some of the causes that clinical history seeks to discover. And while it is acknowledged that clinical history cannot be the solely approach,[77] it is essential for achieving an accurate diagnosis and remedy.[78]

Clinical history and medical diagnoses are just a descriptive metaphor that tells us that history matters. But does history matter in antitrust? Why should antitrust policy care about the origins of dominance?

[B] Diagnoses

As in the antitrust doctor metaphor, the origins of dominance cannot be the only benchmark for analyzing anticompetitive conduct. But at the same time, we cannot do without knowing about what makes the firm dominant.[79] In this respect, Robert Bork captures the central ground for this inquiry. To neglect the *route* by which dominance has been gained is a fundamental error "since inferences about economic effects of market shares properly flow from the origins of those shares."[80]

In terms of economic effects, the origins of dominance are important for distinguishing procompetitive from anticompetitive conduct. It is not only dominance as a threshold that matters but also as an instrument to carry out any serious assessment of alleged anticompetitive behavior. If the origins of dominance are

74. For an account of these, *see* Volmar, E. Keith. "Clinical History and Clinical Correlation" *in* E. Raouf Nakhleh (ed.) *Error Reduction and Prevention in Surgical Pathology*. New York: Springer, 2015: 85-101.
75. Alvord, Ellsworth C., et al. "The Multiple Causes of Multiple Sclerosis: The Importance of Age of Infections in Childhood." *The Journal of Child Neurology* 2.4 (1987): 313-21.
76. Stein, Paul D., et al. "Pulmonary Embolism as a Cause of Death in Patients Who Died with Cancer." *The American Journal of Medicine* 119.2 (2006): 163-165.
77. Blanca-Lopez, N. et al. "Value of the Clinical History in the Diagnosis of Urticaria/Angioedema Induced by NSAIDs with Cross Intolerance." *Clinical & Experimental Allergy* 43 (2013): 85-91.
78. Loy, Clement T. and Les Irwig. "Accuracy of Diagnostic Tests Read with and without Clinical Information: A Systematic Review." *Journal of the American Medical Association*, 292.13 (2004): 1602-1609; Carney, Patricia A., et al. "Use of Clinical History Affects Accuracy of Interpretive Performance of Screening Mammography." *Journal of Clinical Epidemiology* 65.2 (2012): 219-230.
79. Schumpeter writes "Our mind will never be at rest until we have assembled in one model causes, mechanisms, and effects, and can show how it works. *And in this sense the question of causation is the Fundamental Question.*" (emphasis added) *See* Schumpeter, Joseph A. *Business Cycles: A Theoretical, Historical and Statistical Analysis of the Capitalist Process*. New York, Toronto and London: McGraw-Hill Book Company, 1939, at p. 25.
80. Bork, Robert. *The Antitrust Paradox: A Policy at War with Itself*. Simon & Schuster, [1978] 1993, at p. 164.

competition on the merits, then the agency or the court has a second story to work with: dominance should be deemed good for consumer welfare from a process perspective.[81]

The origins of firm dominance plausibly determine the conditions under which its market power will be exercised. This can again be understood with a metaphor.

Consider an authoritarian regime in which political power rests with one person (analogous to a dominant firm). The authoritarian regime can derive its power from sources such as taxes from the people, resource rents (oil, gas, diamonds, etc.), strategic rents (aid from allies) and debt from foreign loans. For example, taxes from the people would require the autocrat to empower them and thereby increase the "risk" of authoritarian decay (e.g., China), while resource-rents-based autocracies indicate a much different trajectory: authoritarian regimes based on oil have hardly see transitions to democracy (e.g., of Kuwait or Venezuela). Of course, these conditions are not destiny but characteristics that enrich the view and understanding of autocratic regimes and their evolution (dominance).[82]

As Geroski and Jacquemin argued in a seminal article, much of the competitive outcome (*t*) between rivals derives from variations in the "initial conditions" or history (*t*-1) that arise from original strategic choices. This is a competition that takes place *for* the market in the form of R&D, investment or location choice.[83] As in the case of the earlier doctor metaphor, the accurate diagnosis of a particular disease will strongly depend on knowing the patient's clinical history. In this regard, focusing the attention on the strategic maneuvering that causes firm dominance enables inferring with a greater degree of accuracy the economic effects of firm dominance and its behavior in the market. In other words, understanding *why* dominance exists in the first place sheds light as to why competition takes place the way it does and it will allow competition policy makers as well as enforcers to adopt more robust decisions. The way in which that movement has taken place is thus crucial for the assessment of dominance and for understanding whether such positions can be sustained or will persist by themselves.

As in the case of an authoritarian regime, an inherited disease or a case of malnutrition, the origins of dominance give information that test the strength or fragility of the dominant firm. For example, Richard Posner has explained that the less capital investment the creation of a monopoly requires, the less secure it is. On the contrary, where the intensity of investment to achieve a dominant position is high, the dominant firm "will have no incentive to engage in exclusionary conduct, since it is costly, unless his monopoly were fragile, that is, vulnerable to new entry."[84]

81. Röller, Lars-Hendrik. "Exploitative Abuses." ESMT, *Business Brief No. BB-107-002* (2007): 3-15.
82. Wenar, Leif. *Blood Oil: Tyrants, Violence, and the Rules That Run the World*. Oxford University Press, 2015, at pp. 23-27.
83. Geroski, Paul A. and Alexis Jacquemin. "Dominant Firms and Their Alleged Decline." *International Journal of Industrial Organization* 2.1 (1984): 1-27.
84. Posner, Richard A. *Antitrust Law*. University of Chicago Press, 2009, at p. 249.

[C] Remedies

Following on with the doctor metaphor, the causes of the suspected disease (dominance) do not only help in carrying out an accurate diagnosis, but its effects spill over to the potential remedies to be applied. In this sense, David Sappington and Gregory Sidak have for instance argued in favor of a different treatment of dominant firms owned and supported by the state. In their view, state-owned enterprises (SOEs) must be subject to a different standard of antitrust liability because these firms are generally nonprofit-maximizing firms. As such, their incentives to engage in abusive conduct are greater than those of profit-maximizing firms.[85]

In terms of policy, incorporating the origins of dominance helps designing appropriate antitrust enforcement standards. Focusing on the *route* to dominance will allow agencies and the EU Courts to abandon the general anticompetitive nature with which dominance associated and be able to also include procompetitive considerations where the *means* for obtaining a dominant position are socially productive.[86]

Due to the limited resources of competition agencies, some authors have argued that the relevance of the origins of dominance should be read in terms of enforcement priorities and timing.[87] In short, the point that intervention against dominant firms in which their market power comes from investments on an innovative product should be carefully considered as opposed to a scenario in which dominance has been inherited from the state. In particular, the risk of hampering the competitive process, however one might define it, would seem higher in the investment-caused dominance scenario than in the inherited dominance scenario.[88]

Lastly, it should be recalled that the origins of dominance, together with dominance itself, are not just a threshold triggering the applicability of Article 102 TFEU's application. As discussed above, the causes that led to the creation of dominant firms are part of the competitive process. They cannot be left outside of any analysis of functioning of markets nor of the enforcement that seeks to protect them.[89] The origins of market power bring a fundamental contribution to understanding of competition.[90] Indeed, from an economic-based approach, the origins of firm dominance ultimately

85. Sappington, David E.M. and J. Gregory Sidak. "Competition Law for State-Owned Enterprises." *Antitrust Law Journal* 71.2 (2003): 479-523.
86. Posner, Richard A. *Antitrust Law*. University of Chicago Press, 2009, at p. 249.
87. Venit, James. "Cooperation, Initiative and Regulation—A Cross Cultural Inquiry" *in* Claus-Dieter Ehlermann and Mel Marquis (eds.) *European Competition Law Annual 2007: A Reformed Approach to Article 82 EC*. Bloomsbury Publishing, 2008.
88. Bork, Robert. *The Antitrust Paradox: A Policy at War with Itself*. Simon & Schuster, [1978] 1993, at p. 196: "efficiency based monopolies are always better for consumers than any alternative antitrust can produce. The firm is better left alone."
89. Schumpeter, Joseph A. *Business Cycles: A Theoretical, Historical and Statistical Analysis of the Capitalist Process*. New York, Toronto and London: McGraw-Hill Book Company, 1939, at p. 15, and at p. 20: "We cannot stress this point sufficiently. General history (social, political, and cultural), economic history, and more particularly industrial history are not only indispensable but really the most important contributors to the understanding of our problem
90. All other materials and methods, statistical and theoretical, are only subservient to them and worse than useless without them."

serve to discover the economic effects that dominance has in the competitive process and thus help improve any antitrust assessments of single-firm behavior.[91]

At this stage of the discussion, it is too early to balance the strengths and weaknesses of the analytical intuitions set out above. It is sufficient for now to highlight that inquiring into the origins of dominant firms will cast possible doubts about the one-size-fits-all concept of dominance and its negative effect on the competitive process.

In business strategy literature, this idea is not new;[92] it is just a logical or common sense-based reflection. Alfred Marshall had already advised at the time that the US had recently adopted the SA that "to denounce [monopolies] without discrimination would be to repeat the error which our forefathers made."[93] More than a hundred years later, the EU Courts are trapped within this error where once dominance is identified, its capabilities, merits, efficiencies or inefficiencies are not even brought into the analysis of unilateral conduct.

Where competition law is enforced to correct market imperfections it should be a logical requirement to understand where markets come from. This is particularly the case in abuse of dominance cases. We corroborate this proposition through the study of the origins of dominance and its impact in the competitive process.

§1.04 SEVEN CONVENTIONAL ORIGINS OF DOMINANCE

[A] Review of the Literature

As discussed above, many scholars have shown a keen interest in inquiring into the origins of market power, and some have drawn particular inferences about their impact in the competitive process. Those initiatives stem from a variety of areas of knowledge: economics, business strategy and legal scholarship. However, there is no cohesive framework in the field of competition law that discusses this literature. Based on that literature, we conclude this section with the identification of seven possible origins of firm dominance.

91. Kaplow, Louis. "Market Definition, Market Power." *International Journal of Industrial Organization* 43 (2015): 148-161.
92. Christos Pitelis and Teece use the black-box concept to criticize that the IO literature has largely overlooked the analysis of decision-making, innovation, resources, capabilities and strategies of the firms, treating them as homogenous agents. *See* Pitelis, Christos N. and David J. Teece. "Cross-Border Market Co-creation, Dynamic Capabilities and the Entrepreneurial Theory of the Multinational Enterprise." *Industrial and Corporate Change* 19.4 (2010): 1247-1270.
93. Marshall, Alfred. 1890. "'Some Aspects of Competition.' The Address of the President of Section F-- Economic Science and Statistics--of the British Association, at the Sixtieth Meeting, Held at Leeds, in September, 1890." *Journal of the Royal Statistical Society* 53.4 (1890): 612-643, 641.

[1] Economic Literature

The question of how firms acquire market power[94] has been a traditional line of economic inquiry. Already as early as 1622, Gerard de Malynes proposed a definition of monopoly by reference to its origins. A monopoly is found in "the Princes grant or letters Patents."[95]
In this regard, it is noteworthy that most traditional economists generally considered the State as the main source of monopoly power. Adam Smith, for instance, understood that the main restraints of competition were the exclusive privileges of guilds and corporations granted by the state and regulated companies.[96] The Penny Cyclopedia entry on monopoly of 1839 states that: "It seems then that the word monopoly was never used in English law, except when there was a royal grant authorizing some one or more persons only to deal in or sell a certain commodity or Article."[97]

The emergence of large-scale private corporations like railroads spurred among classic economists a novel cause of inquiry. First described as natural monopolies by Thomas Malthus, these monopolies were seen in its origins as the opposite to state endowments.[98] In the words of John Stuart Mill, natural monopolies are "those which are created by circumstances, and not by law."[99] However, not only natural monopolies were seen as opposite to the state but also considered as the efficient side of market power. In Edwin Chadwick's description of competition *for* the market, it was the larger scale of Parisian bakers that had led to an advancement of "the art of baking" (innovation), better quality and lower production costs than those of the bakeries in London.[100]

The recurrent interest to inquire into the causes of firm dominance was not exclusive of classical economists. Neoclassical economists, and in particular those working in the field of industrial organization ("IO"), have continued with the tradition.[101] The particular reference to the State as the main source of monopoly is still

94. Market power as an economic concept, not as dominance in the sense of EU competition law.
95. De Malynes, Gerard. *The Maintenance of Free Trade*, London, 1622, *available at* http://name.umdl.umich.edu/A06789.0001.001.
96. Smith, Adams. *An Inquiry into the Nature and Causes of the Wealth of Nations.* Econlib [1776] 2009, at Book I, Chapter 10, part II and Book V, Chapter 1, part III. "The exclusive privilege of an incorporated trade necessarily restrains the competition, in the town where it is established, to those who are free of the trade." And when discussing regulated companies "The terms of admission into the Hamburgh Company are now said to be quite easy, and the directors either have it not their power to subject the trade to any burdensome restraint or regulations" and "the clothiers and free traders of the West of England [had] complained of them to parliament as of monopolists who confined the trade and oppressed the manufactures of the country."
97. The passage is retrieved from the quote *in* Stigler, George J. "The Economists and the Problem of Monopoly." *University of Chicago Law Occasional Paper* No. 19 (1983): 3-22, at 6.
98. *See generally*, Mosca, Manuela. "On the Origins of the Concept of Natural Monopoly: Economies of Scale and Competition." *The European Journal of the History of Economic Thought* 15.2 (2008): 317-353, providing a historical view on the concept and discussions about natural monopolies.
99. Mill, John S. *Principles of Political Economy*. Econlib, [1848] 2009, at II.15.9.
100. Chadwick, Edwin. "Results of Different Principles of Legislation and Administration in Europe; of Competition for the Field, as Compared with Competition within the field, of Service." *Journal of the Statistical Society of London* 22.3(1859): 381-420.
101. Cabral, Luis. *Introduction to Industrial Organization*. MIT Press, 2000.

a recurrent theme,[102] but other sources like natural monopolies, internal growth, innovation or luck have gained traction and deeper understanding in modern economics.

Regarding natural monopolies, economists like Jean Tirole have set out definitions and descriptions of their features. An industry is a natural monopoly if it is economical for a single firm to supply a product or service.[103] Although the definition of natural monopoly is built by reference to the characteristics of an industry, it is also noted that firm behavior could also change the boundaries of the industry. Natural monopolies can thus be transient and dependent on the opportunities for exploitation. Markets that were once (*t*-1) natural monopolies could have evolved into atomistic markets due to advancements in technology, new business models or regulation. The opposite is also true. As Paul Joskow notes, the analysis of the factors that naturally lead a market to evolve into a natural monopoly market raises fundamental questions about the dynamics of the competitive process.[104]

Other scholars, like Paul Belleflamme and Martin Peitz, have sought to divide the origins of market power between exogenous and endogenous causes. In the case of endogenous causes, they discuss advertisement and product differentiation strategies. In contrast, consumers' inertia in their purchasing behavior is seen as an exogenous source of market power (such as search and switching costs). Nevertheless, consumer inertia can also be considered as an endogenous source where the firm's conduct is capable of altering or even creating new consumer choices and preferences.[105] Other authors, like Tibor Scitovsky, argue that, apart from the natural, state and predatory behavior causes, the main origin of monopoly power is to be found in superior knowledge and earlier knowledge. It is the particular knowledge of the firm that assumes out the homogeneity of the different economic agents.[106]

Less orthodox economists have also dissected some of the origins of dominant firms. Ludwig von Mises describes consumers' previous experience or snobbishness as a source of monopoly,[107] and together with Israel Kirzner considers that the exclusive ownership of an essential production factor can confer a monopoly.[108] Their main concern is that economists' unrestrained use of the perfect competition model has diverted attention from the main task of economics. That is, from the analysis of the

102. Shenoy, Sudha R. "The Sources of Monopoly." *New Individualist Review* 4 (1966): 41-44.
103. Tirole, Jean. *The Theory of Industrial Organization*. MIT Press, 1988.
104. Joskow, Paul L. "Regulation of Natural Monopolies" *in* A. Mitchell Polinsky and Steven Shavell (eds.) *Handbook of Law and Economics*, Vol. 2, 2007: 1229-1348, 1239.
105. Belleflamme, Paul and Martin Peitz. *Industrial Organization: Markets and Strategies*. Cambridge University Press, 2015, at pp. 107-192.
106. Scitovsky, Tibor. "The Benefits of Asymmetric Markets." *The Journal of Economic Perspectives* 4.1 (1990): 135-148.
107. von Mises, Ludwig. *Human Action. A Treatise on Economics.* Ludwig von Mises Institute, [1949] 199, at p. 361.
108. Kirzner, Israel M. *Competition and Entrepreneurship*. The University of Chicago Press, 1973, at p. 22. However, Kirzner advances that the essential function of competition, entrepreneurship, cannot be monopolized as it resides within the ingenuity of all economic actors. *Id.* at p. 62.

market process, and, in this particular stance, from the factors that may competitively lead a market to give birth to a position of market power.[109]

Of particular interest for their clarity are the *routes* to monopoly that Harold Demsetz portrays. The first of these routes is the buying of government protection that "follows a circuitous path through fifty state capitals and Washington DC." The second route is investment in new techniques, business models and entrepreneurship. This investment can eventually lead to a dominant position, in which case the route shows that monopolization can hardly be attached to a social cost. The third and last route is to acquire exclusive control over resources that are "essential" to the production of a good.[110]

Some contemporary economists have also highlighted that luck can also play a fundamental role in the appearance of market leaders. The literature is not as prolific as that relating to state-created monopolies or natural monopolies, but it gives interesting insights. The reason for this is that the economic literature is mostly concerned with the elaboration of predictive models where luck becomes an impediment factor. But, as Dennis Mueller contends, "chance events" necessarily play a role in the evolution of markets.[111] In support of this view, Oliver Williamson considers that competition policy and enforcement cannot disregard the uncertainty of the competitive process, where peculiar positions of market dominance can be the result of pure luck or accident.[112]

[2] Strategic Management Literature

An important shortcoming in the economic literature has been to assume that all firms are equal. In turn, this assumption has permeated competition policy under the influence of the IO literature, and thus has plausibly prevented the EU Courts from treating dominant firms in different ways—at least so in a clear or structured manner.[113] This black-box treatment of the dominant firm is however "at odds with much of the competitive strategy literature, which emphasizes differences in the abilities and desires of firms to exploit technological opportunities."[114]

109. von Mises, Ludwig. *Human Action. A Treatise on Economics.* Ludwig von Mises Institute, [1949] 1998, at p. 353.
110. Demsetz, Harold. "Economics as a Guide to Antitrust Regulation." *The Journal of Law and Economics* 19.2 (1976): 371-384, 381-382.
111. Mueller, Dennis C. "First-Mover Advantages and Path Dependence." *International Journal of Industrial Organization* 15.6 (1997): 827-850, 845.
112. Williamson, Oliver E. "Dominant Firms and the Monopoly Problem: Market Failure Considerations." *Harvard Law Review* 85.8 (1972): 1512-1531.
113. Waller, Spencer Weber. "The Language of Law and the Language of Business." *Case Western Law Review* 52.1 (2001): 283-338, arguing that antitrust adopted economics as its primary source of a principled discussion and regrettably split away from the general fields of business and corporate law.
114. Gilbert, Richard J. "Looking for Mr. Schumpeter: Where Are We in the Competition Innovation Debate?" *in* Adam B. Jaffe et al. (eds.) *Innovation Policy and the Economy*, 2006: 159-215.

The EU Courts should neither be blind to the insights that strategic management literature (SML) can provide, nor view it with suspicion.[115] This claim might seem counterintuitive since antitrust is primarily concerned with consumer welfare,[116] while SML arguably focuses on producer welfare.[117] Nevertheless, we consider that incorporating insights from SML would complement antitrust policy as their cores are fundamentally aligned.[118]

Indeed, SML scholars have, for the obvious reasons, inquired about the set of idiosyncratic resources that allow the firm to build up and sustain competitive advantage;[119] that is precisely what competition policy on abuse of dominance is allegedly concerned with: *how* acquiring competitive advantage shapes the competitive process and *when* the use of that advantage might be detrimental to competition.[120] In short, as others before us have previously argued, looking into SML will provide with a fuller understanding of the competitive process.[121]

The number of resources that could lead to positions of dominance is virtually indefinite, but they all seem to point to a fundamental core: intangible resources and capabilities. These include, firm reputation, experience, innovation capability (as opposed to a specific technology), lead-time, etc. As Teece and others have highlighted, the ability of the firm to coordinate/integrate, to learn and to reconfigure are the source of the competitive advantage of the firms. These three roles are comprised in the concept of "managerial and organizational processes."[122]

115. Porter, Michael. "The Contributions of Industrial Organization to Strategic Management." *Academy of Management Review* 6.4 (1981): 609-620.
116. Without prejudice to all positive and normative discussions regarding the objectives of competition law as well as all possible interpretations of what consumer welfare means. For an account of these in EU competition law, *see* Daskalova, Victoria. "Consumer Welfare in EU Competition Law: What Is It (Not) about?" *The Competition Law Review* 11.1 (2015): 131-160.
117. Oberholzer-Gee, Felix and Dennis A. Yao. "Antitrust-What Role for Strategic Management Expertise." *Boston University Law Review* 90 (2010): 1457-1477.
118. Geroski, Paul A. "Thinking Creatively about Markets." *International Journal of Industrial Organization* 16.6 (1998): 677-695, 693: "we should be interested in the way that private sector agents draw market boundaries. [And] thinking about market boundaries is a fundamental part of the process of innovation. ... to meet the demand for help in identifying markets from antitrust authorities ... ."
119. *See, e.g.*, Porter, Michel. *Competitive Advantage: Creating and Sustaining Superior Performance*, New York: Free Press, [1985] 2004; and Teece, David J., Gary Pisano, and Amy Shuen. "Dynamic Capabilities and Strategic Management." *Strategic Management Journal* 18.7 (1997): 509-533.
120. In this respect, there is a growing interest for the SML in the field of antitrust. *See, e.g.*, Hawker, Norman W. and Thomas N. Edmonds. "Strategic Management Concepts for Antitrust: Cooperation, Stakeholders and Sustainability." *The Antitrust Bulletin* 59.4 (2014): 769-788; and Greene, Hilary and Dennis A. Yao. "The Influences of Strategic Management on Antitrust Discourse." *The Antitrust Bulletin* 59.4 (2014): 789-825.
121. Yao, Dennis A., Commissioner, Federal Trade Commission. *Prepared Remarks Before the Illinois State Bar Association and Chicago Bar Association* (Dec. 2, 1992), arguing that the world of business strategy has the potential to bring insights relevant to antitrust analysis providing a fuller picture of competition.
122. Teece, David J., Gary Pisano and Amy Shuen. "Dynamic Capabilities and Strategic Management." *Strategic Management Journal* 18.7 (1997): 509-533, at 518, n. 31: unlike what mainstream economics tells us "fixed assets, like plant and equipment which can be purchased off-the-shelf by all industry participants, cannot be the source of a firm's competitive advantage."

For SML scholars, creating added value together with the ability of the firm to capture that added value is one of the main objectives of the firm.[123] A fundamental question of timing arises thereafter. Is the first-mover or the late entrant that is more likely to succeed and eventually gain a position of dominance? What about chronological sequences of entry timing?[124]

Strategic management scholars, and to a lesser extent some economists,[125] have extensively researched into the effects of entry order and timing since the publication of Marvin Lieberman and David Montgomery's seminal article on first-mover advantages.[126] How much does it matter to be the first in the market? Advantages linked to being the first in the market do not come alone, and drawbacks or disadvantages also come with being the first firm in the market.[127] To identify patterns in the failures and successes of entrants a historical analysis of market evolution is needed. It is in carrying this historical/process-oriented approach that SML has largely regarded intangible resources as bestowing sustained competitive advantage, rather than tangible resources.[128]

[3] Legal Scholarship

Legal scholars have been less interested in discussing the origins of dominance. For legal scholars in the EU dominance is a "veil." This is due to the structure of Article 102 TFEU that requires finding dominance before finding anticompetitive unilateral behavior but creates separate compartments between dominance and abuse. This compartmentalization has proven controversial and inadequate as shown by the artificial finding of dominance in the *Rambus* case with the objective of bringing under Article 102 TFEU what was an anticompetitive acquisition of dominance, rather than an abuse of dominance in the first place.[129]

Although ideas such as internal growth, exclusive rights or mergers and acquisitions are occasionally discussed, these are subject to the normative framework of

123. Peteraf, Margaret A. "The Cornerstones of Competitive Advantage: A Resource-Based View." *Strategic Management Journal* 14.3 (1993): 179-191, 186.
124. Lieberman, Marvin B. and David B. Montgomery. "Conundra and Progress: Research on Entry Order and Performance." *Long Range Planning* 46.4-5 (2013): 312-324.
125. Schmalensee, Richard. "Product Differentiation Advantages of Pioneering Brands." *The American Economic Review* 72.3 (1982): 349-365; Smiley, Robert H. and S Abraham Ravid. "The Importance of Being First: Learning Price and Strategy." *The Quarterly Journal of Economics* 98.2(1983): 353-362; and Mueller, Dennis C. "First-Mover Advantages and Path Dependence." *International Journal of Industrial Organization* 15.6 (1997): 827-850.
126. Lieberman, Marvin B. and David B. Montgomery. "First-Mover Advantages." *Strategic Management Journal* 9(S1) (1988): 41-58.
127. Hultink, Erik J., et al. "Launch Decisions and New Product Success: An Empirical Comparison of Consumer and Industrial Products." *Journal of Product Innovation Management* 17.1 (2000): 5-23; Lieberman, Marvin B. and David B. Montgomery. "First-Mover (Dis)Advantages: Retrospective and Link with the Resource-Based View." *Strategic Management Journal* 19.12 (1998): 1111-1125; Suarez, Fernando and Gianvito Lanzolla. "The Half-Truth of First-Mover Advantage." *Harvard Business Review* (April, 2005).
128. Barney, Jay B. "Resource-Based Theories of Competitive Advantage: A Ten-Year Retrospective on the Resource-Based View." *Journal of Management* 27.6 (2001): 643-650.
129. Commission Decision, Case COMP/38.636, *Rambus*. *See* Chapter 8 for a detailed discussion.

Articles 101, 102, 106 TFEU and the European Union Merger Regulation.[130] Claus-Dieter Ehlermann, for instance, has reduced the normative applicability of Article 102 TFEU to instances in which dominance is the result of internal growth through competitiveness and commercial success. It is further contended that competition law already distinguishes between dominance acquired through the state, in which case Article 106 TFEU together with Article 102 TFEU apply. However, the literature is scarce about whether the state origins of firm dominance affect the *substantive* application of competition rules.[131]

The discussion of excessive pricing abuses is perhaps one of a few areas where the origins of dominance have played a more prominent role in the discussion. Massimo Motta and Alexandre De Streel claim that enforcement action in the field of excessive pricing should be limited to situations in which dominance is the result of predatory behavior, or of monopoly or near-monopoly due to "current or past exclusive special rights."[132] Following the same line of thought, John Fingleton finds that government encumbered dominance is better rewarded than dominance won via competition.[133] On the contrary, Emil Paulis views the proxy of special rights encumbering dominant positions as too restrictive to the freedom of action of competition agencies.[134] The discussion is critical given that the origins of firm dominance can determine the extent of the concept of abuse.

In contrast, in the United States, scholars have more readily discussed the origins of dominance. This is because §2 of the SA declares unlawful conduct that leads to dominant positions and case law on the anticompetitive acquisition of dominance exists.[135] Furthermore, the imposition of divestitures as a remedy to monopolization offenses under §2 of the SA has led American scholars to discuss the merits of dominance, and thus, inevitably, its origins.

Of particular interest in this respect are the discussions of Posner and Bork in the context of divestitures as an appropriate remedy to monopolization offenses. In their view the courts have been misled by disregarding the origins of market power, in particular where the industry under scrutiny shows high concentration levels. Bork remarks that while antitrust had historically dealt with market power according to the means by which it was achieved, the fear of "bigness" led the courts to forget the

130. Council Regulation (EC) No 139/2004 of 20 January 2004 on the control of concentrations between undertakings (the EC Merger Regulation), *OJ* L 24, 29.01.2004, p. 1-22.
131. Ehlermann, Claus-Dieter. "Managing Monopolies: The Role of the State in Controlling Market Dominance in the European Community." *European Competition Law Review* 14.2 (1993): 61-69.
132. Motta, Massimo and Alexandre de Streel. "Excessive Pricing in Competition Law: Never Say Never?" *in* Konkurrensverket (ed.) *The Pros and Cons of High Prices*, 2007: 14-46.
133. Fingleton, John. "De-Monopolising Ireland" *in* Claus-Dieter Ehlermann and Isabela Atanasiu (eds.) *European Competition Law Annual 2003: What Is an Abuse of a Dominant Position?* Bloomsbury Publishing (2006), at pp. 36-38.
134. Paulis, Emil. "Article 82 EC and Exploitative Conduct" *in* Claus-Dieter Ehlermann and Isabela Atanasiu (eds.) *European Competition Law Annual 2003: What is an Abuse of a Dominant Position?* Bloomsbury Publishing, 2006: 515-524.
135. *United States v. Aluminum Co. of America (Alcoa)*, 148 Fed. 2d 416 (2d Cir. 1945); *Verizon Communications Inc. v. Law Offices of Curtis V. Trinko, LLP*, 540 U.S. 398 (2004). *See* Chapter 8 for a comparative discussion.

relevance of the routes to dominance. In particular the ability of a firm's management is fundamental for internal growth and divestiture affecting this source of power is a clear loss to consumers.[136] Posner identifies a number of sources of dominance: patents and copyright,[137] state-created monopolies, the incompetency of national authorities granting exclusive rights, and superior management. Unilateral predatory behavior can also be a cause of dominance. However, Posner's view is that such strategy is rarely profitable because the firm will need to recover at some future point in time the losses incurred, and that action will thereafter attract new entry. But, when the anticompetitive behavior does not imply a profit loss, such as the fraudulent acquisition of a patent or the blowing up a competitor's plant, those actions are simply better dealt with by laws other than competition law.[138]

[B] The Seven Conventional Origins of Dominance

In reviewing the literature, we submit that the following origins of dominance deserve a systematic consideration in the analysis of single-firm behavior under Article 102 TFEU. What follows is an outline of such origins. Each chapter of this book investigates in-depth the literature, the case law and how should EU competition law enforcement be fine-tuned to adequately incorporate the origins of firm dominance into the analysis of single-firm behavior.

[1] Statutory Dominance

The State is predominantly the cause of firm dominance most discussed across the literature, be it economic, legal or philosophical.[139] A state-endowed monopoly is a firm that currently owes its position of dominance to the discretionary choice of a State. Classical examples of statutory dominance are firms that enjoy an exclusive or special right, receive particular protection from the state in the form of funding or regulation, or are simply state-owned companies. In short, these are firms that still operate in a market protected by the State. A less orthodox, but equally important example, are those firms that have been granted a particular favor by the State, normally against outside competition through explicit protectionist measures or subtler geoeconomic strategies.

[2] Historical Operators

Firms that once enjoyed a statutory monopoly are now *historical operators*. The source of dominance is the *legacy* of the state. Historical operators compete in a market that is

136. Bork, Robert. *The Antitrust Paradox: A Policy at War with Itself*. Simon & Schuster, [1978] 1993, at pp. 164 and 194-195.
137. Posner, Richard A. *Antitrust Law*. University of Chicago Press, 2009, at pp. 81-82.
138. *Id.* at pp. 195, 209, 210 and 259.
139. Aristotle. *Politics*. Book I, Section 1259a.

currently open to competition, but their creation brought about by the state was concomitant on the emergence of the market. Examples of historical operators can be found in liberalized industries, such as the telecommunications or transport industries. Firms occupying legacy positions are said to have a special footprint in the competitive process as their market power was obtained in the absence of any competitive process.

[3] Natural Monopolies

In the past, natural monopolies were regarded among economists as an efficient source of dominance, but it is also in modern times the reason for much of the existing regulation. A natural monopoly is any market that is currently more efficiently served by one undertaking alone. An example of this is the exploitation of a mine. Ignoring the analysis of whether a firm is a natural monopoly can lead to an inadequate application of competition rules where regulation would seem more suitable.

[4] Investments

In an uncertain "evenly rotating economy" firms need to invest to discover consumer wants and serve them. Those investment efforts undertaken in a competitive environment might lead a firm to acquire a position of SMP when they are successful. Importantly, when investments are misdirected they also provide useful information to all market participants. They are an important fuel for the competitive process that crystalize in new products but also in extended capacity. Regrettably, investments leading to dominance have tended to be "water under the bridge" in the enforcement of Article 102 TFEU.

[5] Intangible Resources

A firm might acquire dominance as a result of building up over path- and time-dependent processes a series of intangible resources. These are firm-specific and as a result they are difficult to copy or transfer, as opposed to tangible resources like specific technological products. Examples of intangible resources are timing (such as time compression (dis)economies), reputation, experience, innovation capabilities, or managerial processes.

[6] Accident and Luck

Accident and luck are two sides of the same coin: the fortuitous appearance of a dominant firm in the market. Accident or luck is the least referred origin of dominance accounted for in the literature. The relevance of any fortuitous event as the cause of dominance presupposes acknowledging that the competitive process is a discovery and tortuous process in which competition authorities' action must carefully distinguish defects in the competitive process from dissatisfaction with random outcomes.

[7] Anticompetitive Behavior on the Road to Dominance

Anticompetitive behavior may also lead dominant positions. Although the wording of Article 102 TFEU only outlaws anticompetitive unilateral conduct carried out by an *already* dominant firm, this does not mean that *in fact* anticompetitive conduct cannot create dominance. This very fact, together with existing literature and jurisprudence on monopolization in the US, will justify a discussion regarding the (de-)merits of such a void in Article 102 TFEU.

§1.05 LIMITS OF THE INQUIRY

[A] Merger Control

One source of dominance missing from this list is mergers and acquisitions. The choice to leave this source out is nevertheless clear: since the entry into force of the first merger regulation in 1990, mergers and acquisitions are dealt with under the merger control regulation.

This does not impede the author from drawing insights from merger control, and in particular, to consider the different thresholds that EU competition law applies in the context of Article 102 and merger control proceedings. Even if they use the same wording they mean different consequences, and it is contended that the different origins of market power have played a role, maybe inadvertently, in designing different thresholds of "liability."[140] This evident disparity clearly signals toward the need to incorporate the analysis of the causes of dominance into the competitive assessment of any theory of harm.

[B] Categorical Approach

It is conceded that one of the main weaknesses of this approach is to "pigeonhole" the analysis of the origins of dominance. Admittedly, in many cases, the origins of dominance will be a mix of some or even all of the causes outlined above. It may thus be over-simplistic to consider that in all cases there is a single cause or origin. However, this approach brings added value, if only to offer analytical proxies in a state of complete conceptual indeterminacy. The "pigeonhole" approach allows for a systematic analysis of the case law and is endorsed by the literature discussed. This approach should not divert the reader's attention from the main objective of this book: to understand that the economic effects of market power derive from the origins of such power.

Despite the streamlined discussion, the analysis of the origins of the dominant firm eventually requires analyzing the facts and particular circumstances of each case

140. Vickers, John. "How Does the Prohibition of Abuse of Dominance Fit with the Rest of Competition Policy?" *in* Claus-Dieter Ehlermann and Isabela Atanasiu (eds.) *European Competition Law Annual 2003: What Is an Abuse of a Dominant Position?* Bloomsbury Publishing, 2006.

to discover the economic effects of a dominant firm. At the same time, it requires caution as in the complex reality of markets it is equally complex to pinpoint *all* the relevant causes that lead to particular outcomes.[141] Our ambition is to provide an initial platform for reflection that seeks a more complete explanation of the functioning of markets, and certainly not to rigidly frame markets and its participants.[142]

141. Hayek, Friedrich A. "The Pretence of Knowledge." *The American Economic Review* 79.6 (1989): 3-7.

142. Baird, Charles W. "The Economics of Time and Ignorance: A Review." *The Review of Austrian Economics* 1.1 (1987): 189-206, 193-194: "In order to explain it completely, the analyst would have to know all the antecedent conditions and all the relevant chains of cause and effect that gave rise to the event. Such is, as the authors convincingly demonstrate, impossible. Even neoclassical economists deny the possibility of explanation in such a radical sense. The best that can be done is to come up with an explanation that makes the event more intelligible than it would be without that explanation."

CHAPTER 2
Statutory Dominance: The State at the Origin of Market Power

§2.01 INTRODUCTION

This chapter discusses the abusive behavior of dominant undertakings that owe their market positions to a discretionary choice of the State. In other words, it focuses on the situation in which the position of dominance occupied by the undertaking is not due to its market activity but to a deliberate decision of the State to promote it and protect it. Whether by operation of the law, or other statutory means, the dominant firm thus faces limited competition in the market.[1] We refer to this type of dominant firm as "*statutory dominance.*" In contrast, dominant firms that derive their market power from other sources are referred in this chapter as "*other dominant firms.*"

The phenomenon of statutory dominance is not new. In fact, the social choice problem of monopoly versus competition is rather old and remains unsettled. A quick look at history shows a never-ending succession of cycles dealing with this choice: at times society has favored monopolies and restrained competition, and at other times it has favored competition and restrained monopolies.[2] Thus, while in 1624 the English Statue of Monopolies prohibited the power to grant monopolies by the Crown, several decades later the magnitude of exclusive privileges granted by government was so pervasive that it led Adam Smith to denounce them in 1776 as "a sort of enlarged monopolies" that kept up the price of goods above the "natural price."[3]

Although the EU has progressively embraced the free market system, statutory monopolies remain a positive reality. In a certain way, Europe's history of statism is still being written. EU Member States continue to promote, back, finance and protect

1. Commission Decision, Case COMP/37.685, *GVG/FS Italian Railway*, §84.
2. *See* Machlup, Fritz, *The Political Economy of Monopoly - Business Labor and Government Policies*. Baltimore: The Johns Hopkins Press. [1952] 1967, at pp. 180ff.
3. Smith, Adam. *An Inquiry into the Nature and Causes of the Wealth of Nations*. Econlib [1776] 2009, at I.7.28.

firms. For example, the taxi industry, protected by statutory barriers, remains unchallenged despite the continuous market efforts of firms like Uber or Lyft to open the market. In response to these competitive forces, statutory dominant firms may in turn abuse their market positions. They can do so by either hindering the emergence of market-created competitors or by expanding the boundaries of their protected markets.

In this regard, the purpose of this chapter is to show why the statutory origins of dominance should be taken into account as an independent liability factor under Article 102 TFEU, even if EU law has certain provisions dealing with this phenomenon (such as Article 106(1) TFEU or State aid provisions). Otherwise, EU competition law displays a loophole that leaves severe anticompetitive situations insulated from remediation. This situation would all the more be surprising, given that the EU Courts' reluctance to look into the origins of dominance is rationalized on the ground that EU law must treat dominant positions harshly.

Furthermore, this discussion deserves to be put in perspective with evolutions in the global market place where state capitalism is resurgent.[4] In today's trade system, planned or hybrid economies such as China or Russia enjoy access to the markets of unplanned economies such as the EU or the US. Economic power and influence are coming back to the central authority of the state.[5] State capitalism is not the return to a socialist central planning economy but "a system in which the state dominates markets primarily for political gain."[6] Among its actors, one finds national corporations, privately owned national champions and sovereign wealth funds.[7] Statutory dominant firms like China's aluminum monopoly or Russia's gas monopoly enjoy competitive advantages over private-sector rivals that threaten to distort competitive markets. This array of statutory undertakings has gained significant degrees of market power that is in turn leveraged into more open economies to advance certain national objectives.

The interest in the statutory origins of dominant firms is not ours alone. Admittedly aware of the competitive asymmetry between statutory and other dominant firms, the CJEU in *Post Danmark I* required for the first time that the legal origins of a dominant firm be taken into account when assessing abuses of market power under Article 102 TFEU.[8] *Post Danmark I* thus brings a major shift to the jurisprudence, often blind to the sources of market power.

Against this background, the structure of this chapter is as follows. Section 2.02 lays out the general defining attributes of statutory dominance. Section 2.03 describes how EU Member States have historically supported the creation of statutory dominant

4. *The Economist*, "The Rise of State Capitalism" (Jan. 21, 2012).
5. Bremmer, Ian. "State Capitalism Comes of Age: The End of the Free Market?" *Foreign Affairs* 88.3 (2009): 40-55.
6. Bremmer, Ian. "The End of the Free Market: Who Wins the War Between States and Corporations?" *European View* 9.2 (2010): 249-252.
7. Bremmer, Ian. "State Capitalism Comes of Age: The End of the Free Market?" *Foreign Affairs* 88.3 (2009): 40-55.
8. CJEU, Case C-209/10, *Post Danmark I*, ECLI:EU:C:2012:172, §23. *See also* the Guidance Paper showing a concern regarding abuses by statutory dominant firms: "In particular, the Commission will be more likely to find such an abuse in sectors where activities are protected by a legal monopoly." *See* Guidance Paper, n. 39.

firms. Section 2.04 explains why Article 102 TFEU might be independently applied from other Treaty provisions that implicitly deal with statutory dominance and argues that the pervasive lack of interest to discuss the statutory origins is due to a deliberate judicial choice. Section 2.05 puts forward the legal and economic reasons that support, from a process perspective, taking into account the statutory origins of dominance. Section 2.06 contends that, although *Post Danmark I* brings a positive turning point in the assessment of single-firm conduct, the EU Courts have failed to advance what this means for the enforcement of Article 102 TFEU. We then propose a framework of analysis that explores four different paths to incorporate the statutory origins of dominance into the analysis of abusive conduct. Section 7 explores how Article 102 TFEU can apply to foreign statutory dominant firms. In particular, it examines the phenomenon of Chinese-backed monopolies that compete against other firms in unplanned economies. Section 8 concludes.

§2.02 A CONCEPTUAL NOTE

Our proposed concept of statutory dominance uncovers three characteristics that inform the competitive process. *First*, the market power enjoyed by the firm is not the result of an *ex ante* competitive process.

This is different from other settings where State intervention is at play but where a process of competition is institutionalized, like in publicly organized tender procedures[9] or in the innovative race to secure an intellectual property right. In these cases, even though the State is an important actor in creating frameworks of appropriability,[10] there will be competition *for* the market in *t*-1. If such process is unhampered[11] this will tend to provide a competitive outcome in $t + 1$.

On the contrary, the absence of an *ex ante* competitive process shows that statutory dominance is not a competitive temporal outcome. Rather, statutory dominance is an exogenous and coercive interference of the State in the competitive process. Statutory dominance arises from the *discretionary use of state powers* and does not arise from competition.[12] In short, it corresponds to the situation of SMP described by the US Supreme Court in *Standard Oil*, "[a] monopoly is an institution, or allowance by the

9. Publicly organized tender must ensure *ex ante* competition by treating "economic operators equally and without discrimination and shall act in a transparent and proportionate manner." *See* Directive 2014/24/EU of the European Parliament and of the Council of 26 February 2014 on public procurement and repealing Directive 2004/18/EC Text with EEA relevance, *OJ* L 94, 28.3.2014, pp. 65-242, Article 18.
10. Baker, Jonathan. "Evaluating Appropriability Defenses for the Exclusionary Conduct of Dominant Firms in Innovative Industries." *Antitrust Law Journal* 80.1 (2016): 431-461.
11. *See* Chapter 8 for a discussion of anticompetitive acquisitions of market power. In the domain of public procurement, authorities shall also design mechanisms that prevent collusion between market participants; *see* Amaral, Miguel, Stéphane Saussier and Anne Yvrande-Billon. "Auction Procedures and Competition in Public Services: The Case of Urban Public Transport in France and London." *Utilities Policy* 17.2 (2009): 166-175.
12. CJEU, Case C-13/77, *SA GB-INNO-BM v. ATAB*, ECLI:EU:C:1977:185, §41 holding that in defining exclusive or special rights what matters is that these were granted to the recipient with no possibility for other firms to opt for it.

king, by his grant, commission, or otherwise." This monopoly is what restricts others in their lawful trade.[13]

Statutory dominance is thus truly in tension with competition. As von Mises describes, "The great monopoly problem mankind has to face today is not an outgrowth of the operation of the market economy. It is a product of purposive action on the part of governments. It is not one of the evils inherent in capitalism as the demagogues' trumpet. It is, on the contrary, the fruit of policies hostile to capitalism."[14] The restrain and lesser efficiency that come with it are liable to distort private incentives to compete and prevent competition from delivering its full benefits.

Second, statutory dominance also means that when the State supports a firm, this particular firm faces little if no competition at all. In other words, this firm operates in a market protected by diverse statutory barriers that either completely prevent entry or only allow competition to play a very limited role. These statutory barriers may consist either of *de iure* entitlements like the grant of an exclusive right by legislative act, for example by simply creating the tobacco or salt statutory monopolies; or of subtler statutory measures that effectively confer a firm a dominant market position, for example, by facilitating mergers between preferred firms under "public policy" considerations that would otherwise have been prohibited by the relevant authority.[15]

Irrespective of whether the discretionary form in which the State confers market power, the statutory dominant firm truly enjoys "the best of all monopoly profits [:] a quiet life."[16] Observe that our concept of statutory dominance is purely consequential: we avoid distinguishing between undertakings providing services of general economic interest, undertakings enjoying exclusive or special rights, SOEs or private undertakings, etc.[17]

Third, and lastly, statutory dominance can only be dismantled by the state itself. This separates statutory dominance from cases in which an undertaking holds IPR, which do not necessarily confer a dominant position,[18] have a clear limited duration

---

13. *Standard Oil Co. v. United States*, 221 U.S. 1 (1911), at 51, citing pre-neoclassical economist Lord Coke ((3 Inst. 181, c. 85): "*A monopoly is an institution, or allowance by the king* by his grant, commission, or otherwise to any person or persons, bodies politic or corporate, of or for the sole buying, selling, making, working, or using of anything, whereby any person or persons, bodies politic or corporate, are sought to be restrained of any freedom or liberty that they had before, or *hindered in their lawful trade.*" (emphasis added)
14. von Mises, Ludwig. *Human Action. A Treatise on Economics.* Ludwig von Mises Institute, [1949] 1989, at 363.
15. Reader, David. "At a Crossroads in EU Merger Control: Can a Rethink on Foreign Takeovers Address the Imbalances of Globalisation?" *European Competition and Regulatory Law Review* 1.2 (2017): 127-138. More generally, *see* Rothbard, Murray N. *Power & Market: Government and the Economy.* Ludwig von Mises Institute, [1970] 2006.
16. Hicks, John R. "Annual Survey of Economic Theory: The Theory of Monopoly." *Econometrica* 3.1(1935): 1-20, 8.
17. In this chapter we rely on an extensive definition that gives little importance to the form in which the state confers market power. Consequently, our focus turns onto the inescapable will of the state that creates and supports dominant positions thus bypassing or interfering with the normal competitive process.
18. Rato, Miguel and Nicolas Petit. "Abuse of Dominance in Technology-Enabled Markets: Established Standards Reconsidered?" *European Competition Journal* 9.1 (2013): 1-65.

and can be disrupted by novel inventions. On the contrary, when the State discretionarily thrusts market power upon a firm this is likely to endure unless another act of government (which can include decisions taken by competition authorities) dismantles it or subjects it to market forces.

§2.03 STATUTORY DOMINANCE: THE STATE AND THE MARKET

During the seventeenth and eighteenth centuries, the predominant mercantilist system of political economy in Europe meant that governments largely and openly intervened in markets.[19] Among the main policies pursued by mercantilist States was the establishment or protection of monopolies "over local and colonial markets."[20] The establishment of monopolies was the logical consequence of a policy aimed at building State power. Power was the end in itself of the mercantilist policy, and wealth was rather a means of achieving such power.[21]

At the same time, this dynamic between nations and the market prompted the emergence of a "rent seeking society."[22] Companies would help the Crown amassing richness, collecting taxes or advancing political endeavors in exchange for a fenced position of market power. This system provided a comfortable way for the State to incorporate monopoly rents into the treasury and expand the power of the state into an increasingly globalized market.

The mercantilist era was contemporary of the emergence of international commerce, and the ability to decide who had the monopoly power on trade routes was an effective means to build up State power. Thus, among the first and most important companies that benefitted from the protection of the state were trading companies like the East India companies, which held a monopoly to trade with the Far East.[23] As some historians have put it, "the Dutch empire in Asia was the possession of a company, not of the Dutch state."[24] That was the Dutch East India Company (Vereenigde

19. This section is not an exhaustive historical review of state creations of market power. It is rather an illustration of the fact that European states have at different times in history interfered with the free market mechanism to establish monopolies or protect certain undertakings against competition. Furthermore, they continue to do so.
20. Lahaye, Laura. "Mercantilism." *The Concise Encyclopedia of Economics*. Library of Economics and Liberty, 2008, *available at* http://www.econlib.org/library/Enc/Mercantilism.html.
21. For a divergent view, *see* Viner, Jacob. "Power Versus Plenty as Objectives of Foreign Policy in the Seventeenth and Eighteenth Centuries." *World Politics* 1.1 (1948): 1-29, arguing that not only power but *also* wealth was an end in itself of mercantilism.
22. Ekelund Jr., Robert B. and Robert D. Tollison. *Mercantilism as a Rent-Seeking Society: Economic Regulation in Historical Perspective*. College Station, Texas: Texas A&M University Press (1981).
23. Rothbard, Murray N. *An Austrian Perspective on the History of Economic Thought, vol. 1, Economic Thought Before Adam Smith*. Ludwig von Mises Institute, 1995.
24. De Vries, Jan. "The Netherlands in the New World: The Legacy of European Fiscal, Monetary, and Trading Institutions for New World Development from the Seventeenth to the Nineteenth Centuries," *in* Michael D. Bordo and Roberto Cortés-Condo (eds.) *Transferring Wealth and Power from the Old World to the New World: Monetary and Fiscal Institutions in the 17th through the 19th Centuries*. Cambridge: Cambridge University Press, 2001: 100-139, at 117.

Oost-Indische Compagnie). For the Spanish Crown, the rents derived from royal trade monopolies were "far greater" than from other traditional income revenues.[25]

In Europe, dominance was thus not the result of the spontaneous interplay of market processes, but the result of willful design of and protection by the state. Not surprisingly, the usage of the word monopoly in the seventeenth and eighteenth centuries was "a label for a special privilege granted by the monarch."[26] In some instances, the State owned the monopoly firm, in others it gave preference to its domestic firm.[27] European States thus created tobacco monopolies, monopolized salt and sugar, banks, telecommunications services (telephone, telegraph, broadcasting, etc.), airlines, and "without exception every country," monopolized the postal service.[28] Many pedestrian industries were also statutory. These would include, for instance, the Spanish monopoly in the manufacturing of playing cards of the Real Fábrica de Madrid that lasted until the early nineteenth century,[29] or the Tsarist monopoly on the manufacture of solid oak coffins during the ruling of Peter the Great.[30]

With the growing influence of *laissez-faire* economics, the mercantilist system gradually faded. This notwithstanding, in the nineteenth and early twentieth century governments remained active participants in the economy. Fiscal purposes and building state power remained driving forces behind the State's intervention in the economy.[31]

Ex post facto, some economists tried to rationalize intervention by reference to theories of "ruinous competition." The premise was that free competition would invite wasteful overinvestment in the race to secure market power.[32] The theory somewhat helped displacing the advocacy efforts of other economists who favored the selective mechanism of the competitive process. Instead of letting firms compete *for* the field leading to the selection of the most efficient firm,[33] states stepped in to either create or select and control the winning firm. Particularly, the State would grant monopoly power in industries considered of strategic or public importance.

---

25. For an interesting account of the fiscal relevance that statutory monopolies had in colonial times, *see, generally*, Bordo, Michael D. and Roberto Cortés-Condo (eds.) *Transferring Wealth and Power from the Old to the New World: Monetary and Fiscal Institutions in the 17th through the 19th Centuries*. Cambridge University Press, 2006, at pp. 157, 195, 288 and 422.
26. Brozen, Yale. "Is Government the Source of Monopoly?" *The Intercollegiate Review* 5.2 (1968): 67-78, 68.
27. Fox, Eleanor M. and Deborah Healey. "When the State Harms Competition - The Role for Competition Law." *Antitrust Law Journal* 79.3 (2014): 769-820, 771.
28. von Mises, Ludwig. *Human Action. A Treatise on Economics*. Ludwig von Mises Institute [1949] 1998, at p. 366.
29. Denning, Trevor. *The Playing-Cards of Spain: A Guide for Historians and Collectors*. Fairleigh Dickinson University Press, 1996.
30. Massie, Robert K. *Peter the Great: His Life and World*. Random House, 2012, at p. 388, describing that oak coffins started selling for four times their original price after the state took over the market.
31. von Mises, Ludwig. *Human Action. A Treatise on Economics*. Ludwig von Mises Institute, [1949] 1998, at p. 366.
32. Jones, Eliot. "Is Competition in Industry Ruinous?" *The Quarterly Journal of Economics* 34.3 (1920): 473-519.
33. Chadwick, Edwin. "Results of Different Principles of Legislation and Administration in Europe; of Competition for the Field, as Compared with Competition within the field, of Service." *Journal of the Statistical Society of London* 22.3 (1859): 381-420.

Paradoxically, despite trustification and bigness being considered as evil, the State's interference with market processes created the market power that the State disapproved of itself.[34]

In Europe the production of fertilizer in Germany and of sulphur and citrus products in Italy was limited to avoid so-called ruinous competition.[35] The interest of the state was so great to maintain monopoly that the Greek government even mandated the destruction of certain vines.[36] The US economy was not exempt from government interference. Although some commentators have described statutory dominance as an "extraordinary" phenomenon,[37] some monopolies in the nineteenth century were state-created.[38] In fact, before the US Sherman Antitrust Act was enacted in 1890, some of the first antitrust legislative proposals were aimed at limiting the power of the State to grant monopoly. The State of New York proposed, "that the Congress do not grant monopolies" and Massachusetts, New Hampshire and Rhode Island, "that the Congress erect no company of merchants with exclusive advantages of commerce." However, the proposals were finally abandoned.[39]

The creation and support of *statutory* monopolies is what places monopoly, understood as "a privilege granted by the monarch," and competition at odds with one another. It shelters the statutory firm from competition and harms consumers.[40] von Mises puts this brightly: "almost all of these instances of monopoly prices are the outgrowth of government interference with business. They were not created by the interplay of the factors operating on a free market. They are not products of capitalism, but precisely of the endeavors to counteract the forces determining the height of the market prices. It is a distortion of fact to speak of monopoly capitalism. It would be more appropriate to speak of monopoly interventionism or of monopoly statism."[41]

34. Friedman, David D. *The Machinery of Freedom: Guide to a Radical Capitalism*. Open Court Publishing Company, 1989, at 36; Morgan, Mary S. "Competing Notions of 'Competition' in Late-Nineteenth Century American Economics." *Economic History Working Papers*, 1.92 (1992): 1-49; and Epstein, Richard A. *Free Markets under Siege: Cartels, Politics, and Social Welfare*. Hoover Press, 2008, at p. 71 emphasizing that the struggle is "between competition and *state-created* monopoly."
35. Notz, William. "Monopolies in the Ancient Orient." *Bibliotecha Sacra* IV (1917): 254-283, 280-281.
36. *Id.*
37. On the contrary, the *ordinary* monopoly is that which is not backed by the power of the state. *See* Epstein, Richard A. "Justified Monopolies: Regulating Pharmaceuticals and Telecommunications." *Case Western Reserve Law Review* 56.103 (2005): 103-134, at 107; and Sappington, David E.M. and J. Gregory Sidak. "Competition Law for State-Owned Enterprises." *Antitrust Law Journal* 71.2 (2003): 479-523, at 481.
38. Bamzai, Aditya. "The Wasteful Duplication Thesis in Natural Monopoly Regulation." *The University of Chicago Law Review* 71.4 (2004): 1525-1547, at 1530; and Brozen, Yale. "Is Government the Source of Monopoly?" *The Intercollegiate Review* 5.2 (1968): 67-78.
39. Letwin, William. *Law and Economic Policy in America: The Evolution of the Sherman Antitrust Act*. University of Chicago Press, 1981.
40. Business and Industry Advisory Committee's contribution to OECD, *State Owned Enterprises and the Principle of Competitive Neutrality*, DAF/COMP(2009)37 289, at p. 292.
41. von Mises, Ludwig. *Human Action. A Treatise on Economics*. Ludwig von Mises Institute, [1949] 1998, at 677.

Statutory dominance is neither an old economic phenomenon, nor one restricted to sectors of the economy conventionally labeled as natural monopolies.[42] In 1968 the UK government created ICL, a national champion composed of British computer manufacturers with the objective of establishing a market leader that would defy IBM. The venture failed, and Fujitsu eventually acquired ICL in 2002.[43] Despite the unsuccessful challenge, other State interferences with the competitive process brought more fruitful results. Europe's determination "to resist and to match American technological 'imperialism'"[44] led, in December 1970, France, Germany and the UK to create Airbus, an Economic Interest Group of European aviation firms. The goal was to achieve "unilateral industry domination" by outcompeting Boeing and other American aircraft manufacturers.[45]

Similarly, the intervention of the State in the creation of statutory market power is particularly notable in sectors of the economy that are generally considered "strategic," such as transportation[46] or energy. The story behind the merger between Gaz de France and GDF Suez illustrates this point. In reaction to a hostile acquisition of GDF Suez by the Italian energy company Enel, the French government actively promoted and defended the merger between GDF Suez and Gaz de France. The takeover by Enel would have endangered French "economic and political power."[47] The European Commission eventually cleared the merger subject to several structural remedies.

---

42. Buendía, Jose Luís. *Exclusive Rights and State Monopolies under EC Law. Article 86 (Former Article 90) of the EC Treaty*. Oxford, 2000, at 25: "It is difficult to find in the real world clear examples of natural monopolies whose exclusivity does not depend to a certain extent on the will of the State." *See* Chapter 4 explaining why theories of natural monopoly were not the driving force behind early State interventionism.
43. Glynn, Sean and Alan Booth. *Modern Britain: An Economic and Social History*. Burns & Oates, 1996, at 258-259. Interestingly, the world's first modern computer was built and made commercially available in the United Kingdom in 1948 and 1951, respectively. Other national champions in the computer sector that failed to displace IBM are Bull SAS in France and Olivetti in Italy. *See also* OECD, *Competition Policy, Industrial Policy and National Champions*, DAF/COMP/GF(2009)9, at p. 30.
44. Nau, Henry. *International Politics and International Technology*. Johns Hopkins University Press, 1974, at 12, *quoted in* Golich, Vicki L. "From Competition to Collaboration: The Challenge of Commercial-Class Aircraft Manufacturing." *International Organization* 46.4 (1992): 899-934.
45. Golich, Vicki L. "From Competition to Collaboration: The Challenge of Commercial-Class Aircraft Manufacturing." *International Organization* 46.4 (1992): 899-934, 918. Some commentators have described the difficulties put by the Commission to clear the merger between Boeing and McDonnell-Douglas (two American aircraft manufacturers) as protectionist. *See* Reader, David. "At a Crossroads in EU Merger Control: Can a Rethink on Foreign Takeovers Address the Imbalances of Globalisation?" *European Competition and Regulatory Law Review* 1.2 (2017): 127-138. However, the motivations behind the Commission's Decision (*see* Case COMP/IV/M.877, *Boeing/McDonnell Douglas*) are not clear enough to be considered protectionist. The Commission conditioned the merger approval to the suspension for ten years of exclusive supply contracts that Boeing had concluded with several US airlines. The lack of motivation as to the relationship between the merger and the exclusive supply agreements could have intensified the claims of protectionism. *See* Gifford, Daniel J. and E. Thomas Sullivan. "Can International Antitrust Be Saved for the Post-Boeing Merger World? A Proposal to Minimize International Conflict and to Rescue Antitrust from Misuse." *The Antitrust Bulletin* 45.1 (2000): 55-118, 116.
46. *Id.* at 914.
47. Thomas, Ashley Anne. *Balancing Power through the Market: Government Intervention in Cross-Border Mergers & Acquisitions*. Georgetown University PhD Thesis, 2009, at p. 383.

Europe continues to write its own story of "monopoly statism." For example, Governments' will to shape industries and to participate in the economy has led to the retention of certain authority over merger control policy.[48] In 2007 the International Competition Network presented a report on abuse of dominance that addressed, among other issues, "state-created" or "state-enabled monopolies." The report shows that statutory dominance is still a pervasive phenomenon across Europe. Postal services, the lottery, airport infrastructures, insurance, ports, public transport, commodities (energies, money, sugar, etc.), tobacco, alcohol retailing, gambling, etc., are the most commonly cited examples of sectors where the State is behind the creation of SMP.[49]

With this background, the following section explores what is the role left for Article 102 TFEU to deal with abusive conduct of statutory dominant firms.

§2.04 THE INDEPENDENT BUT UNDIFFERENTIATED APPLICATION OF ARTICLE 102 TFEU TO STATUTORY DOMINANT FIRMS

The TFEU contains several provisions that indirectly deal with instances of statutory market power. These provisions attach potential sole liability to the State or joint liability to the State and the statutory firm for its anticompetitive behavior. Consequently, when facing accusations of abusive conduct statutory dominant firms have often claimed Article 102 TFEU to be either inapplicable or limitedly applicable, hence trying to swift liability to the State that supports them. This claim notwithstanding, the EU Courts have clarified that Article 102 TFEU may independently apply to statutory dominant firms (§2.04[A]).

Keeping in mind this clarification, Article 102 TFEU case law has made a deliberate judicial policy not to discuss the origins of dominance. Under this policy, any dominant firm's ability to advance redeeming justifications for its market position is closed (§2.04[B]). While this policy may look adverse to dominant firms, it has the collateral effect of preventing any consideration of the anticompetitive nature of statutory dominant positions, thus creating an enforcement paradox beneficial to statutory dominant firms (§2.04[C]).

48. OECD, *Competition Policy, Industrial Policy and National Champions*, DAF/COMP/GF(2009)9, at p. 27 describing this type of interference as "*heavy-handed* government intervention" (emphasis added).
49. ICN, Unilateral Conduct Working Group. "Report on the Objectives of Unilateral Conduct Laws, Assessment of Dominance/Substantial Market Power, and State-Created Monopolies." *6th Annual Conference of the International Competition Network (ICN)—Moscow* (2007): 1-99. As Eucken wrote, it is often that "the state first encourages the formation of private economic power and then becomes partially dependent on it." *See also* Eucken, Walter. "What Kind of Economic and Social System" *in* Alan Peacock and Hans Willgerodt (eds.) *Germany's Social Market Economy: Origins and Evolution*, 1989: 27-45, 33.

[A] The Independent Application of Article 102 TFEU

Unlike in other competition law regimes,[50] the TFEU contains certain provisions that *limit* the ability of its Member States to enforce particular measures that could distort competition. These provisions, Articles 106(1) TFEU and Articles 107 and 108 TFEU ("State aid provisions"), cover a range of statutory monopoly situations. We now turn to discuss how the case law of the EU Courts has prevented statutory firms from escaping Article 102 TFEU liability by claiming the applicability of Article 106(1) TFEU (§2.04[A][1]) and State aid provisions (§2.04[A][2]).

[1] Article 106(1) TFEU and Article 102 TFEU

Article 106(1) TFEU prohibits Member States to enact or maintain in force any measure contrary to the rules of competition. It also subjects undertakings enjoying exclusive or special rights to the very same rules.

Although Article 106(1) TFEU is a provision addressed to the Member States of the EU, the EU Courts have in numerous occasions applied it in conjunction with Article 102 TFEU. The joint application of both articles arises when a dominant firm enjoying an exclusive or special right adopts an abusive course of conduct forced *or* encouraged by the EU Member State. In such scenarios, the statutory undertaking may either scape antirust liability or share responsibility with the EU Member State that granted the exclusive or special rights.

Despite the fact that Articles 102 and 106(1) TFEU do not prohibit the *mere* creation of a dominant position by the grant of exclusive or special rights,[51] the EU Courts have limited the freedom of action of statutory firms to such an extent that the firm must cease its operations.

A particular example of this is the "automatic-abuse" doctrine whereby "a Member State is in breach of the prohibition contained in [Articles 106(1) and 102 TFEU] only if the undertaking in question, *merely by exercising the exclusive right granted to it*, cannot avoid abusing its dominant position"[52] or "is manifestly not in a position to satisfy the demand prevailing on the market."[53]

---

50. This chapter does not directly discuss state-imposed or state-induced anticompetitive behavior. For an excellent worldwide overview of State anticompetitive conduct, *see* Fox, Eleanor M. and Deborah Healey. "When the State Harms Competition - The Role for Competition Law." *Antitrust Law Journal* 79.3 (2014): 769-820.
51. *See, e.g.,* Case C-155/73, *Giuseppe Sacchi,* ECLI:EU:C:1974:40, §8; Case C-311/84, SA *Centre belge d'études de marché - Télémarketing (CBEM) v. SA Compagnie luxembourgeoise de télédiffusion (CLT) and SA Information publicité Benelux (IPB),* ECLI:EU:C:1985:394, §17; §35; Case C-320/91, *Régie des Postes v. Corbeau,* ECLI:EU:C:1993:198, §11; *or* Case C-266/96 *Corsica Ferries France v. Gruppo Antichi Ormeggiatori del Porto di Genova and Others,* ECLI: EU:C:1998:306, §40.
52. CJEU, Case C-41/90, *Höfner and Elser v. Macrotron,* ECLI:EU:C:1991:161, at §29.
53. *Id.* §31. In *Höfner,* the German Federal Office of Employment enjoyed an exclusive right of employment procurement. Despite the exclusive right, other firms started offering specialized employment procurement services for business executives. In reaction to private initiative, the German Federal Office of Employment set up a special agency dedicated to the placement of business executives. In this situation, the German Regional Court asked the CJEU whether the

The resulting effect of the automatic-abuse doctrine is that the statutory monopoly must cease its operations when they *inevitably* lead to abusive behavior.

This doctrine reveals an understanding of a competitive process in which the State should rather be a referee than an active participant with prerogatives in the market.[54] This appears to be an adequate competition policy since empirical evidence largely supports that selection by the market is more efficient than selection by the State.[55] This is particularly the case if anticompetitive conduct on the road to monopoly is prevented.[56]

At this point, an obvious question arises: if Article 106(1) TFEU already deals stringently with State interferences in the competitive process, is there any space left for the *autonomous* application of Article 102 TFEU against undertakings that benefit from the State's intercession?

In response to this question, the Court of Justice has consistently ruled that Article 102 TFEU can apply, independently of Article 106(1) TFEU, to abusive behavior by statutory dominant firms.[57]

In *Telemarketing*,[58] Telemarketing claimed that Compagnie Luxembourgeoise and its subsidiary Information Publicité had abusively refused to sell telemarketing spots. Until 1984, by virtue of an agreement between Compagnie Luxembourgeoise and Telemarketing, Belgian consumers wanting to buy products advertised on TV over the phone would use Telemarketing's telephone lines and telephonists. However, after the expiration of the agreement, Compagnie Luxembourgeoise informed Telemarketing that advertising spots involving an invitation to make a telephone call would only be admitted if the telephone number displayed was that of its subsidiary Information Publicité.[59] Telemarketing filed a complaint before the Belgian national court that was then referred to the Court of Justice.

The Belgian national court had doubts as to whether Article 102 TFEU could apply to Compagnie Luxembourgeoise given that it had a statutory monopoly in the advertising market. The Court of Justice concluded *first* that Article 102 TFEU also applies to a firm whose dominant position "is brought about or encouraged by reason

monopoly of employment procurement of business executives granted to the public employment agency constitutes an abusive behavior. *See also* Case C-179/90, *Merci convenzionali porto di Genova SpA v. Siderurgica Gabrielli SpA*, ECLI:EU:C:1991:464.

54. This chapter does not discuss state-imposed or state-induced anticompetitive behavior. For an excellent worldwide overview of State anticompetitive conduct, *see* Fox, Eleanor M. and Deborah Healey. "When the State Harms Competition - The Role for Competition Law." *Antitrust Law Journal* 79.3 (2014): 769-820.
55. OECD, *Roundtable on Competition Policy, Industrial Policy and National Champions*, DAF/COMP/GF(2009)9, at p. 14.
56. *See* Chapter 8.
57. CJEU, Joined Cases C-359/95P and C-379/95P *Commission and France v. Ladbroke Racing*, ECLI:EU:C:1997:531, §§33-34 and case law cited.
58. CJEU, Case C-311/84, *SA Centre belge d'études de marché - Télémarketing (CBEM) v. SA Compagnie luxembourgeoise de télédiffusion (CLT) and SA Information publicité Benelux (IPB)*, ECLI:EU:C:1985:394.
59. Telemarketing constitutes a market separate from television advertising. It is an open market where extensive competition is possible. *See* CJEU, Case C-311/84, *SA Centre belge d'études de marché - Télémarketing (CBEM) v. SA Compagnie luxembourgeoise de télédiffusion (CLT) and SA Information publicité Benelux (IPB)*, ECLI:EU:C:1985:394, §7.

of provisions laid down by law" irrespective of whether the provision allows "no competition or only very limited competition on that market."[60] *Second*, that a dominant firm would abuse its position by reserving "without objective necessity" an ancillary activity for its subsidiary when that activity is open to competition.[61]

This position was further clarified in the *RTT* judgment. In *RTT*, GB Inno, an independent and market-created firm wanted to sell non-approved telephones. However, RTT enjoyed a statutory monopoly over the Belgian telegraph and telephone lines and the supply and approval of authorized telephones. In reaction to GB Inno's objective, RTT filed a cease and desist action before the Belgian national court to prevent GB Inno from entering the market. Only equipment supplied or approved by RTT could be sold and connected to the network.[62] GB Inno counter claimed that RTT's cease and desist action was an abuse of its legal monopoly. Once again, the national court stayed the proceedings and requested clarification on the interpretation of Articles 102 and 106(1) TFEU.

The Court of Justice held that Article 102 TFEU applies to statutory dominant firms when their abusive behavior is taken "on their own initiative." An extension of RTT's monopoly onto the market of telephone equipment could constitute abusive conduct under Article 102 TFEU, *or* under Articles 102 and 106(1) TFEU when that extension results from a state measure. It finally found that a law that granted *both* the monopoly over the telecom network *and* the approval of authorized telephones that connected to its network breached Articles 102 and 106(1) TFEU.[63]

A similar situation came up in *Corbeau*.[64] Here, Mr. Corbeau was criminally prosecuted for breaching Belgian legislation on the postal monopoly by undertaking the collection and distribution of mail by noon next day in the Belgian city of Liège and the surroundings areas. Mr. Corbeau's entrepreneurial behavior defied of the statutory postal monopoly held by the Belgian Régie des Postes. The Court of Justice once again clarified that "Article [102 TFEU] applies only to anti-competitive conduct engaged in by undertakings *on their own initiative*, not to measures adopted"[65] or encouraged by the State.[66] The exclusion of Mr. Corbeau's services could not be legally justified as long as the economic equilibrium of the public service obligation of the Régie des Postes was not compromised.[67]

The precedent set in *Telemarketing*, *RTT* and *Corbeau* is seminal. It prevents statutory dominant firms from escaping or reducing antitrust liability by claiming the

---

60. *Id.* §§16-18.
61. *Id.* §27.
62. CJEU, Case C-18/88, *RTT/GB-Inno-BM*, ECLI:EU:C:1991:474, §15.
63. *Id.* at §22: "It is the extension of the monopoly in the establishment and operation of the telephone network to the market in telephone equipment, without any objective justification, which is prohibited as such by Article [102], *or* by Article [106(1)] in conjunction with Article [102]." (emphasis added)
64. CJEU, Case C-320/91, *Régie des Postes v. Corbeau*, ECLI:EU:C:1993:198, §18.
65. CJEU, Case C-18/88, *RTT/GB-Inno-BM*, ECLI:EU:C:1991:474, §20; and CJEU, Case C-320/91, *Régie des Postes v. Corbeau*, ECLI:EU:C:1993:198, §10.
66. CJEU, Case C-13/77, *SA GB-INNO-BM v. ATAB*, ECLI:EU:C:1977:185, §34.
67. CJEU, Case C-320/91, *Régie des Postes v. Corbeau*, ECLI:EU:C:1993:198, §18.

inapplicability of the rules of competition or by shifting responsibility to the Member State that had granted them exclusive rights.

[2] State Aid Law

Articles 107 TFEU and 108 TFEU establish a system of state aid control. These provisions limit the ability of Member States to subsidize market activities by obliging Member States to request approval before the Commission to grant aid.[68]

Similarly, State aid provisions do not prevent the independent application of Article 102 TFEU to dominant firms that owe their market power to any advantages granted by the State. This is of particular relevance in the presence of cross-subsidies, where a state-owned undertaking in a dominant position uses revenues of its reserved market to compete in an "*open market.*"[69] While the transfer of those revenues can be considered state aid, it can also be the case that cross-subsidization amounts to an abuse of market power. *GT-Link A/S* illustrates this point.

In *GT-Link A/S* the Court was referred a preliminary question concerning the harbor duties that DSB, the state-owned Danish railway company, charged GT-Link for the use of the port of Gesder, owned by DSB. The Court held that when DSB charged "unusually low" prices for its own ferry services compared to those charged by competitor ferry companies this could constitute evidence that DSB cross-subsidized its own ferry activities with the profits from its statutory dominant position in port management activities.[70] Such behavior constituted abusive conduct in as much as it was paramount to applying dissimilar conditions to equivalent trading partners.

[B] The Undifferentiated Application of Article 102 TFEU

The cases where the independent application of Article 102 TFEU to statutory dominant firms has been clarified relate to the joint application of Articles 102 and 106(1) TFEU. This legal backdrop might have numbed competition enforcement against the statutory source of market power when independently applying Article 102 TFEU. In other words, it seems as if in the process of reasserting antitrust liability against anticompetitive behavior by statutory dominant firms, the EU Courts and the Commission

68. There is state aid when a Member State confers a *selective advantage*. The advantage must distort or threaten to distort competition. It is thus unnecessary that the advantage be a subsidy in the strict sense of the word but that it has the *effect* of mitigating charges normally included in the budget of that undertaking. *See, e.g.*, CJEU, Case C-387/92, *Banco Exterior de España v. Ayuntamiento de Valencia*, ECLI:EU:C:1994:100, §13; Case C-39/94, *SFEI and others*, ECLI:EU:C:1996:285, §58; Case C-241/94, *France v. Commission*, ECLI:EU:C:1996:353 §19; *and* Case C-6/12, *P Oy*, ECLI:EU:C:2013:525.

69. For the purposes of our discussion, the term "open market" refers to any market where the state has not created a position of SMP.

70. CJEU, Case C-242/95, *GT-Link A/S and De Danske Statsbaner (DSB)*, ECLI:EU:C:1997:376, §§41-43. Discussing this issue, *see* Kronenberger, Vincent. "A Model of the Transformation Process of Statutory Monopolies in European Community Law: From Practice to Theory." *European Business Organization Law Review* 2.2 (2001): 301-338.

decidedly relinquished the opportunity to discuss whether the behavior of these firms deserved a differentiated treatment under Article 102 TFEU alone.

Through a selection of three emblematic cases (*Telemarketing*, *Irish Sugar* and *Compagnie Maritime Belge*),[71] we test the following hypothesis: that the lack of discussion about the statutory origins of dominance reflects a judicial choice (§2.04[B][1]). This deliberate judicial choice results in an enforcement paradox (§2.04[B][2]), which has the subsequent effect of making competition policy ambiguous as to its objectives (§2.04[B][3]).[72] The latter two points are clearly observed in the enforcement and competition policy regarding the postal sector in which statutory positions of dominance abound.

[1] A Judicial Choice

The *first illustration* is the Commission's intervention in *Telemarketing*. In support of the argument that Article 102 TFEU applied also to statutory dominant firms the Commission claimed that dominance "refers to a factual situation independent of the reasons giving rise to that situation."[73] Thus, the statutory origins of Compagnie Luxembourgeoise could not provide it with a safe harbor. However, once antitrust liability had been asserted, neither the Court nor the Commission seemed interested in taking the argument a step further to examine whether the statutory origins of dominance need to be taken into account when enforcing Article 102 TFEU.

However, instead of developing a differentiated approach by looking into the evident statutory origins of dominance (and what this meant for the competitive process), the *Telemarketing* Court simply followed its precedent on abusive conduct by non-statutory dominant firms set in *Commercial Solvents*.[74] The Court concluded that absent any objective necessity, a firm abuses its dominant position if it reserves to

71. As it will become more apparent, other cases discussed in this chapter similarly show that the EU Courts decidedly chose not to explicitly incorporate the statutory origins of dominance in their analyses.
72. Section 2.06 of this chapter explores the extent to which *Post Danmark I* and *Post Danmark II* depart from this judicial choice.
73. CJEU, Case C-311/84, *SA Centre Belge d'études de marché - Télémarketing (CBEM) v. SA Compagnie luxembourgeoise de télédiffusion (CLT) and SA Information publicité Benelux (IPB)*, ECLI:EU:C:1985:394, §15.
74. Commercial Solvents was accused of abusing its dominant position for refusing to supply the raw material aminobutanol to Zoja, a firm specialized in processing nitropropane and aminobutanol into ethambutol, which is used as an anti-tuberculosis drug. Zoja had cancelled its supply agreement with Commercial Solvents, and finding no other better alternatives tried to come back to Commercial Solvents, who refused to supply nitropropane and aminobutanol as it had decided to start processing them itself into derivatives like ethambutol. Remarkably, while the Court acknowledged that competitive position of Zoja, the defendant, "entirely depends" on its technology and know-how that it has acquired in processing nitropropane and aminobutanol into ethambutol; nowhere in the judgment the Court considers that Commercial Solvents' position has been competitively acquired. *Commercial Solvents*, and subsequent case law relating to investor dominant firms, where their market position is the result of a competitive process, would need to be reassessed under this premise. *See* CJEU, Joined Cases 6 and 7/73, *Istituto Chemioterapico Italiano SpA and Commercial Solvents v. Commission*, ECLI: EU:C:1974:18 at p. 232.

itself, or to a subsidiary of the same group, an ancillary activity which could be carried out by another undertaking on a neighboring market.[75]

Such an approach partially shows that the Court viewed Commercial Solvents' dominant position as a similar situation to that of Compagnie Luxembourgeoise irrespective of the fact that Commercial Solvent's position was the result of investments undertaken in competition.[76]

A *second illustration* is *Compagnie Maritime Belge*. This case shows in an explicit manner the judicial choice not to look into the statutory origins of dominance. The statutory monopoly at issue relates to one of the oldest trades: a trade company by the name of Cewal (Associated Central West Africa Lines). Cewal is a shipping conference operating the liner trade route between European North Sea ports and Zaire (now the RDC) and Angola. One of its members is Compagnie Maritime Belge.

Since their inception, shipping companies have established common freight rates and regulated capacity under the auspices of government intervention. This has earned them exemptions from antitrust rules and regulatory protection under the premise that without those agreements ruinous competition would ensue.[77] In fact, at the time of *Compagnie Maritime Belge*, EU Council Regulation 4056/86 granted a block exemption to liner shipping conferences allowing them to cooperate fixing rates. Furthermore, Cewal had concluded an agreement with the Zairian authorities that granted Cewal exclusivity to transport all cargoes from and to Zaire. As a result, Cewal was the only shipping conference that could serve sea trade between European North Sea ports and Zaire (now the RDC). Therein lied the origin of its "superdominance"[78] and the impediment for other conferences to serve the same market. Only "outsiders" (i.e., non-conference companies) could attempt to enter the statutorily safeguarded market.

Against this background, the Commission found that Cewal had abused its collective dominant position by repeatedly requesting the Zairian authorities to comply with the exclusivity agreement. In essence, Cewal sought that the Zairian authorities revoked the entry permission they had unilaterally granted to the outsider undertaking Grimaldi & Cobelfret. The Commission also found that Cewal's tariffs were selectively discriminatory against Grimaldi & Cobelfret.

Interestingly, Compagnie Maritime Belge appealed the decision by the Commission and sought to divert antitrust liability under Article 106(1) TFEU by claiming it had been granted a legal monopoly. As such, Compagnie Maritime Belge argued that its requests to the Zairian authorities were simply aimed at enforcing that right.

---

75. AG Van Gerven in *PTT* followed the same unwarranted rationale. In *PTT*, the Dutch postal operator extended its statutory dominance in the market for postal services below 500 grams into the postal market opened to competition. AG Van Gerven opined that Commercial Solvents and PTT related to a "similar situation." *See* Opinion of AG Van Gerven in Joined Cases C-48 and 66/90, *Netherlands and PTT Nederland v. Commission*, ECLI:EU:C:1991:390, §42. The Court annulled the Decision of the Commission on procedural grounds (namely, for not respecting the rights of defense), and did not examine the issue. *See* CJEU, Joined Cases C-48/90 and 66/90, *Netherlands and PTT Nederland v. Commission*, ECLI:EU:C:1992:63.
76. *See* Chapter 5 for a critique.
77. OECD, *Competition Issues in Liner Shipping*, DAF/COMP/WP2(2015)3.
78. Opinion of AG Fennelly in Joined Cases C-395/96 P and C-396/96 P, *Compagnie Maritime Belge v. Commission*, ECLI:EU:C:1998:518, §137.

Despite the evident statutory origins (either at EU or Zairian level) the Court of Justice did not explicitly address this claim. Instead, it contented itself with remembering that irrespective of the reasons that led a firm to acquire a dominant position, the dominant firm has a special responsibility not to impair competition.[79] Although the agreement was not considered anticompetitive, the Court concluded, Cewal abused its dominant position by requesting its enforcement.

In his opinion, AG Fennelly made the same judicial choice. Adopting a stringently formalistic standpoint, he concluded that Cewal's conduct was simply not of the sort that Article 106(1) TFEU was meant to cover since it could not be said that the exclusivity agreement was an exclusive right as such.[80] In other words, even if the Zairian state was partially behind the limited competition, the discussion about the statutory origins could not ensue because Cewal's right did not fall within the (narrow) category of an exclusive or special right.

The Court of Justice maintained its judicial choice when it examined Cewal's second abuse. This consisted of a deliberate change of Cewal's publicly announced tariffs on the same dates and for the same routes that Grimaldi & Cobelfret operated. Compagnie Maritime Belge argued that the targeted tariffs were not anticompetitive since they were above any measure of cost that could be regarded as predatory. The Court rejected the plea.

Although the Court observed that Regulation 4056/86 already permitted price fixing as an exception, it continued that it was "not necessary ... to rule generally on the circumstances in which a liner conference may legitimately, on a case by case basis, adopt lower prices than those of its advertised tariff in order to compete with a competitor who quotes lower prices, or to decide on the exact scope of the expression 'uniform or common freight rates' in Article 1(3)(b) of Regulation No 4056/86." For the Court of Justice, it was "sufficient to recall that the conduct at issue here is that of a conference having a share of over 90% of the market in question and only one competitor" and that Compagnie Maritime Belge had admitted "that the purpose of the conduct complained of was to eliminate G&C from the market."[81]

With those conclusive statements it is unsurprising that the Court of Justice chose not to discuss the more complex question of whether the statutory position of Cewal had an effect on its findings.

A *third* and last example might be found in the *Irish Sugar* case. In 1933 the Irish Government set up the Irish Sugar Company which was not only protected from competition but also received substantial government funding. Even when Ireland accessed the European Union, Irish Sugar was thereafter (re)allocated the entire quota for the production of sugar for Ireland in accordance with the European Common

79. CJEU, Joined Cases C-395/96 P and C-396/96 P, *Compagnie Maritime Belge* v. *Commission*, ECLI:EU:C:2000:132, §§37 and 85.
80. Opinion of AG Fennelly in *id.*, ECLI:EU:C:1998:518, §§80-86.
81. CJEU, Joined Cases C-395/96 P and C-396/96 P, *Compagnie Maritime Belge v. Commission*, ECLI:EU:C:2000:132, §§118-119. Ibáñez Colomo explains the outcome of the case in terms of the weight the EU Courts placed on the subjective element of exclusionary intent. *See* Ibáñez Colomo, Pablo. "The Law on Abuses of Dominance and the System of Judicial Remedies." *Yearbook of European Law* 32.1 (2013): 389-431.

Agricultural Policy (CAP).[82] As a result, it continued to benefit from this privilege despite its privatization in 1991. The CAP together with the Irish government created a statutory position of market power.

Against this background, the Commission found that Irish Sugar had abused its dominant position by selectively low pricing customers, engaging in price discrimination and granting a series of selective, exclusivity and fidelity rebates. The Commission was aware of the fact that Irish Sugar's position of dominance was partially due to the statutory barriers, but it held that this fact could "not dispense it from the obligation not to act abusively."[83] However, instead of exploring the possibility that the statutory origins of market power could modify thresholds of antitrust liability, the Commission settled with indirectly reaffirming the independent liability of statutory dominance under Article 102 TFEU.[84]

[2] The Enforcement Paradox

The paradox that arises from the judicial choice not to look into the origins of dominance is clearly seen in the enforcement of Article 102 TFEU in the postal sector.

In *Deutsche Post I* the German postal operator enjoyed "a statutory exclusive right" to carry postal mail of letters and catalogues weighing less than 200 grams.[85] Deutsche Post subsequently expanded its activities and started providing parcel delivery services, which is open to competition.

UPS, a private undertaking providing parcel services, complained that Deutsche Post was using revenues from its reserved market to finance below-cost selling in parcel services, which unlike the reserved market, is open to competition. This leveraging of rents allowed Deutsche Post to carry a below-cost pricing strategy that prevented other firms from competing in a market open to competition. The Commission found that Deutsche Post had abused its dominant position by failing to cover the incremental costs of providing the parcel delivery service. In other words, Deutsche Post drove competition away from the parcel services market by covering its losses in

82. The CAP is designed to support agricultural production within the Community. This entails, among many others, the production of sugar.
83. Commission Decision, Case COMP/IV/34.621, 35.059/F-3, *Irish Sugar*, §115; and GC, Case T-228/97, *Irish Sugar v. Commission*, ECLI:EU:T:1999:246, §112. Admittedly, still the Court goes into the origins to hold that *even* holding statutory monopoly does not confer immunity from Article 102 TFEU liability.
84. *See* Commission Decision, Case COMP/IV/34.621, 35.059/F-3, *Irish Sugar*, §149 establishing the rebates system as abusive in light of *Hoffmann-La Roche*'s statement that competition is already weakened by the mere presence of the dominant undertaking, and that the causes behind market cannot grant antitrust immunity; and GC, Case T-228/97, *Irish Sugar v. Commission*, ECLI:EU:T:1999:246, §111. Almost ten years before *Irish Sugar*, the Commission found that British Sugar, the legal monopoly in the production of beet sugar in the United Kingdom, abused its dominant position. In particular, British Sugar refused to supply, applied unprofitable margins, discriminated Napier Brown against some of its customers, and granted "group commitment" bonuses, to drive Napier Brown out from the British retail sugar market. The Commission however did not mention the origins of the dominant firm in its assessment. *See* Commission Decision, Case COMP/IV/30.178, *Napier Brown – British Sugar*.
85. Commission Decision, Case COMP/35.141, *Deutsche Post I*, §2.

the parcel services market with the revenues it derived from its reserved mail services market.

In a footnote, the Commission sketched out the preliminary intuition of a theory of harm applicable to statutory dominant firms. Due to the existence of a "reserved area these economies of scope are not available to competitors."[86] However, the Commission avoided discussing the clarification that the "reserved area" was a unique characteristic that made its theory only applicable to statutory dominant firms. It simply explained that the reserved area is a "likely and permanent source of funding."[87]

In *UPS Europe*, UPS appealed the acquisition of joint control of DHL by Deutsche Post before the General Court. UPS complained that the acquisition was contrary to competition rules. In particular, it argued that Deutsche Post was abusing its statutory position of dominance by using resources from its reserved market to finance the acquisition. To use profits derived from a market where Deutsche Post is protected by the State "to acquire control of a company on a competitive market is *not based on normal business performance and thus is unfair and distorts competition*"[88] (emphasis added).

The Commission replied to UPS viewpoint that "the interpretation of article [102 TFEU] does not depend on whether a dominant position has been conferred by law or acquired otherwise."[89] Companies to which Member States have granted an exclusive right are not prevented from expanding into other areas The General Court followed the same reasoning.[90] Hence, it held that "the mere fact that [Deutsche Post] used those funds to acquire joint control of an undertaking active in a neighboring market open to competition does not in itself, even if the source of those funds was the reserved market raise any problem from the standpoint of the competition rules and cannot therefore constitute an infringement of Article [102 TFEU]."[91] The General Court however conceded that there could be abusive conduct if the applicant were to provide evidence that the funds used by Deutsche Post "derived from abusive behavior on its reserved market.[92]

Comparatively, both cases illustrate the untenable paradox created by the reluctance to look at the origins of dominance. In our view, in *Deutsche Post I*, the anticompetitive effect of its pricing behavior in the parcel delivery market is derived from the fact that Deutsche Post can use the economies of scale and scope of the postal service that are the result of statutory protection in the parcel delivery market.[93] That is, they are statutory advantages that are closed to other firms. As Sappington and Sidak write, the statutory monopoly "truncates the range of services that an entrant can offer

86. Commission Decision, Case COMP/35.141, *Deutsche Post I*, §32 and n. 17.
87. *Id.* §6.
88. GC, Case T-175/99, *UPS Europe SA v. Commission*, ECLI:EU:T:2002:78, §41.
89. *Id.* §§ 46 and 47.
90. Assuming, *arguendo*, that Deutsche Post's funds came indeed from profits made in its reserved market. *See id.* §58.
91. *Id.* §61.
92. *Id.* §§ 55 and 61.
93. Sappington, David E.M. and J. Gregory Sidak. "Competition Law for State-Owned Enterprises." *Antitrust Law Journal* 71.2 (2003): 479-523, at 512.

in competition with [it]." However, in *UPS Europe*, the Commission rejected that Article 102 TFEU could be interpreted differently in cases dealing with statutory positions of dominance.

Moreover, from a process perspective, the Court's reasoning in *UPS Europe* presents certain inconsistency. Whether the resources employed by Deutsche Post to acquire joint control DHL are the result of abusive conduct or statutory rents, both cases are closely similar. The acquisition could be abusive because UPS did not have the *competitive* opportunity to secure the same funds that the statutory monopoly holds today. "It opens the way to an allocation of wealth in accordance with the ability of a person or group to gain control of the State apparatus."[94]

In the *first* scenario, where profits are gained by anticompetitive conduct, it is appropriate that those illegitimate funds do not subsidize further activities of the firm because they are not the result of the competitive process. In the *second* scenario, "statutory rents" have been gained because the state protects the market power of the firm to extract those rents. By allowing any use of those rents to acquire competitors in other markets the statutory dominant firm spills over other markets and continues to upset the competitive process.[95]

As we shall explore in the following section (*see* section 2.05), the statutory dominant firm distorts market investments by non-statutory firms. In an acquisition setting such as the one in *UPS Express*, the price at which the statutory dominant firm can acquire joint control of DHL distorts the competitive process by which the natural price is arrived at.

The acquisition of football player Neymar by the state-backed football club PSG for EUR 222 million illustrates this point.[96] As the Spanish President of LaLiga declared, "[T]he problem is that Neymar is being taken by a financially-doped team that competes with an advantage. The problem is the state-backed clubs, they need to be stopped."[97]

[3] A Policy Paradox

The divergent approach in *Deutsche Post* and *UPS/TNT* inevitably leads to ambiguous statements of competition policy.

On the one hand, the Commission seemingly favors a certain degree of differentiation in its Guidance Paper. It claims that the likelihood of finding anticompetitive effects is higher when the firm is a "legal monopoly." The legal monopoly "may use the

94. Rothbard, Murray N. *Power & Market: Government and the Economy*. Ludwig von Mises Institute, [1970] 2006, at 209.
95. Poillot-Peruzzetto, Sylvaine. "Nouvel apport concernant les entreprises gérant un service d'intérêt économique général." *Contrats Concurrence Consommation* 6 (2002): 98.
96. Whether the Financial Fair Play rules are potentially unlawful, *see* Petit, Nicolas. "'Financial Fair Play' or 'Oligopoleague' of Football Clubs?: A Preliminary Review under European Union Competition Law." *SSRN* (Jun. 16, 2014).
97. *Quoted in* "Spanish league wants EU to referee Neymar transfer saga." Politico (Aug. 3, 2017), *available at* https://www.politico.eu/article/neymar-antitrust-complaint-la-liga-psg-transfer/.

profits gained in the monopoly market to cross-subsidize its activities in another market."[98] This statement is however relegated to a footnote.

In a clearer manner, the Commission's Postal Sector Notice[99] recognizes the need for a differentiated approach. It states that a postal operator that uses the advantages of the reserved area to subsidize activities open to competition "is likely to distort competition."[100] On the contrary, "cross-subsidisation between non-reserved activities is not in itself abusive."[101]

Notwithstanding these policy claims, the Commission has also rejected the differentiated approach—as it explicitly did in *UPS Express*. In its submissions to the OECD roundtable on state-owned undertakings, the Commission claimed that the presence of a state-owned dominant firm raises an "interesting debate" as to its incentives to behave anticompetitively, but not to establish different theories of anticompetitive harm.[102]

[C] Summation

The limitations imposed by Articles 106(1) and 107 TFEU show that the EU legislature saw an impediment to the competitive process in the *statutory* creation and protection of positions of market power. This is unlike Article 102 TFEU that does not prohibit the acquisition of market power, but the abusive exercise of that power. Given this, it is surprising that in applying Article 102 TFEU the statutory origins of the dominant firm are removed from the analysis.

It is not far-fetched to advance that the existence of Article 106(1) TFEU (and to a lesser extent Article 107 TFEU) has generally diverted the EU Courts and Commission's attention from the statutory origins of certain dominant firms. Yet, many Article 102 TFEU cases that fall short of Article 106(1) TFEU or State aid provisions have a statutory dominance component.

As history illustrates, dominant firms in Europe where mostly created or protected by the state at the time when EU competition laws made their first appearance. *Telemarketing*, *Irish Sugar* and *Compagnie Maritime Belge* represent clear examples of a judicial choice not to discuss whether the differences between statutory and "other" positions of dominance deserved a different analysis of conduct. It is not implausible that the EU Courts and the Commission were more concerned with asserting Article 102 TFEU liability against statutory dominance than developing a differentiated analysis of abuse for those cases. This is regrettable.

While the position of market power is indeed a factual situation, the reasons that give rise to it are not simple factual observations. On the contrary, those reasons have

98. Guidance Paper, §63, n. 2.
99. Notice from the Commission on the application of the competition rules to the postal sector and on the assessment of certain State measures relating to postal services. *OJ* C 39, 06.02.1998, p. 2-18.
100. *Id.* §3.3.
101. *Id.* §3.2.
102. OECD, *State Owned Enterprises and the Principle of Competitive Neutrality*, DAF/COMP(2009)37, European Commission Submission at p. 237.

an effect on the competitive dynamics of the market in which the statutory firm is dominant. Hence, a blind spot in the case law arises with the potential to create enforcement and policy paradoxes as those revealed in the postal sector.

Therefore, while the limitations on statutory action imposed by Article 106(1) TFEU and state aid law are welcome in a process-oriented approach to competition enforcement, Article 102 TFEU cannot remain indifferent to the origins of a statutory dominant firm (as well as to other causes of market power). But, why should the application of Article 102 TFEU take into account the statutory origins of the dominant firm?

We seek to provide an answer in the following section, but AG Tesauro's Opinion in *Terminal Equipment* provides a first and high-level reason for it. There is a "fundamental contradiction" in the Treaty that enounces as its political-economy principle a system of free competition, but yet allows Member States to take economic-policy decisions that go against that same principle by allowing the creation of statutory monopolies. It is "obvious" that a statutory monopoly "is not in complete harmony with a system based on free competition."[103]

§2.05 OPENING THE BLACK BOX: STATUTORY DOMINANCE MATTERS

In this section, we examine why the statutory origins of dominant firms should be taken into account in the independent application of Article 102 TFEU from a process-perspective approach.[104]

When the State creates a statutory firm, it upsets the opportunity to participate in the competitive process *initially* (§2.05[A]) and *prospectively* (§2.05[B]). These are both sides of the same coin as the initial attributes of the competitive process (t-1) necessarily affect the conditions under which competition will develop (t and $t+1$). The privilege, support, aid, protection, etc., that the statutory firm received is responsible for limiting economic activities in the free market. Unlike where the existence of a dominant position created by investment efforts or entrepreneurial insight will provide signs of a competitive market,[105] statutory dominance provides no such hints and presumably indicates a risk of a skewed competitive process. This differentiation in no way prejudices the rules governing the system of property ownership (§2.05[C]), but simply demands a particular attention in the enforcement of Article 102 TFEU (§2.05[D]).

103. Opinion of AG Tesauro in Case C-202/88, *France v. Commission*, ECLI:EU:C:1990:64, §§11 and 24.
104. Motta, Massimo and Alexandre de Streel. "Excessive Pricing in Competition Law: Never Say Never?" *in* Konkurrensverket (ed.) *The Pros and Cons of High Prices*, 2007: 14-46, at p. 26, writing that "dominant firms should be treated in a different way according to the source of its market power."
105. *See* Chapters 5 and 6.

[A] An Initial Perspective

From an *initial perspective* (*t*-1), the statutory dominant firm is not the result of the competitive process. On the contrary, it is the result of an external decision by the State that affects the ordinary functioning of markets.

Hayek's work helps us understand this. The competitive process through which a firm might acquire SMP is important because it is a discovery process. Competition tells us "which goods are scarce, however, or which things are goods, or how scarce or valuable they are." Each case of these cases is a "preliminary outcome of the market process that inform[s] individuals where it is worthwhile to search."[106] It is a process *toward* the free market price, *toward* "the most value-productive point."[107] By way of contrast, when the State creates a position of dominance it bypasses the process of competition. As imperfect as the competitive process may be, its circumvention prevents both consumers and firms from engaging in useful and unbounded interactions that result in the creation of knowledge and a "spontaneous order" superior to the State's selection.[108] This is because the State is unable to acquire all knowledge in society which is decentralized.[109]

In a certain way, a statutory dominant firm is an extension of the power of the State onto the market. Legitimized in the use of violence,[110] the State may use that power to upset the conditions prevailing in market by suppressing the amount of *private and voluntary* interactions that fuel the competitive process.[111] Here lies a fundamental difference between the statutory monopoly and the other dominant firms that tends to be largely ignored. The statutory firm is itself a "coercive monopoly" established by government intervention.[112] It is the result "from the abrogation of laissez-faire and from the introduction of the opposite principle—the principle of statism."[113] The statutory firm is an extension of such power and entails a disruption of the competitive process. It is not in harmony a system of free competition.

This means that many of the benefits of the discovery process itself are lost. The statutory dominant firm has bypassed the competitive process, preventing the establishment of a free market price (and choice) and putting consumers and firms at a

106. Hayek, Friedrich A. "Competition as a Discovery Procedure." *The Quarterly Journal of Austrian Economics* 5.3 ([1968] 2002): 9-23, 13.
107. Rothbard, Murray N. *Power & Market: Government and the Economy*. Ludwig von Mises Institute, [1970] 2006, 44.
108. Hayek, Friedrich A. *Law, Legislation and Liberty*, (Vol. 1) *Rules and Order*. Routledge, [1973] 1998.
109. Hayek, Friedrich A. "The Pretence of Knowledge." *The American Economic Review* 79.6 (1989): 3-7.
110. Weber, Max. *Politics as a Vocation*. New York: Oxford University Press, [1921] 1946, 1-48, at 4: "a state is a human community that (successfully) claims the monopoly of the legitimate use of physical force within a given territory."
111. Buchanan, James M. "What Should Economists Do?" *Southern Economic Journal* 30.3 (1964): 213-222, at 219: the market "is not a means toward the accomplishment of anything. It is the institutional embodiment of voluntary exchange processes that are entered by individuals."
112. Rand, Ayn. "Antitrust: The Rule of Unreason." *The Objectivist Newsletter* 1.2 (1962).
113. Branden, Nathaniel. "Monopolies and Laissez-Fake Capitalism." *The Objectivist Newsletter* 1.6 (1962), at p. 23.

disadvantaged position by protecting the statutory firm against the competitive forces of the free market.

This is not a surprising finding. Ordoliberal thinkers already showed particular concerns with statutory monopolies. Trade and industrial privileges that originate positions of market power are a "violent process of imposition" that need to be abolished.[114] It was considered that the State could not in any account be allowed to confer any privileges, whatever their form, as such interference prevents the most important function of a free market: entrepreneurship.[115] Although not all ordoliberal thinkers put the same emphasis on the damaging effects of statutory dominance, most of them maintained strong concerns about it.[116]

A reflection of the strong ordoliberal views against statutory dominance is the Spaak Report, a pivotal document setting the principles underpinning the creation of the internal market. It stated: "It should, however, be borne in mind that *the most flagrant discriminatory practices* are carried out by sellers upon government instructions or *with government assistance*" (emphasis added).[117] This is a view which economist Frank Knight adhered to when he expressed concerns about the role of enterprise monopoly being "enormously exaggerated" while the main and worst part is monopoly that rests on government intervention.[118]

Indeed, while competition generally secures the selection of the most efficient firms, statutory market power is at best a discordant note in the competitive process, and at worst an inefficient state of affairs.[119] Unlike in market selection, there is no consistent evidence in economic history or theory that supports governments' ability to efficiently pick firms. This does not mean that government cannot create winners, but

114. Böhm, Franz. "Rule of Law in a Market Economy" *in* Alan Peacock and Hans Willgerodt (eds.) *Germany's Social Market Economy: Origins and Evolution.* 1989: 46-67, at 56.
115. *Id.* 59.
116. Razeen Sally for instance criticized Walter Eucken's work for underestimating the creation and promotion of monopoly by discriminating acts of government. Sally, Razeen. "Ordoliberalism and the Social Market: Classical Political Economy from Germany." *New Political Economy* 1.2 (1996): 233-257, at 237. *See also* Vanberg, Viktor J. *The Freiburg School: Walter Eucken and Ordoliberalism.* No. 04/11. Freiburg discussion papers on constitutional economics (2004).
117. Intergovernmental Committee established by the Messina Conference. "Report of the Heads of Delegation to the Foreign Ministers" (Brussels, Apr. 21, 1956), at 46. The report is also known as the "Spaak Report," *available at* https://www.cvce.eu/en/obj/report_of_the_heads_of_delegation_to_the_foreign_ministers_brussels_21_april_1956-en-4dd69921-433b-4bc0-acec-808f72fec9ae.html.
118. Knight, Frank H. "The Meaning of Freedom." *Ethics* 52.1 (1941): 86-109, at 103.
119. The press commentary in the United Kingdom, after government in the 1890s had suppressed private messenger companies is revealing of the coercive nature of statutory dominance and its irreconcilable status with competition. The state actions to protect the postal monopoly where "machinations of a red-tape-entangled, slow-moving, *competition-fearing*, monopoly-enjoying, thick-skinned Government department." It is "highly entertaining to see this sluggish and somnolent department thus goaded by private competition into clumsy and reluctant imitation." *See* The Times, March 21 and March 27, 1891, *quoted in* Coase, Ronald H. "The British Post Office and the Messenger Companies." *The Journal of Law & Economics* 4 (1961): 12-65, at 32; *see also* Hayek, Friedrich A. *Law, Legislation and Liberty*, (Vol. 3) *The Political Order of a Free People.* Routledge, [1979] 1998. Hayek goes as far as arguing that government monopoly on issuing money is an example of monopoly used to "enhance the powers of government."

that the "winner" is neither the most efficient one nor the result of a competitive process.[120]

[B] The Prospective Process

Prospectively (t and $t+1$), the privileged[121] advantages that the statutory firm enjoys are unavailable to other firms. Unlike with other dominant firms the monopolized factor is the right to enter the industry. Indeed, when equality of opportunity has been secured at the starting point (t-1) the resulting preliminary outcome would be "just or at least not unjust."[122] However, in the case of statutory dominance the opposite is true. As competitors must overcome or avoid the imposed statutory disadvantage this results in an injustice.

As such the presence of statutory firms imposes other negative externalities in the competitive process. For example, statutory positions of market power discourage private investment in the incontestable industry where the statutory firm operates.[123] The idea that an industry might be *forced* to compete with or be replaced by a statutory monopoly lowers competitive investments.[124] Firms will renege from competing against the statutory dominant firm, either in its protected market or in other open markets where it can make use of its statutory advantages.[125]

At the same time, this eliminates or limits to a great extent the possibility for waves of "creative destruction" to displace statutory monopolistic positions. Adam Smith already saw this when he wrote that statutory monopolies would last only "as long as the regulations of police which gave occasion to them" that would otherwise occur where a market-created dominant firm exists.[126] A particularly clear example of this is the statutory monopoly of taxi services imposed by the States under claims of

120. OECD, Roundtable on Competition Policy, Industrial Policy and National Champions, DAF/COMP/GF(2009)9.
121. *See*, prīvĭlēgĭum, ii, n. privus-lex: *a bill* or *law in favor of* or *against an individual, in* Thomas Lewis, Charlton and Charles Short. *A Latin Dictionary*. Oxford: Clarendon Press (1879).
122. Rawls, John. "Constitutional Liberty and the Concept of Justice" *in* Samuel Freeman (ed.) *Collected Papers*. Harvard University Press (1999): 73-95, at n. 5 discussing market competitiveness. "Given a just system, one need not complain or worry about particular outcomes."
123. OECD, *State Owned Enterprises and the Principle of Competitive Neutrality*. DAF/COMP(2009)37, at pp. 292 and 449.
124. Rothbard, Murray N. *Power & Market: Government and the Economy*. Ludwig von Mises Institute, [1970] 2006, at 218.
125. Epstein, Richard A. "Hayekian Socialism." *Maryland Law Review* 58.7 (1999): 271-299. The resulting problem is evident. In order to compete a non-statutory firm must be "not merely superior [to the statutory firm], but so much superior that its customers are willing to forgo their share of that money." *See also* Friedman, David D. *The Machinery of Freedom: Guide to a Radical Capitalism*. Open Court Publishing Company, 1989, at p. 32.
126. Smith, Adam. *An Inquiry into the Nature and Causes of the Wealth of Nations*. Econlib [1776] 2009, Book I, 7.29, discussing the natural and market price of commodities.

"destructive or excessive competition."[127] Its resilience has continuously prevented the "spontaneous liberalization" of the industry.[128]

Competitive efforts might not only decrease or be for naught but also be misdirected. Indeed, an additional negative externality that the statutory firm imposes on the competitive process is that it incentivizes *rent*-seeking instead of *profit*-seeking behavior.[129] Since statutory firms are beneficiaries of certain privileges that were unobtainable on a free market,[130] disadvantaged potential or actual competitors are incentivized to direct their efforts to securing the same or different privileges. At the same time, statutory dominant firms might turn their efforts to the state that granted them their advantages: *rent*-profiting calls for *rent*-seeking when privileges are put in peril.[131] In both cases, this comes to the detriment of competitive efforts to participate in the competitive process that rewards participants with profits. Rent-seeking becomes undesirable in an open market economy as it further obstructs the free competitive process by recourse to governmental intervention.[132]

When competition is seen as a dynamic process, *profits* are a direct consequence of markets uncertainty and imperfect information. As Teece and Mary Coleman argue, they are "benign sources of rent from an antitrust perspective."[133] They fuel the competitive process by incentivizing firms to engage in the uncertain discovery of consumer wants.[134] On the contrary, here *rents* are a direct consequence of competitive

127. Dempsey, Paul S. "Taxi Industry Regulation, Deregulation, and Reregulation: The Paradox of Market Failure." *Transportation Law Journal* 24 (1996): 73-120, 116.
128. Geradin, Damien. "Uber and the Rule of Law: Should Spontaneous Liberalization Be Applauded or Criticized?" *Competition Policy International* (2015).
129. Although Ricardian rents and Schumpeterian rents are opposed to the idea of monopoly rents, we prefer the term profit to encompass both Ricardian and Schumpeterian rents because the wording easily differentiates benign from unwarranted sources. Ricardian rents are the natural return to the scarce asset and serve to cover the firm's initial investment. Schumpeterian rents are the temporary return to a successful innovation, which is no more than a return on the investment that led to that innovation.
130. Branden, Nathaniel. "Monopolies and Laissez-Fake Capitalism." *The Objectivist Newsletter* 1.6 (1962), at p. 23.
131. This was partially what Cewal did when it sought that the Zairian authorities actively enforced their agreement. *See* discussion above about *Compagnie Maritime Belge*.
132. Tullock, Gordon. "The Welfare Costs of Tariffs, Monopolies, and Theft." *Western Economic Journal* 5.3 (1967): 224-232, arguing that expenditures seeking government to establish protective tariffs "are purely wasteful from the standpoint of society as a whole; they are not spent in increasing wealth ... "; *see also* Bhagwati, Jagdish N. "Lobbying and Welfare." *Journal of Public Economics* 14.3 (1980): 355-363, arguing in favor of certain welfare effects in limited scenarios.
133. Teece, David J. and Mary Coleman. "The Meaning of Monopoly: Antitrust Analysis in High-Technology Industries" *The Antitrust Bulletin* 43 (1998): 801-857, 818, 833.
134. *See* Chapter 5.

asymmetry imposed by the State.[135] They are not the result of a more efficient combination of factors of production, but the result of government protection.[136]

The existence of statutory dominance would require competition policy to strongly adhere to a principle of equality of opportunity. Thus, when competitive disadvantages are the result of State action and not the normal competitive process, the statutory firm must be stringently constrained so its behavior does not lead to a spill-effect of its statutory advantages over other markets.

But even more, from a pragmatic perspective the solution to restore equal conditions lies within the state itself. While government can do little against enterprise monopoly, for when it arises it does as a natural transitory element of the competitive process, the situation is different when dealing with state-created monopolies. As the creator or supporter of such advantage, it is the only one with the power to disarm or limit its power.[137]

[C] *Quid* of Article 345 TFEU?

Article 345 TFEU states that "The Treaties shall in no way prejudice the rules in Member States governing the system of property ownership." This treaty provision has been read as forbidding any distinction between state and private ownership in the application of competition rules to any entity engaged in an economic activity.[138] It could thus appear that Article 345 TFEU is an impediment to taking into account the statutory origins of firm dominance.

However, the dichotomy between private and public undertakings is yet of little importance here. Indeed, the principle of equal treatment requires that public and private undertakings be in comparable situations.[139] Our definition of statutory dominance makes no differentiation between public or private undertakings. It is the discretionary support that the State gives to the undertaking that requires differentiation based on the discriminatory favor that the statutory firm receives against other undertakings. As we have seen, the interference of the State in the selection and support of dominant firms reveals particularities to the competitive process that cannot be left aside in the assessment of abusive conduct. Whether public or private, Article

135. Dilorenzo, Thomas J. "Property Rights, Information Costs, and the Economics of Rent Seeking." *Journal of Institutional and Theoretical Economics (JITE) / Zeitschrift Für Die Gesamte Staatswissenschaft*, 144.2 (1988): 318-332 and Littlechild, Stephen C. "Misleading Calculations of the Social Costs of Monopoly Power." *The Economic Journal* 91.362 (1981): 348-363.

136. *See* Buchanan, James M. "Rent Seeking and Profit Seeking" *in* Buchanan, James M., Robert D. Tollison and Gordon Tullock (eds.) *Toward a Theory of the Rent-Seeking Society*. Texas: A&M University Press, 1980: 55-68.

137. Hayek, Friedrich A. *The Constitution of Liberty*. The University of Chicago Press, [1978] 2011, at p. 382.

138. For an extended discussion, *see* Akkermans, Bram and Eveline Ramaekers. "Article 345 TFEU (ex Article 295 EC), Its Meanings and Interpretations." *European Law Journal* 16.3 (2010): 292-314.

139. CJEU, Joined Cases C-188 to 190/80, *France, Italy and United Kingdom v. Commission*, ECLI:EU:C:1982:134, at §21 *and* Opinion of AG Reischl in Joined Cases C-188 to 190/80, *France, Italy and United Kingdom v. Commission*, ECLI:EU:C:1982:134, at 2588.

345 TFEU does not provide any succor to the dominant firm in the application of competition rules.[140]

[D] Summation

In the same way as the actions of government need to be rigidly defined, for the state holds the monopoly of physical force, the actions of a statutory dominant firm need particular restrain to maintain a free competitive market economy. A more effective industrial policy and antitrust enforcement should aim at dismantling statutory barriers to entrepreneurship, rather than erect new ones by creating or protecting statutory positions of dominance.[141] As such, the application of Article 102 TFEU must take account of this noncompetitive background.[142]

§2.06 THE *POST DANMARK* SAGA: AN INCOMPLETE GAME CHANGER?

The Court of Justice in *Post Danmark I* and *Post Danmark II* seems to have established a turning point in their previous judicial choice not to look into the origins of firm dominance. In a nutshell, the *Post Danmark I* Court ruled: "When the existence of a dominant position has its origins in a former legal monopoly, that fact has to be taken into account."[143]

In this section, we *first* analyze the extent of the judicial policy change brought by *Post Danmark I* and *Post Danmark II*. We claim that the change is welcome but incomplete (§2.06[A]). *Second*, since the *Post Danmark* judgments provide scarce guidance on how the legal origins of a firm should affect the enforcement of Article 102 TFEU we argue that the guiding principle should be that of equality of opportunity (§2.06[B]). *Thirdly*, we advance four different ways of incorporating the statutory origins of dominance into the analysis of abusive behavior in Article 102 TFEU (§2.06[C]). More particularly, this last subsection suggests a different cost analysis for anticompetitive conduct, the imposition of a "proactive approach" toward facilitating entry, a serious incorporation of "less efficient" competitors in the analysis of exclusionary behavior and a limitation of objective justifications.

140. CJEU, Case C-367/98, *Commission v. Portuguese Republic*, ECLI:EU:C:2002:326, §48, dealing with the Sate's ownership of "golden shares" to avoid foreign takeovers, or CJEU, Case C-163/99, *Portugal v. Commission*, ECLI:EU:C:2001:189, §58-59, holding that quantitative and discriminatory rebates granted by a dominant firm are anticompetitive has nothing to do with the public or private nature of that firm.
141. OECD, Competition Policy, Industrial Policy and National Champions, DAF/COMP/GF(2009)9.
142. *See* Article 4 of the Treaty establishing the European Community (Nice consolidated version) *OJ* C 325, 24/12/2002, p. 0041-0041: "the activities of the Member States and the Community shall [adopt an economic policy based on] and conducted in accordance with the principle of an open market economy with free competition."
143. CJEU, Case C-209/10, *Post Danmark I*, ECLI:EU:C:2012:172, §23.

[A] The *Post Danmark* Saga: A Turning Point and a Word of Caution

[1] A Turning Point

In *Post Danmark I* the Court of Justice explicitly departed for the first time from its judicial choice to not look into the statutory origins of dominance under Article 102 TFEU. It ruled in an obiter dictum that "when the existence of a dominant position has its *origins in a former legal monopoly, that fact has to be taken into account.*"[144] (emphasis added).

At the time when the abuse took place, Post Danmark enjoyed a statutory monopoly in the delivery of addressed letters and parcels. Post Danmark also used its mailing network, developed under the auspices of a legal monopoly, to deliver unaddressed mail. The market for unaddressed mail (such as advertising flyers) is a market open to competition where Post Danmark competes with Forbruger-Kontakt (FK). In this context, Post Danmark was accused of abusing its dominant position by practicing selective price discounts to the main customers of FK.

The Danish competition authority had found the selective discounts to be abusive despite the fact that the prices charged were not below a measure of costs considered to be predatory (in the AKZO sense).[145] Post Danmark appealed the decision and the Danish Supreme Court of Justice referred to the EU Court. In particular, the referring court asked whether charging selectively low prices to a certain customer amounts to an abuse when the price "is lower than the average total costs attributed to the business activity concerned, but higher than the total incremental costs pertaining to the latter."[146]

The Court of Justice answered negatively. Selective pricing cannot be considered abusive "simply because" the price charged was lower than the ATC but higher than the AIC.[147] The Court explained that "to the extent that a dominant undertaking sets its prices at a level covering the great bulk of the costs ... attributable to the supply of the goods or services in question, it will, as a general rule, be possible for a competitor *as efficient as that undertaking* to compete with those prices without suffering losses that are unsustainable in the long term" (emphasis added).[148]

144. *Id.* §23. *Post Danmark I* was decided in a Grand Chamber composition. The obiter dictum seems at odds with the facts of the case. Post Danmark still enjoyed a statutory monopoly at the time it had abused that position. A more facts-based construed principle should have avoided introducing the word "*former.*" This factual mismatch does not detract value to the enunciated principle.
145. *See* CJEU, Case C-62/86, *AKZO v. Commission* ECLI:EU:C:1991:286, §§71-72. In particular, the Danish competition authority could not establish an exclusionary intent from Post Danmark.
146. CJEU, Case C-209/10, *Post Danmark I*, ECLI:EU:C:2012:172, §19.
147. *Id.* §37.
148. CJEU, Case C-209/10, *Post Danmark I*, ECLI:EU:C:2012:172, §38. *Variable costs* (VC) are the costs that vary with the output. In essence they answer the question of how much it costs to produce an extra unit. *Average variable cost* (AVC) is the firm's variable costs divided by the total quantity of output of the same product. *Average total cost* (ATC) is the firm's total cost of production divided by the total quantity of output produced. According to the findings in AKZO, a dominant firm that prices below AVC will always (per se) abuse its dominant position.

Notwithstanding its obiter dictum, the *Post Danmark I* court did not explain how the principle has to be taken into account. Nor did the Court clarify whether its analysis of anticompetitive foreclosure based on the AIC was a differentiated price-cost test for behavior by statutory dominant firms. (We will return to this point when reassessing theories of liability.)[149]

It was in *Post Danmark II* that the Court of Justice took the opportunity to explore how the statutory position of Post Danmark affected the analysis of the rebates it had granted.

In essence, the Court of Justice was asked under which conditions a system of standardized retroactive and conditional rebates as implemented by Post Danmark constituted an abuse of a dominant position, and what relevance did the as-efficient competitor (AEC) test had in that regard.[150]

The retroactive rebate meant that when purchasers exceeded the mailing threshold established a year in advance, they would enjoy a rebate not only to the excess of the threshold but also to all mailings during that year. That is, if Customer A would purchase 10 units in excess of a 100 units threshold, it would receive a rebate of x% over all 110 units, and not only over the 10 units in excess.

In deciding that Post Danmark's retroactive rebates were abusive, the Court of Justice took the "statutory monopoly"[151] of Post Danmark twice into account. The opinion of AG Kokott in *Post Danmark II*, amply cited by the Court, followed the same rationale. Aside from market shares, to establish exclusionary effects of the conduct account must be taken of "the origin of the dominant undertaking's position and any existing statutory monopoly which it has over all or some of the market."[152]

This meant, *first*, that the statutory monopoly of Post Danmark lowered the threshold to find antitrust liability for statutory dominant firms. The Court highlighted that competition on the market was limited due to Post Danmark's structural advantages conferred by its "statutory monopoly" and its large market share that made it an unavoidable trading partner.[153] In these circumstances, the Court held that the retroactive rebates tended "*to make it more difficult* for those customers to obtain supplies from competing undertakings produc[ing] an anti-competitive exclusionary effect"[154] (emphasis added).

Thus, and *second*, the *Post Danmark II* Court established that the AEC test[155] is of "no relevance" in markets where the dominant firm has a "very large market share" *and* enjoys "structural advantages conferred, *inter alia*, by that undertaking's statutory

Pricing above ATC will not be considered predatory pricing. Prices below ATC but above AVC will only be considered abusive if there is evidence that they form part of a plan to eliminate a competitor.

149. *See* Section 6 *infra*.
150. The referring court further asked what degree of probability and seriousness was required for the rebates to be deemed abusive and whether foreclosure effect must be appreciable.
151. CJEU, Case C-23/14, *Post Danmark II*, ECLI:EU:C:2015:651, §§4, 14, 35, 39 and 59.
152. Opinion of AG Kokott in Case C-23/14, *Post Danmark II*, ECLI:EU:C:2015:343, §42.
153. CJEU, Case C-23/14, *Post Danmark II*, ECLI:EU:C:2015:651, §§39-41.
154. *Id.*, §42.
155. The AEC test examines whether the pricing practices of a dominant undertaking could drive an equally efficient competitor from the market.

monopoly."[156] Moreover, the Court considered that in in such circumstances, "the presence of a less efficient competitor might contribute to intensifying the competitive pressure on that market."[157]

[2] A Word of Caution

The *Post Danmark I* Court introduced the principle that the legal origins of dominant firms must be taken into account. But it left unanswered how to operationalize it. The *Post Danmark II* Court *seemingly* sought to give it some content by lowering the threshold to find antitrust liability against statutory dominant firms. But, however welcoming such findings are, both judgments show that the reluctance to orderly discuss the origins of statutory dominance continues to be anchored in the enforcement of Article 102 TFEU.

This can be seen in the Court's reference to *Tomra* in *Post Danmark II* to support the conclusion that making the life of competitors "more difficult" can determine the anticompetitive effect of the conduct.[158] First, Tomra is, unlike Post Danmark, a firm originating in the entrepreneurship endeavor of two Norwegian brothers. Second, the *Tomra* Court never sets an exclusionary standard as low as "making it more difficult" for competing undertakings.[159]

The dangers of the continuing reluctance cannot be emphasized strongly enough. If the lower standards set by *Post Danmark II* (i.e., making entry more difficult or excluding less efficient competitors) are not clearly linked to situations of statutory dominance, other dominant firms would be treated equally.[160] However, the *ex ante* process giving birth to a dominant firm affects the competitive dynamics of the market *ex post*. We have seen this clearly in the case of statutory dominance, and we will explore this phenomenon further in the remaining chapters.

---

156. CJEU, Case C-23/14, *Post Danmark II*, ECLI:EU:C:2015:651, §59. On the one hand, the "large market share" requirement tells little about the market power of the undertaking. It is a requirement devoid of any meaningful content. On the other hand, it is remarkable that the only structural advantage mentioned by the court relates to the statutory monopoly of *Post Danmark*. In a similar line, *see* Petit, Nicolas. "Rebates and Article 102 TFEU: The European Commission's Duty to Apply the Guidance Paper." *Competition Law & Policy Debate* 2.1 (2016): 4-12.
157. CJEU, Case C-23/14, *Post Danmark II*, ECLI:EU:C:2015:651, §60.
158. *Id.* §42, citing Case C-549/10 P, *Tomra Systems and Others v. Commission*, EU:C:2012:221, §72.
159. CJEU, C-549/10 P, *Tomra Systems and Others v. Commission*, EU:C:2012:221, §72. For an extended discussion, *see* Chapter 5.
160. The General Court's judgment in *Intel* could be said to have made an erroneous transposition of this lower standard when it declared that Intel's abuse of market power made it more difficult for its competitor AMD to enter the market. *See* GC, Case T-286/09, *Intel v. Commission*, ECLI:EU:T:2014:547, §169. *See also* Commission Decision, Case COMP/39.740, *Google Search (Shopping)*, §331 and Chapter 5 for an extended discussion.

[B] Transposing the Principle of Equality of Opportunity as a *Guiding Principle*

[1] The Common Place of Equality of Opportunity in the Case Law

We argue that, in light of the effects that statutory dominance has on the competitive process the EU Courts introduced the principle of "*equality of opportunity*" in their enforcement of Article 106(1) TFEU and rules relating to the implementation of liberalization directives (failure of EU Member States to act).

In the emblematic *Terminals Equipment* case,[161] France sought to annul the Commission's directive on competition in the markets in telecommunications terminal equipment.[162] The French government claimed that, among others,[163] the Commission had exceeded its competences by mandating in Article 6 of the said Directive a separation between the undertaking providing terminal telecommunications equipment and the undertaking drawing the specifications for such equipment. The Court rejected the French plea holding that "*a system of undistorted competition,* as laid down in the Treaty, *can be guaranteed only if equality of opportunity is secured as between the various economic operators*" (emphasis added).[164] Article 6 had the virtue of maintaining this equality of opportunity by preventing a statutory undertaking from enjoying both complementary competences: the design of specifications and the marketing of the equipment having to comply with those.[165]

The application of the principle of equality of opportunity sought to correct a competitive disadvantage that *originated* in national legislation. This can be seen in the *ISIS Multimedia* case,[166] a case that while it does not concern the application of competition rules, it has been consistently quoted in Article 102 TFEU cases dealing with historical operators.[167]

In *ISIS*, the Court of Justice held that German national law regulating the fees in connection with telephone numbers discriminated between *new* operators and the

161. CJEU, Case C-202/88, *France v. Commission*, ECLI:EU:C:1991:120. *See also* CJEU, Case C-462/99, *Connect Austria*, ECLI:EU:C:2003:297, §83. *See* Marty, Frédéric. "As-Efficient Competitor Test in Exclusionary Prices Strategies: Does Post-Danmark Really Pave the Way Towards a More Economic Approach?" *GREDEG Working Papers Series* No. 2013-26, at 24, misidentifying *Connect Austria* as the case that introduced the concept of equality of opportunity.
162. Commission Directive 88/301/EEC of 16 May 1988 on "Competition in the Markets in Telecommunications Terminal Equipment," *OJ* L 131, 1988, p. 73.
163. The CJEU declared invalid Articles 2, 7 and 9.
164. CJEU, Case C-202/88, *France v. Commission*, ECLI:EU:C:1991:120, at §51.
165. For a detailed analysis of the *Terminals Equipment* case, *see* Larouche, Pierre. *Competition Law and Regulation in European Telecommunications*. Oxford and Portland: Hart Publishing, 2000, at pp. 48 et seq.
166. CJEU, Case C-327/03, *ISIS Multimedia and Firma 02*, ECLI:EU:C:2005:622. *See also* CJEU, Case C-462/99, *Connect Austria*, ECLI:EU:C:2003:297.
167. *See* Chapter 3 for a discussion concerning historical operators.

historical operator Deutsche Telekom.[168] Whereas Deutsche Telekom only had to pay for the allocation of new telephone numbers and had not paid any charge for those during its previous statutory monopoly, new operators willing to enter the market were by reason of the German law obliged to pay "upon allocation of the first number."[169] If the allocation of telephone numbers was a precondition of entry, German national law (and not the legacy advantages of Deutsche Telekom) distorted competition by not securing an equality of opportunity between *new* operators and the *historical* operator.[170]

Of seminal importance is the Court's judgment in *Greek Lignite*. Until the liberalization of the energy market, DEI enjoyed the statutory right to produce, transport and distribute electricity in Greece. At the same time, DEI is the beneficiary of a statutory exclusive right for the exploitation of lignite in the Greek region of Arcadia. The Commission found that the Greek government had breached Article 106(1) TFEU together with Article 102 TFEU by conferring or maintaining DEI's exclusive right over lignite. This right placed DEI's competitors at a disadvantage when accessing first class combustibles for the generation of electricity as they had unequal opportunities, and at the same time, it allowed DEI to maintain its dominant position in the market for wholesale electricity.

DEI appealed the decision, but the Court of Justice upheld the decision of the Commission. It concluded that "if inequality of opportunity between economic operators, and thus distorted competition, is the result of a State measure, such a measure constitutes an infringement of Article [106(1) TFEU] read together with Article [102 TFEU]."[171] In these circumstances, the Court ruled that to find a joint infringement of Articles 106(1) TFEU and 102, "all that is necessary is for the Commission to identify a potential or actual anti-competitive consequence liable to result from the State measure at issue."[172]

[2] Equality of Opportunity as a Guiding Principle in Case of Statutory Dominance

The question of equality or fairness in the context of antitrust proceedings has stimulated discussion in the antitrust community.[173] The ideal has even garnered it the

168. The German national law was an implementation of Directive 97/13/EC of the European Parliament and of the Council of 10 April 1997 on "A Common Framework for General Authorisations and Individual Licenses in the Field of Telecommunications Services," *OJ* L 117, 1997, p. 15.
169. CJEU, Case C-327/03, *ISIS Multimedia and Firma 02*, ECLI:EU:C:2005:622, §42.
170. *Id.* §§37-39 and 43-44.
171. CJEU, Case C-553/12 P, *Commission v. DEI*, ECLI:EU:C:2014:2083, §44.
172. *Id.* §46. Similarly, AG Wathelet opined that "*merely ... the risk* of abuse" is sufficient to trigger the application of Article 106(1) TFEU (emphasis added). *See* Opinion of AG Wathelet in Case C-553/12 P, *Commission v. DEI*, ECLI:EU:C:2013:807, §55.
173. Ezrachi, A. and Maurice E. Stucke. "The Fight over Antitrust's Soul." *Journal of European Competition Law & Practice* (2017): 1-2; and Lamadrid de Pablo, Alfonso. "Competition Law as Fairness." *Journal of European Competition Law & Practice* 8.3 (2017): 147-148.

somewhat derogative label of "hipster antitrust"[174] and has been virtually rejected as an overarching principle of enforcement.[175]

The most appropriate answer in this debate is to be found in the middle. We neither support a complete rejection nor an absolute adherence to the principle.[176] Positions of statutory dominance provide a middle ground for its application. The same is true for historical operators, although the principle must operate here with limitations.[177]

In the context of statutory dominance, there are two ramifications to the application of the principle of equality of opportunity. The *first* one is that the creation of market power by the state will always entail an inequality of opportunity for other undertakings. Thus, if as established in *Greek Lignite*, when inequality of opportunity arises or has the potential to arise from the exercise of an exclusive or special right, such measure constitutes an infringement of Article 106(1) TFEU, then it follows that virtually any creation of a dominant position by the grant of exclusive or special rights will breach Article 106(1) TFEU together with Article 102 TFEU. As we explained above, *statutory measures* hamper competition by creating unequal prospective conditions of competition. This raises several interesting questions, such as whether the theory of automatic abuse under Articles 102 and 106 TFEU should be proactively enforced to reduce the number of statutory created positions of dominance. However, this is not the focus of our current inquiry.

The *second* ramification of this principle, which is relevant to our inquiry, is related to the limited degree of freedom that the statutory dominant firm enjoys when it seeks to expand its activities beyond its statutory market or to protect its position. The willful creation of a dominant position by the State is not the result or efficient outcome of any competitive process. The support the statutory firm receives can be a competitive advantage inaccessible to any free market undertaking.

There is "inequality" and *inequality*.[178]

The *first* is the "inequality" that arises from within the competitive process. As in any process, which is inherently dynamic, in movement, the passing of time dictates that there will be winners and losers. Winners may be thus in a better position than losers to seize new opportunities resulting in evident inequalities: access to a larger base of consumers, investments, publicity, etc. This is the inequality inherent to the *dynamic process* of the free market. Other firms may want to imitate them or aspire to

174. Joshua D. Wright introduced the concept on Twitter; *see* Daly, Angela. "Beyond 'Hipster Antitrust': A Critical Perspective on the European Commission's Google Decision." *European Competition and Regulation Law Review* 1.3 (2017): 188-192.
175. Dolmans, Maurits and Wanjie LIN. "Fairness and Competition Law: A Fairness Paradox." *Concurrences* 4 (2017): 1-20.
176. Faulhaber, Gerald R. "Cross-Subsidy Analysis with More than Two Services." *Journal of Competition Law and Economics* 1.3 (2005): 441-448, at 443: "subsidy analysis focuses on fairness issues, as well as the potential for competitive entry (perhaps restricted in practice by regulation)."
177. *See* Chapter 3 for a discussion on the application of the principle of equality of opportunity to historical operators.
178. *See* Taleb, Nassim Nicholas. *Skin in the Game: Hidden Asymmetries in Daily Life.* Allen Lande, 2018, at pp. 128-131.

be them, and it is accepted they are not an odd or alien element to the process, but a fundamental part of it.[179] The set of incumbency advantages are available at "the start" of the process. Its introduction as a possible theory of harm or aggravating circumstance of antitrust liability goes against the competitive process itself.

Now, the *second* type of *inequality* is alien to the competitive process; it does not arise from within. This is the case of the statutory dominant firm which as has been shown is an exogenous imposition to the process. As such the position of market power is unwarranted and upsets the competitive process dynamics. Monopoly is at odds with competition here, and statutory dominance behavior must be subordinated to laxer thresholds of antitrust liability that neutralize its statutory advantages.

The principle of equality of opportunity must be constrained so it does not magnify the competitive process paradox.[180]

In an open market, firms continuously depart from different initial positions as the process of competition yields different temporal outcomes. An indiscriminate application of the principle of equality of opportunity would subvert the competitive process itself. It would require the State to constantly intervene in the process to reestablish some set of initial conditions. The generalized application of this principle in the context of antitrust is a "wholly illusory ideal"[181] and an attack against the competitive process. It would entail punishing a position of dominance that is the result of investment efforts or superior entrepreneurial insight, when the purpose of competition is exactly to do better than anyone else.

Thus, to protect the competitive process, in their analysis of abusive conduct the EU Courts must account for the fact that in the presence of a statutory monopoly the ability to enter into an industry or even create a competing product is limited by the state, and that the *statutory* advantages that accrue to the dominant firm can be extended over other markets where the firms compete in competition with the impossibility or imposed difficulty to secure those same advantages.[182]

[C] How to Incorporate the Statutory Origins of Firm Dominance in the Analysis of Abusive Conduct

As discussed, the principle of equality of opportunity is a guiding principle that serves to highlight potential exogenous inequalities deriving from statutory dominant firm conduct. As such, the Commission and the EU Courts cannot simply refer to it as a shortcut for establishing antitrust liability under Article 102 TFEU. First, they must

179. As well as one that arises from within but in breach of the rules that dictate the game. That is the case of an abuse of a dominant position or the case of an unlawful acquisition of market power. *See* Chapter 8 for a discussion.
180. *See*, similarly, Chapter 5.
181. Hayek, Friedrich A. *Law, Legislation and Liberty*, (Vol. 2) *The Mirage of Social Justice*. Routledge, [1976] 1998, at p. 85.
182. Akyürek-Kievits, H.E. "The Application of Article 86 of the EEC Treaty to State Monopolies" in J.H.V. Stuyck and A.J. Vossestein (eds.) *State Entrepreneurship, National Monopolies and European Community Law*, at p. 98.

establish what is the statutory advantage that the dominant firm uses, and then either elaborate or adapt the theory of harm in order to address the problematic.

We now turn to exploring four different paths to incorporate the statutory origins of dominance into the analysis of abusive behavior in Article 102 TFEU. In particular we advance, *first*, a different cost analysis for anticompetitive conduct; *second*, the imposition of a "proactive approach" toward facilitating entry; *third*, a serious incorporation of "less efficient" competitors in analysis of exclusionary behavior; and *lastly*, a limitation of objective justifications.

[1] Leveraging Statutory Advantages: A Cost Benchmark

A statutory dominant firm enjoys the comfort of knowing that its position is protected or supported by the state. This gives the statutory firm a privileged advantage to attack other markets.[183] It is not surprising that, albeit inadvertently, most of the abuse of dominance cases against statutory dominant undertakings relate to such behavior, often labeled as cross-subsidy.[184]

Under the overarching concept of cross-subsidization we consider all those practices whereby the statutory dominant firm achieves a competitive advantage over its rivals in an open market by virtue of statutory dominance. Here, the competitive peculiarity, as described before, is that non-statutory firms are denied or hindered to achieve those advantages that the statutory firm enjoys.[185] The underlying negative effect on the competitive process is the spillover of statutory disturbances into open markets. Any price-cost analysis in line with equality of opportunity should be able to capture this phenomenon in all instances. *Post Danmark I* provides a good reference for discussion.

The *Post Danmark I* Court considered that Post Danmark's pricing policy "*may* not be considered to amount to an exclusionary abuse merely because the price that undertaking charges one of those customers is lower than the average total costs attributed to the activity concerned, but higher than the average incremental costs pertaining to that activity." The conclusion that Post Danmark could not set prices below AIC is correct, but certainly incomplete. The question that remains is whether the threshold of antitrust liability was suitable to the statutory position of dominance that Post Danmark enjoyed. We do not think so.

When a statutory monopoly enters an open market, it can use its statutory advantages to upset the competitive process. It is not difficult to see that this scenario is fundamentally different from that of other dominant firms which, having gained a position of market power in an open competitive process on their merits, decide to enter a new market or become multiproduct firms. FK, Post Danmark's competitor in

183. This also gives the firm an incentive to live a quiet life in its non-contestable part of the market.
184. Faulhaber, Gerald R. "Cross-Subsidy Analysis with More than Two Services." *Journal of Competition Law and Economics* 1.3 (2005): 441-448, at 442: "It is only under conditions of regulation, in which a government authority establishes prices and restricts entry that the question of cross-subsidy arises."
185. Sappington, David E.M. and J. Gregory Sidak. "Competition Law for State-Owned Enterprises." *Antitrust Law Journal* 71.2 (2003): 479-523, 485.

the open market for unaddressed mail, did not enjoy the opportunity to gain any competitive advantages in the market of addressed mail.

A price-cost analysis in line with the peculiarities of statutory dominant firms would need to answer the following question: what would be the cost at which Post Danmark could provide the service of unaddressed mail on a stand-alone basis had it not had the possibility to rely on its statutory monopoly?

The stand-alone cost standard is the cost for a multi-service firm of providing one of its services alone.[186] It captures the highest possible cost that any efficient entrant would need to support if it cannot rely on other economies. In our view,[187] such standard provides a more appropriate economic tool to determine whether the prices charged by Post Danmark, a statutory monopoly, were abusive. This is unlike the AIC standard endorsed by the Court of Justice in *Post Danmark I*, which was also employed by the Commission in *Deutsche Post*.[188]

The stand-alone threshold includes those costs that are common to the set of services provided, "even if the costs are not incremental to the production of any one of the products individually."[189] Thus, assuming that the postal network distribution is a common cost, this would not constitute a part of the incremental cost of either addressed or unaddressed mail. Only when there are no synergies between distinct services the incremental cost would be the same as the stand-alone cost. In other words, the prices charged by Post Danmark would be anticompetitive if they were below the stand-alone cost of providing the unaddressed mail service, and not the incremental cost. This price-cost analysis would neutralize the advantages that it derives from having been vested the privilege of statutory market power and establish a level competitive field in markets open to competition.

On the other hand, it should be emphasized that the standard based on incremental costs should be left to assess single-firm behavior by statutory dominant firms and, to a limited extent, to historical operators and anticompetitively acquired dominance.[190] This way dominant firms will not be prevented from realizing

186. In *Deutsche Post* the price charged was already below AIC. This could explain why the Commission did not consider the laxer threshold of predation that a combinatorial form of incremental cost test would have allowed for. It is possible the Commission used the AIC cost benchmark because network capacity costs were "an additional burden" rather than an advantage for the undertaking. *See* Commission Decision, Case COMP/35.141, *Deutsche Post I* §10; *see also* Post Danmark, *Comments to DG Competition discussion paper on the application of Article 82 of the Treaty to exclusionary abuses, available at* http://ec.europa.eu/competition/antitrust/art82/032.pdf.

187. This was also the opinion delivered by AG Mengozzi in the same case. *See* Opinion of AG Mengozzi in Case C-209/10, *Post Danmark I*, ECLI:EU:C:2011:342, §§111-114; *see also* Faulhaber, Gerald R. "Cross-Subsidization: Pricing in Public Enterprises." *The American Economic Review* 65.5 (1975): 966-977.

188. Faulhaber, Gerald R. "Cross-Subsidy Analysis with More than Two Services." *Journal of Competition Law and Economics* 1.3 (2005): 441-448.

189. Sappington, David E.M. and J. Gregory Sidak. "Competition Law for State-Owned Enterprises." *Antitrust Law Journal* 71.2 (2003): 479-523, 489.

190. In the case of historical operators, so long as the legacy advantages subsist (*see* Chapter 3). For anticompetitively acquired dominance, so long as the result of applying such test is to neutralize the anticompetitively acquired market power (*see* Chapter 8).

economies or synergies between services, which they gained in efficient competition against other firms.

With this in mind, it is regrettable that the *Post Danmark I* Court did not seize the opportunity to establish a differentiating rule for statutory monopolies[191] once it had taken the step and ruled that legal origins of the dominant firm must be taken into account. Had the Court adopted a stand-alone cost standard for cases dealing with statutory monopoly positions this would have allowed for a better protection of the competitive process.

[2] A Proactive Approach Toward Facilitating Entry

It has been occasionally argued that dominant firms are subject to excessive thresholds of antitrust liability that are akin to placing them under the obligation to help their competitors. Theories of harm relating to a refusal to supply or to deal with a competitor are often portrayed as an example.[192] While requiring that dominant firms adopt an attitude that could be categorized as "helping competitors" goes against the competitive process itself,[193] this is not true when dealing with statutory dominant firms.

In *GVG/FS*, the Commission found that Ferrovie dello Stato (FS), the Italian railway, had abused its "statutory monopoly"[194] by denying GVG, a potential competitor, access to the train paths on the Domodossola-Milan route. Namely, FS had withheld information that was necessary to allow GVG to prepare an adequate business plan to provide cross-border rail passenger transport services. By withholding that information FS was capable to extend its statutory dominant position on the market for the access to infrastructure to the market for the provision of cross-border rail passenger transport.[195] This, the Commission held, constituted an abusive conduct.

A cursory reading of the *GVG/FS* decision would leave the impression that FS refused to provide some necessary information for GVG to compete—*à la Microsoft*—on the basis that GVG did not have a safety certificate. However, a more detailed reading shows that the Commission knowingly went a step further.[196]

The Commission considered that FS "should have taken a *proactive approach.*" This meant that "FS should have informed GVG that it is FS (Infrastruttura) itself which

191. Bien, Florian and Matthias Krah. "The Ruling of the CJEU in Post Danmark: Putting an End to Selective Price Cuts as an Abuse under TFEU Article 102 and Turning Towards a More Economic Approach." *European Competition Law Review* 10 (2012): 482-487.
192. Ridyard, Derek. "Compulsory Access under EC Competition Law - A New Doctrine of 'Convenient Facilities' and the Case for Price Regulation." *European Competition Law Review* 25 (2004): 669-673.
193. *See* Chapter 5.
194. Commission Decision, Case COMP/37.685, *GVG/FS Italian Railway*, §§82, 115, 116 and n. 65. The number of times that the Commission used the term "statutory monopoly" is remarkable. The Commission also considered that the railways are an essential facility, and that the duplication of the long-distance railway is prohibitive in terms of costs and that it is *impossible* to get the right of way.
195. *Id.* §124.
196. In fact, the Commission did not impose a fine due to the novelty of the case.

grants the safety certificate and *advised it of what is required to obtain such a certificate*" instead of refusing to provide on the basis of technical requirements[197] (emphasis added). In other words, the abuse was not so much about the refusal, but the (lack of) proactive help FS should have given to GVG to allow it to prepare a valid and competitive offer.

This "proactive approach" is reminiscent of the threshold of liability the EU Courts established in *Compagnie Maritime Belge* and *Post Danmark II*. In *Compagnie Maritime Belge*, the General Court ruled that since Cewal's agreement with the Zairian authorities included a provision for a possible derogation of Cewal's exclusivity, Cewal was "*under a duty to make reasonable use of the right* of veto conferred on it by the agreement in respect of third parties' access to the market"[198] (emphasis added). As we discussed, the Court eventually concluded that by *actively participating* in its implementation, Cewal had abused its position of dominance.[199] In a similar way, the *Post Danmark II* Court ruled that making the life of competitors "more difficult" could determine the anticompetitive effect of the rebates at issue.[200]

This threshold of liability is welcome *but* deserves caution and differentiation in its application. Namely, the "proactive approach" liability theory established by the Commission in *GVG/FS* must be restricted to statutory positions of dominance.[201] That is, its application must be directed to lowering *statutory* barriers to entry.[202] Only then, it is entirely appropriate and in line with the protection of the competitive process.[203]

A controlled application is fundamental since the explicit lack of interest in the origins of dominance leads the Commission to place all firms in a dominant position within the same box. Indeed, the Commission held in *GVG/FS* (following *Telemarketing*) that a dominant firm extending its position onto other markets may be abusive

197. Commission Decision, Case COMP/37.685, *GVG/FS Italian Railway*, §127.
198. GC, Joined Cases T-24/93 and T-25/93, T-26/93 and 28/93, *Compagnie Maritime Belge and Others v. Commission*, ECLI:EU:T:1996:139, §§104 and 108.
199. *Id.*, §109.
200. CJEU, Case C-23/14, *Post Danmark II*, ECLI:EU:C:2015:651, §42, citing Case C-549/10 P, *Tomra Systems and Others v. Commission*, EU:C:2012:221, §72.
201. This finding would be contrary to the *Stena Sealink* saga. In its 1992 *Stena Sealink*, the Commission stated that the obligation of nondiscrimination (meaning that the dominant firm is obliged to treat its competitors as users of its facility on equal terms as its own operations) applies irrespective of "whether dominance results from the ownership of a facility or from other factors." *See* Commission Decision, Case COMP/IV/34.174, *Stena Sealink/B&I - Holyhead*: Interim Measures (Jun. 11, 1992), §15. In its 1993 decision, the Commission did not review the merits of the complainant's argument that Stena Sealink "had relied on its exclusive rights to protect" its position as a ferry operator, and also received aid from government. Eventually Sealink was obliged to alter its sailing times, in a decision more affected by the natural monopoly characteristics of the port market. *See* Commission Decision, Case COMP/IV/34.689, *Sea Containers/Stena Sealink* (Dec. 21, 1993).
202. Commission Decision, Case COMP/37.685, *GVG/FS Italian Railway*, at §164, establishing that FS' remedies are appropriate since they dismantle existing entry barriers for international rail passenger services.
203. Eisenach, Jeffrey A. "Broadband Competition in the Internet Ecosystem." *American Enterprise Institute Working Papers* 35845 (2012).

"*even where the dominant position is due* not to the activity of the undertaking itself but to ... *provisions laid down by law* ... " (emphasis added).[204]

[3] Non-contestable Markets and Less Efficient Competitors

In *Post Danmark II* Post Danmark held 95% of the bulk mail market, of which 70% was covered by a statutory privilege. Analyzing the exclusionary effect of Post Danmark's rebates, the Court emphasized that Post Danmark's statutory monopoly constituted a non-contestable share of the demand. Since the retroactive rebates included the non-contestable share of the demand, customers would be strongly induced to reach the purchasing threshold (presumably established above 70%) so they could benefit from the discounts.[205] To compete with those terms, other providers of bulk mail would thus need to grant a rebate in the contestable share that would compensate the customer for the loss made in the non-contestable share.

For example, if customer A would purchase 10 units in excess of a 100 units threshold, assuming a retroactive rebate offered by Post Danmark of 6% and p = EUR 1 per unit,[206] customer A would pay EUR 103.4 in total. For a competitor to match the EUR 6.6 effective discount, and assuming that the 100 units correspond to the 70% statutory share, that competitor would have to offer 10 units at the price of 3.4 units. Assuming the average cost of serving each unit of both Post Danmark and its competitor to be ATC = EUR 0.4, a competitor would have to sell at loss to compete (i.e., EUR 3.4 for 10 units, where the ATC would be EUR 4).

This means that even an "equally efficient" competitor could be evinced from the market even if Post Danmark did not price below costs. Indeed, Post Danmark could spread the EUR 6.6 rebate over 110 units and need not incur below-cost pricing.

Now, the key element in *Post Danmark II* is, in our view, the correspondence between the non-contestable share of the demand with the share of the market under the control of a statutory monopoly. Such correspondence is concisely captured by AG Kokott in her opinion. Post Danmark's statutory monopoly originates from the fact that the non-contestable share was "*closed to competition from the outset.*"[207] In other words, competitors did not have the opportunity to compete for the non-contestable share of the demand and thus become truly as scale efficient as Post Danmark.

From a competitive process perspective, it is in this respect, we submit, that the protection of "less efficient" competitors suggested by both AG Kokott and the Court should be understood. That is, enforcing Article 102 TFEU to prevent the exclusion of

---

204. Commission Decision, Case COMP/37.685, *GVG/FS Italian Railway*, §141. The use of the word "even" reveals once again that the enforcement of Article 102 TFEU is more preoccupied with asserting liability against statutory dominant firms than in asserting liability *and* incorporating its differentiating attributes.
205. CJEU, Case C-23/14, *Post Danmark II*, ECLI:EU:C:2015:651, §35.
206. Post Danmark granted rebates between 6% and 16%. *See* Opinion of AG Kokott in Case C-23/14, *Post Danmark II*, ECLI:EU:C:2015:343, §38.
207. Opinion of AG Kokott in Case C-23/14, *Post Danmark II*, ECLI:EU:C:2015:343, §45.

competitors that were foreclosed by statutory means to compete "from the outset."[208] Other abuses than rebates should follow the same rationale.

[4] *Reducing the Range of Objective Justifications*

Lastly, we suggest that the balancing of justifications be made by taking due account of the statutory origins of dominance. The decision of the Commission in *OPCOM* provides an example of how this would work in practice.

In 2015, the Commission found the Romanian power exchange, OPCOM, to have abused its dominant position. The Romanian government set up OPCOM in 2001 as a subsidiary of Transelectrica, which was also set up by the government in 2000. OPCOM is a power exchange facilitating electricity trading at wholesale level in Romania by bringing multiple buyers and sellers together. The Commission found that OPCOM abused its dominant position by requesting, in a discriminatory manner, a value added tax (VAT) registration from foreign undertakings wishing to purchase electricity.

The Commission concluded that the abusive VAT requirement was an autonomous decision of OPCOM and a discriminatory practice on the grounds of nationality. In effect, the Romanian legislation did not require purchasers to have a registered VAT to buy electricity in the power exchange. Moreover, EU buyers are not exempted from VAT when buying from a Romanian seller. Simply, under the reverse charge mechanism,[209] they pay VAT to the tax authorities in their country of residence.[210] Therefore, OPCOM cannot collect the VAT from a foreign buyer, but it has to pay VAT to the seller of electricity. Although OPCOM can recover the VAT from the Romanian tax authorities later on, this setting creates a temporary but effectively negative cash-flow mismatch when the purchase of electricity by foreign firms exceeds the sale of electricity to Romanian firms. OPCOM thus claimed as an objective justification that requiring VAT registrations allowed to prevent a cash-flow mismatch estimated at EUR 22 million if the Romanian authorities would, in a worst-case scenario, only refund it after nine months.[211]

At the time of the abuse the wholesale market consisted of regulated and competitive segments. Since 2009 only state-owned producers of electricity were obliged by government to sell their output on the power exchange. Output by

---

208. In his regard, *Intel* purports an artificial division of the contestable and non-contestable share of the demand since competition was not statutorily closed or hampered from the outset, but rather was made possible through the investment efforts Intel realized in the first place. *See* Chapter 5 for a critique of the non-contestable share of the market construction.
209. Under Article 38 of the EU VAT Directive (and Article 132(1) of the Romanian Fiscal Code) in the case of the supply of electricity through the electricity distribution system, if the buyer is located in a different EU Member State than the seller, the seller does not pay VAT to the seller. However, the buyer must pay VAT to the relevant authorities where it is registered. It is called "reverse charge mechanism" since it reverses the tax liability from the seller to the buyer. *See* Council Directive 2006/112/EC of 28 November 2006 on the common system of value added tax *OJ* L 347, 11.12.2006, p. 1-118, *and* Commission Decision, Case COMP/39.984, *Romanian Power Exchange/OPCOM*, §69.
210. Commission Decision, Case COMP/39.984, *Romanian Power Exchange/OPCOM*, §168.
211. *Id.* §204-207.

state-owned firms accounted for 90% of the electricity production. This nonetheless, and before 2012, electricity could be traded in the competitive segment by way of bilateral agreements, brokers or the power exchange. However, by virtue of government action, since 2012 all the electricity trading in the "competitive" segment has to take place in the power exchange. This statutory decision placed OPCOM as the only power exchange and the only trading platform. OPCOM holds a statutory monopoly that has only increased its market power since its governmental creation by more government action.[212]

The Commission found that due to the creation of OPCOM's legal monopoly the risk and level of a potential mismatch was significantly reduced. This is because, with the exception of bilaterally concluded agreements on the basis of a letter from the energy regulator, *all* electricity transactions have to occur via OPCOM. Because of this statutory limitation the potential VAT mismatch is reduced significantly.[213] In other words, it is because OPCOM has a statutory monopoly that it can be completely sure that virtually all electricity transactions, both sales and purchases, will occur on its platform and nowhere else.

This finding rests on the very accurate idea that statutory market power is generally irremovable except by another act of government. Likely, it is based on the premise that the Romanian government coerced market players to transact through OPCOM. This degree of certainty the statutory monopoly enjoys is unlike any to be found in a market where competition has not been removed or hindered by an act of the State.

Interestingly, it shall be noted that the rejection of the objective justification followed the same logic as a recoupment test for predatory pricing.

OPCOM's behavior could not be objectively justified because the Commission noted OPCOM would certainly recover the mismatch. In other words, had OPCOM not been able to recoup the mismatch, it seems that the VAT registration requirement could have been justified.

Transposing the logic to predatory pricing abuses, a firm that is unable to recoup cannot be found guilty of anticompetitive behavior. On the contrary, consumers would have benefitted from lower prices for a certain period and the competitive process would have constrained the firm to price higher to recover those loses *ex post*. Unlike firms that owe their position of dominance to other causes than the state, a statutory dominant firm has a manifest ability to recoup its losses. It can raise its prices in its reserved market without attracting entry.[214]

---

212. "The only exception to the rule that all electricity transaction have to go via OPCOM relates to import and export transactions which—on the basis of a letter from the Energy Regulator—may be concluded bilaterally between two traders without the involvement of OPCOM." *See id.* §208.
213. *Id.* §§208-209.
214. Sappington, David E.M. and J. Gregory Sidak. "Competition Law for State-Owned Enterprises." *Antitrust Law Journal* 71.2 (2003): 479-523, 514-515 and n. 122. *See also* Chapter 3 for a discussion on why the recoupment requirement for predatory pricing is in line with the protection of the competitive *process*.

§2.07 THE APPLICATION OF ARTICLE 102 TFEU TO FOREIGN STATUTORY DOMINANCE

The EU Courts and the European Commission have struggled to differentiate statutory dominance from other causes of market power. The rulings in *Post Danmark I* and *Post Danmark II* have left the door open to such differentiation and have thus implicitly endorsed the Guidance Paper. Under the premise that EU competition law can treat differently statutory positions of dominance, the question that naturally arises is whether foreign statutory positions of dominance fall within the same category. The concept "foreign" refers to the support that any undertaking might receive from a state not member to the EU.

As a matter of consistency between standards, EU competition law should take into account the possibility that positions of dominance arise from *foreign* statutory support.

This is not a minor affair or question to discuss. As we have seen, the competitive dynamic between market-created undertakings and state-supported undertakings reveals an important competitive asymmetry that competition policy can help to correct. This competitive asymmetry is magnified in an increasingly globalized economy where many of its actors are firms supported by their respective governments. The growing use of geoeconomics to advance political objectives as an alternative to other means, such as war, has led to an increase of state-supported undertakings. It is thus not a matter of discrimination on the grounds of nationality, but rather a proposal that seeks to place the origins of market power at the center of any analysis of exclusionary conduct under Article 102 TFEU.

In this respect, the increasingly global competitive arena presents the EU Courts and the Commission with an opportunity to clarify and unify principles of application to firms that enjoy a statutory position of dominance, irrespective of their nationality. Our modestly narrow focus in this section is placed upon foreign statutory companies, with particular attention to dominant firms backed by the Chinese and Russian governments. The large amount of Chinese supported entities and its explicit industrial policy aimed at disadvantaging foreign competitors, make Chinese-backed companies a most suitable choice for study. Russia-supported undertakings pose a significant challenge as well in terms of proximity to the EU as evinced in the *Gazprom* case.[215]

We are aware that this competitive asymmetry can occur within the EU as well. Statutory dominant firms can operate in other Member States where the state in question does not interfere with the creation of market power. In particular, this "unbalanced market structure"[216] is the result of different levels of liberalization achieved by EU Member States. This situation continues to benefit statutory monopolies penetrating or investing in Member States where the liberalization of markets is

215. Case COMP/39.816, *Upstream gas supplies in Central and Eastern Europe (Gazprom)*. The decision does not discuss the statutory dominance of Gazprom.
216. Kronenberger, Vincent. 2001. "A Model of the Transformation Process of Statutory Monopolies in European Community Law: From Practice to Theory." *European Business Organization Law Review* 2 (2): 301-338, 338.

more advanced.[217] We briefly examine this scenario, in as much as in terms of substance all the above sections have implicitly covered it.

[A] Geoeconomics and Global Competition

In a globalized market any strong domestic economy *naturally* projects itself outside its national frontiers. But, in more recent years, economic means are increasingly being used in an *active* manner as tools to advance national objectives. The paradigm of international trade is thus changing. It is no longer about the natural projection or passive protection of a state's economy, but about the *strategic use* of economics to achieve geopolitical objectives.

At a general level, this embroiling of the state in economic affairs in a foreign arena has been described as "geoeconomics." Geoeconomics is "[t]he use of economic instruments to promote and defend national interests, and to produce beneficial geopolitical results; and the effects of other nations' economic actions on a country's geopolitical goals."[218]

Geoeconomics is not new. As we outlined above, during the mercantilist era states created and protected trade monopolies to compete in the international "arena." However, they did so on equal footing. The English, Dutch, Portuguese, French and Spanish crowns all embraced a mercantilist policy and thus protected their monopolies. Trading monopolies were created "with the specific intent to further state interests." European nations competed against each other, and so they did *their* trading companies.[219]

But the mercantilist era of trade statutory monopolies was not the only form of geoeconomics. In a similar manner, states embracing an open market economy may use their policies to serve their own geopolitical interests.[220] The state's number of economic instruments is virtually indefinite, and so are its goals.[221]

Today, in the global competitive arena there is a major unbalance of forces between statist or state capitalist economies like China or Russia and free market economies like the EU. For the latter, the tools that the free market offers limit the creation of statutory positions of dominance in the EU. An open market economy that protects the competitive process places the creation of statutory market power at odds with its system of free competition.[222] For the former, it is a return to the mercantilist

217. *Id.*
218. Blackwill, Robert D. and Jennifer M. Harris. *War by Other Means. Geoeconomics and Statecraft.* Harvard University Press, 2016, at p. 20.
219. Erikson, Emily. *Between Monopoly and Free Trade: The English East India Company, 1600-1757.* Princeton University Press, 2014, at p. viii.
220. Blackwill, Robert D. and Jennifer M. Harris. *War by Other Means. Geoeconomics and Statecraft.* Harvard University Press, 2016, at p. 32.
221. *See* Martiningui, Ana and Richard Youngs (eds.). *Challenges for European Foreign Policy in 2012. What Kind of Geo-economic Europe?* Fride, 2011.
222. CJEU, Case C-198/01, *Consorzio Industrie Fiammiferi (CIF) and Autorità Garante della Concorrenza e del Mercato*, ECLI:EU:C:2003:430, §47: "since the Treaty of Maastricht entered into force, the EC Treaty has expressly provided that in the context of their economic policy the

era where statutory dominance is a natural extension of State power. Thus, undertakings that are born and raised in a free market economy, find themselves competing against undertakings that are created and/or supported by more statist economies.

More importantly, foreign statutory monopolies in open market economies are much like "trojan horses" that interfere with the competitive process.[223] The phenomenon of foreign statutory market power is not negligible. Yet, there is a certain blindness in European competition policy as to the problem that it actually poses.[224] Chinese statutory firms (SOE, state-owned investment vehicles, state-backed or subsidized companies, local monopolies, etc.) are increasingly venturing into other markets "as a result of coordinated, state-financed campaigns."[225] While China's "Go Global" policy places government at the center of the internationalization of Chinese firms, Europe sees government as interference to internationalization.[226]

In the international competitive arena, firms are increasingly sensing an unlevel playing field when competing against Chinese statutory firms. "They are perceived to have the blank check book of the Chinese state at their disposal."[227] Aside from traditional sectors like energy or natural resources,[228] China pursues a strong mercantilist policy in the field of innovation designed to acquire foreign technology through state-owned investment vehicles, government aid, or pushing for the development of Chinese-only standards obstructing the entry of foreign firms to its markets.[229] As the Mercator Institute for China Studies reveals, the implementation of Beijing's "*Made in China 2025*" policy endorses a strong statist plan "so as to benefit and facilitate the economic dominance of Chinese enterprises and to disadvantage foreign competitors."[230]

---

activities of the Member States must observe the principle of an open market economy with free competition (*see* Articles 3a(1) and 102a of the EC Treaty (now Article 4(1) EC and Article 98 EC))."

223. Petit, Nicolas. "Chinese State Capitalism and Western Antitrust Policy." *Concurrences* 4 (2016): 69-79, using the term "Trojan horse" to refer to the infiltration of Chinese economic governance through a "mega-wave" of mergers and acquisitions. *See also* Bremmer, Ian. "The End of the Free Market: Who Wins the War Between States and Corporations?" *European View* 9.2 (2010): 249-252.
224. *Id.*
225. Blackwill, Robert D. and Jennifer M. Harris. *War by Other Means. Geoeconomics and Statecraft.* Harvard University Press, 2016, at p. 50.
226. United Nations Conference on Trade and Development, *World Investment Report 2017*, UNCTAD/WIR/2017, *available at* http://unctad.org/en/PublicationsLibrary/wir2017_en.pdf.
227. Freeman III, Charles W. "The Commercial and Economic Relationship" *in* David Shambaugh (ed.) *Tangled Titans: The United States and China.* Rowman & Littlefield Publishers, 2012, at p. 202.
228. Bräutigam, Deborah and Tang Xiaoyang. "Economic Statecraft in China's New Overseas Special Economic Zones: Soft Power, Business or Resource Security?" *International Affairs* 88.4 (2012): 799-816; and Alon, Ilan, Hua Wang, Jun Shen and Wenxian Zhang. "Chinese State-Owned Enterprises Go Global." *Journal of Business Strategy* 35.6 (2014): 3-18.
229. Atkinson, Robert D., Nigel Cory and Stephen J. Ezell. "Stopping China's Mercantilism. A Doctrine of Constructive, Alliance-Backed Confrontation." *ITIF* (March 2017): 1-66.
230. Wübbeke, Jost, et al. "Made in China 2025: The Making of a High-Tech Superpower and Consequences for Industrial Countries." *Mercator Institute for China Studies* 2 (2016).

[B] Abuse of Foreign Statutory Dominance

Our findings above (*see* section 2.05) apply in the same manner to foreign statutory positions of dominance. After all, foreign statutory dominant firms continue to be dominant firms that are fundamentally at odds with the competitive process. However, the question remains as to what peculiarities of foreign statutory dominance could affect the enforcement of Article 102 TFEU as suggested above (*see* section 2.06).

When statist economies interfere with market forces, neutralizing the exercise of such power might be difficult even for other sovereign nations. As Bremmer has put it, statist capitalism is by "its very nature ... exclusionary; it promotes state goals at the expense of outsiders."[231]

In EU competition law this difficulty to neutralize foreign statutory dominance is normatively evident. The European Commission does not have the power to limit the creation of foreign statutory dominance under Article 106(1) TFEU or State aid provisions. Indeed, both provisions are directed against measures by EU Member States.[232]

This notwithstanding, if the enforcement of Article 102 TFEU follows the mandate of *Post Danmark I* and truly aims at discussing the statutory origins of dominance, whether foreign or not,[233] the nationality of the undertaking is irrelevant. What matters is the statutory source of market power of the undertaking. This is not about crony protectionism. It is about ensuring a truly free and competitive market (as an alternative to state capitalism), where, it shall be reminded, competition law is just one tool among many others. The objective is to vigorously enforce competition law against any anticompetitive behavior of any statutory dominant firm.

Indeed, this is what the EU Courts indirectly did in *Compagnie Maritime Belge*. If one foregoes the formalistic analysis of AG Fennelly in *Compagnie Maritime Belge*, the agreement Cewal and the Zairian authorities had concluded, subtly granted or secured a statutory position of dominance in Cewal's trade route. That is why Compagnie Maritime Belge (belonging to the Cewal shipping conference) claimed, in light of the principle of international comity, that neither the conclusion of the agreement with Zaire nor the exercise of the rights conferred by it could be subject to Article 102 TFEU. Generally, under the principle of international comity, a State must refrain from judging acts of another State carried out in its own territory.[234]

The General Court responded that the only conduct being judged was not the conclusion of an agreement between the Zairian government and Cewal, but the

231. Bremmer, Ian. "The End of the Free Market: Who Wins the War Between States and Corporations?" *European View* 9.2 (2010): 249-252, at 251.
232. To our knowledge, the EU Courts have not discussed this issue.
233. Guidelines on the application of EEC competition rules in the telecommunications sector (1991/C 233/02) *OJ* C 233, 6.9.1991, p. 2-26, §18: "... competition rules apply in a non-discriminatory manner to EEC undertakings and to non-EEC ones which have access to the EEC market."
234. GC, Joined Cases T-24/93 and T-25/93, T-26/93 and 28/93, *Compagnie Maritime Belge and Others v. Commission*, ECLI:EU:T:1996:139, §88.

unilateral behavior of the latter. Whether Cewal is the holder of an exclusive right or a concession is not enough to exclude the existence of abusive behavior.[235]

Another noteworthy scenario is the application of Article 102 TFEU to acquisitions subsidized by foreign State funds. The pervasive wave of acquisitions by Chinese-backed companies[236] could face a setback if the Commission and the EU Courts took due account of the statutory origins of those resources. As advocated above, this would require a reassessment of *UPS Express* whereby Article 102 TFEU could catch not only a purchase of assets with "abusive rents" but also with "statutory rents."[237]

Importantly, statutory foreign dominant firms will not necessarily be disadvantaged if they cannot find antitrust exoneration in Article 106(1) TFEU, or any other provision when their behavior is mandated by the state. Lacking an example from the EU judicature the following application of US antitrust law serves as an example.

In *Vitamin C*,[238] the US Court of Appeals was bound to rule over foreign mandated anticompetitive conduct. In 2005, purchasers of Vitamin C brought an antitrust action under Section 1 against Chinese manufacturers for conspiring to fix prices and the supply of Vitamin C between 2001 and 2005. The market power of the Chinese vitamins producers was the result of a state-enforced cartel. The cartel was yet another step of the Chinese government to facilitate industry-wide consolidation initiated in the 1990s to prevent a fall in Vitamin C prices, that ultimately led Chinese suppliers to capture 60% of the worldwide market in 2001.

For the first time,[239] the Chinese government (Chinese Ministry of Commerce) filed an amicus curia to support the Chinese manufacturers' submission. In short, the Chinese government explicated, and the Court deferred, that Chinese regulations "*mandated*" that they coordinate prices and limit supply.[240] The Court held that "Recognizing China's strong interest in its protectionist economic policies and given the direct conflict between Chinese policy and our antitrust laws, we conclude that China's 'interests outweigh whatever antitrust enforcement interests the United States may have in this case as a matter of law.'"[241]

The involvement of the Chinese government to defend the cartel-like behavior of Chinese manufacturers raises fundamental questions of geoeconomics and deference

235. *Id.* §84.
236. Yoshida, Junko. "Lurking Behind Every M&A Is China." *EE Times* (Dec. 13, 2016).
237. Opinion of AG Stix-Hackl in Joined Cases C-34/01 to C-38/01, *Enirisorse SpA v. Ministero delle Finanze*, ECLI:EU:C:2002:643, §62: "If one regards the selective allocation of State funds to a particular undertaking as the grant of an exclusive right to that undertaking, with the consequence that such a grant itself gives the undertaking a dominant position, the law on State aid is deprived of all effect."
238. *In re: Vitamin C Antitrust Litigation*, 837 F.3d 175 (2d Cir. 2016).
239. Wang, Dingding Tina. "When Antitrust Met WTO: Why US Courts Should Consider US-China WTO Disputes in Deciding Antitrust Cases Involving Chinese Exports." *Columbia Law Review* (2012): 1096-1142.
240. *In re: Vitamin C Antitrust Litigation*, 837 F.3d 175 (2d Cir. 2016), at 191: "Deferring to the Ministry's explanation of what is legally required under its system is all the more important where, as here, the record evidence shows a clear disparity between China's economic regulatory regime and our own."
241. *In re: Vitamin C Antitrust Litigation*, 837 F.3d 175 (2d Cir. 2016), at 194.

toward different economic systems. In the US, the balance titled in favor of China's industrial policy interests over US' antitrust interests. It remains to be seen how the European Commission and the EU Courts will solve such an issue that is likely to arise in the near future. Surely, a balancing exercise will be required, and the different settings of each case will determine its outcome.[242]

§2.08 CONCLUSION

Although Article 102 TFEU is not the only solution to the problem of statutory market power,[243] it can be used as an effective tool to prevent its abuse and extension into other markets. The benefits that can be thus achieved are of paramount importance to free markets and they cannot compare to those efforts against "other" dominant firms.[244] Looking into the statutory origins of firm dominance obliges us to reconsider thresholds of antitrust liability where equality of opportunity should become a guiding principle. Furthermore, exploring statutory dominance has provided us with a first glance as to how the competitive process is affected in different ways by the origins of firm dominance.

242. *See, e.g.*, *In re Maxwell Commc'n Corp.*, 93 F.3d 1036 (2d Cir. 1996), at 1046: "Comity, in the legal sense, is neither a matter of absolute obligation, on the one hand, nor of mere courtesy and good will, upon the other."

243. *See* Sokol, D. Daniel. "Limiting Anticompetitive Government Interventions that Benefit Special Interests." *George Mason Law Review* 17 (2009): 119-190.

244. Hayek, Friedrich A. *Law, Legislation and Liberty*, (Vol. 3) *The Political Order of a Free People*. Routledge, [1979] 1998, at p. 88.

CHAPTER 3

Historical Operators: The Legacy of the State

§3.01 INTRODUCTION

As we showed in the previous Chapter, States have ever since their existence established monopolies for the provision of certain goods and services. Fiscal purposes, building state power and theories of ruinous competition led States to create monopolies.[1] But, the creation of statutory monopolies came at the expense of the competitive process. As Adam Smith constantly recalled, the main restraints of competition were the exclusive privileges of guilds and corporations granted by the State and regulated companies.[2]

Following on the preceding Chapter, our research question for this chapter is not one relating to *current* statutory monopolies. It is about *former* statutory monopolies and their footprint in the competitive process now that they have become "*historical operators*." How much of the statutory restraints to competition remain once markets

1. *See, e.g.*, Bordo, Michael D. and Roberto Cortés-Condo (eds.). *Transferring Wealth and Power from the Old World to the New World: Monetary and Fiscal Institutions in the 17th through the 19th Centuries*. Cambridge: Cambridge University Press, 2001. As an illustration of the concerns for ruinous competition in the US, *Addyston Pipe and Steel Co. v. United States*, 175 U.S. 211 (1899) upheld the defense of "ruinous competition" in the framework of a cartel in the steel pipes manufacturers industry. For an extended review of the literature and US case law on "ruinous competition," *see* Hovenkamp, Herbert. *Enterprise and American Law, 1836-1937*. Harvard University Press, 1991, at pp. 311-322.
2. Smith, Adam. *An Inquiry into the Nature and Causes of the Wealth of Nations*. Econlib [1776] 2009, Book I, Chapter 10, Part II *and* Book V, Chapter 1, Part III. "The exclusive privilege of an incorporated trade necessarily restrains the competition, in the town where it is established, to those who are free of the trade." And when discussing regulated companies "The terms of admission into the Hamburgh Company are now said to be quite easy, and the directors either have it not their power to subject the trade to any burdensome restraint or regulations" and "the clothiers and free traders of the West of England [had] complained of them to parliament as of monopolists who confined the trade and oppressed the manufactures of the country."

are open and *former* statutory monopolies become *historical* operators that face competition?

One can intuit that in the presence of former statutory monopolies, history matters.[3] Not surprisingly, the legacy effect of former statutory monopolies is manifest in the Commission's efforts to "level the playing field." Similar statements abound. For instance, the concept of "competitive neutrality" strongly advocated by the Organisation for Economic Co-operation and Development (OECD) is concerned with positions of dominance where the State is at its origins.[4] Their distinguishable *historic* position has also put them at the forefront of the Commission's enforcement priorities. In the energy market, for example, competition rules are to be actively enforced "in particular where legacy advantages of historical operators act as a barrier to entry."[5]

These statements bring to surface what was an open secret. The enforcement of competition law against historical operators has been going on ever since they started facing competition. Historical operators purportedly have a distinct footprint in the competitive process: a distinguishable legacy position that originates in the State and in a market that was closed to competition. To these we dedicate the following pages.

In particular, this chapter aims to discover whether the EU Courts have treated historical operators in a distinctive manner through quasi-automatic findings of dominance, the establishment of different anticompetitive foreclosure tests or specific theories of harm. In other words, we seek to corroborate the extent and manner in which the statutory legacy of these firms has been incorporated into the analysis of abusive behavior. Although the linkage with regulation is unavoidable, we should underline that our inquiry is only concerned with the treatment of historical operators under competition law, and more in particular, under Article 102 TFEU.

In short, this chapter addresses a simple question: is there and should there be, from an antitrust perspective, a *lex specialis* for historical operators?

The remainder of this chapter is structured as follows. Section 3.02 explains why the term "*historical operator*" is preferred to the concept of incumbent. Section 3.03 is a short reminder of *Post Danmark* and proposes to draw an analytical dividing line between the before and after *Post Danmark I* case law.[6] Section 3.04 analyzes and puts forward an orderly structure of the competitive variables that the case law pre-*Post Danmark I* has factored in their analyses of historical operator's unilateral behavior. Section 3.05 analyzes whether post-*Post Danmark I* case law has made a more diligent effort to take into account the historical origins of former legal monopolies. Section 3.06

3. Sewel, William H. "Three Temporalities: Toward a Sociology of the Event." *The Historic Turn in the Human Sciences* (1990): 1-30, at 16: "what has happened at an earlier point in time will affect the possible outcomes of a sequence of events occurring at a later point in time."
4. OECD, *Competitive Neutrality: Maintaining a Level Playing Field Between Public and Private Business*, 2012, at p. 15: "Competitive neutrality is also concerned with the competitive position of government-influenced private entities (*e.g.*, licensed operators, *legacy rights, recently privatised companies, national champions*, or where the state is a relevant shareholder)" (emphasis added).
5. Communication from the Commission on Making the Internal Energy Market Work, COM/2012/0663 final, at §3.1.2.
6. For language economy, we use the term case law to refer to both decisions of the EU Commission as well as judgments rendered by the CJEU.

discusses the termination date of the "historical operator tag" and how it affects its incentives to behave anticompetitively. Section 3.07 concludes.

§3.02 UNIFYING TERMINOLOGY

Before turning to the core of our inquiry, a conceptual and terminological clarification is in order.

The English translation of the case law of the EU Courts and Commission refer to historical operators as "*incumbents*." These are the incumbent telecom operator,[7] the incumbent gas supplier,[8] etc. Some strands of the literature on market regulation do so as well. But as will be explained, it is better and more accurate to use the concept "historical operator" over that of "incumbent."

First, using the term "*historical operator*" as a literal translation of the French version of the case law of the EU Courts ("*opérateur historique*") is more expressive and orderly.[9] It underlines the State origins and legacy component of these positions of dominance. It also accurately conveys the idea that antitrust agencies and courts are trying to capture: that the firm used to be a state-created and sustained monopoly. A historical operator thus need not necessarily be the monopolist in a network. It simply is the firm that came to life as a result of State intervention, concomitantly opened a new market and subsequently, after liberalization or privatization, faced competition.

Second, using the term incumbent in the sense of a state-created monopoly can be mischievous.[10] The concept of incumbency comes from IO and was progressively introduced to replace the concept of monopoly to capture the strategies that the firm could use to either accommodate or deter market entry.[11] In short, whatever its origins, in the IO literature an incumbent is a firm that is already established in the market and that faces potential competition. The distinction is not void because, as will be shown, the effects of incumbency in the process depend on more than just being a firm already established in the market.[12]

In this sense, historical operators can be categorized as a particular type of incumbent firm that faces either actual or potential competition. But, although this incumbent-entrant dynamic is fundamental to the competitive process, the historical operator displays a particularity. These are undertakings that emerged under the impetus of the State and in the absence of competition *for* the market. Historical operators came to life under State ownership or protection and functioned in a closed market. However, subject to several processes of liberalization or privatization they

7. CJEU, Case C-280/08 P, *Deutsche Telekom v. Commission*, ECLI:EU:C:2010:603.
8. GC, Case T-370/09, *GDF Suez SA v. Commission*, EU:T:2012:333.
9. *See* the French version of CJEU, Case C-280/08 P, *Deutsche Telekom*, EU:C:2010:603, and GC, Case T-370/09, *GDF Suez SA v. Commission*, EU:T:2012:333.
10. CJEU, Case C-544/03, *Mobistar and Belgacom Mobile*, ECLI:EU:C:2005:518, at §49, where the English version translates "*opérateur historique*" into "*traditional operator*."
11. Reinganum, Jennifer F. "Uncertain Innovation and the Persistence of Monopoly." *The American Economic Review* 73:4 (1983): 741-748.
12. Chen, P.L., Charles Williams and Rajshree Agarwal. "Growing Pains: Pre-entry Experience and the Challenge of Transition to Incumbency." *Strategic Management Journal* 276 ((July 2011) 2012): 252–276, 256.

now face constraints in an open market.[13] As such, there is usually only one historical operator in each country, but several possible incumbents in the same country. Now, after liberalization has taken place, the national historical operator competes with either new entrants or historical operators from other countries.

In conclusion, historical operators, also referred to as former legal monopolies, are the dominant incumbents we dedicate this chapter.

§3.03 THE *POST DANMARK* OBITER DICTUM: A REMINDER

As explained in the preceding chapter,[14] *Post Danmark* still enjoyed a statutory monopoly at the time of its abusive conduct. This notwithstanding, *Post Danmark I* and *II* are essential to the application of Article 102 TFEU to historical operators.

The *Post Danmark I* Court established that "when the existence of a dominant position has its origins in *a former legal monopoly*, that fact has to be taken into account" (emphasis added).[15]

Post Danmark II took explicit account of the fact that Post Danmark's position in the non-contestable part of the market was *still* protected by a statutory monopoly.[16] Interestingly, the Court did not refer to the *Post Danmark I* obiter dictum. AG Kokott did. In her Opinion, she contended that the origins of dominant firms, in a generic way, needed to be taken into account when analyzing the anticompetitive effects of unilateral conduct.

The case law that came after *Post Danmark I* explicitly accounted for its obiter dictum, i.e., to take into account the fact that some dominant firms were former legal monopolies.[17] At an agency level, the Commission found that *Slovak Telekom* had abused its dominant position by refusing to supply access to its local loop and by engaging in margin squeeze pricing. At the EU Courts' level, the GC took into account of the state origins of the polish telecom operator in *Orange Polska*. Has the *Post Danmark I* principle (re)-shaped the enforcement of Article 102 TFEU? We examine this question under section 3.05.

It is noteworthy that the *Post Danmark I* obiter dictum was not endorsed by any reference to previous case law. However, a careful reading of the pre-*Post Danmark I* case law against historical operators shows that both the EU Courts and Commission did take the origins of these dominant firms into account. In the following section (§3.04), we seek to demonstrate this and explain *how* the EU Courts and Commission factored the origins of former legal monopolies in their analyses.

13. *See*, for instance, in the field of telecommunications, Bacache, Maya, Marc Bourreau and Germain Gaudin. "Dynamic Entry and Investment in New Infrastructures: Empirical Evidence from the Fixed Broadband Industry." *Review of Industrial Organization* 44.2 (2014): 179-209, clarifying that in their particular research "incumbents [are] the historical fixed-line operators or former monopolies."
14. *See* Chapter 2 for a detailed analysis of the *Post Danmark* saga.
15. CJEU, Case C-209/10, *Post Danmark I*, ECLI:EU:C:2012:172, §23.
16. *Id.* §§35 and 39 where the Court explains, following AG Kokott (*see* Opinion of AG Kokott in Case C-23/14, *Post Danmark II*, ECLI:EU:C:2015:343, §38), that the suction effect of the rebate scheme was exacerbated by Post Danmark's existing statutory monopoly.
17. CJEU, Case C-209/10, *Post Danmark I*, ECLI:EU:C:2012:172, §23.

§3.04 HISTORICAL OPERATORS BEFORE *POST DANMARK I*

This section reviews the case law to understand how the concept of historical operator plays a role in competition analysis. The structure that follows is in itself and attempt to bring out the particularities of historical operators under a common general framework.[18] To that end, section 3.04[A] is empirical: it reviews how historical operators are described in the case law. The following sections are more analytical. Section 3.04[B] discusses the case law against the background that both the economic and strategy literature provide, in which the statutory origins of historical operators have been said to have a particular imprint in the competitive process. Sections 3.04[C] and 3.04[D] explain why legacy advantages and entry timing dynamics are essential to the competitive process. Section 3.04[E] addresses how the incentives to invest and innovate of historical operators can change the way in which competition law is enforced. Section 3.04[F] concludes.

This section will show that the case law exhibits the underlying assumption that historical operators deserve special consideration. Nevertheless, that very same case law fails to explain in a consistent, or otherwise structured manner, *how* the fact that the dominant firm is a historical operator plays a role in the analysis of single-firm behavior. The opposite is true. The relevance of historical operators and their statutory legacy overlaps at different levels of the analysis, which tends to be merely descriptive, and generally in a scattered, non-cohesive and unidirectional manner.

[A] Describing Historical Operators

Several cases at both agency and the EU Courts level discuss how historical operators developed their firm capabilities shielded from competition and/or with public resources. These firms rose to dominance not because they outcompeted other firms in the market, but because they were the only firms in their respective geographical territories. They were born dominant, and their origins were generally founded on or supported with public resources.

In 2003, the Commission took its first decision against the abusive behavior of a historical operator in a market open to competition in *Deutsche Telekom*. The Commission recalled in its decision that the network of Deutsche Telekom, the historical telecommunications operator in Germany, had been built using public resources. Deutsche Telekom had enjoyed a legal monopoly the rents of which were used to strengthen its position. Only after liberalization Deutsche Telekom became a *former* legal monopoly and started facing entry.[19]

Following *Deutsche Telekom*, other cases distilled the same descriptive stories. In *Wanadoo*, the EU Courts and Commission emphasized that France Télécom occupied "a special position on the market" as the historical telecommunications operator in

18. While the dissection of the principles and tests of antitrust liability is purely positive (what the Commission and the EU Courts have said), the structure under which they are presented and the analytical discussion is fundamentally normative (how it ought to be).
19. Commission Decision, Case COMP/37.451, 37.578, 37.579, *Deutsche Telekom*, §§6, 7 and 13.

France.[20] And, although the case related to the predatory prices that its subsidiary Wanadoo was charging, the General Court considered that such relationship could not be separated from the assessment of Wanadoo's conduct.[21]

In *Telefónica*, the Commission emphasized that Telefónica had rolled out its network while protected by exclusive rights and that it could use its legal monopoly rents to fund other investments.[22] The assessment of Telefónica's dominant position and margin squeeze abuse is colored with numerous references to its position as a historical operator and the legacy advantages it enjoyed. The Commission insisted on the fact that these where obtained after decades under the protection of the state that "shielded [Telefónica] from competition."[23] In numerous occasions the Commission stressed that Telefónica's network loops were "funded by monopoly rents" during its time as a legal monopoly[24] and that its infrastructure was "inherited from the former legal monopoly."[25]

Several other cases involving historical operators follow the same pattern described above. In *Distrigaz*,[26] the Commission highlighted that Distrigas, the Belgian distributor of natural gas, maintained its inherited position of dominance even many years after liberalization.[27] In *TeliaSonera*, the Court of Justice held that "the competitive structure is also still highly influenced by the former monopolistic structure."[28] In *Orange Polska*, the Commission not only considered that Orange Polska had rolled out its infrastructure with state subsidies and had "for decades" funded its investments through monopoly rents, but also that "preferential governmental policy" and "State funds" had shielded it from competition.[29]

However, not all cases involving historical operators have described the State origins of historical operators. Generally, cases involving historical operators in the energy sector say little as to the State origins of these undertakings.[30] The fact that most of these cases have been addressed under commitment decisions can explain why the origin of dominant firms has not been prominently described.[31] A notable exception to

20. GC, Case T-340/03, *France Télécom v.* Commission, ECLI:EU:T:2007:22, §68.
21. *Id.* §§69-70.
22. Commission Decision, Case COMP/38.784, *Wanadoo España v. Telefónica*, §1.
23. *Id.* §303.
24. Commission Decision, Case COMP/38.784, *Wanadoo España v. Telefónica*, §167.
25. *Id.* at §43 (inherited), §70 (inherited), §167 (monopoly rents), §241 (inherited), §256 (monopoly rents), §273 (inherited), §301 (monopoly rents), §625 (monopoly rents), and §632 (monopoly rents).
26. Commission Decision, Case COMP/37.966, *Distrigaz*.
27. The Imperial Continental Gas Association, a UK firm of private foundation, founded Distrigas. Nevertheless, it operated in Belgium under a protected regime.
28. CJEU, Case C-52/09, *TeliaSonera*, ECLI:EU:C:2011:83, §109.
29. Commission Decision, Case COMP/39.525, *Telekomunikacja Polska* (commonly known as "*Orange Polska*"), §§1, 645, 674 and 809.
30. Commission Decisions, Case COMP/39.388, *German Electricity Wholesale Market*; and Case COMP/39.389, *German Electricity Balancing Market* ("*E.ON AG*"). This has not prevented the Commission from imposing stringent structural remedies in several cases involving energy historical energy operators. For instance, in *E.ON AG*, the Commission ordered the divestiture of approximately 5,000 MW of E.ON's generating capacity and of its transmission system business. E.ON AG was the result of a merger between VEBA AG, founded in 1929 by the State of Prussia.
31. Commission Decision, Case COMP/39.315, *ENI*. Commission Decision, Case COMP/39.402, *RWE Gas Foreclosure*.

this can be found in *Gaz de France*. In its preliminary assessment the Commission found that a substantial part of GDF's import capacity "had generally been reserved for historical reasons and had not been assigned to GDF Suez by any transparent or non-discriminatory procedure."[32]

Except for commitments decisions, the case law shows a certain concern with the legacy effects of former legal monopolies in the competitive process. From an economic perspective this concern seems *a priori* warranted. As regulated environments necessitate of different foreclosure rules than those developed for open competitive markets,[33] the same is true when the effects of State intervention persist after the opening of markets. Once the statutory monopoly becomes a *historical* operator, the market does not reboot and build up from a tabula rasa, but the legacy effects of the historical operator can be sustained over time. In this situation, it seems reasonable that analysis of single-firm conduct under Article 102 TFEU takes the legacy effects (its advantages *and* disadvantages) into account.

[B] The Absence of Competition *for* the Market and State Resources

With this backdrop, there are two *ex ante* competitive variables that play a role in the way competition currently takes place. Although described in passing in the case law, we seek to uncover them by putting forward two explicit frameworks and teachings from economics, strategy and morals. *First* (section 3.04[B][1]), the existence of a non-competitive environment conducive to dominant positions, i.e., the absence of competition *for* the market. *Second* (section 3.04[B][2]), the fact that those dominant positions were not only shielded from competition but also funded by State resources.

[1] The Absence of Competition for (and in) the Market

The term competition for the market has been used to define pre-entry competitive dynamics. It is often called "winner-takes-all" competition to become the dominant standard.[34]

While competition for the market and winner-takes-all scenarios mean that the market will select a winner from a pool of *n* firms, in the case of historical operators the opposite competitive scenario is true. As discussed in the preceding Chapter, the initial cycle of competition is either inexistent or weak and tilted by the State in favor of a single firm. This means that the origin and sustainability of historical operators is not forged in a competitive arena against other actual or potential firms. Put differently, the statutory monopolist has not "*won*" its position against other firms. It is not the fittest

32. Commission Decision, Case COMP/39.316, *Gaz de France*, §28.
33. Laffont, Jean-Jacques and Jean Tirole. *Competition in Telecommunications*. MIT Press, 2001, at p. 136, discussing fair and reasonable access mandates: "Regulatory rules can change the private and social costs and benefits of foreclosure."
34. Besen, Stanley M. and Joseph Farrell. "Choosing How to Compete: Strategies and Tactics in Standardization." *The Journal of Economic Perspectives* 8.2 (1994): 117-131.

survivor. Quite to the contrary, the State selects a "*winner*" (the former legal monopoly) from a pool of just one firm and bans (by granting a legal monopoly) any other firm from entering the market.

This *ex ante* noncompetitive dynamic has several consequences in the way competition will eventually develop in the market where the statutory monopoly becomes *historical*. We explain *why*.

First, economists and strategists have argued that competition for the market can act as an efficient substitute for competition in the market when entry in the competition for the market (*t*-1) is free.[35] However, preventing competition to act as a Darwinian disciplining mechanism in selecting the most efficient firms decreases productive efficiency, which will in turn result in higher prices and lower welfare.[36]

The benefits that competition for the market would bring about are thus lost. In fact, extensive economic research strongly suggests that overall former legal monopolies are less efficient and less profitable than otherwise comparable firms.[37] Among other possible explanations for this, the management literature has consistently remarked that the lack of entrants *for* the market is a fundamental factor that is positively correlated to a firm's performance.[38] Their existence and persistence in the market is not the result of effective competition for the market and the provision of superior products or services.[39]

Second, as Jean-Jacques Laffont and Tirole emphasize, "in the absence of competition for the market, 'winning' generates no information."[40] The process of competition for the market reveals information on price, costs and the competitive dynamics, which in turn enrich the regulator's and other firm's understanding of the market. The statutory reduction or elimination of competition for the market impedes the reduction of information asymmetries between the historical operator and new entrants.[41] On the contrary, when entry is free, new firms are faced with uncertainties

35. Demsetz, Harold. "Why Regulate Utilities?" *The Journal of Law and Economics* 11.1 (1968): 55-65. Etro, Federico. *Competition, Innovation and Antitrust. A Theory of Market Leaders and Its Policy Implications*. Springer, 2007.
36. Motta, Massimo. *Competition Policy. Theory and Practice.* Cambridge University Press, 2004, at p. 51.
37. Megginson, William L. and Jeffry M. Netter. "From State to Market: A Survey of Empirical Studies on Privatization." *Journal of Economic Literature* 39.2 (2001): 321-389.
38. Bayus, Barry L. and Rajshree Agarwal. "The Role of Pre-entry Experience, Entry Timing, and Product Technology Strategies in Explaining Firm Survival." *Management Science* 53.12 (2007): 1887-1902. *See* Chapter 6 for a detailed discussion on pre-entry experience and other intangible resources.
39. Demsetz, Harold. "Industry Structure, Market Rivalry, and Public Policy." *The Journal of Law & Economics* 16.1 (1973): 1-9.
40. Laffont, Jean-Jacques and Jean Tirole. *Competition in Telecommunications*. MIT Press, 2001 at p. 49.
41. For example, information asymmetries are very strong in the postal sector where new entrants face the cost-benefit uncertainty of serving end-users in remote areas. *See* Costa, Carlos. "On the Use of Reverse Auctions to Designate Universal Postal Service Providers" *in* Michael A. Crew and Paul R. Kleindorfer (eds.) *Multi-modal Competition and the Future of Mail*. Edward Elgar Publishing, 2012, at p. 296.

that the historical operator has left behind due to the lead-time of the monopoly period in the industry protected from competition.[42]

Relatedly, the lack of information prevalent at a governmental level can also indirectly affect new entry. For instance, during ENI's legal monopoly in the supply and distribution of energy in Italy, ENI was responsible for designing national energy policy. However, after liberalization, and due to the lack of insufficient experience and expertise on energy policy at an independent governmental level, ENI maintained this role and designed the country's energy policy in line with its own corporate strategy impeding a true open market.[43]

Third, empirical research has corroborated that the lack of pre-entry experience, i.e., experience in related markets gained before entry, is negatively correlated to firm survival.[44] A firm wanting to enter and survive in an industry will be more likely to exit if it has no prior experience.[45] In the case of historical operators, pre-entry experience of national competitors would be thus limited to adjacent markets that could develop without the former legal monopolistic market, to other national historical operators that could leverage their experience, or to historical operators coming from other States. This notwithstanding, it should be noted that the advantage given by pre-entry experience process may be undermined when disruptive technologies arise rendering previous knowledge obsolete or irrelevant.[46]

Lastly, the literature has emphasized that the long absence of competition for the market worsens the ability of the firm to react in the face of competition. This organizational-inertia inhibits the ability of the historical operator to respond to the novelty of competitive threats or changes in technology.[47] While this would suggest an increased vulnerability of the historical operator's position, it also provides interesting insights as to the incentives of historical operators to keep their statutory ties or safeguard their legacy advantage by recourse to the State that granted them, as the ENI example above could indicate. The inability to respond with new products or processes would incentivize the firm to behave anticompetitively to not lose its position (exclusion) or reap the most of its legacy before it fades away (exploitation).[48]

42. Robinson, William T. and Sungwook Min. "Is the First to Market the First to Fail? Empirical Evidence for Industrial Goods Businesses." *Journal of Marketing Research* 39.1 (2002): 120-128, showing that, for industrial good services, the longer the lead-time of monopoly the higher the risk of failure from future entrants.
43. Skalamera, Morena. "Italy's Path to Gas Liberalisation: Corporate Power, Monopoly Distortions and the Russia Factor." *Contemporary Italian Politics* 7.2 (2015): 161-184.
44. Qian, Lihong, Rajshree Agarwal, and Glenn Hoetker. "Configuration of Value Chain Activities: The Effect of Pre-entry Capabilities, Transaction Hazards, and Industry evolution on Decisions to Internalize." *Organization Science* 23.5 (2012): 1330-1349.
45. Carrol, Glenn R., et al. "The Fates of *de novo* and *de alio* Producers in the American Automobile Industry 1885–1981." *Strategic Management Journal* 17.S1 (1996): 117-137. *See also* Chapter 6.
46. Klepper, Steven and Kenneth L. Simons. "Dominance by Birthright: Entry of Prior Radio Producers and Competitive Ramifications in the US Television Receiver Industry." *Strategic Management Journal* 21.10-11 (2000): 997-1016. *See* Chapter 6 for an extended discussion.
47. Lieberman, Marvin B. and David B. Montgomery. "First-Mover Advantages." *Strategic Management Journal* 9(S1) (1988): 41-58, 48.
48. We discuss this in section 3.06 of this chapter.

[2] State Funding

State funding is a reinforcing variable of the effects that the long-sustained absence of competition for the market has in the firm and its transition to a competitive market.[49] In essence, State funding means that the State is unlikely to allow the former monopolist to go bankrupt. Therefore, the historical investment risks for the firm were low.[50] As an extension to this, the risk of financial distress was not part of the business culture and could have imprinted a damaging behavioral inertia in the firm: a remaining sense within the firm of national champion that deserves to be protected. In this respect, the inertia effects of State funding on the investment risks historical operators now face can be even seen in the enforcement of State aid law. After liberalization, the Commission would allow Member States to compensate historical operators for the investments made when the market was closed to competition and became noneconomical as a result of the opening of the industry (stranded costs);[51] even if these were "intrinsically less efficient than ... potential entrants."[52]

Along the lines of distributive justice, some authors have argued that monopoly rents that were the result State funding ought to be redistributed when the market opens to competition. The historical operator who has benefited from *public* resources should counterweigh its position and share the benefits of such protection with new entrants.[53]

In sum, the analysis of these competitive variables suggests that competition in the presence of a historical operator is strongly dependent on the State origins of the dominant firm. We turn now to examine *how* the Commission and the Courts have factored them in their analyses and how alive is the process paradox against historical operators.[54]

---

49. Motta, Massimo. *Competition Policy. Theory and Practice*. Cambridge University Press, 2004, at p. 51 argues that state funding, together with the State-created absence of competition for the market, have detrimental effects for welfare as it mitigates the selective forces of the competitive process.
50. For a review of the literature, *see* Megginson, William L. and Jeffry M. Netter. "From State to Market: A Survey of Empirical Studies on Privatization." *Journal of Economic Literature* 39.2 (2001): 321-389.
51. Commission Decision, Case COMP/SA N 161/04, *Portugal Custos ociosos em Portugal*. In the same line, *see, e.g.*, Commission Decision, Case COMP/SA N 691/2009, *Hungarian stranded cost compensation scheme* and Commission Decision, Case COMP/SA 18.989, *Stranded costs compensations in Poland*.
52. Commission Communication relating to "The Methodology for Analysing State Aid Linked to Stranded Costs," *OJ* L 27, 30.1.1997, p. 20.
53. Frohlich, Norman and Joe A. Oppenheimer. "Ethical Problems When Moving to Markets: Gaining Efficiency While Keeping an Eye on Distributive Justice" *in* Arieh A. Ullmann and Alfred Lewis (eds.) *Privatization and Entrepreneurship: The Managerial Challenge in Central and Eastern Europe*. Psychology Press, 1997.
54. Although we are concerned with other historical operators than telecommunication operators, especially in the energy industry, liberalization has taken place at a slower pace. Further, enforcement of competition law is generally achieved through settlement decisions that generally lack any relevant substantial discussion. Unlike in other sectors, the opening of the telecommunications market to competition has happened faster. The insights gained from the analysis of the case law against telecom operators are thus useful for future cases against historical operators in other industries.

[C] Historical Advantages and Equality of Opportunity

The Commission describes the advantages that accrued to historical operators in the absence of competition and State funding as "*historical advantages*."[55] These historical advantages have found place in its enforcement priorities that promotes an active enforcement of the competition rules "in particular where *legacy advantages of historical operators act as a barrier to entry*"[56] (emphasis added).

Our inquiry turns now to discover *how* the Commission and the EU Courts have weighted these advantages in their analyses of single-firm conduct. The bottom line is that the principle of equality of opportunity (§3.04[C][1]) has been the main tool used to counteract those "*historical advantages*" (§3.04[C][2]). This is surprising, if not contradictory, once one realizes that the principle of equality of opportunity has played no visible role in the enforcement of Article 102 TFEU against statutory positions of dominance.

[1] Equality of Opportunity in Article 102 TFEU

As explained in the preceding Chapter, the EU Courts crafted the principle of "equality of opportunity" in the enforcement of competition rules in the application of Article 106 TFEU and rules relating to the national implementation of liberalization directives. For the first time, in 1988, the Court in *Terminals Equipment* held that "*a system of undistorted competition*, as laid down in the Treaty, *can be guaranteed only if equality of opportunity is secured* as between the various economic operators."[57] (emphasis added) This principle, which remained constrained to cases involving EU Member States' failure to act or cases related to the enforcement of Article 106 TFEU, first spilled over a "pure" Article 102 TFEU case in *Deutsche Telekom*.

In *Deutsche Telekom* the Commission found that the German historical telecom operator Deutsche Telekom had charged unfair prices for wholesale access to the local loop to its downstream competitors.[58] This unfair pricing took the form of a margin

55. The literature often refers to them as "incumbency advantages," but for the reasons we explained above, we will maintain the terminology offered by the Commission (interchangeably "historical advantages" or "legacy advantages"). Nevertheless, in some cases, it is unclear what "history" means. For example, in *Wanado*, there seems to be two possible readings of the concept of historicity. First, Wanadoo was a subsidiary of France Télécom who was the long established and former telecommunications operator in France. Or second, historicity meant being the first in the market. *See* Commission Decision, Case COMP/38.233, *Wanadoo Interactive*, §348.
56. Communication from the Commission on "Making the Internal Energy Market Work," COM/2012/0663 final, at §3.1.2.
57. CJEU, Case C-202/88, *France v. Commission* ("*Terminals Equipment*"), ECLI:EU:C:1991:120, at §51.
58. The local loop is the circuit that connects the final user's premises to the main distribution frame owned and controlled by the historical operators. In view of the lack of competition on the local network the EU issued a regulation mandating historical operators to provide unbundled access to the local loop. *See*, for instance, Regulation (EC) No. 2887/2000 of the European Parliament and of the Council of 18 December 2000 on unbundled access to the local loop, *OJ* L 336, 30.12.2000, p. 4-8.

squeeze. The price that Deutsche Telekom's competitors had to pay for accessing the local network to be able to provide Internet access was higher than the retail Internet access prices Deutsche Telekom charged to its final consumers. This prevented Deutsche Telekom's competitors from realizing any profits in the market for Internet access and obliged them to cross-subsidize their costs from other charges, and in particular from telephone calls. The Commission imposed a fine of EUR 12.6 million on Deutsche Telekom, despite the fact that the German Regulatory Authority controlled the setting of wholesale prices and had itself previously considered that the price difference "was not so significant as to deprive competitors of *any opportunity*."[59] (emphasis added)

Deutsche Telekom appealed the decision before the GC and subsequently to the CJEU.[60] Deutsche Telekom's appeal sought safe harbor in the German Regulatory Authority control over the wholesale price and assessment of Deutsche Telekom's competitors' *opportunities*.[61] In particular, Deutsche Telekom argued that the Commission should have computed the additional charges generated by call services into the retail monthly subscription since unbundled access to the network is a wholesale product in respect of calls and connections.[62] However, in the eyes of the EU Courts, the principle of "*equality of opportunity*"[63] between operators was not safeguarded if Deutsche Telekom's downstream competitors were obliged to cross-subsidize charges, i.e., to use the benefits from telephone calls to cover the losses of Internet access services. Both the General Court and the Court of Justice thus equated anticompetitive effects with the inequality of opportunity caused by Deutsche Telekom's former legal monopoly. This meant that Deutsche Telekom was forced to use a pricing strategy that would correct the competitive asymmetry originating from its historical advantages.[64]

The *Deutsche Telekom* court thus essentially legitimized the application of the principle of equality of opportunity as a benchmark to assess its antitrust theory of liability. Since then other cases involving historical operators have followed suit.[65] To answer the question whether such theory of liability is warranted, we need to examine if it is in line with the view that competition is a process.

---

59. GC, Case T-271/03, *Deutsche Telekom v. Commission*, ECLI:EU:T:2008:101, §117.
60. CJEU, Case C-280/08 P, *Deutsche Telekom v. Commission*, ECLI:EU:C:2010:603; and GC, Case T-271/03, *Deutsche Telekom v. Commission*, ECLI:EU:T:2008:101.
61. Even if the regulatory authority had control on dictating wholesale access prices, the EU Courts held that Deutsche Telekom could still influence its retail prices to avoid a price squeeze by means of charging higher prices consumer. This is a worrying finding that could only find justification in a long-run perspective, when the future benefits of having numerous competitors would outweigh the current losses incurred in by consumers. Such finding however would require a prospective assessment that the EU Courts did not perform, and that looked more like a faith-based consideration rather than a facts-based analysis. *See* CJEU, Case C-280/08 P, *Deutsche Telekom v. Commission*, ECLI:EU:C:2010:603, §182.
    Id. §§180-182.
62. GC, Case T-271/03, *Deutsche Telekom v. Commission*, ECLI:EU:T:2008:101, §§154-164.
63. CJEU, Case C-280/08 P, *Deutsche Telekom v. Commission*, ECLI:EU:C:2010:603, §230.
64. McMahon, Kathryn. "The Regulation of a Margin Squeeze in the European Union and the Intersection of Competition Law and Sector-Specific Regulation 10.2 (2014): 167-204, 190.
65. GC, Case T-336/07, *Telefónica v. Commission*, ECLI:EU:T:2012:172, §204.

[2] Equality of Opportunity and the Process of Competition

The origins of the principle. First, it is important to stress, as already explained,[66] that the application of the principle of equality of opportunity sought to correct a competitive disadvantage that *originated* in national legislation. Let us recall that in *ISIS Multimedia*[67] the Court of Justice held that German national law regulating the fees in connection with telephone numbers discriminated between *new* operators and the historical operator Deutsche Telekom. Whereas Deutsche Telekom only had to pay for the allocation of new telephone numbers and had not paid any charge for those during its legal monopoly, new operators willing to enter the market were by reason of the German law obliged to pay "*upon allocation of the first number.*"[68] If the allocation of telephone numbers was a precondition of entry, German national law (and not the legacy advantages of Deutsche Telekom) distorted competition by not securing an equality of opportunity between *new* and the *historical* operator.[69]

While in *ISIS Multimedia* the *source* of the inequality of opportunity laid within national legislation, in *Deutsche Telekom* the *source* of inequality was found in the historical advantages of the undertaking alone. These historical advantages put the firm under the obligation to offset them once the market was open to competition.[70]

Are these situations in fact so different that the import of the principle should be prevented? Is this principle a useful antitrust standard to assess other than the unilateral behavior of a statutory monopoly (or the behavior of a State itself)?[71]

From a formal perspective, one would be rapidly inclined to support a differentiated treatment. But upon a more careful reflection they show fundamental similarity. They are both the result of a State measure[72] that comes about from the same non-competitive scenario: the absence of competition for the market.

Despite this similarity, the remedy is necessarily different. In the former scenario the application of Article 106 TFEU in conjunction with Article 102 TFEU would oblige the Member State to eliminate the external competitive distortion enshrined in a legal provision. Whereas, in the latter scenario, the effectiveness of the principle would require counteracting the legacy advantages that had become part of the historical operator resources and capabilities. These differences require that the EU Courts fine-tune the application of the principle in several ways. We explore these in turn.

Unidirectional application. The principle of equality of opportunity has played against the historical operator. The Commission and the Courts have however disregarded the other side of the story. That is, historical operators might also be fraught

66. *See* Chapter 2.
67. CJEU, Case C-327/03, *ISIS Multimedia and Firma 02 ("ISIS Multimedia")*, ECLI:EU:C:2005:622. *See also* CJEU, Case C-462/99, *Connect Austria*, ECLI:EU:C:2003:297.
68. CJEU, Case C-327/03, *ISIS Multimedia*, ECLI:EU:C:2005:622, §42.
69. *Id.* §§43-44.
70. *See* Chapter 5 for a discussion concerning the neutralization of incumbency advantages and GC, Case T-232/06, *Evropaïki Dynamiki v. Commission*, ECLI:EU:T:2011:443.
71. Hay, George A. and Kathryn McMahon. "The Diverging Approach to Price Squeezes in the United States and Europe." *Journal of Competition Law and Economics* 8.2 (2012): 259-296, at 276.
72. In this sense, *see* CJEU, Case C-553/12, *Commission v. DEI*, ECLI:EU:C:2014:2083, §44.

with legacy *disadvantages* or regulatory obligations that can dissipate or eliminate the possible advantages. The application of the principle of opportunity is regrettably skewed in this respect. Overall, the Commission and EU Courts have foregone an analysis of the regulatory burdens that the historical operator has to comply with, thereby placing it (all things remaining equal) at a competitive disadvantage.

The unidirectional application of the principle highlights the existence of our process paradox. The EU Courts have sought the protection of the process of competition but made no holistic attempt to discover what causes are responsible for a current state of the market. The *Deutsche Telekom* case again serves as an illustration.[73] On the one hand, the EU Courts considered that the slow growth of market shares of Deutsche Telekom's competitors was due to some distortive advantage that Deutsche Telekom derived from its historicity as a statutory monopoly.[74] But on the other hand, it neither inquired into disadvantages that the historical operator might have had to deal with, nor did it consider other plausible explanations even when other geographical markets showed lower degrees of market share growth.[75]

If we agree that the principle of equality of opportunity is a useful tool to benchmark historical operators' behavior, this is not only because they enjoy legacy advantages, but also because they themselves can be locked-in in old infrastructures or investments that have not yet been amortized—let alone subsisting regulatory obligations. For instance, when an industry is highly innovative, legacy might turn into a historical disadvantage to compete in the wake of technological innovations when previous heavy investments have not yet been paid off.[76]

Limiting the principle. The process paradox is further amplified if the EU Courts were to make an indiscriminate application of such principle to any dominant firm; that is, irrespective of the sources of its market power. We must strongly reject such spillover effect.

Some commentators have argued that equality of opportunity is a principle of universal applicability to Article 102 TFEU cases.[77] For instance, Wouter Wils refers to support his conclusion to the *IMS Health* case. But a careful reading of the judgment shows that the only explicit reference to this principle was put forward up by AzyX (a

73. GC, Case T-271/03, *Deutsche Telekom v. Commission*, ECLI:EU:T:2008:101, § 235: "*Given that, until the entry of a first competitor* on the market for retail access services, in 1998, *the applicant had a monopoly on that retail market*, the anti-competitive effect which the Commission is required to demonstrate relates to the possible barriers which the applicant's pricing practices could have created for the growth of competition in that market." (emphasis added)
74. Rousseva, Ekaterina and Mel Marquis "Hell Freezes Over: A Climate Change for assessing Exclusionary Conduct under Article 102 TFEU." *Journal of European Competition Law & Practice* 4 (2012): 32-50, at 45.
75. Expressing a similar view, *see* Hay, George A. and Kathryn McMahon. "The Diverging Approach to Price Squeezes in the United States and Europe." *Journal of Competition Law and Economics* 8.2 (2012): 259-296, at 279.
76. In the same line, Opinion of AG Mazák in Case C-52/09, *TeliaSonera*, ECLI:EU:C:2010:483, §27: "the vertically integrated undertakings may also find themselves burdened with old infrastructure which requires maintenance and often one is dealing with industries with considerable technological innovation where the incumbent must innovate in order to compete."
77. Wils, Wouter P.J. "The Judgment of the EU General Court in Intel and the So-Called 'More Economic Approach' to Abuse of Dominance." *World Competition: Law and Economics Review* 37.4 (2014): 405-434.

third party to the proceedings) to describe what it thought the objectives of Article 102 TFEU are. Nowhere in the judgment the Court includes the principle of equality of opportunity.[78] Furthermore, references in *Deutsche Telekom* or *Telefónica* in support of the application of the principle only relate to the enforcement of Article 106 TFEU or the implementation of regulatory obligations in the context of liberalization processes.

On the other side of the spectrum, Pierre Larouche and Maarten Peter Schinkel have expressed discomfort with the introduction of this principle into the enforcement of Article 102 TFEU. In their view, it would mean that *all* dominant firms must behave in such a manner so as to allow its competitors to "replicate its business strategy and methods."[79]

Their concern is genuine. An unrestrained application of the principle would have negative consequences if the origins of market power did not form part of the assessment of anticompetitive behavior. In the case of historical operators, the *origins* of their advantages relate to a particular competitive scenario: the absence of competition for the market as designed by the State. To transpose an "*equality of opportunity*" obligation to nonhistorical operators would disregard competition as a process. In a market characterized by competition *for* the market, an application of the principle of equality of opportunity could mitigate the selective forces of the market. It would create an artificial competitive arena which is not the result of the competitive process the EU courts want to protect.[80] These selective forces of the market are however inexistent in the context of historical operators and thus the application of the principle in this context would not *a priori* to collide with a process perspective.

It is unclear whether the EU Courts in *Deutsche Telekom* limited the applicability of the principle of equality of opportunity to any undertaking that "*has a dominant position largely as a result of the legal monopoly it enjoyed before the liberalisation*"[81] (emphasis added). However, the *fact* remains that the EU Court's case law on abuse of dominance has (so far) only recourse to the principle of equality of opportunity as a benchmark to assess anticompetitive behavior by historical operators—at least in an explicit way.

This notwithstanding, the lack of clarity in the application of this principle by the EU Courts might explain why the Commission eventually resorted, *for the first time* outside a "historical operator case" to the principle of equality of opportunity to find Google's behavior abusive in the *Google Shopping* case.[82]

78. CJEU, Case C-481/01 P(R), *NDC Health v. Commission*, ECLI:EU:C:2002:223, §§80-85.
79. Larouche, Pierre and Maarten Pieter Schinkel. "Continental Drift in the Treatment of Dominant Firms. Article 102 TFEU to Section 2 Sherman Act." *TILEC Discussion Paper No. 2013-020* (2013): 1-33, at 20, nn. 50 and 51, discussing the principle of equality of opportunity in light of *Deutsche Telekom*.
80. Similarly, *see* Mariniello, Mario, Damien Neven and Jorge Padilla. "Antitrust, Regulatory Capture and Economic Integration." *Bruegel Policy Contribution*, 2015/11, at n. 11. *See also* Fumagalli, Chiara and Massimo Motta. "A Simple Theory of Predation." *Journal of Law and Economics* 56.3 (2013): 595-631, arguing that in the early stages of market development below-cost prices "might well be consistent with a different interpretation, that is, competition for the market."
81. CJEU, Case C-280/08 P, *Deutsche Telekom v. Commission*, ECLI:EU:C:2010:603, §234.
82. *See* Commission Decision, Case COMP/39.740, *Google Search (Shopping)*, §331. *See* Chapter 5 for an extended discussion.

The application of this principle has relied however on yet another misconception that the historical advantages that the historical operator enjoys will last indefinitely.[83]

[D] First-Movers and Adjacent Markets

[1] What Is the Story?

The absence of competition for the market coupled with the legacy advantages of historical operators has spurred concerns regarding the potential advantage of a historical operator as a first-mover in other markets. Due to its position as a historical operator, the firm may be the first one to enter new dependent or adjacent markets of the formerly State-protected industry.

This concern is not abstract. The most illustrative example of this proposition is *Wanadoo*. Wanadoo was accused of predatory pricing in the market for the provision of ADSL services in France. The ADSL market was at that time a *new* market dependent on the upstream market where France Télécom, the parent company of Wanadoo, was the historical operator. In its decision, the Commission found that Wanadoo could pioneer this new market, *not* because it "provid[ed] an objectively better service than its competitors," but simply because it benefited from its position as the subsidiary of the dominant historical operator.[84] In such circumstances, it stated that "the chronological *sequence of entry into the market is far from neutral*"[85] (emphasis added). In other terms, a sequence of entry that begins with a historical operator can negatively affect the way in which competition will further develop in the market.

Telefónica, *TeliaSonera* and *Orange Polska* subsequently followed suit and aimed to address this non-neutral chronological effect. Indeed, the Commission and the EU Courts have taken a strong stance and have ruled that the development of new adjacent markets cannot in any way prevent the application of competition law especially when the pioneering firm is benefitting from its former legal monopoly position.[86] The objective was clearly spelled out in *TeliaSonera*: competition law must apply stringently to prevent the formation of a new competitive structure negatively influenced by a former monopolistic structure.[87]

83. The assumption is a strong one and requires further elaboration as to when the historical operator stops enjoying those legacy advantages. We will revert to this question at the end of this chapter as it effects expand beyond the application of the principle of equality of opportunity.
84. Commission Decision, Case COMP/38.233, *Wanadoo Interactive*, §348. The line of reasoning is in line with the view that the absence of competition for the market secures less efficient outcomes. In this respect, the Commission seemed to import the view of the deregulatory process that historical operators were inefficient undertakings. *See* Opinion of AG Ruiz Jarabo Colomer in Case C-192/08, *TeliaSonera Finland Oyj*, ECLI:EU:C:2009:309, §10, stating that telecommunication operators were inefficient as they were unable to satisfy consumer demands. Not only they conveyed with accuracy the picture of the quiet monopolist life, but their decisions were also *the result of strong political influences rather than the result of market processes.*
85. Commission Decision, Case COMP/38.233, *Wanadoo Interactive*, §352.
86. Commission Decision, Case COMP/38.784, *Wanadoo España v. Telefónica*, §§623-626; CJEU, Case C-52/09, *TeliaSonera*, ECLI:EU:C:2011:83, §108; Commission Decision, Case COMP/39.525, *Telekomunikacja Polska*, §809-810.
87. CJEU, Case C-52/09, *TeliaSonera*, ECLI:EU:C:2011:83, §§108-109.

These decisions show a clear inefficient view of path dependency. Competition law must intervene to prevent the historical operator, who already enjoys a certain set of historical advantages, from also benefiting from pioneering advantages.[88]

The focus of the Commission is thus placed in the disproportionate variation across firms in their pre-entry capabilities where the historical operator is the *only* advantaged firm. For instance, while Telefónica or TeliaSonera could derive rents from its former State-created monopoly, new entrants do not have these legacy rents.

Because of the absence of competition for the market, historical operator companies built up resources and capabilities that can also be used in related markets, such as mobile telephony or high-speed Internet markets. In the telecommunications industry, some of the literature on entrepreneurial economics and management has argued that to create a level playing field between operators it is essential to consider entry timing variables such as first-mover advantages.[89] A more recent study of the telecommunications industry analyzing data of 191 mobile network operators from 49 different European countries revealed that success of historical operators was not correlated to their entry timing position.[90]

In this regard, we must reject generalizing statements such as those which pervasively assume that the first-mover benefits from an advantage solely because it is the first, and not because it provides an objectively better service—*à la Wanadoo*. Such value statements place first-movers under unmerited severe antitrust scrutiny or lower thresholds for finding liability that do not necessarily hold in all circumstances, even so in the case of historical operators. At the same time the EU Courts and the Commission should avoid general statements that consider the last entrant in an "*objectively* less favourable position"[91] (emphasis added). Indeed, for illustration purposes, OTE, the Greek historical operator, became the leading firm (Cosmote) in the mobile market despite entering this market (third mover) several years later, and even if Cosmote paid the same interconnection fees to its parent company as its competitors did.[92]

88. *See* Commission Decision, Case COMP/39.525, *Telekomunikacja Polska*, §865: On top of Orange Polska's historical advantages, its "first mover advantage has increased rivals' costs relative to [Orange Polska] because [Orange Polska] has benefited as a first mover from network externalities, learning by doing cost reduction or customer lock-in effects."
89. Bijwaard, Govert E., Maarten C.W. Janssen and Emiel Maasland. "Early Mover Advantages: An Empirical Analysis of European Mobile Phone Markets." *Telecommunications Policy* 32.3 (2008): 246-261.
90. Jakopin, Nejc M. and Andreas Klein. "First-Mover and Incumbency Advantages in Mobile Telecommunications." *Journal of Business Research* 65.3 (2012): 362-70.
91. GC, Case T-328/03, *O2 (Germany) GmbH & Co OHG v. Commission*, ECLI:EU:T:2006:116, §§107-108, the GC took into account the position of O2 as the last entrant in its counterfactual analysis of the agreement between O2 and T-Mobile. The GC held that O2's "weak[est] competitive position" as a result of being the last entrant was rebalanced by the agreement.
92. Zu Knyphausen-Aufseß, Dodo, Christian Krys and Lars Schweizer. "Attacker's Advantages in a Homogeneous Market: The Case of GSM." *International Journal on Media Management* 4.4 (2002): 212-224.

[2] A Unidirectional Analysis: What About Pioneering Disadvantages?

The introduction of entry timing as a variable of the competitive process is very welcome. As economic theory shows, the chronological sequence of entry is a fundamental part of the competitive process and allows us to understand why markets function the way they do.[93] Nevertheless, the inclusion of entry timing variables cannot be unidirectional. Any possible disadvantages that the pioneer firm will face should also be taken into account. As a corollary, assuming away that this is not a natural monopoly,[94] the protection of the competitive process requires looking into competitors' ability to compete on the market and take advantage of the efforts already incurred in by the pioneer.

In *Wanadoo*, for example, the Commission focused on the fact that benefits from advertising would accrue to the first-mover. However, it disregarded the possibility that late entrants would benefit (or free-ride) on the advertisement efforts incurred by Wanadoo. Thus, new entrants providing ADSL competing services will not have to raise awareness about a new product and its benefits: the first-mover advantage thus disappearing and becoming a first-mover disadvantage.[95]

This limited view of pioneering is also worrying because it can affect other dominant firms that do not owe their positions to statutory action. Our concern is defensible if, as decided in *Wanadoo*, the "*incumbent* solely by reason of ... being in business" places the new entrant at a disadvantage (emphasis added).[96]

As the Commission's decision makes clear, the incumbent does not refer to the historical operator, but to *any* firm that is already established in the market irrespectively of *how* it established itself in the first place. Although incumbency as a barrier to entry is in line with current Commission's enforcement, this Bainian conception seems to be at odds with an understanding of competition as a process.[97] Incumbency as such, i.e., getting established in a market, is the essence of the competitive process and not a barrier to it.[98] We illustrate why with an example.

The learning experience gained by a pioneering firm would in the eyes of the Commission deserve the same type of entry barrier analysis than in the case of a former

93. Geroski, Paul A. and Alexis Jacquemin. "Dominant Firms and Their Alleged Decline." *International Journal of Industrial Organization* 2.1 (1984): 1-27.
94. With regard to historical operators, the Commission has at times remarked that the cost of duplicating the network is an insurmountable barrier to entry, hence pointing in the direction of a natural monopoly structure. *See* Commission Decision, Case COMP/39.525, *Telekomunikacja Polska*, §808. *See* Chapter 4 for a discussion on natural monopolies.
95. In a study of the telecommunications industry, Jakopin and Klein find that new entrants develop more efficient marketing and distribution channels than historical operators. *See* Jakopin, Nejc M. and Andreas Klein. "First-Mover and Incumbency Advantages in Mobile Telecommunications." *Journal of Business Research* 65.3 (2012): 362-370. More generally, *see* Lieberman, Marvin B. and David B. Montgomery. "First-Mover (Dis)Advantages: Retrospective and Link with the Resource-Based View." *Strategic Management Journal* 19.12 (1998): 1111-1125.
96. Commission Decision, Case COMP/38.233, *Wanadoo Interactive*, §337. The wording "incumbent" leads to confounding enforcement efforts if taken by its meaning in IO literature.
97. Bain, Joe S. *Barriers to New Competition, Their Character and Consequences in Manufacturing Industries*. Harvard University Press, 1956.
98. Harbord, David and Tom Hoehn. "Barriers to Entry and Exit in European Competition Policy." *International Review of Law and Economics* 14.4 (1994): 411-435, at 433 conclude that "the

statutory monopoly.[99] This equalization would miss the whole point about market processes.[100] In liberalized markets, where the chronological sequence of entry never had the opportunity to play a role, the emergence of the dominant firm is not the result of any competitive process.[101] The efficiencies derived from market processes would no longer be spontaneous and competition *for* the market (*ex ante*) could no longer act as a replacement for competition *in* the market (*ex post*). On the contrary, in an open market where the dominant firm is an innovator, a learning curve as a barrier to entry ought to have no antitrust relevance.[102] Any firm could have gathered that knowledge in the competitive process *for* the invention.[103]

If this finding equating historical operators with incumbency were to be further corroborated, it would upset the efforts of the Commission and the EU Courts of truly protecting the competitive process. That we shall further explore in the following chapters.[104]

[3] Standing up for Recoupment

In some isolated predatory pricing cases, a certain amount of interest has been devoted to the recoupment of losses. In such cases, the standard inquiry consists of showing whether prices are below some measure of costs.[105] An optional step consists of showing whether the firm could recoup the lost profits before finding an abuse through

Commission frequently finds more barriers to entry than most economists would be willing to admit." *See* Chapter 5 for an in-depth discussion about "incumbency," barriers to entry and the competitive process.

99. *See* Chapter 6 for a discussion on intangible efficiencies and capabilities.
100. Appelbaum, Elie and Chin Lim. "Contestable Markets under Uncertainty." *The Rand Journal of Economics* 16.1 (1985): 28-40.
101. Expressing a similar view, Crane and Miralles discuss that only where the intervals between competition cycles are very long "*incumbency advantages may take a longer time to wear off.*" *See* Crane, Daniel and Graciela Miralles. "Toward a Unified Theory of Exclusionary Vertical Restraints." *Southern California Law Review* 84.3 (2011): 605-660.
102. Porter, Michael, "Strategic Interaction: Some Lessons from Industry Histories for Theory and Antitrust Policy" *in* Steven C. Salop (ed.) *Strategy, Predation, and Antitrust Analysis.* Federal Trade Commission, 1981, at p. 459.
103. Evans, David S. and Vanessa Zhang. "Assessing Unfair Pricing under China's Anti-monopoly Law for Innovation-Intensive Industries." *University of Chicago Coase-Sandor Institute for Law & Economics Research Paper* no. 678 (2014), at 28: "Quite unlike legal monopolies over industries there is significant competition for creating patents and copyrights. *Nothing prevents firms from entering that race. That situation is unlike state-owned enterprises,* for which competition is barred, *and previously state-owned companies that are the beneficiaries to prior entry barriers together with significant network effects.*" (emphasis added)
104. *See*, in particular, Chapters 5 and 6.
105. The Court held in *AKZO* that prices below AVC will (per se) be abusive. Pricing above ATC will not be considered predatory pricing. Prices below ATC but above AVC will only be considered abusive if there is evidence that they form part of a plan to eliminate a competitor. *See* CJEU, Case C-62/86, *AKZO v. Commission* ECLI:EU:C:1991:286.

predatory pricing.[106] We submit that requiring proof of recoupment EU competition enforcement would be more aligned with a process view of competition.[107]

In *Wanadoo* the Commission carried out a recoupment test in answer to the contentions of the defendant.[108] In its analysis, the Commission discussed entry timing effects and other dynamic variables such as market shares evolution. Regarding entry timing, the Commission finds that by "simply" being the first on the market the pioneer will derive diverse advantages. In view of the Commission, these advantages are barriers to entry that competition law should be concerned with.[109] Those pioneering entry barriers together with the historical advantages of Wanadoo make predatory pricing a profitable strategy, the Commission found.

Although the discussion of recoupment is welcome, this one is regrettably tilted. The Commission states from the start of its analysis, "*it is common practice to consider* that early entry into a market confers a major advantage" to that firm (emphasis added).[110] However, it is well known in the management and strategy literature that pioneering does not always confer advantages and that these are by no means inevitable.[111] Pioneers in the field, Lieberman and Montgomery explain that first-movers suffer from free riding and imitation disadvantages.[112] William Boulding and Markus Christen indicate that "vintage effects," i.e., production technology discontinuities, play against the first-mover firm. Successful market creators are generally "less cost efficient than successful followers" and on average there is a pioneering cost disadvantage.[113] The literature thus shows that advantages are "by no means automatic."[114] They depend on the context, which needs in turn to be examined.[115] For example, in new product markets the costs and risks are remarkably high which makes

106. CJEU, Case C-333/94 P, *Tetra Pak International v. Commission*, ECLI:EU:C:1996:436, §44, rejecting Tetra Pak's contention that the possibility of recoupment be a necessary condition to find predatory pricing abuses and ruling that the risk of eliminating competitors suffices to prove predation.
107. This is unlike in the US. (*See generally, Brooke Group Ltd. v. Brown & Williamson Tobacco Corp.*, 509 U.S. 209 (1993) 224: "Recoupment is the ultimate object of an unlawful predatory pricing scheme; it is the means by which a predator profits from predation. Without it, predatory pricing produces lower aggregate prices in the market, and consumer welfare is enhanced.")
108. Commission Decision, Case COMP/38.233, *Wanadoo Interactive*, §§332 et seq.
109. *Id.* §337.
110. Commission Decision, Case COMP/38.233, *Wanadoo Interactive*, §346.
111. Tellis, Gerard J. and Peter N. Golder. "First to Market, First to Fail? Real Causes of Enduring Market Leadership." *MIT Sloan Management Review* 37.2 (1996): 65-75, referring to pioneering success as an unwarranted "motto."
112. Lieberman, Marvin B. and David B. Montgomery. "First-Mover (Dis)Advantages: Retrospective and Link with the Resource-Based View." *Strategic Management Journal* 19 (1998): 1111-1125.
113. Boulding, William and Markus Christen. "Disentangling Pioneering Cost Advantages and Disadvantages." *Marketing Science* 27.4 (2008): 699-716.
114. Lieberman, Marvin B. and David B. Montgomery. "Conundra and Progress: Research on Entry Order and Performance." *Long Range Planning* 46 (2013): 312-324.
115. Suarez, Fernando and Gianvito Lanzolla. "The Role of Environmental Dynamics in Building a First Mover Advantage Theory." *Academy of Management Review* 32.2 (2007): 377-392.

the survival of the pioneer more difficult, while the opposite is true in the presence of incrementally new product markets.[116]

In this regard, the scenario that Fernando Suarez and Gianvito Lonzolla describe regarding the US telecommunications market is of particular relevance. AT&T was the first company to deploy a cellular telephone in 1978, but in 1983 Ameritech, which arose from AT&T's break-up, offered commercial analogue cellular operations as authorized by the Federal Communications Commission (FCC). They report that AT&T was unable to make a profit in the new product spaces due to the strength of later entrants' offerings.[117]

This notwithstanding, even in those cases where several advantages accrue to the first-mover, to consider first-mover advantages as entry barriers would go against the competitive process itself. As a patent is an exceptional *legal* reward to exceptional innovative efforts, first-mover advantages might become the *natural* reward that the market offers for the risks of those firms that dare to create and open markets. And it is *common* economic understanding that the costs that risks impose can be as burdensome as other monetary costs late entrants may face.[118]

Although Wanadoo appealed the decision, the EU Courts did not substantially discuss the necessity of recoupment. Despite this, AG Mazák engaged in a substantial discussion regarding the competitive process and the recoupment requirement.[119] In his opinion, the absence of a recoupment requirement is in contradiction with the EU Courts' understanding of competition as a process. "*Proof of the possibility of recoupment is inherently ex ante and forward-looking.*"[120] In our lexicon, proof of recoupment requires an analysis of t-1 and $t + 1$. This explains why the recoupment analysis of the Commission is tainted with a process perspective. Unfortunately, this is of limited applicability as long as proof of recoupment is not a requirement to find an abuse in predatory pricing cases.

That the requirement of recoupment is not a necessary condition in EU competition law is thus paradoxical if one reads *Wanadoo* and *Deutsche Telekom* together. In the latter case the Court decided to sacrifice consumers' short-term surplus (Deutsche Telekom could have avoided the margin squeeze increasing its retail prices) for the benefits of long-term competition. But, in order to balance both short-term and long-term, in cases of predatory pricing the EU Courts and the Commission need to implement a recoupment test.

116. Min, Sungwook, Manohar U. Kalwani and William T. Robinson. "Market Pioneer and Early Follower Survival Risks: A Contingency Analysis of Really New Versus Incrementally New Product-Markets." *Journal of Marketing* 70 (2006): 15-33.
117. Suarez, Fernando and Gianvito Lanzolla. "The Half-Truth of First-Mover Advantage." *Harvard Business Review* (April 2005).
118. Buchanan, James M. *Cost and Choice: An Inquiry in Economic Theory*. Indianapolis: Liberty Fund, 1999.
119. AG Mazák considered that the GC had not put forward any substantive argument to conclude that *Tetra Pak* was not limited to the particular circumstances of that case. *See* Opinion of AG Mazák in Case C-202/07 P, *France Télécom v. Commission*, ECLI:EU:C:2008:520, §70.
120. Opinion of AG Mazák in Case C-202/07 P, *France Télécom v. Commission*, ECLI:EU:C:2008:520, §76.

In light of the above, we submit that by requiring proof of recoupment, the EU Courts and the Commission would adhere more closely to their own understanding of competition as a process, and competition law as the means to protect it. As described, the requirement to show a probability of recoupment indicates a process perspective of competition: it is only when the subsequent price increase to recoup the losses does not induce entry that the competitive process is damaged.

Proof of recoupment requires an "*inherently ex ante and forward-looking*" analysis. It is submitted that *ex ante* and *ex post* analysis cannot be confined to recoupment tests in instances of predatory pricing. Competitive enhancing behavior needs also to be accounted for from this holistic perspective. In connection to this, we turn to the next question: how do the incentives to innovate or invest relate to the historical operator nature of the dominant firm?

[E] Incentives to Invest and Innovate

The incentives to invest and innovate of a historical operator are essential to advancing our understanding of the competitive process. In particular, the Commission and the EU Courts have understood that the *ex ante* variable of investment incentives, plays a role in the current status of the competitive process (§3.04[E][1]). This notwithstanding, we submit that their assessment has remained incomplete and scarcely engaging ((§3.04[E][2]).

[1] Telefónica and Beyond

The first of the cases dealing with historical operators' incentives is the result of Telefónica's unfair pricing practices in the wholesale market for Internet access.[121] In *Telefónica*, the Commission found that Telefónica's margin between retail and wholesale access pricing would be insufficient for an as efficient competitor to cover the costs. Telefónica argued that its pricing strategy should be assessed under the *Bronner* criteria on refusal to supply.[122] This meant that before finding an abusive margin squeeze the Commission must establish that: (i) Telefónica's infrastructure was "*indispensable*" for the provision of the downstream service; (ii) Telefónica's behavior would eliminate competition in the downstream market; and (iii) Telefónica's behavior would likely lead to consumer harm.

The Commission dismissed the allegations as it considered that the particular circumstances of *Telefónica* were "fundamentally different" from *Bronner*. *First*, Telefónica's regulatory duty to supply access to its network already took into account the incentives of Telefónica to invest and innovate. *Second*, in any event Telefónica's incentives to invest were not at stake because its infrastructure was developed while

121. While the EU Courts decided *Telefónica* after *Post Danmark I*, the decision of the Commission precedes it. This is why we analyze it in this section.
122. CJEU, Case C-7/97, *Bronner*, ECLI:EU:C:1998:569, §§43-46.

"benefiting from special or exclusive rights that *shielded* it *from competition*" (emphasis added).[123] The latter exception, known in the literature as the "Telefónica exception,"[124] is at the core of our inquiry. Its rationale emanates from the legacy advantages of Telefónica's dominance.

Regrettably, the Court of Justice in appeal did not assess the merits of the Commission and parties' incentives narrative. This is a remarkable silence, all the more because the narrative of historical operators' incentives was not a novel issue for the Court.[125]

Indeed, in *KPN*, AG Poiares Maduro had already put up a framework to address the question.[126] In his opinion, a refusal to supply constitutes an abuse if two requirements are met. First, the dominant firm must have obtained the "necessary inputs for a derivative market" shielded from competition. In our words, the dominant firm is a historical operator. Second, access to the necessary input is not regulated by sector-specific regulation.[127] Such an approach is justified for two reasons. First, the *ex ante* potentially deterrent effect on investment and innovation that results from an *ex post* imposition of a duty to supply "*is minimal.*" Second, such an approach would be in line with objectives of market deregulation.

Central to his opinion is the fact that the historical operator owes its position to former statutory action and is not the result of commercial success in rivalrous competition. Thus, where monopoly *rents* are not the fruits of the competitive process but have been achieved through the protection of the State, these must be shared with its competitors. This is further the case if the legacy inputs are necessary to compete in a derivative market.[128]

Other cases that have come after *Telefónica* have either dealt with the incentives narrative of historical operators or have chosen to avoid the discussion. An example of this dichotomy is *TeliaSonera*. On the one hand, even though TeliaSonera had put forward an incentives narrative to force the application of the *Bronner* criteria, the Court of Justice avoided judging the merits of the plea. In short, the Court of Justice

123. Commission Decision, Case COMP/38.784, *Wanadoo España v. Telefónica*, §§303-304.
124. González Díaz, Francisco E. and Jorge Padilla. "The linkLine Judgment - A European Perspective." *GCP Magazine* (Apr. 1, 2009), referring to the particular circumstances the Commission put forward as the "Telefónica exceptions." We borrow this terminology from them.
125. AG Jacobs in *Bronner* already remarked the importance of preserving incentives to innovate. We leave his analysis for later, Chapters 5 and 6, as it relates to the incentives of dominant firms that owe their dominance to their investments and innovations, and not to historical operators. *See* Opinion of AG Jacobs in Case C-7/97, *Bronner*, ECLI:EU:C:1998:264, §§57 and 62-63.
126. *KPN* relates to a preliminary question referred by the Netherlands regarding the telecommunications liberalization process. However, *KPN* allows us to examine the applicability of Article 102 TFEU because its historical dominance origins in a market closed to competition played a fundamental role in AG Poiares Maduro analysis. *See* Opinion of AG Poiares Maduro in Case C-109/03, *KPN*, ECLI:EU:C:2004:437.
127. The CJEU did not address the applicability of Article 102 TFEU in the context of the proceedings.
128. Opinion of AG Poiares Maduro in Case C-109/03, *KPN*, ECLI:EU:C:2004:437, §§53 and 55.

simply ruled that the effectiveness of Article 102 TFEU requires that margin squeeze be an independent form of abuse from a refusal to supply.[129]

Once again, the silence of the Court is in stark contrast[130] with AG Mazák's opinion in the same case. In particular AG Mazák undertook, upfront, the argument rose by the Swedish Competition Authority and the Commission relating to TeliaSonera's "special situation." TeliaSonera's dominant position was "special" because its upstream market position had been *"developed under the protection of special or exclusive rights or has been financed by State resources"*[131] (emphasis added).

In a timeless dialogue with AG Poiares Maduro Opinion in *KPN*, AG Mazák questioned to what extent this second *"Telefónica exception"* ought to lead to a stricter legal standard under Article 102 TFEU. AG Mazák considered that Article 102 TFEU does not make a distinction between the sources of funding. Further, that such differentiation could be difficult to put in practice especially where former statutory monopolies have made "significant improvements" after privatization. This notwithstanding, he concluded, the relevance of the State origins of the dominant firm would depend on the specifics of the case.[132]

In the interim to these proceedings, the exceptions have found a place in the Commission's Guidance Paper. Here the Commission considers "particularly likely" that imposing an obligation to supply will not affect the incentives to invest and innovate of the dominant firm in two scenarios. First, when regulation that balances those incentives already imposes an obligation to supply. Second, where "the upstream market position of the dominant undertaking has been developed under the protection of special or exclusive rights or has been financed by state resources."[133]

After *Telefónica* and *TeliaSonera*, the incentives narrative seems to have been tacitly accepted by the EU Courts. As a result, the Commission continues to revert to it. In *Orange Polska*, the Commission imposed an obligation on Orange Polska to provide access of alternative operators to the local loop. Orange Polska had limited access to its network, established unreasonable terms, provoked delays in contract negotiations and refused to provide information for the connection to local loop.[134] The Commission shortly remarked that an obligation to supply could have deleterious effects on the

129. CJEU, Case C-52/09, *TeliaSonera*, ECLI:EU:C:2011:83, §§54-58; *see* in particular §58 where the Court highlights the need to ensure the effectiveness of Article 102 TFEU. The doctrinal debate is however far from settled, even more if *Post Danmark I* is to be interpreted as setting a "general" safe harbor for dominant firms pricing above cost. *See* Petit, Nicolas. "Price Squeezes with Positive Margins in EU Competition Law: Economic and Legal Anatomy of a Zombie." *Revue du Droit des Industries de Réseau* 2 (2014): 123-128.

130. The CJEU and AG Mazák reached divergent conclusions. In the Opinion of AG Mazák, if there is no regulatory obligation or the product is not indispensable there cannot be an abuse on the basis of an insufficient margin between wholesale and retail prices without a demonstration of anticompetitive effects in the downstream market. *See* Opinion of AG Mazák in Case C-52/09, *TeliaSonera*, ECLI:EU:C:2010:483, §§29 and 30. It is interesting to note that Mazák's Opinion is based on O'Donoghue, Robert and Jorge Padilla, *The Law and Economics of Article 82 EC*. Hart Publishing, 2006.

131. Opinion of AG Mazák in Case C-52/09, *TeliaSonera*, ECLI:EU:C:2010:483, §§17 and 24.

132. *Id.* §29.

133. Guidance Paper, §82.

134. GC, Case T-486/11, *Orange Polska*, ECLI:EU:T:2015:1002, §§28-30.

incentives to invest of a dominant firm. However, it concluded without further analysis that the need to promote competition in the downstream market exceeded the need to preserve Orange Polska's "ex ante incentives to invest in and exploit the upstream infrastructure."[135]

[2] Ex ante Incentives: Analysis for Historical Operators

The silence of the EU Courts in *Telefónica*[136] and *TeliaSonera*[137] regarding the validity or extent of the exceptions was a missed opportunity. The Courts could have shed some light upon the role that particular incentives to invest and innovate of historical operators have for the competitive process.

After *Telefónica*, the Commission continues to miss a balanced approach and deepens the confusion surrounding the analysis of incentives to invest and innovate of historical operators. While in *Telefónica*, the IP strand of the case law was rejected as irrelevant; in *Orange Polska* the references to *IMS*,[138] *Magill*[139] and *Microsoft*[140] are not only inconsistent but also disconcerting.[141] The Commission does not discuss *how* the incentives of Orange Polska were different from those of its competitors. Instead, it simply considers that the regulatory authorities already take such balance into account when they decide to impose supply duties.[142] The lack of substantive discussion also disregards that in vertically integrated firms, incentives to invest and innovate in the downstream market can also be affected.

On the contrary, the discussions in some of the AGs' opinions clearly evince an underlying peculiarity to historical operators that deserves further attention. The attempts of both AGs in *KPN* and *TeliaSonera* are welcome. However, they are still far away from bringing a coherent system for the inclusion of historical operators' incentives in the analysis of abusive conduct. The key question that arises can be

135. Commission Decision, Case COMP/39.525, *Telekomunikacja Polska*, §807.
136. It is important to highlight that the exceptions the Commission brought up in *Telefónica* are a reply to Telefónica's claim that for a margin squeeze to be abusive the conditions for refusal to supply must be satisfied. In this line, *see* O'Donoghue, Robert and Jorge Padilla. *The Law and Economics of Article 102 TFEU*. Hart Publishing, 2013, at p. 579.
137. The point was not substantially discussed in appeal. The GC, simply following *TeliaSonera* (*see* CJEU, Case C-52/09, *TeliaSonera*, ECLI:EU:C:2011:83), held that margin squeeze was a stand-alone abuse and did not assess the merits or rationale of the "Telefónica exceptions." For a critique to both exceptions, *see* Geradin, Damien. "Refusal to Supply and Margin Squeeze: A Discussion of Why the 'Telefónica Exceptions' Are Wrong." *TILEC Discussion Paper* No. 2011-009 (2011).
138. CJEU, Case C-418/01, *IMS Health*, ECLI:EU:C:2004:257.
139. CJEU, Joined Cases C-241/91 P and C-242/91 P, *Radio Telefis Eireann (RTE) and Independent Television Publications Ltd (ITP) v. Commission* ("*Magill*"), ECLI:EU:C:1995:98.
140. GC, Case T-201/04, *Microsoft v. Commission*, ECLI:EU:T:2007:289.
141. Commission Decision, Case COMP/39.525, *Telekomunikacja Polska*, §700.
142. *See* Commission Decision, Case COMP/39.525, *Telekomunikacja Polska*, §807. Perhaps this is an implicit objective sought by the Commission. As Pablo Ibáñez Colomo writes: "There are several examples that show that the Commission and the Court sometimes depart from the relevant substantive standards to ensure that EU competition law has a meaningful role to play in liberalised markets." *See* Ibáñez Colomo, Pablo. "EU Competition Law in the Regulated Network Industries" *in* Jonathan Galloway (ed.) *Intersections of Antitrust: Policy and Regulation*. Oxford University Press, 2016.

articulated as follows, *what if the historical operator had not been shielded from competition and thus developed its dominant infrastructure under normal competitive conditions?*[143]

Some authors have criticized the "*incentives exception*" because it leads to laxer antitrust liability standards for historical operators. Robert O'Donoghue and Jorge Padilla advance several arguments against a general stricter legal standard of antitrust liability when dominance is the result of public funding.[144] First, a verbatim reading of Article 102 TFEU does not allow for such distinction. The Commission already dismissed the State sources of monopoly as irrelevant in *Frankfurt Airport*.[145] Second, it would be difficult to establish the causal link between dominance and public funding. Third, if private funding could not duplicate certain assets then the solution would be "*to regulate natural monopolies created by public funds.*" In a similar line, Damien Geradin deems the exception to be unjustified because it finds no ground in the case law, it is difficult to apply in practice (leading thus to erroneous results), and it ignores adverse effects on future incentives to invest.[146]

We share the views of AG Poiares Maduro in *KPN*. We find some of the claims in the literature overstated *and* reject the incomplete analysis of the EU Courts and Commission.

First, that the literal wording of Article 102 TFEU does not make the distinction does not mean that the possibility is excluded. The EU Courts have already disregarded the literacy of Article 102 TFEU. In *Akzo*,[147] the Court held "*contrary to the literal sense of Article [102 TFEU]*" that there was no need to establish a cause and effect relationship between the dominant position and its abusive exploitation.[148]

Furthermore, the obiter in *Post Danmark I* is enough to counteract the allegation that Article 102 TFEU precludes distinguishing historical operators from other firms. As a matter of fact, previous case law to *Post Danmark I* has already done so, albeit in a scattered, non-cohesive and unidirectional manner. Regrettably, the analysis of incentives does not escape this skewed differentiation.

Thus, *second*, we do not share the shortcut of *Telefónica* and *TeliaSonera* in avoiding an analysis of incentives analysis by tagging the conduct as "margin squeeze." Having a complete story of the competitive process requires recognizing that historical operators' incentives to invest and innovate have their own peculiarities. Not

---

143. Lianos, Ioannis. "Categorical Thinking in Competition Law" *in* Ariel Ezrachi (ed.) *Article 82 EC: Reflections on Its Recent Evolution*. Hart Publishing, 2009, at p. 43.
144. O'Donoghue, Robert and Jorge Padilla. *The Law and Economics of Article 82 EC*. Hart Publishing, 2006, at p. 463. *See also* González Díaz, Francisco E. and Jorge Padilla. "The linkLine Judgment - A European Perspective." *GCP Magazine*, April 1 (2009). It should be noted that the authors represented/advised Telefónica in the proceedings. Similarly, O'Donoghue claims that differentiating dominance according to its sources of market power is akin to opening Pandora's box. *See* Ehlermann, Claus-Dieter and Isabela Atanasiu (eds.) *European Competition Law Annual 2003: What Is an Abuse of a Dominant Position?* Bloomsbury Publishing, 2006, at p. 43.
145. Commission Decision, Case COMP/34.801, *FAG - Flughafen Frankfurt/Main AG*.
146. Geradin, Damien. "Refusal to Supply and Margin Squeeze: A Discussion of Why the 'Telefónica Exceptions' Are Wrong." *TILEC Discussion Paper* No. 2011-009 (2011).
147. CJEU, Case C-62/86, *AKZO v. Commission*, ECLI:EU:C:1991:286.
148. Opinion of AG Lenz in Case C-62/86, *AKZO v. Commission*, ECLI:EU:C:1989:154, §41.

that they do not exist. An *ex ante* analysis, i.e., *t*-1, that looks into the incentives to invest of a historical operator will show that these incentives are fundamentally different from other firms that invested in a competitive environment before arriving to dominance.

It is well established in the literature that the profit expectations for investing and innovating are positively correlated to the *ex ante* incentives to invest and innovate. The larger the probability for the firm to appropriate the benefits of its investment and innovation, the more likely the firm will invest or innovate. On the contrary, if the *ex post* probability of appropriating those benefits its diminished this will decrease the incentives of the firm to invest or innovate.

In connection to this, Phillip Areeda and Herbert Hovenkamp argue in favor of a different treatment. While in the US a refusal to supply will hardly succeed as a monopolization offense, Areeda and Hovenkamp defend that refusals to supply are arguably applicable to statutory monopolies.[149] These firms have not been urged to compete, and thus, there is no risk in turning them upon.

The analysis of incentives requires a backwards assessment as it also requires a prospective inquiry into how future investments will be affected by antitrust enforcement actions.[150] This is the balance the EU Courts and the Commission fail to strike. This means that, in refusal to supply or margin squeeze cases, the conditions of access should reflect *both* historic costs and "the value associated with the new investments."[151]

In the case of a historical operator, the *ex post* probability of appropriating the profits of its investment was high, even after some time of the opening of the market. First, the historical operator knew that the State would never let it go into bankruptcy. This eliminated any uncertainty and risk inherent to the normal process of investment and innovation. Second, the investment or innovative efforts took place in a non-competitive industry, thereby securing the "*win*." And third, its incentives were not profit-driven motivated but, more generally, motivated by a public service obligation. Under these conditions of certainty, the effects of an obligation to supply access, and to do so under fair conditions (to avoid a margin squeeze abuse) has a limited effect as compared to a situation where the dominant firm has not been created by the State.[152]

An obligation to supply access is a sensible position if the access to the facility was fully developed under those conditions However, if the historical operator invests in the facility once the market was open to competition, a careful balance must be struck that accounts both for the historic costs and the value of new investments. Such balance will be more easily found when the abuse takes place at an early point in time

149. Areeda, Phillip and Herbert Hovenkamp. *Antitrust Law*. Little, Brown & Company, 1996.
150. Geradin, Damien. "Refusal to Supply and Margin Squeeze: A Discussion of Why the 'Telefónica Exceptions' Are Wrong." *TILEC Discussion Paper* No. 2011-009 (2011).
151. *See* Draft Commission staff working document, Explanatory note on the Commission Recommendation on regulated access to Next Generation Access Networks, 2008, at p. 11. The proposal was not included in the final text. Further, it considered the analysis of both costs alternatively and not cumulatively as we advance here.
152. Bergman, Mats A. "When Should an Incumbent Be Obliged to Share Its Infrastructure with an Entrant under the General Competition Rules?" *Journal of Industry, Competition and Trade* 5.1 (2005): 5-26.

after the former legal monopoly has turned into a historical operator. As Larouche has argued, imposing asymmetrical obligations *only* on the basis of "historical facts" is unsustainable in the long run.[153] However, it remains a historical fact that must be factored into the analysis of single-firm behavior under Article 102 TFEU.

Indeed, our approach thus sits in between the obligations that the telecommunication liberalization directives imposed in the 1990s. On the one hand, Directive 96/19 attached asymmetric obligations to incumbent operators based on their history. The asymmetric obligations would prevent "a continuation de facto of the current special and exclusive rights."[154] While subsequent Directive 97/33 shifted the reference framework for the application of asymmetric obligations to firms with SMP, namely firms with more than 25% of market share.[155] This shift appears to have arisen in reaction to the opinion of a majority of operators who argued that asymmetrical regulation was incompatible with fair competition.[156]

[F] Competition Between Historical Operators and Effect on Trade

An effect on trade is required to find an abuse of a dominant position. Although commonly underdiscussed,[157] the Commission's analysis of the effect in *Telefónica* and *Orange Polska* reveals a certain degree of inconsistency across legal findings.

On the one hand, the Commission found that historical operators from other countries did not impose a competitive constraint on Telefónica and Orange Polska. Yet, on the other hand, it considered that any conduct of undertakings that had "formerly enjoyed a State monopoly" in its national markets would "generally affect" trade between Member States.[158] The origin of such effect being the historical effects of a State-imposed geographical segregation of the telecommunications market.

153. Larouche, Pierre. *Competition Law and Regulation in European Telecommunications*. Hart Publishing, 2000, at p. 27.
154. Commission Directive 96/19/EC of 13 March 1996 amending Directive 90/388/EEC with regard to the implementation of full competition in telecommunications markets, *OJ* L 074, 22/03/1996, p. 0013–0024, at §13: "Given the imbalance in negotiating power of new entrants compared with the telecommunications organizations whose monopoly position results from their special and exclusive rights ... failure by Member States to adopt the necessary safeguards to prevent such a situation would lead to a continuation de facto of the current special and exclusive rights."
155. Article 4(3) of Directive 97/33/EC of the European Parliament and of the Council of 30 June 1997 on interconnection in Telecommunications with regard to ensuring universal service and interoperability through application of the principles of Open Network Provision (ONP) *OJ* L 199, 26/07/1997, p. 0032–0052.
156. The Consultation on the Green Paper on the Liberalisation of Telecommunication Infrastructure and Cable Television Networks. COM(95) 158 final, 3 May 1995, at p. 11. However, as the Consultation recounts, divergent opinions regarding the imposition of asymmetric obligations existed. *Id.* at p. 15.
157. The analysis of the Commission and EU Courts in cases of abuse of dominance is thin and taken for granted. Arguably, a reason for this is that the EU Courts have lowered the threshold to finding an effect on trade between Member States. *See Michelin I*, where the Court held that to qualify as an abuse the conduct must be just "capable of having that effect." CJEU, Case C-322/81, *Michelin I*, ECLI:EU:C:1983:313, §104.
158. Commission Decision, Case COMP/38.784, *Wanadoo España v. Telefónica*, §695 and 696.

This automatic presumption of effect on trade is partially inconsistent with the finding that historical operators from other countries are not a competitive constraint. It is in contradiction with the belief that legacy advantages need to be taken into account.

For this approach to be fully in line with the competitive process, legacy and potential first-mover advantages of other historical operators, which are competitors in the market, must also be factored in the analysis of anticompetitive effects.[159] As Telefónica argued, the firms that sought access to its network were the German and French historical operators Deutsche Telekom and France Télécom. These firms also benefitted from incumbency advantages and strong financial backing. However, the Commission considered this *"irrelevant"* because the German and French historical operators did not enjoy "a prominent position"[160] (emphasis added). In the same line, the Commission dismissed in *Orange Polska* the claim that historical operators from other Member States could leverage their advantages into other national markets.[161]

The outright rejections in *Telefónica* and *Orange Polska* must be avoided if the focus is to be put on the process of competition, as well as to ensure coherence and consistency across the enforcement of different competition rules.

For instance, relating the enforcement of Article 101 TFEU, in *E.ON/GDF*,[162] the Commission fined both E.ON and GDF EUR 553 million for agreeing to share energy markets. The Commission understood that the agreement could not be exempted under the claim that competition was restricted by the State. The Commission maintained that competition could and did occur between historical operators—even if E.ON still retained certain statutory prerogatives that allowed it to control market access:

> La Commission ne conteste ni l'existence de barrières à l'entrée, ni le fait que *la concurrence transfrontalière* n'était que marginale *entre les opérateurs historiques*. Les deux entreprises sont toutefois des acteurs importants du secteur gazier européen et chacune doit être considérée comme un nouveau concurrent naturel sur le marché de l'autre; autrement dit, elles *constituent des concurrents bien placés qui avaient en principe toutes les chances de réussir leur entrée sur le marché voisin* (emphasis added).[163]

Also, in merger control, the Commission has taken due account of legacy advantages across different markets. For instance, in *EDP/ENI/GDP*, the Commission prohibited the concentration between the historical electricity and gas operators in Portugal. The acquisition of GDP would eliminate a strong potential competitor with strong incentives to enter the wholesale electricity market. GDP would enter the market

159. Arguing the same, *see* Hay, George A. and Kathryn McMahon. "The Diverging Approach to Price Squeezes in the United States and Europe." *Journal of Competition Law and Economics* 8.2 (2012): 259-296, at 294 (discussing about competition between the subsidiaries of "*ex-ante monopolies*").
160. Commission Decision, Case COMP/38.784, *Wanadoo España v. Telefónica*, §§340 and 348. *See also* GC, Case T-340/03, *France Télécom v. Commission*, ECLI:EU:T:2007:22, §§114-116, where the GC chose to focus on the size of France Télécom instead of balancing legacy and first-mover advantages between historical operators.
161. Commission Decision, Case COMP/39.525, *Telekomunikacja Polska*, §886.
162. Commission Decision, Case COMP/39.401, *E.ON/GDF*.
163. *Id.* §240.

as an "*effective competitive force due to the various incumbency advantages* that it could rely on as the major gas supplier in Portugal"[164] (emphasis added).

These decisions, taken in the context of merger control and Article 101 TFEU investigations, are more in line with economic literature than Article 102 TFEU enforcement. The economic literature indeed emphasizes that competition between historical operators is of outmost importance and cannot be overlooked. The know-how, resources and capabilities of historical operators are capable of being transferred across markets, thereby balancing their legacy advantages among different historical operators.[165]

§3.05 HISTORICAL OPERATORS AFTER *POST DANMARK I*

In *Post Danmark I* the Court of Justice ruled that when "a dominant position has its origins in a former legal monopoly, that fact must be taken into account."[166]

This section explores whether *Post Danmark I* obiter was followed in subsequent enforcement initiatives. As discussed, the case law before *Post Danmark I* has not saliently accounted for State historicity in its analyses. However, a closer look into it has revealed that the both the EU Courts, and the Commission (to a greater extent) implicitly factor it in their analyses. Overall, this finding is welcome. However, the non-cohesive, scattered and unidirectional manner in which principles and tests have been applied is still far from equitable enforcement. Have the EU Courts and Commission examined historicity in a more commendable way after the Court of Justice's obiter in *Post Danmark I*?

[A] *Orange Polska*

The appeal brought by Orange Polska gave the General Court the opportunity to implement the CJEU's obiter. In line with *Post Danmark I* it held that "[i]n assessing the proportionality of the fine and, more specifically, the proportionality of the basic amount of the fine, it is essential to take account, first, of the fact that the applicant had a dominant position which owed its origin to the former legal monopoly ... ."[167]

164. Commission Decision, Case COMP/M 3.440, *EDP/ENI/GDP*, at §§340-345 and 362.
165. Whalley, Jason and Peter Curwen. "Incumbency and Market Share within European Mobile Telecommunication Networks." *Telecommunications Policy* 36.3 (2012): 222–236. More generally, *see* Laffont, Jean-Jacques and Jean Tirole. *Competition in Telecommunications*. MIT Press, 2001, at p. 14: "Besides the traditional operators (fixed-link and mobile), other network operators such as cable companies, railroad infrastructure owners, and electricity, gas and water utilities can be efficient providers." As the Commission further illustrated in E.ON/GDF, competition between historical operators goes even further than competition between neighboring historical operators. A subsidiary of GAZPROM (Russian State controlled energy company) and Rockefeller's descendant in Germany, Mobil Erdgas Erdöl, had entered the market and sold natural gas in competition with E.ON, the German historical operator, descendant of VEBA, created by the Prussian state. *See* Commission Decision, Case COMP/39.401, *E.ON/GDF*, at §§29-30.
166. CJEU, Case C-209/10, *Post Danmark I*, ECLI:EU:C:2012:172, §23.
167. GC, Case T-486/11, *Orange Polska v. Commission*, ECLI:EU:T:2015:1002, §§177-178.

The salient manner in which the General Court takes the legacy effects on board is laudable. Nonetheless, it is disconcerting as to the place it occupies in the judgment, and intensifies legal uncertainty in the already-opaque world of fines' setting.

The disconcert stems from the lack of correspondence with the Commission's assessment.[168] The General Court held that the Commission had factored in its assessment of the gravity of the fine the former legal monopoly character of Orange Polska.[169] The Commission imposed a fine of EUR 127 million on Orange Polska for restricting and rendering access to the local loop more difficult.[170] But nowhere did the Commission's calculation of the fine take into account Orange Polska's former legal monopoly origins.

Post *Orange Polska* legal certainty is also at stake. The introduction of historicity as a benchmark for the assessment of fines is novel. Indeed, the Guidelines on the method of setting fines do not foresee such scenario in their proposed methodology.[171] Despite the novelty, the General Court failed to explain how to factor historicity into the proportionality assessment. The only hint the Court left recounted to the special responsibility mantra and the degree of market power of the infringing firm.

The General Court could be suggesting that where the dominant firm has its origins in the State and thus assuming a strong market power, the special responsibility is higher and thus the infringement of competition law rules is more serious.[172] This argument alone would however be incomplete from a process perspective. What matters is not the degree of market power alone but the origin of that market power.

The Court might have framed a policy of higher fines for historical operators in terms of deterrence. If historical operators' incentives to engage in anticompetitive conduct is arguably higher than for other firms,[173] larger fines could act as a deterrent mechanism. The EU Courts' case law supports that deterrence is part of a fine's objective, and in *Orange Polska*, the GC held that the amount of the fine must also "have a sufficiently deterrent effect."[174] The Guidelines on the method of setting fines

168. *Id.* §§182-186.
169. GC, Case T-486/11, *Orange Polska v. Commission*, ECLI:EU:T:2015:1002, §§177 and 182; and CJEU, Case C-123/16 P, *Orange Polska v. Commission*, ECLI:EU:C:2018:590, §86.
170. Among others, the Commission factored in that the Polish regulatory authority had already fined Orange Polska need for the same conduct; the duration and intentional nature of the infringement, Orange Polska's awareness of the illegality and the importance from a social point of view of the affected markets. *See id.* §§179-181.
171. Guidelines on the method of setting fines imposed pursuant to Article 23(2)(a) of Regulation No 1/2003 *OJ* C 210, 1.9.2006, p. 2–5 ("Guidelines on the method of setting fines").
172. CJEU, Case C-52/09, *TeliaSonera*, ECLI:EU:C:2011:83, §81: "Nonetheless the degree of market strength is, as a general rule, significant in relation to the extent of the effects of the conduct of the undertaking concerned rather than in relation to the question of whether the abuse as such exists." *See also* the Guidance Paper, §20: "In general, the stronger the dominant position, the higher the likelihood that conduct protecting that position leads to anti-competitive foreclosure."
173. *See* section 3.06[B] below.
174. GC, Case T-486/11, *Orange Polska v. Commission*, ECLI:EU:T:2015:1002, §176. However, the Court of Justice on appeal did not address this issue. *See* CJEU, Case C-123/16 P, *Orange Polska v. Commission*, ECLI:EU:C:2018:590. Other cases that have explicitly made of deterrence and objective of the imposition of fines include: CJEU, Joined Cases C-100, 101, 102, 103/80 *Musique Diffusion Française v. EC Commission ("Pioneer")*, ECLI:EU:C:1983:158, §106; CJEU,

also hold the principle that fines should be set "at a level which ensures that it has a sufficiently deterrent effect."[175] However, the General Court did not take the opportunity to walk down this road, and has thus left the calculation of fines in a state of further indeterminacy.

[B] *Slovak Telekom*

Slovak Telekom is the first case handed down by the Commission after the *Post Danmark* saga that explicitly acknowledges the need to take the former State origins of dominant firms into account.

The Commission found that the historical operator Slovak Telekom refused to grant unbundled access to its local loops and applied a margin squeeze on alternative operators. Slovak Telekom was already under the regulatory obligation to grant access to the unbundled local loop.

The Commission recalled that the Court in *Post Danmark I* required that the former legal monopoly origins of the dominant firm be taken into account. In a situation, such as Slovak Telekom's, where the dominant position has been acquired under the protection of exclusive rights and financed by state resources, it concludes that an obligation to give access "*may* not have an impact on [its] incentives to invest and innovate"[176] (emphasis added). Those incentives, the Commission concludes, are taken into account under the regulatory framework.

The Commission thus avoided meeting the strict essential facilities test set out in *Bronner*[177] where the application of Article 102 related to the imposition of an obligation to supply an asset in which the undertaking had invested itself. Unlike Bronner, Slovak Telekom's network had been created by the State "under a monopolistic regime."[178]

On appeal, Slovak Telekom argued that disapplying the *Bronner* conditions (namely indispensability of the input) could not be based on the premise that Slovak Telekom's origins were those of a statutory monopoly. It (rightly) pointed out that the Commission previous decisional practice states that the historical nature of a monopoly is irrelevant for the assessment of abusive conduct under Article 102 TFEU. And that in any event, the Commission should have examined how the legal origins of Slovak Telekom justified disregarding the conditions set in *Bronner*.[179]

The General Court confirmed *Post Danmark I obiter* ruling that, is "settled case-law that the existence of a dominant position resulting from a legal monopoly must be taken into consideration in the context of the application of Article 102 TFEU."[180] The GC understood that the reasoning put forward by the Commission

Case 511/06 P, *Archer Daniels Midland Co. v. Commission*, ECLI:EU:C:2009:433, §105; GC, Case T-167/08, *Microsoft v. Commission*, ECLI:EU:T:2012:323, §94.

175. Guidelines on the method of setting fines, §30. *Id.* at §4.
176. Commission Decision, Case COMP/39.523, *Slovak Telekom*, §373.
177. CJEU, C-7/97, *Bronner*, ECLI:EU:C:1998:569, §41.
178. *Id.* §§370 and 373.
179. GC, Case T-851/14, *Slovak Telekom v. Commission*, ECLI:EU:T:2018:929, at §§149 and 160.
180. GC, Case T-851/14, *Slovak Telekom v. Commission*, ECLI:EU:T:2018:929, at §153.

relating to the existence of a preexisting statutory monopoly was sufficient to derogate from the *Bronner* conditions.[181]

A reasoning which was however scarce. As the GC recalls, the Commission only considered it *possible* that the historical condition of Slovak Telekom would mean that the imposition of an obligation to supply or grant access has no impact on its incentives to invest or innovate. The GC considered that enough, since the regulator had already assessed those incentives when imposing access conditions. Indeed, part of the reasons why the regulatory framework-imposed access conditions was that new entrants did not have widespread alternative network infrastructures, given that telecom operators, such as Slovak Telekom, had rolled out theirs protected by exclusive rights and public funds.

§3.06 THE TRANSIENT HISTORICAL POSITION AND INCENTIVES TO BEHAVE ANTICOMPETITIVELY

[A] Sustainability

The due date, the day in which historical operators will be no more, is a question we have been postponing. Not without a reason, for it affects the whole analysis above. For how long will the effects of the absence of competition for the market persist? For how long should equality of opportunity be used as a benchmark to assess single-firm behavior under Article 102 TFEU? For how long will first-mover advantages be a concern and incentives to innovate affected by its legacy position?

The EU Courts and the Commission mechanically assume that legacy advantages are durable. The case law does not make a single reference as to their sustainability or when they will fade away.

In *Slovak Telekom*, the Commission and the GC did not address the defendant's contention that the period during which the SMP analysis was made by the regulator could be different than the period in which the competition analysis is carried out.[182] Incentives are malleable. They are not static. As such, incentives to invest and innovate of the historical dominant firm might have well changed due, for example, to further investments in the network post-liberalization.

Strategy scholars call this a sustainable competitive advantage and have dedicated rivers of ink to research it.[183] We cannot give a complete answer to these questions here as they require an analysis of each historical operator under scrutiny. This notwithstanding, we can put forward a series of questions that competition

181. *Id.* at §166.

182. Commission Decision, Case COMP/39.523, *Slovak Telekom*, §§373-377, and 891-894, and GC, Case T-851/14, *Slovak Telekom v. Commission*, ECLI:EU:T:2018:929, at §§ 161 and 166. Other cases simply do not mention the historical operator nature of the dominant firm. Whether this means that the effects of a statutory dominant position have disappeared would be ill conjecture. *See, e.g.*, GC, Case T-201/11, *Si.Mobil*, ECLI:EU:T:2014:1096; GC, Case T-432/10, *Vivendi*, ECLI:EU:T:2013:538.

183. *See* Chapter 6 for a discussion on the SML. More generally, *see* Porter, Michael E. *Competitive Advantage: Creating and Sustaining Superior Performance*. New York: Free Press, [1985] 2004.

authorities should strive to answer to assess the "due date" of the historical operator character of the dominant firm.

First, when did the historical operator lose the support or protection of the state? The younger the historical operator is, the more probable it is that its legacy effects are stronger, and vice versa.

Second, has the footprint of the historical operator declined or increased *over time*? A simple finding of dominance in the present is not enough. Competition authorities should evaluate the evolution of market position of the dominant firm, as well as that of its competitors. Regression models, such as that of Nejc Jakopin and Andreas Klein, built over a sufficient time frame and accounting for entry timing variables and legacy effects should help to assess the relevance and due dates of the historical operator's footprint in the competitive process.[184]

Third, in case of regulated industries, what is the actual incentive analysis carried out by the regulator? Competition authorities and courts should take the regulator's assessment into consideration, update it to the current market situation and be aware of the different objectives sought by regulators. Simply relying on the regulator's assessment is not enough. Time might have lapsed, and objectives of the regulator may differ from a competition law perspective.

[B] Incentives to Behave Anticompetitively

Lastly, together with the opening of market, the expiration date will also mark the incentives of the firm to engage in anticompetitive conduct. Reducing the probability of entry has a cost for the firm, but in the case of historical operators the risks involved in precommitments that affect *ex post* entry are lower or inexistent so long as the expiration date does not arrive, or entry is not possible.[185]

The risk of precommitments, which have an investment character, is lower before the market is open because the firm is still protected by the State. It will not allow the historical operator to go bankrupt. Furthermore, the introduction of State Aid rules that protect the redundant investments incurred by the historical operator (stranded costs) minimize *ex post* risks. Once the market is open, but the effects of the absence of competition still remain, the undertaking will benefit from the lack of information that potential entrants might need to make their entry decision.[186]

184. This is the approach suggested in Jakopin, Nejc M. and Andreas Klein. "First-Mover and Incumbency Advantages in Mobile Telecommunications." *Journal of Business Research* 65.3 (2012): 362-370, 364. More generally, *see* Caves, Richard E., Michael Fortunato and Pankaj Ghemawat. "The Decline of Dominant Firms, 1905-1929." *The Quarterly Journal of Economics* (1984): 523-546.

185. Appelbaum, Elie and Chin Lim. "Contestable Markets under Uncertainty." *The Rand Journal of Economics* 16.1 (1985): 28-40.

186. Opinion of AG Ruiz Jarabo Colomer *in* Case C-192/08, *TeliaSonera Finland Oyj*, ECLI: EU:C:2009:309, §11: "fragile foundations trembled owing to the existing superiority of the former public operator, *deriving from the rights which it had long enjoyed and from its profound knowledge of the market*" (emphasis added).

The supposed trade-off between the ability of the historical operator to make some decisions early and the ability of new entrants to make their entry decision with more information erodes the longer the market has been closed to competition and the longer its effects persist.[187] The case for predation would follow a similar line of reasoning as that seen in the case of statutory monopolies. So long as legacy and the absence of competition for the market are still sustainable and important enough, the historical operator could rely on the asymmetric investment costs faced by new entrants, where the historical operator developed its resources and capabilities under the umbrella of the State.[188] An example of this would be retroactive rebates that rely on entry fixed costs that the historical operator no longer has to bear because these were subsidized.

The grip that some historical operators might still have on the decision-making process is also part of the ability to minimize risks in their pre-entry strategies. This is a grip that former Commissioner Joaquín Almunia highlighted without mince words. Historical operators "maintain a significant influence on the national decision-making process."[189] Albeit it will still need to be corroborated on a case-by-case basis, the risk has caught the attention of the Commission in *Orange Polska* and *Slovak Telekom* where, in a subtler manner, it held that entry was more difficult because it required overcoming "numerous administrative obstacles."[190]

Exclusionary incentives are however not the end of the story.[191] Exploitation, and in particular, excessive pricing abuses seem more prone to occur where former statutory monopolies still benefit from legacy advantages or the like. Motta and de Streel consider that a firm that owes its position of dominance to the State did not incur in risky investments.[192] This should be sufficient to treat the firm differently and impose liability for exploitative pricing as the risks of chilling innovation or investments are foregone. Higher prices are not the reward of competition *for* the market, that is, the result of a competitive process.[193]

187. Appelbaum, Elie and Chin Lim. "Contestable Markets under Uncertainty." *The Rand Journal of Economics* 16.1 (1985): 28-40.
188. Fumagalli, Chiara and Massimo Motta. "A Simple Theory of Predation." *Journal of Law and Economics* 56.3 (2013): 595-631, 605-606.
189. Almunia, Joaquín. "EU Competition Policy and Sectoral Challenges." *41st Annual Conference on International Antitrust Law and Policy Fordham*, New York (Sept. 12, 2014), *available at* http://europa.eu/rapid/press-release_SPEECH-14-592_en.htm.
190. Commission Decision, Case COMP/39.525, *Telekomunikacja Polska*, §676; and Commission Decision, Case COMP/39523, *Slovak Telekom*, §333.
191. Existing regulatory obligations can change the incentives of the firm to engage in anticompetitive behavior.
192. Motta, Massimo and Alexandre de Streel. "Excessive Pricing in Competition Law: Never Say Never?" *in* Konkurrensverket. *The Pros and Cons of High Prices*, 2007.
193. Röller, Lars-Hendrik. "Exploitative Abuses." ESMT, *Business Brief No. BB-107-002* (2007). Röller proposes as well to take into account whether the dominant position is the result of government actions. *See also* Evans, David S. and Jorge Padilla. "Excessive Prices: Using Economics to Define Administrative Legal Rules." *Journal of Competition Law and Economics* 1.1 (2005): 97-122.

§3.07 CONCLUSION

The Commission and EU Courts have taken the origins of historical operators into account. However, much of this was done in a non-cohesive, scattered and skewed manner, even after the Court of Justice's obiter in *Post Danmark I*. In this chapter, we have sought to discover its implicit application in the Article 102 TFEU case law, structure it in a more cohesive manner and address the shortcomings that evince that the process paradox is still far from resolved.

A related finding is that the Article 102 TFEU case law is absorbing several principles that seemed unique to the enforcement of Article 106 TFEU. Some of them are the level playing field, equality of opportunity and a non-cross-subsidizing principle. We have shown that there are reasons that warrant such approach, but that certain limitations must be put in place.

In this line, the idea of a level playing field and equality of opportunity must be stringently restricted to historical operators and limited both in time and scope. There is a risk of spillover effects of this concept to find abuses of dominance where the dominant firm has its origins in other sources than the State. The risk is tangible. As former Commission's Secretary General Alexander Italianer said in Palo Alto in 2013: "The role of antitrust rules is *to safeguard the level playing field* so that consumers reap the benefits of productivity and innovation."[194] His words have found place in the *Google Shopping* decision, where the apparent underpinning theory of liability is the principle of equality of opportunity.[195] Against this risk, it must be recalled that it is the unlevelled playing field that is the result of a competitive process that fills it with meaning, the existence of a disequilibrium that creates opportunities to innovate and be more efficient than others. Therein lies the process paradox. Lax antitrust thresholds of liability that take over the enforcement of Article 102 TFEU without differentiating the origins of dominant firms' market shares would be ill-conceived.[196]

Lastly, accurate terminology is essential to avoid confusion. As we have seen, the risks of transposing a generic negative view of incumbency stems from the confusion between incumbency originating in the state (historical operators) as opposed to incumbency in the sense that IO literature means. *Wanadoo* is a clear example of this risk, where the Commission conflated the historical operator's footprint in the competitive process with the common value of incumbency. Incumbency, i.e., getting and being established in the market is part of the competitive process and not an

194. Italianer, Alexander. "Prepared Remarks on: Level-Playing Field and Innovation in Technology Markets." Conference on Antitrust in Technology (Jan. 28, 2013). *See also* KADAR, Massimiliano. "European Union Competition Law in the Digital Era." *Zeitschrift für Wettbewerbsrecht* 4 (2015): 342. (Kadar, official at the Directorate General of Competition of the Commission advocates for such similar treatment.)
195. Commission Decision, Case COMP/39.740, *Google Search (Shopping)*, §331. *See* Chapter 5 for a detailed exposition.
196. De Streel, Alexandre. "The Antitrust Activism of the European Commission in the Telecommunications Sector" *in* Philip Lowe, and Mel Marquis (eds.) *European Competition Law Annual 2012: Competition, Regulation and Public Policies*. Bloomsbury Publishing, 2014.

impediment to it. Adequate terminology prevents unconscious spill over from the treatment of legacy effects onto firms that owe their market power positions, and accompanying efficiencies to other sources.

CHAPTER 4

The Natural Monopolist

§4.01 INTRODUCTION

Contemporary economic literature generally discusses natural monopoly in the context of state regulation. At a high level, the main issue of interest is whether and how the State should regulate the only firm providing a certain service. At a technical level, the literature considers questions related to the output and price levels of the natural monopoly firm, the conditions that regulate (compulsory) access to its infrastructure, or the design of bidding mechanisms for the right to operate the regulated monopoly.[1]

By contrast, the economic literature has only marginally discussed natural monopoly as an element of the competitive process. This is not surprising. Most natural monopolies are regulated, leaving little (if no) theoretical space for competition policy to do its job. Yet, a by-product of this is that the application of competition law to *unregulated* natural monopolies has remained virtually unexplored in the economic literature. This is unfortunate. A natural monopoly is a specific market setting in which it is comparatively more efficient that a single firm supplies the entire industry output. Such attributes are unique from an economic perspective. Hence the intuition that natural monopolies require a particular analysis under Article 102 TFEU. This issue is what this chapter seeks to explore.

To that end, this chapter is structured as follows. First, we give an overview of the economic theory of natural monopoly (§4.02). Second, we review the history of several industries ordinarily considered as natural monopolies and call into question whether such monopolies ever originated naturally (§4.03[A]). We then assess the value that the economic concept of natural monopoly has in the description of competition as a *process* (§4.03[B]). Third, in light of our findings, we look at the place that natural

1. Joskow, Paul L. "Regulation of Natural Monopoly" in A. Mitchell Polinsky and Steven Shavell (eds.) *Handbook of Law and Economics* Vol. 2, 2007: 1227-1348; and Ayal, Adi. "Is Monopoly Really Unfair?" *Journal of European Competition Law & Practice* 5.6 (2014): 386-392, at 391.

monopolies occupy in the case law (§4.04[A]). We then discuss how Article 102 TFEU should apply to natural monopolies (§4.04[B]). Lastly, we conclude (§4.05).

§4.02 THE ECONOMIC THEORY OF NATURAL MONOPOLY

Despite its apparent simplicity, the defining attributes of a natural monopoly have generated substantial debate. Several readings of the concept have emerged in the economic literature ever since Malthus used the term for the first time.[2]

Although certain divergences continue to exist,[3] a wide consensus in microeconomics and IO literature now exists on the defining features of a natural monopoly. In this section we review the evolution of the concept and explain the structural reasons that underlie the concept of natural monopoly. This will entitle us to subsequently analyze to what extent the economic concept is adjusted to the competitive reality of markets, and thereafter to understand whether the enforcement of competition law has been influenced by the theory of natural monopoly.

[A] What a Natural Monopoly Is *Not*

A natural monopoly is neither a statutory monopoly nor a public utility. The first economists to inquire into the nature of natural monopolies were deeply aware of the differences between these. In fact, in one of the first definitions of the concept of natural monopoly, John Stuart Mill wrote that natural monopolies are "those which are created by the circumstances, and not by the law."[4]

Mill was aware that there were instances in which the law could subject the natural monopolist to a particular treatment. Perhaps with the aim of highlighting those instances where nature and legal artifice overlapped, Mill described as "practical monopolies" those situations where, being "certain" that only a single firm would exist, government would "subject the business to reasonable conditions for the general advantage, or ... retain such power over it."[5] In his opinion, roads, canals, railroads and gas or water companies were clear examples of practical monopolies.[6]

Indeed, whereas the term natural monopoly is an *economic* concept, the term public utility is a *legal* status granted by government that confers certain privileges.[7] Thus, while a natural monopoly need not be a public utility (because among its differentiating attributes government is not a necessary condition), government may grant the status of a public utility to what it considers a natural monopoly. One reason

2. Mosca, Manuela. "On the Origins of the Concept of Natural Monopoly: Economies of Scale and Competition." *The European Journal of the History of Economic Thought* 15.2 (2008): 317-353.
3. *See, e.g.*, Jamison, Mark A. "A Further Look at Proper Cost Tests for Natural Monopoly." *University of Florida, Public Utility Research Center* (1997): 1-13.
4. Mill, John S. *Principles of Political Economy*. Econlib, [1848] 2009, at II.15.9.
5. *Id.* at V.11.36.
6. *Id.*
7. Cherry, Barbara A. "Historical Mutilation: How Misuse of 'Public Utility' and 'Natural Monopoly' Misdirects US Telecommunications Policy Development." *20th ITS Biennial Conference* (2014): 1-25.

for this may be to allocate to consumers the productive efficiency gains stemming from a natural monopoly.

Despite Mill's efforts, some commentators and policy makers came to conflate both instances of monopoly power. By 1900 public utility and natural monopoly had become interchangeable concepts.[8] It was economist Richard Ely who mainly called for public ownership of infrastructure and preferred the concept of public utility to that of natural monopoly. The former enjoyed "greater popularity" and made it easier to justify intervention on public policy grounds.[9] The term also enjoyed much popularity with "wanna-be" competitors who claimed that competition was too destructive. In a study of the public utility concept, economist Horace Gray remarked that "the public utility status was to be the haven of refuge for all aspiring monopolists who found it too difficult, too costly, or too precarious to secure and maintain monopoly by private action alone ... provided always, of course, that government did not exact too high a price for its favors in the form of restrictive regulation."[10]

The confusion is regrettable because, as Manuela Mosca explains in her review of the origins of the concept, the use of the term "natural" denoted that most classical economists saw it with a favorable eye and considered the other concept of public utility "unnatural."[11]

With this, our interest here is in the economic concept of *natural* monopoly. That is what Posner described as the "unregulated natural monopoly."[12] We now turn to explore what are the attributes that economists have considered to determine the existence of a *natural* monopoly.

[B] Natural Monopoly Is Found in Nature

In the early literature, a natural monopoly was described as the situation of a single firm that had benefited from geographical accidents or "peculiar products of the earth"—as Thomas Malthus wrote.[13] Its defining attribute was deemed to be the

8. Plaiss, Adam. "From Natural Monopoly to Public Utility: Technological Determinism and the Political Economy of Infrastructure in Progressive-Era America." *Technology and Culture* 57.4 (2016): 806-830, 818. Quoting the Mayor of Toledo, Ohio: "all natural monopolies should be publicly owned because ... private ownership of a public utility is a public immorality."
9. *Id.* at 807 and 818; *see also* Ely, Richard T. "Natural Monopolies and the Workingman. A Programme of Social Reform." *The North American Review* 158.448 (1894): 294-303, 296-297: "As it is not a question ... whether we will have competition or not, but only a question whether we shall have private or public monopoly, public monopoly is preferred to irresponsible private monopoly."
10. Gray, Horace M. "The Passing of the Public Utility Concept." *The Journal of Land & Public Utility Economics* 16.1 (1940): 8-20, 9; *see also* Demsetz, Harold. "Why Regulate Utilities?" *The Journal of Law and Economics* 11.1 (1968): 55-65, 63 and 65, recalling that the main driving force behind the regulatory movement in the US was the industry itself.
11. Mosca, Manuela. "On the Origins of the Concept of Natural Monopoly: Economies of Scale and Competition." *The European Journal of the History of Economic Thought* 15.2 (2008): 317-353, 323. In fact, it is unclear whether Ely himself considered natural monopoly a possibility.
12. Posner, Richard A. "Natural Monopoly and Its Regulation." *Stanford Law Review* 21.3 (1968): 548-643, 563.
13. "Peculiar products of the earth ... may be called *natural and necessary monopolies*" (emphasis added). *See* Malthus, Thomas R. "An Inquiry into the Nature and Progress of Rent, and the

scarcity of a particular commodity found in nature.[14] Pointing out to a concrete example, Malthus considered that "certain vineyards in France, which, from the peculiarity of their soil and situation, exclusively yield wine of a certain flavour" could lead to a natural monopoly.[15] Similarly, Ely and other economists considered as good examples of natural monopolies those "derived from *special limitations in the supply of raw materials*." (emphasis added).[16]

Not only products of the earth but also space constraints that physically restrict the presence of multiple firms could lead to situations of natural monopoly.[17] As von Mises explained, a "limited-space monopoly is the outcome of the fact that physical conditions restrict the field of operation in such a way that only one or a few enterprises can enter it."[18] Diamonds and mercury constituted, in von Mises view, examples of natural monopolies.[19] Similarly, economists Arthur Hadley or William Summer contended that physical limitations of space caused the emergence of natural monopoly.[20] As Hadley wrote of railroad transportation and water supply, a natural monopoly exists where "competition is *physically* impossible" (emphasis added). However, he concluded that in most cases there is no natural monopoly.[21]

In his taxonomy of the causes of trusts and monopolies, Francis Walker described a natural monopoly as a single firm in control of a "useful gift of nature such as coal, ore, petroleum, timber, water power, etc."[22] With some possible exceptions, Walker considered that the use of these natural resources contained a "competition-destroying" tendency that would keep only the most powerful corporation in business. This tendency was caused by the decreasing costs with an increased volume of output.[23] Walker did not seem to consider this cost structure as an efficiency enhancing structure since natural monopolies belonged to a different category than what he called

Principles by which it is regulated." *Project Gutenberg eBook* #4336 [1815] 2013, at p. 20. Adam Smith would not use the term natural monopoly but would refer to instances where the "singularity of soil and situation" would impede the supply of "effectual demand" and may, as a result of those natural causes, "operate forever." *See* Smith, Adam. *An Inquiry into the Nature and Causes of the Wealth of Nations*. Econlib [1776] 2009, at I.7.24-25.

14. von Mises, Ludwig. *Human Action. A Treatise on Economics*. Ludwig von Mises Institute, [1949] 1998, at p. 363.
15. Malthus, Thomas R. "An Inquiry into the Nature and Progress of Rent, and the Principles by which It Is Regulated." *Project Gutenberg* eBook #4336, [1815] 2013, at 20.
16. Ely, Richard T., Thomas S. Adams, Max O. Lorenz and Allyn A. Young. *Outlines of Economics*. Macmillan, 1910, at p. 197.
17. While Malthus agreed that the "extent of the earth" was in itself limited and could not be enlarged by human demand, he argued that fact alone was insufficient to create a natural monopoly. Perhaps, he continued, "the term partial monopoly might be fairly applicable." *See* Malthus, Thomas R. "An Inquiry into the Nature and Progress of Rent, and the Principles by which It Is Regulated." *Project Gutenberg eBook* #4336, [1815] 2013, at p. 14.
18. von Mises, Ludwig. *Human Action. A Treatise on Economics*. Ludwig von Mises Institute, [1949] 1998, at p. 371.
19. *Id.*, at p. 363.
20. Summer, William G. *Earth-Hunger and Other Essays*. Transaction Publishers, [1888] 1980, at p. 245.
21. Hadley, Arthur T. *Railroad Transportation: Its History and Its Laws*. GT Putnam's Sons, 1885, at pp. 64 and 103.
22. Walker, Francis. "The Causes of Trusts and Some Remedies for Them." *American Economic Association Quarterly* 11.1 (1910): 290-320, 294.
23. *Id.* 298 and 301.

"efficient monopolies." Therefore, the legal consequences he attached to the former and to the latter varied significantly. On the one hand, in case of a natural monopoly Walker suggested that government impede the acquisition of property rights over natural resources and eventually acquire such right for itself. On the other hand, he suggested that if monopoly rested on superior efficiency the monopoly could continue its course as a public utility.[24]

Although the meaning of natural monopoly due to a fixed supply of natural resources has been virtually superseded,[25] some modern IO scholars still consider it as a possible defining attribute (perhaps as a descriptive shortcut). For example, Belleflamme and Peitz describe a natural monopoly as one that arises from the scarcity of a particular input. Mining could be, for instance, a suitable illustration such natural monopoly where the natural resource of interest (the mine) is limited and leaves no room but for one single firm in the market to exploit it.[26]

[C] Natural Monopoly in Contemporary IO Terms

The law of increasing returns and economies of scale progressively replaced the natural resource condition as the defining attribute of natural monopoly. There are increasing returns to scale if output is larger in proportion to an equal increase of inputs. Ely considered that natural monopoly could arise if a service uses a peculiar spot of land, the service is provided in connection with the plant itself, *and* the returns are in accordance with the law of increasing returns. Marshall preferred to say that industries that followed the law of increasing returns are "indivisible industries," and not monopolies.[27]

The problem with such defining attribute is that most cost functions display increasing returns, at least up to some level of output.[28] Indeed, as soon as there are fixed costs in an industry, at some point of the cost production function a unit increase in input will yield a relatively higher unit increase in output. With this pattern of scale, and if prices of inputs are constant, the average long-run production function will be

24. *Id.* at 306-307 (natural monopoly) and 311 (superior efficiency). Mill on the contrary contended that when monopoly is a natural one then it "cannot be prevented from existing." *See* Mill, John S. *Principles of Political Economy*. Econlib, [1848] 2009, at II.16.2.
25. Mosca, Manuela. "On the Origins of the Concept of Natural Monopoly: Economies of Scale and Competition." *The European Journal of the History of Economic Thought* 15.2 (2008): 317-353, 324.
26. Belleflamme, Paul and Martin Peitz. *Industrial Organization: Markets and Strategies*. Cambridge University Press, 2015, at pp. 5 and 124.
27. Marshall, Alfred. "'Some Aspects of Competition.' The Address of the President of Section F - Economic Science and Statistics--of the British Association, at the Sixtieth Meeting, Held at Leeds, in September, 1890." *Journal of the Royal Statistical Society* 53.4 (1890): 612-643, 628-631.
28. Thomas Adams (economist contemporary of Ely) would argue that the cheapest way of proving railroad transportation would be "limited by its success in directing the largest possible volume of movement through the *fewest possible channels*" (emphasis added), instead of saying "a *single* channel." Adams, Thomas B. "Railway Commissions." *Journal of Social Science* 2 (1870): 233-236, *quoted in* McCraw, Thomas K. *Prophets of Regulation*. Harvard University Press, 1984, at p. 10.

U-shaped. Under this premise, one could have multiple firms exhibiting some level of increasing returns, and no natural monopoly.[29] Francis Edgeworth seemed to be aware of this problematic in his seminal analysis of increasing returns in the railway sector. Although he avoided using the term natural monopoly, he considered that a "monopoly regime" arises when the demand function intersects at some point of the decreasing production cost function.[30]

Against this background, Demsetz was right to observe that the theory of natural monopoly remained "exceedingly unclear."[31] Ely's works provide perhaps the best illustration of the analytical confusion surrounding the theory. On the one hand, Ely contended that large scale "by no means necessarily signifies monopolized production."[32] Yet, on the other hand, Ely wrote that "vast scale" would give an industry an "inherent and irresistible impulse toward monopoly."[33] Both statements are irreconcilable. They call for more work to clarify the significance of economies of scale in defining natural monopoly.

The missing element that would help clarify the theory of natural monopoly was the explicit and cohesive recognition of the range of the demand in the literature. As Edgeworth described, only when a firm had economies of scale *through the entire range of demand* one could infer the existence of a natural monopoly. In this scenario, the average cost curve falls as output increases at any observed output level so that a single firm can produce all the industry's output at the lowest cost.[34] This is what Paul Samuelson meant when he stated that "*persisting* decreasing costs for the firm" (emphasis added) could bring about a "single monopolist."[35] Certainly, this was what Demsetz meant when he wrote that natural monopoly existed if production scale economies make it "it is less costly for one firm to produce a commodity *in a given market* than it is for two or more firms" (emphasis added).[36] (*See* Figure 4.1 below.)

29. Cole, Daniel H. and Peter Grossman (eds.). *The End of a Natural Monopoly: Deregulation and Competition in the Electric Power Industry*. Routledge, 2004, at p. 28.
30. Edgeworth, Francis Y. "Contributions to the Theory of Railway Rates—IV." *The Economic Journal* 23.90 (1913): 206-226, at 213-214.
31. Demsetz, Harold. "Why Regulate Utilities?" *The Journal of Law and Economics* 11.1 (1968): 55-65, at 56.
32. Ely, Richard T. *Monopolies and Trusts. Grosset & Dunlap*, [1900] 1906, at pp. 61 and 162. Ely also criticized Mill for calling land a natural monopoly: "it is misleading to speak of it as a natural monopoly," at pp. 33 and 36.
33. Ely, Richard T. "Social Studies. The Reform of Railway Abuses." *Harper's New Monthly Magazine* 73.436 (1886): 571-578, at 574.
34. Breyer, Stephen G. "Antitrust, Deregulation, and the Newly Liberated Marketplace." *California Law Review* 75.3 (1987): 1005-1047, at 1007.
35. Samuelson, Paul A. *Economics*. [1948] 1964, at 461, *quoted in* Demsetz, Harold. "Why Regulate Utilities?" *The Journal of Law and Economics* 11.1 (1968): 55-65. *See also* McConnell who highlighted economies of scale should be "particularly pronounced" in a natural monopoly scenario. McConnell, C.R. *Elements of Economic Analysis*. New York: McGraw-Hill, 1960, at p. 373, *quoted in* Ulbrich, Holley H. "Natural Monopoly in Principles Textbooks: a Pedagogical Note." *The Journal of Economic Education* 22.2 (1991): 179-182, criticizing the lack of clarity in economic textbooks as to the principles governing the definition of natural monopoly.
36. Demsetz, Harold. "Why Regulate Utilities?" *The Journal of Law and Economics* 11.1 (1968): 55-65, 56.

Figure 4.1 Economies of Scale

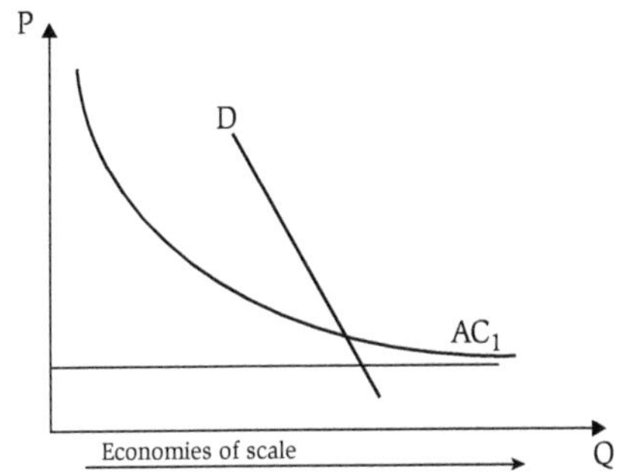

With these advancements in theory, Baumol reassessed the scale-equals-natural-monopoly equation.[37] In his mathematical examination, Baumol proved that scale is neither a sufficient nor a necessary condition to find a natural monopoly, particularly in single-product firms. In other words, one could find instances of natural monopoly even in the absence of scale economies over the whole range of demand.

In Baumol's view, the only necessary condition to determine the existence of a natural monopoly is the strict subadditivity of the cost function. This means that the firm can produce any and all output of the market at a strictly less cost than two or more firms would when producing that output separately. In a natural monopoly industry, it is always cheaper to have one firm [AC_1] produce whatever combination of outputs than having two [AC_2] or more firms producing that combination (*see* Figure 4.2 below), provided that $P \leq MC$.

37. Baumol, William J. "On the Proper Cost Tests for Natural Monopoly in a Multiproduct Industry." *The American Economic Review* 67.5 (1977): 809-822. *Also*, Sharkey, William W. *The Theory of Natural Monopoly*. New York: Cambridge University Press, 1982, at p. 21: "It is evident from the ... general literature survey that the existence or nonexistence of economies of scale is of importance in determining whether any given industry is a natural monopoly. Although the test for economies of scale is an incomplete test of natural monopoly ..., it [is] illuminating to examine the application of this test in a particular industry."

Figure 4.2 Subadditivity

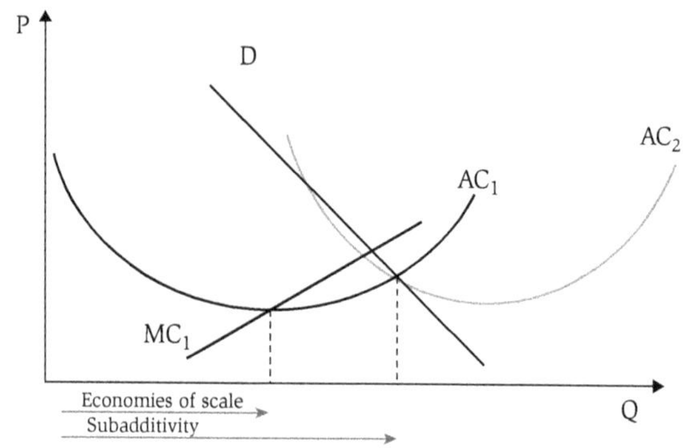

Baumol explained that while economies of scale could be sufficient to prove subadditivity in a firm producing a single output, economies of scale alone did not suffice to determine whether a multiproduct firm is a natural monopoly. Indeed, since scale refers to volume increases of output they alone cannot determine whether it is less costly to produce two or more different outputs together or separately. A multiproduct firm thus requires multiproduct cost complementarity, i.e., economies of scope and economies of scale over certain output range of the products. For example, there might be economies of scope in a vertically integrated firm between infrastructure (e.g., construction of railway tracks) and management (e.g., operation of railway tracks). This point is important. It fits better with day-to-day market facts, where most suppliers are multiproduct firms.

[D] Summation

To close our review of the history of the natural monopoly concept, we would like to insist on two important points. First, classical economists generally thought of monopoly as a natural outcome of competition. Second, it took until the 1970s for economists to offer a cohesive understanding of what "natural monopoly" meant.

With this, we will consider in the rest of this chapter that a natural monopoly means that of a single firm that can meet the entire demand of a product or a given combination of products thereof at the lowest cost than any other arrangement of firms could.

Let us now turn to a more empirical question: how often do natural monopolies arise in practice?

§4.03 THE MARKET REALITY OF NATURAL MONOPOLIES

Are natural monopolies "as rare as Bigfoot sightings"?[38] We look at this controversial question by reviewing the evolution of two industries often labeled "natural monopolies" (§4.03[A]). In light of our findings, we then discuss the shortcomings our existing economic definition of natural monopoly faces when one looks at competition from a process-oriented perspective (§4.03[B]).

[A] Natural Monopolies and Industrial History

Many industries deemed as natural monopolies have in the past been subject to economic regulation.[39] We thus face a difficult question as to whether monopoly would have prevailed absent regulation, as a natural outcome of the competitive process.

James Nelson put it strongly that, in relation to regulated industries, natural monopoly cannot be "traced back through history in a pure form."[40] A more nuanced description is that of Jose Luís Buendía in his book *Exclusive Rights and State Monopolies* in which he claims, "it is difficult to find in the real world clear examples of natural monopolies whose exclusivity does not depend to a certain extent on the will of the State."[41]

It seems clear that regulation generally occurred before any workable theory of natural monopoly was available to the legislator. The natural monopoly argument would have rather come as an *ex post* economic rationalization of what initially was a policy choice based on other considerations like political unification, public health or national security.[42] Even assuming that in the early years of regulation the law of increasing returns was *the* accepted defining attribute of a natural monopoly, one of its major advocates, Ely, would assert that "it has never been proved that" the law of increasing returns operates without limit.[43]

---

38. Carden, Art and Steven Horwitz. "Is Market Failure a Sufficient Condition for Government Intervention." *Library of Economics and Liberty* (Apr. 1, 2013) Blog article, *available at* http://www.econlib.org/library/Columns/y2013/CardenHorwitzmarkets.html.
39. Many of these industries have now been deregulated or reregulated. It is argued that technological advancements have eroded the natural monopoly characteristics of certain industries. *See* Doh, Jonathan P. and Hildy J. Teegen. "Private Investment in Emerging Markets Telecommunications Infrastructure: Global Trends, National Policies, Firm Strategies." *Competition & Change* 7.1 (2003): 39-60, 41.
40. Nelson, James R. "The Role of Competition in the Regulated Industries." *The Antitrust Bulletin* 11.1 (1966): 393-428, 396.
41. Buendía, Jose Luís. *Exclusive Rights and State Monopolies under EC Law. Article 86 (Former Article 90) of the EC Treaty*, Oxford, 2000, at p. 25.
42. Dilorenzo, Thomas J. "The Myth of Natural Monopoly." *The Review of Austrian Economics* 9.2 (1996): 43-58; and Gray, Horace M. "The Passing of the Public Utility Concept." *The Journal of Land & Public Utility Economics* 16.1 (1940): 8-20. The concept of natural monopoly could be seen as a limiting principle to regulation. However, "achieving long-term benefits of any kind through price regulation is hard and should be tried only when markets will likely fail to achieve *society's objectives*." *See* Shelanski, Howard A. "The Case for Rebalancing Antitrust and Regulation." *Michigan Law Review* 109.5 (2011): 683-732, 721-722.
43. Ely, Richard T. *Monopolies and Trusts*. Grosset & Dunlap, [1900] 1906, at p. 65.

In this section we provide a historical overview of two industries commonly said to be evolving naturally toward monopoly (with or without regulation), namely telecommunications and railroad infrastructure. We find that in the US, the introduction of economic regulation suspended an ongoing process of competition, not one of natural monopolization. In Europe, we show that the adoption of economic regulation had even stricter consequences, by nipping an incipient process of competition in the bud.[44] Although history alone cannot provide a full answer to our question,[45] it does serve to cast some doubt about the natural origins of what perhaps would have not become a natural monopoly.

[1] Telecommunications

The telecommunication network was said to be a paradigmatic example of natural monopoly for very long. Competition set off with Graham Bell's patented invention of the telephone system in 1876 and the set-up of the Bell Telephone Company (now AT&T) in the US. In the end, however, regulation put an end to it despite that the market did not seem to evolve toward any *natural* monopoly arrangement.

In the US, after the Bell's telephone patents had expired between 1893 and 1894 competitors rushed into the market. These new firms started by providing services in areas where AT&T did not provide telephone service yet. In just a year, 80 new firms had acquired 5% of the total market share. And by the early 1900s more than 3,000 competitors existed and had acquired 51% of the telephone service in local markets. Moreover, and unlike AT&T until 1922, the large majority of competitors started providing automatic telephone switching, which consumers found more attractive.[46] In this competitive wake, AT&T's returns on investment plummeted from 46% in the 1890s to 8% in 1906.[47]

About twenty years later, AT&T's acquisition of several independent competitors caught the attention of the FTC. In 1913, AT&T settled with the FTC its monopolization claims. By what was called the "Kingsbury Commitment," AT&T agreed to sell its stock on the telegraph company Western Union, not to acquire other competitors and to allow them to interconnect with its system. Importantly, the last commitment was part of AT&T's own objective of becoming a universal service provider (in original terms, a

44. "The English and American maxim is that whatever can be done without government, should be thus done. The continental principle is that whatever can be done by government, should be." *See* Hadley, Arthur T. *Railroad Transportation: Its History and Its Laws*. GT Putnam's Sons, 1885, at p. 187.
45. It goes without saying that a full historical account of the evolution of these industries is outside the scope of this work. Multiple books of (economic) history have been devoted to this at length. We provide here a selected review.
46. Interestingly, AT&T only introduced automatic operation in New York in 1940, where it operated exclusively. *See* Huurdeman, Anton A. *The Worldwide History of Telecommunications*. John Wiley & Sons, 2003, at pp. 231-233 and n. 2.
47. Thierer, Adam D. "Unnatural Monopoly: Critical Moments in the Development of the Bell System Monopoly." *Cato Journal* 14.2 (1994): 267-285, at 269-271. Western Union, which was at that time the leader in the telegraph industry, declined the opportunity to buy the telephone patents thinking the telephone was a fleeting novelty.

"common carrier"). As a result of this interconnection obligation, independent competitors were disincentivized to keep on establishing their own long-distance systems.[48]

Thus, instead of promoting competition the Kingsbury Commitment had the opposite effect. It carved up the markets. Western Union would retain a monopoly in telegraph; AT&T a monopoly over long-distance operations; and unconnected telephone systems that had started to extend telephone services throughout the US remained as local telephone exchanges.[49] In other words, the Kingsbury Commitment strongly thwarted the existing competitive race between unconnected telephone systems to establish competing universal systems.[50] As Mueller explains, "it was the refusal of Bell and the independents to interconnect with each other [what] propelled both systems into the race to achieve universal geographic coverage and universal penetration."[51]

The state-driven consolidation of the telephone industry continued over the next years as a result of different processes at every governmental level (city councils, state legislatures and regulatory commissions and state-wide referendums).[52] Among those, two acts particularly influenced the removal of the remaining competitive rivalry. *First* it was the nationalization of the industry during World War I, from August 1, 1918 until August 1, 1919. This provided AT&T substantial returns. On the one hand, government sanctioned rates allowed AT&T to increase long-distance rate by 20%, which remained after privatization. And on the other hand, government paid AT&T USD 13 million to cover alleged losses.[53] *Second* was the passing of the federal Willis-Graham Act of 1921 granted AT&T antitrust immunity. Despite the evidence that the competitive race to reach universal coverage worked, the Hearing Committee considered that there was "nothing to be gained by local competition in the telephone business"[54] and thus announced that the provision of telephone services was to be preserved from competition.[55]

48. Brock, G.W. The *Telecommunications Industry: The Dynamics of Market Structure*. Cambridge: Harvard University Press, 1981, at p. 156, *quoted in* Thierer, Adam D. "Unnatural Monopoly: Critical Moments in the Development of the Bell System Monopoly." *Cato Journal* 14.2 (1994): 267-285, 267.
49. Huber, Peter William, Michael K. Kellogg and John Throne. *Federal Telecommunications Law*. Aspen Publishers Online, 1999, at pp. 16-17, *quoted in* Thierer, Adam D. "Unnatural Monopoly: Critical Moments in the Development of the Bell System Monopoly." *Cato Journal* 14.2 (1994): 267-285, 273.
50. Mueller, Milton. "Universal Service and the Telecommunications Act: Myth made law." *Communications of the ACM* 40.3 (1997): 39-47.
51. Mueller, Milton. "Universal Service in Telephone History: A Reconstruction." *Telecommunications Policy* 17.5 (1993): 352-369, 359 and 368.
52. *Id.* 359 and 365.
53. Thierer, Adam D. "Unnatural Monopoly: Critical Moments in the Development of the Bell System Monopoly." *Cato Journal* 14.2 (1994): 267-285, at 275-276.
54. H.R. REP. No. 190, 67th Cong., Ist Sess. 1 (1921), at 1, *quoted in* Loeb, G. Hamilton. "The Communications Act Policy toward Competition: A Failure to Communicate." *Duke Law Journal* 1 (1978): 1-56, 14.
55. Loeb, G. Hamilton. "The Communications Act Policy toward Competition: A Failure to Communicate." *Duke Law Journal* 1 (1978): 1-56, 15.

History shows that the emergence of AT&T as a monopoly was rather *unnatural* and that the industry did not tend toward natural monopoly for the provision of a "universal service." On the contrary, rivalry in the US provided a competitive stimulus to deliver universal service, reduced costs and encouraged the introduction of technological advancements (like automatic switching).[56]

Is this interpretation of the competitive process in line with the subadditivity theory of natural monopoly? Although economic research regarding AT&T subadditive cost function reveals mixed results, it is now widely acknowledged that telecommunications are not a natural monopoly.[57]

In 1982, following a monopolization suit brought back in 1974, AT&T agreed to divest its business. The break-up prompted economists to test whether AT&T's cost function was indeed subadditive, i.e., naturally monopolistic. Such an analysis could shed light on whether the benefits derived from the divestiture outweighed the alleged efficiencies of being a single firm in the market.

A way of simplifying the subadditivity analysis, followed by David Evans and James Heckman,[58] was to restrict the range of output where a duopoly configuration is compared to a monopoly configuration. Using AT&T's data and analyzing output levels produced between 1958 and 1977 they reject the possibility that AT&T's cost function was subadditive. However, Abraham Charnes and colleagues, purportedly using the same data but alternative estimation metrics, find the opposite result.[59]

Evans and Heckman rebutted the contradictory findings of Charnes and colleagues as, they had either used different data or different models that made the comparison misleading and impractical. Moreover, they concluded, economic studies on natural monopoly should focus on finding better data rather than "alternative estimation metrics."[60] Richard Shin and John Ying, building on better data and a larger

56. *See* Armstrong, Mark, Simon Cowan and John Vickers. *Regulatory Reform: Economic Analysis and British Experience*. MIT Press, 1994, at p. 201, explaining that these attributes reinforce the possibility that international networks are unlikely to be "severe natural monopolies."

57. Even the local loop (often considered as the last remaining natural monopoly in the telecommunications sector) reveals a more complex reality that casts doubts about its true natural monopoly nature. As Pierre Larouche explains: "nothing prevents the establishment of a number of parallel local loops; with wireless local loops, in particular, the marginal cost of an additional subscriber tends to be low ... nevertheless, even if parallel local loops can be put in place, most subscribers will only use one of them, so that the other(s) remain idle ... only one of them is likely to produce any revenue." *See* Larouche, Pierre. *Competition Law and Regulation in European Telecommunications*. Hart Publishing, 2000, at p. 324.

58. Evans, David S. and James J. Heckman. "A Test for Subadditivity of the Cost Function with an Application to the Bell System." *The American Economic Review* 74.4 (1984): 615-623. Evans and Heckman's paper is a rebuttal to the evidence AT&T brought in the proceedings trying to demonstrate it was a natural monopoly.

59. Charnes, Abraham, William W. Cooper, and Toshiyuki Sueyoshi. "A Goal Programming/Constrained Regression Review of the Bell System Breakup." *Management Science* 34.1 (1988): 1-26. Similarly, Röller shows that gains from divestiture were negative in all years and concluded that AT&T held a natural monopoly. *See* Röller, Lars-Hendrik. "Proper Quadratic Cost Functions with an Application to the Bell System." *The Review of Economics and Statistics* (1990): 202-210.

60. Evans, David S. and James J. Heckman. "Rejoinder - Natural Monopoly and the Bell System: Response to Charnes, Cooper and Sueyoshi." *Management Science* 34.1 (1988): 27-38.

set of observations, showed that of local exchange carriers are not natural monopolies.[61] Their cost structure is not globally subadditive. In their view, these results "suggest that AT&T was also unlikely to be a natural monopoly before its breakup."[62]

The telecommunications industry in *Europe* evolved in a significantly different manner. Notwithstanding the idiosyncrasies of the European States, the industrial history shows a succession of stories with a common underlying theme: after Bell's discovery, competition was given virtually no room for play.

In the UK, the Telegraph Act of 1869 had granted a statutory monopoly on all telegraphic communications to the Post Office. However, the disruptive threat that the telephone system could pose to its monopoly prompted judicial action to clarify whether the telephone was also a telegraph. In a lawsuit brought by the Attorney General the High Court swiftly clarified by 1880 that the telephone fell under that monopoly. This substantially thwarted the competitive process that had just started with Bell's invention in 1876. While the Post Office could license out private companies for over a period of twenty-four years, it kept the right to purchase the license back. As a result, by 1911 the Post Office had bought all remaining licensees and set course of history for a hundred years.[63]

More unswervingly in France, the Government enacted on July 16, 1889 a law whereby the statutory monopoly in telegraph lines was extended to the telephone—thus detained by the Administration des Postes et Télégraphes (PTT).[64] Interestingly, the French Government left the more commercially risky external networks in private hands, such as those connecting with its colonies.[65] Competition had limited time to develop and was stringently constrained.

Indeed, one must highlight that the proposed legislation granting PTT a statutory monopoly over telephone had been publicly debated since 1884. Few entrepreneurs would have taken the risk of starting a business that could eventually be taken over by PTT. Moreover, the Government had enacted on May 6, 1837, a law prohibiting private initiatives to introduce optical telegraph services. Anyone who transmitted "any signal" by telegraph or by any other means without a statutory authorization would not only face a fine but also imprisonment.[66] With this background, by 1880, few firms had

61. Shin, Richard T. and John S. Ying. "Unnatural Monopolies in Local Telephone." *The RAND Journal of Economics* 23.2 (1992): 171-183, at 173: "Given that the number of observations is small relative to the number of parameters being estimated, it is not surprising that the results have oscillated depending on the specification and the estimation technique."
62. *Id.* 179.
63. Liffen, John. "Telegraphy and Telephones." *Industrial Archaeology Review* 35.1 (2013): 22-39. *See also* Huurdeman, Anton A. *The Worldwide History of Telecommunications*. John Wiley & Sons, 2003, at p. 168; and Stumpers, F.L. "The History, Development, and Future of Telecommunications in Europe." *IEEE Communications Magazine* 22.5 (1984): 84-95.
64. Musso, Pierre. "Aux origines de 'l'autonomie' des Télécommunications Françaises, la Loi de 1923." *Réseaux* 12.66 (1994): 99-117.
65. Stumpers, F.L. "The History, Development, and Future of Telecommunications in Europe." *IEEE Communications Magazine* 22.5 (1984): 84-95.
66. This law stayed in force until the EU liberalization directives forced its replacement. *See* Huurdeman, Anton A. *The Worldwide History of Telecommunications*. John Wiley & Sons, 2003, at pp. 39 and 45. The translation of the law, which had only one article, is: "anyone who transmits any signal without authorization from one point to another one whether with the aid

undertaken the risk and the stringent conditions that the authorizations imposed did not allow for the development of competition. The only three private undertakings benefiting from an authorization to enter the market in 1880 where all under control of PTT by 1889.[67]

France and the UK are just examples of how European states left little or virtually no space for competition to develop in the telecommunications industry. By 1913 all trunk lines in Europe were state owned.[68]

This was despite evidence pointing to beneficial competition between operators. Sweden, unlike its European counterparts, had placed no initial obstacles to the development of telephone networks. This led to the establishment of several telecommunication companies like the Stockholm Public Telephone Company.[69] This brought a period of strong competition where Swedish consumers were "the real winners" by having the lowest telephone charges in Europe and the highest teledensity.[70]

As Justice Breyer summarized, "there is now considerable agreement that longlines telecommunications does not possess the characteristics of a natural monopoly."[71] Moreover, we should add, there is compelling evidence from the competitive dynamics of the industry that telecommunications *was* not a natural monopoly in the first place.

[2] Railroads

Despite being commonly regarded as natural monopolies, classical economists like Hadley regarded railroads as a new sort of monopoly, different from legal or natural ones. Railroads were becoming "industrial monopolies" "where the business interests of the parties concerned make competition practically impossible."[72] Hadley considered that this was the result of reckless speculation in the construction of railroads in the US. In a span of three years, between 1880 and 1882, an additional 29,000 miles of railroads were built. "Not more than one third of these were justified by existing

of mechanical telegraphs or by any other means will be subject to imprisonment for a duration of between one month and one year, *and* will be liable to a fine of from 1,000 to 10,000 francs" (emphasis added).

67. Griset, Pascal. "L'Etat et les Télécommunications Internationales au Début du XXème Siécle en France: Un Monopole Stérile." *Histoire, économie et société* 6.2 (1987): 181-207, 191-192. Furthermore, Griset explains, government would use every law and regulation addressing petty problems in telecommunications to reaffirm the statutory monopoly.
68. Millward, Robert. "Business and the State" *in* Geoffrey G. Jones and Jonathan Zeitlin (eds.) *The Oxford Handbook of Business History*. Oxford University Press, 2008: 529-557, 546.
69. Giertz, Eric. "Understanding the Swedish Saga through an Historical Exposé" *in* Eric Giertz, Annika Rickne and Petri Rouvinen (eds.) *Small and Beautiful—The ICT Success of Finland and Sweden*. Verket för innovationssystem-VINNOVA (2015): 62-95.
70. Huurdeman, Anton A. *The Worldwide History of Telecommunications*. John Wiley & Sons, 2003, at pp. 174-176.
71. Breyer, Stephen G. "Antitrust, Deregulation, and the Newly Liberated Marketplace." *California Law Review* 75.3 (1987): 1005-1047, at 1020.
72. Hadley's book, written in 1885, provides a truly contemporary perspective of railroads. Much of what follows in this subsection comes from his book. *See* Hadley, Arthur T. *Railroad Transportation: Its History and Its Laws*. GT Putnam's Sons, 1885, at pp. 65-66.

business. Another third, perhaps, were likely to be profitable at some future date."[73] The excess in output led to a spiral of price decreases that continued even when prices could not cover costs.

As a result, rate competition was widespread and aggressive. This led railroad companies to leave the business, enter price fixing agreements and price discriminate between long and short routes. High prices in short routes (where fewer railroads competed) could subsidize lower rates in long-distance routes where competition was tougher.[74] However, this seemingly "unsustainable" situation knew exceptions, especially in long routes. For example, in the Chicago-Omaha connection demand for the service was so high that three different roads could compete without arriving to a "cut-throat point."[75]

As railroads became critical means of transportation, federal states sought to exert control. In *Munn v. Illinois* the US Supreme Court upheld federal state's power to regulate any business "affected with a public interest," among which were common carriers on railroads.[76] The US Supreme Court did not consider natural monopoly as a cause for the regulation of the railroads. The fact of the matter was that railroads exercised a "sort of public office, and have duties to perform in which the public is interested."[77] Ten years later, in 1887, the *Wabash* Supreme Court judgment removed virtually all federal state's competence to regulate interstate commerce and hand it over to the Senate.[78]

In this context, and after hearing key industry leaders, the Senate Committee on Interstate Commerce had decided to regulate the industry on January 18, 1886.[79] And on February 4, 1887, the Interstate Commerce Commission (ICC) was created. Yet, although some degree of industry consolidation was naturally expected, the ICC's prohibition on price discrimination and contractual coordination encouraged railroad companies to merge.[80] Waiting for the survival of the fittest railroads was not an option.[81]

---

73. Hadley, Arthur T. *Railroad Transportation: Its History and Its Laws*. GT Putnam's Sons, 1885, at p. 52.
74. Langlois, Richard N. "Antitrust: Where Did It Come from and What Did It Mean?" *University of Connecticut. Department of Economics Working Paper Series* 2016-07 (September 2016): 1-54, 20.
75. Hadley, Arthur T. *Railroad Transportation: Its History and Its Laws*. GT Putnam's Sons, 1885, at p. 91.
76. *Munn v. Illinois*, 94 U.S. 113 (1876), at 115 and 130.
77. *Id.* at 130.
78. *Wabash, St. Louis & Pacific Railway Company v. Illinois*, 118 U.S. 557 (1886).
79. Kolko, Gabriel. *Railroads and Regulations, 1877-1916*. Princeton University Press, [1965] 2015, at pp. 36-40, but also conceding at p. 20 that: "the movement for federal regulation of the railroad system was not, in any strict sense, deliberately initiated by the railroads."
80. Langlois, Richard N. "Antitrust: Where Did It Come from and What Did It Mean?" *University of Connecticut. Department of Economics Working Paper Series* 2016-07 (September 2016): 1-54, 25.
81. As a railroad president claimed: "the prevailing contagion of depression and loss, from the effects of ruinous rates, which were uncontrollable from a *lack of adequate protection of railroad interests in the past, is not to be remedied by waiting upon the 'survival of the fittest'*" (emphasis added), *quoted in* Kolko, Gabriel. *Railroads and Regulations, 1877-1916*. Princeton University Press, [1965] 2015, at p. 20.

In Continental Europe, private enterprise was unwilling to start building railroads unless the state took the initiative.[82] Thus, to incentivize railway construction the state would subsidize private companies.[83] However, the existence of private companies should not be confused with competition. In general terms, European States' urgency to build railroads bypassed the competitive process.[84]

In France, railroads were barely open to competition, and the statutory financial backing made their position extremely advantageous—"heads I win, tails you lose."[85] Moreover, prohibiting the construction of parallel routes was the norm in central Europe, as it was the case in Prussia[86] and France (the double railroad connection between Paris and Versailles being an exception to this).[87] In Italy the State had nearly complete public ownership, and Scandinavia owned all the trunk lines.[88]

Despite this general trend in Europe, the UK and Belgium governments allowed market forces to play out for considerably long periods of time. The result was that, despite a tendency to concentration national railway monopolies did not seem to arise, and in some instances competition between similar railroads prospered.

James Foreman-Peck has argued that the UK run a "market test for natural monopoly" in railroads.[89] Unlike in other European countries (where the State pre-empted competition from the early days) in the UK "so many speculators wanted to build railroads [that] Parliament had not the moral courage to refuse them charters."[90] By 1843, 70 companies had built 2,100 miles of tracks, and in 1865 the number of companies had increased to 78 and railway mileage gone up to 11,451.[91] According to Hadley, the stability of the railroad industry in the UK was due to the less dodgy investments undertaken by private companies. While in the UK the main purpose of building railroads was to connect existing business and cities, Americans largely built

82. Hadley, Arthur T. *Railroad Transportation: Its History and Its Laws*. GT Putnam's Sons, 1885, at pp. 188, 193 and 195.
83. Millward, Robert. *Private and Public Enterprise in Europe: Energy, Telecommunications and Transport, 1830-1990*. Cambridge University Press, 2005, at p. 28.
84. Millward, Robert. "Business and the State" *in* Geoffrey G. Jones and Jonathan Zeitlin (eds.) *The Oxford Handbook of Business History*. Oxford University Press, 2008: 529-557, 536.
85. Ekelund Jr., Robert B. and Robert F. Hébert. "Dupuit and the Railroads." *History of Political Economy* 44.1 (2012): 97-111, 99, and at 101: "The French railroads were basically a government-organized cartel."
86. Millward, Robert. *Private and Public Enterprise in Europe: Energy, Telecommunications and Transport, 1830–1990*. Cambridge University Press, 2005, at p. 28.
87. Ekelund Jr., Robert B. and Robert F. Hébert. "Dupuit and the Railroads." *History of Political Economy* 44.1 (2012): 97-111, at 102, n. 7 "The Paris-Versailles railroads merged in 1855 *under government rules and regulations*, including entry control, after initially being given *government* permission to build separate facilities" (emphasis in the original).
88. Millward, Robert. "Business and the State" *in* Geoffrey G. Jones and Jonathan Zeitlin (eds.) *The Oxford Handbook of Business History*. Oxford University Press, 2008: 529-557, 536.
89. Foreman-Peck, James S. "Natural Monopoly and Railway Policy in the Nineteenth Century." *Oxford Economic Papers* 39.4 (1987): 699-718.
90. Hadley, Arthur T. *Railroad Transportation: Its History and Its Laws*. GT Putnam's Sons, 1885, at p. 166.
91. Foreman-Peck, James S. "Natural Monopoly and Railway Policy in the Nineteenth Century." *Oxford Economic Papers* 39.4 (1987): 699-718.

"for the future." Naturally, many of these prospective investments in the supply of railroad transportation did not match a corresponding demand.[92]

Despite the large number of UK railway companies, concentration left the industry in 1907 with thirteen companies owning 88% of the total mileage. In Foreman-Peck's reading, this evolution seemed to indicate that the railway "industry was a regional natural monopoly at least."[93] The UK Board of Trade reached the same conclusion in 1911: "active competition between railway companies of an extensive kind hardly any longer exists."[94] However, as Anthony Arnold and Sean McCartney concentration analysis shows, after the 1870s there were no real advances in industry concentration.[95] This very long period (approximately forty years) did not seem to end in a national natural monopoly. Thus, by the Railways Act of 1921 government merged the remaining 120 companies into four large regional groups.[96]

In Belgium, railroad construction followed in inverse order than in the UK. King Leopold started building railroads in 1833 fearing that the Dutch private initiative would leapfrog him. But when the Belgian State stopped building railroads, competition burst in and a period of intense rivalry brought growth in an otherwise stagnant industry. In twenty years, from 1850 to 1870, private railroad companies increased the existing statutory 350 miles of railroads to 1,750 miles. Private railroad companies did not remain as mere local branches connected to the state railroads but became *rivals* for the same traffic. Although they could not occupy the same physical space as the state railroads, many private railroads were well enough situated to actively compete against each other. This competition was "intolerable" to the Belgian government (but not to the private companies!) because it prevented government from developing "an independent policy." Therefore, to retake influence over railroad transportation, the Belgian government acquired most of the competing lines. By 1885 the Belgian State owned three-quarters of the mileage and had put an end to competition.[97]

Overall, it seems clear that the reasons that led governments to extend their monopoly over railroads were not natural monopoly.[98] The development of railroads took place in the same period where many European States had just become modern states, like Belgium in 1830 or Italy in 1860, and when the old ones, France and

92. Hadley, Arthur T. *Railroad Transportation: Its History and Its Laws*. GT Putnam's Sons, 1885, at p. 147.
93. Foreman-Peck, James S. "Natural Monopoly and Railway Policy in the Nineteenth Century." *Oxford Economic Papers* 39.4 (1987): 699-718, 701.
94. *Quoted in* Arnold, Anthony J. and Sean McCartney. "Rates of Return, Concentration Levels and Strategic Change in the British Railway Industry, 1830-1912." *The Journal of Transport History* 26.1 (2005): 41-60, 47.
95. Arnold, Anthony J. and Sean McCartney. "Rates of Return, Concentration Levels and Strategic Change in the British Railway Industry, 1830-1912." *The Journal of Transport History* 26.1 (2005): 41-60.
96. *Id.* 48.
97. Hadley, Arthur T. *Railroad Transportation: Its History and Its Laws*. GT Putnam's Sons, 1885, at 212-217.
98. Joskow, Paul L. "Regulation of Natural Monopoly" *in* A. Mitchell Polinsky and Steven Shavell (eds.) *Handbook of Law and Economics*, Vol. 2, 2007: 1227-1348, 1248; and *id.* at 1261: "It is hard to argue that the growth of federal regulation at this time reflected a renewed concern about performance problems associated with 'natural monopolies.'"

Germany, were involved in the Franco-Prussian War. Thus, the railroads were crucial to achieve social cohesion within the boundaries of the new states and were pivotal for military purposes.[99] In Europe, the main objective was to increase political influence (in particular military power); or to make up for the lack of entrepreneurial activity (with the exception of the UK). The prevention of certain behavior such as discriminatory pricing was only a subordinate objective in Europe, but the main one in the US in the 1880s.[100]

Following Baumol's theory of subadditivity, most of the empirical research for the US and Europe generally verify that railway infrastructures obtain constant returns to scale. Unsurprisingly, this is particularly true when the infrastructure makes larger use of its capacity. However, there are slight decreasing returns in the case of companies with a larger size.[101] The results seem consistent with the evolution of the industry, although at times competition between competing railroads seemed a possibility. This begets the question as to whether regulation in the early days created a "natural monopoly" or simply accelerated the inevitable outcome of an actual natural monopoly.[102]

[3] Summation

A study of the history of competition in telecommunications and railroads suggests that natural monopoly did not arise naturally.[103] Both in the US and Europe, the State

99. Millward, Robert. "Business and the State" *in* Geoffrey G. Jones and Jonathan Zeitlin (eds.) *The Oxford Handbook of Business History*. Oxford University Press, 2008: 529-557.
100. Hadley, Arthur T. *Railroad Transportation: Its History and Its Laws*. GT Putnam's Sons, 1885, at p. 238.
101. Sánchez Cantos, Pedro. "A Subadditivity Test for the Cost Function of the Principal European Railways." *Transport Reviews* 20.3 (2000): 275-290.
102. Posner, Richard A. "Natural Monopoly and Its Regulation." *Stanford Law Review* 21.3 (1968): 548-643, 636.
103. Other so-called natural monopolies could have been selected, arriving to similar results. Gas pipelines are an interesting example. Pipelines transport gas from an origin market, such as a gas field, to a destination market, such as an industrial area or a local distribution company. They seemingly are a most clear case of a natural monopoly. But as Jeff Makholm explains "despite their cost structure, major gas pipelines face persistent threats of rivalry" and "their market power is challenged by geology, geography, time." As with railroads, governments built every major pipeline in Europe, unlike in the US. In the US, privately built pipelines continue to compete against each other in some regions. However, in Europe, since state-built pipelines could never face competition one may wonder whether absent regulation competition between pipelines could have been a reality. *See* Makholm, Jeff D. *The Political Economy of Pipelines: A Century of Comparative Institutional Development*. University of Chicago Press, 2012, at pp. 14, 17, 21, and 40-42. Another doubtful example of natural monopoly is that of electric utilities. *See*, for instance, Behling, Burton N. *Competition and Monopoly in Public Utility Industries*. Urbana: University of Illinois, 1938, at pp. 19-20 *quoted in* Demsetz, Harold. "Why Regulate Utilities?" *The Journal of Law and Economics* 11.1 (1968): 55-65, 59, showing that in 1900s multiple electric light companies operated in New York, Minesssota and Chicago. Also Primeaux's works argue that all the attributes attached to any conception of natural monopoly failed in the case of electric utilities. In particular, Primeaux shows that the capital costs of electric utilities were not higher than those of other industries and that duopoly firms operated at lower costs than if they did not face competition. *See* Primeaux Jr., Walter J. "Some Problems with Natural Monopoly." *Antitrust Bulletin* 24 (1979): 63-85. More generally, *see* Daniel H.

created monopoly before any industry had become "naturally monopolistic by anyone's definition."[104]

It is difficult to determine if, in those cases, the State thwarted a process the end game of which would have been a natural monopoly. That is an uncertainty that the competitive process aims to discover. But one may at least doubt whether natural monopoly characterized those industries before the state replaced competition with regulation.[105]

That being said, when State regulation took some time to be introduced, market competition persisted without denoting a general tendency toward natural monopoly. The telecommunication industry in the US provides a good example.

By contrast, there were also instances where market competition seemed to lean toward natural monopoly. The evolution of the railroads industry provides a good illustration where connections in the US, France or the UK were only capable of maintaining a single most efficient undertaking. However, some mixed interpretations can also be found. The evolution of the railroad industry also revealed that private undertakings competed with one another in some connections within Belgium or the US.[106]

[B] Natural Monopoly and the Competitive Process

As seen above with telecommunications and railroads, the main flaw of the economic concept of natural monopoly is that it is anchored in a highly static framework of analysis. This has three practical consequences for the application of legal provisions that seek to protect the competitive process, as is arguably the case of Article 102 TFEU.[107]

First, the intuitive appeal of the model describing natural monopoly by reference to subadditivity is fraught with measuring difficulties. Subadditivity requires a theoretical analysis of any and every possible combination of smaller firms and knowing

---

Cole and Peter Grossman (eds.) *The End of a Natural Monopoly: Deregulation and Competition in the Electric Power Industry*. Routledge, 2004. Subadditivity of electricity distribution can nonetheless be found in some markets like Switzerland; and Filippini, Massimo. "Are Municipal Electricity Distribution Utilities Natural Monopolies?" *Annals of Public and Cooperative Economics* 69.2 (1998): 157-174.

104. Hazlett, Thomas W. "The Curious Evolution of Natural Monopoly Theory" *in* Robert W. Poole (ed.) *Unnatural Monopolies: The Case for Deregulating Public Utilities* (1985): 1-25, at 1, *quoted in* Cherry, Barbara A. "Historical Mutilation: How Misuse of 'Public Utility' and 'Natural Monopoly' Misdirects US Telecommunications Policy Development." *20th ITS Biennial Conference* (2014): 1-25, 9.
105. Demsetz, Harold. "Why Regulate Utilities?" *The Journal of Law and Economics* 11.1 (1968): 55-65, 59.
106. Posner, Richard A. "Natural Monopoly and Its Regulation." *Stanford Law Review* 21.3 (1968): 548-643, 636. Empirical analysis continues to be small ever since Baumol provided a definition of natural monopoly and subadditivity; *see also* Reid, Gavin C. "The Theory of Natural Monopoly by William Sharkey." *The Economic Journal* 93.372 (1983): 929-931, 930; and Joskow, Paul L. "Regulation of Natural Monopoly" in A. Mitchell Polinsky and Steven Shavell (eds.) *Handbook of Law and Economics*, Vol. 2, 2007: 1227-1348, 1248.
107. Makholm, Jeff D. *The Political Economy of Pipelines: A Century of Comparative Institutional Development*. University of Chicago Press, 2012, at p. 30.

the behavior of the cost curve over the whole range of demand. Since such complete knowledge is unattainable one cannot be "entirely certain that the firm ... is a natural monopoly."[108] As Baumol and his colleagues acknowledged, subadditivity analysis requires "data that may lie well beyond the range of recorded experience."[109]

We can clearly appreciate this problem in the economic literature dealing with AT&T's break-up. The radically opposite conclusions that eminent scholars have reached about the existence/absence of natural monopoly in the industry have as its most direct cause the quality and extent of the data employed in the analyses.

Second, the reference of analysis is the cost production function of a particular output, or combination of outputs thereof. This means that an empirical test of the natural monopoly hypothesis requires homogeneity of output and an identity of production functions among firms. Thus, the cost function of a firm does not reveal possible competition from other products or services interchangeable to the eyes of consumers.[110] Transportation by train provides a suitable illustration. While it can be argued with a high degree of certainty that a single rail firm connecting two geographical points might be the most efficient cost structure, one cannot emphasize enough that this assessment is strictly limited to the comparison between different cost production functions of a rather homogenous service: the railroads.[111]

But the natural monopoly hypothesis leaves the comparison with other modes of transportation between the same geographical points that pose an actual competitive constraint to the railroad firm—intermodal competition—out of consideration. Thus, a railroad connection between London and Brussels can face competition by an airline connection, or the connection between Brussels and Paris can face competition by road transportation. Although the railroad might be a natural "monopoly" in the sense of having the most effective cost production function for that particular infrastructure, doubts about its actual monopoly power arise in the presence of intermodal competition. This is particularly true with the increase of internationalization of commerce that undermined many so-called natural monopolies.[112] It remains unanswered whether so-called natural monopolies would truly possess SMP if left unprotected by regulatory barriers to entry.[113]

Third, the notion of natural monopoly is explicitly based "on the assumption that the menu of available techniques is fixed (no technological change)."[114] Improvement

108. Sharkey, William W. *The Theory of Natural Monopoly*. New York: Cambridge University Press, 1982, at p. 84.
109. Baumol, William J. "On the Proper Cost Tests for Natural Monopoly in a Multiproduct Industry." *The American Economic Review* 67.5 (1977): 809-822, 809.
110. Coldwell III, Daniel. "The New Theory of Public Utilities: The Case of the Natural Monopoly." *Antitrust Bulletin* 26.1 (1981): 133-144, 140-141.
111. Arnold, Anthony J. and Sean McCartney. "Rates of Return, Concentration Levels and Strategic Change in the British Railway Industry, 1830-1912." *The Journal of Transport History* 26.1 (2005): 41-60.
112. OECD, *Excessive Prices*. DAF/COMP(2011)18, at p. 384.
113. Posner, Richard A. "Natural Monopoly and Its Regulation: A Reply." *Stanford Law Review* 22.3 (1970): 540-546, 541, 543, 545, and at 542 stating: "[w]e take too much for granted in these areas."
114. Baumol, William J. "On the Proper Cost Tests for Natural Monopoly in a Multiproduct Industry." *The American Economic Review* 67.5 (1977): 809-822, 809.

in production costs and the introduction of new products are likewise assumed away. Furthermore, the concept of natural monopoly only has meaning for a particular level of demand. Changes in consumer tastes, goals, or utility are assumed likely assumed away.[115] As Posner has put it, "to embrace regulation because an industry is today a natural monopoly and seems likely to remain so is to gamble dangerously with the future."[116]

The limits of today's technology have been overcome by new technology that increases supplies, broadens the availability of substitutable products and reduces the requirements of a particular output for another. This is—at least partially—what the competitive process is about. The existence today of a natural monopoly is simply the result of advancements in technology that continue to shift production functions and the utility of outputs. Thus, "for fuel we have shifted from wood to coal to petroleum to falling water to uranium and a host of 'unconventional' sources."[117] So long as market power flows from the cost and demand characteristics of the market in which the alleged natural monopoly is present potential competition cannot be ruled out.[118]

§4.04 WHITHER NATURAL MONOPOLIST? A LEGAL ANALYSIS

In this section we explore the place that natural monopolies occupy in the case law (§4.04[A]). We find that no real legal framework of analysis governs unregulated natural monopolies. We therefore move on with a discussion of a proposed analytical framework for unregulated natural monopolies (§4.04[B]).

[A] Natural Monopolies in the Case Law

The EU Courts' and the Commission's thinking about natural monopolies is unclear. In the Article 102 TFEU case law, the references to natural monopoly found in the case law are both elusive and rare. The same holds true of the case law adopted under other EU legal provisions (§4.04[A][1]) Admittedly, however, the jurisprudence may simply prefer a different terminology (§4.04[A][2]) to that offered by mainstream economists (§4.04[A][3]).

115. Brätland, John. "Contestable Market Theory as a Regulatory Framework: An Austrian *Post-mortem*." *The Quarterly Journal of Austrian Economics* 7.3 (2004): 3-28, 23-24.
116. Posner, Richard A. "Natural Monopoly and Its Regulation." *Stanford Law Review* 21.3 (1968): 548-643, 636.
117. Scott, Anthony and Peter Pearse. "Natural Resources in a High-Tech Economy: Scarcity Versus Resourcefulness." *Resources Policy* 18.3 (1992): 154-166, 163.
118. Posner, Richard A. "Natural Monopoly and Its Regulation." *Stanford Law Review* 21.3 (1968): 548-643, 601 and 636. *See also* Joskow, Paul L. "Regulation of Natural Monopoly" *in* A. Mitchell Polinsky and Steven Shavell (eds.) *Handbook of Law and Economics*, Vol. 2, (2007): 1227-1348, 1248, stating that the reality of markets is that "there is not likely to be a bright line between industries that are 'natural monopolies' and those that are (imperfectly) 'competitive.'"

[1] Natural Monopolies

The earliest case law appearance of the concept of natural monopoly dates back to 1974. In *Giuseppe Sacchi*, Italian law organized television broadcasting as a statutory monopoly service. The Italian Government argued that the exclusive right it had granted to RAI (Radio Audizione Italiana) was justified because TV broadcasting constituted a natural monopoly. According to the Italian government, this was due to the nature of the industry that only allowed a limited number of undertakings to provide the service. In turn, the argument of the Italian Government was that since State was not creating a monopoly, the grant of an exclusive right could not be considered incompatible with Articles 102 or 106 TFEU: "*The law* which attributes the operation of something in such a situation to the State *does not therefore create the monopoly but limits itself to reserving it to the State* for the purpose of avoiding its appropriation by private monopolies." (emphasis added)[119]

Unfortunately, the Court did not explicitly address the argument in its decision. By contrast, AG Reischl opined that the existence of a natural monopoly did not preclude the application of Article 102 TFEU. He further considered that cable TV could not be a natural monopoly since its operation was not limited by a number of frequencies, as it is the case with radio.[120] The Commission reached a similar conclusion on the basis of a distinct rationale. Implicitly rejecting the idea that TV was a natural monopoly, it argued that "technical developments" had made available a wider choice of possibilities.[121]

In *Fluggesellschaft v. Eurocontrol*, the Court did not address the issue of natural monopoly, yet its AG gave it some consideration. The case concerned Eurocontrol, an organization tasked by public authorities to perform air control services. In his opinion, AG Tesauro concluded that, although Eurocontrol is not undertaking, the provision of air control services could be deemed a natural monopoly. Two reasons were advanced in support of the natural monopoly point: first, Eurocontrol exercised a "public authority" in air navigation control; second, competition in air control services between two or more firms is not only "undesirable" but also "impractical" in practice.[122]

In *Commission v. Czech Republic*, the Commission brought an action against the Czech Republic for failure to fulfill certain obligations under the Railways Directive 2001/14, where the notion of natural monopoly is explicitly used in relation to railroad infrastructures.[123] Among the failures, the Commission complained that the Czech Republic had not adopted incentives to encourage the railroad infrastructure manager to reduce the costs of providing infrastructure and the level of access charges. The

119. CJEU, Case C-155/73, *Giuseppe Sacchi*, ECLI:EU:C:1974:40, at 419.
120. Opinion of AG Reischl in Case C-155/73, *Giuseppe Sacchi*, ECLI:EU:C:1974:22, at 441.
121. CJEU, Case C-155/73, *Giuseppe Sacchi*, ECLI:EU:C:1974:40, at 414.
122. Opinion of AG Tesauro in Case C-364/92, *SAT Fluggesellschaft v. Eurocontrol*, ECLI:EU:C:1993:878, §13.
123. Directive 2001/14/EC of the European Parliament and of the Council of 26 February 2001 on the allocation of railway infrastructure capacity and the levying of charges for the use of railway infrastructure and safety certification, *OJ* L 75, 15.3.2001, p. 29-46.

Court upheld the complaint without giving any attention to natural monopoly arguments.[124] By contrast, AG Jääskinen opined that the dangers of inefficiency are "inherent in natural monopolies."[125] And this explains the need to actively provide adequate incentives to lower their costs.

In *Portuguese Airports*, the Court considered that airports were likely to enjoy a natural monopoly,[126] and that a system of discounts on landing charges, differentiated according to the origin of the flight, constituted an infringement of Articles 102 TFEU and 106 TFEU. Although the Court did not elaborate on the concept, the Commission had established in the appealed decision that airports are "the only means available to a carrier of providing air transport services to a given town." Importantly, the Court ruled that general objective justifications regarding the procompetitive or neutral nature of quantity rebates are insufficient when the dominant firm, the airport, is "likely to enjoy a natural monopoly."[127]

In *De Staat der Nederlanden v. Essent and others*, AG Jääskinen delivered an opinion concerning certain liberalization measures of the electricity and gas distribution systems in the Netherlands. In his opinion, the concept of natural monopoly played a central role in assessing whether prohibiting energy distribution systems from carrying out unrelated activities constituted a restriction on the free movement of capital.

Energy distribution systems connect the consumer to the national energy transmission system.[128] AG Jääskinen described them as natural monopolies because "they cannot reasonably be duplicated owing to [their] very large economies of scale." From a competition perspective, these natural monopolies constitute an "essential facility" that confers market power to the owner of the distribution system.[129] Thus, in AG Jääskinen opinion, it is justified that *to accomplish the liberalization of a market* "characterised by a natural monopoly," national legislation would prevent the "spill-over of resources" accruing to the natural monopoly onto other markets.[130] It is important to emphasize that the standard of liability does not refer to the natural

124. *Id.* §40; Directive 2012/34/EU of the European Parliament and of the Council of 21 November 2012 establishing a single European railway area, *OJ* L 343, states likewise, at §71.
125. Opinion of AG Jääskinen in Case C-545/10, *Commission v. Czech Republic*, ECLI: EU:C:2012:791, §54.
126. CJEU, Case C-163/99, *Portugal v. Commission*, ECLI:EU:C:2001:189, §53.
127. *Id.* §57. Van der Vijver, Tjarda. "Article 102 TFEU: How to Claim the Application of Objective Justifications in the Case of *prima facie* Dominance Abuses?" *Journal of European Competition Law & Practice* 4.2 (2013): 121-133, at n. 80: "the Court attached great importance to the context of the case, which involved airports with a natural monopoly for most of their activities. The Court took this high level of dominance into account when it ruled that the rebates under investigation were prima facie abusive and could not be justified."
128. Following the energy liberalization directives, part of the Dutch legislation aimed at replacing vertically integrated energy companies by unbundling the distribution system from the marketing and production of energy.
129. Opinion of AG Jääskinen in Joined Cases C-105/12 to C-107/12, *De Staat der Nederlanden v. Essent NV and Essent Nederland BV* (C-105/12), *Eneco Holding NV* (C-106/12), *Delta NV* (C-107/12), ECLI:EU:C:2013:242, §63. Interestingly, AG Jääskinen considered the essentiality of the distribution systems in terms of national security. At §65: "the person controlling the distribution of electricity also controls modern society in all its functions."
130. *Id.* §§100-104.

monopoly character of the industry but to the objectives of liberalizing the EU energy market.

[2] Are "De Facto Monopolies" Natural Monopolies?

Classic economists used the term "natural monopoly" to differentiate it from "legal monopolies." Similarly, the case law seems to draw a distinction between "de jure monopolies" and "de facto monopolies." However, it is subject to discussion whether the Commission and the Court equate "de facto monopolies" with natural monopolies in the economic sense of a single firm being the most efficient industry arrangement. At best, it seems that the characterization of a firm as a de facto monopoly is just a shortcut to describe a *single* firm with SMP in a given market.

Let us look at several cases where the EU Courts' case law and decisional practice talked of de facto monopolies. In *Kali und Salz*, the Court called a firm a de facto monopoly for the first time. The case concerned a cooperation agreement, eventually held anticompetitive, between Kali and Salz and the Société Commerciale des Potasses d'Alsace, who had a statutory monopoly for the sales of potassium salts in France. The Court called the combination a de facto monopoly in the sale of potassium in the Federal republic of Germany, in spite of the fact that Kali und Salz was not the only undertaking involved in that trade (some low-volume imports of potassium salts existed).[131]

In *Glass Containers*, the Commission took a slightly different tack. Noting that Schiedam, a party to an anticompetitive agreement, constituted "one large undertaking," it qualified it as a de facto monopoly. Interestingly, the Commission accepted to talk of a natural monopoly in spite of the fact that Schiedam was not the sole firm in the market. Indeed, Schiedam position was "mitigated" by Glasindustrie Dongen who, as Schiedam, manufactured jars for preserves and bottles for the soft drink industries, and by imports from Germany and Belgium.[132]

In *GVL*, the Commission endorsed a stricter understanding of de facto monopoly, steeped in the concept of a single supplier. GVL, a German copyright collecting society, had refused to conclude management agreements with foreign nonresident artists in Germany. The Commission, finding such refusal abusive, concluded that GVL was a de facto monopoly since it had no competitors.[133]

---

131. Commission Decision, Case COMP/IV/791, *Société Commerciale des Potasses et de l'Azote (SCPA)—Kali und Salz (formerly VDK)*, at 4.
132. Commission Decision, Case COMP/IV/400, *Agreements between manufacturers of glass containers*, §26. The conduct concerned the fair trading rules' or "IFTRA rules" applied by European manufacturers of glass containers that contained certain anticompetitive provisions such as discriminatory prices, publication of individual price and discount lists, as well as other different agreements.
133. Commission Decision, Case COMP/IV/29.839, *GVL*, §47. However, in *BRT v. SABAM*, the Court of Justice avoided employing the term de facto monopoly for the Belgian collecting society, SABAM, as the referring national court described it. Instead, the Court considered that SABAM occupied a "quasi-monopoly" position in the market. *See* CJEU, Case C-127/73, *BRT v. SABAM*, ECLI:EU:C:1974:25, §5.

In *AAMS*, the Commission repeated the equivalence between de facto monopoly and single supplier. It held that the Amministrazione Autonoma dei Monopoli di Stato (AAMS) occupied a de facto monopoly as the "only operator present" in the Italian market for the wholesale distribution of cigarettes. This was despite the fact that import and wholesale distribution of cigarettes had been liberalized.[134]

Besides this, a slightly distinct strand in the case seems to describe a de facto monopoly as the position of a firm holding an indispensable resource. In *Magill*, for example, the Court ruled that TV stations RTE, ITP and BBC enjoyed "by force of circumstance" a de facto monopoly over the information used to elaborate listings for TV programs. This "force of circumstance" meant that TV stations were "the *only* source of such information" simply because they decide their own programming schedules (channel, day, time and title).[135] The Court held that a refusal to supply that information (ultimately protected by national copyright laws) constituted an abuse of dominance.[136]

With this background, the case law has a relatively homogeneous understanding of the concept of a de facto monopoly. There is a de facto monopoly when there is a single supplier in an industry. This is different from de jure monopolies.

Admittedly, as Larouche has argued, a de facto monopoly may simply be what follows a de jure monopoly in a liberalization process.[137] This would seem to be a fair reading of the concept. In *GVS/FS*, a case concerning a refusal to deal and refusal to form an international railroad grouping,[138] the Commission described the Italian national railroad carrier market power in two steps. "Until April 2001, FS had a de jure monopoly for the provision of traction on the Italian rail infrastructure. Since then [when actual liberalization took place], FS has a de facto monopoly for the provision of traction."[139] However right, this interpretation is not entirely convincing. As we have seen, the concept "de facto monopoly" has been largely used in industries that have not undergone any liberalization transition.[140]

134. Commission Decision, Case COMP/IV/36.010, *Amministrazione Autonoma dei Monopoli di Stato*, §31.
135. CJEU, Joined Cases C-241/91 P and C-242/91 P, *Magill*, ECLI:EU:C:1995:98, §47.
136. In this regard, the Guidance Paper of the Commission considers that a natural monopoly can be due to "single-source information" and thus give rise to the indispensability of the input. "In general, an input is likely to be impossible to replicate when it involves a natural monopoly due to scale or scope economies, where there are strong network effects or when it concerns so-called 'single source' information. However, in all cases account should be taken of the dynamic nature of the industry and, in particular whether or not market power can rapidly dissipate." *See* Guidance Paper, §83, n. 3.
137. Larouche, Pierre. *Competition Law and Regulation in European Telecommunications*. Hart Publishing, 2000, at p. 331.
138. *See* Chapter 2 for an extended discussion.
139. Commission Decision, Case COMP/37.685, *GVG/FS Italian Railway*, §110.
140. The EU Courts and the Commission have employed the term "virtual monopoly" in the enforcement of Article 102 TFEU against historical operators in the telecommunications industry. *See* CJEU, Case C-280/08 P, *Deutsche Telekom AG v. Commission*, ECLI: EU:C:2010:603, §276; *and* GC, Case T-336/07, *Telefónica v. Commission*, ECLI:EU:T:2012:172, §413. The Commission considered it was "economically unfeasible or unreasonably difficult in a reasonable time period" to have alternative local loop in the market. It is important to highlight that "economically unsound" is not the same as "unreasonably difficult." The former description points into the direction of natural monopoly, the latter one not. As we have argued

Beyond this seemingly coherent description of a natural monopoly as a single firm, the case law has at times conflated the concept with legal monopolies.[141] Thus, in *Commission v. Portugal*, the General Court established that "*where a Member State prohibits any undertaking*, other than official customs agents for which it has reserved one of the two types of representation, from carrying out the other type of representation as a regular part of its business activity. *Such a prohibition protects official customs agents against any effective competition by other undertakings, and accordingly grants them a de facto monopoly* with regard to customs declarations made on behalf of another person" (emphasis added).[142]

[3] Efficiency and Natural Monopolies

None of the examined cases seems to consider natural monopoly along the lines of Baumol's interpretation. The closest relationship of the case law to economic thinking would be the simple differentiation between statutory and natural monopolies that Mill established in 1848.

---

before, it seems that natural monopoly was not the underlying competitive concern but rather the fact that Telefónica's investments were undertaken in its capacity as a statutory monopoly. *See* Commission Decision, Case COMP/38.784, *Wanadoo España v. Telefónica*, §167, and Chapter 3. Indeed, only railroads and the supply of natural gas (archetypal illustrations of natural monopoly) have been described in the case law as a de facto monopoly. *See* CJEU, Case C-36/92 P, *Samenwerkende Elektriciteits-Produktiebedrijven (SEP) NV v. Commission*, ECLI:EU:C:1994:205, §2; and GC, Case T-39/90, *NV Samenwerkende Elektriciteits-Produktiebedrijven v. Commission*, ECLI:EU:T:1991:71, §3.

141. This confusion between natural and statutory monopolies has also come up in other jurisdictions. Supposedly, former Article 21 of the Japan Antimonopoly Act contained an exemption over so-called natural monopolies: "*The provisions of this Act shall not apply to* such acts relating to the production, sale, or supply as are done in the proper course of business by a person engaging in railway, electricity, gas or *any other business constituting monopoly by the inherent nature of the said business*" (emphasis added). (*See* Japan Antimonopoly Act (AMA). Act on Prohibition of Private Monopolization and Maintenance of Fair Trade (Act No. 54 of Apr. 14, 1947).) However, a report by the Japanese Fair Trade Commission clarified in 1993 that "Article 21 is nothing but a declaratory or confirmative statement saying that since *the monopolistic position of natural monopoly businesses is obtained and maintained through the governments restriction on entry*, and not through the acts of the entrepreneurs, such monopolistic position and resulting monopoly in supply does not constitute a AMA violation. Accordingly, the Article cannot be regarded as an AMA exemption clause in its proper meaning" (emphasis added). *See* OECD, *Application of Competition Policy to the Electricity Sector*, OECD/GD(97)132, Japan's submission, at p. 72. Another alternative reading has sometimes conflated the concept of natural monopoly with what could be regarded as an illegal monopoly. This was the case in *Auditel* concerning the market for measuring TV audience figures. Italian private and public TV channels, as well as advertising agencies and associations, had agreed with Auditel to use exclusively its audience measurements and research. The Commission found this exclusivity agreement to be anticompetitive, which among others put Auditel "in a de facto monopoly position, eliminating all competition." Nevertheless, the Commission established that such a de facto monopoly was short-lived because the anticompetitive agreement that caused it was void. "Since Article 11 of the agreement will be annulled by this decision, Auditel will in future no longer have a monopoly position." *See* Commission Decision, Case COMP/IV/32031, *Auditel*, §35.

142. CJEU, Case C-323/90, *Commission v. Portugal*, ECLI:EU:C:1992:119, §14.

A sensible explanation for this simple understanding could be related to the pace of development of economic theory. Because the economic theory of natural monopoly remained "exceedingly unclear" well into the 1970s, the EU Courts have arguable been unable to provide any workable framework of analysis.[143] Instead of truly examining whether a firm is a natural monopoly and what this means for the enforcement of Article 102 TFEU, the Commission and the EU Courts would have at times "found" a firm with natural monopoly in archetypically regarded monopolistic industries such as railroads, gas or electricity; and in the majority of cases used the term simply as a wording shortcut to describe large market power detained by a single firm.

We could, however, find a possible exception to this simple approach to natural monopoly in *Post Danmark II*.[144] In this case, the referring Danish court asked the Court of Justice about the relevance of the as efficient competitor test to assess the legality of certain rebates. The Court of Justice answered that the test, being "one tool amongst others," was irrelevant whenever "the structure of the market makes the emergence of an as-efficient competitor practically impossible."[145]

Although the Court of Justice did not explicitly refer to situations of natural monopoly, such holding mirrors the market characteristics of a natural monopoly. Clearly, if there is one scenario in which the emergence of an AEC is impossible, it is that of a natural monopoly.[146] A market that is most efficiently served by a single undertaking cannot withstand another as-efficient firm.

This suggested interpretation could be questioned on the basis that the Court of Justice, immediately after, concluded that Article 102 TFEU is also concerned with less efficient competitors.[147] From a process perspective, where competition selects the most efficient firms, how could the Court be concerned with less efficient market arrangements where an actual *natural* monopoly is present?

However, both scenarios are complementary and make sense together from a process-oriented enforcement of competition law. On the one hand, in the case of an actual natural monopoly, it seems irrelevant that courts employ an AEC test when the market is more efficiently served by a single undertaking. In the case of a statutory monopoly (as in *Post Danmark II*), the AEC test might be irrelevant since the firms

143. Similarly, describing the difficulties in turning the theory of two-sided markets into a workable antitrust policy prescription, *see* Auer, Dirk and Nicolas Petit. "Two-Sided Markets and the Challenge of Turning Economic Theory into Antitrust Policy." *The Antitrust Bulletin* 60.4 (2015): 426-461.

144. This is irrespective of the fact that *Post Danmark II* seems to be strongly driven by the *statutory* origins of *Post Danmark*. *See* Chapter 2.

145. CJEU, Case C-23/14, *Post Danmark II*, ECLI:EU:C:2015:651, §§59 and 61.

146. Abundant commentary on *Post Danmark II* overlooks this possibility. *See, e.g.*, Subiotto, Romano, David R. Little and Romi Lepetska. "The Application of Article 102 TFEU by the European Commission and the European Courts." *Journal of European Competition Law & Practice* 3.2 (2012): 175-181; Tóth, András. "CJEU Judgment in *Post Danmark II*: Role of Economic Evidence in Competition Cases." *European Networks Law & Regulation Quarterly* 3 (2015): 266-273; Venit, James S. "Making Sense of *Post Danmark I* and *II*: Keeping the Hell Fires Well Stoked and Burning." *Journal of European Competition Law & Practice* 7.3 (2016): 165-179. Rummel, Per. "Rebate Schemes under Article 102 TFEU: *Post Danmark II*." *Common Market Law Review* 53.4 (2016): 1121-1131.

147. CJEU, Case C-23/14, *Post Danmark II*, ECLI:EU:C:2015:651, §60.

trying to enter the market were initially prevented from acquiring certain competitive advantages that belonged exclusively to the statutory dominant firm.

With this, it is understandable to discard the AEC test when there is a natural monopoly. But this leaves the following question open: if a natural monopoly arises from competition,[148] how should Article 102 TFEU be enforced in an unregulated market that can only support a single firm?

[B] Natural Monopolies and Article 102 TFEU Enforcement

Two policy principles should guide the antitrust analysis of cases featuring a natural monopoly. *First*, the existence of a natural monopoly should provide a defense against charges of exclusionary conduct, though the defense should not be absolute.[149] *Second*, antitrust enforcement should focus on conduct that prevents the emergence of displacing technology with potential to obsolesce the natural monopoly.

[1] Natural Monopoly Defense

The CJEU in *Post Danmark I* made clear that the competitive process entails the departure of less efficient firms from the market. It is not the purpose of Article 102 TFEU to protect less efficient firms from the hardship of market competition. Yet, it remains a possibility that either as-efficient firms compete in the market, or that they might attempt entry in light of the prospects for profit that the market offers.

But, in the presence of a natural monopoly entry by an AEC is an inefficient arrangement. The *Post Danmark II* Court arguably understood this when it held that the AEC test is of no use when the emergence of another as-efficient firm is impossible. Indeed, by definition, a natural monopoly exists when the entire demand can be satisfied at the lowest cost by a single firm. Since increasing the number of firms in the market will only increase the costs of production, "exclusionary" behavior by the natural monopoly can preserve productive efficiency.[150] With this background, antitrust liability of natural monopolists should obtain some relief.[151]

A similar situation arises when a *legal* framework restricts competition to a point where further restriction by an undertaking is impossible. This is what the Court held in *Suiker Unie*. Here, the Court partially annulled the decision of the Commission for not taking due account of the fact that Italian regulations maintaining a uniform price

148. We proceed in the assumption of the existence of a natural monopoly and thus leave aside market definition issues that would be necessary to judge whether a natural monopoly exists in the first place.
149. Woodcock, Ramsi A. "Inconsistency in Antitrust." *University of Miami Law Review* 68.1 (2013): 105-188, arguing that natural monopolies should be exempt from antitrust laws.
150. Elhauge, Einer. "Defining Better Monopolization Standards." *Stanford Law Review* 56.2 (2003): 253-344, at 338.
151. Hamilton, Neil W. and Anne M. Caulfield. "The Defense of Natural Monopoly in Sherman Act Monopolization Cases." *DePaul Law Review* 33.3 (1983): 465-493.

for sugar and restricting imports rendered the anticompetitive behavior of the undertakings irrelevant.[152] As Fernando De La Torre Castillo and Eric Gippini Fournier explain this is "even if the agreement would contain a *prima facie* restriction by object."[153] Thus, aiming for a cohesive framework, one should extend the same analysis in cases of natural monopolies where the "economic fundamentals" already restrict competition and there is no margin for further restriction.[154]

In this regard, it is important to understand that natural monopoly is not a failure of the competitive process, but it represents a part of it. The only way to understand this is by taking a "longer-run view" of the natural monopoly situation. As Kirzner has put forward, if the natural monopoly has been secured in competition then "it represents, as such (and as far as it goes) a step forward in the entrepreneurial process of the market." It is not a market failure, but it rather is the elimination of "inconsistencies between the decisions of consumers and those of the earlier resource owners."[155] Natural monopoly is the second best solution when the ideal of all prices at competitive level is simply unattainable.[156] Competition enforcement would bring no benefit by forcing the market to adopt a more atomistic structure where small firms will have higher production cost structures.[157]

In *Intel* the Court of Justice held that it is up to the dominant firm to establish that its conduct does not hamper the emergence of an as efficient competitor.[158] Likewise, it seems clear that the burden of proving its natural monopoly will rest with the accused undertaking. Unlike those who believe that *Intel* is too generous to the interests of dominant firms,[159] this line of defense is by no means an easy one to discharge. The applicant is indeed required to prove that despite there being a natural monopoly, the larger production costs of any other combination of firms would bring competitive prices. The burden of proof must rest with the applicant. Indeed, while the productive efficiency of a natural monopoly is unambiguous, the price effects of introducing and enforcing competition in the market are uncertain.[160] In other words, the enforcement

152. CJEU, Joined Cases, 40/73-48/73, 50/73, 54/73-56/73, 111/73, 113/73 and 114/73, *Suiker Unie and Others v. Commission*, EU:C:1975:174, §§70-73.
153. De La Torre Castillo, Fernando and Eric Gippini Fournier. *Evidence, Proof and Judicial Review in EU Competition Law*. Edward Elgar Publishing, 2017, at p. 8, n. 20.
154. In such cases Elhauge argues that the proper remedy should be "utility rate regulation" but cautioning that: "distinguishing natural from temporary monopolies is difficult." *See* Elhauge, Einer. "Defining Better Monopolization Standards." *Stanford Law Review* 56.2 (2003): 253-344, 307-308, n. 163.
155. Kirzner, Israel M. *Competition and Entrepreneurship*. The University of Chicago Press, 1973, at pp. 22-23.
156. Posner, Richard A. "Natural Monopoly and Its Regulation." *Stanford Law Review* 21.3 (1968): 548-643, 560-561.
157. Liebowitz, Stan J. and Stephen E. Margolis. "Should Technology Choice Be a Concern of Antitrust Policy?" *Harvard Journal of Law & Technology* 9.2 (1996): 283-318, 301.
158. CJEU, Case C-413/14 P, *Intel v. Commission*, ECLI:EU:C:2017:632, §§138 and 139.
159. The complexity of establishing a natural monopoly is commensurate with the stricter threshold of liability whereby the exclusion of an as efficient competitor will not suffice to establish liability under Article 102 TFEU.
160. Hamilton, Neil W. and Anne M. Caulfield. "The Defense of Natural Monopoly in Sherman Act Monopolization Cases." *DePaul Law Review* 33.3 (1983): 465-493, 497.

of Article 102 TFEU against the natural monopolist should favor productive efficiency against allocative efficiency in order to reduce type I errors.[161]

Relatedly, one could argue, Article 102 TFEU might be used to regulate exploitative behavior. This would allow for an optimal productive efficiency with natural monopoly while reducing the ability to profit from that power. In this setting, the costs of enforcement must be taken into account.

However, reducing the profits the natural monopolist can charge is at odds with the competitive process. They incentivize entrepreneurs to take risks in the competitive process of discovering consumer needs or wants. They are both the reward to the successful discoverer, and the signal for future competitors to enter the market or create new ones. On the contrary, any natural monopoly defense must be dismissed where the natural monopoly position has been achieved by anticompetitive means.[162] In other words, the fact that natural monopoly is the inevitable *outcome* cannot exempt the winning firm from anticompetitive behavior in the race to secure it.[163] A process-oriented approach[164] would require that EU competition law take into account either the competitive or anticompetitive origins of the natural monopoly.[165]

The question remains as to why a natural monopolist would take action to exclude competitors when it should not need to.

[2] The "More Efficient" Firm Framework

Not without reason, several commentators have argued that antitrust laws can do little about natural monopolies.[166] Their claims focus closely on competition *in* the market. That is, in the emergence of a competitor as efficient as the incumbent in providing the same product. However, the possibility remains that an entrant will be more cost efficient than the natural monopolist or that it will produce a new technology that will

161. Demsetz, Harold. "Why Regulate Utilities?" *The Journal of Law and Economics* 11.1 (1968): 55-65, 59-60: "we have no theory that allows us to deduce from the observable the degree of concentration in a particular market whether or not price and output are competitive."
162. Ohlhausen, Hon Maureen K. "The Elusive Role of Competition in the Standard-Setting Antitrust Debate." *Stanford Technology Law Review* 20.93 (2017): 93-142.
163. In the enforcement of Section 2 of the SA, natural monopoly is a "commonly rejected" defense when put forward to justify anticompetitive conduct to achieve that monopoly. *See* Elhauge, Einer. "Defining Better Monopolization Standards." *Stanford Law Review* 56.2 (2003): 253-344, at 256.
164. For a divergent opinion revealing a strictly outcome-oriented approach to natural monopoly, *see* Baker, Jonathan B. "Preserving a Political Bargain: The Political Economy of the Non-interventionist Challenge to Monopolization Enforcement." *Antitrust Law Journal* 76.3 (2010): 605-652, 631; Woodcock, Ramsi A. "Inconsistency in Antitrust." *University of Miami Law Review* 68.1 (2013): 105-188, 155.
165. *See* Chapter 8 for an extended discussion on the anticompetitive origins of dominance.
166. Posner, Richard A. "Natural Monopoly and Its Regulation: A Reply." *Stanford Law Review* 22.3 (1970): 540-546, at 542: "the antitrust laws provide no answer to the problem of the monopolist's inadequate output." *See also* PELKMANS, Jacques. "Making EU network markets competitive." *Oxford Review of Economic Policy* 17.3 (2001): 432-456, at 438, suggesting that EU competition only matters when natural monopoly is absent, there being space for competition *in* the market.

render the existing market outmoded.[167] There is always space for competitors to bring up a niche market for which there is consumer demand.[168]

Putting forward the importance of competition for the market has an impact in the assessment of natural monopoly itself. In industries where technology evolves rapidly, the characterization of a firm as a natural monopoly should be limited, as it tends to be problematic.[169] This seems to be the viewpoint of the Commission's Guidance Paper where it must pay close attention to the "dynamic nature of the industry" in the presence of a so-described natural monopoly.[170]

If competition enforcement must at times express a policy preference between conduct that favors competition *in* the market and competition *for* the market, in the case of natural monopolies this balance clearly tilts in favor of the latter, namely the replacement of the existing natural monopoly.[171]

As the resource savings of the natural monopoly are unambiguous, the applicant must prove that the alleged anticompetitive behavior is preventing the emergence of a more efficient firm. This would closely resemble to Chadwick or Demsetz's competition for the franchise to operate a regulated monopoly, where every given period the competent authority would compare the tenders submitted by the participants and select the most efficient one.[172]

§4.05 CONCLUSION

Economists strived for more than a hundred years to find a cohesive concept for natural monopoly. However, the extent to which today's natural monopolies would have come to exist if State intervention had left the competitive process free of interference remains unclear. It is somewhat unsurprising that the EU Courts have been unable to

167. Sidak, J. Gregory and David J. Teece. "Dynamic Competition in Antitrust Law." *Journal of Competition Law and Economics* 5.4 (2009): 581-631, 600.
168. Liebowitz, Stan J. and Stephen E. Margolis. "Should Technology Choice Be a Concern of Antitrust Policy?" *Harvard Journal of Law & Technology* 9.2 (1996): 283-318, 307.
169. Hamilton, Neil W. and Anne M. Caulfield. "The Defense of Natural Monopoly in Sherman Act Monopolization Cases." *DePaul Law Review* 33.3 (1983): 465-493, 485.
170. Guidance Paper, §83, n. 3.
171. The EU Courts have not explicitly formulated this trade-off. On the contrary, the US Courts are explicitly aware. A reason for this could be that Section 2 of the Sherman Act is fundamentally concerned with the means by which monopoly power is acquired. *See*, for instance, *Omega Satellite Prods. Co. v. City of Indianapolis*, 694 F.2d 119 (7th Cir. 1982), at 127, in relation to cable television and its apparent natural monopoly characteristics, the Court recalled that "the antitrust laws protect competition not only in, but for, the market—that is, competition to be the firm to enjoy a natural monopoly, and *by a modest extension competition to replace the existing natural monopolist*" (emphasis added, citation omitted).
172. Chadwick, Edwin. "Results of Different Principles of Legislation and Administration in Europe; of Competition for the Field, as Compared with Competition within the field, of Service." *Journal of the Statistical Society of London*, 22.3 (1859): 381-420; and Demsetz, Harold. "Why Regulate Utilities?" *The Journal of Law and Economics* 11.1 (1968): 55-65.

provide a coherent definition and a framework of analysis for such situations. Perhaps, as Nelson wrote, natural monopoly is simply "one of the most unfortunate phrases ever introduced into law or economics."[173]

173. Nelson, James R. "The Role of Competition in the Regulated Industries." *Antitrust Bulletin* 11.1 (1966): 393-428, 395.

CHAPTER 5

The Investor Dominant Firm

§5.01 INTRODUCTION

An investment is a diversion of a firm's current resources predicated on the calculus that future benefits will offset its present costs.[1] We call the firm that acquires SMP through those investments the "*investor dominant firm*."[2] This chapter analyzes the role that investments leading to dominance have had in the enforcement of Article 102 TFEU. It then shows how a process-perspective approach could improve if it were to take into account the investor origins of dominant firms.

In a free market, investments made under uncertainty are an igniting mechanism of the competitive process.[3] In economic terms, investment need not necessarily be reduced to a "technical" advancement that brings new products, new processes or new business models. Investment is also necessary to expand output of the same product, as it is the case of a firm that builds a larger manufacturing site to meet an increase in demand.[4]

1. Knight, Frank H. *Risk, Uncertainty and Profit*. New York: Augustus M. Kelly, [1921] 1964, at p. 58; and Hayek, Friedrich A. *Law, Legislation and Liberty*, (Vol. 2) *The Mirage of Social Justice*. Routledge, [1976] 1998, at pp. 98-99.
2. For instance, the "incomplete contract literature ... focuses only on the market power arising from past investments." *See* Zingales, Luigi. "Towards a Political Theory of the Firm." *Journal of Economic Perspectives* 31.3 (2017): 113-130, 118-119. In Schumpeter's understanding of how economic progress is achieved, the first stage is the investment, the second stage, the innovation, and the third stage is diffusion of that innovation. Applying that framework of analysis to study the impact of merger control on innovation, *see* Ormosi, Peter, Anna Rita Bennato, Steve Davies and Franco Mariuzzo. "Feasibility Study on the Microeconomic Impact of Enforcement of Competition Policies on Innovation." *Luxembourg: Publications Office of the European Union*, 2017, *available at* http://ec.europa.eu/competition/publications/reports/kd0417860enn.pdf.
3. Knight, Frank H. *Risk, Uncertainty and Profit*. New York: Augustus M. Kelly, [1921] 1964, at pp. 160-161 explaining that a technical process is as a source of income that "is produced in the first place in the same way, by the investment of present resources (in research and experiment)."
4. *Id.* at p. 371; *see also* Belleflamme, Paul and Martin Peitz. *Industrial Organization: Markets and Strategies*. Cambridge University Press, 2015, at pp. 405-411, discussing investment in capacity.

Although investment in capacity plays a crucial role in more traditional or less innovative markets,[5] other less traditional markets such as those relating to data analytics, cloud service providers or artificial intelligence may as well require large investments in capacity (e.g., memory storage or computational power). This was for instance Google's strategy to outcompete e-mail service providers: to offer an e-mail service that constantly increased its storage capacity. Whichever may be in each particular case, it is a successful investment effort that leads the investor to the acquisition of titles to income.[6]

Eventually, either of both will lead to a property right from which the firm derives an income that might offset the costs.

However, it is important to acknowledge that an investment may not be successful *stricto sensu* for the investor. An investment may fail. Despite this, the fact of the matter remains that in the process of competition an investment is a step toward the discovery of needs. A "failed" investment has the potential to reveal certain data that was previously unknown to market participants.[7] For example, the "failed" investment can tell whether consumers are not interested in a particular piece of technology or whether there is no more demand for a particular existing product. Thus, malinvestments are in themselves *also* drivers of the continuous adjustment that the competitive process allows.[8]

Against this background, this chapter is structured as follows. Section 2 examines the place that the investor dominant firm has in the enforcement of Article 102 TFEU. In particular, this section shows through a selection of heterogeneous cases and judicial constructs that EU competition law belittles, disregards or even views investments efforts as an impediment to competition. Section 5.03 advances an economic framework that explains *why* investments leading to market power are a positive element of the competitive process. In line with that framework, section 5.04 explores *how* the enforcement of Article 102 TFEU against investor dominant firms should change in order to accommodate an approach in line with the objective of protecting the competitive *process*. Section 5.05 concludes.

---

5. Kaplow, Louis and Carl Shapiro. "Antitrust" *in* A. Mitchell Polinsky and Steven Shavell (eds.) *Handbook of Law and Economics*, Vol. 2, 2007: 1073-1225, at 1117 and 1192, arguing that in traditional markets investment in capacity can be the most important dimension of competition in the long run.
6. Schumpeter, Joseph A. *Business Cycles: A Theoretical, Historical and Statistical Analysis of the Capitalist Process*. New York, Toronto and London: McGraw-Hill Book Company, 1939, at p. 70. As we explained in Chapter 1, we do not discuss the possibility of acquiring dominance by merger or acquisition, which arguably under Schumpeter's definition could be seen as another type of investment.
7. Lieberman, Marvin B. "The Learning Curve and Pricing in the Chemical Processing Industries." *The RAND Journal of Economics* 15.2 (1984): 213-228.
8. Schumpeter, Joseph A. *Business Cycles: A Theoretical, Historical and Statistical Analysis of the Capitalist Process*. New York Toronto London: McGraw-Hill Book Company, 1939, at p. 146. On a more contemporary note, *see* Mcardle, Megan. *The Up Side of Down: Why Failing Well Is the Key to Success*. Penguin, 2015.

§5.02 THE PLACE OF INVESTMENT EFFORTS IN ARTICLE 102 TFEU

This section examines the place that investments have in Article 102 TFEU. *First*, it looks into a selection of heterogeneous cases to show how the case law is consistent across years in its neglect of investments (5.02[A]). And *second*, it points to two doctrinal constructs that epitomize a disinterest for the past, and in particular for past investment efforts (5.02[B]).

[A] A General Look into the Place of Investments in Article 102 TFEU Case Law

In this chronological and heterogeneous selection of Article 102 TFEU we show that both the EU Courts and the Commission have explicitly neglected the value of the investments undertaken by the dominant firm. That said, the reader should be reminded that the number of cases that do not discuss investments leading to dominance, or simply mention them in passing, is substantial.[9]

[1] United Brands and the Forgotten Paragraph

In *United Brands*, the Commission found that United Brands abused its dominant position by, among others, charging excessive prices for its bananas. United Brands appealed before the Court of Justice and contended that its financial performance was nothing but the result of "a normal return on its investments."[10] However, the Court's discussion regarding the investments undertaken by United Brands took another path.

The Court considered that the exceptionally large investments that United Brand had made created an important barrier to entry since its competitors would have to create and run another banana plantation. The Court was fundamentally concerned that in attempting to enter the market competitors would fail and be unable to recover their costs.[11] On the contrary, the Court never considered that United Brands itself was proof that such investments could be overcome, and that failure is part of the competitive process.

9. CJEU, Case C-62/86, *AKZO v. Commission*, ECLI:EU:C:1991:286, §122, establishing that the amount of capital investment required renders market entry "not easy"; CJEU, Case C-322/81, *Michelin I*, ECLI:EU:C:1983:313, §55, acknowledging that Michelin has a lead on investment and research over its competitors but leaving this description out of the assessment of the rebates; and CJEU, Case C-163/99, *Portugal v. Commission*, ECLI:EU:C:2001:189, §§55 and 57, where the applicant claimed that the use of quantity discounts was to promote an intense use of the airports and aimed at deploying an strategic reinvestment, and the Court regarded such argumentation generic and insufficient in a situation where the airports "are likely to enjoy a natural monopoly" (*see* Chapter 4 for a discussion on the lack of clarity that the concept natural monopoly has in the case law); *see also* Commission Decision, Case COMP/37.507, *AstraZeneca*, §§520 and 562, where the Commission equates pioneering to the negative idea of gatekeeper and belittles the continued investment efforts of AstraZeneca.
10. CJEU, Case C-27/76, *United Brands v. Commission*, ECLI:EU:C:1978:22, at p. 237.
11. *Id.* §122.

The *United Brands* Court is often cited to explain what the Court considers an excessive price. A price is excessive when it has no reasonable relation to its economic value, the Court held.[12] However, the paragraph that precedes the Court's test seems to have been overlooked in the literature.

In that "*forgotten paragraph*" the Court holds that a dominant firm cannot "reap trading benefits which it would not have reaped if there had been normal and sufficiently effective competition."[13] In other words, a dominant firm cannot profit from the benefits of its investment, and it should price its goods "*as if*" it had no market power. In this manner, the Court sets a baseline of antitrust liability that disregards the investments leading to dominance.

The "as if" standard, reminiscent of the ordoliberal school of thought,[14] is in tension with the competitive *process* of discovery and hence in tension with the investments efforts of all its participants. The dominant firm, or the EU Courts, would need to establish a counterfactual describing how competition would have been.[15] However, this would either entail the (artificial) assumption that the investment in capacity or innovation had never occurred, or a guess as to how any ideal of competition would have been where change, by definition, would be unwelcome. Whichever solution is followed, both would in essence neglect competition as an ongoing process as well as the benefits and incentives that it provides.

[2] Commercial Solvents and the Protection of a Rival's Investments

In *Commercial Solvents* the Court found that Commercial Solvents had abused its dominant position by refusing to supply to Zoja the raw material aminobutanol. Zoja, a firm specialized in processing aminobutanol into ethambutol had cancelled its supply agreement with Commercial Solvents.[16] But after rescinding its contract, Zoja did not manage to find better supply alternatives and tried to reinstate its contract with Commercial Solvents. Commercial Solvents then refused to supply mainly because after Zoja's contractual termination it had decided to start processing itself the raw substances into derivatives like ethambutol. This notwithstanding, the Court found Commercial Solvents' refusal to sell abusive.

---

12. *Id.* §250. The Court has provided further guidance in CJEU, Case C-177/16, *Biedrība "Autortiesību un komunicēšanās konsultāciju aģentūra - Latvijas Autoru apvienība" v. Konkurences padome*, ECLI:EU:C:2017:689.
13. CJEU, Case C-27/76, *United Brands v. Commission*, ECLI:EU:C:1978:22, §249.
14. The "as if" standard was the solution advanced by the ordoliberal thinker Miksch as a solution to the problem of monopoly power. Instead of costly governmental intervention aimed at divesting monopoly positions the dominant firm was given a standard of behavior to abide by. However, as Gerber explains, not all ordoliberal thinkers were sympathetic about the standard. Gerber, David J. *Law and Competition in the Twentieth Century Europe. Protecting Prometheus*. Oxford, 2003, at pp. 251-253.
15. Herrera Anchústegui, Ignacio. *Buyer Power in EU Competition Law*. Concurrences, 2017, at p. 95. Inexplicably, Herrera Anchústegui does not discuss *United Brands* in this context.
16. Zoja also processes another substance: nitropropane. Ethambutol was used in the manufacturing of anti-tuberculosis drugs.

The case is important because it shows how from the early days of enforcement of Article 102 TFEU, the EU Courts have disregarded the dominant firm's investments and at times protected the businesses of competitors instead of the competitive process.[17] This asymmetry between the value of investments undertaken by the dominant firm and its competitors has led to an incomplete understanding of competition as a process.

In its analysis, the Court of Justice emphasized that Zoja's market position "entirely depends" on its technology and know-how that it has acquired in processing aminobutanol into ethambutol. As such, the imposition of a duty to reinstate the supply on Commercial Solvents would protect Zoja's investments on its technology and know-how.[18] However, the Court of Justice completely waived away the investments made by Commercial Solvents in the first place and disregarded that Zoja's opportunity to operate was the result of the investment efforts undertaken in competition by the dominant firm in the first place.[19] The "test" of liability designed by the Court was a simple leveraging infringement. A dominant firm that "with the object of reserving such raw material for manufacturing its own derivatives, refuses to supply a customer, which is itself a manufacturer of these derivatives, and therefore risks eliminating all competition on the part of this customer, is abusing its dominant position within the meaning of Article [102]."[20]

The Court thus holds that Article 102 TFEU not only could be used to facilitate competing firms to operate in a derivative market, *but also*, to limit dominant firms like Commercial Solvents in their freedom to provide a derivative product. Certainly, obliging the dominant firm to sell its product to a downstream firm is a means to achieve a limitation of the market power of the dominant firm in the adjacent market.

[3] Microsoft and the Echoes of United Brands and Commercial Solvents

In *Microsoft*, Sun Microsystems complained to the Commission that Microsoft refused to provide certain interoperability information. This information enabled Sun's work group servers to attain a sufficient degree of interoperability with personal computers (PCs) running the Windows Operating System (OS). Without that information, the Commission and the General Court found, that Sun and other firms could not compete

17. CJEU, Joined Cases 6 and 7/73, *Istituto Chemioterapico Italiano SpA and Commercial Solvents v. Commission*, ECLI:EU:C:1974:18, §25.
18. As in *Commercial Solvents*, the Commission considered in *IMS Health* interim measures decision that due to IMS Health refusal to license its 1,860 brick structure NDC's "substantial investments" were lost. The only way to make NDC's "unsustainable financial position" was for it to make use of the brick structure. *See* Commission Decision, Case COMP/38.044, *NDC Health/IMS Health: Interim measures*, §191.
19. The industry however praised Commercial Solvents for pioneering the production of acetone and butanol by fermentation processes. *See* Lehman Brothers Collection. *Contemporary Business Archives. Commercial Solvents Corp.* Harvard Business School, *available at* https://www.library.hbs.edu/hc/lehman/.
20. CJEU, Joined Cases 6 and 7/73, *Istituto Chemioterapico Italiano SpA and Commercial Solvents v. Commission*, ECLI:EU:C:1974:18, §25.

on an "equal footing."[21] Further, both the Commission and the GC concluded that refusing to license an intellectual property right would also be abusive when it impeded the emergence of a "technical development."[22]

As a result, the Commission mandated Microsoft to license its interoperability data and ordered Microsoft's that the remuneration from the licensing "should not reflect the '*strategic value*' stemming from Microsoft's power in the client PC operating system market or in the work group server operating systems market" (emphasis added).[23] Moreover, the licensing terms "should not create disincentives to compete with Microsoft, or unnecessarily restrain the ability of the beneficiaries to innovate" and should remain "sufficiently predictable [because] implementing the specifications will indeed constitute a *significant investment*" (emphasis added).[24]

It suffices for now to highlight two important points. *First*, the prohibition to include a "strategic value" in the licensing terms divorces the investments that led Microsoft in the first place to innovate and acquire market power from the calculus of remuneration.[25] In other words, the Commission considered that the licensing terms should be set at a competitive level akin to the *United Brands* benchmark as "if there had been normal and sufficiently effective competition."[26] *Second*, and relatedly, while the Commission held that the licensing terms should take due account of rivals incentives to invest, the Commission did not include a minimum safeguard of Microsoft's *ex ante* and *ex post* incentives to invest.[27] The licensing framework that the Commission established was concerned with the protection of Microsoft's rivals, à la *Commercial Solvents*, and that is that.[28]

21. GC, Case T-201/04, *Microsoft v. Commission*, ECLI:EU:T:2007:289, §§230, 374, 390 and 421. On its own initiative, the Commission also investigated whether Microsoft's tying of Windows Media Player to Windows OS constituted another abuse. The Commission found the tying abusive and the General Court upheld the decision on its entirety.
22. *Id.* §647.
23. Commission Decision, Case COMP/37.792, *Microsoft*, §1008 (ii).
24. *Id.* §1008 (iii) and (iv).
25. Ridyard, Derek. "Compulsory Access under EC Competition Law-A New Doctrine of 'Convenient Facilities' and the Case for Price Regulation." *European Competition Law Review* 25 (2004): 669-673.
26. CJEU, Case C-27/76, *United Brands v. Commission*, ECLI:EU:C:1978:22, §249.
27. The Commission had considered these incentives previously (*see* Commission Decision, Case COMP/37.792, *Microsoft*, §§709-742), but failed to include them as a part of the terms imposed by Microsoft to access its interoperability information.
28. If at any point, the General Court held that the incentives to invest of the dominant firm were to be analyzed as a possible objective justification and not as part of the refusal to supply test itself. *See* GC, Case T-201/04, *Microsoft v. Commission*, ECLI:EU:T:2007:289, §659. In a similar fashion, (i.e., disregarding the investments of the dominant firm but protecting those of its competitors) the Commission in Intel concluded that "[t]he emergence of AMD as a competitive threat to Intel was dependent on the availability of investors willing to finance risky investments in research and development as well as AMD production facilities. *Such investments are only undertaken when there is a prospect of an adequate return*" (emphasis added). *See* Commission Decision, Case COMP/37.990, *Intel*, §1613.

[4] Intel, Moore's "Law" and Endogenous Change

The *Intel* decision illustrates the marginal role that investments have in the assessment of abusive behavior.[29]

The Commission found that Intel abused its dominant position by granting anticompetitive rebates to purchasers of its x86 microprocessors. In its assessment of both market power and abuse, the Commission described Intel as the industry leader for ten years. Intel's investments in production, R&D and marketing made it a must-have brand. Importantly, these *competitive* efforts put forward by Intel are nowhere described as competitive achievements. In parallel, the Commission describes the investments that Intel's competitors must undertake as barriers to entry since Intel does not need to incur them as an established player.[30]

Among other claims, Intel argued that the falling prices of microprocessors evidenced an intense competition in the industry. In Intel's view this finding was incompatible with the finding of a dominant position. The Commission rejected the argument in a way that disparaged Intel's investment efforts. Thus, it held that innovation, technological progress and the lower prices that come with these are simply "an intrinsic feature of this industry ... irrespective of the state of competition."[31] Put differently, the Commission seems to suggest that prices would have fallen as the result of some inevitable exogenous rule, independent of a firm's behavior.[32] The Commission portrayed Moore's Law as an exogenous force that made prices fall, irrespective of the state of competition.[33]

However, Moore's "Law" is not a law. It is a social construct made to organize the innovation efforts of market participants. That is, in a nutshell, a *forecast* of a cost reduction and an increase in computational power of microprocessors in an exponential manner.

Unlike in neoclassical frameworks in which technological change is given as an exogenous variable,[34] the reality of markets is that technological progress does not simply happen. Technological innovation must be carried out by a firm, which in turn

29. The decision is of further interest because the Commission issued it a few months after publishing the Guidance Paper on Article 102 TFEU. This, notwithstanding, the Guidance Paper was not applicable to the case since the proceedings had started in July 2007, that is, two years before the publication of the Guidance Paper. The Commission initiated its proceedings on Jul. 26, 2007, and the Guidance Paper was published in February 2009. It is important to note, however, that the modernization process to bring a more-economic approach to the enforcement of Article 102 TFEU had already started long before the Commission initiated its proceedings against Intel.
30. Commission Decision, Case COMP/37.990, *Intel*, §§853-866.
31. *Id.* §§907 and 908.
32. This finding is reminiscent of the largely abandoned economic structure-conduct-performance paradigm where behavior of the firm is the result of the structure of the market.
33. Commission Decision, Case COMP/37.990, *Intel*, §908.
34. Aizcorbe, Ana. "Moore's Law, Competition, and Intel's Productivity in the Mid-1990s." *The American Economic Review* 95.2 (2005): 305-308, at 306: "Suppose the quality of chips evolves at an exogenous rate *q* that is determined by Moore's Law." Exogenous meaning that change originates from sources outside the firm.

affects, among others, (microprocessor) costs and eventually prices.[35] It is possible that Moore's law acted to a certain degree as a self-reinforcing mechanism of expectations around which Intel, AMD or other firms developed their technical plans, but as Professor Kenneth Flamm puts it, "there was nothing inevitable about Moore's Law — no underlying technical or physics-based reason for the phenomenon."[36]

As economist Paul Romer argues, a large part of technological change is *endogenous* in that it results from a firm "intentional investment decisions" that respond to market incentives.[37] This is a market reality that even Robert Solow's famous model of exogenous growth acknowledged but dismissed because of the measurement problems it posed. He writes, "Of course this is not meant to suggest that the observed rate of technical progress would have persisted even if the rate of investment had been much smaller or had fallen to zero. Obviously much, perhaps nearly all, innovation must be embodied in new plant and equipment to be realized at all."[38]

Turning back to *Intel*, a claim such as lower prices and technological progress are an "intrinsic feature" of the microprocessor industry empties Intel's risky investments of any competitive value and its effects in growth.[39] This, in turn, leads to the paradoxical implication that a dominant firm should not be able to "reap the trading benefits" of its entrepreneurial action since innovation and technological change are not a result of "intentional investment decisions." We shall explore further ahead the consequences of leaving investment outside of the picture.

[5] Google Shopping and Investments as an Entry Barrier

In *Google Shopping*, the Commission found that Google abused its position of dominance in the market of general search services by leveraging its position into the market of comparison shopping services.[40] Google leverages its dominance by positioning and displaying its own comparison shopping service, i.e., Google Shopping, in a more favorable manner than competing comparison services. The Commission held that Google's favorable treatment of its own product was anticompetitive because "equality of opportunity" was not achieved.

35. Jorgenson, Dale. "Information Technology and the U.S. Economy." *The American Economic Review* 91.1 (2001): 1-32.
36. Flamm, Kenneth. "Moore's Law and the Economics of Semiconductor Price Trends" *in* National Research Council (ed.) *Productivity and Cyclicality in Semiconductors: Trends, Implications, and Questions—Report of a Symposium.* Washington, DC: The National Academies Press (2004), at 166.
37. Romer, Paul M. "Endogenous Technological Change." *Journal of Political Economy* 98.5, Part 2 (1990): S71-S102, S77.
38. Solow, Robert M. "Technical Change and the Aggregate Production Function." *The Review of Economics and Statistics* 39.3 (1957): 312-320, 316-317.
39. Romer, Paul M. "Endogenous Technological Change." *Journal of Political Economy* 98.5, Part 2 (1990): S71-S102, at S89.
40. For a discussion regarding the market definition, *see* Broos, Sébastien and Jorge Marcos Ramos. "Competing Business Models and Two-Sidedness: An Application to the Google Shopping Case." *The Antitrust Bulletin* 62.2 (2017): 382-399.

In its decision, the Commission depicts investments that competitors of Google have to make as barriers to entry. Moreover, since Google continues to invest in its search engine competitors "would have no choice but to attempt to match these investments."[41] These would in turn be higher than Google's because newcomers would have to face scale and network externalities that Google already benefits from.[42] Thus, while the Commission seems to praise Microsoft's investments in Bing, as well as other competitor's,[43] it portrays Google's investments as barriers to entry created by Google.

Whether investments are what led Google to be preferred above other web browsers, the Commission decided this does not change the assessment of abuse. As the Court of Justice already held in *Continental Can*, that "the reasons or the causes for which Google has a dominant position on the national markets for general search services are irrelevant."[44] Thus, because of the division in the assessment between dominance and abuse, Google's investments are swept under the rug when the Commission outlines its theory of harm.

In this regard, it is unsurprising that only once again investments efforts come up in the decision. The Commission vaguely argued, without more substantiation, that Google's unfavorable treatment is "*likely* to reduce the incentives ... to invest in developing innovative services, improving the relevance of their existing services and creating new types of services" (emphasis added). Furthermore, competitors trying to compensate their discrimination by using paid sources of online traffic like advertisement "this will also reduce the revenue available to invest."[45]

Three important points can be taken from the *Google Shopping* decision. *First*, investments made by dominant firms create barriers to entry. This is in line with the Guidance Paper's assessment of market power. *Second*, the compartmentalized assessment of dominance and abuse prevents the investor origins of the dominant firm from informing the theory of harm. *Third*, the Commission readily finds that conduct by a dominant undertaking has a negative impact on incentives to innovate of the competitors of the dominant firm. On the contrary, past investments undertaken by the dominant firm are disregarded, and its future incentives to invest are readily dismissed.

[B] Doctrinal Constructs and Investment Myopia

In what follows we explore two doctrinal constructs that epitomize the EU Courts' disinterest for past investments and the origins of dominant firms. The *first* construct is the dichotomy between the existence and the exercise of an intellectual property right. The *second* construct is the existence of different legal tests for different types of property in refusal to deal cases.

---

41. Commission Decision, Case COMP/39.740, *Google Search (Shopping)*, §291.
42. *Id.* §270.
43. *Id.* §§286 and 583. The names of those "other competitors" appear redacted in the pubic version of the decision.
44. *Id.* §315.
45. *Id.* §595.

[1] *The Existence and Exercise Dichotomy*

The disconnection between investment efforts and the subsequent acquisition of market power is particularly evident in the application of Article 102 TFEU limiting IPR. We posit that the source of such disconnection is however to be found in the artificial distinction the Court of Justice drew in *Consten and Grundig* between the existence and the exercise of an intellectual property right and that still remains unrevised.

In *Consten and Grundig*,[46] Consten had been appointed as the exclusive distributor of Grundig electronic products and their spare parts in France. Under this distribution agreement, Consten undertook not to carry competing products, to order a minimum quantity of Grundig products, to provide appropriate publicity, to set up a repairs shop and to carry out the guarantee and after sales service. In exchange, Grundig would grant Consten the retail rights, and would not import itself directly or indirectly in the area covered by the contract. More importantly to our purposes here, Consten was authorized to use Grundig's trademark GINT and register it in its own name in France. When the contract ceased Consten would transfer the trademark GINT to Grundig. Despite the absolute territorial protection, another company, UNEF, bought products from Grundig in Germany and started reselling them in France. Consten brought actions against UNEF for unfair competition and trademark infringement, and UNEF counteracted by lodging a complaint before the Commission on the basis of Article 101 TFEU. The Commission found that the contract and the agreement concerning the registration and use of the trademark GINT infringed Article 101 TFEU. Consten and Grundig appealed to the Court of Justice.

The Court considered the agreement concerning the GINT trademark was intended to be an obstacle to parallel imports and thus restrict competition. To avoid interfering with the systems of *property* of the Member States, (as back then trademarks rights were under the exclusive competence of Member States) the Court explained that the application of Article 101 only limited the *exercise* of the right but did not affect the grant of the right.[47] The Court gave further content in *Deutsche Grammophon* to its argument advanced in *Consten and Grundig*. In the context of the application of the rules of Articles 36, 101 and 102 TFEU, it held that "the Treaty does not affect the existence of rights" recognized in EU Member States "with regard to industrial and commercial property." But, "the *exercise* of such rights may nevertheless fall within the prohibitions."[48]

Valentine Korah explains that "the [Court] used the distinction between the existence and exercise of property rights" to develop the doctrine of exhaustion.[49] The objective was to prevent the fragmentation of the internal market that IP rights could create under the exclusive competence of Member States while not interfering with

46. CJEU, Joined Cases C-56/60 and C-58/60, *Consten and Grundig v. Commission*, ECLI: EU:C:1966:41.
47. *Id.* at pp. 345-346.
48. CJEU, Case C-78/70, *Deutsche Grammophon and METRO*, ECLI:EU:C:1971:59, §11.
49. Korah, Valentine. "The Interface Between Intellectual Property and Antitrust: The European Experience." *Antitrust Law Journal* 69.3 (2002): 801-839, 805. A discussion on the issue of exhaustion and the application of Articles 30-36 TFEU is outside the scope of inquiry.

their systems of property.[50] The Court would "only interfere" with the exercise of that right but not with its existence. Thus, the Court was effectively holding that once Grundig products had been placed on the market with its consent, Consten could not use the trademark to prevent UNEF's parallel importations from Germany.

Regrettably, this philosophical separation between the existence of an intellectual property right and its exercise has made antitrust enforcement against investor dominant firms myopic.[51] This means that enforcement of Article 102 TFEU veers toward an *ex post* narrative of anticompetitive harm that overlooks the *ex ante* competitive process. Thus, by the time the property owner exercises its rights, the competitive investments that led to the creation (existence) of market power are "water under the bridge."[52] As Korah explains, the overriding policy of the internal market integration and the national character of the IP system "trumped the rationale for intellectual property rights—the need to induce or reward investment in research and development, etc."[53]

Interestingly, the perverse effects that this dichotomy has on investments leading to market power are in stark contrast with the Court's description of competition as a process in *Consten and Grundig*: "the principle of freedom of competition concerns the *various stages and manifestations of competition*" (emphasis added).

In a certain way, the existence and exercise dichotomy is analogous to the separation of dominance from the abuse in the analysis of anticompetitive effects. How can the Court assess harm to the competitive *process* without considering its various stages and manifestations? This is the process paradox the Court, perhaps inadvertently, steps in, and we address in sections 5.04 and 5.05.

[2] The Unwarranted Asymmetry Between Intellectual and Physical Property in Refusal to Deal Cases

The existence and exercise dichotomy subsists. Importantly, the effects that this dichotomy has had in the enforcement of Article 102 TFEU go beyond conduct related to intellectual property. The line of cases relating to refusal to deal shows this. Here, the

50. Venit, James S. "EEC Patent Licensing Revisited: The Commission's Patent License Regulation." *The Antitrust Bulletin* 30.2 (1985): 457-526, at 469.
51. Despite multiple evidences to the contrary, and for ease of exposition, we assume that the IP is a proxy for market power. *See* Gilbert, Richard J. "Mobility Barriers and the Value of Incumbency" *in* Richard Schmalensee and Robert D. Willig (eds.) *Handbook of Industrial Organization*, Vol. 1, 1989: 475-535, at 499: "patents are rarely of sufficient scope to block competing technologies and hence their value in entry prevention is limited." *See also* Bostyn, Sven and Nicolas Petit. "Patent = Monopoly: A Legal Fiction." *Working Paper Series. University of Liverpool* (2013) 1-19; and Kobayashi, Bruce H. "Spilled Ink or Economic Progress? The Supreme Court's Decision in *Illinois Tool Works v. Independent Ink.*" *The Antitrust Bulletin* 53.1 (2008): 5-33.
52. Korah, Valentine. "The Interface Between Intellectual Property and Antitrust: The European Experience." *Antitrust Law Journal* 69.3 (2002): 801-839, 803.
53. *Id.* 805. Only the European sui generis protection of databases makes explicitly dependent on the grant of intellectual property that the individual makes a *"substantial investment"* in its creation. *See* Article 7(1) of Directive 96/9/EC of 11 March 1996 on the legal protection of databases, *OJ* L 77, 1996, p. 20.I.

EU Courts missed the forest for the trees. By differentiating in a formalistic manner between different types of property, the EU Courts assumed away, once again, the value of the investments involved in the creation of any property.

As described above, *Commercial Solvents* denotes an early disinterest for investments leading to dominance in the enforcement of Article 102 TFEU. However, it was not until *Magill* and *Bronner* that the EU Courts introduced two different legal tests contingent on the type of property involved in the refusal.[54]

The *first* of these tests relates to IPR, such as patents. Here, the controlling standard is found in *Magill*[55] and *IMS Health*[56] and *Microsoft*.[57] The second one relates to "other" property rights, such as physical infrastructures. Here, the controlling legal test is found in *Bronner*.[58]

In *Bronner*, claimant Bronner sought access to the nation-wide home-delivery network of newspapers owned by Mediaprint. Bronner claimed that by refusing to grant access, Mediaprint was abusing its dominance in the market for the distribution of daily newspapers. Bronner argued that it could not start its own home-delivery system because it lacked a sufficient number of newspaper subscribers.

The Court rejected Bronner's contention. Mediaprint's home-delivery network was not indispensable because there were other methods of newspaper delivery available. Furthermore, there seemed to be no legal, economic or technical obstacles that impeded or made "unreasonably difficult" the establishment of such a new network. With this background, the Court formulates a legal test that was absent in *Commercial Solvents* to deal with refusals to supply of "other" property than intellectual property. A dominant firm commits an abuse by refusing to supply if: (i) access to the service in itself is indispensable to allow the claimant to carry its business;[59] (ii) the refusal is "*likely* to eliminate *all* competition" "on the part of the person requesting the service" (emphasis added); and (iii) the refusal is not objectively justified.[60]

The *Bronner legal test* differs from the test applied by the Court in cases relating to intellectual property.

In *Magill*, the Commission found that a group of broadcasting companies (ITP, RTE and BBC) were abusing their dominant position by refusing to grant licenses for

54. Other refusals to deal cases came after *Commercial Solvents*. For example, in *Volvo v. Veng*, and in *CICRA v. Renault*, the Court held that a refusal to supply spare parts to independent repairers was in principle permissible unless accompanied by other abusive conduct. Such as if the refusal was arbitrary, if the prices for spare parts were set at an unfair level or if the refusal was accompanied by a decision to no longer produce spare parts for a particular model. *See* CJEU, Case C-238/87, *Volvo v. Veng*, ECLI:EU:C:1988:477, §9; and CJEU, Case C-53/87, *CICRA and Others v. Renault*, ECLI:EU:C:1988:472, §18.
55. CJEU, Joined Cases C-241/91 P and C-242/91, *Magill*, ECLI:EU:C:1995:98; GC, Case T-69/89, *Radio Telefis Eireann v. Commission* ("GC, *Magill*"), ECLI:EU:T:1991:39.
56. CJEU, Case C-418/01, *IMS Health*, ECLI:EU:C:2004:257.
57. GC, Case T-201/04, *Microsoft v. Commission*, ECLI:EU:T:2007:289.
58. CJEU, Case C-7/97, *Bronner*, ECLI:EU:C:1998:569.
59. The first time the requirement of indispensability is explicitly mentioned in the case law is in *Télémarketing*. *See* Case C-311/84, SA *Centre belge d'études de marché - Télémarketing (CBEM) v. SA Compagnie luxembourgeoise de télédiffusion (CLT) and SA Information publicité Benelux (IPB)*, ECLI:EU:C:1985:394, §26; *and* Chapter 2.
60. CJEU, Case C-7/97, *Bronner*, §41.

the publication of their respective weekly TV listings. These TV listings were protected under Irish law by copyright, which the Commission submitted should not exist because they were not in themselves secret, innovative or related to any research. The Commission held that the refusal was abusive because Magill was unable to introduce in the market *a new product*.[61] The new product consisted of a weekly TV guide instead of the daily TV listings that ITP, RTE and BBC published. The Commission further argued that the refusal abusively allowed ITP, RTE and BBC to keep for themselves the derivative market for weekly TV guides, and that such conduct fell outside the scope of the specific subject-matter of that intellectual property.[62]

The EU Courts upheld the decision. In a more orderly manner than the Commission had done in its decision, the EU Courts fleshed out a legal test to determine when a refusal to license intellectual property is abusive. First, access to the property is indispensable for the appearance of a new product for which there is a potential consumer demand; second the refusal allows the defendant to reserve the secondary market for itself by excluding all competition on that market; and third, there was no objective justification for the refusal.[63] In reaching this conclusion it seems that the Court considered the submission by the Commission that the copyright was not the result of any particular competitive activity.[64] However, it remains unclear that this important consideration transcended the legal test.

The legal test in *Magill* contains an element that the Court in *Bronner* did not include, that is, that the input in question must be indispensable for the production of *a new product*. Yet, the *Bronner* Court left the possibility open that the standard set in the case law relating to intellectual property right could be applicable to "the exercise of any property right whatever."[65] If that were the case, this would mean that the standard(s) set in *Magill* and later on in *IMS Health* or *Microsoft* could be transposed to analyze other types of property. The Court of Justice in *IMS Health* subsequently corroborated the "new product condition" in intellectual property cases.

IMS Health is an American company that provides healthcare information to pharmaceutical companies. The information relates to doctors' prescriptions and pharmacies' sales of medicines. To gather and analyze this information IMS uses a "brick system." Simply, every brick is a geographical meaningful division of any territory chosen by IMS. In the case at hand, NDC Health, a competitor of IMS, sought to use IMS' brick structure of Germany comprising a *copyrighted* structure consisting of 1,860 bricks and a derived structure of 2,847 bricks.[66] IMS' initiated proceedings to

61. Commission Decision, Case COMP/IV/31.851, *Magill TV Guide/ITP, BBC and RTE*, §23.
62. *Id.*
63. CJEU, Joined Cases C-241/91 P and C-242/91 P, *Magill*, ECLI:EU:C:1995:98.
64. *Id.* §§46 and 71.
65. CJEU, Case C-7/97, *Bronner*, ECLI:EU:C:1998:569, §41.
66. NDC also filed a complaint before the Commission. As in *Commercial Solvents*, the Commission found in *IMS Health* interim measures decision that due to IMS Health refusal to license its 1,860 brick structure NDC's "substantial investments" were lost. The only way to get NDC's out of its "unsustainable financial position" was for it to make use of the 1,860 brick structure. *See* Commission Decision, Case COMP/38.044, *NDC Health/IMS Health: Interim measures*, §191. IMS Health appealed the interim measures decision but eventually withdrew its application because the Commission had in the meantime withdrawn it.

obtain an injunction prohibiting any unlawful use of its 1.860 brick structure. The hearing court, the Landgericht Frankfurt am Main, decided to stay proceedings and ask the Court of Justice in what circumstances did a refusal to grant a license constitute an abuse of dominance.

The *IMS Health* Court upheld the legal test in *Magill* and emphasized the importance of the new product condition. In particular, the Court ruled that that condition serves to balance the interest in protecting intellectual property right and the interest in protecting free competition. Therefore, a refusal can only be abusive when the potential licensee "does not intend to limit itself essentially to duplicating the goods or services already offered on the secondary market by the owner of the intellectual property right but intends to produce new goods or services not offered by the owner of the right and for which there is a potential consumer demand."[67]

In spite of the ruling of the CJEU in *IMS Health*, the GC in *Microsoft* subsequently expanded the new product condition.

It is clear that the test applicable to a refusal to license intellectual property is different from that applicable to other types of property. By requiring a "new product" *Magill* and *IMS* established a stricter legal test for refusals to deal intellectual property than the *Bronner* test for tangible property.[68]

The *Microsoft* Court was aware of this asymmetry. In fact, it upheld the decision of the Commission to proceed "on the premise that, so far as it relates to the interoperability information, *the conduct at issue in the present case might not be a mere refusal* to supply a product or a service indispensable to the exercise of a specific activity *but a refusal to license intellectual property rights, and thus chose the strictest legal test* and therefore the one most favourable to Microsoft" (emphasis added).[69]

However, the General Court made the strictest legal test more flexible. First, it modified the "new product" condition for the "technical development" condition. Second, the requirement in both *Magill* and *IMS Health, and Bronner* that "all competition" be "likely" eliminated disappeared. This was in fact one of Microsoft's arguments. Likelihood as meaning high probability, and not mere capability should be the standard. The standard General Court, in one of the most disturbing sentences in the case law, held that "Microsoft's complaint is purely one of terminology and is wholly irrelevant."[70] Thus, while the legal test in *Magill* and *IMS* is clearly stricter than that of *Bronner*, it is unclear whether the same can be said of *Microsoft's* legal test.

67. CJEU, Case C-418/01, *IMS Health*, ECLI:EU:C:2004:257, §§48-49.
68. Highlighting the same point, *see* Geradin, Damien. "Limiting the Scope of Article 82 of the EC Treaty: What Can the EU Learn from the US Supreme Court's Judgment in *Trinko* in the Wake of *Microsoft, IMS*, and *Deutsche Telekom*?" *Common Market Law Review* 41.6 (2004): 1519-1553; and Ritter, Cyril. "Refusal to Deal and Essential Facilities: Does Intellectual Property Require Special Deference Compared to Tangible Property." *World Competition* 28.3 (2005): 281-298.
69. GC, Case T-201/04, *Microsoft v. Commission*, ECLI:EU:T:2007:289, §284. *See also* §289 where the GC held that trade secrets "must be treated as equivalent as intellectual property rights."
70. *Id.* §§439 and 561 *and* at §456, the Commission similarly contended that "*the expressions 'risk', 'possibility' and 'likelihood'* used by the Court of Justice in its case law on abusive refusals to supply *have the same meaning*" (emphasis added). This trend to disregard likelihood or capability as different thresholds to determine anticompetitive harm continues in the decisional practice of the Commission against investor dominant firms. In *Google Shopping*, the Commission considered Google's unfavorable treatment of competitors as "capable of having, or likely

This notwithstanding, in establishing these different legal standards the EU Courts have avoided a discussion (at least an explicit one) around the investments leading to dominance. This is particularly striking because imposing an obligation to deal is one of the most coercive limitations on property and freedom of contract that antitrust rules may impose on a dominant firm.

Thus, it is unsurprising that the General Court in *Microsoft* went as far as to consider Microsoft's right to exclude others from its competitively acquired trade secrets as an "*artificial* advantage" (emphasis added) that needs to be addressed with compulsory dealing. The importance that Microsoft's investments had in developing those trade secrets and in achieving its position of dominance was relegated to the assessment of objective justifications. In particular, the General Court held that the assessment of the technical development condition only concerned the impact of Microsoft's refusal on the incentives to innovate of its competitors.[71]

Only, AG Jacobs in *Bronner* pointed to a tension between competition law and the competitive process. In his opinion, when imposing an obligation to supply the Court has to take into account that the firm must make an appropriate return on investment that is related to the level of risk involved.[72] AG Jacobs nuanced his opinion with two observations. First, that a substantial investment would be particularly true in relation to intellectual property. Second, that the advantage the dominant firm has might be the result of the creation of a facility that "took place under *non-competitive conditions*, for example, partly through public funding." While we sympathize with the latter nuance, this one is in partial contradiction with the first. Other property than intellectual property can require substantial investments as well. By reducing the relationship between investments and competition to intellectual property AG Jacobs maintained the division between types of property. This is to the detriment of the competitive process under which that property, either intellectual or other, arose in the first place.[73]

From a process perspective, this formalistic asymmetry is unwarranted. Property rights, whether they relate to intellectual or tangible property, protect by way of exclusivity the investment realized in its acquisition. If competition is seen as a

to have" anticompetitive effects, without establishing which of the standards was applicable. *See* Commission Decision, Case COMP/39.740, *Google Search (Shopping)*, §§341, 342, 589, 590, 592, 606, 608, 609, 626, 636, 638, 641 and 737.

71. GC, Case T-201/04, *Microsoft v. Commission*, ECLI:EU:T:2007:289, §§659. Interestingly, the General Court talks here of the "new product" condition and not of a technical development.
72. Opinion of AG Jacobs in Case C-7/97, *Bronner*, ECLI:EU:C:1998:569, §§62 and 64.
73. An explanation to this could be that AG Jacobs had in mind only infrastructures developed by statutory monopolies and not by other firms in an open market. However, this is only a conjuncture. In its Guidance Paper, the Commission draws a dividing line between the incentives to invest of an investor dominant firm and a statutory dominant firm. It says that when dominance "has been developed under the protection of special or exclusive rights or has been financed by state resources" it may be clear that imposing an obligation to supply is not capable of having negative effects on the firm. *See* Guidance Paper, §82.

process, Article 102 TFEU must take due account of the investment efforts leading to dominance,[74] irrespective of the type of property involved.[75]

§5.03 INVESTMENTS, MARKET UNCERTAINTY AND THE COMPETITIVE PROCESS

This section advances a general theoretical background that explains why investments leading to market power are part of the competitive process.

Investment would be virtually costless in a world where the future is perfectly certain.[76] But such a world is illusory. On the contrary, it is generally accepted that the competitive process is fraught with uncertainty and that investments are a valuable instrument to diminish that uncertainty.[77] At a general level, when a firm decides to invest in capacity the firm is forecasting that there will be an increase in demand for the product that it already provides. Once the investment in capacity is realized the firm and other market participants will know how precise its forecast was. Similarly, when a firm invests in a new technology the firm forecasts the development of new needs. Once the investment comes to fruition with the launching of a new product the firm will know whether consumers are interested in its new product and the firm will make the corresponding profits or losses. During this process, competitors of the investor dominant firm will also receive valuable information that they can use to adjust their competitive behavior.

Despite this inherent characteristic of markets, we have seen that both the EU Courts and the Commission disregard investments in the enforcement of Article 102 TFEU. This has two related consequences. The *first* one is that once the successful investor dominant firm has dissipated the uncertainty the vast majority of investments that failed in the process are often neglected in any assessment of anticompetitive

74. The Guidance Paper could be said to closely follow the case law regarding investor dominant firms and its doctrinal constructs. The Guidance Paper considers investments as barriers to entry created by "the own conduct" of the firm. When positive references appear, they are relegated to the analysis of objective justifications. In other words, only once the abuse has been established investments may play a role. Only in the assessment of refusals to supply the Commission appears more flexible and cautions that an obligation to supply *might* undermine the dominant firm's incentives to invest. *See* Guidance Paper, §§46 and 89 (objective justification), and §75 (incentives to invest in refusal to supply). This is in strong contrast with the EAGCP Report. Here, the importance to safeguard incentives to invest is emphasized within all theories of harm and not relegated to efficiency justifications in limited scenarios. *See* Gual, Jordi, Martin Hellwig, Anne Perrot, Michele Polo, Patrick Rey, Klaus Schmidt, and Rune Stenbacka. "An Economic Approach to Article 82. Report to the European Commission by the European Advisory Group on Competition Policy." *EAGCP*, 2005.
75. The symmetry need not neglect the unique features of each property right. *See* Wright, Joshua D. and Douglas H. Ginsburg. "Whither Symmetry? Antitrust Analysis of Intellectual Property Rights at the FTC and DOJ." *George Mason University Law and Economics Research Paper Series* 13-71 (2013): 1-23, 2.
76. Knight, Frank H. *Risk, Uncertainty and Profit*. New York: Augustus M. Kelly, [1921] 1964, at p. 169.
77. *Id.* at p. 172.

behavior.[78] In other words, the competitive race for dominance does not count, and so neither do the investments that were deployed in this *ex ante* process. Consequently, and *second*, the value of the investment incurred by the successful firm (eventually and perhaps only momentarily dominant firm) tends to be taken for granted or even considered as a barrier to entry in abuse of dominance cases. Put differently, since the competition *for* dominance does not count, the winning firm is not granted the consideration it deserves as a natural and efficient outcome of that process. This is paradoxical.

Past investment efforts are an important part of the competitive process itself. As one commentator has put it: "the size distribution of firms and the spread of efficiency across them will reflect past investment and growth."[79]

Admittedly, a snapshot of today's market might suffice to convey the idea that the investment cost was eventually low or high. However, this snapshot is simply a relative assessment done by reference to an *ex post facto* situation of dissipated uncertainty. A more comprehensive evaluation of any investment effort should take into account the uncertainty and risk borne at the time when the investment took place. As a result, the emergence of an investor dominant firm can be then reconsidered as a procompetitive *temporal*[80] outcome.

Adam Smith already mentioned this a long time ago: the perils of establishing a new trade at "own risk and expence (*sic*)" need to be recompensed with the "easiest and most *natural* way," that is, "a monopoly of the trade for a number of years" (emphasis added).[81]

Due to the division between dominance and abuse, EU competition law does not understand this. Instead, any exercise of SMP is compared against an *ex post facto* ideal where investments undertaken *ex ante* are no longer part of the equation.

The theory goes as follows.

If there is monopoly power, then prices equal Pm, such that Pm > MC. This gives rise to monopoly profits and an alleged deadweight loss. But, and here comes the *ex post facto* ideal, *if* the market were "competitive," prices would equal Pc such that Pc = MC = AC. This snapshot model shows itself an "imperfect" situation where the choice seems obviously in favor of the "competitive" ideal. However, this is nothing

78. Rosenberg, Nathan. "Uncertainty and Technological Change" *in* Nathan Rosenberg (ed.) *Studies on Science and the Innovation Process: Selected Works of Nathan Rosenberg.* World Scientific Publishing Co. Pte. Ltd (2009): 153-172.
79. Hughes, Alan. "Competition Policy and the Competitive Process: Europe in the 1990s." *Metroeconomica* 43.12 (1992): 1-46, 3. As Knight argues, the first part of the problem as to how much of today's income has to be diverted to further social welfare "is solved in the market by *competition between present goods and the prospective fruits of their investment*" (emphasis added). *See* Knight, Frank H. *Risk, Uncertainty and Profit.* New York: Augustus M. Kelly, [1921] 1964, at pp. 58 and 371.
80. Knight, Frank H. *Risk, Uncertainty and Profit*. New York: Augustus M. Kelly, [1921] 1964, at pp. 170, n. 1 and 342. *See also* Opinion of AG Jacobs in Case C-7/97, *Bronner*, ECLI:EU:C:1998:569, §63 where AG Jacobs considered that the copyrighted TV listings in *Magill* provided a "permanent barrier" to entry due to the relatively short life of program guides.
81. Smith, Adam. *An Inquiry into the Nature and Causes of the Wealth of Nations*. Econlib, [1776] 2009, Book I, Ch.7, V.1.119.

but a "nirvana approach"[82] that places the investor dominant firm under unwarranted scrutiny.

Figure 5.1 Output before and after Investment

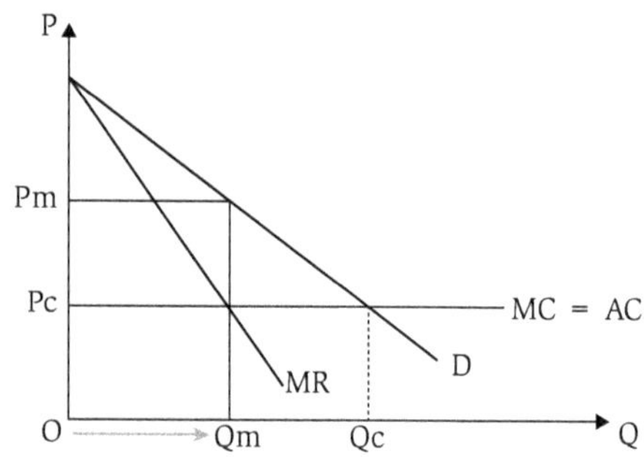

Without a process perspective, the nirvana approach foregoes that the competitive equilibrium, Qc (competitive quantity), would only be achieved if every competitor or firm had the same idea at the same time and thus invested in that idea to put it in the marketplace. When comparing the real world to this nirvana, one risks condemning the real world for resulting in a "monopoly price," Pm, instead of making the right comparison.[83] This one should ask, how much output did the market provide *before* the investment in capacity or new product was realized? The answer as shown in the Figure 5.1 is O, which is simply the *ex ante* point in time *t*-1 where the new product or the increased capacity did not exist and hence it equaled O. In other words, without investment there would be no new product or new capacity.

When quantity (or price) is measured against the background of the competitive *process*, one sees that it is the investment carried by the firm what leads to Qm, depicted in the Figure 5.1 by the gray arrow (O→Qm). The investor "monopoly" quantity (or price) is the competitive result of an output expansion. It is not an abstract "monopoly quantity" or "monopoly price."

AG Jacobs was implicitly aware of the nirvana problem in *Bronner*. The distribution network that Mediaprint had was an "*efficient* facility" that could not be expropriated. Mediaprint invested in an open market in creating a distribution network with resources derived from its newspaper business. Unlike the creation of certain facilities that "took place under *non-competitive conditions*"[84] (emphasis added), Mediaprint did so in the face of risk and uncertainty (emphasis added).

82. Demsetz, Harold. "Information and Efficiency: Another Viewpoint." *The Journal of Law and Economics* 12.1 (1969): 1-22.
83. Posner, Richard A. "Natural Monopoly and Its Regulation." *Stanford Law Review* 21.3 (1969): 548-643, at 559: "In attempting to determine the degree to which monopoly prices can reasonably be deemed excessive, it is improper to compare returns under monopoly with returns under fully competitive condition."
84. Opinion of AG Jacobs in Case C-7/97, *Bronner*, ECLI:EU:C:1998:569, §66.

Accounting for an *ex ante* narrative it rather seems that there is more consumer surplus to customers of the new product (or same product yet unavailable until investment in capacity) than there was before. Importantly, in the presence of a new product customers of the previous product will still benefit from it or be able to switch until the firms that competed with the now-monopolist (or new firms) enter the market or invest in a new discovery [→]. On the contrary, leaving out the *ex ante* investments can lead Article 102 TFEU to fall prey of a nirvana fallacy where O→Qm is assumed away.

In this regard, assuming away the *ex ante* investment risks establishing theories of antitrust liability (excessive prices, discrimination, rebates, refusals to deal, etc.) that are disconnected or at odds with the "propelling factor" of the competitive process. Schumpeter was indeed weary of criticisms levied against Alcoa's alleged monopoly and its costs and profits structure. "Argument from costs and profits in criticism of this 'monopoly' must take it for granted that a multitude of competing firms would have been about equally successful in cost-reducing research, in the economical development of the productive apparatus, in teaching new uses for the product and in avoiding wasteful breakdowns. This is, in fact, being assumed by criticism of this kind, i.e., the propelling factor of modern capitalism is being assumed away."[85]

Due to this uncertainty, not all market participants are willing to employ their current valuable resources to discover new opportunities or increase capacity.[86] Thus, the market incentivizes individuals to invest by rewarding them with the fruits of a successful discovery and eventually SMP.[87] This would not only justify being very cautious with "exploitative" conduct but also with conduct of the investor dominant firm that makes use of its efficient market power to compete against other firms.

The right to exclude, embedded in any property right,[88] is in this respect essential to protect incentives to invest. At the extreme, as some commentators have argued, without it market participants would wait for others to run the costs and risks of the investment, thus creating a situation in which investment terminates and the economy stagnates.[89]

The separation between the origins and the exercise of market power can also have perverse effects on future investments of all market participants. This can be easily seen when comparing a statutory dominant firm with an investor dominant firm. As Larouche explains, it would be "legitimate to ignore the externality" on investment

85. Schumpeter, Joseph A. *Capitalism, Socialism and Democracy*. Routledge, [1943] 2003, at 101-103 and n. 20.
86. Report from the European Commission. *Final Report of the Sector Inquiry on Capacity Mechanisms*, COM (2016) 752 final, at 5.
87. Regarding patents, Mises writes that "If the government objects to monopoly prices for new inventions, it should stop granting patents. It would be absurd to grant patents and then to deprive them of any value by forcing the patentee to sell at the competitive price." *See* von Mises, Ludwig. *Human Action. A Treatise on Economics.* Ludwig von Mises Institute, [1949] 1998, at pp. 760-761.
88. Demsetz, Harold. "Toward a Theory of Property Rights." *The American Economic Review*, 57.2 (1967): 347-359, at 354: "Private ownership implies ... the right of the owner to exclude others."
89. Ahlborn, Christian, David S. Evans and A. Jorge Padilla. "The Logic & Limits of the Exceptional Circumstances Test in *Magill* and *IMS Health*." *Fordham International Law Journal* 28.4 (2004): 1109-1156, 1131.

incentives imposed on statutory dominant firms given that their "*rent* arose out of incumbency" (emphasis added).[90] Since no investment incentives were at play at the time when the firm was thrust upon its statutory position, competition law enforcement could be used, as we have argued before, to level a playing field unlevelled by the coercive and exogenous force of the state.[91] On the contrary, the incentive to invest in a free market needs to be preserved because investments are undertaken in an uncertain and risky competitive process.[92] The expropriation of market power efficiently acquired in the competitive process will negatively affect any firm's investment plans, and not only those of the dominant firm, by downgrading scale of investments or suppressing them altogether.[93]

Overall, the problem of leaving investment efforts outside of any assessment of antitrust liability is that it risks placing Article 102 TFEU at the service of the "common man" and disservice of the competitive process. This "common man" is José Ortega y Gasset's rightful description of a new kind of man who "finding himself in a world so excellent, technically and socially, believes that it has been produced by nature, and never thinks of the personal efforts of highly-endowed individuals which the creation of this new world presupposed. Still less will he admit the notion that all these facilities still require the support of certain difficult human virtues, the least failure of which would cause the rapid disappearance of the whole magnificent edifice."[94] The investment efforts of the firm, which may be the cause of both some degree of market power and well-being cannot remain alien, as to the common man, to the enforcement of Article 102 TFEU. The contrary would only reveal a neglect of the competitive process where the common man imagines that his "role is limited to demanding these benefits peremptorily, as if they were natural rights."[95]

90. Larouche, Pierre. "Europe and Investment in Infrastructure, with Emphasis on Electronic Communications" *in* G. Arts, W. Dicke and L. Hancher (eds.), *New Perspectives on Investment in Infrastructures.* WRR Studies, Amsterdam: Amsterdam University Press, 2008, 241-270, at 247.
91. Larouche talks about "a 'fat-trimming' phase" when "it could be argued that the fat, i.e., the monopoly rent, was actually being redistributed." *Id.* at p. 247. *See also* Chapters 2 and 3.
92. Motta, Massimo. *Competition Policy: Theory and Practice.* Cambridge University Press, 2004, at pp. 67-68.
93. Hayek, Friedrich A. *Law, Legislation and Liberty,* (Vol. 2) *The Mirage of Social Justice.* Routledge, [1976] 1998, at p. 71. The general willingness in EU competition law to oblige a dominant firm to share its resources ("to allow third-party access") might be partially driven by the widespread presence of statutory dominant firms or historical operators. *See also* Geradin, Damien. "The Opening of State Monopolies to Competition: Main Issues of the Liberalization Process" *in* Damien Geradin (ed.) *The Liberalization of State Monopolies in the European Union and Beyond,* Kluwer (2000): 181-205, 183-184.
94. Ortega Y Gasset, José. *The Revolt of the Masses.* New York: W.W. Norton, 1932, at pp. 63-64.
95. *Id.* at p. 65. Ortega continues: "In the disturbances caused by scarcity of food, the mob goes in search of bread, and the means it employs is generally to wreck the bakeries. This may serve as a symbol of the attitude adopted, on a greater and more complicated scale, by the masses of today towards the civilisation by which they are supported." *See also* Ortega Y Gasset, José. "Meditación de la Técnica." *Ensimismamiento y Alteración. Meditación de la Técnica y Otros Ensayos.* Alianza Editorial, [1933] 2014, at pp. 127-128. As if aspirins, smartphones or cars were not products that required an investment to be discovered and produced but were to be found as a rock or a plant are found in nature.

§5.04 A PROCESS-ORIENTED APPROACH TO ARTICLE 102 TFEU AND INVESTOR DOMINANT FIRMS

In this section we develop the arguments outlined before explaining *how* the enforcement of Article 102 TFEU could be improved to better accommodate an approach in line with the objective of protecting the process of competition.

[A] Depropertization and the Competitive Process

There has been some commentary against the property asymmetry in refusal to deal cases. Commentators argue that the preferential treatment that intellectual property enjoys in EU competition law is unwarranted. However, instead of advocating that other types of property be treated under the same stricter principles, they contend that the stricter test should be abandoned.[96] Here we contend that while the asymmetry is indeed unwarranted, a laxer test would only be in detriment of the competitive process that competition law is meant to protect. This symmetry does not mean that the EU Courts should ignore the unique features of intellectual property or those of the physical infrastructure at stake.[97] It rather means that the EU Courts take due account of the investments that went in discovering consumer needs.

From a process perspective, the reasons in favor of the principle of symmetry in line with a stricter legal test seem clear. In a free market, property rights enable the competitive process by encouraging firms to invest in their acquisition. Whether they are intellectual or other property rights, these are the result of a particular investment activity in competition that cannot be neglected. There is nothing more paradoxical than to promote competition but to turn down those successful firms that have been urged to compete.[98]

Let us depict the competitive process as a time line with an investor dominant firm (*see* Figure 5.2 below).[99]

During some time in the *ex ante* competitive process (*t*-1) a number of *n* firms compete under uncertainty to bring to the market a new product. From all the paths that the competitive process offered [Y', Y'', ..., *n*] the market choses the firm that invested in product Y. The market went from providing X, to also providing Y. The firm that now provides Y is depicted in the case law in a snapshot (*t*) of the current time line as a dominant firm. However, we have preferred to call it the "*investor dominant firm*" to take due account of its competitive origins (*t*-1). We only know, from an *ex post*

96. Ritter, Cyril. "Refusal to Deal and Essential Facilities: Does Intellectual Property Require Special Deference Compared to Tangible Property." *World Competition* 28.3 (2005): 281-298.
97. Wright, Joshua D. and Douglas H. Ginsburg. "Whither Symmetry? Antitrust Analysis of Intellectual Property Rights at the FTC and DOJ." *George Mason University Law and Economics Research Paper Series* 13-71 (2013): 1-23.
98. *United States v. Alcoa*, 148 F.2d 416 (2d Cir. 1945), at 430: "The successful competitor, having been urged to compete, must not be turned upon when he wins."
99. This timeline, here abstracted in three periods for ease of exposition, is a continuum of events that occur without interruption in any market.

perspective, that our investor dominant firm could surmount the risks and uncertainties of the process with its investment, and that it did not acquire its market position by a state endowment, luck or anticompetitive behavior. The competitive process, yet, does not end there. As a result of the successful investment of the investor dominant firm (and *not in spite of*!),[100] *and* as well as those made in failed paths [Y', Y'', ..., *n*], the market discovers new opportunities and methods of competition. Importantly, however, how many of those new paths [Z, Z', Z'', ..., *n*], and which among those will succeed will, once again, only be revealed *ex post*. Put differently, when market participants have tinkered enough, aggressively tried and failed, a successful investment comes to fruition: Z.

Figure 5.2 Competitive Tinkering Process

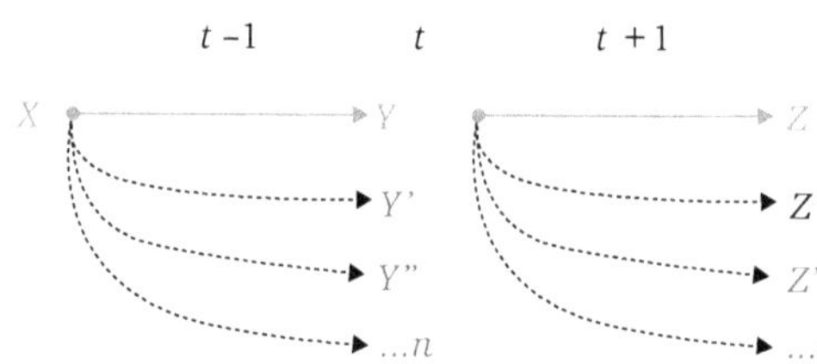

The special responsibility that investor dominant firms have to actively provide access[101] eliminates property rights. That is, the right to exclude others.[102] As certain ordoliberal thinkers would propose eliminating monopoly power in itself, an obligation to deal is a "significant interference with private property" only experienced in "wartime."[103]

Some antitrust commentators seemingly in favor of this depropertization trend claim that the right to exclude others is simply one among other sticks in the bundle of rights that comes with property.[104] But as Merrill points out, the right to exclude others is the *conditio sine quae non* the remaining rights cannot succeed. It is from the right to exclude others that one can derive other "incidents of ownership."[105] It is not a

100. A dominant position weakens the competitive structure with its mere presence. CJEU, *Hoffman-La Roche*, §§91 and 107; Commission Decision, Case COMP/39.740, *Google Search (Shopping)*, §332.
101. Commission Decision, Case COMP/37.792, *Microsoft*, §§33 and 747.
102. Demsetz, Harold. "Toward a Theory of Property Rights." *The American Economic Review*, 57.2 (1967): 347-359 and Landes, William M. and Richard A. Posner. *The Economic Structure of Intellectual Property Law*. Harvard University Press, 2009, at p. 12, describing property rights as "a legally enforceable power to exclude others from using a resource ... and so with no need to make contracts with would-be users of the resource forbidding their use."
103. Gerber, David J. *Law and Competition in the Twentieth Century Europe. Protecting Prometheus*. Oxford, 2003, at p. 252.
104. Crane, Daniel A. "Intellectual Liability." *Texas Law Review* 88.2 (2009): 253-300, 272.
105. Merrill, Thomas W. "Property and the Right to Exclude." *Nebraska Law Review* 77.4 (1998): 730-755, 742.

matter of balancing the right to exclude with other rights derived from property,[106] but rather a matter of necessity and sufficiency for property rights to exist.

More important is that the protection of property rights in a competitive market is based on the premise that "without property, that is, without the right to exclude others, there can be no gift-giving, no contractual exchange, or no inheritance."[107] In a free market where information is imperfect individuals invest in order to discover and satisfy consumers' wants. For example, IPR are the result of a competitive process to discover what the legislator considers an innovative step by reference to the existing art.

In general, property rights ensure investments by signaling the investor firm that if his current resources were eventually transformed into Y, these will continue to belong to him. Thus, irrespective of the type of property, "without [it] markets would collapse, as parties would have nothing to trade" and nothing to compete for.[108] Regimes with communist policies where private property is a privilege suffer indeed from a lack of competition.[109] As some commentators have described, rivalrous competition "requires institutions that promote the linkage between *resource creation and rewards*. That is, vigorous competition requires institutions that protect the property rights that firms and individuals have in" in their creations.[110]

Property rights thus do not only allow competition but they are the "foundation of efficient markets."[111] From a static perspective, property rights do allocate scarce resources to those users that value it the most. From a process perspective, they tell firms what part of their current resources to invest in providing future consumer wants. In other words, property rights allow for the "efficient allocation of resources over time."[112] As explained above, investments are an important fuel for the competitive

106. In an astute manner, Crane speaks of patents and copyrights as intellectual rights, and not as intellectual *property* rights. It does so to include under such label both property and liability rights.

107. Merrill, Thomas W. "Property and the Right to Exclude II." *Brigham-Kanner Property Rights Conference Journal* 3 (2014): 1-25, 5.

108. Meese, Alan J. "Property, Aspen, and Refusals to Deal." *Antitrust Law Journal* 73.1 (2005): 81-114, 81. *FAG Flughafen* is the first case dealing with property and competition law. FAG is the company that owns and operates Frankfurt airport. Here the Commission obliged FAG to grant access to its monopoly on ramp-handling. FAG's property was not an absolute right and the public policy of competition allowed its curtailment. Although the Commission did not consider it relevant, FAG's origins of market power were statutory. *See* Commission Decision, Case COMP/IV/34.801, *FAG Ð Flughafen Frankfurt/Main AG*, §§89-92. Likewise, defendants in *Google Shopping* raised a defense based on property rights that was ultimately rejected. The Commission considered that the (never-heard-of) "right of users to receive information from competing comparison shopping services" justified the restriction of Google's rights to dispose of its property in its advantage. Thus, not even considering that competing alternatives existed even if they were unfavorably displayed or positioned. *See* Commission Decision, Case COMP/39.740, *Google Search (Shopping)*, §§667-669.

109. Hayek, Friedrich A. *The Road to Serfdom: Text and Documents: The Definitive Edition*. Routledge, [1944] 2014.

110. Hunt, Shelby D. and Dennis B. Arnett. "Competition as an Evolutionary Process and Antitrust Policy." *Journal of Public Policy & Marketing* 20.1 (2001): 15-26, 23.

111. Spulber, Daniel F. "Competition Policy and the Incentive to Innovate: The Dynamic Effects of *Microsoft* v. *Commission*." *Yale Journal on Regulation* 25.2 (2008): 247-301, 268.

112. *Id*.

process and the growth it delivers. Without the ability to exclude other firms would not divert current valuable resources to future avenues where the firm is unable to benefit from its investment.[113]

Unfortunately, aside from AG Jacobs' Opinion in *Bronner*, one must look into the jurisprudence on the other side of the Atlantic to find a positive recognition of dominance linked to investment efforts. In *Trinko*, a case concerning a refusal to access, the US Supreme Court understood that monopoly power acquired by investing in infrastructure is a natural way and element of the competitive process. The property is "uniquely suited to serve their customers." Thus, it held that to oblige firms "to share the source of their advantage is in some tension with the underlying purpose of antitrust law, since it may lessen the incentive for the monopolist, the rival, or both to invest in those economically beneficial facilities."[114]

In a similar fashion, the Guidelines on the application of Article 101(3) TFEU take due account of the uncertainty of the competitive process, irrespective of the type of property involved. Simply, "the more uncertain the success of the product covered by the agreement, the more a restriction may be required to ensure that the efficiencies will materialise."[115] Likewise, the TTBER Guidelines explain that "the risk facing the parties and the sunk investment that must be committed may thus lead to the agreement falling outside Article 101(1) or fulfilling the conditions of Article 101(3), as the case may be, for the period of time required to recoup the investment."[116]

Although we believe that the concept of restriction is imprudent because absent such "restriction" there would be no product at all, and thus no possible further "restrictions," it is welcome that both Guidelines capture that when past investments are brought into the analysis the view of the deadweight loss that market power imposes is attenuated or redeemed, and that the formalistic boundary between different types of property is hence dissolved.

The Commission itself in the context of an agreement between competitors binds the analysis of imposing an obligation to supply to the *ex ante* competitive process. "Nor should a competitor have immediate access to [a firm's] improvements *without bearing either the risk or the financial investment which each party has borne*" (emphasis added).[117] Importantly, this assessment is done under Article 101(1) TFEU,

113. Etro, Federico. *Competition, Innovation, and Antitrust: A Theory of Market Leaders and Its Policy Implications*. Springer, 2007, at p. 187: "In high-tech sectors (hardware, software, pharmaceuticals, biotechnology) firms compete mainly by innovating. This is possible as long as there are well defined intellectual property rights (IPRs), and especially patents, protecting their innovations and investments, which is ultimately what leads to technological progress in our economies."
114. *Verizon Communications Inc. v. Law Offices of Curtis V. Trinko, LLP*, 540 U.S. 398, (2004).
115. Communication from the Commission—Guidelines on the application of Article 81(3) of the Treaty, *OJ* C 101, 27.4.2004, p. 97-118, at §80.
116. Communication from the Commission—Guidelines on the application of Article 101 of the Treaty on the Functioning of the European Union to Technology Transfer Agreements, *OJ* C 89, 28.3.2014, p. 3-50, at §8.
117. Commission Decision, Case COMP/IV/32.009, *Elopak/Metal Box-Odin*, §34. (The case concerned the agreement between Elopak and Metal Box to establish and to jointly own Odin. The Commission considered that the parties' licensing obligations in case of Odin's dissolution did not infringe Article 101(1) TFEU. The following restrictions are not caught by Article 101(1):

and not at a subsequent stage of objective justifications (i.e., under Article 101(3) TFEU) as the EU Courts and the Commission have done in the context of Article 102 TFEU.

The value that the competitive process delivers in the form of a successful investment should not be overridden by the prospects of a competitor's better use of that investment in the first place. This would be akin to encouraging a firm to invest in an uncertain project on the basis of property over the returns to that investment, but then dismantling the property itself by distributing the benefits of the investment among participants that lost in the race or did not even participate in the process.[118] As Hayek argues, there is "no moral claim to something that would not exist but for the decision of others to risk their resources on its creation." Directing investment to points where they most enhance productivity is the most effective and important way of advancing welfare.[119]

While the three conditions of the *Bronner*, *Magill-IMS Health* and *Microsoft* legal tests are "highly speculative,"[120] there is nothing speculative about the fruitful investment efforts of the dominant firm. On the contrary, a firm that seeks coercive access is in itself acknowledging the enhanced productivity created by the investment efforts of

"(a) the obligation on each parent, for five years after break-up of Odin (or sale by one party of its shares), not to allow a competitor of the other parent to use that other parent's know-how or improvements made by Odin, and (b) the provision giving the seller right of first refusal in the event of a further sale. Such provisions are a necessary result of the creation of Odin without which the two parents could not reasonably be expected to cooperate.") The importance of this counterfactual was also highlighted by the GC in *O2 (Germany)*. Here the GC annulled the decision of the Commission for having failed to examine, among others, the significant investments necessary for O2 to roll out its own 3G network. Competitors O2 and T-Mobile had notified to the Commission a cooperation agreement for the deployment of 3G on the German market. The Commission exempted most of the agreement, but it declared that national roaming between network operators restricted competition. "National roaming at wholesale level will lead to a greater uniformity of conditions at retail level, given the fact that the underlying network coverage, quality and transmission speeds are likely to be similar" (Commission Decision, Case COMP/38.369, *T-Mobile Deutschland/O2 Germany: Network Sharing Rahmenvertrag*, §111). O2 appealed the decision. The GC found that the Commission's counterfactual analysis (i.e., whether the deployment of 3G would have been possible in the absence of the agreement) "could not [take] for granted" that O2 would have been entirely or partially present in the 3G market. On the contrary, the Commission should have envisaged the possibility that absent the agreement O2 would have been not been present in the market. GC, Case T-328/03, *O2 (Germany) GmbH & Co. OHG v. Commission*, ECLI:EU:T:2006:116.

118. Notice that in *Bronner* and *IMS Health* the facts of the cases did not relate to an adjacent or related market, but to the same market where the firm was dominant. On the contrary, the refusal to supply in *Commercial Solvents*, *Magill* or *Microsoft* allowed them to use their competitively acquired market power to keep on competing and enter new markets. The General Court in *Microsoft* was strongly concerned with this possibility. In the assessment of the fine, it held that, "Since Microsoft is very likely to maintain its dominant position on the client PC operating systems market, at least over the coming years, it cannot be precluded that it will have other opportunities to use leveraging vis-à-vis other adjacent markets." *See* GC, Case T-201/04, *Microsoft v. Commission*, ECLI:EU:T:2007:289, §1363.
119. Hayek, Friedrich A. *Law, Legislation and Liberty*, (Vol. 2) *The Mirage of Social Justice.* Routledge, [1976] 1998, at pp. 98-99.
120. Spulber, Daniel F. "Competition Policy and the Incentive to Innovate: The Dynamic Effects of *Microsoft* v. *Commission*." *Yale Journal on Regulation* 25.2 (2008): 247-301, 259.

the dominant firm. However, an obligation incumbent upon investor dominant firms to actively supply the resource is akin to neglecting that value.

This does not mean that antitrust laws should protect market power. But it also does not mean that antitrust laws should aim at dismantling the competitive advantages of the dominant firm. A competitive advantage in the market shall last as long as the competitive process allows for, no less and no more. In this respect a refusal to supply is not an "artificial" advantage but the natural consequence of a free market founded on property rights.[121]

An obligation to supply also has negative effects on the incentives to invest. To the investment costs of prospecting the uncertain market, the not yet dominant firm will have to add the costs of having to share its resources. When those certain costs of providing access outweigh the benefits of an uncertain investment effort, the firm will not direct its investment toward that point that perhaps most enhanced productivity.[122] By diminishing the incentives to invest on innovation or infrastructures, an obligation to supply is thus likely to distort the competitive process.[123]

Moreover, an obligation to supply also disincentivizes investments on new paths that do not require access to the resources of the investor dominant firm. In other words, imposing an obligation to supply distorts the process of competition by signaling in a noncompetitive manner where investment efforts are the easiest but not necessarily the most needed or wanted.

Coming back to the competitive timeline in the presence of an investor dominant firm, this means that competition authorities would be opening an easy path represented by [→ Z'] that allowed firms to free-ride on the risks, uncertainty and investments borne by the dominant firm (*t*-1), on the (strong) assumption that this action is not provoking a reduction in the investments on other paths and thus preventing or delaying the emergence of a truly competitive outcome represented by [→ Z] (*see* Figure 5.3 below). However, this is "a task in which governments notoriously fail, for reasons inherent in non-competitive bureaucratic organizations."[124]

121. Opinion of AG Jacobs in Case C-7/97, *Bronner*, ECLI:EU:C:1998:569, at §57: "the mere fact that by retaining a facility for its own use a dominant undertaking retains an advantage over a competitor cannot justify requiring access to it."
122. Spulber, Daniel F. "Competition Policy and the Incentive to Innovate: The Dynamic Effects of *Microsoft* v. *Commission*." *Yale Journal on Regulation* 25.2 (2008): 247-301, 274.
123. *See* Taleb, Nassim Nicholas. *Skin in the Game: Hidden Asymmetries in Daily Life*. Allen Lande, 2018, at p. 145: "As I have explained in Antifragile, too high a rate of mutation prevents locking-in the benefits of previous changes: evolution (and progress) requires some, but not too frequent variation."
124. Hayek, Friedrich A. *Law, Legislation and Liberty*, (Vol. 2) *The Mirage of Social Justice*. Routledge, [1976] 1998, at p. 99.

Figure 5.3 Statutory Effect in the Tinkering Process

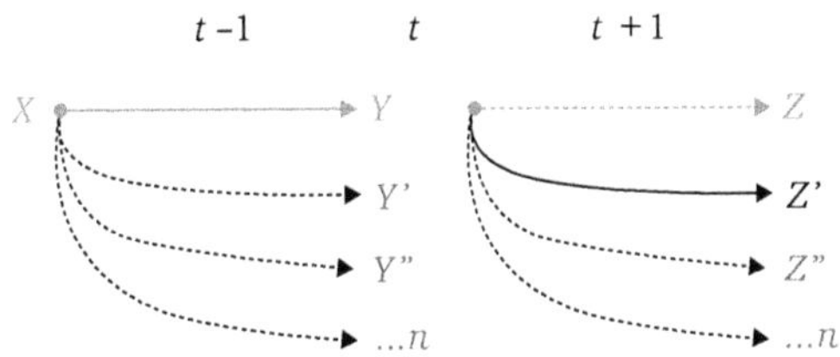

In a certain way, imposing an obligation to supply represents the fear that the competitive process will end if access is not provided. The reason for this is that the snapshot of the market tends to be binary: either the competitor seeking access succeeds with intervention with the relevant competition authority or competition will cease. But the opposite is true. The relationship between investments and the competitive process is a "continuing force" that should not be dismantled by policies that entice firms into rent-seeking activities.[125]

As numerous commentators have explained, the introduction of a new product condition [→ … *n*] in *Magill* and *IMS Health* is not only the most speculative element of the test but also one fraught with measuring impossibilities. In such conditions, the benefit of the doubt should go to the investor dominant firms whose efficiencies are a bird in hand and not two in the bush.[126]

It is thus unsurprising that the General Court held that Microsoft could not sufficiently establish which specific technologies and products would significantly suffer from fewer innovation efforts as a result of the refusal to supply.[127] But it is likewise unsurprising that the Commission in *Google Shopping* referred in a similar "vaguely"[128] manner to the investment incentives of Google competitors being affected by the unfavorable treatment Google dispensed them.[129]

[B] The Misleading Non-contestable Share of the Demand

The objective of this subsection is to reexamine the theory underpinning all-units rebates by taking into account the investor origins of the dominant firm. The current more-economic approach to all-units rebates is not necessarily in line with a process

125. Baumol, William. *The Free Market Innovation Machine: Analysing the Growth Miracle of Capitalism*. Princeton University Press, 2002, at p. 295.
126. Carlton, Dennis W. "A General Analysis of Exclusionary Conduct and Refusal to Deal—Why Aspen and Kodak Are Misguided." *Antitrust Law Journal* 68.3 (2001): 659-683, 675.
127. GC, Case T-201/04, *Microsoft v. Commission*, ECLI:EU:T:2007:289, §698.
128. The *Microsoft* General Court held that "Microsoft merely put forward vague, general and theoretical arguments on that point." *See* GC, Case T-201/04, *Microsoft v. Commission*, ECLI:EU:T:2007:289, §698.
129. Commission Decision, Case COMP/39.740, *Google Search (Shopping)*, §595.

perspective. More in particular, it is advanced that the division between contestable and incontestable market shares is unwarranted from a process perspective.[130]

All-units rebates are called like this because they apply on *all units* purchased conditioned upon the attainment of a certain percentage, volume or exclusivity threshold. For example, a firm would grant a 10% discount on all units purchased by customer A if this customer A buys more than 80% of its needs from the firm. Thus, if customer A buys 90 units (meaning 90% of its requirements) it the seller will apply a 10% discount not over the 10 extra units, but over all 90 units.

[1] The "Old" Leveraging Theory

Since *Hoffmann-La Roche*, the case law relating to all-units rebates has aimed at preventing the dominant firm from making use of its competitively acquired market power. It was in *Hoffmann-La Roche* that the Court minted the belief that "the very presence" of a dominant firm weakens the degree of competition or its structure.[131] *Michelin I*,[132] *BPB*,[133] *Michelin II*,[134] *British Airways*,[135] *Tomra*[136] or the overturned *Intel* judgment[137] subsequently upheld such belief that facilitated a narrative of anticompetitive behavior. Since competition is already damaged, little do the additional negative effects of the conduct matter—if at all. Not surprisingly, the stringent per se approach to exclusivity rebates had so long been maintained for almost forty years, until the Court of Justice judgment in *Intel*.

In appearance, *Hoffmann-La Roche* eluded any explicit articulation of its anticompetitive theory. A superficial reading of both the decision and the judgment suggested that all-units rebates were abusive in themselves. While it is certain that it lacked any "economic" anticompetitive theory, *Hoffmann-La Roche* was motivated by the clear objective of preventing the dominant firm from leveraging its efficiencies.

In *Hoffmann-La Roche*, the Commission itself virtually praised Roche's leadership position.[138] It held that Roche provides to its customers a "regular and rapid supply" despite the expiry of its patents for the manufacturing of vitamins. Roche's "constant improvement of manufacturing methods and strict analytical control ... is

130. *See* Chapter 2 explaining why the division between contestable and incontestable market shares *is not* artificially construed in the case of statutory dominant firms.
131. CJEU, Case 85/76, *Hoffmann-La Roche v. Commission*, ECLI:EU:C:1979:36, §§6, 51, 91, 107, 120 and 123.
132. CJEU, Case C-322/81, *Michelin I*, ECLI:EU:C:1983:313, §70.
133. GC, Case T-65/89, *BPB Industries and British Gypsum* ("*BPB*"), ECLI:EU:T:1993:31, §§90 and 118.
134. GC, Case T-203/01, *Michelin v. Commission* ("*Michelin II*"), ECLI:EU:T:2003:250, §54.
135. CJEU, Case 95/04 P, *British Airways v. Commission* (CJEU, "*British Airways*"), ECLI:EU:C:2007:166, §66; *and* GC, Case T-219/99, *British Airways v. Commission* ("GC, British Airways"), ECLI:EU:T:2003:343, §241.
136. CJEU, Case C-549/10 P, *Tomra Systems ASA and Others v. Commission* (CJEU, "*Tomra*"), ECLI:EU:C:2012:221, §17; *and* GC, Case T-155/06, *Tomra Systems ASA and Others v. Commission* (GC, "*Tomra*"), ECLI:EU:T:2010:370, §§38 and 206.
137. GC, Case T-286/09, *Intel*, ECLI:EU:T:2014:547.
138. CJEU, Case 85/76, *Hoffmann-La Roche v. Commission*, ECLI:EU:C:1979:36, at 484, *Hoffmann-La Roche*'s leadership is "the expression of an obvious truth."

known throughout the world for quality and service."[139] *However*, according to the Commission, Roche's evil was "to take advantage of the technological knowledge acquired in the manufacture and use of synthetic vitamins so as to strengthen its dominant position."[140] Little it mattered that Roche's prices had progressively declined over the years and quantities served gone up. The decline in prices that Roche's all-units rebate schemes provided was the result of "a price policy designed to forestall [competitive] pressure"[141] based "on the supply of all or a very large proportion of a customer's requirements."[142] Simply, the Court held, a dominant firm cannot use all-units rebate contracts because they restrict a customer's freedom of choice and prevents other firms from accessing the market.[143]

The lack of an economic theory underpinning the *Hoffmann-La Roche* case law on all-units rebates remained in subsequent case law until the *Tomra* and *Intel* decisions where the Commission *articulated* a leveraging theory in economic terms.[144] In both cases the Commission acknowledged it could close up the investigation on the grounds of *Hoffmann-La Roche*'s but decided to seek an economic foundation for its approach. As will be shown, however "economic," this leveraging theory brings nothing new. And, although the Court of Justice has "further clarified" *Hoffmann-La Roche* in *Intel*,[145] the leveraging theory seems alive and well.[146]

[2] The "More-Economic" Leveraging Theory

Tomra produces reverse vending machines (RVMs). Retail outlets (mainly large supermarket groups) use these automated machines to collect empty returnable or refillable drink containers as well as other disposable containers. Prokent, a former competitor of Tomra, complained to the Commission about Tomra's commercial practices that had put it out of the market. In its decision, the Commission found Tomra was abusing its dominant position by concluding contracts that contained exclusivity clauses, quantity commitments leading to de facto total or partial exclusivity and all-units rebate schemes (called by the Commission "retroactive"). Through these retroactive rebates Tomra offered its customers discounts on *all units* purchased

139. Commission Decision, Case COMP/IV/29.020, *Vitamins* (commonly known as "*Hoffmann-La Roche*"), §8.
140. CJEU, Case 85/76, *Hoffmann-La Roche v. Commission*, ECLI:EU:C:1979:36, at 486.
141. *Id.* §§74, 76, 78 and p. 492; while at pp. 498 and 499, the Commission establishes that *Hoffmann-La Roche* was not exposed to any effective competition. *See also* Commission Decision, Case COMP/IV/29.020, *Vitamins* (*Hoffmann-La Roche*), §22.
142. Commission Decision, Case COMP/IV/29.020, *Vitamins* (*Hoffmann-La Roche*), §22.
143. *Id.*
144. Before *Tomra* and *Intel*, the Commission or the Courts had "never looked seriously at the ability of competitors to profitably match the pricing strategy of the dominant firm." *See* Heimler, Alberto. "Below-Cost Pricing and Loyalty-Inducing Discounts: Are They Restrictive and, If So, When?" *Competition Policy International* 1.2 (2005): 149-172, 159.
145. CJEU, Case C-413/14 P, *Intel v. Commission*, ECLI:EU:C:2017:632, §138.
146. The leveraging theory underpins other cases than all-units rebates. As the General Court in *Microsoft* clearly explains, the refusal to deal (and so the tying abuse) are simply part of a general leveraging infringement. *See* GC, Case T-201/04, *Microsoft v. Commission*, ECLI: EU:T:2007:289, §1344.

conditioned upon the attainment of a threshold based on a certain percentage, volume or outright exclusivity.

In *Tomra*, the Commission *prospectively* advanced its economic articulation of the leveraging theory. Under this theory the Commission divided the market between the contestable and the non-contestable share of the demand for RVM. The market share covered by Tomra's agreements is the non-contestable share.[147]

With this market division the Commission was able to rationalize the leverage of Tomra's market power in economic terms. That is, a leverage that resulted in potential "suction" effects of Tomra's rebates.[148] The rebates were anticompetitive because the prices competitors had to offer to a customer's contestable demand were "very low" or "even negative."[149] Prokent and other competitors would have to compensate the customer not only for the rebate applied on the contestable units but also on the non-contestable units that the customer had already purchased from Tomra. Hence, if Tomra would grant a 10% discount on all units purchased if customer A buys more than 80% of its needs (100 units) from it, Tomra's competitors would not only have to offer a 10% discount on the remaining 20 units, but also compensate for the loss of the rebate over the units that customer had already purchased or committed to purchase from Tomra. If the price per unit is EUR 1, for 79 units, the customer would have to pay EUR 79, while for 80 units, the customer would have to pay EUR 72. From the artificial division of the market,[150] it would seem as if the price of the last unit bought to reach the threshold, (the eightieth unit) was negative, i.e., EUR -8.

Importantly, on appeal, both Courts partially modified the definition of the non-contestable share of the demand. While the Commission had defined it as the quantity purchased by Tomra's customers "under the anticompetitive agreements," the General Court seemingly considered the non-contestable share of the demand as an "inherent" characteristic of a dominant firm who being an "unavoidable trading partner" serves a substantial and non-substitutable part of the demand.[151]

---

147. In its more-economic analysis, the Commission observed that the all-units rebates allowed Tomra to maintain a stable market share, which never fell below 66% of the market. In comparison to Tomra's, the market shares of its competitors were at their lowest when the all-units rebates were in place. In fact, the Commission also considered as strong evidence that complainant Prokent had filed for bankruptcy and exited the market. *However*, the Commission did not discuss why other competitors like Bevesys had increased their market share in the meantime. The Commission observed that Tomra's rivals sold more RVM machines, whenever the portion of total demand covered by the exclusivity agreements was smaller. *See* Commission Decision, Case COMP/38.113, *Tomra*, §163, n. 335.
148. Geradin claims that that the Commission "did not apply a suction effect test" in *Tomra*. *See* Geradin, Damien. "A Proposed Test for Separating Pro-Competitive Conditional Rebates from Anti-competitive Ones." *World Competition* 32 (2009): 41-70, at n. 65. The economic assessment presented by defendants was a response to the Commission's (ambiguous) analysis of suction effects. *See also* Maier-Rigaud, Frank and Dovile Vaigauskaite. "Prokent/Tomra, a Textbook Case? Abuse of Dominance under Perfect Information." *Competition Policy Newsletter* 2 (2006): 19-24, 22.
149. Commission Decision, Case COMP/38.113, *Tomra*, §§165 and186.
150. Note that the Commission accompanied the explanation of the suction effect with the words "From that perspective." *See id.* §165.
151. GC, Case T-155/06, *Tomra*, ECLI:EU:T:2010:370, §269; and CJEU, Case C-549/10 P, *Tomra*, ECLI:EU:C:2012:221, §79.

The prospective character of *Tomra* makes the decision unclear as to whether the Commission embraced a more-economic approach or maintained the *Hoffmann-La Roche* formalistic approach. The Commission itself acknowledged in its decision it could have closed up the investigation against Tomra by simply resorting to *Hoffmann-La Roche, Michelin II* or *British Airways*. In light of those judgments it would be enough to show that rebates are capable of having the effect of restricting competition.[152] However, from the EU Courts' perspective the approach would seem clearer. As the General Court clarifies, the decision was not primarily based on showing that competitors would have to offer very low or negative prices to compensate the rebate loss.[153] Logically thus both Courts held that "competitors should be able to compete on the merits for the entire market and not just for a part of it."[154]

Similar to *Tomra*, the *Intel* decision advanced a leveraging theory sustained by the division of a market between the non-contestable and contestable shares of the demand. After receiving a complaint from Intel's main competitor AMD, the Commission found Intel had abused its dominant position in the x86 CPU microprocessors market by granting all-units rebates to major computer manufacturers (OEMs) like Dell, HP, Lenovo and NEC. The Commission considered that absent objective justifications the rebates would "in themselves" be sufficient to proof an abuse[155] in a market where the degree of competition is already weakened.[156] Despite this, the Commission complemented its analysis with an assessment of the "capability or likelihood" of Intel's rebates to anticompetitively foreclose the market.[157] However, unlike in *Tomra*, the Commission adopted a more process-oriented approach by establishing an AEC standard to determine anticompetitive foreclosure.

The analysis of a leveraging abuse is done by referencing to the "more-economic" approach of dividing the market between a contestable and a non-contestable share of the demand. On the one hand, the Commission considered Intel an "unavoidable trading partner" that benefits in its trading from the noncontestable share of demand of OEMs for x86 CPU microprocessors. On the other hand, the contestable share of the market corresponded to the amount of purchases a customer could realistically switch to another firm.[158]

In the Commission's view, the all-units rebates enable Intel to use the non-contestable share "as leverage to decrease the price for the elastic or 'contestable' share of demand."[159] Intel's rebates are anticompetitive if they are capable or likely to drive a competitor as efficient as Intel from the market. The Commission then clarifies what this means. That is, all-unit rebates would be capable of foreclosing an as efficient

152. Commission Decision, Case COMP/38.113, *Tomra*, §322. The Commission itself acknowledges it closed the investigation by simply resorting to *Hoffmann-La Roche, Michelin II* or *British Airways*. In light of those judgments, it would be enough to show that rebates are capable of having the effect of restricting competition.
153. GC, Case T-155/06, *Tomra*, ECLI:EU:T:2010:370, §258.
154. *Id.* §241; *see also* CJEU, Case C-549/10 P, *Tomra*, ECLI:EU:C:2012:221, §42.
155. Commission Decision, Case COMP/37.990, *Intel*, §925.
156. *Id.* §914.
157. *Id.* §925.
158. *Id.* §1009.
159. *Id.* §§1005 and 1010.

competitor if the *effective price* for x86 microprocessors is below average avoidable costs,[160] where the effective price is the average price of the *contestable* units.

Under appeal, the General Court contented itself with the economic version of "leveraging rebates theory"[161] but rejected the process approach. Since Intel's all-units rebates allowed it to use its non-contestable share of the market to secure the contestable share, this was enough to finding an infringement of Article 102 TFEU. The rebating instrument is thus in itself anticompetitive and "it is unnecessary to undertake an analysis of the actual effects" on as efficient competitors.[162]

In this last regard, the Court of Justice has overturned the General Court in *Intel* and "further clarified" *Hoffmann-La Roche.*[163] In line with *Post Danmark I*, the *Intel* Court ruled that the competitive process entails less efficient firms exiting the market. In other words, Article 102 TFEU cannot be used as a barrier to exit for less efficient firms. This is most welcome. The argument of foreclosure alone cannot simply justify liability under Article 102 TFEU for every contract won by a seller will foreclose a part of the demand to its competitors.[164] The General Court will have to reassess whether Intel's all-units rebates are capable of foreclosing an as efficient competitor.[165] Regrettably, it seems that the leveraging theory is alive and well.

[3] Incumbency Advantages: A Process Perspective

The more-economic leveraging theory is an idealistic construct that, with difficulty, can be reconciled with an understanding of competition as a process.

It is an idealistic construct because the division between contestability and non-contestability is an artificial one, aimed at providing "equality of opportunity" for competing firms in the contestable share and preventing the mobilization of incumbency advantages.[166] This is why the price cost analysis is done by reference to the

160. *Id.* §§1006 and 1037. Setting the measure of viable costs at the average avoidable costs allows taking account of the high fixed costs involved in the manufacturing of microprocessors.
161. Petit, Nicolas. "Intel, Leveraging Rebates and the Goals of Article 102 TFEU." *European Competition Journal* 11.1 (2015): 26-68.
162. *See* GC, Case T-286/09, *Intel*, ECLI:EU:T:2014:547, §§103 and 145, where the General Court ruled it unnecessary to show that competitors had to offer negative prices.
163. CJEU, Case C-413/14 P, *Intel v. Commission*, ECLI:EU:C:2017:632, §138.
164. *Barry Wright Corp. v. ITT Grinnell Corp.*, 724 F.2d 227 (1st Cir. 1983), at 236: "virtually every contract to buy 'forecloses' or 'excludes' alternative sellers from some portion of the market, namely the portion consisting of what was bought."
165. CJEU, Case C-413/14 P, *Intel v. Commission*, ECLI:EU:C:2017:632, §§138 and 139. The Court "clarifies" *Hoffmann-La Roche* by recourse to a procedural scheme. It is only when the dominant firm "submits, during the administrative procedure, on the basis of supporting evidence, that its conduct was not capable of restricting competition" that the Commission must "assess the possible existence of a strategy aiming to exclude competitors that are at least as efficient as the dominant undertaking from the market." This is critical since neither the Commission nor the General Court can dismiss an effects-based analysis by simply stating that rebates are per se anticompetitive.
166. *See, e.g.*, the idealistic benchmark set by the Commission it its *Guidance Paper*, §36: "*If competitors can compete on equal terms for each individual customer's entire demand*, exclusive purchasing obligations are generally unlikely to hamper effective competition." (emphasis added)

"effective price" that the competitor would have to match and not by reference to the average price of all-units actually sold. The framework thus wrongly turns to judging a cost structure devoid of any efficiencies derived from the non-contestable part of the market.[167]

The risk of such leveraging theory is that if competitors cannot compete on equal terms, rebates, exclusivity contracts, and other theories of harm will by extension impose fast antitrust liability on dominant firms on an incessant basis.[168]

Competition *is* a destabilizing process where equality of opportunity could only be achieved by constantly resetting the race and thus distorting the process itself. The economic leveraging theory is simply a sophisticated shell of the theory underpinning the progeny of *Hoffmann-La Roche*. That is, to establish equality of opportunity as the lynchpin theory of anticompetitive rebates by forbidding the dominant firm to mobilize incumbency advantages that are the result of a competitive process.

Thus seen, the economic theory rests on a generalized negative view of incumbency. This means that the incumbent dominant firm cannot rely on its already overcome entry investment when it tries to lure buyers to buy its product because the entrant has not yet incurred those costs. It is the leveraging theory, in full, that must be revised.

Current theories of *anticompetitive* foreclosure—for not every exclusion is anticompetitive—appear to adopt a negative view to incumbent market power. That is unequivocally the case when the EU Courts attach a special responsibility to the dominant firm and limit its freedom of action by considering anticompetitive practices that would be irreproachable if carried out by a nondominant firm. Competitors of dominant firms know this. As former AMD's Chairman at the time, Hector Ruiz, stated at the beginning of proceedings against Intel rebates are "just business. But for a monopolist, this is illegal."[169] But this is likewise the case when the more-economic leveraging theory bases anticompetitive harm on an "undue" mobilization of incumbency advantages.

Early described as barriers to entry by Gilbert, these incumbency advantages are *profits* "that a firm can earn as a sole consequence of being established in an

167. This would be, in Posner's words, "a superficial analysis." As he explains, "a firm that can spread its fixed costs over more sales, in however many markets, is more efficient than a firm with a smaller output," *see* Posner, Richard A. "Natural Monopoly and Its Regulation." *Stanford Law Review* 21.3 (1968): 548-643, at 613. The same "as efficient as" analysis is done in vertical foreclosure. It is based on the revenue and cost structure of only the downstream arm of the dominant firm. *See, e.g.*, Commission Decision, Case COMP/39.523, *Slovak Telekom*, at §922.

168. *See, e.g.*, Commission Decision, Case COMP/39.740, *Google Search*, §339: "Customers and users should have the opportunity to benefit from whatever degree of competition is possible on the market and competitors should be able to compete on the merits for the entire market and not just for a part of it."

169. Bayot, Jennifer. "Intel Accused of Antitrust Violations." *The New York Times* (Jun. 29, 2005), *available at* http://www.nytimes.com/2005/06/29/business/worldbusiness/intel-accused-of-antitrust-violations.html.

industry."[170] Since only the incumbent can mobilize these profits, they represent in themselves a competitive disadvantage to the entrant. While in the presence of an investor dominant firm incumbency advantages represent a natural asymmetry that arises from the competitive process the division between contestability and incontestability shares wants to neutralize it.

The story advanced is the following one. All-units rebates may be abusive because firms differ in terms of reputation, productive capacity or variances in the product portfolio that allows the dominant firm to become the de facto exclusive supplier.[171] These significant asymmetries prevent other firms that are equally efficient in terms of production costs from competing on "roughly equal" terms.[172] The Guidance Paper is clear in this regard. "If competitors can compete on equal terms for each individual customer's entire demand, exclusive purchasing obligations are generally unlikely to hamper effective competition."[173] On the contrary, one could add, exclusivity discounts granted by a dominant firm enjoying significant asymmetries will significantly restrict competition. Thus, as a way to ensure competitive neutrality *Intel* and *Tomra* neutralize the incumbent's advantage by declaring anticompetitive rebate schemes that allow the dominant firm to make use of those natural asymmetries.[174]

This negative view of incumbency is repeatedly stressed in the Commission's decisional practice. Intel's incumbency advantage lies in its "must-stock" status that provides it with "additional market power" and "significant leverage."[175] Intel's incumbency advantage is its "legacy advantage" that imposes on new entrants or already competitors a barrier they need to overcome.[176] Tomra's incumbency advantages are its larger product portfolio, a denser service network, or an established reputation.[177] Other cases than rebates also echo this concern with incumbency advantages.[178] The incumbency advantage of AstraZeneca, found guilty of abusing its

170. Gilbert, Richard J. "Mobility Barriers and the Value of Incumbency" *in* Richard Schmalensee and Robert D. Willig (eds.) *Handbook of Industrial Organization*, Vol. 1, 1989: 475-535, 478. Gilbert uses both terms, rents and profits, interchangeably. *See* our discussion on profits versus rents terminology in Chapter 2.
171. Hewitt, Gary. "Background Note" *in* OECD, *Loyalty and Fidelity Discounts and Rebates, Roundtable on Competition Policy*. DAFFE/COMP(2002)21: 19-48, 21.
172. *Id.*
173. Guidance Paper, §36.
174. Taylor, Simon. "The Challenge of Competitive Neutrality in Public Procurement and Competition Policy: The UK Health Sector as Case Study." *Competition Policy International* 7 (2011): 2-8, writes, "Incumbency advantage is a common barrier to competitive neutrality."
175. Commission Decision, Case COMP/37.990, *Intel*, §§870 and 881.
176. *Id.* §887.
177. Commission Decision, Case COMP/38.113, *Tomra*, §277.
178. In *Microsoft*, the Commission and the Court considered Microsoft's property over its interoperability information an "*artificial* advantage" that the refusal to supply allows it to keep (emphasis added). It is remarkable that the Court uses the word "*artificial*" instead of "*competitive* advantage" or "*natural* advantage" to describe Microsoft's position. This allows the General Court to consider unnecessary to factor in the analysis the fact that consumers never claimed they had been forced to adopt a Windows work server group. The GC simply ruled: "Microsoft cannot rely on [this fact]." GC, Case T-201/04, *Microsoft v. Commission*, ECLI:EU:T:2007:289, §§653 and 662.

dominant position by misleading the regulatory authorities and withdrawing drug-marketing authorizations, is that new entrants generally have to invest more in promotion than the incumbent.[179]

Aside from the Commission, some economists have also attached an anticompetitive value to incumbency. In a series of papers, Chiara Fumagalli and Motta show that their models of foreclosure rely on the incumbency advantages of the dominant firm.[180] Foreclosure is anticompetitive because incumbency advantages do not correspond to the narrow view of "productive efficiency" that their AEC test purports.[181] Thus, by mobilizing incumbency advantages the dominant firm can even foreclose a firm that is "as efficient," or even "more efficient," than the dominant firm itself.[182] Rebates are anticompetitive because if the incumbent did not benefit from any incumbency advantages (if they were on *equal* footing) then the rival could profitably enter the market. As Alberto Heimler writes, "the exclusionary nature of discounts is related entirely to the inability of competitors to spread discounts over the same turnover as the dominant firm."[183]

Fumagalli and Motta's stylized models only give us a picture of a competitive story in dire need of a process perspective. On the one hand, their picture looks to an *ex post* game where the incumbent takes advantage of its particular position, at times reinforced by first-mover offerings which lock-in potential customers. But on the other, their papers disregard the *ex ante* games when the dominant firm competed to become an incumbent. In other words, their papers, and likewise the decisional practice of the EU courts and the Commission, forego the possibility that incumbency advantages can be the result of particular investments to resolve market uncertainties and thus be welfare enhancing.[184] The seminal question is avoided: *did* the incumbent incur a cost to achieve incumbency advantages?[185]

---

179. Commission Decision, Case COMP/37.507, *AstraZeneca*, §585.
180. Fumagalli, Chiara and Massimo Motta. "A Simple Theory of Predation." *The Journal of Law and Economics* 56.3 (2013): 595-631; and Fumagalli, Chiara and Massimo Motta. "On the Use of Price-Cost Tests in Loyalty Discounts and Exclusive Dealing Arrangements: Which Implications from Economic Theory Should Be Drawn?" *Antitrust Law Journal* 81.2 (2017): 537.
181. *See* Choné, Philippe and Laurent Linnemer. "Nonlinear Pricing and Exclusion: II. Must-Stock Products." *The RAND Journal of Economics* 47.3 (2016): 631-660.
182. To be consistent with a process perspective, anticompetitive foreclosure can only be established if the foreclosed rival were *more efficient at the same scale* as the dominant firm. Otherwise, the contestable/non-contestable theory would be nothing than a social construct designed to create fake incumbency positions, i.e., to sanction any dominant firm. Moreover, when two firms are equally efficient it would not be a problem that society prefers one or the other.
183. Heimler, Alberto. "Below-Cost Pricing and Loyalty-Inducing Discounts: Are They Restrictive and, If So, When?" *Competition Policy International* 1.2 (2005): 149-172, 158 and 165.
184. Gilbert, Richard J. "Mobility Barriers and the Value of Incumbency" *in* Richard Schmalensee and Robert D. Willig (eds.) *Handbook of Industrial Organization*, Vol. 1, 1989: 475-535.
185. In our view, Stigler's definition of a barrier to entry is not fully in line with a process perspective of competition. Stigler writes "a barrier to entry may be defined as a cost of producing (at some or every rate of output) that must be borne by a firm which seeks to enter the industry but is not borne by firms already in the industry." *See* Stigler, George J. *The Organization of Industry*. University of Chicago Press, 1968, at p. 67. However, the process perspective we advocate for would require that natural antitrust-relevant barriers to entry be also defined by reference to *ex ante* periods. Hence, instead of using the present tense for a cost that "*is* not borne" by the

The natural cost asymmetries are difficulties that *all* firms in a free market had or have to overcome to enter the industry. When a firm competes and eventually becomes an incumbent it has surmounted those hurdles by benefiting consumers, not only by means of producing a (new) product but also by reducing uncertainties, learning curve, transaction costs through distribution networks, risk aversion problems, etc.

Those incumbency advantages, which also benefit consumers and are the result of a competitive process, are part of the efficiencies the dominant undertaking shall have at its disposition.[186] As Demsetz argues, "in the presence of such costs, consumers will find it useful to rely on a firm's experience and reputation, or more correctly, on its history or on the fact that it has made sizeable investments specific to this industry."[187] Incumbency profits are simply another driver of the competitive process and antitrust authorities should be weary to implement theories aiming at neutralizing them.[188] They are natural and unavoidable by-products of a well-functioning market rewarding entrepreneurial activity.

In some way, to forbid a dominant undertaking from using those efficient advantages would be to fall back onto the insubstantial distinction between the existence and exercise of property rights. Rebates can represent savings that are more difficult to measure such as lower inventory costs promotional costs.[189] Dominance thus may be a threshold of liability, but it is also an indicator of how markets function and should not be detached from any analysis of conduct.

Paradoxically, in the context of public procurement the EU Courts have grasped the importance of not interfering with competitively acquired incumbency advantages.

Public procurement rules are by necessity concerned with the rules that govern the competitive *process*. Thus, when the rules of the tender abide by the requirements set in the Directives, the winner becomes—one would allow the simplification—the temporary dominant firm in that market, until a new tender procedure is issued and competition for a new temporary dominant firm reopened. In *Evropaïki Dynamiki*[190] the General Court held that the competitive advantages derived from the incumbent's previous relationship with the contracting authority are a natural consequence of the

---

incumbent, a barrier to entry might be antitrust-relevant if a similar cost of producing that must be borne by any firm that seeks to enter *was* not borne by the incumbent firms. Dennis Carlton and Jeffrey Perloff similarly adapt Stigler's definition: "a long-run barrier to entry is a cost that must be incurred by a new entrant that incumbent do not (or *have not had to*) bear" (emphasis added). *See* Carlton, Dennis W. and Jeffrey Perloff. *Modern Industrial Organization*. Addison-Wesley, 1999, at 77 and n. 12.

186. Bork, Robert. *The Antitrust Paradox: A Policy at War with Itself*. Simon & Schuster, [1978] 1993, at p. 195: "If everything that makes entry more difficult is viewed as a barrier, and if barriers are bad, then efficiency is evil. That conclusion is inconsistent with consumer-oriented policy."
187. Demsetz, Harold. "Barriers to Entry." *The American Economic Review* 72.1 (1982): 47-57, at 50.
188. Gans, Joshua S. "When Is Static Analysis a Sufficient Proxy for Dynamic Considerations? Reconsidering Antitrust and Innovation." *Innovation Policy and the Economy* 11.1 (2011): 55-78, 56.
189. Carlton, Dennis W. "A General Analysis of Exclusionary Conduct and Refusal to Deal—Why Aspen and Kodak Are Misguided." *Antitrust Law Journal* 68 (2001): 659-683. In Carlton's view all-units rebates are a normal method of competition and antirust liability should "should be used rarely and apply only to extreme pricing conditions." *See also* Chapter 6 discussing non-quantifiable resources.
190. GC, Case T-232/06, *Evropaïki Dynamiki v. Commission*, ECLI:EU:T:2011:443.

competitive process. As long as those advantages are not the result of "any conduct on the part of the contracting authority" they are an "*inherent de facto* advantage" that warrants no neutralization (emphasis added).[191]

As with any process which is affected by its own history, the winner of the first contest will have a competitive advantage over the rest of competitors once the new competition for the market reopens, for instance, learning-by-doing or reputation effects.[192] These advantages, from an *ex post* perspective, are apparently unavailable to the competitors of the previous temporary dominant firm. But from an *ex ante* perspective, all participating firms were potential candidates to benefit from incumbency advantages. The tender, however, selected the most adequate firm, who as a reward for better satisfying customers' needs benefits from providing those needs and enjoying incumbency advantages.

Yet, the division between contestable and incontestable shares deployed so as to carry out a price-cost analysis of the "effective price" does precisely the opposite. It prevents the dominant firm and its customers from mobilizing *competitive* incumbency advantages. It creates a false incumbency position.[193]

This is why we believe it worrying that even the *Intel* Court did not attempt to modify *Hoffman-La Roche*'s holding that whether customers are pleased with the rebates or are misled into them makes no difference in the assessment of anticompetitive effects.[194] Such shortcut avoids discovering that loyalty is often a reflection of lower real cost of transacting, industry-specific investments, or a reputable history. If the value of incumbency was thus analyzed, one would discover that customers go to the firm that offers the best deal, and that unless they are being misled, the Commission will not be better placed to make the assessment than those that spend their actual money in securing rebates based on exclusivity. "A reputable history is an asset to the firm possessing it and to the buyer who relies on it because information is not free."[195] If rationality is predicated from the dominant firm, as the Commission did in *Tomra* to

191. *Id.* §76, upheld by the CJEU, Case C-597/11 P, *Evropaïki Dynamiki v. Commission*, ECLI: EU:C:2012:616. *See similarly*, GC, Case T-345/03, *Evropaïki Dynamiki v. Commission*, ECLI: EU:T:2008:67, §70.
192. *See* Chapter 6 for a discussion about how reputation, experience and other intangible resources need to be built over path and time dependent processes.
193. *See* Chapter 3 discussing the substantial difference between a historical operator and an incumbent.
194. CJEU, Case 85/76, *Hoffmann-La Roche v. Commission*, ECLI:EU:C:1979:36, §89: a dominant firm that "ties purchasers - even if it does so at their request" by an exclusive obligation abuses that position of market power. Commission Decision, Case COMP/37.990, *Intel*, §1624 and n. 1935, reinstates this holding. *See* Glazer, Kenneth L. and Brian R. Henry. "Coercive *vs.* Incentivizing Conduct: A Way out of the Section 2 Impasse." *Antitrust* 18.1 (2003): 45-51, explaining that incentivizing behavior, such as rebates, should be analyzed under a predatory pricing framework even when exclusivity is attached to it.
195. Demsetz, Harold. "Barriers to Entry." *The American Economic Review* 72.1 (1982): 47-57, at 51: "Firms with less experience can gain a foothold when the price older firms would need to receive, if they are to increase their sales, rises sufficiently to offset the value to consumers of their longer experience."

reject the economic analysis presented by the defendants,[196] so it should be predicated of its customers.[197]

An analysis of all-units rebates would be more *process*-oriented, if the price-cost analysis was done by reference to all-units and rejected the artificial distinction between contestability and incontestability. All-units rebates cannot be anticompetitive unless, and at least if, the price on all units sold after all discounts are taken is below the dominant's firm average variable cost (AVC).[198]

[4] A Simple Process Comparative and a Pragmatic Approach

The "more-economic" leveraging theory remains a limiting principle to the vacuity of *Hoffman-La Roche*. In markets where the firm's market power is statutory in origin, both the EU Courts and the Commission have presumptively upheld the existence of a dominant position with little analysis. Statutory monopolies are "by virtue of that fact, in a dominant position." This is "even if the services provided under a monopoly are linked to a product which is itself in competition with other products."[199] This hastened conclusion could be explained by the desire of the EU institutions to constrain the market power yielded by statutory firms.

In *Post Danmark II*, the Court of Justice tied the non-contestable share of the market to Post Danmark's statutory monopoly. The suction effect of the rebates "is enhanced" by the fact that *Post Danmark* can leverage its non-contestable share of the market, which the Court emphasized is "covered by Post Danmark's statutory monopoly."[200] Yet, it remains uncertain whether the *Post Danmark II* restricted the application of the leveraging theory to the statutory origins of the firm. The contestability division thus risks being reasserted if the different origins of market power are not explicitly accounted for.[201]

This notwithstanding, the leveraging theory articulated through the division of contestable and non-contestable shares can find a realistic rationale in the presence of a statutory dominant firm. We illustrate this with the following example.

Let us compare two scenarios. The *first scenario* represents a dominant firm enjoying a non-contestable market share due to the discretionary protection of the State. Let us denote this statutory undertaking as Firm A. Firm A grants all-units rebates

196. Commission Decision, Case COMP/38.113, *Prokent/Tomra*, §§373 and 387.
197. *Id.* §§152 and 181, where the Commission acknowledges that customers extracted different commitments from Tomra that benefitted them better than those offered at first.
198. Areeda, Phillip and Herbert Hovenkamp. *Fundamentals of Antitrust Law*. Wolters Kluwer, 2011, (2017 supplement), at 7-87. The same approach is contained in DOJ, "Competition and Monopoly: Single-Firm Conduct under Section 2 of The Sherman Act" (2008, Report), (withdrawn without replacement on Nov. 05, 2009), at 116-117.
199. GC, Case T-229/94, *Deutsche Bahn*, ECLI:EU:T:1997:155, §§51 and 57.
200. *See* CJEU, Case C-23/14, *Post Danmark II*, ECLI:EU:C:2015:651, at §35 (following the Opinion of AG Kokott in Case C-23/14, *Post Danmark II*, ECLI:EU:C:2015:343, §38): "That suction effect is further enhanced by the fact that, in the case in the main proceedings, the rebates applied without distinction both to the contestable part of demand and to the non-contestable part of demand, that is to say, in the latter case, to addressed advertising mail weighing less than 50 grams covered by Post Danmark's statutory monopoly."
201. CJEU, Case C-209/10, *Post Danmark I*, ECLI:EU:C:2012:172, §23.

that affect the contestable share of the market. However, an as efficient market entrant Firm B cannot parallel these rebates because it does not have access to the non-contestable market under the grip of statutory Firm A. The *second scenario* represents an investor dominant Firm AA. Firm AA, eventually enjoys a non-contestable market because it has acquired it through a competitive process that yields efficient outcomes. Unlike Firm B in the first scenario, Firm B in the second scenario had the opportunity to achieve, at *t*-1, the non-contestable share by competing more efficiently than Firm AA. When either Firm A or Firm AA leverages the non-contestable share into the contestable market one sees a much different competitive scenario. While the incontestable rents of A are due to a non-competitive endowment by the State in *scenario 1*, the non-contestable profits of Firm AA are the result of the very competitive process that competition law seeks to protect in *scenario 2*. The *apparent* effects on an isolated outcome might be the same, i.e., Firm B will not be able to compete in the contestable market. However, the effects on the competitive process are not.[202] A retrospective look into the competitive process shows Firm A always in the market (for its position is asserted by the State); while the existence of Firm AA (for its entry depends on the *ex post* expected profits yielded by its investment) is the result of the competitive process itself, and its incumbency advantages a reward to its entrepreneurial behavior.[203]

Thus, on the one hand, the division of a market between contestable and non-contestable shares is alien to the competitive process in the case of dominant firms whose position in the "non-contestable" share market is due to their investment efforts in a competitive process.[204] On the other hand, the division and accompanying leveraging theory seem fitting to a process perspective in *scenario 1* with the presence of a statutory dominant firm.

---

202. Baker & Mckenzie. Response to DG Competition's Article 82 Consultation available at ec.europa.eu/competition/antitrust/art82/076.pdf. ("Many, if not most, dominant undertakings will have certain non-replicable advantages and economies of scale are a natural part of almost all industrial sectors. It is not the purpose of Article 82 to protect an entrant that has made a commercial miscalculation by choosing to enter at an inefficient scale or enter a market where it cannot replicate the dominant undertaking's advantages. Once again, this would result in inefficient competitors, as opposed to the competitive process, being protected by antitrust policy.")
203. As an extreme example, one could think for instance of the case of an intellectual property right on drug X in the pharmaceutical sector owned by a dominant undertaking. The revenues coming from selling X not only allow the firm to recover its investment and reward the firm for its entrepreneurial action but they will also be used to subsidize the emergence of new products in new markets. The dominant firm uses the profits obtained from drug X to further invest and innovate, which in turn might bring a new monopoly to the firm and a new drug Y for consumers. In *AstraZeneca* the Commission emphasized that in dynamic sectors, such as the pharmaceutical industry, a dominant company needs to invest regularly if it wants to preserve its market position. *See* Commission Decision, Case COMP/37.507, *AstraZeneca*, §514.
204. Rato, Miguel and Nicolas Petit. "Abuse of Dominance in Technology-Enabled Markets: Established Standards Reconsidered?" *European Competition Journal* 9.1 (2013): 1-65, at 14: if "vigorous competition has taken place ex ante, then the market position of the allegedly dominant firm is nothing but a competitive outcome. This should prevent a finding of dominance, and the emergence of the ensuing special responsibility borne by dominant firms." Yet, we do not claim that dominance is inexistent or a helpful threshold. Rather, that the theories of antitrust liability need to take due account of the origins of market power.

Alternatively, an all-units price-cost analysis is more administrable and certain than resource-intensive and unclear guesses as to which portions of demand are contestable. Yet, it should not be the only justification. The OECD[205] and the DOJ[206] have underlined the difficulty in establishing the contestable share of the market. The difficulty partially strikes at the heart of the process of competition that is in constant change, despite some commentators describing the market as a "textbook case."[207] This is why some commentators have advanced a partial solution. Instead of establishing a fixed number, the contestable share of the demand should be seen "as a random variable" that considers "a range of values for the contestable demand."[208] All things considered, if there is a non-contestable market share that can be clearly delineated and is more administrable is that of the statutory monopoly.

A final qualification is in order. The AEC framework we have advanced is nothing but a tool that serves to frame the discussion and to bring upfront the investments undertaken in the competitive process. Markets are complex realities that do not function as textbook case studies. Whether in the presence of rebates or other business practices, to constrain the amount of possibilities that competitors have to a cost-benefit analysis risks to lead to a narrow and incomplete understanding of the competitive process.[209] As Richard Epstein writes, "complex industrial practices do not have just one consequence, either positive or negative"[210] and economic actors do not have just one way of reacting.

[C] Incumbency Disadvantages: *Google Shopping* and Beyond

A dominant firm that is not obliged to give access to its input *and* can use its *competitive* advantages should be entitled to give access to competitors on less favorable conditions.[211] If not, as Petit puts it in a driving metaphor, this would be analogous to "prohibiting speeding above 120 km/h [less favorable conditions but access], yet

205. OECD, Executive Summary of the Roundtable on Fidelity Rebates held at the 125th meeting of the Competition Committee of the OECD, DAF/COMP/M(2016)1/ANN4/FINAL/en/pdf.
206. DOJ, "Competition and Monopoly: Single-Firm Conduct under Section 2 of The Sherman Act" (2008, Report) (withdrawn without replacement on Nov. 05, 2009).
207. Maier-Rigaud, Frank and Dovile Vaigauskaite. "Prokent/Tomra, a Textbook Case? Abuse of Dominance under Perfect Information." *Competition Policy Newsletter* 2 (2006): 19-24.
208. Choné, Philippe and Laurent Linnemer. "Nonlinear Pricing and Exclusion: II. Must-Stock Products." *The RAND Journal of Economics* 47.3 (2016): 631-660, 653.
209. *See* Chapter 6 emphasizing the critical importance of non-quantifiable efficiencies.
210. Epstein, Richard A. "Monopoly Dominance or Level Playing Field? The New Antitrust Paradox." *The University of Chicago Law Review* 72.1 (2005): 49-72, 58.
211. Hayek, Friedrich A. *Law, Legislation and Liberty*, (Vol. 2) *The Mirage of Social Justice*. Routledge, [1976] 1998, at p. 72, explaining that the ability to determine the price of any resource that is the result of an investment in competitive conditions, "is necessary consequence of the recognition of private property in particular things, and cannot be eliminated without abandoning the institution of private property. There is in this respect no difference between a manufacturer, or merchant who has built up a unique organization, or acquired a uniquely suitable site, and a painter who limits his output to what will bring him the largest income. There exists no more an argument in justice, or a moral case, against such a monopolist making a monopoly profit than there is against anyone who decides that he will work no more than he finds worth his while."

tolerating it above 150km/h [no access at all]."[212] However, as long as an obligation to supply and to neutralize competitive advantages lure behind investor dominant firms speeding at 120km/h will still be prohibited.[213]

The decision of *Google Shopping* is thus a predictable outcome. Here, the Commission held that irrespective of the reasons that caused its dominant position, Google abuses its position if it treats its comparison shopping service, Google Shopping, more favorably than those of its competitors. Google's favorable treatment consists in increasing search traffic from Google's general search results pages to Google Shopping. It does so by positioning Google Shopping as a first result to certain queries and by displaying Google Shopping results with richer graphical features that include pictures and price information.[214] Whether such behavior is likely to benefit Google is outside of the scope of our inquiry. What interests us here is the misguided legal theory underpinning the *Google Shopping* decision: equality of opportunity.[215]

The Commission's description of its theory of harm is arguably an amalgamation of principled statements without apparent rhyme or reason.[216] The dominant firm has a special responsibility. The dominant firm weakens the competitive process with its mere presence. The dominant firm can abuse its position by impacting an effective competitive structure. It can also abuse its position by extending that position into neighboring markets or by adopting conduct that is unobjectionable if adopted by nondominant undertakings. The list of abuses in Article 102 TFEU is not exhaustive. The origins of dominance play no role in the assessment of abusive conduct. The dominant firm can provide an objective justification for its conduct. The Commission then "concludes" that Google's abuse is to treat its own service more favorably. It dedicates a hundred pages to explain *how* Google favors its service, and *how* this benefits Google. However, aside from this amalgamation of principles, the Commission never explains in a cogent manner *why* Google's behavior is anticompetitive. In other words, if one were to replace the word "abusive conduct" with "competitive conduct" the decision would make equal sense.

But, among the enumerated principles, we have explicitly omitted one. The purpose is to bring it to the forefront, under the spotlight.

According to the Commission in *Google Shopping*, "a system of undistorted competition can be guaranteed only if equality of opportunity is secured as between the various economic operators."[217] This is, without a doubt, a milestone in the policy of

212. Petit, Nicolas. "The Future of the Court of Justice in EU Competition Law—New Role and Responsibilities" *in* Court of Justice of the EU (ed.) *The Court of Justice and the Construction of Europe: Analyses and Perspectives on Sixty Years of Case-Law*. Nomos Verlagsgesellschaft, 2013, at p. 16 and Petit, Nicolas. "Theories of Self-Preferencing under Article 102 TFEU: A Reply to Bo Vesterdorf." *SSRN* (2015): 1-18, 8.
213. For an excellent exposition, *see* Ibáñez Colomo, Pablo. "Exclusionary Discrimination under Article 102 TFEU." *Common Market Law Review* 51.1 (2014): 141-163, at 154: arguing that if "dominant firms are entitled, as a rule, to deal with whom they please, [this] implies by definition that they should also be entitled, as a rule, to favour their own activities over those of rivals."
214. Commission Decision, Case COMP/39.740, *Google Search (Shopping)*, §397.
215. *Id.* §331.
216. *Id.* §§331-345.
217. *Id.* §331.

aggressive enforcement of Article 102 TFEU. As explained in Chapters 2 and 3, the principle of equality of opportunity originated in the application of Article 106 TFEU. Thereafter, it appeared in Article 102 TFEU cases involving statutory monopolies or historical operators. Now, in *Google Shopping*, a firm that is neither one nor the other, an investor dominant firm is for the *first time* subject to this standard of liability.

The Commission seems to have been aware of its novel step. There are three reasons that emanate from the decision that compel us to understand so. *First*, the Commission stated that Google's origins could not inform the assessment of the abuse in two occasions. The Commission seemingly sought active confirmation on this point from Google in the assessment of dominance. "Google does not contest" that "the reasons or the causes for which Google has a dominant position ... are irrelevant."[218] Interestingly, no reference to *Post Danmark I* obiter on the statutory origins of certain dominant firms is found in the decision.

Second, the references to the case law allegedly supporting the inclusion of the principle of equality of opportunity do not include references to Article 106 TFEU cases, but *only* to Article 102 TFEU cases that involved historical operators. That is, *Deutsche Telekom* and *Telefónica*.[219] This is unlike the same case law that based the introduction of the principle of equality of opportunity on Article 106 TFEU case law.[220]

Third, the word discrimination is absent from the decision. This suggests that finding a favorable treatment of one's own property abusive is subject to the unclear and flexible contours of what "equality of opportunity" means. This, in turn, leaves the ambiguous effects that discrimination has on the competitive process outside of the analysis.

In the context of Article 102 TFEU, the principle of equality of opportunity can be generally understood as imposing an obligation upon investor dominant firms to ensure a level playing field. As we have maintained before, the strict application of this principle to firms other than statutory monopolies,[221] or its cautious application to historical operators,[222] cannot be imposed on firms that owe their positions of market power to their investment efforts. This would be akin to mistakenly impose on investor dominant firms the same obligations as those that are incumbent upon states.[223] The purpose of competition rules cannot interfere with the incentives of firms that lead them to offer more or better products than its competitors on the premise that their

218. *Id.* §§315 and 338.
219. Case C-280/08 P, *Deutsche Telecom v. Commission*, EU:C:2010:603, §230; Case T-336/07, *Telefónica v. Commission*, EU:T:2012:172, §204.
220. *See* Chapter 3.
221. *See* Chapter 2.
222. *See* Chapter 3.
223. Temple Lang, John. "Commonly Accepted Errors and Misunderstandings in European Competition Law–Abuse of Dominance, and Patent Licensing." *19th St.Gallen International Competition Law Forum ICF* (2012).

success creates an unlevelled playing field.[224] Thus, there is a paradoxical contradiction between the objective of competition law, which is to protect the competitive process, and a competition policy that obliges the dominant firm not to use in its favor the advantages it has competitively acquired in that process.[225]

Furthermore, the "new" obligation incumbent upon investor dominant firms to ensure a level playing field can have the perverse effect of placing that dominant firm at a disadvantage vis-à-vis nondominant firms.[226] Note moreover that incumbency can be a disadvantage itself. This incumbency disadvantage is so considerable that it has led the EU Courts to rule that a dominant firm might be prevented from "the right to adopt a course of conduct or take measures which are not in themselves abuses and which would even be unobjectionable if adopted or taken by non-dominant undertakings."[227] This *artificial* incumbency disadvantage has the potential of distorting the competitive process.

As long as Article 102 TFEU cannot catch anticompetitive conduct leading to the acquisition of dominance,[228] a nondominant firm could unlawfully acquire dominance in an already monopolized or an adjacent market by resorting to anticompetitive practices, such as exclusionary contracting or predation, which the dominant firm cannot meet.

Let us draw a stylized example: a market where a dominant Firm A has a 60% market share, a nondominant Firm B has a 40% of market share, and 5 customers have an equal market distribution of 20% share each. If instead of Firm A, Firm B was the first to lure away another customer with an exclusionary contract, this would grant it an extra 20% of the market.[229] In this situation, Firm B will acquire dominance in an allegedly "competitive" manner because Firm A cannot meet the same contractual conditions: exclusivity appears to be anticompetitive for the dominant firm.[230]

Another example would be a nondominant firm that engages in predatory pricing in adjacent markets to those of the dominant firm.[231] This may either require deeper pockets than its rivals, or "instant scalable markets" that will easily tip in favor of first

224. CJEU, Case C-209/10, *Post Danmark I*, ECLI:EU:C:2012:172, §22: The competitive process entails a "departure from the market or the marginalization of competitors that are less efficient and so less attractive to consumers from the point of view of, among other things, price, choice, quality or innovation."
225. Easterbrook, Frank H. "Limits of Antitrust." *Texas Law Review* 63.1 (1984): 1-40, 1-2.
226. Guidance Paper, §20, acknowledging that a competitor can pose a significant competitive constrain even if it is not dominant.
227. *See, e.g.*, GC, Case T-340/03, *France Télécom v. Commission*, ECLI:EU:T:2007:22, §186; *and* GC, Case T-111/96 *ITT Promedia v. Commission*, ECLI:EU:T:1998:183, §139.
228. *See* Chapter 8 for an extended discussion on anticompetitive conduct on the road to dominance.
229. In the predation model of Fumagalli, Chiara and Massimo Motta. "A Simple Theory of Predation." *The Journal of Law and Economics* 56.3 (2013): 595-631, the first-mover advantage is only available to the incumbent dominant firm. However, nothing impedes that the new entrant or incumbent nondominant firm enjoys that advantage instead.
230. If exclusionary contracts were anticompetitive, anticompetitive harm does not depend on the excluding firm being a monopoly, *see* Rasmusen, Eric B., J. Mark Ramseyer and John S. Wiley Jr. "Naked Exclusion." *The American Economic Review* 81.5 (1991): 1137-1145, 1144.
231. Tor, Avishalom. "Unilateral, Anticompetitive Acquisitions of Dominance or Monopoly Power." *Antitrust Law Journal* 76.3 (2010): 847-872, 868.

and most aggressive player.[232] In the latter case, being the first firm to deploy such strategy can be a short-term rational strategy that will tip the market in favor of the violator. In those markets, the dominant firm could be unable to acquire market power if it competes against a nondominant rival that resorts to predatory pricing to win that market. Little seems to matter in EU competition policy that the nondominant firm is less efficient than the disadvantaged dominant firm.[233] Predatory pricing by a non-dominant firm can thus drive an efficient dominant undertaking out of the market (or prevent its expansion into other markets) because the latter is incapable of meeting competition and the former's behavior cannot fall under Article 102 TFEU.[234]

This can have an even more perverse effect than the difficulty of distinguishing anticompetitive from procompetitive conduct. Since the adjacent market has given rise to a new position of SMP, the firm will eventually enjoy incumbency advantages that are not the result of procompetitive conduct. Once the market has inefficiently tipped it will then be difficult to restore it to its precompetitive scenario.[235]

The Commission has endorsed this artificial incumbency disadvantage in its Guidance Paper. Here, the Commission purposively decided to leave out the meeting competition defense in the context of predatory pricing. On the contrary, the Discussion Paper at least stated that "in case the conduct concerns pricing below AAC the meeting competition defense can *normally* not be applied"[236] (emphasis added). Here "the key word is 'normally'"[237] as it seems to envisage particular situations where pricing below costs for the dominant firm could be permissible. If Article 102 TFEU cannot catch anticompetitive conduct leading to dominance, an investor dominant firm should be able to justify its conduct by simply claiming that it is meeting (not beating) the behavior of a rival, even if such prices were below any measure of cost.[238]

Thus, the special responsibility incumbent upon the investor dominant firm has the perverse effect of distorting the competitive process itself. It gives the nondominant firm an "undeserved leg up" under the false premise of leveling the playing field.[239] As

232. Liebowitz, Stan J. and Stephen E. Margolis. *Winners, Losers & Microsoft; Competition and Antitrust in High Technology*. Independent Institute, 2001, at p. 137; *also*, Devlin, Alan. "Analyzing Monopoly Power Ex Ante." *NYU Journal of Law & Business* 5 (2009): 153-209.
233. Gelamn, Judith R. and Steven C. Salop. "Judo Economics: Capacity Limitation and Coupon Competition." *The Bell Journal of Economics* 14.2 (1983): 315-325. Although not in the context of the acquisition of market power, Gelman and Salop discuss how small firms can use its rival's large size to its advantage.
234. *Sensu contrario, see* CJEU, Case C-62/86, *AKZO v. Commission*, ECLI:EU:C:1991:286, §72: "Predatory prices can drive from the market undertakings which are perhaps as efficient as the dominant undertakings but which, because of their smaller financial resources, are incapable of withstanding the competition waged against them."
235. Gavil, Andrew I., William E. Kovacic, Jonathan B. Baker and Joshua Wright. *Antitrust Law in Perspective: Cases, Concepts and Problems in Competition Policy*. West Academic Publishing, 2017, at p. 1100.
236. Guidance Paper, §83.
237. Simpson, Claire. "Dominant Firms and Selective Discounting in the EU: When Is 'Meeting Competition' a Defence?" *European Competition Journal* 12.1 (2016): 1-27, 24-25.
238. This point is also made by Gal, Michal, "Below-Cost Price Alignment: Meeting or Beating Competition?" *New York University Law and Economics Working Papers* Paper 95 (2007): 1-15, 11-14.
239. Epstein, Richard A. "Monopoly Dominance or Level Playing Field? The New Antitrust Paradox." *The University of Chicago Law Review* 72.1 (2005): 49-72, 61.

Ioannis Kokkoris argues, what it is clear is that, "non-dominant firms can also have an adverse impact on consumer welfare by adopting unilateral acts."[240] This incumbency disadvantage complicates the task of distinguishing anticompetitive behavior from that that belongs to the competitive process even more.[241] If the dominant firm cannot have recourse to the business justification of a "normal business practice" nothing seems to separate competitive from anticompetitive conduct.

§5.05 CONCLUSION

Generally, a dynamic analysis simply is "the analysis of sequences in time"[242] such as the relationship among t-1, *t* and *t*+1. A dynamic analysis of competition is the analysis of the process of competition itself and not of a single snapshot. However, despite aiming at protecting the competitive process, the EU Courts and the Commission make snapshot analyses of abusive behavior by investor dominant firms. Exploitative abuses, obligations to deal or leveraging theories suffer from an oversight where the investment efforts that led to a dominant position are bygones and paradoxically regarded as barriers to competition.[243] Dominance may be a threshold of liability, but it is also an indicator of how markets function and should inform any analysis of the effects of single-firm behavior.

240. Kokkoris writes: "the fact that [this conduct] cannot be addressed by Article 82 is surprising and worrying." Kokkoris proposes that competition law provisions catch anticompetitive conduct, even if it does not lead to dominance. *See* Kokkoris, Ioannis. *A Gap in the Enforcement of Article 82*. British Institute of International and Comparative Law, 2009, at p. 60.
241. Wright, Joshua D. "Antitrust Law and Competition for Distribution." *Yale Journal on Regulation* 23.2 (2006): 169-208.
242. Schumpeter, Joseph A. *Capitalism, Socialism and Democracy*. Routledge, [1943] 2003, at p. 103.
243. Kaplow, Louis and Carl Shapiro. "Antitrust" *in* A. Mitchell Polinsky and Steven Shavell (eds.) *Handbook of Law and Economics*, Elsevier, Vol. 2, 2007: 1077-1225, 1201. This oversight may be partially due to the absence of investment opportunities in models of perfect competition where there is no space for new profit opportunities or the discovery of new wants to be served. *See* Barry, Norman. "The Tradition of Spontaneous Order." *Literature of Liberty* 5.2 (1982): 7-58.

CHAPTER 6

The Intangible Dominant Firm

§6.01 INTRODUCTION

In the preceding chapters, we have looked into the black box of the dominant firm. This has led us to track the different sources of the SMP that dominant firms hold. In turn, this has provided support to the idea that antitrust laws should not treat dominant firms uniformly. Arguably, the means by which firms reach a dominant position not only differentiates them but also impacts the competitive process in different ways.

In this chapter, we carry on with that analysis. This time, we explore the extent to which intangible capabilities can propel a firm to a position of market dominance and how these might affect the assessment of abusive behavior. To that end, we draw heavily on the SML. Given the little interest received by SML in antitrust scholarship, some preliminary words on this field of the literature are in order. SML posits that firms are heterogeneous because they develop over time a set of internal capabilities that allows them to enjoy a competitive advantage. Firms possess and combine these capabilities in different ways to create value and are thus heterogeneous even when they provide the "same" service or sell the "same" product.

Of direct relevance to our inquiry is the fact that in SML, many of these capabilities are intangible. Examples of intangible capabilities are a firm's reputation, its organizational culture and business model, its tacit knowledge or experience, or its learning abilities. As such, they are difficult to quantify and are non-tradable in the market. In other words, the competitive edge that intangible capabilities provide will be lost or substantially diminished once they are outside the firm.

Intangibles offer added value to the customers of the firm that possess them and are generally deemed to be a source of efficiency.[1] From the customer's perspective, a

1. David J. Teece, one of the major exponents of contemporary SML, explains, "it is no longer in product markets but in intangibles assets where [competitive] advantage is built and defended." *See* Teece, David J. "Capturing Value from Knowledge Assets: The New Economy, Markets for Know-How, and Intangible Assets." *California Management Review* 40.3 (1998): 55-79, 77.

customer purchasing from the dominant firm does not only carry a simple price/cost analysis. Indeed, he might also consider those intangible resources that come tacitly with the deal, such as reputational effects. From the firm's perspective, when a firm improves a product or develops a new one it does not start from scratch. Rather, it draws on the experience that it has accumulated over the years.

Against this background, this chapter proceeds in two steps. To start, we review SML, to describe how intangible resources can be a critical source of competitive advantage. On that basis, we point out the main elements of SML that can improve our understanding of how the competitive *process* operates (§6.02). Then, we discuss how the enforcement of Article 102 TFEU should integrate the teachings of SML in order to take into account the intangible origins of firm dominance (§6.03).

§6.02 WHY ARE SOME FIRMS MORE SUCCESSFUL THAN OTHERS? A STRATEGIC MANAGEMENT PERSPECTIVE

This section explores SML in search of insights on why some firms are more successful than others. We first generally review what SML has to say on why intangible resources can give a firm a competitive advantage (6.02[A] and [B]). We then specifically focus on some of the SML insights about intangible resources that could improve our understanding of the competitive *process* (6.02[C]). Lastly, we conclude (6.02[D]).

[A] Intangible Resources

Why are some firms more successful than others even if they face the same economic forces?

SML offers a tentative answer. Certain unique capabilities of individual firms or firm-units are what thrust some firms ahead of others.[2] Thus, unlike mainstream economics, the main unit of analysis of contemporary SML is the firm and not the structure of the market.[3]

SML has developed different approaches to studying how resources and capabilities of a firm might explain differences in performance. These approaches include

2. Rumelt, Richard P. "How Much Does Industry Matter?" *Strategic Management Journal* 12.3 (1991): 167-185.
3. In this sense, transaction cost economics is an important exception to mainstream economics. *See* Coase, Ronald H. "The Nature of the Firm." *Economica* 4.16 (1937): 386-405; and Williamson, Oliver E. *Markets and Hierarchies. Analysis and Antitrust Implications*. New York: Free Press, 1975. On the contrary, some early and influential strategy and management scholars, like Michael Porter, built their research upon the structure-conduct-performance paradigm used in neoclassical economics, while accepting that firms could also influence industry structure. *See* Porter, Michael E. *Competitive Strategy: Techniques for Analyzing Industries and Competition*. New York: Free Press, [1980] 2004. More generally, *see* Rumelt, Richard P., Dan Schendel and David J. Teece. "Strategic Management and Economics." *Strategic Management Journal* 12 (1991): 5-29, examining the parallel and related evolution of IO and strategic management.

the resource-based view,[4] dynamic capabilities theory,[5] and the knowledge-based view.[6,7] These approaches are generally different methods of describing a firm's resources rather than a "new" theory of competitive advantage.[8] Yet, the notion that firms are heterogeneous and can derive competitive advantages from their unique combination of internal resources remains a common assumption in the inquiry.[9]

Firm resources include tangible resources, such as physical resources like plants and equipment, and intangible resources, such as knowledge, information, managerial know-how, organizational culture, learning, and so on.

Notably, the literature has largely regarded intangible resources to bestow sustained competitive advantage, rather than tangible resources.[10] Hiroyuki Itami and Thomas Roehl claim that only a firm that develops "invisible assets" such as customer loyalty, positive reputation, accumulated consumer information, or technological know-how (as opposed to a particular technology)[11] are sources of competitive advantage.[12] Teece considers that intangible resources are a critical source of competitive advantage, among which knowledge resources are the most important.[13] This is

4. Initially developed by Wernerfelt, Birger. "A Resource-Based View of the Firm." *Strategic Management Journal* 5.2 (1984): 171-180; Barney, Jay B. "Firm Resources and Sustained Competitive Advantage." *Journal of Management* 17.1 (1991): 99-120; and Peteraf, Margaret A. "The Cornerstones of Competitive Advantage: A Resource-Based View." *Strategic Management Journal* 14.3 (1993).
5. *See, generally*, Dierickx, Ingemar and Karel Cool. "Asset Stock Accumulation and Sustainability of Competitive Advantage." *Management Science* 35.12 (1989), 1504-1511; Teece, David J., Gary Pisano and Amy Shuen. "Dynamic Capabilities and Strategic Management." *Strategic Management Journal* 18.7 (1997): 509-533, defining dynamic capabilities as "the firm's ability to integrate, build, and reconfigure internal and external competences to address rapidly changing environments"; and Helfat, Constance E. "Know-How and Asset Complementarity and Dynamic Capability Accumulation: The Case of R&D." *Strategic Management Journal* (1997): 339-360.
6. *See generally* Kogut, Bruce and Udo Zander. "Knowledge of the Firm, Combinative Capabilities, and the Replication of Technology." *Organization Science* 3.3 (1992): 383-397; Spender, J.-C. "Making Knowledge the Basis of a Dynamic Theory of the Firm." *Strategic Management Journal* 17.S2 (1996): 45-62; and Grant, Robert M. "Toward a Knowledge-Based Theory of the Firm." *Strategic Management Journal* 17.S2 (1996): 109-122.
7. This chapter defines SML as encompassing the resource-based view, dynamic capabilities theory, and the knowledge-based view.
8. Barney, Jay B. and Asli M. Arikan. "The Resource-Based View: Origins and Implications" *in* Michael A. Hitt, R. Edward Freeman and Jeffrey S. Harrison (eds.) *The Blackwell Handbook of Strategic Management*. Wiley-Blackwell, 2001: 124-187.
9. Peteraf, Margaret A. "The Cornerstones of Competitive Advantage: A Resource-Based View." *Strategic Management Journal* 14.3 (1993): 179-191.
10. Barney, Jay B. "Resource-Based Theories of Competitive Advantage: A Ten-Year Retrospective on the Resource-Based View." *Journal of Management* 27.6 (2001): 643-650. This does not mean that tangible and intangible resources are to be found as separate constructs within firms, but will often be bundled together. *See* Ray, Gautam, Jay B. Barney and Waleed A. Muhanna. "Capabilities, Business Processes, and Competitive Advantage: Choosing the Dependent Variable in Empirical Tests of the Resource-Based View." *Strategic Management Journal* 25.1 (2004): 23-37.
11. Dierickx, Ingemar and Karel Cool. "Asset Stock Accumulation and Sustainability of Competitive Advantage." *Management Science* 35.12 (1989), 1504-1511, drawing this important distinction.
12. Itami, Hiroyuki and Thomas W. Roehl. *Mobilizing Invisible Assets*. Harvard University Press, [1991] 2009.
13. Teece, David J. "Strategies for Managing Knowledge Assets: The Role of Firm Structure and Industrial Context." *Long Range Planning* 33.1 (2000): 35-54.

particularly true because intangible resources are generally affected by increasing returns and positive feedback loops. This means that reputation, knowledge, customer loyalty or producer-learning make the firm become more efficient as time goes by and experience builds up.[14] Intangible resources substantially drive asymmetries in performance—for example, proactiveness, teamwork, ability to resolve problems and a learning capability.[15]

Empirical studies have validated the critical importance of intangible resources as sources of competitive advantage. Richard Hall addressed a survey to 847 CEOs in the UK to test the hypothesis. Respondents to the survey claimed that company reputation, product reputation and employee know-how were the most important contributors to their firm's success. Moreover, the most important intangible resources were also considered to have the longest replacement periods. This meant that the *time* it would take the company to build the resource from scratch was positively correlated to its relevance. As such, company reputation scored the highest replacement period with a replacement average period of 10.8 years.[16]

Michael Michalisin and colleagues considered that even though the nature of intangible resources makes them difficult to quantify, they could still be perceived by market participants. In this regard, the higher ratio between market value (i.e., perception) to book value (i.e., accounting) could serve as a good proxy to estimate a firm's competitive edge.[17] Drawing from a randomly selected 100 American firms based on *Fortune 500* and *The Service 500* directories, Michalisin and his colleagues observed that reputation and know-how were correlated to firm performance and were associated with returns above the median of the industry.[18]

Other empirical studies have focused on particular intangibles. For instance, Peter Roberts and Grahame Dowling focused on the impact of reputation on future financial performance. To test the hypothesis, Roberts and Dowling based their analysis on data retrieved from Fortune's *America's Most Admired Corporations* between 1984 and 1998,[19] and linked each firm-year observation to data on profitability, market-to-book value (market value divided by total shareholder's equity) and firm size (total sales). Their results consistently suggested that firms have "a greater chance

---

14. Teece, David J. "Capturing Value from Knowledge Assets: The New Economy, Markets for Know-How, and Intangible Assets." *California Management Review* 40.3 (1998): 55-79.
15. Connor, Tom. "The Resource-Based View of Strategy and Its Value to Practising Managers." *Strategic Change* 11.6 (2002): 307-316.
16. Hall, Richard. "The Strategic Analysis of Intangible Resources." *Strategic Management Journal* 13.2 (1992): 135-144.
17. Hall, Richard. "A Framework Linking Intangible Resources and Capabilities to Sustainable Competitive Advantage." *Strategic Management Journal* 14.8 (1993): 607-618, testing his proposed framework of analysis with six companies. The key identified intangible resources were company reputation, product reputation, employee know-how, perception of quality standards and the ability to manage change.
18. At a statistically significant level, *see* Michalisin, Michael D., Douglas M. Kline and Robert D. Smith. "Intangible Strategic Assets and Firm Performance: A Multi-industry Study of the Resource-Based View." *Journal of Business Strategies* 17.2 (2000): 93-117.
19. The survey determines the overall reputation of each firm and covers Fortune 1000 firms. Roberts and Dowling dataset consisted of 3,141 observations, and not the complete 4,444 firm-year observations, to discard from the sample firms that did not report two consecutive years of data.

of sustaining superior performance over time if they also possess relatively good reputations."[20] Similarly, Rajendra Srivastava and colleagues emphasized that a substantial proportion of the market value of firms listed in *Fortune 500* lied in intangible assets (around 70%). such as reputation, know-how (particularly in relation to customers' needs) or the ability to innovate.[21]

[B] The Inimitability of Intangible Resources

Why might intangible resources become sources of sustained competitive advantage?

The SML, building on the work of Jay Barney, generally considers intangible assets to be sources of competitive advantage because they are: (i) *valuable*, they improve the efficiency and effectiveness of the firm; (ii) *rare*, actual or potential competitors do not *possess* them; (iii) *imperfectly imitable* or *inimitable*, actual or potential competitors cannot *obtain* them; and (iv) there are *no strategic substitutes*.[22]

From a competitive process perspective, the most important of those parameters is arguably the third. While the first two conditions (value and rareness) provide the firm with the opportunity to gain an advantage,[23] the condition of inimitability allows the firm to sustain that advantage and make use of those resources. And inimitability can be generally predicated from intangible resources.

Resources are inimitable when the ability to obtain the resource is, individually or in combination, dependent on historical conditions, the resource exhibits time compression (dis)economies, the link between the resources and the success is causally ambiguous and the resource is socially complex.[24]

Let us focus on each of those elements successively.

First, one cannot explain firm performance independent of its unique history. The ability of a firm to possess and exploit valuable resources depends on its unique "time and place." The performance of a firm might not only depend on the industry structure, but also on the trajectory that the firm has followed in the process and that places it where it is.[25] This historical view of the firm has often been described as path dependence to describe that it is the distinctive path through history of the firm what eventually determines its success or failure.[26]

---

20. Roberts, Peter W. and Grahame R. Dowling. "Corporate Reputation and Sustained Superior Financial Performance." *Strategic Management Journal* 23.12 (2002): 1077-1093.
21. Srivastava, Rajendra K., Tasadduq A. Shervani and Liam Fahey. "Market-Based Assets and Shareholder Value: A Framework for Analysis." *The Journal of Marketing* (1998): 2-18.
22. Barney, Jay B. "Firm Resources and Sustained Competitive Advantage." *Journal of Management* 17.1 (1991): 99-120.
23. As we explained in Chapter 5, market uncertainty dissipated with investment explains the efficient origins of some dominant firms (so-called investor dominant firms).
24. Barney, Jay B. "Firm Resources and Sustained Competitive Advantage." *Journal of Management* 17.1 (1991): 99-120. Dierickx, Ingemar and Karel Cool. "Asset Stock Accumulation and Sustainability of Competitive Advantage." *Management Science* 35.12 (1989): 1504-1511.
25. Barney, Jay B. "Firm Resources and Sustained Competitive Advantage." *Journal of Management* 17.1 (1991): 99-120, 107-108.
26. *See generally* Liebowitz, Stan J. and Stephen E. Margolis. *The Economics of QWERTY: History, Theory, and Policy*. NYU Press, 2002.

Second, the idea of time compression diseconomies means that it requires time to develop the resources that make a firm successful. That is, time is a necessary and non-replaceable function to develop certain firm-related efficiencies. Resources are the cumulative result of specific behaviors over time, and as such the firm that has honed them over time enjoys a time compression economy. On the contrary, to the competitors of the intangible dominant firm these are time compression diseconomies.[27] Competitors must run faster than the successful firm to catch up because the firm tends to become more efficient over time.[28]

Intangible resources belong to this category of firm efficiencies that are necessarily dependent on the passage of time since they need to be cultivated over time. For example, loyalty and reputation must be earned "through *a history* of honest dealings"[29] (emphasis added).

As a result, many intangible resources are generally non-tradable. Non-tradability implies that intangible resources will be built and remain in the firm and generally lose or diminish their value if transferred outside the firm. This imperfect mobility, characteristic of intangible resources, not only determines firm heterogeneity but is also a "cornerstone" of competitive advantage.[30]

Economists outside the strategic management field have also underscored this important insight. Kenneth Arrow submits that intangible resources like trust "have real, practical economic value; they increase the efficiency of the system, enable you to produce more goods or more of whatever values you hold in high esteem. But they are not commodities for which trade on the open market is technically possible or even meaningful."[31] Likewise, Williamson points out that nonphysical resources like specialized training and learning-by-doing economies are rarely tradable.[32] Being non-transferable the firm necessarily accumulates them internally through experience on a learning-by-doing basis.[33] As such, they exhibit positive feedback loops that make the firm building them more efficient as time goes by.[34]

27. Dierickx, Ingemar and Karel Cool. "Asset Stock Accumulation and Sustainability of Competitive Advantage." *Management Science* 35.12 (1989): 1504-1511, 1505 and 1506.
28. Malerba, Franco, et al. "Competition and Industrial Policies in a 'History Friendly' Model of the Evolution of the Computer Industry." *International Journal of Industrial Organization* 19.5 (2001): 635-664.
29. Dierickx, Ingemar and Karel Cool. "Asset Stock Accumulation and Sustainability of Competitive Advantage." *Management Science* 35.12 (1989): 1504-1511, 1505; *see also* Dowling, Grahame R. "Defining and Measuring Corporate Reputations." *European Management Review* 13.3 (2016): 207-223.
30. Peteraf, Margaret A. "The Cornerstones of Competitive Advantage: A Resource-Based View." *Strategic Management Journal* 14.3 (1993): 179-191, 185-186.
31. Arrow, Kenneth J. *The Limits of Organization*. New York: WW Norton & Company, 1974, at p. 23.
32. Williamson, Oliver E. "Transaction-Cost Economics: The Governance of Contractual Relations." *The Journal of Law and Economics* 22.2 (1979): 233-261, at 240. It is not surprising that Williamson paid close attention to these issues as his research on transaction cost economics places the firm at the heart of the inquiry.
33. Dierickx, Ingemar and Karel Cool. "Asset Stock Accumulation and Sustainability of Competitive Advantage." *Management Science* 35.12 (1989): 1504-1511, 1505.
34. Porter, Michael E. "Strategic Interaction: Some Lessons from Industry Histories for Theory and Antitrust Policy" *in* Steven C. Salop (ed.) *Strategy, Predation, and Antitrust Analysis*. Federal Trade Commission, 1981: 449-506, 457.

When a firm acquires another, it will be certain that it has acquired any IPR the target company has. However, it "cannot be certain that he will retain the intangible resources of know-how, culture, or networks which can ultimately 'walk away'."[35] Therefore, while IPR have at times been described as intangible resources, it is the ability to innovate, and not the particular technology, that is truly intangible and generally inimitable.

Relatedly, knowledge or know-how by its own nature cannot be easily purchased and must be built over time within the firm. This is particularly true of organizational knowledge.[36] As evolutionary economists Richard Nelson and Sidley Winter posit, the routine of the successful firm "may involve so much idiosyncratic and 'impacted' tacit knowledge that even successful replication is problematic, let alone imitation from a distance."[37] On the contrary, personal knowledge (embedded in talented personnel) can be hired away.[38]

Third, when the link between resources (and combination thereof) and performance is poorly understood, causal ambiguity exists. Since the exact factors responsible for superior performance are ambiguous their imitation and mobility are strongly limited.[39] The answer to the question "What are the actions that competing firms should take to be as successful as the dominant firm?" is ambiguous.

It is key to recognize that the intangible dominant firm might as well have an incomplete understanding of the reasons for its own success. Moreover, since information about causality could eventually be diffused, imperfect imitability will be further assured when *all* firms (both the rivals and the more superior firm) have an imperfect understanding of the link between resources and success.[40]

Economists outside of the strategic management field have also stressed this ambiguity problem. For example, Demsetz described that when dealing with large and complex enterprises, "it may be very difficult for these firms to understand the reasons for this difference in performance or to know to which inputs to attribute the

35. Hall, Richard. "The Strategic Analysis of Intangible Resources." *Strategic Management Journal* 13.2 (1992): 135-144.
36. Teece, David J. "Strategies for Managing Knowledge Assets: The Role of Firm Structure and Industrial Context." *Long Range Planning* 33.1 (2000): 35-54, 36. *See also* at 44 arguing that competitive advantage "depends upon the creation and exploitation of difficult-to-replicate non-tradable assets."
37. Nelson, Richard R. and Sidney G. Winter. *An Evolutionary Theory of Economic Change*. The Belknap Press of Harvard University Press, 1982, at p. 124.
38. Teece, David J. "Strategies for Managing Knowledge Assets: The Role of Firm Structure and Industrial Context." *Long Range Planning* 33.1 (2000): 35-54.
39. Lippman, Steven A. and Richard P. Rumelt. "Uncertain Imitability: An Analysis of Interfirm Differences in Efficiency under Competition." *The Bell Journal of Economics* (1982): 418-438; Reed, Richard and Robert J. Defillippi. "Causal Ambiguity, Barriers to Imitation, and Sustainable Competitive Advantage." *Academy of Management Review* 15.1 (1990): 88-102; Fernández, Esteban, José M. Montes and Camilo J. Vázquez. "Typology and Strategic Analysis of Intangible Resources: A Resource-Based Approach." *Technovation* 20.2 (2000): 81-92.
40. Barney, Jay B. "Firm Resources and Sustained Competitive Advantage." *Journal of Management* 17.1 (1991): 99-120, 109.

performance of the successful firm. It is not easy to ascertain just why G.M. and I.B.M. perform better than their competitors."[41]

Lastly, the ambiguity problem leads us to the closely related issue of social complexity. Intangible resources, such as the relationship between managers, the firm's reputation among customers, or the culture of the firm, are socially complex.[42]

Unlike physical technology, these socially complex resources cannot be reverse-engineered or easily imitated.[43] Thus, competing firms observing that certain social relationships among employees improve a firm's efficiency cannot systematically recreate those conditions in their organizations.[44] Consequently, when the successful exploitation of a technology involves socially complex firm resources, the mere possession of the same technology need not necessarily be linked to its successful exploitation.[45]

Social complexity also implies that a company's success rarely lies in an individual. On the contrary, success is the result of complex individual interactions within an organizational and evolutionary routine. Simply poaching talented personnel from the successful firm will often prove an unsuccessful strategy.[46] It is the organizational capabilities of the firm that make it more efficient than the sum of its parts.[47]

[C] Intangible Dominance and the Cumulative Characteristic of the Competitive Process

The preceding examination of intangible resources and their characteristic inimitability highlights the inevitable effect that *ex ante* processes have in subsequent firm performance. Firm dominance might arise because intangible resources are inimitable efficiencies that *accumulate* over preceding processes that are path dependent, causally ambiguous and socially complex.[48]

The managerial implication from these insights is clear. Firms should focus on building those idiosyncratic skills and resources.[49] But what public policy implication

41. Demsetz, Harold. "Industry Structure, Market Rivalry, and Public Policy." *The Journal of Law and Economics* 16.1 (1973): 1-9, 2.
42. Itami, Hiroyuki and Thomas W. Roehl. *Mobilizing Invisible Assets*. Harvard University Press, [1991] 2009, 23. The complexity and ambiguity of organizational culture is illustrated by the often-used phrase "organization's chemistry."
43. Nelson, Richard R. and Sidney G. Winter. *An Evolutionary Theory of Economic Change*. The Belknap Press of Harvard University Press, 1982, at p. 123.
44. Barney, Jay B. "Firm Resources and Sustained Competitive Advantage." *Journal of Management* 17.1 (1991): 99-120, 110.
45. *Id.*
46. Fernández, Esteban, José M. Montes and Camilo J. Vázquez. "Typology and Strategic Analysis of Intangible Resources: A Resource-Based Approach." *Technovation* 20.2 (2000): 81-92, 87.
47. Chandler, Alfred D. *Strategy and Structure: Chapters in the History of the Industrial Enterprise*. MIT Press, 1990, at p. 15.
48. Barney, Jay B. "Resource-Based Theories of Competitive Advantage: A Ten-Year Retrospective on the Resource-Based View." *Journal of Management* 27.6 (2001): 643-650.
49. Dierickx, Ingemar and Karel Cool. "Asset Stock Accumulation and Sustainability of Competitive Advantage." *Management Science* 35.12 (1989): 1504-1511.

can we draw from this point? How should these findings improve our understanding of the competitive process?

In this section, we reexamine these four teachings from the literature to improve our understanding of how competition works as an efficient process in selecting dominant firms. In this context, we further explore how *path dependencies* and *time compression economies* are important and are generally efficient features of the competitive process.

[1] Path Dependence and Reputation

The concept of path dependence can be described with a casual aphorism: "history matters."

A series of papers in the 1980s by Brian Arthur and Paul David triggered the study of path dependence. Arthur's theory suggested that in selection processes with increasing returns "small events" could lead to the selection and lock-in of less efficient outcomes among competing technologies. As the particular technology leapfrogs its competitors, thanks to razor-thin (random) events, the payoff of adopting the technology could change considerably and be thrust to dominate the market.[50] An often-cited example of this phenomenon is the QWERTY keyboard configuration.

In the early days of the typewriting industry (1860s), Sholes, the owner of the typewriter patent, arranged his keyboard to prevent the type bars from getting jammed when struck in close succession. Those keys more likely to be struck in close succession were placed at opposite sides of the machine. This arrangement gave rise to the QWERTY configuration.

In what became to be known as "the economics of QWERTY," David followed Arthurs' theory to demonstrate that the typewriting industry had been prematurely locked-in "*on the wrong*" keyboard configuration (emphasis original). The reason for this was that QWERTY benefited from "*technical interrelatedness*, *economies of scale*, and *quasi-irreversibility* of investment."

In David's view, QWERTY was an inefficient path "*prematurely*" selected over the allegedly better keyboard configuration patented by August Dvorak—the Dvorak Simplified Keyboard (DSK). In support of the more efficient DSK solution, David claimed a study from the Navy "had shown that the increased efficiency obtained with DSK would amortize the cost of retraining a group of typists within the first ten days of their subsequent full-time employment."[51] And that was that.

In response to David's paper, Stan Liebowitz and Stephen Margolis sought to undertake a detailed historical record of the industry.[52] They found that much of the QWERTY-DSK story put forward by David did not survive scrutiny. First, the evidence

50. Arthur, W. Brian. "On Competing Technologies and Historical Small Events: The Dynamics of Choice under Increasing Returns." *IIASA Working Paper* WP-83-90 (1983).
51. David, Paul A. "Clio and the Economics of QWERTY." *The American Economic Review* 75.2 (1985): 332-337, 336.
52. Liebowitz, Stan J. and Stephen E. Margolis. "The Fable of the Keys." *The Journal of Law and Economics* 33.1 (1990): 1-25.

of the Navy study had many possible biases to be conclusive and affect its credibility.[53] Furthermore, even studies carried out by Dvorak himself showed mixed results.[54]

Second, Liebowitz and Margolis' review of the ergonomics literature found no significant support to conclude that Dvorak's configuration was superior to QWERTY.

Third, there was vigorous competition among producers of typewriters. This excluded the possibility that QWERTY was the only solutions available. In fact, as David accounts Sholes was the fifty-second person to invent the typewriter.[55]

Fourth, and relatedly, typing competitions of speed were a fairly common event at that time. Although the results of the contests cannot be standardized to be compared to one another their existence shows that more than just a "small event" caused QWERTY's dominance.

Although David wrote several articles in response to Liebowitz and Margolis' critic, he did not rebut the historical correctness of their research. Instead, David's papers are rather a repositioning of his views and refinement of the *theory* and accompanying definitions.[56] On the one hand, in his 1985 paper David concluded to believe that "there are many more QWERTY worlds lying out there in the past."[57] In general terms, this meant that he believed path-dependent market failures to abound. However, in 1997, David seemed to recognize that the inefficiency story was a tactic to get attention: "What is the subject that jolts economists even more than mention of Sex? Inefficiency! So, I would have to produce a story involving an economic process ... that would be judged to be no better for some, and for others definitely worse than a feasible alternative."[58] Later on, in 2007, David clarified that path dependence does not necessarily imply "the existence or non-existence of 'market failure'."[59]

These clarifications are welcome. Indeed, path-dependent process might result in either efficient or inefficient outcomes. However, to simply conclude that a certain lock-in is a market failure one must present a historical comparative.[60] Such an analysis

53. Liebowitz and Margolis identify several methodological flaws. In particular, the selection of the study groups was based on unclear parameters (most certainly non-random), and there were inconsistent measurements that artificially reduced the measured values in typing-speed on QWERTY. Furthermore, there were also strong potential conflicts of interest. August Dvorak was Lieutenant Commander, and "the Navy's top expert in the analysis of time and motion studies during World War II." *See* Liebowitz, Stan J. and Stephen E. Margolis. "The Fable of the Keys." *The Journal of Law and Economics* 33.1 (1990): 1-25, 10-12.

54. *Id.* at 9: The "study really establishes only that to find studies in which students learning to type on Qwerty appear to have progressed less rapidly in terms of calendar Dvorak's students did on his keyboard." Dvorak's studies also compared students of different ages and abilities.

55. David, Paul A. "Clio and the Economics of QWERTY." *The American economic review* 75.2 (1985): 332-337, 333 and 334.

56. Durlauf, Steven N. "Complexity and Empirical Economics." *The Economic Journal* 115.504 (2005): 225-243.

57. David, Paul A. "Clio and the Economics of QWERTY." *The American economic review* 75.2 (1985): 332-337, 336.

58. David, Paul A. "Path Dependence and the Quest for Historical Economics: One More Chorus of the Ballad of QWERTY." *Discussion Papers in Economic and Social History No. 20* (November 1997): 1-48, 9.

59. David, Paul A. "Path Dependence: A Foundational Concept for Historical Social Science." *Cliometrica* 1.2 (2007): 91-114, 103.

60. Sydow, Jörg, Georg Schreyögg and Jochen Koch. "Organizational Path Dependence: Opening the Black Box." *Academy of Management Review* 34.4 (2009): 689-709.

must explain why it was foreseeable and feasible that at time *t*-1 a more-efficient market path was taken. On the contrary, there can be no market inefficiency if at that time the market could not have done better with the available information at hand.[61] To do otherwise would be to judge the market outcome under the nirvana approach where the ideal norm is compared to some alleged "imperfection" instead of comparing real alternative arrangements.[62]

The strength of path dependency remains an empirical question.[63] However, as explored in SML, intangible resources can generally be regarded as *efficient* path-dependent cumulative experiences that tend to provide competitive advantage due to their imperfect inimitability. Reputation or knowledge cannot be traded in the market but must be built *over time*.[64] As such, intangible resources allow the firm to perform more efficiently over time due to their positive self-reinforcing nature.[65]

Think about knowledge. The more Google's search algorithm learns about search preferences (knowledge), the easier it becomes for Google to offer better results. As Sidak and Teece casually put it, "success breeds success."[66] This does not mean that *other* technologies will be unable to come and disrupt Google's algorithm. It emphasizes that while a firm trying to compete on the same terms as Google might find itself at an inevitable disadvantage this will not constitute an antitrust-relevant market failure.

Similarly, in a context of path dependence, the reputation of a firm is an efficient source of market power. In a world of imperfect information and uncertainty, reputation summarizes information about the firm's past actions, and thus, the benefits the customer can expect to derive from the intangible dominant firm.[67] Indeed, reputation

61. Liebowitz, Stan J. and Stephen E. Margolis. "Path Dependence, Lock-in, and History." *The Journal of Law, Economics, & Organization* 11.1 (1995): 205-226.
62. *See* Chapter 5 further discussing the pitfalls of EU competition enforcement under the nirvana approach (Demsetz, Harold. "Information and Efficiency: Another Viewpoint." *The Journal of Law & Economics* 12.1 (1969): 1-22). *See also* Chapter 8 for a discussion on the anticompetitive acquisition of dominance as an area where EU competition displays an enforcement gap which is not aligned with its objective of protecting the competitive process.
63. Sidak, J. Gregory and David J. Teece. "Dynamic Competition in Antitrust Law." *Journal of Competition Law and Economics* 5.4 (2009): 581-631, 617, 608, emphasizing that the firm's learning builds on previous experiences.
64. Teece, David J., Gary Pisano and Amy Shuen. "Dynamic Capabilities and Strategic Management." *Strategic Management Journal* 18.7 (1997): 509-533, 528.
65. Vergne, Jean-Philippe and Rodolphe Durand. "The Path of Most Persistence: An Evolutionary Perspective on Path Dependence and Dynamic Capabilities." *Organization Studies* 32.3 (2011): 365-382.
66. Sidak, J. Gregory and David J. Teece. "Dynamic Competition in Antitrust Law." *Journal of Competition Law & Economics* 5.4 (2009): 581-631, 608. As Sidak and Teece rightly point out, the increased probability of further success also holds in the case of "*cumulative* technological advances" (emphasis added).
67. Roberts and Dowling follow Fombrun's definition reputations is "a perceptual representation of a company's past actions and future prospects that describe the firm's overall appeal to all its key constituents when compared to other leading rivals." *See* Fombrun, Charles. *Reputation*. John Wiley & Sons, 1996, at p. 72, *quoted in* Roberts, Peter W. and Grahame R. Dowling. "Corporate Reputation and Sustained Superior Financial Performance." *Strategic Management Journal* 23.12 (2002): 1077-1093, 1078. *See also* Teece, David J., Gary Pisano and Amy Shuen. "Dynamic Capabilities and Strategic Management." *Strategic Management Journal* 18.7 (1997): 509-533, 521.

can only be built over time, and thus, it is determined by the value of the firm's previous choices.[68]

Reputation is critical in a dynamic setting like a competitive process. If a market participant sells its product only once, it would be more profitable to behave dishonestly. For example, the firm could disguise its product to be of more quality than it actually is and/or to inflate its price without fear of subsequent retaliation as the market was just that one transaction. However, in a market where the process of acquiring a position of market power takes time and is dependent on previous paths, future rewards will generally discipline the prospective dominant firm to not behave dishonestly. Reputation is thus valuable to present and future customers because it signals the underlying quality of the firm. Such quality need not only represent the technological superiority of a firm's product or services but might also include lower contractual hazards of enforcement and monitoring the transaction.[69]

These intangible benefits, which are a source of market efficiency, might determine the success of a firm that need not be technologically superior in quantifiable terms. Thus, for example, when Godiva, the Belgian chocolate manufacturer, decided to enter the East European and Middle Eastern markets, it did so more successfully than other multinational rivals like Nestlé and Milka because of the long and strong trust-based relationships it had with Ülker, a Turkish food manufacturer.[70]

[2] Time Compression and Experience

A firm wanting to compete (by imitation) with the intangible dominant firm needs time to develop those resources that the dominant firm has already built up. When time compression diseconomies are large, the dominant firm will sustain its unique source of competitive advantage for a longer time.

A snapshot look into a market will often forego time compression effects and paint the intangible resources of the dominant firm as a market failure. Static antitrust enforcement will fright seeing that competitors are at a disadvantage vis-à-vis the successful dominant firm because they do not have the same resources (!). On the contrary, a process-oriented perspective looks into time compression effects to show that the dominant firm also built resources that necessarily required time to become a source of efficiency. In other words, they were also a diseconomy for the firm when it started developing but developed as a source of efficiency as time went by.

68. Podolny and Phillips explain that reputation and status are both derived from past added value. It is in this respect that "market exchanges are not only important as conduits of resources and goods, but as determinants of identity." *See* Podolny, Joel M. and Damon J. Phillips. "The Dynamics of Organizational Status." *Industrial and Corporate Change* 5.2 (1996): 453-471, 453-454.
69. Roberts, Peter W. and Grahame R. Dowling. "Corporate Reputation and Sustained Superior Financial Performance." *Strategic management journal* 23.12 (2002): 1077-1093.
70. Kamasak, Rifat. "The Contribution of Tangible and Intangible Resources, and Capabilities to a Firm's Profitability and Market Performance." *European Journal of Management and Business Economics* 26.2 (2017): 252-275.

This is important because the wording employed in the literature can hide the dynamic nature of these effects. It is not the first firm that "*possesses*" certain resources that succeeds (*t*). Rather, it is the first firm that manages to *build up over time* certain resources that eventually acquires a competitive advantage. Similarly, one cannot simply state that a market has "tilted" in favor of a particular firm. Rather, it is the firm that *progresses toward* successful entry, and it is that process that can help explain the observed outcome.

Freek Vermeulen explains this dynamic with an evocative and easy-to-relate example. As a kid he used to play the cello. Every Saturday morning, he would attend his cello lessons where he would show his teacher how he had progressed and eventually get a new piece to study. He would usually practice three hours a week: 30 minutes per day for six days. Yet, sometimes, he would miss his routine and try to catch up on Friday by practicing three hours in a row. Unsurprisingly, compressing those three hours in one day never worked.[71] It takes time. There is no shortcut. But once the ability to play the cello has been developed, one may give a concert.

Intangible resources are like cello practice. They tend to exhibit compression (dis)economies because they need particular paces and rhythms of time to develop.[72] Those firms that have not yet developed the resource cannot simply compress time and develop them on equal terms as the intangible dominant firm. For example, a firm investing the same amount in research one year as the leading firm spent over the past *n* years will not suffice it to catch up. *It requires time to do it right*, not only a correspondingly proportionate investment. This might explain why crash R&D programs tend to be less effective than R&D programs that are developed over longer periods of time.[73]

When the pace of experience is too fast, managers will tend to be unable to lock-in that experience and convert it into a meaningful advantage. In the context of M&A, Kathleen Eisenhardt and Jeffrey Martin explain that "too many acquisitions done too frequently impaired managers' ability to absorb the lessons of any particular acquisition."[74]

---

71. Vermeulen, Freek. "Slow and Steady Wins the Growth Race." *Harvard Business Review* (February 2009).
72. Vermeulen, Freek and Harry Barkema. "Pace, Rhythm, and Scope: Process Dependence in Building a Profitable Multinational Corporation." *Strategic Management Journal* 23.7 (2002): 637-653; and Eisenhardt, Kathleen M. and Jeffrey A. Martin. "Dynamic Capabilities: What Are They?" *Strategic Management Journal* (2000): 1105-1121.
73. Dierickx, Ingemar and Karel Cool. "Asset Stock Accumulation and Sustainability of Competitive Advantage." *Management Science* 35.12 (1989), 1504-1511; and Cool, Karel, Ingemar Dierickx and Gonçalo Pacheco de Almeida. "Diseconomies of Time Compression." *INSEAD Faculty & Research Working Paper* 78/ST (2012).
74. Eisenhardt, Kathleen M. and Jeffrey A. Martin. "Dynamic Capabilities: What Are They?" *Strategic Management Journal* (2000): 1105-1121; and Vermeulen, Freek and Harry Barkema. "Pace, Rhythm, and Scope: Process Dependence in Building a Profitable Multinational Corporation." *Strategic Management Journal* 23.7 (2002): 637-653. Relatedly, Taleb explains that too-high rates of change prevent the lock-in of the benefits of previous changes. *See* Taleb, Nassim Nicholas. *Antifragile: Things that Gain from Disorder.* Random House Incorporated, 2012, and *Skin in the Game: Hidden Asymmetries in Daily Life.* Allen Lande, 2018, at p. 145.

In a study concerning fertility clinics, Kannan Srikanth and Mihaela Stan analyzed data of successful in-vitro fertilization cases of all UK clinics from 1998 to 2006.[75] Srikanth and Stan showed that compressing the accumulation of experience negatively impacted learning. Moreover, the results also showed that time compression further impaired the ability of fertility clinics to deal with complex cases. Success was a measure of live-birth events at a clinic per year. Experience accumulation was represented by the number of years since each firm was set up. Since success decreases abruptly after age 35, complexity was measured by reference to the number of female patients above that age treated in the clinic. Interestingly, time compression diseconomies were mitigated when the clinic had a nurse or physician in charge of coordinating the different fertility specialists involved in the treatment of a patient.[76] Thus, this shows that firms within the same industry can be subject to different levels of time compression diseconomies depending on the managerial resources they decide to deploy.[77]

An intangible dominant firm that has overcome time compression diseconomies validates the existence superior unseen efficiencies. As Edith Penrose explains, superior firms that have *accumulated* valuable experience and take advantage of those intangible efficiencies "are not 'monopolistic' in a restrictive sense, nor are they easily removable—they are corollaries of size, experience, and successful past."[78]

[D] Summation

Firms are heterogeneous in the resources they have developed over time. Among those resources intangible capabilities are often unseen efficiencies that might be critical enough so as to confer significant competitive advantages.

As long as intangible resources remain unseen, certain elements of the competitive process will remain misunderstood. Hence, apparent "market failures" will thus mistakenly seek to be corrected. It is in this regard that the historicity of the firm, affected by path-dependence and the accumulation of economies over time, is deemed critical to understand firm performance.[79]

75. All UK clinics are obliged to report data to the UK Human Fertilization and Embryology Authority.
76. In-vitro fertilization requires different medical personnel at different stages of the process: gynecologist, embryologist, endocrinologist and nursing.
77. Srikanth, Kannan and Mihaela Stan. "Taking Time to Do It Right: The Impact of Time-Compressing Experience Accumulation on Organizational Quality Outcomes" *in* Proceedings of the 35th DRUID Celebration Conference 2013 in Barcelona (2013): 1-31.
78. Penrose, Edith T. *The Theory of the Growth of the Firm*. Oxford University Press, [1959] 2009, at p. 192. This in stark contrast with mainstream economics that consider a firm's learning curve as efficiency enhancing but continue to describe it as a barrier to entry. *See, e.g.*, Cabral, Luis and Michael H. Riordan. "The Learning Curve, Predation, Antitrust, and Welfare." *The Journal of Industrial Economics* 45.2 (1997): 155-169, 167: "However, it is noteworthy that a learning curve creates a barrier to entry. Firm A has an advantage over an entrant because it has already moved down its learning curve."
79. This is in stark contrast to IO literature where the firm and the market are largely seen in ahistorical terms. *See* Greene, Hilary and Dennis A. Yao. "The Influences of Strategic Management on Antitrust Discourse." *The Antitrust Bulletin* 59.4 (2014): 789-825, 796-797.

§6.03 INTANGIBLE RESOURCES AND UNILATERAL FIRM BEHAVIOR

The insights of the process-oriented approach of SML have remained somewhat disconnected from antitrust policy. Some scholars have rightly aimed at downplaying market structure as a determinant of innovation. If competition is a path and time dependent process where firms accumulate different resources, then it is rather a firm's resources that have a strong influence on "the rate and direction of innovation."[80]

Other strategy scholars have examined the value of the strategic management insights in the context of market definition or the assessment of horizontal mergers. For example, Guilherme Monteiro and Nicolai Foss explain that by focusing on demand substitutability in the delineation of antitrust markets, one could wrongfully disregard a firm's resources to compete, which belong to the supply side function.[81] This creates an unwarranted separation between market definition and the identification of potential competition, and incidentally of the assessment of dominance.[82]

A similar separation occurs between the Commission's enquiry into the intangible resources of the dominant firm and the assessment of anticompetitive behavior. Indeed, while experience, reputation, know-how or innovation record and capabilities are used to describe a firm's market power, their descriptive character does not bear on the substantive analysis of behavior. Once they have been used to place a firm under severe antitrust scrutiny they are bygones.

In this section, we explore how the enforcement of Article 102 TFEU against dominant firms would be more process-oriented if it were to take those intangible resources into account in the assessment of anticompetitive behavior.[83]

[A] *Competitive* Asymmetries

As we saw in Chapter 5, mainstream economics (and contestability theory in particular) sees a market failure in need of correction in a situation in which entrants must incur a sunk cost that the dominant firm does not. In other words, symmetry between an incumbent and a potential entrant guarantees market contestability and requires no intervention.

80. Sidak, J. Gregory and David J. Teece. "Dynamic Competition in Antitrust Law." *Journal of Competition Law and Economics* 5.4 (2009): 581-631, 590.

81. Monteiro, Guilherme Fowler A. and Nicolai Foss. "Resources and Market Definition: Rethinking the 'Hypothetical Monopolist' from a Resource-Based Perspective." *Managerial and Decision Economics* 39.3 (2018): 346-353. *See also* Greene, Hilary and Dennis A. Yao. "The Influences of Strategic Management on Antitrust Discourse." *The Antitrust Bulletin* 59.4 (2014): 789-825.

82. Broos, Sébastien and Jorge Marcos Ramos. "Competing Business Models and Two-Sidedness: An Application to the Google Shopping Case." *The Antitrust Bulletin* 62.2 (2017): 382-399, 399: "competition authorities ought to focus also on supply side substitution in defining the boundaries of the relevant market. The supply side should not only play the role of 'potential competition' once market shares have been calculated on the basis of demand-consumer substitution."

83. Barney, Jay B. "Competence Explanations of Economic Profits in Strategic Management" *in* Jerome Ellig (ed.) *Dynamic Competition and Public Policy: Technology, Innovation, and Antitrust Issues*. Cambridge University Press, 2001.

On the other hand, strategic management scholars have identified that most resources create an asymmetry between the incumbent and the potential entrant because they are the result of cumulative path and time dependent processes.[84] Put differently, the competitive process is about asymmetry forged in cumulative advances. Resources that the dominant firm has developed and accumulated over time cannot be expected from potential entrants. Paradoxically, however, it is their possession that fuels the competitive process.[85] EU competition enforcement fails to see this.

In a historical account of the microchip industry, Gonçalo Pacheco and Peter Zemsky showed that Intel had been revealing information to its rivals about its microprocessor technology up until 1985. Intel's strategy had the effect of incentivizing rivals to adopt a "wait-and-imitate" behavior. This was particularly the case with AMD, which developed its technology based on Intel's specifications.[86] A competition authority would be generally pleased with such state of affairs for it diminished asymmetry in technological information and experience. However, *homogeneity* in technological knowledge only decreased competitive pressure under the illusion of a structurally competitive market.

In 1985, with the introduction of the i386 microprocessor, Intel stopped sharing its new designs. Initially this caused AMD to lag between four and five years behind Intel to bring microprocessors to market by way of reverse-engineer. By way of comparison, under the "wait-and-imitate" strategy AMD's development time was two years. However, after several years of reverse engineering, AMD abandoned its strategy and in 1996, it launched its own first microprocessor K5, and a year later the K6. By the end of 1998, 37% of the sub-USD 1,000 computers' category sold in the US came with AMD.[87] Intel's decision to stop disclosing its microprocessor technology prompted an "aggressive competition for the first time in years."[88]

When competitive advantage revolves around non-tradable resources, such as experience, managerial capabilities, or know-how, competitors are constrained to build it.[89] This insight places certain competition theories of harm, such as refusals to supply, under duress. Imposing an obligation to supply an intangible resource will not close the competitive gap between the entrant and the incumbent. Intangible resources

84. Lockett, Andy and Steve Thompson. "The Resource-Based View and Economics." *Journal of Management* 27.6 (2001): 723-754, 746-747.
85. Sidak, J. Gregory and David J. Teece. "Dynamic Competition in Antitrust Law." *Journal of Competition Law and Economics* 5.4 (2009): 581-631, 608.
86. Pacheco de Almeida, Gonçalo and Peter B. Zemsky. "Some Like It Free: Innovators' Strategic Use of Disclosure to Slow Down Competition." *Strategic Management Journal* 33.7 (2012): 773-793.
87. *Id. See also* Chapter 5, explaining how imposing an obligation to supply diverts the competitive process.
88. Malik, Om. "Intel's Revenge." *Forbes* (Jan. 14, 1999). Conversely, the regulatory obligation incumbent upon AT&T to provide access to its network put an end the existing rivalrous competition to provide universal access in the US. *See* Chapter 4 for a discussion of AT&T's creation of a "natural monopoly."
89. Dierickx, Ingemar and Karel Cool. "Asset Stock Accumulation and Sustainability of Competitive Advantage." *Management Science* 35.12 (1989): 1504-1511, 1509.

cannot be shared and transferred without losing their superiority.[90] Superior performance is unique to the firm. It is inseparable from the firm as it is the result of complex and cumulative path and time-dependent processes. Thus, an obligation to *share* the intangible input will destroy the capabilities that are a critical source of efficiency and have little impact in the success of potential entrants.[91] Furthermore, obliging to share what is not the actual source of competitive advantage could anesthetize true rivalrous competition and encourage a "wait-and-imitate" strategy instead of encouraging firms to develop their unique source of competitive advantage.

[B] The Expansion of Intangible Dominance and *Google Shopping*

Competition policy is concerned with the expansion of dominant firms into other markets. As the Commission consistently emphasized in its *Google Shopping* decision, "the *use* of a dominant position on one market to extend that dominant position to one or more adjacent markets can constitute an abuse" (emphasis added).[92]

This concern seems to exist because the expansion of a dominant firm into other markets is regarded as a "vicious circle"[93] rather than a "virtuous circle." Because a dominant company can use its market power to increase the odds of success in a new market, this places its rivals at a disadvantage.

While we have argued that such concern is particularly warranted in the case of statutory monopolies,[94] we have likewise cautioned against it in the presence of an investor dominant firm.[95] Now, looking into the intangible sources of market power further supports our claim in the latter sense. That is, the use of intangible market power to expand that power into other markets is a *virtuous* competitive cycle.

To support the virtuous nature of such expansion one must look into the origins of dominance. Theories like self-favoring, discrimination or tying remain incomplete without asking also whether the market power being *used* is the result of an efficient allocation of scarce resources. To ask this question is to scrutinize a firm behavior in a

90. Woodcock, Ramsi A. "Inconsistency in Antitrust." *University of Miami Law Review* 68.1 (2013): 105-188, 141-142, n. 88, calling this phenomenon of essential inputs that lose its superiority if shared "the problem of natural monopoly."
91. Demsetz argues that when teams of employees, knowledge, reputation or goodwill constitute a firm's source of superior performance the only "solution" is to acquire the firm itself. *See* Demsetz, Harold. "Industry Structure, Market Rivalry, and Public Policy." *The Journal of Law and Economics* 16.1 (1973): 1-9, 2. Even if transferring or sharing those intangible resources may improve the position of the complainant, sharing destroys a degree of efficiency for the sake of some equality of outcome.
92. Commission Decision, Case COMP/39.740, *Google Search (Shopping)*, §649, *also* §§334, 652 and 727.
93. De Streel, Alexandre. "Remedies in the European Electronic Communications Sector" *in* Damien Geradin (ed.) *Remedies in Network Industries: EC Competition Law vs Sector-specific regulation*. Antwerp: Intersentia, 2004, at p. 94.
94. *See* Chapter 2.
95. *See* Chapter 5.

process-oriented manner where history matters[96] and requires taking into account the sources of market power.

When the dominant firm uses its intangible resources to build up competitive advantage in another market the answer seems clear. The ability to leverage within a firm from one part of their business to another is an essential driver of competition, not an anticompetitive behavior. From a process perspective, where resources are accumulated over path- and time-dependent processes and imitation is unlikely due to causal ambiguity, to hinder the dominant firm in the use of its resource base to enter new products is radically at odds with the competitive process.[97] *Ad absurdum*, the opposite rationale would require the dominant firm to forget all skills and capabilities developed *ex ante* that could help it gain an advantage over its rivals in any subsequent competition.

In the Commission's assessment of Google's leverage into the online shopping comparison market, it does not matter that Google's success in search is the result of the accumulation of data over time,[98] that consumers confidently rely on Google's reputation to deliver relevant search results,[99] or that it constantly invests more than its competitors to improve its services.[100] All these efficiencies achieved and accumulated over time are bygones in the Commission's final conclusion that Google must treat its rivals as it treats its own subsidiary. The Commission thus turns a blind eye on the competitive process when it concludes in *Google Shopping* that "the reasons or the causes for which Google has a dominant position on the national markets for general search services are irrelevant."[101]

But, to require under Article 102 TFEU that an intangible dominant firm treat one of its business units in the same manner as rivals is to neglect that exchange inside the firm necessarily occurs in a different manner than outside the firm.[102] As we have explored above, and Teece and his colleagues summarize, "the very essence of most capabilities/competences is that they cannot be readily assembled through markets."[103]

This is particularly true of intangible resources that need to be built and accumulated over time within the firm and as a result are generally non-tradable.[104] An intangible dominant firm that exploits its resources behaves in an efficient and effective manner. If it were not to, those idiosyncratic resources that the firm has developed over time would remain underutilized and negatively affect total welfare.[105]

96. Lockett, Andy and Steve Thompson. "The Resource-Based View and Economics." *Journal of Management* 27.6 (2001): 723-754, 2001 726.
97. *Id.* 740.
98. Commission Decision, Case COMP/39.740, *Google Search (Shopping)*, §§286 and 287.
99. *Id.* §§312 and 538.
100. *Id.* §291.
101. *Id.* §315.
102. Teece, David J., Gary Pisano and Amy Shuen. "Dynamic Capabilities and Strategic Management." *Strategic Management Journal* 18.7 (1997): 509-533, 517.
103. *Id.*
104. This is unless the firm or business unit is bought. *See id.* 518.
105. *See* Barney, Jay B. "Firm Resources and Sustained Competitive Advantage." *Journal of Management* 17.1 (1991): 99-120, 116: "In this sense, the higher levels of performance that accrue to a firm with resource advantages are due to the efficiency of these firms in exploiting

It is the ability that intangible dominant firms have to take those intangible resources and leverage them onto new markets that drives competition and innovation.[106] Abundant empirical research shows that the specific pre-entry knowledge and experience firms have built up is key for the successful development of new products in the same or related industries.[107] This is the case in the US automobile, tire, television, and penicillin industries. Steven Klepper showed that the evolution toward oligopoly in these industries selected firms with prior experience.[108] Marco Fontana et al. concluded that also pre-entry experience in related industries like semiconductors is crucial for the survival of start-ups in the US telecommunications industry.[109] Similarly, Klepper and Kenneth Simons showed that firms with experience manufacturing radios were the firms that dominated the US television receiver industry and exhibited higher rates of innovation.[110]

The anticompetitive effects question should thus address whether in using its market power the dominant firm is preventing a more efficient market arrangement than that of the dominant firm *and* its accompanying efficiencies. Likewise, it would also be incumbent on the applicant to demonstrate that the expansion of market power is the expansion of inefficiency. Only a historical look into the paths and choices

---

those advantages, rather than to efforts of firms to create imperfectly competitive conditions that fail to maximize social welfare." *See also* Oberholzer-Gee, Felix and Dennis A. Yao. "Antitrust-What Role for Strategic Management Expertise." *Boston University Law Review* 90 (2010): 1457-1477, 1475. Relatedly, Larouche and Schinkel explain that from a dynamic perspective competition on the merits does not only include innovative products or processes, "but also marketing or business methods." *See* Larouche, Pierre and Maarten Pieter Schinkel. "Continental Drift in the Treatment of Dominant Firms: Article 102 TFEU in Contrast to § 2 Sherman Act." *TILEC Discussion Paper No. 2013-020* (2013): 1-33, 21.

106. Barney, Jay B. "Competence Explanations of Economic Profits in Strategic Management" *in* Jerome Ellig (ed.) *Dynamic Competition and Public Policy: Technology, Innovation, and Antitrust Issues*. Cambridge University Press, 2001.

107. Most of this research concerns US industries due to the large industry and firm population size, a relatively more stable environment compared to Europe during the twentieth century, and the ease to obtain consistent time series. *See* Buenstorf, Guido. "Evolution on the Shoulders of Giants: Entrepreneurship and Firm Survival in the German Laser Industry." *Review of Industrial organization* 30.3 (2007): 179-202, 180. Buenstorf's analysis suggests that in the German laser industry technological knowledge was a less important determinant of successful entry than knowledge about market opportunities and customer needs. Indeed, academic start-ups (assumedly possessing greater technological knowledge) were less long-lived than entrants with market and customer experience.

108. Klepper considered firms as "experienced entrants if they produced the new product in the same organization (with the same name) in which they produced products prior to entry, enabling them to tap into the physical, human, and organizational capital of their firms." *See* Klepper, Steven. "Firm Survival and the Evolution of Oligopoly." *RAND Journal of Economics* (2002): 37-61, 42-43.

109. The reason why semiconductors and the telecommunication industries are related is that semiconductor components incorporate in their chips entire parts of the telecommunication system. *See* Fontana, Roberto, Franco Malerba and Astrid Marinoni. "Pre-entry Experience, Technological Complementarities, and the Survival of De-Novo Entrants. Evidence from the US Telecommunications Industry." *Economics of Innovation and New Technology* 25.6 (2016): 573-593.

110. Klepper, Steven and Kenneth L. Simons. "Dominance by Birthright: Entry of Prior Radio Producers and Competitive Ramifications in the US Television Receiver Industry." *Strategic Management Journal* (2000): 997-1016.

undertaken in the market will provide, on a case-by-case basis, an answer to that question.

[C] The Limits of Centralized Knowledge: *Michelin I* and *Intel*

Technological superiority might be insufficient to challenge the intangible dominant firm. Thus, the present outcome (*t*) is not necessarily the result of the firm's current behavior but it is simply a reflection of the pattern of successful entry into a market. This pattern, according to SML, results in the accumulation of path- and time-dependent resources that are both difficult to disentangle and to quantify. They are a source of efficiency.[111]

In this regard, the intangible nature of certain resources should caution antitrust enforcers against rushed findings of anticompetitive effects. Being unquantifiable does not mean being irrelevant. And quite to the contrary, we have shown that intangible resources are efficient sources of competitive advantage even if they are difficult to quantify or to delineate. Customers choosing between dominant firm A and firm B might chose dominant firm A, even if the *visible* cost to pay for the product of firm B is lower (assuming some production cost advantage) simply because it *perceives* the added value (experience, reputation, potential for innovation, preferred business model, etc.) of transacting with dominant firm A.[112]

This notwithstanding, the EU Courts and the Commission have generally explicitly relinquished to consider the relevance of these perceptions. Indeed, the EU Courts and the Commission have consistently held that a dominant undertaking that enters into an exclusivity agreement "even if it does so at [the] request" of its customers abuses its dominant position.[113] *Michelin I* and *Intel* are two prominent examples of the separation between a firm's intangible resources and the assessment of unilateral behavior.[114]

---

111. Itami, Hiroyuki and Thomas W. Roehl. *Mobilizing Invisible Assets*. Harvard University Press, 1991.
112. Tadelis, Steven. "Reputation and Feedback Systems in Online Platform Markets." *Annual Review of Economics* 8 (2016): 321-340.
113. *See*, CJEU, Case 85/76, *Hoffmann-La Roche v. Commission*, §89; Case C-62/86, *AKZO v. Commission* ECLI:EU:C:1991:286, §§149-150; Case C-552/03 P, *Unilever Bestfoods (formerly Van den Bergh Foods Ltd.) v. Commission*, ECLI:EU:C:2006:607, §92; GC, Case T-155/06, *Tomra*, ECLI:EU:T:2010:370, §208; Case T-286/09, *Intel*, ECLI:EU:T:2014:547, §§72, 123, and 787.
114. *Van Den Bergh Foods* also exemplifies this separation. The Commission explained that HB had a long-established know-how which it had acquired from its extended experience. In fact, the Commission concluded, no other rival "has this degree of relevant knowledge and experience." However, the Commission did not take these intangible resources into account in the analysis of HB's abusive behavior; namely inducing ice-cream retailers to enter into an agreement whereby HB provides a freezer cabinet to store impulse ice-cream subject to a condition of exclusivity. Even if that practice was normal commercial usage and beneficial to both contracting parties, the Commission once again stated that these considerations could "not be unreservedly accepted in a case ... where, because of the dominant position of a firm, the degree of competition is already weakened." *See* Commission Decision, Cases COMP/IV/34.073, IV/34.395 and IV/35.436, *Van den Bergh Foods Limited*, §260 (intangible resources) and §267 (weakened degree of competition).

[1] **Michelin I**

In *Michelin I*,[115] the Commission found that Michelin had abused its dominant position in the tire market by granting a series of individualized and retroactive rebates to its dealers. The rebate scheme, which was not clearly confirmed in writing,[116] "tied" tire dealers to Michelin and foreclosed rivals tire manufacturers.

Before carrying out the assessment of Michelin's rebates, the Commission highlighted in its description of the business context several intangible resources that Michelin possessed. Michelin's basic patents had expired, and it had since 1956 granted manufacturing rights to other firms. Moreover, Michelin "has a special *degree of know-how*" and pursues "an active policy of *research and innovation.*" The experience and innovation capabilities have permitted Michelin to reach new categories of consumers. Further, the Commission emphasized that reputation is critical in the tire market. "It is only after *several years' experience* with tires of a given make that consumers [of lorry tires] can make up their minds on a tire's reliability." This allows well-established brands like Michelin to maintain a strong position.[117] Stocking Michelin tires is commercially prestigious.[118] Lastly, the Commission acknowledged that Michelin's commercial and technical service provides an added value to its customers who receive diverse technical advice, such as the type of tire that must be fitted, recommended tire pressure, checks of tires and state of the vehicles, etc. This service also benefits Michelin who can collect information about competing brands used by its customers. This "*market knowledge* ... rivals that of the specialized trade."[119]

On the whole, one may rightfully characterize Michelin as an intangible dominant firm. However, this descriptive analysis does not bear on the substantive analysis of the abusive character of the rebates. The Commission puts aside all these unquantifiable efficiencies and concludes that competition is not "operating effectively."[120] What "effective" means to the Commission is unclear, but it seems that product reliability, reputation, experience, technical service, and innovative efforts do not form part of its conception. Absent all these unquantifiable efficiencies, the Commission could easily conclude that "dealers would never accept" such rebate scheme if it were imposed by other manufacturers.[121] A straightforward conclusion indeed in the

115. Commission Decision, Case COMP/IV.29.491, *Bandengroothandel Frieschebrug BV/NV Nederlandsche Banden-Industrie Michelin* (*Michelin I*).
116. Following the idea that unilateral behavior by a dominant firm may be abusive even if that conduct is irreproachable when carried by a nondominant firm, the Commission considered that it did "not of course have any objections of principle to the purely oral notification of terms of sale." However, if this method is applied by an undertaking in a dominant position and the terms are complex leading to possible misunderstandings, "this combination of factors amounts to abusive conduct." *See* Commission Decision, Case COMP/IV.29.491, *Michelin I*, §47. In the Commission's eyes, these rebates were not "normal competition" even if they were a common practice in the sector.
117. Commission Decision, Case COMP/IV.29.491, *Michelin I*, §12.
118. *Id.* §35.
119. *Id.* §19.
120. *Id.* §35.
121. *Id.* §48.

absence of said efficiencies. Why would retailers otherwise agree? The Commission did not seek to provide an answer since it had already closed the door to possible intangible explanations.

[2] Intel

Intel had requested the Commission to take into account several documents that allegedly contained important evidence to fully assess the effects of Intel's rebates. Intel claimed these documents showed that AMD had limited ability to compete with Intel and lacked "reputational advantages" vis-à-vis its customers.[122] However, the Commission concluded that the requested documents did not contain "exculpatory evidence" and that Intel's description of the documents was incorrect.[123] Stating that abusive behavior is an objective concept, the Commission concluded that these documents could not "by their very nature ... be considered exculpatory for Intel [since they] relate to questions of AMD's performance."[124] In other words, if there was any market failure this was not AMD's lack of ability to invest in capacity or a reputational disadvantage vis-à-vis its customers.

One cannot properly assess the weight of each claim since the information contained in those documents is partially redacted or unavailable in its entirety. This notwithstanding, the Commission itself included in the assessment of Intel's dominance that "OEMs generally need to have branded computers with Intel x86 CPUs *to satisfy their customers' needs or preferences.*"[125] And quoting the internal document of one OEM the Commission concluded that "[t]he Intel brand has *a stronger reputation* in the professional market than AMD."

Customer's preferences and reputation effects aided the Commission to describe Intel as an "unavoidable trading partner," thus placing it under severe antitrust scrutiny.[126] However, the Commission considered them irrelevant in its assessment of rebates. Following the settled case law, the Commission emphasized that it was unnecessary to take into account the reasons why OEMs might have required the rebates themselves.[127] Reputation effects or customer preferences had no place in the substantive assessment of Intel's behavior.

Paradoxically, this formalistic approach to Intel's rebates is in stark contradiction with the Commission's own assessment that "it is not for the Commission to make absolute judgments on the technical performance of the products at stake, or relative

122. Commission Decision, Case COMP/37.990, *Intel*, §§77, 78 and 80.
123. *Id.* §§64, 77, 78 and 80.
124. *Id.* §65.
125. *Id.* §890.
126. *Id.* §§890-892. We do not discuss here questions concerning investment in capacity. *See* Chapter 5 for a discussion on Intel's investment efforts regarded as relevant antitrust barriers to entry.
127. Indeed the Commission repeated in several occasions that "an undertaking which is in a dominant position on a market and ties purchasers – <u>even if it does so at their request</u> – by an obligation or promise on their part to obtain all or most of their requirements exclusively from the said undertaking" (*Sic*). *See* Commission Decision, Case COMP/ 37.990, *Intel*, §§964 and 1769; *see also id.* §920, without emphasis.

judgments on the comparative performance of AMD and Intel products, either across the board or within certain segments. *OEMs are the best-placed to come to the soundest judgment as regards their supply needs, and the most appropriate products to fulfill those needs*"[128] (emphasis added).

Indeed, a process-oriented enforcement of Article 102 TFEU cannot simply disregard decentralized information but must be taken into account. Whereas the Commission was right to claim in *Intel* that that OEMs were the best-placed to determine their supply needs, (indirectly thus making a product judgment between alternatives), the Commission could not maintain that OEMs' request or acceptance of an exclusivity condition was irrelevant in the assessment of anticompetitive behavior without incurring in a contradiction. Firms transacting in the market under scrutiny own the risk of the transaction and as such they will commonly take into account the intangible benefits of contracting with a given firm. If competitive success depends to a large extent on the intangible resources of each firm, one should be careful to readily find anticompetitive effects where firms are unsuccessful or simply less successful than the intangible dominant firm.

The EU Courts and the Commission should start truly questioning *why* customers enter into or demand exclusivity agreements from the dominant firm, rather than jump into rushed conclusions of (ab-)use of market power.

§6.04 CONCLUSION

Intangible resources are generally inimitable because they depend on historical conditions (path dependence), they need to be built up inside the firm over long periods of time (they are firm-specific and are generally non-tradable), and they are socially complex. They tell us that much of what the firm does is determined by its capabilities and not just by the structure of the market; and that competition is an ongoing process where all market participants learn and accumulate experience. As a surgeon director naturally capitalizes on his previous idiosyncratic experience, know-how or reputation to successfully perform a novel surgery process, when a dominant firm capitalizes on its intangible resources to enter into new markets it behaves in an efficient and effective manner. The enforcement of competition law would benefit from taking into account the intangible origins of dominant firms.

128. *Id.* §1698.

CHAPTER 7

The Lucky Monopolist

§7.01 INTRODUCTION

In August 2004, emerging from the African coast, Hurricane Charley struck the southwest coast of Florida. The hurricane storm carrying winds at up to 130kts (240 km/h) was responsible for numerous deaths and caused USD 15 billion in damage.[1] It also upset the *normal* free market situation and unexpectedly put some of its actors in an advantageous position. In Orlando, a gas station started selling bags of ice cubes at five times the price before the Hurricane disabled the electricity network powering up refrigerators. Contractors offered a homeowner to clear two trees off his roof for USD 23,000. And a family whose house had been destroyed were charged USD 110 per night for a motel room that before the hurricane went for USD 39.[2]

An accident for some and a lucky punch for others, the illustration of Hurricane Charley shows in a simple way that market processes can be strongly affected by unforeseen events. Randomness gains the upper hand over efficient, defective firm behavior or even State intervention. However, its impact in the market suggests that we differentiate efficient and defective competitive processes from dissatisfaction with *lucky* outcomes. And, in the particular field of competition law, we distinguish dominant firms whose market power is the result of "an unusual sequence of fortuitous events."[3] The main question that this chapter is set to answer is whether competition law should be concerned with dominance outcomes caused by random or fortuitous events and how it should handle it. We call this dominant firm the lucky monopolist.

1. Franklin, James L., et al. "Atlantic Hurricane Season of 2004." *Monthly Weather Review* 134.3 (2006): 981-1025.
2. Treaster, Joseph B. "Hurricane Charley: The Economics; With Storm Gone, Floridians Are Hit With Price Gouging." *New York Times*, August 18, 2004.
3. Williamson, Oliver E. "Dominant Firms and the Monopoly Problem: Market Failure Considerations." *Harvard Law Review* 85.8 (1972): 1512-1531.

§7.02 THE PASSIVE ACQUISITION OF DOMINANCE

[A] Who Is the Lucky Monopolist?

The lucky monopolist is not the dominant firm whose power comes from the State or from natural efficiencies. It is also not one that comes from unparalleled investment efforts or from inimitable management ability. Its SMP is not the result of anticompetitive conduct. Then, who is this lucky monopolist? It is the undertaking that profits from "simple, blind, dumb luck."[4] It is the undertaking whose market power results from a random or accidental event.

I want to define what we mean by luck, accident or randomness. These are terms that we will use interchangeably for they all mean the same thing in the context of this chapter.

In short, by luck, accident or randomness, we refer to those events that: (1) are outside the knowledge of the economic actor or its ability to determine the timing of the event; (2) do not require the firm to incur any cost to secure their market position; they are exogenous to the cost functions of the firm; and (3) are meaningful enough to thrust a firm to a position of dominance among existing firms.[5] We explain these features in turn.

First, uncertainty is ubiquitous. Hence, market processes are not free from the opportunities or risks that lucky or accidental events can generate. "By 'uncertain' knowledge, let me explain, I do not mean merely to distinguish what is known for certain from what is only probable. ... These are matters for which] there is no scientific basis on which to form any calculable probability whatever. We simply do not know."[6]

Economic actors do not have access to "infinitely detailed prior knowledge" of the set of circumstances that might affect their prospects.[7] Human action is bound by limited knowledge and business decisions might prove themselves to be wrong speculations if the market develops differently.[8] *Ex ante*, the limited knowledge of economic actors produces indeterminacy as to what the future will bring.[9] With *ex post* detailed knowledge of fortuitous events, it might be easy to tell a story that narrates why the market developed in such an unexpected manner.

---

4. Breyer, Stephen G. "The Problem of the Honest Monopolist." *Antitrust Law Journal* 44.2 (1975): 194-201.
5. Hao Ma gives a similar description of pure luck. Pure luck "refers to the situation where factors exogenous to the firm give raise to competitive advantage spontaneously." *See* Ma, Hao. "Competitive Advantage: What's Luck Got to Do with It?" *Management Decision* 40.6 (2002): 525-536, 526.
6. Keynes, John. M. "The General Theory of Employment." *The Quarterly Journal of Economics* 51.2 (1937): 209-223, 213-214.
7. Arthur, W. Brian. "Competing Technologies, Increasing Returns, and Lock-in by Historical Events." *The Economic Journal* 99.394 (1989): 116-131, 118.
8. von Mises, Ludwig. "Comments about the Mathematical Treatment of Economic Problems." *Journal of Libertarian Studies* 1.2 (1977): 97-100. *See also* Hayek, Friedrich A. "The Pretence of Knowledge." *The American Economic Review* 79.6 (1989): 3-7.
9. *See* Chapter 6 for a discussion on path dependency and efficient outcomes under uncertainty.

Second, *luck is costless*. Not only is it unknown but it is also exogenous to the cost functions of the firm. It is spontaneous. It neither requires the firm to invest nor an adaptive effort from the firm to acquire market power.[10] The lucky monopolist is, paraphrasing Judge Learned Hand, the "passive beneficiary" of a chance event.[11] Thus, the benefits that it derives are not the result of entrepreneurial profits because it did not act deliberately.[12]

Third, the random shock must be meaningful enough so as to confer SMP. On the contrary, luck can also explain why market shares are just that, the result of a random event, rather than the ability to behave monopolistically.

The gas station in Orlando started selling bags of ice cubes for USD 10 instead of USD 2 because a hurricane thrust the gas station with enough market power to set prices five times higher. On the one hand, Hurricane Charley brought unforeseen opportunities to the gas station at no cost. On the other, it also brought unforeseen hazards to the formerly competing gas stations or the electricity network operators.

[B] The Relevance of Luck for Dominance

The economic literature on stochastic determinants of firm growth maintains that increases in firm size *are* driven by random shocks.[13] In an effort to explain industry concentration, Frederic Scherer writes, "Why do concentrated firm size distributions arise from initial conditions that seemingly give each firm an equal chance? The answer, in a word, is luck."[14]

As early as 1950, Armen Alchian described luck as a way of achieving economic success. In the absence of any adaptive behavior of the firm (motivation, rationality and foresight) we can find that it is the environment that *adopts* "appropriate" survivors.[15] Richard Mancke construed a model in which the differences between firms' profit rates were positively correlated with "chance-caused" events at previous points in time. Luck can also be a sensible explanation to observed differences in firm

---

10. Alchian, Armen A. "Uncertainty, Evolution, and Economic Theory." *Journal of Political Economy* 58.3 (1950): 211-221 (removing any "adaptive calculus" from the firm helps assessing role of luck in the market).
11. *United States v. Aluminum Co. of America* ("*Alcoa*"), 148 Fed. 2d 416 (2d Cir. 1945), at 430.
12. Kirzner, Israel M. *Perception, Opportunity, and Profit: Studies in the Theory of Entrepreneurship*. Chicago: University of Chicago Press, 1979, recognizing the role of luck and surprise in the discovery process of competition, but requiring that the firm acts entrepreneurially.
13. An area that was pioneered by Robert Gibrat. Gibrat's law consists of two components explaining firm growth: first, a stochastic component that depends on the known probability distribution of the growth rates, and second, a purely random component dependent on chance. *See* Gibrat, Robert. *Les inegalités économiques*. Paris: Recueil Sirey, 1931. *See also* Chin, Andrew. "Antitrust by Chance: A Unified Theory of Horizontal Merger Doctrine." *The Yale Law Journal* 106.4 (1997): 1165-1195, an early exponent of luck also applying Gibrat's framework to the analysis of horizontal mergers.
14. Scherer, Frederic M. *Industrial Market Structure and Economic Performance*. Houghton Mifflin, 1980, at p. 146.
15. Such "apparently unrealistic" assumption, Alchian writes, "aids in assessing the role of luck and chance in the operation of our economic system." *See* Alchian, Armen A. "Uncertainty, Evolution, and Economic Theory." *Journal of Political Economy* 58.3 (1950): 211-221, 214.

performance together with other, more prevalent, IO explanations.[16] Models of Schumpeterian competition, like that of Richard Nelson and Sidney Winter, argue that the more competitive an industry is, the more luck will be the principal factor that separates "winners from near-winners."[17] Steven Lippman and Richard Rumelt focus on firm entry and explain heterogeneity among firms as randomly generated. Some firms are just luckier than others.[18] And Geroski cautioned econometricians against deceptive unexpected shocks. An unexpected shock which "may be surprising to an econometrician may not, in fact, be very surprising to the managers of the firm it happens to."[19]

Whether random events are the *only* cause of superiority cannot be proved or disproved here. The economic literature has itself not solved this question as several competing theories of firm growth show.[20] However, unobserved variations in luck cannot be the exclusive explanation to all firm differences and growth.[21]

This notwithstanding, the extant literature serves us to underscore that dominance may result from an "unusual run of luck" and that this phenomenon at least warrants particular consideration.[22] After all, if a firm's market power can be determined by a random event, then an appropriate way to think about antitrust policy is to consider how lucky dominance outcomes should be dealt with, and the consequences of doing so.

The fact that more "mainstream" antitrust economics have not looked into this phenomenon should not detract us from our inquiry. Classical economists have not extensively researched luck as a cause of market power because the classical model of monopoly ignores the opportunity costs in setting up monopoly.[23] The classical model indicates that monopoly profit is simply the difference between monopoly revenue and

---

16. Mancke, Richard B. "Causes of Interfirm Profitability Differences: A New Interpretation of the Evidence." *The Quarterly Journal of Economics* 88.2 (1974): 182-193.
17. Nelson, Richard R. and Sidney G. Winter. "Forces Generating and Limiting Concentration under Schumpeterian Competition." *The Bell Journal of Economics* 9.2 (1978): 524-548.
18. Lippman, Steven A. and Richard P. Rumelt. "Uncertain Imitability: An Analysis of Interfirm Differences in Efficiency under Competition." *The Bell Journal of Economics* 13.2 (1982): 418-438.
19. Geroski, Paul A. "The Growth of Firms in Theory and in Practice." *CEPR* Discussion Paper No. 2092 (2002): 1-30.
20. The main theories of firm growth are developed in classical economics (firm growth is part of the quest of classical economists to find the optimum size of the firm), behavioral economics (firm growth is related to the maximization of the utility of management rather than maximization of the firm's value) stochastic economists (increases in firm size are driven by random shocks) and learning/capabilities theory (growth of the firm is related to its ability to learn and adapt to new market circumstances). For a detailed review of competing theories, *see* Teruel Carrizosa, Mercedes. *Firm Growth, Persistence and Multiplicity of Equilibria: An Analysis of Spanish Manufacturing and Service Industries*. PhD thesis, 2006.
21. Caves, Richard E., Bradley T. Gale and Michael E. Porter. "Interfirm Profitability Differences: Comment." *The Quarterly Journal of Economics* 91.4 (1977): 667-675.
22. For a review of the literature on stochastic growth models, *see* Sutton, John. "Gibrat's Legacy." *Journal of Economic Literature* 35 (1997): 40-59.
23. Demsetz explains this by comparing a costly acquired dominant position (by acquisition of its competitors' assets) to a firm that has not incurred any cost in securing its dominant position (by pure luck). *See* Demsetz, Harold. "The Problem of Monopolization." *Working Paper* #243 (June 1982). In a process-oriented fashion, John Sutton explains that maximizing models will decree that, in a natural monopoly scenario, only one firm enters because there is only space for one

the cost of producing the output that yields this revenue. But it does not tell whether it pays off to create a monopoly. As Demsetz writes, "it mistakenly ignores the opportunity cost to monopolization, the value of securable competitive rents."[24] In the case of a lucky dominant firm, this foregone analysis is fundamental.[25]

The lucky monopolist did not incur any costs to secure its position of dominance. This is unlike the case of a firm that acquires competitive assets from its competitors or invests heavily in R&D. Since the cost of acquiring control over prices is zero, the optimal output of the lucky monopolist differs from that of the dominant firm that costly secured its position.[26] Thus, the firm that finds monopoly through pure luck will surely be wealthier than the firm that secures monopoly at some positive cost.[27] The larger profits that the lucky monopolist derives are not the reflection of a return to investment or time-scale economies.

Now, does the lucky dominant firm believe its monopoly is worth maintaining? One could argue that, "if it were not worth buying neither would it be worth maintaining if acquired at no cost."[28] In such a scenario, the lucky monopolist might exploit its position without fear of attracting entry for it knows its dominant position is not worth maintaining at some positive cost.[29]

The case law has also explicitly considered luck as a credible source of SMP. In the EU, the Commission condemned a refusal to supply in the context of the 1972 oil crisis. It considered that exogenous market events had put British Petroleum in a position of dominance vis-à-vis its customers.[30] In the United States, the *Grinnell* Court ruled in favor of the legality of a monopoly resulting from "historical accident."[31] Whether by "historical accident" the Supreme Court had random processes giving birth

firm, but "will be silent on the selection mechanism that choses the lucky firm from among potential entrants." *See* Sutton, John. "Gibrat's Legacy." *Journal of Economic Literature* 35 (1997): 40-59, n. 7.

24. Demsetz, Harold. "The Problem of Monopolization." *Working Paper* #243 (June 1982).
25. Other reasons exist. Randomness diminishes the value of more conventional economic models, hindrances the predictability of economic changes and impairs the ability of policy makers to improve the effectiveness of the market. To explain a phenomenon (such as dominance) as a random outcome is to forsake control.
26. Knight, Frank H. *Risk, Uncertainty and Profit.* New York: Augustus M. Kelly, [1921] 1964, at p. 337: "Discovery of new natural wealth may result from pure accident, in which case its value is all pure profit."
27. Demsetz, Harold. "The Problem of Monopolization." *Working Paper* #243 (June 1982).
28. *Id.*
29. In the alternative, that is, if the dominant firm considers that it is worth maintaining, it will be concerned that high prices attract entry. Furthermore, it might engage in exclusionary practices to put potential competitors at bay when the accidental event has not erected insurmountable barriers to entry.
30. Commission Decision, Case COMP/IV/28.841, *ABG Oil Companies operating in the Netherlands* ("*British Petroleum*").
31. *United States v. Grinnell Corp.*, 384 U.S. 563 (1966), at 570-71. As Lande explains, the language employed by Justice Scalia in *Trinko* is even more pro-monopoly than *Grinnell*. *See* Lande, Robert H. "A Traditional and Textualist Analysis of the Goals of Antitrust: Efficiency, Preventing Theft from Consumers, and Consumer Choice." *Fordham Law Review* 81 (2012): 2349-2403, 2380.

to monopoly positions in mind is something that remains uncertain.[32] This notwithstanding, we are in favor of considering the lucky monopolist as a relevant antitrust phenomenon. After all, it remains a monopoly, and thus it has a certain degree of control over the market[33]—however temporal this control may be.

Process-oriented claims could find this statement overly static. Prospectively, it could be argued that a dominant position acquired by luck is an ephemeral episode. Surely, this could be the case in certain situations. As when heavy rains burst the banks of a river that will soon return to its riverbed, the market will correct the lucky monopolist's power. Market forces will select the most efficient firms and discard the inefficient ones.[34]

But process-oriented claims cannot be solely concerned with how markets will evolve. They also require understanding how markets arrived at the situation that we observe. A position of dominance resulting from a pure chance event shows that its position can be disregarded as a competitive outcome.

The process paradox of EU competition enforcement lies here: it disregards past events that can explain current market conditions in a more accurate way. A random event may have shaped the way the market currently functions. How long its effects will last, i.e., how long the lucky monopolist will retain its position and its incentives to maintain it, will strongly depend on the extent of the accident and industry in which it occurs. Its origin cannot imply superior efficiency or consumer choice.[35]

In his dissent in *Eastman Kodak*, Justice Scalia stated that while "circumstantial power" could injure some consumers, such "a brief perturbation in competitive conditions [is] not the sort of thing the antitrust laws do or should worry about."[36] Is the lucky monopolist akin to a "brief perturbation" that antitrust laws should ignore? Admittedly no.

The *Kodak* majority condemned Kodak under a per se rule of illegality for tying spare parts to aftermarket services. Justice Scalia dissented and considered that Kodak's monopoly position in the aftermarket was circumstantial in that it derived from Kodak's equipment. That is, the power that every manufacturer possesses over the parts uniquely associated with the main product that it provides. Thus, consumers who have invested in equipment "will tolerate some level of service-price increases before changing equipment brands."[37] But this "circumstantial leverage" is ubiquitous (as when the refrigerator breaks down and the customer prefers to fix it than to buy a

32. The meaning of this concept is certainly obscure.
33. Breyer, Stephen G. "The Problem of the Honest Monopolist." *Antitrust Law Journal* 44.2 (1975): 194-201.
34. Lopatka, John E. "Stephen Breyer and Modern Antitrust: A Snug Fit." *The Antitrust Bulletin* 40.1 (1995): 1-97, arguing that Chicago School scholars would not be concerned about position of dominance acquired by chance because market forces would determine its maintenance or disappearance through superior efficiencies or inefficiencies.
35. Demsetz writes "monopoly may also come to a person by luck and this might very well give raise to inefficiency." *See* Demsetz, Harold. "The Problem of Monopolization." *Working Paper* #243 (June 1982).
36. Justice Scalia, dissenting, *Eastman Kodak Co. v. Image Technical Services, Inc*, 504 U.S. 451 (1992), at 498.
37. *Id.* at 497.

new one) and rational consumers will generally factor in their purchase a rough expected cost of aftermarket support. This simply is a "'brief perturbation' in competitive conditions"[38] that has nothing to do with the accidental origins of the lucky monopolist but with normal market conditions.

On the one hand, we may find an "*irreversible*" outcome of dominance caused by a "brief [but lucky!] perturbation." Imagine that all nuclear power plants in France except for one would suffer irreparable damage due to a series of earthquakes. The permanence of the lucky monopolist would last long enough so as to consider it *irreversible*: the industry would not look the same in the foreseeable future. Market forces alone are insufficient to upset the lucky monopolist. In this sense, it has been argued elsewhere that a lucky dominant firm should be an actionable manifestation of market failure.[39]

On the other hand, the lucky monopolist might find itself in an "*ephemeral*" position of dominance. Suppose a snow avalanche has collapsed roads and other transport ways so that the inhabitants of a village can only do their groceries in one supermarket. At some early point in time snow ploughs will remove the snow or the sun will melt it away. The villagers will in short time be able to do their groceries in other groceries stores. The lucky monopolist can thus be a short-lived phenomenon or an entrenched outcome that is not dependent on superior efficiencies to maintain its randomly acquired position of market power.

[C] Discovering the Lucky Monopolist

By definition, a chance event is unexpected, uncertain. Economic actors do not know that it will happen and when it will occur. It follows that a lucky position of dominance cannot be prevented from arising. This simple finding is telling. Antitrust authorities that put negative emphasis on the mere presence of dominant firms would be ill advised to prevent their random emergence.

This point aside, the opportunity to restrain potential anticompetitive behavior comes thus into place. But for that, we must first discover which dominant firm has been randomly selected.

Some scholars have argued that the courts would be incapable of identifying a monopoly born of luck or that the risk of error costs would be very high.[40] Stephen Breyer, Associate Justice of the Supreme Court of the United States, considers that the main difficulty would lie in overcoming human biases. What the dominant firm will deem to be skill, its competitors will think of it as luck. ("I am skillful; you are lucky.")[41] Einer Elhauge does not dismiss luck as a cause of market power, but

38. *Id.* at 498. The example of the refrigerator is Justice Scalia's.
39. Williamson, Oliver E. "Dominant Firms and the Monopoly Problem: Market Failure Considerations." *Harvard Law Review* 85.8 (1972): 1512-1531.
40. Lopatka, John E. and William H. Page. "Posner's Program for the Antitrust Division: A Twenty-Five Year Perspective." *SMU Law Review* 48 (1994): 1713-1747, at 1731 writing that "accidental monopolies" are virtually impossible to identify and the risks of error costs are high.
41. Breyer, Stephen G. "The Problem of the Honest Monopolist." *Antitrust Law Journal* 44.2 (1975): 194-201.

considers that examples of accidental acquisitions of market power are difficult to think of.[42]

On the other hand, scholars from different disciplines have argued that lucky positions of dominance can be inferred when there is no other apparent source of market power. Nobel laureate Oliver Williamson maintains that dominance should be presumed to be the result of a "chance event failure" unless IPR, scale, predatory behavior or superior management claims can be supported.[43] Nassim Taleb, a probability theorist, argues that the only reason why markets work "is because they allow people to be lucky."[44] And strategy scholars like Jay Barney have highlighted that economists have not yet developed "rigorous methods" that reject luck as the cause of sustained competitive advantage.[45]

Both strands of the literature have their merits, but we find ourselves seeking to strike a balance between these opposing views. The reasons are twofold. First, failure to systematically neglect "unobservable factors" like luck could bias assessments of market power.[46] We therefore discard the outright rejection of the lucky monopolist hypothesis on the basis of identification difficulties. Second, we also discard outright presumptions in favor of luck as an explanation for firm dominance.

How to assess this? Both probability theory and empirical observation can provide a middle ground solution to either discover or reject the lucky monopolist conjecture.

In a somewhat unnoticed paper, several economists at the US FTC provided a framework based on probability theory to determine the extent to which dominance may have originated from random events.[47] If we accept luck as a ubiquitous factor in the market, in any competitive process there is a probability p of any firm being randomly selected from a pool of equally competitive firms. Let us assume the existence of two homogeneous firms: A and B; they sell the same good which

42. Elhauge, Einer. "Defining Better Monopolization Standards." *Stanford Law Review* 56.2 (2003): 253-344, 261.
43. Williamson, Oliver E. "Antitrust Enforcement and the Modern Corporation" in Victor R. Fuchs (ed.) *Economic Research: Retrospect and Prospect, Volume 3, Policy Issues and Research Opportunities in Industrial Organization*. NBER, 1972: 16-33, 21.
44. Taleb, Nassim Nicholas. *The Black Swan: The Impact of the Highly Improbable*. Random House, 2010, at p. xxv. Taleb argues that "The reason free markets work is because they allow people to be lucky, thanks to aggressive trial and error, not by giving rewards or 'incentives' for skill. The strategy is, then, to tinker as much as possible and try to collect as many Black Swan opportunities as you can." While we certainly agree with Taleb that uncertainty is what makes free markets work as they do (*see* Chapter 5), we are not concerned with that "tinkering-driven luck" which is the result of a *positive acquisition cost*.
45. Barney, Jay B. "On Flipping Coins and Making Technology Choices: Luck as an Explanation of Technological Foresight and Oversight" *in* Raghu Garud, Praveen Rattan Nayyar and Zur Baruch Shapira (eds.) *Technological Innovation: Oversights and Foresights*. Cambridge University Press, 1997.
46. Jacobson, Robert. "Unobservable Effects and Business Performance." *Marketing Science* 9.1 (1990): 74-85. *See* Chapter 6 for a discussion regarding unseen, unquantifiable but perceived efficiencies giving rise to firm dominance.
47. What follows draws from their research and applies our process-paradox framework (t-1, t, and t+1) to it. *See* Herman, Douglas A., Shawn W. Ulrick and Seth B. Sacher. "Dominance Thresholds: A Cautionary Note." *The Antitrust Bulletin* 59.4 (2014): 855-893. We borrow from Ulrick and Sacher the terminology of "thinly" and "thickly traded" markets.

consumers see as perfectly interchangeable. Let us observe, at *t*, that Firm A has a market share of 75% and Firm B 25%, and that their market shares are the result of having sold 3 and 1 goods, respectively. Now, at *t*-1 (the competitive process where A and B realized 4 transactions) there is a probability *p* of A's market share being the result of a pure chance event rather than the result of a fringe competitive advantage.

Now, following the law of large numbers, the probability that A's 75% market share is the result of a pure chance event (as in a tossing coins contest) will be higher the less frequent the transactions are. Thus, in the presence of homogenous firms, the more "thinly traded" a market is, the higher is the probability that luck is a determinant of market share. On the contrary, the assumption of homogenous firms would weaken if in a "thickly traded" market the observed differences in firm performance would persist. Luck would no longer be a determinant of market share but rather the existence of an unobserved competitive advantage at *t*-1. For example, that Firm A was better located for three-quarters of potential consumers.

We acknowledge that market shares are not determinants of market power. An analysis of barriers to entry and expansion would thus remain necessary. This is not our task here. This notwithstanding, the random choice of Firm A over Firm B could define the short-term or long-term viability of Firm B given the existence of minimum efficient scale, lock-in effects or inertia patterns, etc. The chance event must, correspondingly, be determining enough to grant the firm with market power at no cost for Firm A.

Retrospectively, lucky events can and should be thoroughly examined as an alternative explanation of firm dominance. However, whether the chance event is determining enough it can only be assessed on a case-by-case basis.[48] Heuristically, in the presence of thinly traded markets a word of caution against direct correlations between market shares and market power is advised.[49]

Empirically, tracing luck as a source of firm dominance is akin to composing a story in which a chance event is the pivotal element to it. Williamson strongly argued in favor of an examination of unanticipated events to assess randomly created positions of dominance; the chance event that upset the *status quo* of an industry structure at a point in time.[50] Natural disasters, like Hurricane Charley, or man-made accidents like the Volkswagen diesel scandal are easy to discover and to attach causality.[51] A holistic observation of both *ex ante* and *ex post* market conditions is sufficient to uncover this

48. Demsetz, Harold. "Industry structure, market rivalry, and public policy." *The Journal of Law & Economics* 16.1 (1973): 1-9, at 3: "Superior performance can be attributed to the combination of great uncertainty plus luck or atypical insight by the management of a firm. It is not until the experiments are actually tried that we learn which succeed and which fail."
49. Herman, Douglas A., Shawn W. Ulrick and Seth B. Sacher. "Dominance Thresholds: A Cautionary Note." *The Antitrust Bulletin* 59.4 (2014): 855-893.
50. Williamson, Oliver E. "Antitrust Enforcement and the Modern Corporation" *in* Victor R. Fuchs (ed.) *Economic Research: Retrospect and Prospect, Volume 3, Policy Issues and Research Opportunities in Industrial Organization*. NBER, 1972: 16-33, at 19, arguing that randomly created positions of dominance must be considered as market failures.
51. Arkansas Code of 2010, §4-88-303, "Protection of Consumers from Price Gouging and Unfair Pricing Practices During and Shortly After a State of Emergency."

with a high degree of certainty. We describe some more examples in the following section.

Lastly, we chose to limit chance events to the description given above: they must be uncertain, they are outside the cost function of the firm and are meaningful enough. Probability and observation are sufficient tools to make the traceability of these chance events a sound and administrable delimitation. Thus, we chose not to deal with other fanciful lucky punches, like the inheritance of an unexpectedly appreciated good, like getting ahold of the total supply of coltan before its essentiality to manufacture electronic devices becomes known.[52]

Now, if luck is an important variable in the market, why should competition law account for it? How should it do so? We provide some opening answers to these related questions below.

§7.03 THE LUCKY MONOPOLIST UNDER ANTITRUST SCRUTINY

[A] A Window for Opportunistic Behavior

If, as argued by Chicagoan scholars, only superior efficiency and governmental action can maintain a monopoly, the random origin of such position should be left alone. Market forces will swiftly deal with it.[53] Even more, in the presence of higher prices or restricted output these will accelerate entry. Monopoly profits will attract back former competitors of the lucky monopolist, and the market will be reinstated to a more competitive structure.

We do not necessarily disagree with such a proposition.[54] That is, if we assume that no barriers to entry exist and that an infinite queue of efficient competitors awaits to rush into the market at the slightest deviation from some measure of cost.[55] But we must not disregard that abusively opportunistic behavior can occur between periods of luck-encumbered dominance and its final erosion.[56]

52. Demsetz, Harold. "The Problem of Monopolization." *Working Paper* #243 (June 1982).
53. Posner, Richard A. "Oligopoly and the Antitrust Laws: A Suggested Approach." *Stanford Law Review* 21 (1968): 1562-1606, at 1597, suggesting that monopolies that are not supported by the state, superior skill, predatory practices or a natural monopoly market are likely to be short-lived. Structural remedies against short-lived monopolies seem therefore "inappropriate to cure transitory market imperfections."
54. Williamson, Oliver E. "Economies as an Antitrust Defense Revisited." *University of Pennsylvania Law Review* 125.4 (1977): 699-736, 731-733, arguing, against Posner's proposition, that a chance event failure can be determining enough so as to warrant the imposition of antitrust structural remedies.
55. Baumol, William J., John C. Panzar and Robert D. Willig. *Contestable Markets and the Theory of Industry Structure*. 1988. Geroski and Jacquemin strongly criticized this assumption. *See* Geroski, Paul A. and Alexis Jacquemin. "Dominant Firms and Their Alleged Decline." *International Journal of Industrial Organization* 2.1 (1984): 1-27.
56. Worcester, Dean A. Jr. "Why 'Dominant Firms' Decline." *Journal of Political Economy*, 65.4 (1957): 338-346, at 346: "The burden of this article is that it may be fruitful to look for the exploitation of short-run opportunities in trying to assess the development of monopolistic and oligopolistic practices."

We define this opportunistic conduct as any unilateral behavior to take advantage of an *unforeseen* and *exogenous* opportunity to charge monopoly prices, withhold output or raise artificial barriers to entry. Following Posner's description, "another name for opportunism is—monopoly."[57]

Transaction cost economics supports the view that opportunistic behavior is likely to occur in the presence of uncertainty. The research carried by Alchian and his colleagues[58] and by Williamson explains that the law of contracts can cope with the problem of opportunism by closing those windows that allow firms to behave in such way.[59] Businesses and contracts should be designed to avoid information costs and thus reduce the exposure of market participants to opportunistic behavior.[60] For example, the uncertainty inherent to incomplete contracts should be minimized to prevent the contractor from taking advantage of a contractually *unforeseen* contingency.[61] Contract law, however, cannot prevent the emergence of market power. Further, it only diminishes the emergence of windows for opportunistic behavior in the context of contractual relationships.

Anticompetitive opportunism is particularly acute when market power has been acquired by chance, at no cost. Significant and unforeseen changes in the competitive environment open the window to opportunistic behavior.[62] The degree and type of uncertainty involved increases the probability opportunism,[63] and the uncertainty about the preservation of market power only exacerbate this. The unpredicted nature of the event means that it is especially difficult for the firm to assess where it will be at any time in the future,[64] and thus it will seek to profit before the previous market structure is reinstated and/or prevent its reinstauration.

57. Posner, Richard A. *Economic Analysis of Law*. Aspen Publishers, 2011, at p. 118.
58. Klein, Benjamin, Robert G. Crawford and Armen Alchian, "Vertical Integration, Appropriable Rents, and the Competitive Contracting Process." *Journal of Law and Economics* 21.2 (1978): 297-326.
59. Williamson, Oliver E. "Transaction-Cost Economics: The Governance of Contractual Relations." *The Journal of Law and Economics* 22.2 (1979): 233-261.
60. Williamson, Oliver E. *Market and Hierarchies: Analysis and Antitrust Implications*. New York: Free Press, 1975.
61. Meese, Alan J. "Monopolization, Exclusion, and the Theory of the Firm." *Minnesota Law Review* 89 (2004): 743-847, 774, 785-787 and 827, discussing how perfect competition models viewed nonstandard contracts, which went beyond "spot" market situations as a departure from the "moment-to-moment atomistic rivalry." Transaction cost economics helped in understanding that nonstandard contracts had efficiencies like preventing opportunistic behavior that the model of perfect competition assumed away.
62. In a similar fashion, Petit argues that, in the presence of procompetitive legal or market disruptions, firms in an oligopolistic market might overcome the procompetitive effect of the disruption by engaging in collusive behavior to reestablish their predisruption collusive equilibrium. A theory of liability concerning an abuse of collective dominance would require proving: "(i) pre-existing collusion; (ii) disruption; (iii) re-pricing strategy; (iv) post-disruption return to collusive equilibria." *See* Petit, Nicolas. "Re-Pricing Through Disruption in Oligopolies with Tacit Collusion: A Framework for Abuse of Collective Dominance" *in OECD Hearing on Oligopoly Markets*, DAF/COMP/WD (2015) 52.
63. Riegg, Ryan M. "Opportunism, Uncertainty, and Relational Contracting - Antitrust Rules in the Film Industry." *UCLA Law*, Working Paper (2008).
64. Geroski, Paul A. "The Growth of Firms in Theory and in Practice." *CEPR* Discussion Paper No.2092 (2002): 1-30, 5.

The Competition and Markets Authority ("CMA") in the United Kingdom has shown concern in this respect. In the presence of sunk costs and significant changes in the environment, like an unforeseen supply shock or an accident of nature, the possibility of opportunistic bargaining by firms raised to dominance is introduced.[65] In unforeseen troubled waters, opportunism is king and must be discouraged.

Assuming, in line of the Chicago tradition, that the lucky monopolist is ephemeral, the lucky monopolist will have stronger incentives to exploit its position at t and to behave competitively at $t+1$. It is difficult to argue that an accidental monopoly will behave, *artificially*, in a competitive manner both at t and $t+1$. The costs of engaging in exploitation are zero for the lucky monopolist who need not exclude competitors beforehand, irrespective of whether this was done on competition on the merits or by anticompetitive conduct. The costs of exclusion are not zero, as in the exploitation case, but they are lower than when a firm has acquired its position by incurring a certain cost since the lucky monopolist is a costlessly achieved position.

Because costs of exploitation and exclusion are necessarily lower or inexistent, the incentives to behave anticompetitively are higher. Firms prefer low-cost strategies to achieve their business goals. The same can be predicated of firms engaging in anticompetitive conduct. The more cost-effective the latter is, the higher the probability is that the firm will engage in it. Some authors have referred to this correlation between costs and incentives as situations of "cheap exclusion." They are cheap because they are "low-cost exclusionary strategies" and because they lack "any redeeming qualities."[66]

This notwithstanding, reputation efficiencies might offset opportunistic behavior incentives. The dominant firm, knowing that its condition is transient, will fear retaliation from consumers once the market reboots to the structure previous to the chance event.[67]

Competition policy is thus faced with a trade-off: either to accept exploitative or exclusionary conduct to accelerate the reestablishment of a competitive market or to prevent the lucky monopolist from engaging in exploitation for it will harm consumers (e.g., excessive prices) and presumably difficult transition to competitive market conditions (e.g., long-term exclusivity contracts signed in the aftermath of the lucky event). The trade-off must be faced by reference to the *ex ante* market conditions and the meaningfulness of the chance event (which in turn will determine the degree of market power) and reputational effects.

Where *ex ante* market conditions (i.e., previous to the chance event) showed the existence of a vigorous competitive market and the chance event has not made those conditions irreversible, the likelihood of reentry will be high and both exploitative and

65. Dobson, Paul, Michael Waterson and Alex Chu. "The Welfare Consequences of the Exercise of Buyer Power." *OFT*, Research Paper 16 (September 1998).
66. Creighton, Susan A., D. Bruce Hoffman, Thomas G. Krattenmaker and Ernest A. Nagata. "Cheap Exclusion." *Antitrust Law Journal* 72.3 (2005): 975-995. The authors only focus on the abusive behavior, but we extend their premise to the costs of acquiring a dominant position. We discuss opportunistic behavior in the sense Creighton et al. in the context of anticompetitive acquisitions of market power through SSOs. *See* Chapter 8 for an extended discussion.
67. *See* Chapter 6 for a discussion about reputation effects.

exclusionary abuses are a primary concern. But, if the *ex ante* market conditions showcased a lessened competitive market environment and the chance event has made conditions irreversible, exploitative abuses should be prioritized.

With this backdrop, the story that emerges is that dominance by luck increases the incentives of the dominant firm to behave opportunistically thus leading to "suboptimal results."[68] Luck creates an unexpected and unwarranted window of opportunity to "seek with *guile*."[69] The petrol station in Orlando had not created the situation resulting in a reduction of supply,[70] but it can be argued that it took opportunity of its sudden position of market power to raise prices. The question that antitrust laws need to address is whether those prices were just the result of the natural scarcity or rather the result of opportunistic behavior of the firm.

[B] Luck and Article 102 TFEU Case Law

The EU Courts and the Commission have not explicitly considered chance events. However, some of its case law transpires an aversion for positions of market power created by noneconomic considerations. In particular, we uncover two luck-related situations that have made its way into the analysis of anticompetitive conduct. First, there are unforeseen events that place a firm in a position of market power. Second, there is the case of erroneously *granted* monopolies.

[1] Unforeseen Events

In October 1973, the Organization of Arab Petroleum Exporting Countries (OAPEC) imposed an export embargo on oil.[71] The sudden decision[72] was their response to the US and Europe for their support to Israel in the Yom Kippur war. In Europe, the oil shock particularly affected the Netherlands who saw a cessation of oil shipments from

68. Haskel, Michael A. "The Benign Time Assumption's Role in the Application of 2 of the Sherman Antitrust Act." *Quinnipiac Law Review* 24 (2005): 265-299, 272.
69. Williamson, Oliver E. *The Economic Institutions of Capitalism. Firms, Markets Relational Contracting*. New York: The Free Press, 1985, at p. 47.
70. Posner draws a difference between *created* shortages and *natural* shortages that can determine the bargaining power of the parties to a contract. He contrasts the case of the increases in prices of gas stations to the *Alaska Packers' Ass'n v. Domenico* case, where a man who had hired seamen for a trip to fish for salmon in Alaska, was asked higher wages than agreed when the boat arrived in Alaskan waters. Posner writes, "the seamen, *created* the shortage by refusing to work." Interestingly, Posner does not discuss whether *natural* shortages can serve to behave opportunistically. *See* Posner, Richard A. *Economic Analysis of Law*. Aspen Publishers, 2011, at pp. 147-148.
71. US Department of State. "Oil Embargo Against the U.S. and Israel in 1973". *Office of the Historian, available at* https://history.state.gov/milestones/1969-1976/oil-embargo.
72. Yergin, Daniel. *The Prize: The Epic Quest for Oil, Money & Power*. Simon and Schuster, 2011. On September 26, 1973, Japanese Prime Minister Kakuei Tanaka said, "Regarding the energy crisis, an oil crisis ten years from now is clearly seen." Yergin writes: "It was more like ten days."

the Middle East.[73] It revealed how external noneconomic events could have a devastating effect on the economy. As such, antitrust did not remain alien to its effects on market competitiveness.

In *British Petroleum (ABG Oil Companies)*,[74] the Commission accused British Petroleum (BP) of abusing its dominant position during the oil embargo crisis in the Netherlands (from November 1973 to March 1974). BP, a refiner of petroleum, had significantly and disproportionately reduced its supplies to ABG by reference to what other BP customers were supplied at that time. ABG is a purchasing cooperative that imports, exports and deals at wholesale in petroleum products in the Netherlands.

In its decision, the Commission takes account of the unexpected market situation created by the oil embargo. It considers that BP enjoyed a position of dominance despite there being another six strong refineries competitors. BP's "*found itself in position to control production and distribution in a substantial proportion of the market.*"[75] This is an unusual understating of how dominant positions are created and one that recalls very much to Judge Learned Hand's wording of a "thrust upon" monopoly in *Alcoa*.[76]

A combination of luck and incumbency effects[77] thrust BP to a position of dominance. "This was because of their special relationships with the oil-producing countries of the Middle East [BP was originally an Anglo-Persian company: the Anglo-Persian oil company, founded in 1808]. *Such a sudden shortage especially one that was not brought about by economic considerations*, [i.e., luck or accident] *led to a restriction of both actual and potential competition among the small group of companies concerned, a restriction that was particularly marked at the level of distribution*" (emphasis added).[78] BP costumers had thus become suddenly dependent on BP for the supply of oil.

The reduction and disproportion in supply was assessed by reference to a long enough period previous to the oil shock. This helped to provide a realistic representation of commercial relationships between BP and its customers. Remarkably, the Commission took into account the uncertainty created by the sudden shortage and decided on this ground not to impose a fine on BP.[79]

---

73. The Editors of Encyclopædia Britannica. "Arab Oil Embargo. International Relations [1973]." *Encyclopædia Britannica* (Jun. 16, 2016), *available at* https://www.britannica.com/topic/Arab-oil-embargo.
74. Commission Decision, Case COMP/IV/28.841, *ABG Oil Companies operating in the Netherlands*.
75. *Id.*, at p. 8.
76. *United States v. Aluminum Co. of America* ("*Alcoa*"), 148 F.2d 416, 430 (2d Cir. 1945), at 429.
77. Interestingly, BP was at the time of the proceedings a state-owned company. The company would only start its privatization in 1979. This fact however did not play a visible role in the decision.
78. Commission Decision, Case COMP/IV/28.841, *ABG Oil Companies operating in the Netherlands*, at p. 9.
79. Quite to the contrary, Posner considers that opportunistic breach of a contract should be remedied by "throwing the book at him." *See* Posner, Richard A. *Economic Analysis of Law*. Aspen Publishers, 2011, at p. 149.

However, BP appealed, and the Court of Justice annulled the decision.[80] The Court rightly considered that there could be no abuse since the commercial relationship between BP and ABG had changed before the oil crisis. ABG was no longer a traditional customer but an occasional one and thus no longer commercially dependent on BP.[81] The Court did not call the Commission's analysis of an accidentally created dominant position into question.

The analysis of the Commission regarding market power is welcome, as it is the silence of the Court. Accidental events can have a strong impact in the market competitiveness. These can last a few months as the oil shock in the Netherlands or have a more lasting or irreversible effect.

In this latter sense, it has been elsewhere discussed that the Fukushima earthquake had a determining effect regarding market power in the German energy sector.

Before Fukushima, Germany had been a strong advocate of nuclear policy. In 2012, the Fukushima accident prompted a "sudden, unexpected and significant" decision taken by the German government: to permanently close all the eight pre-1981 nuclear plants. If the accident had not occurred, the nuclear plants would not have been closed.[82]

A traditional look at market shares would have revealed little change in market power. The biggest energy suppliers in Germany, RWE and EON, did not experience a significant change in their market shares. However, market power measures carried out by Luigi Grossi and others showed an increase by almost 50% in the Residual Supply Index variable after the nuclear plants were shut down.[83] This indicates that market power plays a major role after the nuclear plants were closed. As suggested above, in the face of an irreversible outcome (i.e., the permanent closure), their estimates suggested strong price increases which were not caused by a shift in the supply schedule between different energy sources but by unilateral exercise of market power.[84]

[2] Wrongly Granted Monopolies

An accidentally originated monopoly can also arise from a default in regulation. For example, a mistakenly awarded concession or a wrongly granted patent could put a firm in a lucky position of dominance. *Windsurfing International* is a first example of how the EU Courts have acted against accidental monopolies.

80. CJEU, Case C-77/77, *British Petroleum v. Commission*, ECLI:EU:C:1978:141. The case is better known for the collective dominance part. *See* Kellezi, Pranvera. "Abuse Below the Threshold of Dominance" in M.O. Mackendrot, B.C. Gallego and S. Enchelmaier, S. (eds.) *Abuse of Dominant Position: New Interpretation, New Enforcement Mechanisms?* Springer, 2008, at p. 77.
81. CJEU, Case C-77/77, *British Petroleum v. Commission*, ECLI:EU:C:1978:141, §§32-33.
82. Grossi, Luigi, Sven Heim and Michael Waterson. "A Vision of the European Energy Future? The Impact of the German Response to the Fukushima Earthquake." *ZEW - Centre for European Economic Research* Discussion Paper No. 14-051 (2014): 1-45.
83. The Residual Supply Index indicates the degree of market power and accounts for the dynamics of the demand side. *See id.*16.
84. *Id.* at 18-21.

Windsurfing International ("Windsurfing") had concluded several licensing agreements based on a patent relating to a rig for a sailboard. The licensing agreements contained a number of anticompetitive provisions. Among others, licensees could only sell complete sailboards comprising a board and a rig together and had to seek approval from WSI before selling new board models. More importantly, however, was inclusion of a no-challenge clause that prevented licensees from challenging the validity of the licensed patent.

The Commission considers in its decision that no-challenge clauses prevented licensees from removing "wrongly granted monopolies" in the form of a patent.[85] Patent validity challenges are essential to a free system of competition because they eliminate detrimental market power. Windsurfing appealed the decision and the Court upheld the Commission's finding. Although the Court did not explicitly equate patent with monopoly,[86] it ruled "the removal of a monopoly perhaps wrongly granted to the licensor [which] must prevail over any other consideration" to be in the public interest.[87]

Following *Windsurfing*, the Court ruled in *Lundbeck* that a patent granted in error could constitute an obstacle to economic activity.[88] And in *AstraZeneca*, the EU Courts reinforced the special responsibility of a dominant firm that acquires a patent by error. The GC held that the dominant firm must "at the very least" inform the public authorities about the unlawfully granted exclusive right.[89] Against the same background, the Commission and the GC consider patent challenges to be an essential part of the competitive process in the pharmaceutical industry.[90] Similarly, the TTBER Guidelines indicate that in the interest of undistorted competition invalid IPR should be eliminated.[91]

The unlawfulness of no-challenge clauses shows a strong concern for the permanence of accidental monopolies arising from a default in the regulatory system. Challenging patents is not only an expression of potential competition but also a mechanism to purge the free market system from unmerited market power.

However, there is a point missing in the discussion. Namely, this is, whether the exercise of market power in the context of a wrongfully granted patent should be

85. Commission Decision, Case COMP/IV/29.395, *Windsurfing International* ("*Windsurfing*"), at p. 15. *See also* CJEU, Case C-193/83, *Windsurfing v.* Commission, ECLI:EU:C:1986:75, at §91: "[T]he public interest in ensuring an essentially free system of competition and therefore in *the removal of a monopoly perhaps wrongly granted to the licensor must prevail over any other consideration*" (emphasis added).
86. As Nicolas Petit explains, the degree of confusion that the EU Courts have regarding the relationship between market power and the intellectual property right is "spectacular." *See* Petit, Nicolas, "The Antitrust and Intellectual Property Intersection in European Union Law" *in* Roger D. Blair and Daniel Sokol (eds.) *Handbook of Antitrust, Intellectual Property and High Tech.* Cambridge University, 2017.
87. CJEU, Case C-193/83, *Windsurfing v.* Commission, ECLI:EU:C:1986:75, §92.
88. GC, Case T-472/13, *Lundbeck*, ECLI:EU:T:2016:449, §390; *see also* Opinion of Advocate General Wathelet *in* Case C-170/13, *Huawei Techs. Co. v. ZTE Corp.*, ECLI:EU:C:2015:477, §95.
89. GC, Case T-321/05, *AstraZeneca v. Commission*, ECLI:EU:T:2010:266, §358.
90. Commission Decision, Case COMP/39.226, *Lundbeck*, §1037.
91. Communication from the Commission—Guidelines on the application of Article 101 of the Treaty on the Functioning of the European Union to Technology Transfer Agreements, *OJ* C 89, 28.3.2014, p. 3–50, at §§134 and 138.

assessed differently than in the context of valid patents or anticompetitively acquired patents.[92] There are two possible scenarios that deserve such differentiation.[93] First, when the owner of the invalid patent knew at the time of the abuse that its patent was wrongly granted. Second, when the owner of the invalid patent did not know at the time of the abuse that its patent was invalid.

The first scenario requires consciousness about invalidity and intent to exploit the accidentally created monopoly. In other words, proving that the firm knew about the error made by the granting authority and sought to take advantage thereafter. For example, in the presence of strong information asymmetries, where potential licensees are unaware of the error, refusing to license the patent would artificially maintain an accidental position of dominance. In a counterfactual, the license would diminish information asymmetries and put the accidental position of dominance in danger by giving information to the licensee about the invalidity of the patent. Anticompetitive effects of such conduct would positively differ from a "classical" refusal to supply case. In this case, there are no countervailing efficiencies or objective justifications. The object of the refusal to supply is clear: the maintenance of an erroneously created monopoly.

The second scenario requires that the lucky monopolist did not know about the invalidity at the time of the abuse. The accident would operate as an objective justification to the conduct of the owner of the invalid patent. This situation should prompt an analogous application of the accident defense foreseen in US jurisprudence to excuse monopolization cases.

[3] The Luck Defenses

In the context of Section 2 of the SA the defendant accused of having acquired a monopoly position through other means than skill, foresight or industry, can resort to luck or the rival's bad luck as explanations.[94]

This luck defense has two variants. The first, relates to the idea that a lucky monopolist is a legitimate position of market power. As the *Alcoa* court advanced, if Alcoa's power would have been acquired because it had been "thrust upon," then Alcoa would not have monopolized the ingot market.[95] Its monopoly position would be

92. *See* Chapter 8.
93. We acknowledge that in both scenarios the requirement that the patent is finally revoked is a necessary condition for adapting thresholds of antitrust liability to wrongly granted monopolies. However, *see* GC, Case T-691/14, *Servier and others v. Commission*, ECLI:EU:T:2018:922, at §§244-245, where the General Court clarified that since patents are national, neither the Court nor the Commission can have jurisdiction to rule on the validity of a patent.
94. Markovits, Richard S. *Economics and the Interpretation and Application of U.S. and E.U. Antitrust Law: Volume I Basic Concepts and Economics-Based Legal Analyses of Oligopolistic and Predatory Conduct.* SpringerLink: Bücher. Springer Berlin Heidelberg, 2014, at p. 82.
95. *Alcoa*, 148 F.2d 416, 430 (2d Cir. 1945), at 429. *See also* at 432: "[N]o monopolist monopolizes unconscious of what he is doing." For an excellent discussion on the case, *see* Winerman, Marc and William E. Kovacic. "Learned Hand, Alcoa, and the Reluctant Application of the Sherman Act." *Antitrust Law Journal* 79.1 (2013): 295-348, showing evidence that Judge Hand struggled with finding the right answers to the questions brought up in *Alcoa*.

a legitimate one because Alcoa was simply the "passive beneficiary" of monopoly power.[96] Unfortunately for Alcoa, Judge Hand found that Alcoa had monopolized the ingot market because it continued to expand output in response to increases in the demand for ingot while such strategy was not "inevitable."[97] Alcoa's achievement of power was a deliberate choice.[98]

The second variant resorts to luck as a rationalization for apparent anticompetitive effects of a conduct. In *Aspen Skiing*, the Supreme Court ruled that one "*must draw a distinction here between practices which tend to exclude or restrict competition* on the one hand and the success of a business which reflects only a superior product, a well-run business, *or luck*"[99] (emphasis added). Notwithstanding that luck could explain the foreclosure of competition, the Court imposed on Aspen Skiing, the owner of a ski mountain, Section 2 liability for refusing to deal with a competitor's mountain, Aspen Highlands.[100]

There is no similar case in EU competition law. While the recurrent principle of "competition on the merits" comes close to "superior product" or "well-run business" explanations, it would fail to catch luck justifications. As the case law on Article 102 TFEU stands, the possibility of introducing a luck defense seems arduous. The difficulty can be realized in the way EU Courts and Commission regularly overlook other explanations for decreases in market shares of a dominant firm's rivals.

In *Deutsche Telekom*, the Court dismissed the application of a "reasonably efficient competitor" test that would look at the rival's costs of Deutsche Telekom. The application of the "as efficient competitor" test was deemed to be sufficient to proof the existence of a margin squeeze. However, as some authors have rightly argued, incorporating the rival's costs in the analysis as a complementary tool would diminish wrong imputations of margin squeeze cases.[101] Furthermore, incorporating the rival's costs in the analysis would diminish the imputation of exclusionary effects that are just the result of a stochastic variable.

The *Intel* court is also a paradigmatic example of the reluctance of the EU Courts to look for other explanations of market outcomes. During the period when Intel's loyalty rebates were in place, AMD's market share and expenditures in R&D increased,

96. *Alcoa*, 148 F.2d 416, 430 (2d Cir. 1945), at 430.
97. *Id.* at 431.
98. Joliet, René. *Monopolization and Abuse of Dominant Position: A Comparative Study of American and European Approaches to the Control of Economic Power*. Collection scientifique de la Faculté de Droit de l'Université de Liège [1970] 1975, at p. 55.
99. *Aspen Skiing Co. v. Aspen Highlands Skiing Corp.*, 472 U.S. 585 (1985), at 596.
100. In particular, Aspen Skiing decided to terminate a cooperation agreement whereby Aspen Skiing and Highlands sold joint ski tickets to the mountains they owned in the same area. Aspen Skiing owned three of those mountains and Highlands owned a fourth.
101. Geradin, Damien and Robert O'Donoghue. "The Concurrent Application of Competition Law and Regulation: The Case of Margin Squeeze Abuses in the Telecommunications Sector." *Journal of Competition Law and Economics* 1 (2005): 355-425, 392-393, explaining that the CMA of the UK has on the contrary looked at rivals' costs in complementarity with those of the dominant firm to determine whether foreclosure is due to the abusive behavior of the dominant firm or rather its rivals' inability to compete.

and the price of x86 CPUs decreased. Despite this, the General Court lightly concluded that AMD's growth "might have been greater" had Intel's rebates not been in place.[102]

As some scholars have argued, decreases in market share of a dominant firm's competitors can also be explained by reference to their "ineptitude" to compete in the market.[103] In this regard, the CMA of the UK has, contrary to the EU Courts, looked at rivals' costs in complementarity with those of the dominant firm to determine whether foreclosure is due to the abusive behavior of the dominant firm or rather its rivals' inability to compete.[104]

By considering all the relevant competitive circumstances,[105] and thus including the need to look into a monopolist rivals' cost structure, the space for luck explanations of market outcomes is narrowed down and so the probability of both false positives (wrong finding of abuse) and false negatives (wrong acquittal of abuse) reduced. The acquisition of monopoly power by luck or accident of its competitors cannot thus be neglected in the appraisal of anticompetitive conduct.

[C] Price Gouging (Regulation)

At the EU level, it is well-known that Article 102 TFEU condemns excessive pricing as abusive behavior. Further, that both the CJEU and national competition authorities have found abusive pricing conduct which is unfair.[106] Quite to the contrary, in the US, and in particular since *Trinko,* it is widely recognized that Section 2 of the SA has no power to regulate above-cost pricing by a dominant firm. It is the "opportunity to charge monopoly prices is what attracts 'business acumen' in the first place."[107]

This notwithstanding, it is less notorious on the European side of the Atlantic that, at US Federal Level, thirty-four States and the District of Columbia have enacted regulation against excessive prices.[108] These Federal statutes apply in situations of national emergency or the occurrence of an accident. Further, in 2013, US Congress passed a bill protecting consumers from price gouging of gasoline and entrusted the FTC with its enforcement.[109] These statutes and bill aim at preventing opportunistic behavior caused by an accidental event. This is why we deal with them here.

102. GC, Case T-286/09, *Intel*, ECLI:EU:T:2014:547, §186.
103. Williamson, Oliver E. "Antitrust Enforcement and the Modern Corporation" *in* Victor R. Fuchs (ed.) *Economic Research: Retrospect and Prospect, Volume 3, Policy Issues and Research Opportunities in Industrial Organization*. NBER, 1972: 16-33, 19.
104. OFCOM decision, Case CW/00760/03/04, *Investigation against BT about potential anti-competitive exclusionary behaviour.*
105. CJEU, Case C-413/14 P, *Intel v. Commission*, ECLI:EU:C:2017:632, §119.
106. Either pure excessive pricing cases like Case COMP/40.394, *Aspen* (not yet decided), or hybrid cases like CJEU, Case C-27/76, *United Brands v. Commission*, ECLI:EU:C:1978:22.
107. *Verizon Communications Inc. v. Law Offices of Curtis V. Trinko, LLP*, 540 U.S. 398 (2004) at 407.
108. For a complete list of these, *see* Giberson, Michael. "List of State Anti-Price Gouging Laws" (Nov. 3, 2012), *available at* https://knowledgeproblem.com/2012/11/03/list-of-price-gouging-laws/.
109. H.R. 2070 - Federal Price Gouging Prevention Act of 2013.

Among others, the New York General Business Law Code clearly states this concern. "During periods of abnormal disruption of the market ... or other extraordinary adverse circumstances, some parties within the chain of distribution of consumer goods [take] *unfair advantage* of consumers by charging *grossly excessive prices*" (emphasis added).[110] And in Arkansas, the law is as clear as to declare it unlawful to sell goods or services for a price of more than 10% above the price charged immediately prior to the proclamation of a state emergency.[111]

Anti-price gouging regulations follow the maxima that public emergencies require modifying the existing order.[112] The existing order in the US is that monopoly prices are what attract business acumen. Not surprisingly, former FTC Chairwoman Deborah Platt Majoras stated that gasoline price gouging legislation "likely will do consumers more harm than good." Further, the President's Council of Economic Advisers considered regarding the same piece of legislation that it would only exacerbate shortages, "create an unnecessary regulatory regime with potentially high litigation costs and great uncertainty" which "would deter investment in new supply, increasing prices in the long run."[113]

This concern is not unjustified. Accidents can create shortages of different products and services and eventually leave few firms in the market to provide them. Scarcity and the prices that normally follow are the natural response of the market to an efficient allocation of those products and services. As acknowledged above, price-gouging regulation can distort market responses where high prices induce entry (assuming the existence of other firms) and, overtime reestablish the market to its former structure and conditions (assuming that no tacit collusion occurs).[114]

However, we want to reposition the discussion along the lines of opportunistic behavior.[115] Not all price increases are the result of increased costs or a readjusted measure of scarcity. In other words, not all rents derived from a lucky position of dominance are Ricardian rents, i.e., generated by the scarcity of the resource.[116] As in

110. Ney York General Business Law of 2014, 396-r.
111. Arkansas Code Ann. § 4-88-303 -4-88-305.
112. Dillbary, Shahar J. "Emergencies, Body Parts and Price Gouging" *in* Austin Sarat (ed.) *Sovereignty, Emergency, Legality*, Cambridge University Press, 2010, at p. 166.
113. A White Paper on The Economic Consequences of Gasoline "Price Gouging" Legislation (Jun. 20, 2007), *available at* https://georgewbush-whitehouse.archives.gov/cea/text/Price_Gouging_WP_062007.html.
114. Montgomery, David, Robert A. Baron and Mary K. Weisskopf. "Potential Effects of Proposed Price Gouging Legislation on the Cost and Severity of Gasoline Supply Interruptions" *Journal of Competition Law and Economics* 3.3 (2007): 357-397. *See* also Rubin, Janice E. "'Price Gouging,' the Antitrust Laws, and Vertical Integration in the Petroleum Industry: How They Are Related." *Congressional Research Service Report* RS22262 (May 28, 2008), at 6, stating that price-gouging laws are "the flip side" to the marketplace competition that sets prices.
115. Idaho Code §48-603(19). Idaho's statute, under Title 48 "Monopolies and Trade Practices" states that it is an unfair method of competition to "tak[e] advantage of a disaster or emergency" to charge excessive prices.
116. *See Chapter* 2 for a discussion on the preferred use of the term profit to encompass both Ricardian and Schumpeterian rents. Sanderson and Winter also captured this point. However, they prefer the term profit or pure rent to identify the unlawful exercise of market power: "One needs to know the source of a high accounting return to a firm, *i.e.*, whether the high return is due to exclusionary activity, luck, the return to genuine business acumen, or talent in meeting a buyer's needs, or Ricardian rents, or scarcity rents, before the high return can be labeled

the above example of the energy supply in Germany, they can also be the result of lucky increase in market power. That is the case in which price increases are not due to the exacerbated costs *and* risks of doing business in a troubled market.[117] In this respect, the North Carolina law is welcome because it explicitly accounts for price increases that are correlated to an increase in costs.[118] This leaves space for market forces to work while preventing opportunistic behavior.[119]

In this context, the EU Courts found in *AKKA/LAA* that to decide whether a price is excessive, the difference between the actual price and the comparative benchmark "must persist for a certain length of time and must not be temporary or episodic."[120] While such finding is mostly welcome as it sets an important limit to excessive pricing enforcement, it could also leave opportunistic behavior by a lucky dominant firm unaddressed. (This is aside from the more obvious question as to how long does "temporary or episodic" mean.)

Indeed, although high prices may be beneficial if they attract entry, over the short-term they also impose "a rationing scheme."[121] In the presence of a lucky monopolist, the question EU competition enforcement should ask is concerned with how many consumers would be better off by way of reducing prices. Suppose a local supplier of bottled water is the only one remaining in an area affected by a disaster and that the previous cost of supplying those bottles was EUR 3. The accident has increased costs of supply by EUR 1. The supply is not simply scarce but monopolized. Taking advantage of the sudden situation, the local supplier decides to sell water bottles for EUR 10 each. While it is true that some consumers will be able to pay for them, and thus satisfy their needs, *more* consumers would be better off if the prices were lower.[122] If ten consumers were better off because they could purchase at EUR 10, a more just

---

'profit' and be used to infer the exercise of market power." *See* Sanderson, Margaret and Ralph A. Winter. "Profits Versus Rents in Antitrust Analysis: An Application to the Canadian Waste Services Merger." *Antitrust Law Journal* 70.2 (2002): 485-511, 511.

117. Snyder, Jeremy. "What's the Matter with Price Gouging?" *Business Ethics Quarterly* 19.2 (2009): 275-293.

118. North Carolina General Statute of 2011, §75-38. Among others, *see also* New York General Business Law of 2014, §396-r(3)(b)(ii) and Idaho Code of 2011, §48-603(19)(b). It has been argued that this safe harbor does not confer much protection to the defendant. *See* Brewer, Michael. "Planning Disaster: Price Gouging Statutes and the Shortages They Create." *Brooklyn Law Review* 72.3 (2007): 1101-1137, 1115, citing *People v. Beach Boys Equip. Co.*, 709 N.Y.S. 2d 729, where the defendant's claim that the high prices to which it was selling energy generators was correlated to additional costs imposed by its supplier was rejected by the court.

119. Note that the major critique offered by Montgomery et al. is that some of the price gouging legislation imposes artificial prices caps that can prevent suppliers from accounting for increased costs of doing business. *See* Montgomery, David, Robert A. Baron and Mary K. Weisskopf. "Potential Effects of Proposed Price Gouging Legislation on the Cost and Severity of Gasoline Supply Interruptions." *Journal of Competition Law and Economics* 3.3 (2007): 357-397, 362, 378 and 380.

120. CJEU, Case C-177/16, *Biedrība 'Autortiesību un komunicēšanās konsultāciju aģentūra – Latvijas Autoru apvienība' v. Konkurences padome* ("*AKKA/LAA*"), ECLI:EU:C:2017:689, §56.

121. Snyder, Jeremy. "What's the Matter with Price Gouging?" *Business Ethics Quarterly* 19.2 (2009): 275-293. *See also* Zwolinski, Matt. "The Ethics of Price Gouging." *Business Ethics Quarterly* 18.3 (2008): 347-378, arguing that price gouging is not morally reprehensible.

122. This is a point missing *in* Brewer, Michael. "Planning Disaster: Price Gouging Statutes and the Shortages They Create." *Brooklyn Law Review* 72.3 (2007): 1101-1137.

scenario would be that of twenty consumers purchasing at EUR 5 instead. Absent economies of scale (i.e., the price to which the seller bought himself the pack does not diminish as purchased units increase) the producer would have lower profits (EUR 1 per sold bottle instead of EUR 6), but consumer welfare would be larger.

That profits would be lower in the presence of labeling excessive pricing conduct as abusive is certain. However, the argument of reward for success loses its strength in the case of a lucky monopolist.[123] Its position and the rents it derive thereof are not the result of past investments or innovations.[124] Certainly, the risks of staying in a distressed market should be accounted for and prices adjusted in accordance. Yet, always bear in mind that "*unexpected* superior economic returns are just that, unexpected, a surprise, and a manifestation of a firm's good luck, not of its ability to accurately anticipate the future value of a strategy."[125] Only the latter, to anticipate and capture the value of a strategy, is the lynchpin of the *competitive* process.

§7.04 CONCLUSION

In the words of Nobel price recipient Jean Tirole, if a firm "dominates simply because of luck of circumstance, that skews competition unfairly."[126]

EU competition enforcement priorities should track firms that have a long-standing in the market. This would prevent discouraging other firms from entering the market knowing they would reap the benefits of their acquired monopoly for a sufficient period of time. On the contrary, suing firms after little time of success might discourage other firms from competing. The introduction of luck as a source of firm dominance alters this scenario.[127] The change in the competitive structure is not the result of better products or improved processes of manufacturing which lower prices. Enforcers know that before the chance event a more competitive structure thrived and could be again reinstated by policing the lucky monopolist. Preventing the emergence of opportunistic behavior should be a priority in this respect. Accordingly, competition enforcement should draw a distinction between firms that arrive to monopoly through luck from those that arrive through superior skill,[128] with less fear for over enforcement or deterring efficient entry.

123. Breyer, Stephen G. "The Problem of the Honest Monopolist." *Antitrust Law Journal* 44.2 (1975): 194-201.
124. Evans, David S. and Jorge Padilla. "Excessive Prices: Using Economics to Define Administrative Legal Rules" *Journal of Competition Law and Economics* 1.1 (2005): 97-122.
125. Barney, Jay B. "Strategic Factor Markets: Expectations, Luck, and Business Strategy." *Management Science* 32.10 (1986): 1231-1241.
126. Tirole, Jean. "Market Failures and Public Policy," *available at* https://bfi.uchicago.edu/news/feature-story/regulation-and-market-power.
127. Breyer, Stephen G. "The Problem of the Honest Monopolist." *Antitrust Law Journal* 44.2 (1975): 194-201, 198.
128. Evans, David S. and Keith N. Hylton. "The Lawful Acquisition and Exercise of Monopoly Power and Its Implications for the Objectives of Antitrust." *Competition Policy International* 4.2 (2008): 203-241 at 220.

CHAPTER 8

The Anticompetitive Road to Dominance*

§8.01 INTRODUCTION

Generally, a US monopolization offense requires an *ex post* finding of market power.[1] Section 2 of the SA case law analyzes whether the allegedly anticompetitive conduct leads to the *acquisition*, maintenance or increase of monopoly power.[2] On the contrary, EU competition law requires an *ex ante* finding of a dominant position.[3] Article 102 TFEU case law analyzes whether an *already* dominant firm behaves anticompetitively. This means that unilateral conduct of firms without *ex ante* dominance will escape liability under EU competition rules. This gap exists independently of whether unilateral anticompetitive conduct leads to the attainment of a dominant position or not.[4]

Article 102 TFEU displays an enforcement gap that seems paradoxical in EU competition law. As shown in previous chapters, both the EU Courts and the European

* This chapter adopts a *comparative analysis* between Section 2 of the US SA and Article 102 TFEU to examine unilateral anticompetitive conduct that leads to the acquisition of SMP.

1. *United States v. Grinnell Corp.*, 384 U.S. 563 (1966), at 570-71. Section 2 SA also declares unlawful the "attempt to monopolize," which would not require proof of an increase in market power. In *Spectrum Sports*, the Supreme Court established the prevailing test of the offense of attempt to monopolize. An attempt to monopolize does not require the plaintiff to prove that the defendant has monopoly power as a result of certain predatory or anticompetitive conduct. Anticompetitive conduct, "a dangerous probability of achieving monopoly power," and "a specific intent to monopolize," suffice to prove a violation of Section 2 SA. *See Spectrum Sports, Inc. v. McQuillan*, 506 U.S. 447 (1993), at 456 and 459. More generally, *see Schine Chain Theatres, Inc. v. United States*, 334 U.S. 110 (May 3, 1948), at 130: "Monopoly power is not condemned by the Act only when it was unlawfully obtained. The mere existence of the power to monopolize, together with the purpose or intent to do so, constitutes an evil at which the Act is aimed."
2. The Sherman Antitrust Act of 1890 (SA, 26 Stat 209, 15 U.S.C. §§1-7), §2.
3. The TFEU makes unlawful "[a]ny abuse ... of a dominant position." Consolidated Version of the Treaty on the Functioning of the European Union - Article 102, May 9, 2008, *OJ* C 115, 2008, 89.
4. Melamed highlights this fundamental difference in his comment to Kaplow's view of market power. *See* Melamed, Douglas. "Response. Antitrust Law Is Not That Complicated." *Harvard Law Review Forum* 130 (2017): 163-172, 169-170. *See* also Kaplow, Louis. "On the Relevance of Market Power." *Harvard Law Review* 130.5 (2017): 1303-1407.

Commission are committed to the protection of the competitive process. And it is clear from their case law that dominance is perceived as an impediment to and not a component of competition. A research question consequently arises: *to what extent is EU competition law concerned with anticompetitively acquired dominance?*

To reveal the existence of this process paradox we compare Section 2 SA with the Article 102 TFEU case law on anticompetitive behavior on the road to dominance. This road to dominance is simply the process that leads a firm to acquire a position of SMP, be it a monopoly in US antitrust law or a dominant position in EU competition law. The reason for this comparative inquiry by reference to Section 2 SA is simple. As explained by Judge Rose in *American Can Co.*,[5] it is the precise wording of Section 2 that allowed Congress to deal with anticompetitive behavior that occurred on the road to dominance. "If such illegitimate attempts [to acquire dominance] were effectively prevented, the occasions on which it would become necessary to deal with size and power ... might never be necessary to deal with them at all."[6]

Importantly, however, our inquiry into the anticompetitive road to dominance does not discuss theories of incipiency.[7] We are not concerned with conduct that may have an effect on competition "before the harm to competition is effected,"[8] that is, before SMP actually ensues. Rather, in the anticompetitive road to dominance, dominance must be the outcome of anticompetitive behavior.[9]

To discuss these issues, we rely on two specific concepts. First, we refer to the process through which a nondominant firm anticompetitively acquires a position of SMP as the "anticompetitive road to dominance or monopoly."[10] Second, the dominant firm that originates from this anticompetitive behavior as an "*unworthy dominant or monopoly firm*."

To verify the existence of a process paradox in the anticompetitive road to dominance, the remainder of this chapter is structured as follows. First, we explain how the wording and general application of Section 2 of the SA and Article 102 TFEU has given rise to different ways of understanding the anticompetitive road to monopoly (§8.02). Second, we explore the different treatment that the case law has given to unworthy acquisitions of market power as opposed to the exercise of that power (§8.03). Third, in line with the overarching theme of this book, we advance a simple

5. *U.S. v. American Can* Co, 230 F. 859 (D. Md. 1916).
6. Also stating: "The problem presented by size and power is one of such far-reaching difficulty that Congress has said, while it does not see how to deal with them when acquired in the legitimate expansion of a lawful business, it will prevent their illegitimate and unnatural acquirement by any attempt to restrain trade or monopolize industry." *See U.S. v. American Can Co*, 230 F. 859 (D. Md. 1916), at 902.
7. Section 2, which makes unlawful an "attempt to monopolize," is also referred as an incipiency statute.
8. *Standard Fashion Co. v. Magrane Houston Co.*, 258, U.S. 346 (1922), at 356-357.
9. Likewise, we are not concerned with conduct that "tends to create a monopoly," as assessed under Section 7 of the Clayton Act or under the EUMR. For a short discussion on incipiency and Section 7 of the Clayton Act, *see* Salop, Steven C. "Symposium on Mergers and Antitrust." *The Journal of Economic Perspectives* 1.2 (1987): 3-12. For a more detailed discussion, *see* Lande, Robert H. "Resurrecting Incipiency: From *Von's Grocery* to Consumer Choice." *Antitrust Law Journal* 68.3 (2001): 875-898.
10. Röller, Lars-Hendrik. "Exploitative Abuses." ESMT, *Business Brief No. BB-107-002* (2007): 3-15.

framework of antitrust liability to anticompetitive acquisitions of firm dominance under Article 102 TFEU (§8.04). Lastly, we conclude (§8.05).

§8.02 SECTION 2 SA AND ARTICLE 102 TFEU ON THE ROAD TO MONOPOLY

In the following section we examine why the text of Section 2 SA can catch anticompetitive conduct on the road to monopoly while the text of Article 102 TFEU cannot. Then we describe policy changes in the interpretation of both provisions on both sides of the Atlantic. On the one hand, antitrust policy under Section 2 SA seems to have lost interest in anticompetitive acquisition of market power. On the other hand, more recent case law at the EU level shows an increasing concern with the enforcement gap of Article 102 TFEU.

[A] A Threshold Misjudgment

The concept of monopoly in US antitrust law is analogous to the concept of monopoly used in microeconomic models. Monopoly serves to designate a firm that has a SMP demonstrated by its ability to maximize profits by charging a price above its marginal cost. Conceptually, a monopoly position is to Section 2 of SA what a dominant position is to Article 102 TFEU. Thus, for general antitrust purposes, monopoly power, dominance and market power are "*qualitatively*" similar.[11] This notwithstanding, US antitrust law tolerates higher degrees of market power than EU competition law.[12] This "*quantitative*" distinction among degrees of market power does not alter the fact that they are qualitatively similar.

Some commentators have argued that this distinction is barely noticeable in practice as the thresholds for monopolization are much higher than those for finding dominance. This would suggest that Article 102 TFEU is catching conduct performed by a firm without actual market power under US-monopoly standards. However, such construction rests on an unadjusted or illogical comparison of both legal systems. Under Section 2, "monopoly" level can trigger liability if further monopolization occurs through anticompetitive behavior. Under Article 102, "dominance" level can trigger liability if abused by way of exclusionary or exploitative behavior. Qualitatively, both,

11. Krattenmaker, Thomas G., Robert H. Lande, and Steven C. Salop. "Monopoly Power and Market Power in Antitrust Law." *Georgetown Law Journal* 76.2 (1987): 241-270.
12. Generally, in the US monopolization is rarely found if the defendant's market share is below 70%. *See Exxon Corp. v. Berwick Bay Real Estates Partners*, 748 F.2d 937 (5th Cir. 1984), at 940. In the EU, firms with a market share below 40% are unlikely to be dominant. *See* Guidance Paper, §14. In *British Airways*, the EU Courts upheld the Commission's decision that British airways had abused its dominant position that covered 39.7% of the market for air travel agency services. *See* GC, Case T-219/99, *British Airways v. Commission*, ECLI:EU:T:2003:343, §211. On the opposite side of the spectrum, *see* CJEU, Case T-79/12, *Cisco Systems and Messagenet v. Commission*, ECLI:EU:T:2013:635. Cisco claimed that the Commission should have prohibited Microsoft's acquisition of Skype, among others, because of the large market shares in video. The GC rejected Cisco's allegations and held at §69, that "high market shares are not necessarily indicative of market power."

"monopoly" and "dominance" are concerned with SMP. Quantitatively, however, their relevance for US and EU antitrust regimes is a matter of degree. While Section 2 jurisprudence reveals a higher quantitative threshold, Article 102 case law reveals a lower quantitative threshold. These are post-threshold levels of market power.[13]

Post-threshold levels of market power are rather a question of policy choice and enforcement priorities, most probably based on different perceptions of market forces and the efficacy and time these will take in displacing or eroding SMP. However, it is not a denial of the qualitative existence of market power.[14] The post-threshold levels of market power that each system is willing to "tolerate" vary, and correspondingly the pre-threshold levels (those before monopoly or dominance is achieved) vary accordingly. If for EU competition law more than a post-threshold of 50% is not permissible (as triggering Article 102 TFEU liability), it should mean that for EU competition law anticompetitively acquiring such "dominance *degree*" should be a matter of concern. Thus, the question whether Article 102 TFEU should catch anticompetitive conduct on the road to monopoly cannot be rejected by reference to Section 2 SA higher post-threshold levels.

This nonetheless, the acquisition of post-threshold levels of market power seems to be out of reach for Article 102 TFEU insofar as it only applies to firms that *already* have a position of dominance. The wording and structure of this Article shows a particular legislative intent in this regard.

As René Joliet illustrated, Article 102 TFEU is about regulating market power and is not concerned with the methods of its acquisition. In other words, whether a firm acquires a position of dominance as a result of certain behavior or not, such behavior cannot fall under Article 102 TFEU.

In the case law, two judgments exemplify Joliet's concerns. *First*, *Continental Can*. Here, the Commission resorted to Article 102 TFEU to quash an acquisition by Continental Can because neither the Treaty nor secondary EU law contained any provision expressly dealing with the control of concentrations. The Court, on appeal, then upheld the Commission's decision. Since Continental Can already had a dominant position, Article 102 TFEU could be used to prevent the acquisition of a competing firm that led to the strengthening of Continental Can's market power. Yet, the CJEU inadvertently ruled that the existence of a legislative gap regarding merger control could not justify the application of Article 102 TFEU to mergers or acquisitions where at least one of the undertakings did not enjoy a position of dominance at the time of the transaction.[15] *Second*, *Michelin I*, where the CJEU established that irrespective of the reasons that lead to a dominant firm to acquire such position, the dominant firm has a

13. We borrow the terminology from, Tor, Avishalom. "Unilateral, Anticompetitive Acquisitions of Dominance or Monopoly Power." *Antitrust Law Journal* 76.3 (2010): 847-872.
14. In fact, any departure from perfect competition results in some degree of market power.
15. CJEU, Case C-6/72, *Europemballage Corporation and Continental Can Company v. Commission* ("*Continental Can*"), ECLI:EU:C:1973:22, §26; *see also* GC, Case T-87/05, *EDP v. Commission*, ECLI:EU:T:2005:333, §§45-49.

special responsibility not to impair competition.[16] The *Michelin I* obiter, that has ever since permeated the EU case law, expanded from the *Continental Can* court. In *Continental Can* the merger was the means through which Continental strengthened its dominant position. Article 102 TFEU could apply to quash those means.[17] But *Michelin* expanded such interpretation. Article 102 TFEU now imposed a special responsibility on *every* dominant firm regardless of the means by which that position was achieved in the first place.

[B] The Paradoxical Irrelevance of Market Power in Article 102 TFEU

Despite *Continental Can*, the finding of an abuse under Article 102 TFEU does not require finding that such the alleged abuse leads to the maintenance or the strengthening of SMP. As the CJEU has consistently held since *Michelin*, a dominant undertaking abuses its position if its behavior "tends to remove or restrict the buyer's freedom to choose his sources of supply, to bar competitors from access to the market, to apply dissimilar conditions to equivalent transactions with other trading parties *or to strengthen the dominant position by distorting competition*" (emphasis added). What is often underappreciated here is that the CJEU formulates the abuse test as a set of alternatives. The strengthening of a dominant position is only one among other standards to decide whether a conduct is or is not anticompetitive.[18]

Importantly, this multifaceted notion can exist because Article 102 TFEU does not require a link of causation between dominance and abuse.[19] As the CJEU established in *Hoffmann-La Roche*,[20] confirmed in *Continental Can*[21] and clearly remarked in *Astra-Zeneca*: "an abuse of a dominant position does not necessarily have to consist in the use of the economic power conferred by a dominant position."[22] The lack of causation implies, first, that the dominant firm need not necessarily strengthen its position to be found in a situation of abuse. And secondly, that it is possible for the dominant firm to abuse its position without actually relying on that position. This multifaceted notion results in easier findings of abusive behavior, albeit, "abuses" that may be unrelated to the protection of the competitive process. This is confusing since, as we said elsewhere,

16. CJEU, Case C-322/81, *Michelin I*, ECLI:EU:C:1983:313, §57; Case C-6/72, *Continental Can*, §27; CJEU, Case C-395/96 P, *Compagnie maritime Belge transports and Others v. Commission*, ECLI:EU:C:2000:132, §37; *and* GC, Case T-210/01, *General Electric v. Commission*, ECLI: EU:T:2005:456, §549.
17. CJEU, Case C-6/72, *Continental Can*, ECLI:EU:C:1973:22, §27.
18. Only in application of Article 102 TFEU to mergers and acquisitions one may find that the strengthening of a dominant position has played a tangible role. *See id.*, §26: "Abuse may therefore occur if an undertaking in a dominant position strengthens such position in a way that the degree of dominance reached substantially fetters competition."
19. Whish, Richard, and David Bailey. *Competition Law*. Oxford University Press, USA, 2015, at pp. 214-215.
20. CJEU, Case C-6/72, *Continental Can*, ECLI:EU:C:1973:22, §27.
21. CJEU, Case 85/76, *Hoffmann-La Roche v. Commission*, §91.
22. GC, Case T-321/05, *AstraZeneca v. Commission*, ECLI:EU:T:2010:266, §354.

it is the way in which dominance is acquired, i.e., the causes of market power, what matters in terms of economic effects and understanding of the competitive process.[23]

That the EU Courts have taken such an approach is not surprising. As Joliet describes, none of the examples listed in Article 102 TFEU "relates to practices by which market domination can be achieved or maintained."[24] On the contrary, they relate to how that power is exercised, irrespective of the features and origins of the dominant firm under scrutiny.[25] Within the EU competition rules, only Article 101 TFEU catches the creation of a position of market power by way of restrictive agreements; and Articles 106 and 107 TFEU limit the State in building up market power.[26]

Despite this long-standing case law and the clear wording of Article 102 TFEU, the more recent case law at both the EU Courts and the Commission levels shows a novel interest in the anticompetitive road to dominance. In *Rambus*, the unlawful acquisition of market power in a standard-setting process led the Commission to claim that Rambus' excessive prices were the result of market power anticompetitively obtained. And while *Post Danmark I* recalled that Article 102 TFEU does not prevent an undertaking from acquiring a dominant position, the Court added implicitly that such position be acquired "on its own merits."[27] The consequences to draw from that obiter about the origins of the dominant firm be taken into account are not fully understood.[28] We shall return to these considerations further ahead.

[C] Market Power at the Center of Monopolization Offenses in US Antitrust Laws

Much to the contrary, it is established US case law that Section 2 requires the plaintiff to show that the defendant acquired a significant degree of market power through anticompetitive means.[29] In other terms, *how* monopoly power is acquired is a decisive inquiry in determining the legality of monopoly power.[30] The effect that must be proven is the anticompetitive acquisition, maintenance or strengthening of monopoly power. Although partially revamped by subsequent case law for its broad definition of

23. Bork, Robert. *The Antitrust Paradox: A Policy at War with Itself*. Simon & Schuster, [1978] 1993, at p. 164; and Röller, Lars-Hendrik. "Exploitative Abuses." ESMT, *Business Brief No. BB-107-002* (2007): 3-15, 9.
24. Joliet, René. *A Comparative Study of American and European Approaches to the Control of Economic Power*. Collection scientifique de la Faculté de Droit de l'Université de Liège [1970] 1975, at p. 247.
25. *See also* Petit, Nicolas, "Intel, Leveraging Rebates and the Goals of Article 102 TFEU." *European Competition Journal* 11.1 (2015): 26-68, 56-57.
26. *See* Chapter 2.
27. CJEU, Case C-209/10, *Post Danmark I*, ECLI:EU:C:2012:172, §20. *See also* CJEU, Case C-52/09, *TeliaSonera*, ECLI:EU:C:2011:83, §24.
28. CJEU, Case C-209/10, *Post Danmark I*, ECLI:EU:C:2012:172, §23.
29. *See, e.g., United States v. Grinnell Corp.*, 384 U.S. 563 (1966) *and Verizon Communications Inc. v. Law Offices of Curtis V. Trinko, LLP*, 540 U.S. 398 (2004).
30. *United States v. Aluminum Co. of America* ("*Alcoa*"), 148 F.2d 416 (2d Cir. 1945), at 429: "[T]he origin of a monopoly may be critical in determining its legality."

monopolization,[31] the Court's opinion in *Alcoa* still voices the importance of such inquiry. "[T]he only question is whether [Alcoa's monopoly] falls within the exception established in favour of those who do not seek, but cannot avoid the control of the market."[32]

US antitrust enforcement vilifies two scenarios of monopoly power. *First*, where a firm that is already a monopoly maintains or strengthens market power as a result of certain unilateral anticompetitive conduct. In *Lorain Journal v. United Sates*, the Supreme Court referred to this idea: a firm "*already enjoying* a substantial monopoly in its area, violates ... §2 when it uses its monopoly to destroy threatened competition" (emphasis added).[33] *Second*, a nondominant firm monopolizes if it *acquires monopoly* as a result of unilateral anticompetitive conduct. This was the scenario encountered in *American Can Co.* where American Can's power had its origin in unlawful acts. Namely, the acquisition of can manufacture plants with the objective of suppressing competition.[34]

These two scenarios have received more or less enforcement interest since the SA was enacted in 1890. The initial policy of Section 2 SA was strongly directed against the emergence of monopolies. Motivated by Congress' fundamental concern with the emergence of monopoly power, Section 2 SA was initially used to prevent firms from acquiring a monopoly in the first place. The 1911 *Standard Oil* case is a paradigmatic example in this respect.[35]

Standard Oil was accused of monopolizing the oil industry by combining the capital stock of various oil firms. Defendants claimed that Section 2 *only* caught unlawful means to acquire monopoly but that once monopoly was acquired it could not be found unlawful. Since Government had been too slow in preventing the emergence of monopoly there was no room for the application of Section 2 *a posteriori*. The Supreme Court, adopting the rule of reason,[36] rejected this view. It held that if Standard Oil's interpretation were true unlawful means of combination not attacked by the Government *before* monopoly power came to existence would be beyond the reach of the law. "Undoubtedly, the words 'to monopolize' and 'monopolize' as used in the section reach *every act bringing about the prohibited results*."[37] (emphasis added).

31. *United States v. Grinnell Corp.*, 384 U.S. 563.
32. *United States v. Aluminum Co. of America* ("*Alcoa*"), 148 Fed. 2d 416 (2d Cir. 1945), at 431.
33. *Lorain Journal v. United States*, 342 U.S. 143, 154 (1951), at 155. Lorain, an "already" dominant newspaper firm, was found guilty of monopolization for refusing to sell advertising space to merchants that already purchased advertising space on competing radios.
34. *U.S. v. American Can Co*, 230 F. 859 (D. Md. 1916), at 877: "There was no other conceivable reason, than the desire to suppress competition, for buying plants which it obviously would not pay to run, and at prices which in most cases far exceeded the cost of fitting up, with brand new and up-to-date machinery, factories capable of turning out several if not many times as many cans in the same time." Yet, Justice Rose concluded that, as those illegal acts had taken place around fifteen years ago, and since then market conditions had changed, the can industry could not simply be put back to where it was in 1901. Dissolving American Can would only destroy a "finely adjusted ... industrial machine" that is able to satisfy all consumer needs. *Id.* at 897 and 903.
35. Similarly, *see United States v. American Tobacco* Co., 221 U.S. 106 (May 29, 1911).
36. *Standard Oil Co. v. United States*, 221 U.S. 1 (1911).
37. *Id.* at 61. *See* also *Rambus, Inc. v. Infineon Techs. AG*, 330 F.Supp.2d 679 (E.D. Va. 2004), at 697: "antitrust law historically has been concerned with the risk of one or a small number of

By contrast, most modern US antitrust enforcement efforts are now directed toward firms that already have monopoly power and that either maintain or augment it by anticompetitive means. This change in direction is perhaps the combination of several factors. First, the decreasing number of statutory monopolies in the US economy.[38] Second, and consequently, a more-economic approach to market power.[39] Third, certain oblivion of the legislative history and early jurisprudence of Section 2 SA.[40] As a result, US courts have reexamined the often-held view that monopoly power was an anticompetitive outcome of the competitive process.

The judgments in *Grinnell*[41] and *Trinko* clearly emphasize that market power can be the result of procompetitive practices and that "monopoly power ... is an important element of the free-market system. The opportunity to charge monopoly prices ... is what attracts 'business acumen' in the first place."[42] Thus, most modern Section 2 enforcement actions have taken place against already monopolistic firms.[43]

Yet, at the same time, the FTC has taken broader enforcement action against illegal acquisitions of monopoly power under Section 5 of the FTC Act.[44] Section 5 of the FTC Act is designed for unilateral anticompetitive conduct by nondominant firms that creates market power but not monopoly.[45] As former Director of the FTC Bureau of Economics Michael Salinger explains, Section 5 of the FTC Act can serve to fill the gap and lower the threshold for intervention.[46]

---

participants capturing the economic power of an industry-wide standard and turning the SSO into a source of exclusionary power."

38. Sappington, David E.M. and J. Gregory Sidak. "Competition Law for State-Owned Enterprises." *Antitrust Law Journal* 71.2 (2003): 479-523, 481.
39. That is, a departure from Judge Learned Hand's finding that: "[N]o monopolist monopolizes unconscious of what he is doing" *See United States v. Aluminum Co. of America* ("*Alcoa*") 148 F.2d 416 (2d Cir. 1945) at 430. Alcoa's increase of production from 42 million pounds of ingot to 327 proved that Alcoa's monopoly was designed, sought after. Little did matter that Alcoa's output expansion would have been considered efficient under any economic standards. Possibly, as Avishalom Tor writes, the reduced interest to police unilateral anticompetitive acquisitions of monopoly may "stem from the perception that its anticompetitive effects are often insignificant, given the limited market power" of the not yet monopoly firm. As we shall see, this is not always the case. *See* Tor, Avishalom. "Unilateral, Anticompetitive Acquisitions of Dominance or Monopoly Power." *Antitrust Law Journal* 76.3 (2010): 847-872, 848.
40. *See* First, Harry and Spencer Weber Waller. "Antitrust's Democracy Deficit." *Fordham Law Review* 81.5 (2013): 2543-2574, arguing that the prevailing error cost approach in antitrust analysis, which is unempirical and disregards accuracy benefits, together with today's rule of reason, is what reduces antitrust enforcement.
41. *United States v. Grinnell Corp.*, 384 U.S. 563. For a less "charitable reading" of *Grinnel, see* Elhauge, Einer. "Defining Better Monopolization Standards." *Stanford Law Review* 56.2 (2003): 253-344 at 261, arguing that the *Grinnell* court "did not really think willfulness was distinct from using business acumen." Elhauge refers to a footnote where the Supreme Court writes, "since ... monopoly power was consciously acquired, [there is] no reason ... to show that their dominance is due to skill, acumen, and the like." *United States v. Grinnell Corp*, 384 U.S. 563, 577, n. 7.
42. *Verizon Communications Inc. v. Law Offices of Curtis V. Trinko, LLP*, 540 U.S. 398 (2004).
43. Tor, Avishalom. "Unilateral, Anticompetitive Acquisitions of Dominance or Monopoly Power." *Antitrust Law Journal* 76.3 (2010): 847-872.
44. Federal Trade Commission Act of 1914, ch. 311, 38 Stat. 717 (1914), codified as amended at 15 U.S.C. §§41-58. ("FTC Act").
45. 15 U.S.C. §§ 41-58, Federal Trade Commission Act.
46. Salinger, Michael. "Remarks at the FTC Workshop on Section 5." (Oct. 17, 2008), at p. 86: "Section 5 should not be used as a lesser version of Sherman Sections 1 and 2, but instead it

The lower degree of market power required by Section 5 FTC Act brings it closer to the degree of market power that makes Article 102 TFEU enforceable against dominant firms.

Unilateral anticompetitive acquisitions of monopoly power continue to find room in the enforcement actions of US antitrust agencies and private parties' litigation. This is unlike EU competition enforcement where unilateral anticompetitive acquisitions of dominance do not fall under Article 102 TFEU. By contrasting US and EU case law, we see that Article 102 TFEU should be reformed if the protection of the competitive process is the goal underpinning EU competition law. The harm that this type of behavior can have in the market (competition *for* dominance) can far exceed the harm generated by mere incremental increases in already existing monopoly power (competition *in* dominated markets). This can be understood with a simple example. In the first case, the deadweight loss created by the anticompetitive acquisition of SMP moves the firm from 0 to 1 without the redeeming virtues of an efficiently acquired monopoly. In the second case, the *existing* deadweight loss is the result of investments or business acumen that can outweigh the deadweight loss. The firm increasing its SMP moves instead from 1 to 1.1 but the anticompetitive impact is simply 0.1, as the remaining 1 is outweighed by its redeeming virtues. That is what we described in Chapter 5 as the gray arrow [O→ Qm] (see Figure 8.1 below).

Figure 8.1 Output before and after Investment

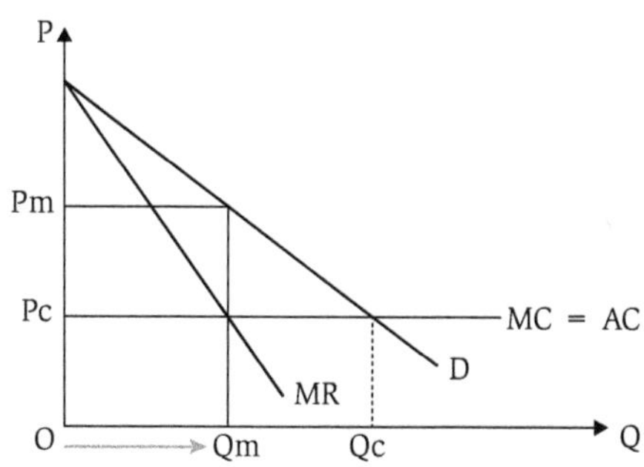

§8.03 THE ANTICOMPETITIVE ACQUISITION OF MONOPOLY POWER AND EXERCISE OF THAT POWER

At a stylized level, two scenarios of unilateral anticompetitive conduct on the road to dominance are conceivable. The *first* deals with the acquisition of dominance as a result of anticompetitive conduct. This path suggests that a nondominant firm has hindered the competitive process to acquire a dominant position. A counterfactual analysis should show with a reasonable degree of probability that if the nondominant

should be used for cases that fall in the cracks between Sections 1 and 2." *available at* https://www.ftc.gov/sites/default/files/documents/public_events/section-5-ftc-act-competition-statute/transcript.pdf.

firm had not engaged in anticompetitive conduct it would not have acquired dominance. The second is concerned with the exercise of unlawfully acquired dominance. This scenario suggests that the behavior of unlawful dominant firms be closely scrutinized and subject to different tests of antitrust liability.[47]

This bifurcated structure is sharper at a theoretical level than at a practical one. Indeed, both US and EU case law show somewhat different enforcement principles and tests of antitrust liability. Section 2 case law is at its core concerned with the first scenario of enforcement, which has given birth to a strand of jurisprudence dealing with anticompetitive acquisitions of monopoly. On the contrary, Article 102 TFEU has only focused on the anticompetitive exercise of unworthy dominance. Albeit, it has done so scantily, restrained by its early jurisprudence holding that abuses of dominance need not be connected to the means by which dominance was acquired in the first place.

Table 8.1 Streamlined Representation of Enforcement Scenarios

	Road to SMP	*Exercise of SMP*
Section 2 SA	YES	NO/YES
Article 102 TFEU	NO	YES

In this section, we examine different theories of competitive harm on the road to dominance and how anticompetitively acquired dominance can be reconciled with the competitive process.

[A] The Road to and Exercise of SMP

In *Standard Oil* the question revolved around the unlawful *acquisition* of monopoly. Defendants contended that Section 2 was inapplicable because they had already acquired monopoly power. Although the *Standard Oil* court rejected the defendant's view, the Supreme Court reexamined a similar but more multifaceted situation in *Walker Process v. Food Machinery*.[48] In *Walker Process* the Supreme Court had to rule not only on the unlawful *acquisition* of market power by Food Machinery but *also* about its *exercise*.

In a patent infringement suit filed by Food Machinery against Walker Process, Walker counterclaimed that Food Machinery had fraudulently acquired and maintained the asserted patent. The mere existence of such patent, Walker claimed, had

47. *Intergraph Corp. v. Intel Corp.*, 195 F.3d 1346, 1353 (Fed. Cir.1999): "[t]he antitrust law has consistently recognized that a producer's advantageous or *dominant market position based on superiority of a commercial product and ensuing demand is not the illegal use of monopoly power* prohibited by the Sherman Act" (emphasis added). It thus follows from such holding that those monopolies whose market power is derived from other than competition on the merits may deserve a different antitrust consideration.

48. *Walker Process Equipment, Inc. v. Food Machinery & Chemical Corp.*, 382 U.S. 172 (1965). The District Court dismissed Food Machinery's complaint and Walker's Section 2 counterclaim.

deprived it of business "that it would have otherwise enjoyed." The Supreme Court had to clarify "whether the maintenance and enforcement of a patent obtained by fraud on the Patent Office may be the basis of an action under §2 of the Sherman Act."

The Supreme Court held that enforcing a patent procured by fraud on the Patent Office might violate Section 2 provided that the illegal patent gave its holder exclusionary power.[49] By requiring that the plaintiff prove the acquisition of exclusionary power, the Court rightly rejected a per se condemnation under Section 2 of fraudulent patent acquisitions. This could not be the case, for example, if the unlawfully patented invention had other effective substitutes in the market. A monopolization offense under Section 2 thus requires that the defendant acquires monopoly power. The claimant must prove that the illegally acquired patent grants its holder SMP.[50]

Walker Process did not only establish that the fraudulent acquisition of a patent can constitute a monopolization offense, but it also establishes a limit to the exercise of that power. Exceptionally, antitrust can be enforced against actions carried within the scope of the patent when the latter has been unlawfully acquired.[51] As explained by the Supreme Court in *Actavis*, actions that are within the scope of the patent are, in principle, not subject to antitrust scrutiny. However, this rule has two exceptions. First, antitrust can intervene in the presence of sham litigation.[52] And secondly, when the litigation involves a patent procured by fraud on the Patent Office as in *Walker Process*.[53]

Patents procured by "intentional fraud" are a "special class of patents."[54] The market power that comes with them is not the result of superior product, business acumen or historic accident. Thus, while antitrust actions against patent monopolies can chill the innovation process, as Justice Harlan opined, "antitrust remedies should be allowed room for full play" when market power has been illegally acquired.[55] In the presence of an unlawful monopoly based on an IP right, the chilling effects on innovation emanate precisely from the unchallenged presence of an unlawfully

49. *Id.* at 174.
50. *Id.* at 178-179. In the context of copyrighted works, the District Court in Xerox clarified that the road to monopoly matters for the breadth of conduct a dominant firm can engage in. CSU claimed that Xerox violated the SA for engaging in price discrimination between Independent Service Organizations (ISOs) and end-consumers. Since ISOs were charged much higher prices than end-users, CSU claimed that Xerox was in fact preventing ISOs from selling spare parts. The district court held that unless a copyright is unlawfully acquired a refusal to sell or license its copyrighted expression is not unlawful exclusionary conduct. *See CSU, L.L.C. v. Xerox Corp. (In re Independent Serv. Orgs. Antitrust Litig.)*, 203 F.3d 1322 (Fed. Cir. 2000). Subsequently, *see United States v. Grinnell Corp.*, 384 U.S. 563, at 571. The *Grinnell* court would reinstate that §2 offenses require proving that the defendant acquired, maintained or augmented monopoly power that is not result of superior product, business acumen or historic accident. In seemingly contradiction, the court writes in n. 7 that since "monopoly power was consciously acquired" the Court had no reason to reach that "dominance is due to skill, acumen, and the like."
51. *FTC v. Actavis, Inc.*, 133 S. Ct. 2223, 2227, 186 L. Ed. 2d 343 (2013), 2232.
52. *Professional Real Estate Investors, Inc. v. Columbia Pictures Industries, Inc.*, 508 U.S. 49, 113 S. Ct. 1920, 123 L. Ed. 2d 611 (1993), at 60-61.
53. *FTC v. Actavis, Inc.*, 133 S. Ct. 2223, 2227, 186 L. Ed. 2d 343 (2013).
54. *Walker Process Equipment, Inc. v. Food Machinery & Chemical Corp.*, 382 U.S. 172 (1965), at 177.
55. *Id.* at 180 (Justice Harlan concurring opinion).

acquired monopoly.[56] Unlawfully secured patents, as representations of market power, harm the competitive process because either monopoly or the inefficiencies imposed by unlawful behavior on market participants in the road to dominance (*t*-1) should not have occurred in the first place.[57]

The relationship between the acquisition and exercise of unlawfully acquired market power is clearly identified in *Berkey Photo v. Eastman Kodak*.[58] Berkey is a competitor of Kodak in the market for converting exposed film into finished prints or movies. Kodak is at the same time Berkey's supplier of film, which Berkey resells to its customers. In a monopolization claim brought by Berkey, the Court held that Kodak had monopolized the photofinishing market by leveraging its long-standing monopoly power over the film and camera markets.

The Court of Appeals engaged in a substantial discussion regarding the demerits of an unlawfully acquired monopoly by a nondominant firm.[59] Affirming conceived fundamental Section 2 doctrine, the *Berkey Kodak* Court recalls that "[t]he statement in *Alcoa* that even well-behaved monopolies are forbidden by §2 must be read carefully in context. Its rightful meaning is that, if monopoly power has been *acquired* or maintained through improper means, the fact that the power has not been used to extract improper benefits provides no succor to the monopolist." "*Unlawfully acquired power remains anathema even when kept dormant*" (emphasis added).[60]

It remains "*anathema*" because it is the unlawful conduct that brought about the monopoly power that Section 2 wants to prevent. That is, the anticompetitive creation of a deadweight loss. The District Court went on to discuss that excessive prices are not in themselves anticompetitive conduct. Although the SA was intended to correct those, this is only when monopoly is acquired through unlawful means. It is not the exercise of monopoly power, in the form of excessive prices in this case, that is anticompetitive,

56. Justice White, in concurring opinion, reaches a similar conclusion in the context of Section 1 violations. The scenario that he describes relates to collusion between patent applicants aimed at preventing prior art being known by the Patent Office. Such collusion would allow them to secure a monopoly grant from the Patent Office, which in Justice White's opinion "runs afoul of the Sherman Act's prohibitions against conspiracies in restraint of trade — if not bad per se, then such agreements are at least presumptively bad." *See United States v. Singer Mfg. Co*, 374 U.S. 174, 200 (1963). *See also American Cyanamid Company v. FTC*, 363 F.2d 757 (6th Cir. 1966), the Court finds that a patent obtained by fraud can be subject to a compulsory licensing remedy under Section 5 of the FTC Act.
57. For a different view, *see Brunswick Corp. v. Riegel Textile Corp.*, 752 F.2d 261 (7th Cir. 1984), holding that no harm to competition results when a firm acquires a lawful patent monopoly because the patent monopoly would exist either way. At 266: "the transfer of a valid patent has no antitrust significance," because it "merely shifts a lawful monopoly into different hands." The approach of the court shows a total disregard for the competitive process by solely focusing on the outcome.
58. *Berkey Photo, Inc. v. Eastman Kodak Co.*, 603 F.2d 263 (2d Cir. 1979).
59. This, notwithstanding that *Berkey Kodak* relates to the acquisition of market power in another market by an *already* dominant firm.
60. *Berkey Photo, Inc. v. Eastman Kodak Co.*, 603 F.2d 263 (2d Cir. 1979), at 275-276. This finding of the Court is remarkable and seemingly contradictory. The Court in repeated occasions established that much of Kodak's success was without doubt due to its innovative efforts. However, it did not draw any difference between unlawfully and lawfully acquired monopoly power: "[A] firm with a legitimately achieved monopoly may not ... employ its market position as a lever to create—or attempt to create—a monopoly in another market."

but the anticompetitive conduct that led the firm to acquire control over prices in the first place. It is "the taint of an impure origin"[61] that deprives the unlawful monopoly, under the US antitrust laws, from "the fruits" of its previous anticompetitive conduct.[62]

The forceful and clear statements by the US courts reveal that Section 2 is fundamentally process-oriented. What we mean with this is that its enforcement is not about monopoly power in the vacuum,[63] but concerned with *how* monopoly is acquired. The existence and exercise of monopoly power are inevitably linked to one another. It is the unlawful acquisition of that power that matters for the competitive process, and its profitable exercise a subordinate reason for intervention.[64]

In Europe, the Article 102 TFEU distinction between acquisition and exercise of unlawfully acquired patents can be somewhat found in *AstraZeneca*.[65] Here, the pharmaceutical firm AstraZeneca had made misleading representations to several patent authorities to acquire supplementary patent certificates (SPCs). These SPCs, the Commission and EU Courts held, unduly expanded the time of protection that AstraZeneca already had for its patented product Losec—a drug used to treat different gastrointestinal conditions.

First, AstraZeneca contended that the mere *acquisition*, even if unlawful, of SPCs could not constitute an abuse alone. An abuse requires that such rights be *exercised* knowing that they are invalid. The Commission argued that misrepresentations before national authorities "*that create* or shield market power may inflict severe public harm" (emphasis added).[66] Second, it claimed that what matters are "the effects on competition," irrespective of whether the case relates to the acquisition of an IP license or the acquisition of an SPC.[67]

The General Court, upheld by the Court of Justice, ruled that Article 102 TFEU does not require "that an exclusive right obtained as a result of misleading representations has been enforced" for there to be an abuse of dominance.[68] Going even further, the GC ruled that an abuse can occur even if the dominant firm does not secure the exclusive right, as long as "representations are actually liable to lead the public authorities to grant the exclusive right applied for."[69]

AstraZeneca is relevant to our inquiry for two reasons. First, because the Court and the Commission consider that the acquisition of market power can be an abuse

61. *Id.* at 296 (interpreting *Alcoa*).
62. *Schine Chain Theatres, Inc. v. United States*, 334 U.S. 110 (May 3, 1948), at 129.
63. *Standard Oil Co. v. United States*, 221 U.S. 1 (1911), at 62.
64. *Intergraph Corp. v. Intel Corp.*, 195 F.3d 1346 (Fed. Cir.1999), at 1353: "The antitrust law has consistently recognized that a producer's advantageous or *dominant market position based on superiority of a commercial product* and ensuing demand *is not the illegal use of monopoly power* prohibited by the Sherman Act." (emphasis added)
65. CJEU, Case C-457/10 P, *AstraZeneca v. Commission*, ECLI:EU:C:2012:770; and GC, Case T-321/05, *AstraZeneca v. Commission*, ECLI:EU:T:2010:266. Although the discussion ensued against the backdrop of abusive behavior by an already dominant firm, it is worth examining—not least because both defendant and the Commission referred to US case law in their arguments.
66. GC, Case T-321/05, *AstraZeneca v. Commission*, ECLI:EU:T:2010:266, §329.
67. *Id.* §336.
68. *Id.* §362.
69. *Id.* §§331 and 377.

independent of its subsequent exercise. However, the acquisition of market power is simply an "extension" of an existing SMP, i.e., dominance. *Only* the Commission seems to plead, perhaps inadvertently, in favor of anticompetitive conduct in the *ex novo* "creation" of dominance. "In the Commission's view, *misrepresentations* that distort national authorities' decision-making in ways *that create* or shield *market power* may inflict severe public harm" (emphasis added).[70] The case is however too unclear to derive any definitive conclusions as to whether the Commission had an anticompetitive-road-to-dominance theory in mind.[71]

Second, *AstraZeneca* is helpful because it draws a distinction between the anticompetitive effects derived from acquisitions of dominance from those that stem from maintenance or strengthening claims.[72]

The classical anticompetitive story tells that a firm eliminates or reduces competition through anticompetitive means and thereafter enjoys the benefits of larger market power. The *creation* of dominance has precisely that *effect*, and the question that must be answered is whether the creation comes at the expense of the competitive process. The question of what constitutes anticompetitive misleading behavior is thus at the center of the inquiry. And this is a difficult question because not every misleading behavior has anticompetitive *effects*.

Taken literally, the EU Courts' finding is that even misrepresentations that are "*liable to lead* the public authorities to grant the exclusive right" are abusive. In other words, plaintiffs need not show that market power was indeed acquired through misrepresentations. We object to this standard if transposed to the *creation* of dominance. In our view, the competitive process is too uncertain to derive anticompetitive *effects* from potential acquisitions of dominance. The risk of false positives would be high enough to dampen the competitive process, particularly in markets prone to competition *for* the field. It is thus our submission, that if the EU Courts were to give a "monopolization" reading to Article 102 TFEU, this standard should be rejected and replaced by a standard that equates anticompetitive effects with the actual acquisition of dominance. In short, this means that misleading behavior requires the *acquisition* of market power that results in the exclusion of competitors or in an increase in power over price.

It is thus welcoming that the Commission emphasizes that what matters are "the effects on competition." However, the Commission and the Courts are wrong to

70. *Id.* §329.
71. Interestingly, *see* Guidance Paper, §30, where the Commission's view that: "*exclusionary conduct which* maintains, *creates* or strengthens a market position approaching that of a monopoly can normally not be justified on the grounds that it also creates efficiency gains" (emphasis added).
72. In the US, the FTC found that *Biovail Corp.* had infringed Section 5 of the FTC Act by engaging in unlawful acts that *maintained* its monopoly in the market for Tiazac, a drug used to treat high blood pressure. Those acts included the acquisition and wrongful listing of a patent in the Orange Book to prevent the entry of the generic version, Andrx, of Tiazac. *See Biovail Corp.*, FTC Docket No. C-4060 (Oct. 2, 2002) (consent order). *See also Bristol-Myers Squibb Co.*, FTC Docket No. C-4076 (Apr. 14, 2003) (consent order), regarding similar anticompetitive listings with the aim of delaying generic entry.

separate the "effects on competition" from the means by which market power is acquired.

While the outcome might look the same (the creation or maintenance of market power) the harm to competition is different if looked at from a process perspective. The fraudulent acquisition of an IP license, or an IP right as in *Walker Process*, will thrust the nondominant firm to a position of dominance (from $0 \rightarrow 1$). Importantly, such behavior eliminates a more important degree of competition in the market, than when an already dominant firm simply secures its efficient position or strengthens it by unlawfully acquiring an SPC or engaging in another type of anticompetitive conduct (from $1 \rightarrow 1.1$). The "effects on competition" are different when looked through the glass of *ex ante* conduct leading to market power. In the first scenario, society has to bear the burden of a deadweight loss that is not the result of the competitive process. In the second scenario, the deadweight loss is redeemed by its procompetitive origins, and only the subsequent anticompetitive increase is inefficient. The enforcement gap of Article 102 TFEU is thus disturbing in that higher degrees of anticompetitive effects would escape liability.

[B] Deception in a Standard-Setting Process

The relevance of anticompetitively acquired dominance for the competitive process is best captured in a series of cases involving unilateral deceptive conduct before Standard Setting Organizations (SSOs).

SSOs set industry standards. Consensus of members is required for the adoption of a standard. SSO members are industry players. Among them, some own technology that may become essential for the development of the standard. Thus, before adopting a standard, SSO members are often required to disclose whether they hold any patents or pending patent applications that they believe are essential for the implementation of a standard.[73] Once the SSO adopts the standard and thus the technology that it will read upon, the owner of the patent required to implement the standard *may* gain SMP *if* the standard effectively eliminates substitute technologies.[74]

The standard-setting process is both a collaborative and competitive process. Often, several technologies vigorously compete to be incorporated into the standard but do so in a cooperative and organized way under the rules set by the SSOs. Notwithstanding the cooperative element, its members may seek to deceive the SSO and its members to see their technology adopted instead of others. Such anticompetitive behavior can entitle a nondominant firm to anticompetitively acquire dominance or monopoly. We proceed under such assumption.[75]

73. This will depend on the Intellectual Property Policies of the particular SSO.
74. Larouche, Pierre and Florian Schuett. "Repeated Interaction in Standard Setting." *TILEC Discussion Paper* No. 2016-010, *CentER Discussion Paper* No. 2016-021 (2016): 1-37.
75. As we have discussed before, the acquisition of a patent, or a standard essential patent, need not lead to the acquisition of dominance or monopoly power. *See* Chapter 5, Bostyn, Sven and Nicolas Petit. "Patent = Monopoly: A Legal Fiction." (2013) and Kobayashi, Bruce H. "Spilled Ink or Economic Progress? The Supreme Court's Decision in *Illinois Tool Works v. Independent Ink*." *The Antitrust Bulletin* 53.1 (2008): 5-33.

Against this backdrop, both public enforcement and private litigation in the US have given birth to a strand of jurisprudence concerned with the unlawful acquisition of monopoly power in the context of standard-setting processes. The EU has timidly followed suit. The first of these enforcement actions took place against Dell under Section 5 of the FTC Act *In re. Dell.* Thereafter, several other cases followed, *Rambus* being the most relevant case for our inquiry for it was tried at both sides of the Atlantic.

[1] In re. Dell: Stiglerian and Bainian Market Power

Dell is a member of the Video Electronics Standards Association ("VESA"), an SSO grouping all major US computer manufacturers. In the context of selecting a standard for computer bus designs, which carry information between computer's CPU and the computer's peripheral devices, Dell failed to disclose the existence of its '481 patent. Some months after VESA had adopted the VL-bus standard, Dell informed computer manufacturers that by implementing the VL-bus design in their computers they were infringing its '481 patent. The FTC entered into a consent order with Dell declaring that by failing to disclose the existence of the '481 patent Dell breached Section 5 of the FTC Act.

On several occasions, following the disclosure policies established by VESA, a Dell representative certified that the proposal did not infringe any known patent of Dell. The FTC found that by failing to disclose its '481 patent Dell had unlawfully acquired market power. There was evidence on the record that if Dell had disclosed the existence of its '481 patent, VESA "would have implemented a different non-proprietary design."[76] As a result of Dell's failure to disclose (acquisition) and its subsequent enforcement actions (exercise) the industry's acceptance of the standard was hindered, uncertainty concerning the acceptance of the VL-bus standard raised Dell's rivals' costs and the industry's willingness to participate to standard-setting process were chilled. Commissioner Azcuenaga dissented.

The dissent serves as a baseline to discuss both the unlawful acquisition of market power as a stand-alone offense (i.e., unlawful monopoly does not require its exercise to trigger a monopolization claim) and the contours of the concept of deception. In her statement, Commissioner Azcuenaga rejected the FTC's view that Dell had acquired market power. The anticompetitive effects put forward by the FTC "do not necessarily translate into higher prices of computers for consumers, restricted output of computers in any relevant geographic market."

Her reasoning is not convincing because the Dissent's description of monopoly power is limited to a Stiglerian conception of market power. That is, market power described as the ability to control price and output. It wrongly dismisses a Bainian conception of monopoly power as the ability to raise its rivals' costs.[77] In this respect, the FTC's allegations of anticompetitive effects relate to the acquisition of Bainian market power. The uncertainty created by the deceptive conduct and enforcement

---

76. FTC, Consent Order, *In re. Dell Computer Corporation*, Docket C-3658 (May 20, 1996), at p. 624.
77. Krattenmaker, Thomas G., Robert H. Lande and Steven C. Salop. "Monopoly Power and Market Power in Antitrust Law." *Georgetown Law Journal* 76.2 (1987): 241-270.

threats of Dell "raised the costs of implementing" the VL-bus standard and "of developing competing bus designs" thus foreclosing competitor's ability to compete.[78] By deceiving the SSO Dell acquired unlawful market power. Because Dell deceived the rules of the competitive process and thus raised its rival's costs its behavior was deemed anticompetitive.

Importantly, the remedies imposed by the FTC are directed at the source of unlawfully acquired market power. Dell was prevented from enforcing its '481 patent in any way. The FTC further ordered that for a period of ten years Dell would cease and desist from enforcing "any patent rights" that where intentionally undisclosed in a standard-setting process.[79] Dell could not seek any royalties from its patent since the FTC had proof to believe that the SSO would have, absent Dell's deception, chosen a non-proprietary standard. Imposing such remedy, the FTC, de facto, dismantled the unlawfully acquired market power, and restored the competitive process.[80]

Rightly, however, the dissent opinion remarks that the FTC did not consider the "intentional" element in the acquisition of market power.[81] It is "intentional fraud," as in *Walker Process*, that triggers liability under Section 2. The Dissent thus considered that the FTC was stretching "established monopolization theory" by condemning Dell.

Intent in the context of a standard-setting process is fundamental as the number of patents that involved in the selected standard can be very large. In particular, participants to the standardization process can own very large patent portfolios and be ignorant as to the ownership of a patent that can potentially be essential to the implementation of the standard. On the other hand, when it comes to searching the same portfolio to enforce the (forgotten) patent, the size of the portfolio seems to pose fewer impediments.[82] In balancing both possibilities, and due to the disruptive effects of antitrust enforcement, negligence in failing to disclose a patent is not sufficient. Negligence is a far cry away from intentional fraud and punishing the former with the same severity as the latter could have negative effects in standard-setting processes.

[2] Rambus and the Anticompetitive Road to Monopoly on Both Sides of the Atlantic

Rambus features a similar anticompetitive deception story as *In re. Dell*. Interestingly, Rambus' conduct gave raise to antitrust proceedings both in the US and the EU. In a clear manner, both enforcement actions show the divergent approach to unilateral anticompetitive acquisitions of monopoly under Section 2 SA and dominance under

78. FTC, Consent Order, *In re. Dell Computer Corporation*, Docket C-3658 (May 20, 1996), at p. 618.
79. *Id.* at pp. 620-62.
80. *Id.* at pp. 616 and 624, and n. 5.
81. *Id.* Dissent Opinion, at p. 632.
82. Kipnis, Jason. "Beating the System: Abuses of the Standards Adoption Process." *IEEE Communications Magazine* 38.7 (2000): 102-105.

Article 102 TFEU. On the one hand, the FTC[83] and DC Federal Circuit[84] focused on the unlawful acquisition of monopoly power and the causal link between anticompetitive conduct and the emergence of such power. On the other hand, the EU Commission focused its analysis on the anticompetitive exercise of unlawfully acquired dominance, with little emphasis on its unlawful acquisition and causal link. While the DC Federal Circuit would set aside the FTC's monopolization findings, the EU Commission would settle the case by adopting an Article 9 decision.

In the early 1990s the computer hardware industry was facing a memory bottleneck problem. In short, this meant that the speed of computers' physical memory was slower than CPUs. This prevented CPUs from realizing its speeds of data processing as CPUs can only compute as fast as the memory can be accessed. In this industrial context, Rambus filed a patent application claiming the invention of a faster architecture for dynamic random access memory ("DRAM").

After failing to establish its proprietary DRAM technology as a de facto standard,[85] Rambus joined the Joint Electron Device Engineering Council ("JEDEC"), an SSO that, among others, was in the process of selecting a standard that would solve the memory bottleneck problem. It then became apparent to Rambus that JEDEC was committed to developing a synchronous DRAM standard ("SDRAM") and Double Data Rate SDRAM (together "the SDRAM standards"), that would rely on as many as possible non-proprietary technologies. Despite such efforts, even if Rambus' DRAM technology would not be selected as the industry standard, Rambus' CEO believed that JEDEC's selected SDRAM technology would infringe some claims of Rambus' patents. Further, that where JEDEC's technology did not infringe Rambus' patents, Rambus could introduce additional or amended claims to its original patent so that it would cover features of the SDRAM standards.[86]

The FTC issued a monopolization complaint under Section 2 alleging that Rambus had deceived JEDEC by failing to disclose its patents and other pending patent applications that would cover technologies incorporated into JEDEC's memory standards. The FTC established that but for Rambus' deceptive conduct, "JEDEC *either* would have excluded Rambus' patented technologies from the JEDEC DRAM standards ['the first scenario'], *or* would have demanded RAND assurances, with an opportunity for *ex ante* licensing negotiations ['the second scenario']" (emphasis added).[87] The DC District Circuit reversed the FTC's decision. The first scenario did not meet a sufficient level of causation. And the second scenario did not involve a monopolization claim.

83. FTC, *In the Matter of Rambus, Inc.* Docket No. 9302 ("FTC, *Rambus*").
84. *Rambus, Inc. v. FTC.*, 522 F.3d 456 (D.C. Cir. 2008), at 469: "The critical question is whether Rambus engaged in exclusionary conduct, and thereby acquired its monopoly power in the relevant markets unlawfully." Cert. denied, 129 S. Ct. 1318 (2009).
85. *See* FTC, *Rambus*, at 8; and FTC, Administrative Complaint, *In the Matter of Rambus, Inc.* Docket No. 9302 ("FTC, Administrative Complaint, *Rambus*") (Jun. 18, 2002), §39.
86. *See* FTC, Administrative Complaint, *Rambus*, §§42-46. Rambus business plan stated, §44: "Rambus expects the patents will be issued largely as filed and that companies will not be able to develop Rambus-compatible or Rambus-like technology without infringing on multiple fundamental claims of the patents ... Rambus' patents are likely to have significant applications other than for the Rambus Interface."
87. FTC, *Rambus*, at 74, 77 and 118-119.

We find both findings by the District Circuit unconvincing. In contrast, we find that the European Commission came closer in *Rambus*[88] to protecting the competitive process by partially analyzing the concepts of dominance and abuse together.

First scenario: JEDEC would have excluded Rambus' patented technologies

In the first scenario, the District Circuit correctly assumed, as a matter of law, that failure to disclose would support a monopolization claim for it harmed the "competitive process."[89] As *In re. Dell*, Rambus' deception would have created a monopoly position that did not exist in the first place. However, the District Court concluded that the FTC had not met the threshold to prove a causal link between Rambus' behavior and the creation of monopoly.

In *Microsoft*, the DC District Circuit had required unilateral behavior to be "reasonably capable of contributing significantly to a defendant's continued monopoly power."[90] Thus, following *Microsoft*,[91] the FTC considered that Rambus' deception "contributed significantly" to the creation of its monopoly.[92] This notwithstanding, and without discussing *Microsoft*'s merits, the DC Circuit established a higher causation threshold: a "but-for-world." To prove causation, likelihood that JEDEC would have adopted Rambus' technology must be removed. Since the FTC had "expressly left open the likelihood that JEDEC would have standardized Rambus' technologies even if Rambus had disclosed its intellectual property" the bar to prove causation was not met.[93]

In essence, the DC Circuit ruled that both scenarios are mutually exclusive. Such finding is only convincing if the circumvention of a price constraint imposed by a FRAND commitment is not regarded as an unlawful acquisition or extension of monopoly power. We turn to these issues now.

Second scenario: JEDEC would have demanded (F)RAND assurances

Regarding the second scenario, where absent Rambus' deception its technology would have been selected when subjected to FRAND terms, the District Court held that it did not involve any monopolization. The District Court held that "an otherwise lawful monopolist's use of deception simply to obtain higher prices normally has no particular tendency to exclude rivals and thus to diminish competition."[94]

The District Court's analysis seems erroneous for two reasons. First, by relying on *NYNEX*, the District Court ignored that market power is not only restricted to the ability to exclude competitors, but it can also reveal itself as the ability to gain control over

88. Commission Decision, Case COMP/38.636, *Rambus*.
89. Quoting *Microsoft*, the DC. Cir., equated harm to competition as harm to the competitive process, at 463. *See United States v. Microsoft Corp.*, 253 F.3d 34 (D.C. Cir. 2001), at 58.
90. *Id.* at 79.
91. FTC, *Rambus*, at 80.
92. FTC, *Rambus*, at 31.
93. *Rambus Inc. v. FTC*, 522 F.3d 456 (D.C. Cir. 2008), at 466.
94. *Id.* at 464.

price.[95] Second, and relatedly, concealing its patents was a way for Rambus to dodge a possible *ex ante* discussion of its prices that could have undermined its ability to be selected in the first place. The District Court thus wrongfully disregarded Rambus' *ex ante* price as a parameter of competition that could affect the creation of a monopoly for Rambus.

Our first critique turns to the District Court's neglect of the fact that market power is not only restricted to the ability to exclude competitors but to "gain power over price."[96] Further, that by relying on *NYNEX* it only exacerbates the error. The District Court ruled that Rambus' monopoly lawfully existed before its technology was selected, any deceptive conduct leading to an increase in royalties would fall under *NYNEX*'s protection.

In *NYNEX*, the New York Telephone Company had circumvented the regulatory power that limited its ability to control prices by, allegedly, fraudulently changing from a low-cost supplier (Discon) to a high-cost supplier (AT&T) for the service of removing outdated telephone switching equipment. As a result of those higher costs, the New York Telephone Company had to charge higher prices, which were in turn approved by the regulator. Artificially higher prices were thus passed on to consumers while the New York Telephone Company would increase its profits as a result of AT&T's subsequent grant of a special rebate at the end of the year. Discon refused to play the "rebate game" and thus was driven out of business.

But the District Court application of *NYNEX's* principle is misplaced. The *NYNEX* Court did not establish a per se rule of legality in relation to deception by lawful monopolists. *NYNEX* only addressed whether the type of conduct had to be subject to a rule of *per se* illegality. Eventually, it refused "to apply the *per se* rule."[97] Thus, applying *NYNEX* principle, the *Rambus* court should have applied a rule of reason to establish whether Rambus' deception constituted unlawful monopolization.[98]

95. Krattenmaker, Thomas G. and Steven C. Salop. "Anticompetitive Exclusion: Raising Rivals' Costs to Achieve Power over Price." *The Yale Law Journal* 96.2 (1986): 209-293.
96. *Id.* at 242. This point disproves the views of Geradin and Miguel Rato that "if dominance could be found to exist ex ante the standard being adopted, *it is not easy to see how the ambush would have strengthened the IPR owner's dominance*" (emphasis added). *See* Geradin, Damien and Miguel Rato. "Can Standard-Setting Lead to Exploitative Abuse? A Dissonant View on Patent Hold-Up, Royalty Stacking and the Meaning of FRAND." *European Competition Journal* 3.1 (2007): 101-161, at 160.
97. *NYNEX Corp. v. Discon, Inc*, 525 U.S. 128, 130 (1998), at 137-138: "To apply the per se rule here ... would transform cases involving business behavior that is improper for various reasons, say, cases involving nepotism or personal pique, into treble-damages antitrust cases." This misplaced use of NYNEX is also raised in Cary, George S., et al. "The Case for Antitrust Law to Police the Patent Holdup Problem in Standard Setting." *Antitrust Law Journal* 77.3 (2011): 913-946, 922.
98. The Court makes this clear when citing Areeda and Hovenkamp, "[I]n the presence of substantial market power, some kinds of tortious behavior could anticompetitively create or sustain a monopoly, [but] it is wrong categorically to condemn such practices ... or categorically to excuse them." *See* US, *NYNEX Corp. v. Discon, Inc*, 525 U.S. 128, 130 (1998), at 137, *citing* Areeda, Phillip and Herbert Hovenkamp. *Antitrust Law*. Little, Brown & Company, 1995, at p. 80.

The District Court in *Rambus* must have accounted for the fact that NYNEX's subsidiary, New York Telephone Company, was, unlike Rambus, a regulated monopoly[99] and that the New York Telephone Company's deception was not conducted in a framework of cooperation between competitors, unlike the more distinct standard-setting process in *Rambus*. NYNEX's deception was not at the heart of the dispute. Rather, it was the competitive freedom to switch from one supplier to that led the Supreme Court to reject a per se rule of illegality for such conduct.[100]

While the *NYNEX* principle of competitive freedom to switch suppliers is welcome, the general rule established in *NYNEX* that a lawful monopoly should charge as much as it wants is incomplete.[101] It is true that the prospects of charging monopoly prices are an important driver of competition.[102] However, at the same time, once deception is what causes the ability of the firm to charge higher prices, there is an unlawful acquisition of market power over price.[103] In our view, competition law should intervene when deception entitles the firm market power to control price.

In the context of JEDEC's standardization process it was assumed that the cost of the selected and patented technology would always be FRAND. If alternative technologies existed, being FRAND (price) an assumed competitive parameter among all rivals, quality would have been a stronger parameter of competition determining the winner. However, Rambus' circumvention of the FRAND commitment reintroduces price as a parameter of competition in the selection of the technology. Thus, even if Rambus' technology was superior in terms of quality, absent its FRAND commitment the market might have deemed its price too high to select Rambus' technology. Thus, a competitive process unaffected by a FRAND mechanism terms could have pushed Rambus into the background.[104] In other words, FRAND worked as a mechanism that adjusted Rambus' prices to the market equilibrium given the qualities of its product. Absent FRAND and the cooperative nature of the SSO, the competitive process could have

99. *See* Culley, Daniel, Malik Dhanani and Maurits Dolmans. "Learning from Rambus—How to Tame Those Troublesome Trolls." *Antitrust Bulletin* 57.1 (2012): 117-160, at n. 29.
100. Making the same point, *see* Wallace, Joel M. "'*Rambus v. FTC*' in the Context of Standard-Setting Organizations, Antitrust, and the Patent Hold-up Problem." *Berkeley Technology Law Journal* 24.1 (2009): 661-693, at 686. Also, it should be recalled that the Supreme Court's decision was strongly influenced by the fear that antitrust treble damages would create over-deterrence, and discourage firms from changing suppliers. *See NYNEX Corp. v. Discon, Inc*, 525 U.S. 128, 130 (1998), at 138; *see also*, highlighting this point, Kovacic, William E. "The Intellectual DNA of Modern US Competition Law for Dominant Firm Conduct: The Chicago/Harvard Double Helix." *Columbia Business Law Review* (2007): 1-80, 62.
101. *See also Berkey Photo, Inc. v. Eastman Kodak Co.*, 603 F.2d 263 (2d Cir. 1979), at 294: "If a firm has taken no action to destroy competition it may be unfair to deprive it of the ordinary opportunity to set prices at a profit-maximizing level."
102. *See Verizon Communications Inc. v. Law Offices of Curtis V. Trinko, LLP*, 540 U.S. 398 (2004), at 407: "The mere possession of monopoly power, and the concomitant charging of monopoly prices, is not only not unlawful; it is an important element of the free-market system."
103. "Market power is the ability to raise prices above those that would be charged in a competitive market." *See NCAA v. Board of Regents of Univ. of Okla*, 468 U.S. 85, 109 (1984) at n. 38.
104. The European Commission made a similar assertion in its preliminary investigation into Rambus's conduct. "The Commission took the preliminary view that there was wide-ranging evidence that the industry was concerned about costs associated with any DRAM interface technology." It "concluded that users were willing to forego increases in performance in order to keep costs down." *See* Commission Decision, Case COMP/38.636, *Rambus*, §§44-45.

selected a different product than it would have arisen under the SSO's vigilance.[105] Let us explain this with a simple numerical example.

Assume that Rambus' technology would be sold at EUR 10 if it committed to FRAND terms, but that absent FRAND Rambus would sell its technology at EUR 12 (there is no price cap). Assume that the next best alternative technology would be sold on the market at EUR 10 without FRAND and at EUR 9 with FRAND. Assume that the implementers' reservation price is EUR 10. Then, if Rambus' technology was superior, implementers would be willing to pay an extra EUR 1, i.e., up to EUR 10, for Rambus' technology. In a FRAND world, the SSO would select Rambus' technology. However, if FRAND no longer restraints price, the implementers' reservation price is below Rambus' own valuation, and having the choice between different technologies priced at EUR 10 and EUR 12, they would choose EUR 10 because the additional EUR 2 would not be worth Rambus' technological superiority.[106] In such scenario, JEDEC would have not selected Rambus' technology.

The only way for Rambus to be *selected* and claim royalties to the level it desired was by deceiving JEDEC and locking in the industry into a standard that made its patents essential to implement it. In a de facto standardization process, without SSO imposed rules and a cooperative environment, Rambus may have not won the process if it was unwilling to lower its valuation or if it took it too long to adjust prices. On the contrary, deception hid the real costs the industry would have to bear and created market power that did not exist because if these costs were revealed to the market Rambus' technology would not have been selected. Eventually, Rambus might have gone out of business. Thus, Rambus could have in fact created market power by circumventing JEDEC's IPR policy.[107]

As a matter of fact, before joining JEDEC, Rambus had tried to license its DRAM technology. The FTC considered that "Rambus attempted to position RDRAM as the *de facto* standard." However, it failed to do so because manufacturers were reluctant to pay the royalties and licensing fees that Rambus demanded. The FTC, however, only discussed this point in the description of the industry evolution, and, mistakenly, did not include it in its assessment of the second scenario of monopolization.[108] As shown

105. Shapiro, Carl. "Setting Compatibility Standards: Cooperation or Collusion?" *in* Rochelle C. Dreyfuss, Diane L. Zimmerman, and Harry First (eds.) *Expanding the Bounds of Intellectual Property*. Oxford University Press, 2001, at p. 88.
106. This is the case, for instance, when technology is marketed too early and consumers are not yet willing the pay the price set by the seller. Knight, Shawn. "Technology Before Its Time: 9 Products That Were Too Early to Market," *Techspot* [Blog] (Oct. 11, 2013), *available at* http://www.techspot.com/article/723-tech-ahead-of-its-time/.
107. *See* Raymon, Neil. "Price Ceilings, Product Quality and Consumer Welfare." *Journal of Economics* 46.4 (1986): 369-395. We acknowledge that the example only considers FRAND as a cap for high prices and does not consider the possibility that FRAND can also prevent too low prices. In fact, RDRAM failed to achieve significant market success, however, at least in part because manufacturers were reluctant to pay royalties and licensing fees to Rambus. This point was mentioned in the description of the industry evolution but did not form part of the FTC's assessment of monopolization.
108. *See* FTC, *Rambus*, at p. 8. This, notwithstanding, the FTC did engage in a discussion relating to Rambus's technology costs if it had disclosed its patents to JEDEC, i.e., in a FRAND world. Even then, it found that "Rambus failed to demonstrate that alternatives would have been more expensive." *Id.* at pp. 81-96.

above, Rambus' misrepresentation could have obscured the costs for its rivals of implementing its technology. This would, in turn, as explained in *Broadcom v. Qualcomm*, "confer an unfair competitive advantage and bias the competitive process in favor of that technology's inclusion in the standard."[109] Rambus acquired market power to charge *ex post* the fees that corresponded to its *ex ante* valuation in a world without FRAND. Had it disclosed its patents before JEDEC and its unwillingness to commit to the FRAND terms, JEDEC would have selected other non-proprietary technology to include in the standard.

This would seem to have been the rationale underpinning the European *Rambus* case. Here, the Commission's analysis focused on "potentially abusive royalties" that Rambus claimed for the use of certain patented technology that was relevant to the DRAM standard. Coining the term "patent ambush" for deceptive nondisclosures in standard-setting processes, the Commission took the view that Rambus' claimed royalties were at a level that absent the patent ambush "it would not have been able to charge."[110]

The European *Rambus* case is of particular interest for it is the first time in which the Commission explicitly links the effects of an abuse to the origins of market power.[111] In other words, it is the "intentionally deceptive" conduct that renders Rambus' royalties excessive. The Commission viewed that "the finding of abuse would rather be conditioned by the [intentionally deceptive] conduct that has necessarily influenced the standard process."[112]

The linkage between the concept of abuse and that of a dominant position is much welcomed. It eliminates the separate analysis of dominance and abuse. This, in turn, helps bridging the process paradox by bringing the origins of market power into the analysis of anticompetitive effects. As shown above, the anticompetitive road to dominance is fundamentally concerned with the competitive process. *Rambus* points

109. *Broadcom v. Qualcomm*, 501 F.3d 297 (3d Cir. 2007), at 313.

110. Commission Decision, Case COMP/38.636, *Rambus*, §28. Furthermore, the commitments offered by Rambus seemed to address the acquisition of dominance as they mirrored, in part, those remedies imposed by the FTC, *In re. Dell*. *See* Commission Decision, Case COMP/38.636, *Rambus*, at §72: "Rambus committed not to charge royalties for the SDRAM and DDR standards that were adopted during the time in which the Commission provisionally considered Rambus may have engaged in intentional deceptive conduct" before JEDEC.

111. Interestingly, in 2002 the Commission explained that it was aware that Article 102 TFEU could be difficult to apply to anticompetitive acquisitions of firm dominance. *See* Brenning, Magdalena. "Competition & Intellectual Property Policy Implications of Late or No IPR Disclosure in Collective Standard-Setting." Speech, Brussels (Jun. 17, 2002), stating that intentional concealment before an SSO "appears difficult to attack it under Article 82," thus leaving a small door open for future action, *available at* http://ec.europa.eu/competition/speeches/text/sp2002_037_en.pdf.

112. Commission Decision, Case COMP/38.636, *Rambus*, §39. Cary and colleagues correctly highlight that under EU Competition law the origins of dominance are not relevant. However, they mistake *Rambus* as one of those cases in which the lack of interest for the origins of dominance allowed the Commission to pursue an excessive pricing theory of harm. The finding of an abuse is conditioned to the deceptive conduct that influences the competitive process. *See* Cary, George S., et al. "The Case for Antitrust Law to Police the Patent Holdup Problem in Standard Setting." *Antitrust Law Journal* 77.3 (2011): 913-946, 943.

to the fact that that *ex ante* games (*t*-1) influence the anticompetitive effects deriving from unilateral conduct in the current competitive arena (*t*).

However, *Rambus* does not come full circle on endorsing a process approach.[113] While the Commission clearly states that Rambus held a dominant position years after JEDEC had adopted the standard,[114] it does not clarify whether Rambus did or did not hold a position of dominance before JEDEC's standardization. At best, the Commission mutters that Rambus did not enjoy such position. Its view was that "save for Rambus' alleged deceit, JEDEC Members were likely to have designed a 'patent-free' standard around Rambus' patents."[115]

But, if Rambus acquired dominance as a result of anticompetitive conduct the anticompetitive effect of excessive royalties would be different than in the case of excessive royalties as a result of the strengthening of an already dominant firm. The Commission would need to prove the existence of excessive royalties by reference to an *ex ante* pricing level. Such pricing level, i.e., the price that Rambus would have been able to charge *ex ante*, would be determined by its market power at that point in time. The price in excess would be thus computed differently if Rambus did or did not have a dominant position at the time before its technology was incorporated in the standard. The difference between Royalty A (non-RAND by deception) and Royalty X (nondominant Rambus) would be greater than the difference between Royalty A (non-RAND by deception) and Royalty Z (dominant Rambus). This means that if Rambus did not have a dominant position, the difference between *ex ante* pricing and *ex post* excessive pricing would have been higher than if Rambus had already been dominant, in which case the difference between *ex ante* pricing and *ex post* excessive pricing would have been lower.

Now, *in arguendo*, let us follow the District Circuit and consider that Rambus' second deception scenario did not create market power by excluding competitors. In other words, in a but-for-world, Rambus would have won with or without deception because Rambus was already dominant. If that was the case, the FTC's alternative finding is worrying because both scenarios are mutually exclusive. On the contrary, the Federal Circuit would have been right to consider that the likelihood standard was not achieved if the FTC placed both scenarios at the same level. On the contrary, one scenario must have been more likely to occur than the other.

A process-oriented inquiry into market power should not simply be concerned with whether Rambus would have won the standard race or not, but rather, how it won

113. The lack of legal analysis is due to the fact that the case was closed by a commitment decision. In our view, the Commission should have issued an Article 7 decision where the theory of harm was fully explained in such a novel case, which went beyond a mere excessive pricing case by relating the anticompetitive origins of dominance to the standard of abuse. Expressing a different opinion, *see* Gautier, Axel and Petit, Nicolas. "Optimal enforcement of competition policy: the commitments procedure under uncertainty." *European Journal of Law and Economics* 45.2 (2018): 195-224, arguing on the contrary that excessive pricing cases bear little legal uncertainty, and thus, a commitments procedure seems a more optimal enforcement priority than an Article 7 prohibition decision.

114. Commission Decision, Case COMP/38.636, *Rambus*, §2.

115. *Id.* §43.

the race and the consequences of doing so for the competitive process.[116] The complete question to be asked is whether Rambus, in the alternative, unlawfully strengthened an existing market power by enabling it to establish non-FRAND terms. This was the case. The creation of that power, as the ability to impose non-FRAND terms, was not the result of efficiency but of mere deception to the established rules of the competitive standard-setting process. Rambus might have not needed to outcompete its rivals because its technology was superior. However, Rambus needed to deceive JEDEC to remove the price constraint preventing it from charging its *ex ante* valuation.[117] Daniel Swanson and Baumol make a similar point when they write that failure to disclose a patent may amount to an antitrust violation, but that this competitive concern will "evaporate" if constrained by FRAND terms. On the contrary, if the firm was unconstrained, it would enjoy "the ability to charge royalties that reflect market power created by standard selection or investments others have made to follow the standard ... and the ability to discriminate against other users of its IP."[118]

In a similar fashion as an SSO, the regulatory authority, that was deceived and thus unwittingly allowed NYNEX to charge artificially inflated prices, is an institution that exogenously influences the competitive process. It dictates norms and regulations that inform an artificial competitive process, not only its structure. While their existence might facilitate anticompetitive opportunistic behavior, this should not—as long as they exist—prevent competition law from being applied to the deceptive creation or strengthening of a dominant position. Quite to the contrary, "cheap" forms of acquiring market power should be at the forefront of the enforcement priorities.[119] A free market is better protected by exposing the problems that state intervention in the market (in the form of government sanctioned SSOs, regulators, etc.) poses to the competitive process, rather than pretending that the state is not, as a matter of fact, a part of it.[120]

---

116. *Rambus, Inc. v. FTC,* 522 F.3d 456 (D.C. Cir. 2008), at 469: "The critical question is whether Rambus engaged in exclusionary conduct, and thereby acquired its monopoly power in the relevant markets unlawfully."
117. This was precisely the concern of Commissioner Azcuenaga dissenting statement in *In re. Dell Computer Corporation,* Docket C-3658 (May 20, 1996), at p. 632. *See also Rambus, Inc. v. Infineon Techs. AG,* 330 F.Supp.2d 679 (E.D.Va.2004), at 697: "Simply put, by hijacking or capturing an SSO, a single industry player can magnify its power and effectuate anticompetitive effects on the market in question."
118. Swanson, Daniel G. and Baumol, William J. "Reasonable and Nondiscriminatory (Rand) Royalties, Standards Selection, and Control of Market Power." *Antitrust Law Journal* 73.1 (2005): 1-58, 54. *See also* Elhauge, Einer. "Disgorgement as an Antitrust Remedy." *Antitrust Law Journal* 76.1 (2009): 79-96, 85 and n. 24. For a divergent opinion, *see* Kobayashi, Bruce H. and Joshua D. Wright. "Federalism, Substantive Preemption, and Limits on Antitrust: An Application to Patent Holdup." *Journal of Competition Law and Economics* 5.3 (2009): 469-516, stating that *NYNEX* was correctly applied by the *Rambus* District Court and that the effectiveness of federal patent law and state law warrants limiting antitrust enforcement against this type of conduct.
119. Creighton, Susan A., D. Bruce Hoffman, Thomas G. Krattenmaker and Ernest A. Nagata. "Cheap Exclusion." *Antitrust Law Journal* 72.3 (2005): 975-996.
120. Another question is whether regulatory authorities should be the only authorities dealing with excessive pricing abuses in this context. We are convinced that this should be the case as they are better equipped to determine what constitutes an excessive price. Their role is to act as price regulators, and thus they have more complete information about the regulated firm and the

Of course, someone could counterargue that competition law is not a torts statute. When "cheating" on competitors, for instance, by signaling an increase in output that will never happen to exclude that competitor is not reproachable from an antitrust and purely *competitive* perspective; on the other hand, where "cheating" occurs in the context of cooperation *and* competition, as in the framework of a standard-setting process, cheating to acquire SMP can be seen as an antitrust offense under a *different* set of norms that are *only* applicable in the absence of the check and balances of self-interested behavior that the competitive market does impose. As "in market transactions, the checks and balances built into the system of commercial exchange are such as to permit more instrumental (or 'self-interested') forms of behavior. In administered transactions, by contrast, these checks and balances are absent ... and thus the institutional context calls for much greater exercise of moral restraint."[121] When deception procures SMP over price *à la Rambus*, then it becomes an antitrust violation.[122] Had it not bypassed the competitive process, it would have been unable to charge undeserved monopoly *rents*, but merited monopoly profits.[123]

[3] Broadcom: Outcomes or Processes?

In the context of private litigation, Broadcom sued Qualcomm for falsely agreeing to abide by ETSI IPR's policy. ETSI is an SSO involved in the selection of technologies to be included in mobile telecommunications' standards. Broadcom alleged that Qualcomm's consent to license its essential mobile technology in FRAND terms was false. The alleged objective of Qualcomm's false consent was to have its technology incorporated in the standard.[124] Had Qualcomm not consented to abide by the ETSI IPRs policy, ETSI would have selected another technology. On appeal, the Court

---

market. We partially share AG Wahl's opinion that in the presence of regulated monopolies, antitrust authorities' intervention should be "mainly confined to cases of error or, more generally, to regulatory failures: cases where the sectoral authority should have intervened and erroneously failed to do so." *See* Opinion of AG Wahl in Case C-177/16, *AKKA/LAA*, ECLI:EU:C:2017:286, §47; *see also* CJEU, Case C-177/16, *AKKA/LAA*, ECLI:EU:C:2017:689. For the US counterpart on the place of antitrust intervention in regulated industries, *see Verizon Communications Inc. v. Law Offices of Curtis v. Trinko, LLP*, 540 U.S. 398 (2004), at 412: "Just as regulatory context may in other cases serve as a basis for implied immunity, *see, e.g., United States v. National Assn. of Securities Dealers, Inc.*, 422 U.S., at 730-735, it may also be a consideration in deciding whether to recognize an expansion of the contours of §2." SSOs, on the contrary, do not have enforcement powers, thus if competition authorities do not intervene, deception or other anticompetitive conduct, that leads to market power, could remain unchallenged. For an opposing view, *see* Kobayashi, Bruce H. and Joshua D. Wright. "The Limits of Antitrust and Patent Holdup: A Reply to Cary et al." *Antitrust Law Journal* 78.2 (2012): 505-526.

121. Heath, Joseph. "An Adversarial Ethic for Business: Or When Sun-Tzu Met the Stakeholder." *Journal of Business Ethics* 72.4 (2007): 359-374; Gauthier, David. "No Need for Morality: The Case of the Competitive Market." *Philosophic Exchange* 13.1 (1982): 41-54.
122. *See* Hovenkamp, Herbert. *The Antitrust Enterprise. Principle and Execution*. Harvard University Press, 2005, at pp. 174-180, discussing torts as antitrust violations.
123. *See* Chapter 2 for a discussion on the bypass of competitive processes and a distinction between rents and profits.
124. Broadcom also claimed Qualcomm discriminated against competitors and customers who were not using chipsets manufactured by Qualcomm but that included its essential technology.

reversed the District Court and declared Qualcomm's conduct an unlawful acquisition of monopoly power that violated Section 2.[125]

The Court established four conditions to establish a monopolization claim. Where "(1) in a consensus-oriented private standard-setting environment, (2) a patent holder's intentionally false promise to license essential proprietary technology on FRAND terms, (3) coupled with an SDO's reliance on that promise when including the technology in a standard, and (4) the patent holder's subsequent breach of that promise, is actionable anticompetitive conduct."[126] Further, the Court went on to deceptive FRAND commitments to the deceptive nondisclosure of IPRs as being both harmful to the competitive process and thus actionable anticompetitive conduct. Somewhat unlike the second prong of the Rambus monopolization claim by the FTC, Qualcomm's false commitment had exclusionary effects because absent the commitment the SSO would not have incorporated Qualcomm's technology into the standard.

Interestingly, the Court of Appeals endorsed a process-oriented analysis that strikingly differs from the more outcome-driven perspective of the District Court. The Court of Appeals focused on the *ex ante* process that led Qualcomm to acquire monopoly power. On the contrary the District Court held that the fact that, as a result of any standardization process, the outcome is the adoption of a standard that eliminates competition, Qualcomm's deception did not alter the *ex post* monopolistic structure of the market.[127] The District Court analysis pays lip service[128] to the reason why competition law protects the process, so that the eventual market power outcome which imposes a deadweight loss on consumers is the result of innovation, investment or business acumen, and not the result of deceptive or fraudulent conduct.

[C] Anticompetitive Behavior *for* Dominance

The line of cases above shows that firms can anticompetitively acquire a position of dominance or monopoly. However, in all these cases the resulting dominant firm had made use of an existing framework established by a third party to gain their market

125. The Court of Appeals held, that FRAND commitments, or lack thereof, are "a key indicator of the cost of implementing a potential technology." The price-setting mechanism, in this particular case, altered by the SSO's IPR policies, orientates the norms under which prices will be set. Thus, by obscuring the costs of the technology in a cooperative environment will disrupt the price-setting mechanism of the market. In other words, "[m]isrepresentations concerning the cost of implementing a given technology may confer an unfair advantage and bias the competitive process in favor of that technology's inclusion in the standard." Such misrepresentations increase the likelihood that, in the absence of monopoly power *ex ante*, the patented technology incorporated in the standard will cause monopoly power. *See Broadcom v. Qualcomm*, 501 F.3d 297 (3d Cir. 2007), at 313.
126. *Broadcom v. Qualcomm*, 501 F.3d 297 (3d Cir. 2007), at 314.
127. "[I]t is the SDO's decision to set a standard for WCDMA technology, not Qualcomm's 'inducement,' that results in the absence of competing WCDMA technologies." *See Broadcom v. Qualcomm*, 501 F.3d 297 (3d Cir. 2007), at 305.
128. The Administrative Law Judge (ALJ) in *Broadcom v. Qualcomm* misjudged a similar outcome situation. In *Broadcom v. Qualcomm*, the Broadcom argued that but for the deception of Qualcomm to the SSO, Qualcomm would have not acquired a monopoly. The ALJ contended that even if that were the case, it did not matter since the end result of the standardization process would be the creation of a monopoly, with or without Qualcomm.

power. Is it possible that in "nonregulated" environments firms anticompetitively acquire dominance? Our short and intuitive answer is yes. If a firm can acquire market power by providing the best product, accident or by sheer business strategy, it seems that unlawful conduct may as well provide a competitive edge that results in a dominant position. Consider for instance the axiomatic example by Posner of the firm that acquires monopoly power by blowing up a competitor's plant or stealing a competitor's trade secrets.[129] While Posner considers that these cases raise little analytical interest because other laws can adequately punish them, we remain unconvinced of the claim that antitrust laws have no room for play.

What all these regulated-market examples have in common is the instant and cheap scalability of market power.[130] It is instant because the dominant position arises from a rapid displacement of its competitors or the incumbent monopoly. And it is cheap because it does not entail a costly or risky strategy to the firm behaving anticompetitively.[131] This instant and cheap scalability however can be found in nonregulated markets and in circumstances less extreme than Posner's caricatural example.

Instant scalability is not a chimera outside nonregulated markets or in the context of rather fanciful anticompetitive behavior like blowing up a competitor's plant. In particular, in winner-takes-all (or most) markets where the emergence of a monopoly or a dominant position is a highly probable outcome, anticompetitive practices during the period of competition *for* dominance may tip the market in favor of the violator. Liebowitz and Margolis document that in the markets for personal finance software and low-end desktop publishing, market shares changed by 50% or 60% within two years; and in the Internet browser market 40% within a similar two-year period interval.[132]

Note again that the concepts of monopoly or dominance simply denote a certain degree of market power.[133] Quantitatively, firms with market power can thus be above or below the threshold that each authority is willing to tolerate. Qualitatively, the firm, unless it departs from a perfect competition scenario, does not acquire market power *ex*

129. Posner, Richard A. *Antitrust Law*. The University of Chicago Press, 2009, at p. 195.
130. We borrow the term of "instant scalability" from Liebowitz, Stan J. and Stephen E. Margolis. "Network Effects and the Microsoft Case" *in* Jerome Ellig (ed.) *Dynamic Competition and Public Policy: Technology, Innovation, and Antitrust Issues*. Cambridge 2001, at p. 163: referring to instant scalability as the characteristic that allows the firm to increase output "very rapidly without the additional costs associated with sudden increases in output." Other unlawful acquisitions of dominance that make use of established procedures could arise in the context of public procurement processes. Here, nevertheless, the strategy might prove less rational as the actor that sets up the tender—normally the State or an infra-State authority—will be able to restore the competitive process by setting up another tender procedure and prohibiting the firm to participate again.
131. Creighton, Susan A., D. Bruce Hoffman, Thomas G. Krattenmaker and Ernest A. Nagata. "Cheap Exclusion." *Antitrust Law Journal* 72.3 (2005): 975-995, 977.
132. Liebowitz, Stan J. and Stephen E. Margolis. "Network Effects and the Microsoft Case" *in* Jerome Ellig (ed.) *Dynamic Competition and Public Policy: Technology, Innovation, and Antitrust Issues*. Cambridge 2001, at p. 184.
133. *See* Shenefield, John H. and Stelzer, Irwin M. *The Antitrust Laws: A Primer*. American Enterprise Institute, 2001, at 37: "Remember that monopoly itself is only a threshold requirement for Section 2 application."

novo but it strengthens or extends its already existing market power. Thus, the higher the degree of market power the stronger the possibility that exclusionary conduct confers a position of dominance or monopoly.

Notwithstanding the above, the set of exclusionary strategies that can materially lead to a position of dominance or monopoly are more limited in a competitive market than in a regulated market.[134]

For example, deception or misrepresentations in a competition-*for*-dominance environment are less likely to be actionable anticompetitive conduct than in a regulated setting. In a standard-setting process, participants will be less aware or ready to defend themselves against possible anticompetitive strategies due to the inherently cooperative nature of the process.[135] Similarly, the regulated market in which market power was unlawfully acquired will prompt market participants to "respect" the monopoly[136] because the dominant position, although unworthy, is vested with a false veil of legitimacy.[137] In contrast, where a firm has anticompetitively secured its dominant position in a competitive market, competitors will be more readily predisposed to fight and challenge that dominant position.[138]

[D] Summation

US antitrust enforcement is commonly described as outcome oriented. This means that, in Section 2 cases, the plaintiff must generally prove the acquisition (maintenance or strengthening) of market power. On the contrary, EU competition law is commonly described as process-oriented, based on the ubiquitous statements by the EU Courts and Commission that the objective of competition law is to protect the competitive process.

While these descriptions are fundamentally correct they lead to wrong conclusions as to how enforcement is truly concerned with the process of competition. As shown by both the wording of Section 2 and its case law, the analysis of outcomes in

134. *Brooke Group Ltd. v. Brown & Williamson Tobacco Corp.*, 509 U.S. 209 (1993), at 225: "[e]ven an act of pure malice by one business competitor against another does not, without more, state a claim under the federal antitrust laws." It is important to note that this is a question of tactics rather than anticompetitive effects. Empirically, it may be possible that larger firms are more likely to undertake a larger set of successful exclusionary tactics. But this would prioritize "tactics over [anticompetitive] harm." *See* Brennan, Timothy J. "Saving Section 2: Reframing U.S. Monopolization Law" *in* Vivek Ghosal and Johan Stennek (eds.) *The Political Economy of Antitrust (Contributions to Economic Analysis, Volume 282)* Emerald Group Publishing Limited, 2007: 417-451, 425.
135. *Broadcom v. Qualcomm*, 501 F.3d 297 (3d Cir. 2007), at 312.
136. *See, e.g.*, GC, Case T-321/05, *AstraZeneca v. Commission*, ECLI:EU:T:2010:266, §362.
137. Competitors of the dominant firm will, assumingly, not infringe the patent, abide by the public regulation, or follow the SSO standard.
138. The FTC made this point in FTC, *Rambus*. *See In the Matter of Rambus, Inc.* Docket No. 9302, at 32-33. In *ITT Promedia*, the Commission refused to hear ITT's claim that Belgacom was abusing its dominant position by spreading "false, misleading and disparaging statements" against ITT. However, the Commission's rejection was because the Brussels Court of Commerce had already granted relief in favour of ITT. (Belgacom was at that time a legal monopoly.) *See* Commission Decision, Case COMP/IV/35.268, *ITT Promedia / Belgacom* (Rejection decision of Dec. 21, 1995), §§8-10.

US antitrust law is as a matter of fact process-oriented. By asking *how* the dominant firm acquired a monopoly in the first place, US courts avoid falling in the trap of condemning monopoly in isolation.[139] On the contrary, while the EU Courts case law prides itself from protecting the process, the wording of Article 102 TFEU and the actual analysis of the EU Courts is fundamentally outcome-oriented in abuse of dominance cases. Little does it matter *how* the firm acquired its dominant position. What matters is that the very existence of dominance is deemed to weaken the competitive structure and thus the firm holding that position has a special responsibility not to weaken it further.

Further, these cases illustrate that competition enforcement paths are bifurcated. While Article 102 TFEU cannot condemn the unlawful acquisition of a dominant position, Section 2 outlaws the anticompetitive acquisition of monopoly power. Unlawful monopoly not only remains *anathema*, but the means by which it is acquired can trigger liability under Section 2. This reveals that the understanding of competition as a process is embedded in Section 2. On the contrary, the wording of Article 102 TFEU literally displays little intention to protect the competitive process.

§8.04 FIXING THE ENFORCEMENT GAP IN ARTICLE 102 TFEU

Could EU competition law integrate the anticompetitive origins of a dominant position into the analysis of a subsequent abuse of that position?

Introducing a more process-oriented proposition in EU competition law, which is at the core of our proposition, is undoubtedly likely to run into difficulties. This is particularly true in the case of an unworthy dominant position. Four questions would need to be addressed. First, are outcomes and processes different? Second, is the CJEU inclined to look at the process? Third, is the irrelevance of causation in the case law of Article 102 TFEU an impediment? And, fourth, is it possible to design remedies that restore competition to its precompetitive state, where rivals may have already exited the market?[140] We explore these questions below.

[A] Differences Between Processes and Outcomes

Notwithstanding that US Section 2 case law "cannot take precedence" over the enforcement of European competition law,[141] the preceding sections reveal that by

139. In the case of *ex novo* acquisitions of market power, this is assessed by reference to the *process* that brought the firm to dominance in the first place.

140. Gavil, Andrew I., William E. Kovacic, Jonathan B. Baker and Joshua Wright. *Antitrust Law in Perspective: Cases, Concepts and Problems in Competition Policy*. West Academic Publishing, 2017, at p. 1100.

141. GC, Joined Cases T-191/98 and T-212/98 to T-214/98, *Atlantic Container Line and Others v. Commission*, ECLI:EU:T:2003:245, §1407: "the Commission cannot be required in its decision to explain why it departs from the legal position adopted under US law ... the position adopted by US law cannot take precedence over that adopted by Community law."

looking into the anticompetitive origins of dominant firms the analysis of anticompetitive conduct is more process-oriented.[142] Bridging the disconnection between dominance and abuse would reinforce that objective.

The anticompetitive origins of a dominant firm clearly expose that anticompetitive process and outcomes are two sides of the same coin. They cannot be disconnected from one and other. At a stylized level, monopoly power is the target of antitrust laws because it imposes a deadweight loss on society. Monopoly power reduces output and increases prices where competition would increase output and reduce prices.[143] Now, overarching idea is that not all deadweight losses are equal. In this context, the origins of a dominant firm provide welcome information on the welfare effects of business behavior. Our understanding of the deadweight loss ceases to be a basic snapshot and turns into a process-oriented movie. As seen in previous chapters, the deadweight loss created by innovative efforts is counteracted and even outweighed by the innovation that lies beneath market power. It is in this sense that, from a process perspective, the investor origins of a dominant firm are superior to the deadweight loss imposed on society by a lucky monopolist.[144]

Now, if there is a cause where the imposed deadweight loss cannot be justified from a process perspective, then it is when that one is unworthy. The anticompetitive acquisition of dominance not only imposes a deadweight loss on society, but it also dissipates all possible redeeming virtues of such SMP. Its undeserving and inefficient origins are proof of an already distorted market and loss of efficiency.[145] It is only in these circumstances where the pervasive statement of the EU Courts that the mere presence of a dominant undertaking weakens the competitive process becomes partially accurate. We should fine-tune that statement. It is the presence of *anticompetitively acquired* dominance that reveals whether the competitive process has been weakened. Anticompetitively acquired dominance, and not just dominance, is thus the central antitrust problem because, as some commentators have put it, "the inefficient acquisition of market power ... harms consumers" and "more fundamentally [because it] subverts the competitive process."[146] As such competition rules aiming at protecting the competitive process should prevent their *unlawful* emergence and establish different tests and thresholds of liability.

As a matter of fact, by focusing on the anticompetitive acquisition or creation of dominance Article 102 TFEU is brought in line with the spirit of other competition law

142. For a divergent view, *see* Devlin, Alan. "Analyzing Monopoly Power Ex Ante." *NYU Journal of Law & Business* 5 (2009): 153-206, arguing in favor of an *ex ante* approach to market power analysis in Section 2 cases.
143. Nothing prevents a monopoly from setting prices at a competitive level. The assumption that a dominant firm imposes a deadweight loss which is larger than some measure of competition, or even perfect competition, is just that: an assumption.
144. *See* Chapter 7.
145. Tor, Avishalom. "Unilateral, Anticompetitive Acquisitions of Dominance or Monopoly Power." *Antitrust Law Journal* 76.3 (2010): 847-872, 855.
146. Farrell, Joseph, John Hayes, Carl Shapiro and Theresa Sullivan. "Standard Setting, Patents, and Hold-Up." *Antitrust Law Journal* 74.3 (2007): 603-670, 609.

provisions.[147] Articles 101, 106 and 107 TFEU and merger control's[148] fundamental concern is whether market power is created through noncompetitive means.[149] Although quantitatively concerned with different degrees of market power, Article 101 TFEU essentially asks whether certain artificially created market power allows firms to fix prices, restrict output or allocate markets;[150] Articles 106 and 107 TFEU ask whether the State confers a competitive advantage to a firm (or group of firms) while denying the same advantage to other similar firms;[151] and the Merger Control regulation essentially asks whether a merger would substantially lessen competition by creating market power.[152]

The unavoidable ensuing question is how to bridge this enforcement gap if Article 102 TFEU is not a monopolization statute.

[B] How to Bridge the Gap?

The straightforward solution would be to amend the Treaty to include a "domination" passage in Article 102 TFEU. Such change, however, seems to fall short of the political support necessary to open a Treaty revision procedure.[153]

---

147. Ortiz Blanco, Luis. *Market Power in EU Antitrust Law*. Bloomsbury Publishing, 2011.
148. Council Regulation (EC) No 139/2004 of 20 January 2004 on the control of concentrations between undertakings (the EC Merger Regulation), *OJ* L 24, 29.01.2004, p. 1-22.
149. *See* Brennan, Timothy J. "Saving Section 2: Reframing U.S. Monopolization Law" *in* Vivek Ghosal and Johan Stennek (eds.) *The Political Economy of Antitrust (Contributions to Economic Analysis, Volume 282)* Emerald Group Publishing Limited, 2007: 417-451, from which the example is taken.
150. CJEU, Case C-6/72, *Continental Can*, ECLI:EU:C:1973:22, §25: "Articles 85 and 86 seek to achieve the same aim on different levels, *viz.* the maintenance of effective competition." The holding seems at odds with the subsequent statement, at §27, that "the means and procedure by which [a dominant position] is achieved" are irrelevant to the application of Article [102 TFEU]. In the context of Article 101 TFEU, *see* Stucke, Maurice E. and Ariel Ezrachi. "Artificial Intelligence & Collusion: When Computers Inhibit Competition." *Oxford Legal Studies Research Paper No. 18/2015; University of Tennessee Legal Studies Research Paper No. 267* (Apr. 8, 2015), at 21, asking the relevant question as to the condemnation of algorithms that allow the creation of market power by collusion: "The question is therefore whether one may condemn and challenge the creation of market conditions which led to sustaining tacit collusion - the creation of a transparent market in which monitoring and punishment mechanisms are present."
151. Friederiszick, Hans W., Lars-Hendrik Röller and Vincent Verouden. "European State Aid Control: An Economic Framework" *in* Paolo Buccirossi (ed.) *Handbook of Antitrust Economics*. The MIT Press, 2006: 625-669.
152. Council Regulation (EC) No. 139/2004 of 20 January 2004 on the control of concentrations between undertakings (the EC Merger Regulation), *OJ* L 24, 29.1.2004, p. 1-22, §§25 and 26: While a significant impediment to effective competition (SIEC) goes "beyond the concept of dominance," SIEC also "generally results from the creation or strengthening of a dominant position."
153. As established in Article 48 of the TEU, which contains the Treaty amendment procedure, the use of the simplified procedure is forbidden when the proposal is aimed to "*increase* the competences conferred on the Union." Being the ordinary procedure thus the only amendment procedure available at this stage renders a potential reform of Article 102 TFEU implausible. For a detailed overview of the revision procedures, *see* Rossi, Lucia Serena. "A New Revision of the EU Treaties after Lisbon?" *in* Lucia S. Rossi and Federico Casolari (eds.) *The EU after Lisbon*. Springer International Publishing, 2014. The ordinary procedure has been used to adopt two

Against this background, we would welcome an initiative intended to integrate the anticompetitive origins of the dominant position into the analysis of abuse. As we have previously maintained and demonstrated, it is the origins of market power that matter in terms of economic effects.[154]

Despite some commentators describing the EU *Rambus* case as a "controversial" decision,[155] we remained convinced that the EU *Rambus* case is praiseworthy. It shows that the Commission is willing to integrate the unlawful acquisition of market power into the assessment of economic effects. In particular, it is Rambus where the "unfair pricing" prohibition makes sense, as well as other exploitative theories of harm. The difficulty of separating procompetitive conduct from exploitative behavior is bridged by reference to *ex ante* anticompetitive conduct.[156]

Lars-Hendrik Röller, the first-appointed Chief Economist at DG COMP, is the major exponent of such approach. His approach not only reveals pragmatism but also a fundamental concern with the competitive process. "By focusing on the road to dominance through anticompetitive behavior, exploitative abuse cases are firmly grounded in the way markets work."[157] In contrast, if a firm acquires dominance competitively, then the subsequent exploitation of such position is just the reward for its *ex ante* conduct.[158] The approach is also supported by Avishalom Tor,[159] and also Motta and de Streel, who consider that a "necessary (but not sufficient) condition" to condemn excessive pricing actions in abuse of dominance cases, is that the origins of the dominant position are due to past and uncondemned anticompetitive behavior.[160]

Importantly, not only the EU *Rambus* decision but also *TeliaSonera* and *Post Danmark I* present an opportunity to include the unlawful origins of the dominant firm into the assessment. In *TeliaSonera* the Court ruled for the first time, "Article 102 TFEU does not prohibit an undertaking from acquiring, *on its own merits*, the dominant position in a market ... " (emphasis added). The Court in *Post Danmark I* gave particular content to the words "*on its own merits*" and seemingly ruled that the legal

protocols. One to increase the number of European Members of Parliament and a second "Protocol on the concerns of the Irish people on the Treaty of Lisbon," *OJ* L 60, 2.3.2013, p. 129-130.

154. Röller, Lars-Hendrik. "Exploitative Abuses." *ESMT, Business Brief No. BB-107-002* (2007): 3-15, 9; and Bork, Robert. *The Antitrust Paradox: A Policy at War with Itself*. Simon & Schuster, [1978] 1993, at p. 169.
155. De La Mano, Miguel, Renato Nazzini and Hans Zenger. "Article 102" *in* Jonathan Faull and Ali Nikpay (eds.) *The EU Law of Competition*, Oxford, 2014, at p. 501.
156. In a Rawlsian way, Lyons states: "our view of fairness comes from the process by which inequality has been generated. If the process is considered fair, the observed inequalities are typically considered fair." *See* Lyons, Bruce. "Inequality and Competition Policy." *CPI* (October 2017):1-6, 3.
157. Röller, Lars-Hendrik. "Exploitative Abuses." *ESMT, Business Brief No. BB-107-002* (2007): 3-15, 10.
158. Elhauge, Einer. "Disgorgement as an Antitrust Remedy." *Antitrust Law Journal* 76.1 (2009): 79-96, 91.
159. Tor, Avishalom. "Unilateral, Anticompetitive Acquisitions of Dominance or Monopoly Power." *Antitrust Law Journal* 76.3 (2010): 847-872, 856.
160. The other conditions are the presence of high and non-transitory barriers and the lack of jurisdiction of sector-specific regulator to solve the matter. *See* Motta, Massimo and Alexandre de Streel. "Excessive Pricing in Competition Law: Never Say Never?" *in* Konkurrensverket (ed.) *The Pros and Cons of High Prices*, 2007: 14-46.

origins of a dominant firm are not on the merits. The implementation of a "merited" acquisition of market power thus leaves the door open to other "non-merited" acquisitions of dominance, like those that are anticompetitive.[161]

Some commentators have pointed in this direction. Ekaterina Rousseva and Mel Marquis write that a possible reading of such statement could be as giving content to the special responsibility to firms that have achieved dominance "by anticompetitive means outside the scope of Article 102." In this latter case, the dominant firm could be "subject to closer scrutiny."[162]

The statement "on its own merits" is however based on a deceiving reference in *TeliaSonera* and *Post Danmark I* to *Michelin*. Quite on the opposite side of the spectrum, the *Michelin I* Court established that dominant firms have the special responsibility not to impair competition, "*irrespective of the reasons* for which it has such a dominant position"[163] (emphasis added). While *Michelin I* is perhaps the most vivid exponent of what we call the black-box treatment of dominance, *TeliaSonera* and, to a greater degree, *Post Danmark I*, break that box by delivering an obiter to take into account the *legal origins* of the dominant firm, and more largely those that are (not) on the merits.[164] However, the CJEU is still reluctant to do so. In its much-awaited answer to a preliminary reference on the concept of "unfair prices" neither the Court of Justice

161. Interestingly, it must be noted that the Spaak Report were aware of the possibility of including a domination statue. However, they concluded it unnecessary as revealed by Article 102 TFEU. The reasons are however unclear from the report. *See* Intergovernmental Committee established by the Messina Conference. "Report of the Heads of Delegation to the Foreign Ministers" (Brussels, Apr. 21, 1956). Some commentators have suggested that the exclusion of a domination provision indicates that the founding members of the European Communities did not side with the more orthodox ordoliberal tradition where monopoly was seen as an evil in and of itself, irrespective of its origins. *See* Akman, Pinar. *The Concept of Abuse in EU Competition Law: Law and Economic Approaches*. Bloomsbury Publishing, 2012, at p. 96.
162. Rousseva, Ekaterina, and Mel Marquis. "Hell Freezes Over: A Climate Change for Assessing Exclusionary Conduct under Article 102 TFEU." *Journal of European Competition Law & Practice* 4.1 (2013): 32-50, 43.
163. CJEU, Case C-322/81, *Michelin v. Commission*, ECLI:EU:C:1983:313, §57.
164. The court refers to *TeliaSonera* and *Michelin I*, where *TeliaSonera* had previously referred to Michelin to introduce the statement "on its own merits." Thus, the contradictory statement lies with *TeliaSonera*, but gains significance in *Post Danmark I* when the Court introduces its obiter. This type of referencing error lingers in the case law and would seem to occur when the court wants to reinterpret the application of competition law principles. As Nicolas Petit shows, the Court of Justice in *Cartes Bancaires*, to determine when an agreement is *restrictive by object*, referred to a sequence of cases that ended up with *Asnef-Equifax and Administración del Estado*, where the Court had established how to determine when an agreement is *restrictive by effect*. *See* Petit, Nicolas, "La rationalisation au long cours de la restriction de concurrence par « objet » dans la jurisprudence de la Cour de justice de l'Union européenne." *Actualité Juridique Contrats d'affaires* October (2015): 422-429; CJEU, Case C-67/13 P *Groupement des cartes bancaires (CB) v. Commission*, ECLI:EU:C:2014:2204, §53 and C-238/05, *Asnef-Equifax, Servicios de Información sobre Solvencia y Crédito, SL, Administración del Estado v. Asociación de Usuarios de Servicios Bancarios (Ausbanc)*, ECLI:EU:C:2006:734, §49. *See also* Petit, Nicolas, "Intel, Leveraging Rebates and the Goals of Article 102 TFEU." *European Competition Journal* 11.1 (2015): 26-68, at 40-52: criticizing "the truly spectacular number of inconsistencies" in the judgment of the General Court in *Intel*.

nor AG Wahl included the anticompetitive origins of a dominant position as a possible scenario of excessive pricing abuses.[165]

[C] Causation and Abuse

Causation is a fundamental requirement to ascertain whether anticompetitive conduct is what significantly contributed the nondominant to acquire dominance in the first place. In the proposed solution to fix the gap in the enforcement of Article 102 TFEU, it is the anticompetitive origins of the dominant firm that render subsequent exploitation or exclusion anticompetitive. Thus, it arises the need to establish a causal link between dominance and abuse.

Since what renders anticompetitive the *ex post* conduct of the dominant undertaking is its anticompetitive origin, it should be necessary to prove that the *ex ante* conduct reasonably appears capable of making a significant contribution to creating dominance.[166]

The requirement we set forth finds some hurdle in *Continental Can*. Here the Court established that the link of causality between dominance and abuse is of no relevance. "[T]he strengthening of the position of an undertaking may be an abuse and prohibited under Article [102] of the Treaty, regardless of the means and procedure by which it is achieved."[167] But the relevance of the origins advanced by the Court in *Post Danmark I* indicates a change in the direction of a more process-oriented approach.

The integration of dominance in the assessment of the abusive conduct could start, as it timidly did in *Rambus*, with those positions of dominance that have been anticompetitively acquired, or legally granted by the state, as the Court advanced in *Post Danmark I*.

The threshold of causation that we propose follows the US *Microsoft* Court: any anticompetitive conduct that *reasonably appears capable* of having created a dominant position.[168] The Court endorsed Areeda and Hovenkamp's view that since "monopoly will almost certainly be grounded in part in factors other than a particular exclusionary act, no government seriously concerned about the evil of monopoly would condition its intervention solely on a clear and genuine chain of causation from an exclusionary act to the presence of monopoly."[169]

Causation is also necessary to impose adequate remedial action requires a counterfactual analysis. Should a court impose structural or behavioral remedies? As Areeda and Hovenkamp write: "more extensive equitable relief, particularly remedies

165. CJEU Case C-177/16, *Biedrība 'Autortiesību un komunicēšanās konsultāciju aģentūra – Latvijas Autoru apvienība' v. Konkurences padome*, ECLI:EU:C:2017:689 *and* AG Wahl Opinion, Case C-177/16, *Biedrība 'Autortiesību un komunicēšanās konsultāciju aģentūra – Latvijas Autoru apvienība' v. Konkurences padome*, ECLI:EU:C:2017:286.
166. *United States v. Microsoft Corp.*, 253 F.3d 34 (D.C. Cir. 2001), at 79.
167. CJEU, Case C-6/72,*Continental Can*, ECLI:EU:C:1973:22, §27. *See also* CJEU, Case 85/76, *Hoffmann-La Roche v. Commission*, ECLI:EU:C:1979:36, §91; GC, Case T-321/05, *AstraZeneca v. Commission*, ECLI:EU:T:2010:266, §267.
168. *United States v. Microsoft Corp.*, 253 F.3d 34 (D.C. Cir. 2001), at 79.
169. Areeda, Phillip and Herbert Hovenkamp. *Antitrust Law*. Little, Brown & Company, 1996, ¶651f, at 82.

such as divestiture designed to eliminate the monopoly altogether, raise more serious questions and require a clearer indication of a significant causal connection between the conduct and creation or maintenance of the market power."[170] The US *Microsoft* Court adopted such standard. "Absent some measure of confidence that there has been an actual loss to competition that needs to be restored, wisdom counsels against adopting radical structural relief."[171]

[D] Causation and Remedial Action

Remedies imposed should relate process and outcomes altogether. In the context of anticompetitively acquired market power, this is fundamental since it may entail the disgorgement of the unlawful monopolist's rents or the structural dismantling of its position to restore the market to its precompetitive situation.[172]

In this connection, the FTC's withdrawn Report on Antitrust Monopoly Law[173] drew a clear distinction between remedies imposed to an unlawful acquisition of monopoly power as that opposed to its maintenance. "In contrast [to a monopoly-maintenance case], in a monopoly-acquisition case, the pre-conduct setting may have been competitive, so eliminating the anticompetitive consequences of the violation might include dismantling the monopoly to restore the competitive environment that would have existed without the violation."[174]

However, Article 102 TFEU is not a domination statute and thus the protection of the competitive process can fall short if remedies cannot be directed against unlawful acquisitions of dominance. It cannot reestablish the market to its *ex ante* competitive conditions. Per Hellstrom, former Chief of Unit C3 in DG COMP, brought up the US/EU remedial dichotomy in the 2007 Section 2 Hearings on Remedies. "It is not really the purpose [of EU competition law] to terminate the illegal monopoly insofar as our Article [102] relates to abusive behaviors. It is more about terminating the abusive behavior and not the dominant position as such."[175] This approach is however regrettable.

171. *United States v. Microsoft Corp.*, 253 F.3d 34 (D.C. Cir. 2001), at 81.
172. *United States v. United Shoe Mach. Corp.*, 391 U.S. 244 (1968) at 250: "[I]n a [Section] 2 case ... it is the duty of the court *to prescribe relief which will terminate the illegal monopoly, deny to the defendant the fruits of its statutory violation*, and ensure that there remain no practices likely to result in monopolization in the future." (emphasis added); *see also United States v. Grinnell Corp.*, 384 U.S. 563 (1966), at 577.
173. US Dep't of Justice, *Justice Department Withdraws Report on Antitrust Monopoly Law* (May 11, 2009) Press Release *available at* https://www.justice.gov/opa/pr/justice-department-withdraws-report-antitrust-monopoly-law.
174. DOJ, "Competition and Monopoly: Single-Firm Conduct Under Section 2 of The Sherman Act" (2008, Report) (withdrawn without replacement on Nov. 05, 2009), Chapter 9: "[I]n a monopoly-maintenance case, conditions before the unlawful conduct may have involved a lawful monopoly, and re-establishing the opportunity for competition would not necessarily produce new competitors or reduce the monopolist's market share."
175. FTC, *Section 2 Hearings. Understanding Single-Firm Behavior: Remedies*. Mar. 28, 2007, at p. 78, *available at* https://www.ftc.gov/sites/default/files/documents/public_events/section-2-sherman-act-single-firm-conduct-related-competition/070328.pdf.

The objective of protecting the competitive process will prove unsuccessful if, in the words of Joliet, remedies under Article 102 TFEU "consist of regulating market power and not restoring workable competitive conditions through structural reorganization of the industry or through injunctions directed against exclusionary practices *which are the cause of market power*"[176] (emphasis added). As expressed by the US Supreme Court, "*[d]ivestiture or dissolution must take account of* the present and future conditions in the particular industry as well as *past violations*"[177] (emphasis added).

Under Article 102 TFEU, the path to imposing appropriate remedies in the presence of an unlawful monopoly requires the abuse of such power. The remedy imposed must then achieve an analogous effect to what a structural remedy would achieve if it were designed to eliminate the unlawful market power. What would be the *competitive* scenario absent the unlawfully acquired dominant position? Remedies in this context thus require a proper assessment of the past conditions of competition and thereafter a counterfactual assessment to reestablish the opportunity for the market to work.[178]

As Röller advocates, in the presence of a legal monopoly the proper policy should be structural remedies like liberalization, open markets, etc., so long as these are available to the authority.[179] However, where an unlawful dominant position is thereafter exploited, behavioral remedies must then be designed to achieve an analogous effect to structural remedies. They must be directed against the "cause of market power" that allows the dominant firm to abuse and profit from its unlawful position.

Some authors have however raised doubts about the effectiveness of such remedial action. Elhauge writes, "that even the best-designed behavioral remedies have difficulty really changing the operation of markets, create perverse incentives, and are hard to administer."[180] It is not surprising thus that in the context of merger control the European Commission (as well as US agencies) have consistently preferred structural remedies against behavioral remedies.

Although remedies will be crafted following a case-by-case analysis it should be remembered that when the cause of market power is anticompetitive behavior, therein lies an impediment to competition. But, as we explained above, the Commission did not carry out such counterfactual in the *Rambus* case. As Gautier and Petit argue, the reason the Commission possibly "under remedied" the case is because it had not addressed the past anticompetitive harm inflicted by Rambus.[181]

---

176. Joliet, René. *A Comparative Study of American and European Approaches to the Control of Economic Power.* Collection scientifique de la Faculté de Droit de l'Université de Liège [1970] 1975, at pp. 249-251 and also pp. 130-131.
177. *Schine Chain Theatres, Inc. v. United States*, 334 U.S. 110 (May 3, 1948), at 128.
178. DOJ, "Competition and Monopoly: Single-Firm Conduct under Section 2 of The Sherman Act" (2008, Report), (withdrawn without replacement on Nov. 05, 2009), Chapter 9.
179. Röller, Lars-Hendrik. "Exploitative Abuses." ESMT, *Business Brief No. BB-107-002* (2007): 3-15.
180. Elhauge, Einer. "Disgorgement as an Antitrust Remedy." *Antitrust Law Journal* 76.1 (2009): 79-96, 88.
181. Gautier, Axel and Nicolas Petit. "Optimal Enforcement of Competition Policy: The Commitments Procedure under Uncertainty." *European Journal of Law and Economics* 45.2 (2018): 195-224.

§8.05 CONCLUSION

"Any departure from perfect competition implies some market power."[182] And *some* market power can be used in anticompetitive ways to obtain *more* market power, and eventually acquire dominance. Competition policy cherishes vigorous competition and the monopolist having been urged to compete must not be turned upon.[183] But the acquisition of monopoly power through anticompetitive practices must be turned down.

The deadweight loss imposed by monopoly power is an unworthy and inefficient concentration of wealth as it was obtained anticompetitively. As it has been shown, anticompetitive behavior on the road to dominance can lead to more inefficient outcomes when the nondominant firm makes use of established competitive frameworks prone to establish a monopoly outcome. For example, we have seen that in a standardization process anticompetitive behavior to acquire dominance can be a rational strategy for a firm.

In the presence of anticompetitively acquired dominance and from a process-oriented perspective, the real problem is not the exploitation of that power, but the more fundamental issue of an inefficient outcome. In this sense, strong structural remedies can aim at restoring the market. However, assuming that structural remedies will not be achieved immediately or that dismantling the dominant firm may be more costly than allowing its preserve, then we need to decide how the dominant firm might exercise its anticompetitively acquired market power. It is in this regard that exploitative abuses recover all the economic relevance.

182. Areeda, Philip E. *Antitrust Law*. Little, Brown & Company, 1978, §635.
183. *United States v. Aluminum Co. of America* ("*Alcoa*"), 148 F.2d 416 (2d Cir. 1945), at 430.

General Conclusion

> In a sense, the whole history of antitrust policy can be read as the judicial quest for a working definition of competition; for before one can decide what the law of monopoly ought to be, it is necessary to form a view of what the process of competition is "really" like.
>
> (Donald Dewey, 1964)

We have sought to exemplify a basic proposition. Analyzing *why* the dominant firm comes into existence is critical to assess the effects of unilateral firm behavior under Article 102 TFEU. The ruling of the Court of Justice in *Post Danmark I* provides partial support for this proposition. It held: "When the existence of a dominant position has its origins in a former legal monopoly, that fact has to be taken into account."[1] The Court did not say how that fact should be taken into account. Neither did the Court say that other origins of firm dominance should be taken into account. However, *Post Danmark I* represents an explicit departure from the long-established principle in Article 102 TFEU enforcement that the reasons for which a firm enjoys dominance are irrelevant.[2]

To exemplify our proposition, we have argued, and we have shown, how other causes than the former legal origins of firm dominance should be taken into account in the assessment of unilateral firm behavior.

Gathering from EU case law, legal, economic and SML, we have proposed a categorization of seven dominant firms' origins. These are: the statutory dominant firm, the historical operator, the natural monopolist, the investor dominant firm, the intangible dominant firm, the lucky monopolist, and the anticompetitively acquired dominance.

We have shown that Article 102 TFEU case law has generally disregarded the reasons as to *why* firm dominance exists in the first place. This is particularly evident in the case of statutory dominance (Chapter 2) and investor dominant firms (Chapter

1. CJEU, Case C-209/10, *Post Danmark I*, ECLI:EU:C:2012:172, §23.
2. CJEU, Case C-322/81, *Michelin I*, ECLI:EU:C:1983:313, §57.

5). Only in the presence of historical operators the EU Courts and the Commission have explicitly looked into the origins of the firm (Chapter 3).

The reasons for this oversight are diverse. For instance, in the case of statutory monopolies, TFEU provisions limiting Member States' behavior in the market have steered Article 102 TFEU enforcement away from the statutory origins of certain dominant firms. In the case of anticompetitively acquired dominance (Chapter 8), the wording of Article 102 TFEU does not catch unilateral anticompetitive conduct leading to dominance. Indeed, unlike Section 2 of the SA, Article 102 TFEU is not a domination provision. And in the case of natural monopolies (Chapter 4), the lack of clarity and distinctly static assessment in the economic literature has produced in the case law a variety of divergent conceptualizations of what it means to be a natural monopolist.

However varied all these reasons might be, they can all be subsumed within the fact that both the EU Courts and the Commission have little interest to explore what the process of competition is "really" like.[3] This leaves us with what we call the process paradox. If the objective of EU competition rules is the protection of the competitive process (Chapter 1), one must "really" examine how that process works.

By looking into the dominant firm we have reminded that competition is a great *imperfect process*. It is, paraphrasing together Winston Churchill and Friedrich A. Hayek, the best of all systems that have been tried to deliver growth, progress, and new discoveries.[4] This reminder is not to advocate a hands-off approach, but rather to emphasize that one cannot assess unilateral firm conduct by reference to an idealistic benchmark.

A simple illustration of this is that of a natural monopolist. Assume there is only one mine of cobalt and that one single firm exploits it most efficiently. A natural monopoly is the best *possible* arrangement. Yet, competition policy would desire that there were ten cobalt mines and that ten different firms mined each of these, so that the suppliers of cobalt would compete and offer lower prices to consumers. However, as a matter of fact, there is only *one* mine and only *one* firm can efficiently operate this mine.

In the competitive process, the investor origins of firm dominance remind us that competition is a risky and uncertain process that advances thanks to the efforts of the entrepreneurial firm. Its present gains are the result of past investments in competition. The competitive or anticompetitive use of those gains cannot be assessed without a look into the past (*t*-1). On the contrary, the statutory origins of a dominant firm tell us that its presence is not the result of a competitive process. As such it benefits from a series of statutory advantages that remain unavailable to other market participants. In turn, the statutory dominant firm can turn greedy and use its *privileged* position to enter yet other open markets. These actions should attract severe antitrust scrutiny,

3. Dewey, Donald. "The Economic Theory of Antitrust: Science or Religion?" *Virginia Law Review* 50.3(1964): 413-434.
4. Churchill, Winston S. *Churchill by Himself*. Rosetta Books, 2013, at p. 574; and Hayek, Friedrich A. "Competition as a Discovery Procedure." *The Quarterly Journal of Austrian Economics* 5.3 [1968] (2002): 9-23.

particularly in a globalized market where firms in open market economies might end up competing against firms backed by planned or hybrid economies.

But these statutory advantages gradually fade when the state stops supporting the firm and it becomes a historical operator. The strength of those advantages must be seriously analyzed to determine the potential anticompetitive effects of unilateral firm conduct. The younger the historical operator is, the stronger those advantages will likely be.

The existence of a natural monopolist or an intangible dominant firm prompts us to think that one cannot have both the scale or intangible efficiencies that make up those firms and the efficiencies that flow from an atomistic conception of competition at the same time.[5] In those circumstances, use of market power is generally not an abuse, but rather the most efficient and effective way a firm can provide and keep on discovering new needs and wants. On the contrary, the lucky monopolist conveys the story that another competitive world was really possible in the past and that the lucky emergence of dominance was costless. One should be weary of unilateral behavior aimed at locking in its lucky position. Lastly, the unworthy dominant firm is a reflection of a thwarted competitive process. Had the firm not behaved anticompetitively, another more efficient dominant firm or firms would have been selected; or, had the firm been selected absent its anticompetitive behavior, its ability to exercise its market power been would have been different.

As a result, the following list of policy proposals relating to the practical introduction of competitive process elements in Article 102 TFEU is recommended:

- The EU Courts and the Commission should look into the origins of the dominant firm. This means asking the following "origins question": *why* is the dominant firm dominant?
- To answer the "origins question," we have put forward a categorization of seven origins that can help the EU Courts and the Commission answer the question. The seven origins are: statutory dominance, historical dominance, natural monopoly, investor dominance, intangible dominance, lucky dominance, and anticompetitively acquired dominance.
- Answering why the dominant firm is dominant will require the EU Courts and the Commission to revisit dominance as a simple threshold of liability.
- The "origins question" is a necessary step to establish anticompetitive *effects*. However, it is neither a sufficient condition to either acquit or find the dominant firm guilty nor a necessary step in cases involving restrictions by object.
- Statutory dominant firm behavior should be closely monitored. The EU Courts and the Commission should adopt a stand-alone cost test in cases involving the leveraging of statutory dominance into other markets. They should also narrow down the range of objective justifications and require from statutory dominant firms that they adopt a "proactive approach" toward facilitating

5. Hovenkamp, Herbert. *The Antitrust Enterprise: Principle and Execution.* Harvard University Press, 2005, at p. 285.

entry. Article 102 TFEU enforcement should similarly take the *foreign* origins of statutory dominance into account.

- The guiding principle of equality of opportunity must be explicitly limited to cases relating to statutory positions of dominance, and only apply in cases involving historical operators if their historical advantages have not yet been eroded.
- In the case of historical operators, the EU Courts and the Commission should take a more balanced approach in their assessments. This means, first, taking into account that legacy disadvantages, such as those imposed by asymmetric regulation or sunk investments, can eliminate or dissipate presumed historical advantages, and how his relationship can affect the incentives to invest and innovate of the firm. Second, abandoning generalized statements *against* first-movers and in favor of late entrants in favor of an effects-based approach that analyzes the actual effects of being first, second, or late in the market. And third, taking actively into account competition between historical operators.
- When analyzing single natural monopoly behavior, the EU Courts and the Commission should replace the "as efficient competitor" test by the "more efficient competitor" test. Likewise, the EU Courts and the Commission should revise their ambiguous description of what constitutes a natural monopoly.
- The EU Courts and the Commission should reexamine their account of investments as a relevant antitrust barrier to entry. In short, investments undertaken in competition are not a relevant antitrust barrier to entry.
- The division of single-product markets into contestable and incontestable market shares should be abandoned in cases involving single-firm behavior by natural monopolies, investor or intangible dominant firms.
- When a dominant firm expands into another market it leverages numerous intangible efficiencies such as experience, know-how, reputation, managerial skills, innovation capabilities, and so on. These "unseen" efficiencies must be taken into account. In this regard, the EU Courts and the Commission should abandon the holding that a customer's request or acceptance of an exclusivity condition is an irrelevant fact.
- Refusal to supply abuses should be abandoned in cases involving natural monopolies, investor or intangible dominant firms. Imposing an obligation to supply negates the *ex ante* competitive process, it contributes to the depropertization of acquired rights, and it negatively affects the incentives to invest for both the dominant firm and its competitors, by *directing* the latter into "the easy way." Furthermore, when dominance rests upon intangible resources, sharing them will destroy their superiority and make everyone worse off. In cases involving historical operators, the incentives analysis done by the regulator cannot be taken at face value.
- The EU Courts and the Commission should abandon guiding principles of enforcement that create incumbency disadvantages preventing natural monopolies, investor dominant firms, and intangible dominant firms, from behaving in the same way as nondominant firms.

- Lucky or accidental events can thrust a firm into a position of dominance and incentivize anticompetitive behavior. As a result, the EU Courts and the Commission should ensure that the restoration to the *ex ante* competitive conditions is not thwarted by the opportunistic behavior of the lucky monopolist.
- Exploitative abuses should investigate whether the position of dominance has been anticompetitively acquired. Consequently, Article 102 TFEU enforcement should establish a causal link between *ex ante* exclusionary conduct leading to a position of dominance and the *ex post* exploitation of that position.

Taking into account the origins of firm dominance is not to open Pandora's box. Rather, it represents an effort to revisit commonly stated dogmas in Article 102 TFEU case law, such as that the mere presence of a dominant firm weakens a competitive structure, that every dominant firm has a special responsibility, or that irreproachable conduct might be deemed abusive if carried out by a dominant firm. In this sense, several practical amendments to bring Article 102 TFEU closer to its objective of protecting the competitive process have been advanced. This means sometimes lowering the thresholds of liability, and at other times heightening that threshold.

In sum, this book is an attempt to improve our understanding of the functioning of the competitive process and thus be better equipped to safeguard it.

Bibliography

Adams, Thomas B. "Railway Commissions." *Journal of Social Science* 2 (1870): 233-236.

Ahlborn, Christian, David S. Evans and A. Jorge Padilla. "The Logic & Limits of the Exceptional Circumstances Test in *Magill* and *IMS Health*." *Fordham International Law Journal* 28.4 (2004): 1109-1156.

Aizcorbe, Ana. "Moore's Law, Competition, and Intel's Productivity in the Mid-1990s." *The American Economic Review* 95.2 (2005): 305-308.

Akkermans, Bram and Eveline Ramaekers. "Article 345 TFEU (ex Article 295 EC), Its Meanings and Interpretations." *European Law Journal* 16.3 (2010): 292-314.

Akman, Pinar. "Searching for the Long-Lost Soul of Article 82 EC." *Oxford Journal of Legal Studies* 29.2 (2009): 267-303.

Akman, Pinar. *The Concept of Abuse in EU Competition Law: Law and Economic Approaches*. Bloomsbury Publishing, 2012.

Akyürek-Kievits, H.E. "The Application of Article 86 of the EEC Treaty to State Monopolies" *in* J.H.V. Stuyck and A.J. Vossestein (eds.) *State Entrepreneurship, National Monopolies and European Community Law*.

Alchian, Armen A. "Uncertainty, Evolution, and Economic Theory." *Journal of Political Economy* 58.3 (1950): 211-221.

Almunia, Joaquín. "EU Competition Policy and Sectoral Challenges." *41st Annual Conference on International Antitrust Law and Policy Fordham*, New York (September 12, 2014), http://europa.eu/rapid/press-release_SPEECH-14-592_en.htm.

Alon, Ilan, Hua Wang, Jun Shen and Wenxian Zhang. "Chinese State-Owned Enterprises Go Global." *Journal of Business Strategy* 35.6 (2014): 3-18.

Alvord, Ellsworth C., et al. "The Multiple Causes of Multiple Sclerosis: The Importance of Age of Infections in Childhood." *The Journal of Child Neurology* 2.4 (1987): 313-21.

Amaral, Miguel, Stéphane Saussier and Anne Yvrande-Billon. "Auction Procedures and Competition in Public Services: The Case of Urban Public Transport in France and London." *Utilities Policy* 17.2 (2009): 166-175.

Andriychuk, Oles. "Rediscovering the Spirit of Competition: On the Normative Value of the Competitive Process." *European Competition Journal*, 6.3 (2010): 575-610.

Appelbaum, Elie and Chin Lim. "Contestable Markets under Uncertainty." *The Rand Journal of Economics* 16.1 (1985): 28-40.

Areeda, Philip E. *Antitrust Law*. Little, Brown & Company, 1978.

Areeda, Philip E. and Herbert Hovenkamp. *Antitrust Law*. Little, Brown & Company, 1996.

Areeda, Philip E. and Herbert Hovenkamp. *Fundamentals of Antitrust Law*. Wolters Kluwer, 2011.

Aristotle. *Politics*.

Armstrong, Mark, Simon Cowan and John Vickers. *Regulatory Reform: Economic Analysis and British Experience*. MIT Press, 1994.

Arnold, Anthony J. and Sean McCartney. "Rates of Return, Concentration Levels and Strategic Change in the British Railway Industry, 1830-1912." *The Journal of Transport History* 26.1 (2005): 41-60.

Arrow, Kenneth J. *The Limits of Organization*. New York: WW Norton & Company, 1974.

Arthur, W. Brian. "On Competing Technologies and Historical Small Events: The Dynamics of Choice under Increasing Returns." *IIASA Working Paper* WP-83-90 (1983).

Arthur, W. Brian. "Competing Technologies, Increasing Returns, and Lock-in by Historical Events." *The Economic Journal* 99.394 (1989): 116-131.

Arthur, W. Brian. "Positive Feedbacks in the Economy." *Scientific American* 262.2 (1990): 92-99.

Atkinson, Robert D., Nigel Cory and Stephen J. Ezell. "Stopping China's Mercantilism. A Doctrine of Constructive, Alliance-Backed Confrontation." *ITIF* (March 2017): 1-66.

Auer, Dirk and Nicolas Petit. "Two-Sided Markets and the Challenge of Turning Economic Theory into Antitrust Policy." *The Antitrust Bulletin* 60.4 (2015): 426-461.

Ayal, Adi. "Is Monopoly Really Unfair?" *Journal of European Competition Law & Practice* 5.6 (2014): 386-392.

Bacache, Maya, Marc Bourreau and Germain Gaudin. "Dynamic Entry and Investment in New Infrastructures: Empirical Evidence from the Fixed Broadband Industry." *Review of Industrial Organization* 44.2 (2014): 179-209.

Bian, Joe S. *Barriers to New Competition, Their Character and Consequences in Manufacturing Industries*. Harvard University Press, 1956.

Baird, Charles W. "The Economics of Time and Ignorance: A Review." *The Review of Austrian Economics* 1.1 (1987): 189-206.

Baker, Jonathan B. "Preserving a Political Bargain: The Political Economy of the Non-Interventionist Challenge to Monopolization Enforcement." *Antitrust Law Journal* 76.3 (2010): 605-652.

Baker, Jonathan B. "Evaluating Appropriability Defenses for the Exclusionary Conduct of Dominant Firms in Innovative Industries" *Antitrust Law Journal* 80.1 (2016): 431-461.

Bamzai, Aditya. “The Wasteful Duplication Thesis in Natural Monopoly Regulation.” *The University of Chicago Law Review* 71.4 (2004): 1525-1547.

Banks, Karen. “Mergers and Partial Mergers under EEC Law.” *Fordham International Law Journal* 11.2 (1987): 255-309.

Barney, Jay B. “Strategic Factor Markets: Expectations, Luck, and Business Strategy.” *Management Science* 32.10 (1986): 1231-1241.

Barney, Jay B. “Firm Resources and Sustained Competitive Advantage.” *Journal of Management* 17.1 (1991): 99-120.

Barney, Jay B. “On Flipping Coins and Making Technology Choices: Luck as an Explanation of Technological Foresight and Oversight” *in* Raghu Garud, Praveen Rattan Nayyar and Zur Baruch Shapira (eds.) *Technological Innovation: Oversights and Foresights*. Cambridge University Press, 1997.

Barney, Jay B. “Competence Explanations of Economic Profits in Strategic Management” *in* Jerome Ellig (ed.) *Dynamic Competition and Public Policy: Technology, Innovation, and Antitrust Issues*. Cambridge University Press, 2001.

Barney, Jay B. “Resource-Based Theories of Competitive Advantage: A Ten-Year Retrospective on the Resource-Based View.” *Journal of Management* 27.6 (2001): 643-650.

Barney, Jay B. and Asli M. Arikan. “The Resource-Based View: Origins and Implications” *in* Michael A. Hitt, R. Edward Freeman and Jeffrey S. Harrison (eds.) *The Blackwell Handbook of Strategic Management*. Wiley-Blackwell, 2001: 124-187.

Barry, Norman. “The Tradition of Spontaneous Order.” *Literature of Liberty*, 5.2 (1982): 7-58.

Baumol, William J. “On the Proper Cost Tests for Natural Monopoly in a Multiproduct Industry.” *The American Economic Review* 67.5 (1977): 809-822.

Baumol, William J., John C. Panzar and Robert D. Willig. *Contestable Markets and the Theory of Industry Structure*. 1988.

Baumol, William J. *The Free-Market Innovation Machine: Analyzing the Growth Miracle of Capitalism*. Princeton University Press, 2002.

Bayus, Barry L. and Rajshree Agarwal. “The Role of Pre-entry Experience, Entry Timing, and Product Technology Strategies in Explaining Firm Survival.” *Management Science* 53.12 (2007): 1887-1902.

Behling, Burton N. *Competition and Monopoly in Public Utility Industries*. Urbana: University of Illinois, 1938.

Belleflamme, Paul and Martin Peitz. *Industrial Organization: Markets and Strategies*. Cambridge University Press, 2015.

Bergman, Mats A. “When Should an Incumbent Be Obliged to Share Its Infrastructure with an Entrant under the General Competition Rules?” *Journal of Industry, Competition and Trade* 5.1 (2005): 5-26.

Besen, Stanley M. and Joseph Farrell. “Choosing How to Compete: Strategies and Tactics in Standardization.” *The Journal of Economic Perspectives* 8.2 (1994): 117-131.

Bhagwati, Jagdish N. “Lobbying and Welfare.” *Journal of Public Economics* 14.3 (1980): 355-363.

Bien, Florian and Matthias Krah. "The Ruling of the CJEU in Post Danmark: Putting an End to Selective Price Cuts as an Abuse under TFEU Article 102 and Turning Towards a More Economic Approach." *European Competition Law Review* 10 (2012): 482-487.

Bijwaard, Govert E., Maarten C.W. Janssen and Emiel Maasland. "Early Mover Advantages: An Empirical Analysis of European Mobile Phone Markets." *Telecommunications Policy* 32.3 (2008): 246-261.

Blackwill, Robert D. and Jennifer M. Harris. *War by Other Means. Geoeconomics and Statecraft*. Harvard University Press, 2016.

Blanca-Lopez, N., et al. "Value of the Clinical History in the Diagnosis of Urticaria/Angioedema Induced by NSAIDs with Cross Intolerance." *Clinical & Experimental Allergy* 43 (2013): 85-91.

Böhm, Franz. "Rule of Law in a Market Economy" *in* Alan Peacock and Hans Willgerodt (eds.) *Germany's Social Market Economy: Origins and Evolution* (1989): 46-67.

Bordo, Michael D. and Roberto Cortés-Condo (eds.). *Transferring Wealth and Power from the Old to the New World: Monetary and Fiscal Institutions in the 17th through the 19th Centuries*. Cambridge: Cambridge University Press, 2006.

Bork, Robert. *The Antitrust Paradox: A Policy at War with Itself*. Simon & Schuster, [1978] 1993.

Bostyn, Sven and Nicolas Petit. "Patent = Monopoly: A Legal Fiction." *Working Paper Series. University of Liverpool* (2013) 1-19.

Boulding, William and Markus Christen. "Disentangling Pioneering Cost Advantages and Disadvantages." *Marketing Science* 27.4 (2008): 699-716.

Branden, Nathaniel. "Monopolies and Laissez-Fake Capitalism." *The Objectivist Newsletter* 1.6 (1962).

Brätland, John. "Contestable Market Theory as a Regulatory Framework: An Austrian Postmortem." *The Quarterly Journal of Austrian Economics* 7.3 (2004): 3-28.

Bräutigam, Deborah and Tang Xiaoyang. "Economic Statecraft in China's New Overseas Special Economic Zones: Soft Power, Business or Resource Security?" *International Affairs* 88.4 (2012): 799-816.

Bremmer, Ian. "State Capitalism Comes of Age: The End of the Free Market?" *Foreign Affairs* 88.3 (2009): 40-55.

Bremmer, Ian. "The End of the Free Market: Who Wins the War Between States and Corporations?" *European View* 9.2 (2010): 249-252.

Brennan, Timothy J. "Saving Section 2: Reframing U.S. Monopolization Law" *in* Vivek Ghosal and Johan Stennek (eds.) *The Political Economy of Antitrust (Contributions to Economic Analysis, Volume 282)* Emerald Group Publishing Limited, 2007: 417-451.

Brenning, Magdalena. "Competition & Intellectual Property Policy Implications of Late or No IPR Disclosure in Collective Standard-Setting." Speech, Brussels (June 17, 2002), http://ec.europa.eu/competition/speeches/text/sp2002_037_en.pdf.

Brewer, Michael. "Planning Disaster: Price Gouging Statutes and the Shortages They Create." *Brooklyn Law Review* 72.3 (2007): 1101-1137.

Breyer, Stephen G. "The Problem of the Honest Monopolist." *Antitrust Law Journal* 44.2 (1975): 194-201.

Breyer, Stephen G. "Antitrust, Deregulation, and the Newly Liberated Marketplace." *California Law Review* 75.3 (1987): 1005-1047.

Brock, G.W. The *Telecommunications Industry: The Dynamics of Market Structure.* Cambridge: Harvard University Press, 1981.

Broos, Sébastien and Jorge Marcos Ramos. "Competing Business Models and Two-Sidedness: An Application to the Google Shopping Case." *The Antitrust Bulletin* 62.2 (2017): 382-399.

Brozen, Yale. "Is Government the Source of Monopoly?" *The Intercollegiate Review* 5.2 (1968): 67-78.

Buchanan, James M. "What Should Economists Do?" *Southern Economic Journal* 30.3 (1964): 213-222.

Buchanan, James M. "Rent Seeking and Profit Seeking" *in* Buchanan, James M., Robert D. Tollison and Gordon Tullock (eds.) *Toward a Theory of the Rent-Seeking Society*. Texas: A&M University Press, 1980.

Buchanan, James M. *Cost and Choice: An Inquiry in Economic Theory*. Indianapolis: Liberty Fund, 1999.

Buendía, Jose Luís. *Exclusive Rights and State Monopolies under EC Law. Article 86 (Former Article 90) of the EC Treaty*. Oxford, 2000.

Buenstorf, Guido. "Evolution on the Shoulders of Giants: Entrepreneurship and Firm Survival in the German Laser Industry." *Review of Industrial Organization* 30.3 (2007): 179-202.

Cabral, Luis and Michael H. Riordan. "The Learning Curve, Predation, Antitrust, and Welfare." *The Journal of Industrial Economics* 45.2 (1997): 155-169.

Cabral, Luis. *Introduction to Industrial Organization*. MIT Press, 2000.

Carden, Art and Steven Horwitz. "Is Market Failure a Sufficient Condition for Government Intervention." *Library of Economics and Liberty* (April 1, 2013), http://www.econlib.org/library/Columns/y2013/CardenHorwitzmarkets.html.

Carlton, Dennis W. and Jeffrey Perloff. *Modern Industrial Organization*. Addison-Wesley, 1999.

Carlton, Dennis W. and Jeffrey Perloff. "A General Analysis of Exclusionary Conduct and Refusal to Deal – Why Aspen and Kodak Are Misguided." *Antitrust Law Journal* 68.3 (2001): 659-683.

Carney, Patricia A., et al. "Use of Clinical History Affects Accuracy of Interpretive Performance of Screening Mammography." *Journal of Clinical Epidemiology* 65.2 (2012): 219-230.

Carrol, Glenn R., et al. "The Fates of *de novo* and *de alio* Producers in the American Automobile Industry 1885–1981." *Strategic Management Journal* 17.S1 (1996): 117-137.

Cary, George S., et al. "The Case for Antitrust Law to Police the Patent Holdup Problem in Standard Setting." *Antitrust Law Journal* 77.3 (2011): 913-946.

Caves, Richard E., Michael Fortunato and Pankaj Ghemawat. "The Decline of Dominant Firms, 1905-1929." *The Quarterly Journal of Economics* (1984): 523-546.

Caves, Richard E., Bradley T. Gale and Michael E. Porter. “Interfirm Profitability Differences: Comment.” *The Quarterly Journal of Economics* 91.4 (1977): 667-675.

Chadwick, Edwin. “Results of Different Principles of Legislation and Administration in Europe; of Competition for the Field, as Compared with Competition within the field, of Service.” *Journal of the Statistical Society of London* 22.3 (1859): 381-420.

Chandler, Alfred D. *Strategy and Structure: Chapters in the History of the Industrial Enterprise*. MIT Press, 1990.

Charnes, Abraham, William W. Cooper and Toshiyuki Sueyoshi. “A Goal Programming/Constrained Regression Review of the Bell System Breakup.” *Management Science* 34.1 (1988): 1-26.

Chen, P.L., Charles Williams and Rajshree Agarwal. “Growing Pains: Pre-entry Experience and the Challenge of Transition to Incumbency.” *Strategic Management Journal* 276 ((July 2011) 2012): 252-276.

Cherry, Barbara A. “Historical Mutilation: How Misuse of ‘Public Utility’ and ‘Natural Monopoly’ Misdirects US Telecommunications Policy Development.” *20th ITS Biennial Conference* (2014): 1-25.

Chin, Andrew. “Antitrust by Chance: A Unified Theory of Horizontal Merger Doctrine.” *The Yale Law Journal* 106.4 (1997): 1165-1195.

Choné, Philippe and Laurent Linnemer. “Nonlinear Pricing and Exclusion: II. Must-Stock Products.” *The RAND Journal of Economics* 47.3 (2016): 631-660.

Churchill, Winston S. *Churchill By Himself*. Rosetta Books, 2013.

Clark, John M. “The Relation Between Statics and Dynamics” *in* Jacob H. Hollander (ed.) *Economic Essays Contributed in Honor of John Bates Clark*, The Macmillan Company, 1927: 46-70.

Clark, John M. *Competition as a Dynamic Process*. Washington, DC: The Brookings Institution, 1961.

Coase, Ronald H. “The Nature of the Firm.” *Economica* 4.16 (1937): 386-405.

Coase, Ronald H. “The British Post Office and the Messenger Companies.” *The Journal of Law & Economics* 4 (1961): 12-65.

Coase, Ronald H. “Industrial Organization: A Proposal for Research” *in* Victor Fuchs (ed.) *Economic Research: Retrospect and Prospect, Volume 3, Policy Issues and Research Opportunities in Industrial Organization*. NBER (1972): 59-73.

Coldwell III, Daniel. “The New Theory of Public Utilities: The Case of the Natural Monopoly.” *Antitrust Bulletin* 26.1 (1981): 133-144.

Cole, Daniel H. and Peter Grossman (eds.). *The End of a Natural Monopoly: Deregulation and Competition in the Electric Power Industry*. Routledge, 2004.

Connor, Tom. “The Resource-Based View of Strategy and Its Value to Practising Managers.” *Strategic Change* 11.6 (2002): 307-316.

Cool, Karel, Ingemar Dierickx and Gonçalo Pacheco de Almeida. “Diseconomies of Time Compression.” *INSEAD Faculty & Research Working Paper* 78/ST (2012).

Costa, Carlos. “On the Use of Reverse Auctions to Designate Universal Postal Service Providers” *in* Michael A. Crew and Paul R. Kleindorfer (eds.) *Multi-modal Competition and the Future of Mail*. Edward Elgar Publishing, 2012.

Crane, Daniel A. “Intellectual Liability.” *Texas Law Review* 88.2 (2009): 253-300.

Crane, Daniel A. and Graciela Miralles. "Toward a Unified Theory of Exclusionary Vertical Restraints." *Southern California Law Review* 84.3 (2011): 605-660.

Creighton, Susan A., D. Bruce Hoffman, Thomas G. Krattenmaker and Ernest A. Nagata. "Cheap Exclusion." *Antitrust Law Journal* 72.3 (2005): 975-995.

Culley, Daniel, Malik Dhanani and Maurits Dolmans. "Learning from Rambus – How to Tame Those Troublesome Trolls." *Antitrust Bulletin* 57.1 (2012): 117-160.

Daly, Angela. "Beyond 'Hipster Antitrust': A Critical Perspective on the European Commission's Google Decision." *European Competition and Regulation Law Review* 1.3 (2017): 188-192.

Darwin, Charles. *The Origins of Species by Means of Natural Selection.* 1859.

Daskalova, Victoria. "Consumer Welfare in EU Competition Law: What Is It (Not) about?" *The Competition Law Review* 11.1 (2015): 131-160.

David, Paul A. "Clio and the Economics of QWERTY." *The American Economic Review* 75.2 (1985): 332-337.

David, Paul A. "Path Dependence: A Foundational Concept for Historical Social Science." *Cliometrica* 1.2 (2007): 91-114.

David, Paul A. "Path Dependence and the Quest for Historical Economics: One More Chorus of the Ballad of QWERTY." *Discussion Papers in Economic and Social History No. 20* (November 1997): 1-48.

De La Mano, Miguel, Renato Nazzini and Hans Zenger. "Article 102" *in* Jonathan Faull and Ali Nikpay (eds.) *The EU Law of Competition* Oxford, 2014.

De La Torre Castillo, Fernando and Eric Gippini Fournier. *Evidence, Proof and Judicial Review in EU Competition Law.* Edward Elgar Publishing, 2017.

De Malynes, Gerard. *The Maintenance of Free Trade.* London, 1622, http://name.umdl.umich.edu/A06789.0001.001.

De Streel, Alexandre. "Remedies in the European Electronic Communications Sector" *in* Damien Geradin (ed.) *Remedies in Network Industries: EC Competition Law vs Sector-specific regulation.* Antwerp: Intersentia, 2004.

De Streel, Alexandre. "The Antitrust Activism of the European Commission in the Telecommunications Sector" *in* Philip Lowe, and Mel Marquis (eds.) *European Competition Law Annual 2012: Competition, Regulation and Public Policies.* Bloomsbury Publishing, 2014.

De Vries, Jan. "The Netherlands in the New World: The Legacy of European Fiscal, Monetary, and Trading Institutions for New World Development from the Seventeenth to the Nineteenth Centuries," *in* Michael D. Bordo and Roberto Cortés-Condo (eds.) *Transferring Wealth and Power from the Old World to the New World: Monetary and Fiscal Institutions in the 17th through the 19th Centuries.* Cambridge: Cambridge University Press, 2001: 100-139.

Dempsey, Paul S. "Taxi Industry Regulation, Deregulation, and Reregulation: The Paradox of Market Failure." *Transportation Law Journal* 24 (1996): 73-120.

Demsetz, Harold. "Toward a Theory of Property Rights." *The American Economic Review,* 57.2 (1967): 347-359.

Demsetz, Harold. "Why Regulate utilities?" *The Journal of Law and Economics* 11.1 (1968): 55-65.

Demsetz, Harold. "Information and Efficiency: Another Viewpoint." *The Journal of Law and Economics* 12.1 (1969): 1-22.
Demsetz, Harold. "Industry Structure, Market Rivalry, and Public Policy." *The Journal of Law and Economics* 16.1 (1973): 1-9.
Demsetz, Harold. "Economics as a Guide to Antitrust Regulation." *Journal of Law and Economics* 19.2 (1976): 371-384.
Demsetz, Harold. "Barriers to Entry." *The American Economic Review* 72.1 (1982): 47-57.
Demsetz, Harold. "The Problem of Monopolization." *Working Paper* #243 (June 1982).
Denning, Trevor. *The Playing-Cards of Spain: A Guide for Historians and Collectors.* Fairleigh Dickinson University Press, 1996.
Devlin, Alan. "Analyzing Monopoly Power Ex Ante." *NYU Journal of Law & Business* 5 (2009): 153-209.
Dewey, Donald. "The Economic Theory of Antitrust: Science or Religion?" *Virginia Law Review* 50.3 (1964): 413-434.
Dierickx, Ingemar and Karel Cool. "Asset Stock Accumulation and Sustainability of Competitive Advantage." *Management Science* 35.12 (1989), 1504-1511.
Dillbary, Shahar J. "Emergencies, Body Parts and Price Gouging" *in* Austin Sarat (ed.) *Sovereignty, Emergency, Legality*. Cambridge University Press, 2010.
Dilorenzo, Thomas J. "Property Rights, Information Costs, and the Economics of Rent Seeking." *Journal of Institutional and Theoretical Economics (JITE) / Zeitschrift Für Die Gesamte Staatswissenschaft* 144.2 (1988): 318-332.
Dilorenzo, Thomas J. "The Myth of Natural Monopoly." The *Review of Austrian Economics* 9.2 (1996): 43-58.
Dobson, Paul, Michael Waterson and Alex Chu. "The Welfare Consequences of the Exercise of Buyer Power." *OFT*, Research Paper 16 (September 1998).
Doh, Jonathan P. and Hildy J. Teegen. "Private Investment in Emerging Markets Telecommunications Infrastructure: Global Trends, National Policies, Firm Strategies." *Competition & Change* 7.1 (2003): 39-60.
Dolmans, Maurits and Wanjie LIN. "Fairness and Competition Law: A Fairness Paradox." *Concurrences* 4 (2017): 1-20.
Dowling, Grahame R. "Defining and Measuring Corporate Reputations." *European Management Review* 13.3 (2016): 207-223.
Durlauf, Steven N. "Complexity and Empirical Economics." *The Economic Journal* 115.504 (2005): 225-243.
Easterbrook, Frank H. "Limits of Antitrust." *Texas Law Review* 63.1 (1984): 1-40.
Edgeworth, Francis Y. "Contributions to the Theory of Railway Rates – IV." *The Economic Journal* 23.90 (1913): 206-226.
Edlin, Aaron and Joseph Farrell. "Freedom to Trade and the Competitive Process." *National Bureau of Economic Research* No. w16818 (2011).
Ehlermann, Claus-Dieter. "Managing Monopolies: The Role of the State in Controlling Market Dominance in the European Community." *European Competition Law Review* 14.2 (1993): 61-69.

Ehlermann, Claus-Dieter and Isabela Atanasiu (eds.) *European Competition Law Annual 2003: What Is an Abuse of a Dominant Position?* Bloomsbury Publishing, 2006.

Ehlermann, Claus-Dieter and Mel Marquis (eds.) *European Competition Law Annual 2007: A Reformed Approach to Article 82 EC.* Bloomsbury Publishing, 2008.

Eisenach, Jeffrey A. "Broadband Competition in the Internet Ecosystem." *American Enterprise Institute Working Papers* 35845 (2012).

Eisenhardt, Kathleen M. and Jeffrey A. Martin. "Dynamic Capabilities: What Are They?" *Strategic Management Journal* (2000): 1105-1121.

Ekelund Jr., Robert B. and Robert D. Tollison. *Mercantilism as a Rent-Seeking Society: Economic Regulation in Historical Perspective.* College Station, Texas: Texas A&M University Press, 1981.

Ekelund Jr., Robert B. and Robert F. Hébert. "Dupuit and the Railroads." *History of Political Economy* 44.1 (2012): 97-111.

Elhauge, Einer. "Defining Better Monopolization Standards." *Stanford Law Review* 56.2 (2003): 253-344.

Elhauge, Einer. "Disgorgement as an Antitrust Remedy." *Antitrust Law Journal* 76.1 (2009): 79-96.

Ely, Richard T. "Social Studies. The Reform of Railway Abuses." *Harper's New Monthly Magazine* 73.436 (1886): 571-578.

Ely, Richard T. "Natural Monopolies and the Workingman. A Programme of Social Reform." *The North American Review* 158.448 (1894): 294-303.

Ely, Richard T. *Monopolies and Trusts.* Grosset & Dunlap, [1900] 1906.

Ely, Richard T., Thomas S. Adams, Max O. Lorenz and Allyn A. Young. *Outlines of Economics*. Macmillan, 1910.

Encyclopædia Britannica. "Arab Oil Embargo. International Relations [1973]." *Encyclopædia Britannica* (June 16, 2016), https://www.britannica.com/topic/Arab-oil-embargo.

Epstein, Richard A. "Hayekian Socialism." *Maryland Law Review* 58.7 (1999): 271-299.

Epstein, Richard A. "Justified Monopolies: Regulating Pharmaceuticals and Telecommunications." *Case Western Reserve Law Review* 56.103 (2005): 103-134.

Epstein, Richard A. "Monopoly Dominance or Level Playing Field? The New Antitrust Paradox." *The University of Chicago Law Review* 72.1 (2005): 49-72.

Epstein, Richard A. *Free Markets under Siege: Cartels, Politics, and Social Welfare.* Hoover Press, 2008.

Erikson, Emily. *Between Monopoly and Free Trade: The English East India Company, 1600-1757*. Princeton University Press, 2014.

Etro, Federico. *Competition, Innovation and Antitrust. A Theory of Market Leaders and Its Policy Implications*. Springer, 2007.

Eucken, Walter. "What Kind of Economic and Social System" *in* Alan Peacock and Hans Willgerodt (eds.) *Germany's Social Market Economy: Origins and Evolution*, 1989: 27-45.

Evans, David S. and James J. Heckman. "A Test for Subadditivity of the Cost Function with an Application to the Bell System." *The American Economic Review* 74.4 (1984): 615-623.

Evans, David S. and James J. Heckman. "Rejoinder - Natural Monopoly and the Bell System: Response to Charnes, Cooper and Sueyoshi." *Management Science* 34.1 (1988): 27-38.

Evans, David S. and Jorge Padilla. "Excessive Prices: Using Economics to Define Administrative Legal Rules." *Journal of Competition Law and Economics* 1.1 (2005): 97-122.

Evans, David S. and Keith N. Hylton. "The Lawful Acquisition and Exercise of Monopoly Power and Its Implications for the Objectives of Antitrust." *Competition Policy International* 4.2 (2008): 203-241.

Evans, David S. and Vanessa Zhang. "Assessing Unfair Pricing under China's Antimonopoly Law for Innovation-Intensive Industries." *University of Chicago Coase-Sandor Institute for Law & Economics Research Paper* No. 678 (2014).

Ezrachi, A. and Maurice E. Stucke. "The Fight over Antitrust's Soul." *Journal of European Competition Law & Practice* (2017): 1-2.

Falcon, Andrea. "Aristotle on Causality" *in* Edward N. Zalta (ed.) *The Stanford Encyclopedia of Philosophy.* Spring 2015 Edition. http://plato.stanford.edu/archives/spr2015/entries/aristotle-causality/.

Farrell, Joseph, John Hayes, Carl Shapiro and Theresa Sullivan. "Standard Setting, Patents, and Hold-Up." *Antitrust Law Journal* 74.3 (2007): 603-670.

Faulhaber, Gerald R. "Cross-Subsidization: Pricing in Public Enterprises." *The American Economic Review* 65.5 (1975): 966-977.

Faulhaber, Gerald R. "Cross-Subsidy Analysis with More than Two Services." *Journal of Competition Law and Economics* 1.3 (2005): 441-448, at 443.

Fernández, Esteban, José M. Montes and Camilo J. Vázquez. "Typology and Strategic Analysis of Intangible Resources: A Resource-Based Approach." *Technovation* 20.2 (2000): 81-92.

Filippini, Massimo. "Are Municipal Electricity Distribution Utilities Natural Monopolies?" *Annals of Public and Cooperative Economics* 69.2 (1998): 157-174.

Fingleton, John. "De-Monopolising Ireland" *in* Claus-Dieter Ehlermann and Isabela Atanasiu (eds.) *European Competition Law Annual 2003: What Is an Abuse of a Dominant Position?* Bloomsbury Publishing, 2006.

First, Harry and Spencer Weber Waller. "Antitrust's Democracy Deficit." *Fordham Law Review* 81.5 (2013): 2543-2574.

Flamm, Kenneth. "Moore's Law and the Economics of Semiconductor Price Trends" *in* National Research Council (ed.) *Productivity and Cyclicality in Semiconductors: Trends, Implications, and Questions – Report of a Symposium. Washington*, DC: The National Academies Press, 2004.

Fombrun, Charles. *Reputation.* John Wiley & Sons, 1996.

Fontana, Roberto, Franco Malerba and Astrid Marinoni. "Pre-entry Experience, Technological Complementarities, and the Survival of De-Novo Entrants. Evidence from the US Telecommunications Industry." *Economics of Innovation and New Technology* 25.6 (2016): 573-593.

Foreman-Peck, James S. "Natural Monopoly and Railway Policy in the Nineteenth Century." *Oxford Economic Papers* 39.4 (1987): 699-718.

Foster, John. "Competitive Selection, Self-Organisation and Joseph A. Schumpeter." *Journal of Evolutionary Economics* 10.3(2000): 311-328.

Fox, Eleanor M. and Deborah Healey. "When the State Harms Competition - The Role for Competition Law." *Antitrust Law Journal* 79.3 (2014): 769-820.

Franklin, James L., et al. "Atlantic Hurricane Season of 2004." *Monthly Weather Review* 134.3 (2006): 981-1025.

Freeman III, Charles W. "The Commercial and Economic Relationship" *in* David Shambaugh (ed.) *Tangled Titans: The United States and China.* Rowman & Littlefield Publishers, 2012.

Friederiszick, Hans W., Lars-Hendrik Röller and Vincent Verouden. "European State Aid Control: An Economic Framework" *in* Paolo Buccirossi (ed.) *Handbook of Antitrust Economics.* The MIT Press, 2006: 625-669.

Friedman, David D. *The Machinery of Freedom: Guide to a Radical Capitalism.* Open Court Publishing Company, 1989.

Friedman, Milton. *Essays in Positive Economics. Part I - The Methodology of Positive Economics.* University of Chicago Press, [1953] 1970: 3-43.

Frohlich, Norman and Joe A. Oppenheimer. "Ethical Problems When Moving to Markets: Gaining Efficiency While Keeping an Eye on Distributive Justice" *in* Arieh A. Ullmann and Alfred Lewis (eds.) *Privatization and Entrepreneurship: The Managerial Challenge in Central and Eastern Europe.* Psychology Press, 1997.

Fumagalli, Chiara and Massimo Motta. "A Simple Theory of Predation." *Journal of Law and Economics* 56.3 (2013): 595-631.

Fumagalli, Chiara and Massimo Motta. "On the Use of Price-Cost Tests in Loyalty Discounts and Exclusive Dealing Arrangements: Which Implications from Economic Theory Should Be Drawn?" *Antitrust Law Journal* 81.2 (2017): 537.

Gal, Michal, "Below-Cost Price Alignment: Meeting or Beating Competition?" *New York University Law and Economics Working Papers* Paper 95 (2007): 1-15.

Gans, Joshua S. "When Is Static Analysis a Sufficient Proxy for Dynamic Considerations? Reconsidering Antitrust and Innovation." *Innovation Policy and the Economy* 11.1 (2011): 55-78.

Gauthier, David. "No Need for Morality: The Case of the Competitive Market." *Philosophic Exchange* 13.1 (1982): 41-54.

Gautier, Axel and Nicolas Petit. "Optimal Enforcement of Competition Policy: The Commitments Procedure under Uncertainty." *European Journal of Law and Economics* 45.2 (2018): 195-224.

Gavil, Andrew I., William E. Kovacic, Jonathan B. Baker and Joshua Wright. *Antitrust Law in Perspective: Cases, Concepts and Problems in Competition Policy*, West Academic Publishing, 2017.

Gelamn, Judith R. and Steven C. Salop. "Judo Economics: Capacity Limitation and Coupon Competition." *The Bell Journal of Economics* 14.2 (1983): 315-325.

Geradin, Damien. "The Opening of State Monopolies to Competition: Main Issues of the Liberalization Process" *in* Damien Geradin (ed.) *The Liberalization of State Monopolies in the European Union and Beyond*, Kluwer (2000): 181-205.

Geradin, Damien. "Limiting the Scope of Article 82 of the EC Treaty: What Can the EU Learn from the US Supreme Court's Judgment in *Trinko* in the Wake of *Microsoft*,

IMS, and *Deutsche Telekom*?" *Common Market Law Review* 41.6 (2004): 1519-1553.

Geradin, Damien and Robert O'Donoghue. "The Concurrent Application of Competition Law and Regulation: The Case of Margin Squeeze Abuses in the Telecommunications Sector." *Journal of Competition Law and Economics* 1 (2005): 355-425.

Geradin, Damien and Miguel Rato. "Can Standard-Setting Lead to Exploitative Abuse? A Dissonant View on Patent Hold-Up, Royalty Stacking and the Meaning of FRAND." *European Competition Journal* 3.1 (2007): 101-161.

Geradin, Damien. "A Proposed Test for Separating Pro-Competitive Conditional Rebates from Anti-competitive Ones." *World Competition* 32 (2009): 41-70.

Geradin, Damien. "Refusal to Supply and Margin Squeeze: A Discussion of Why the 'Telefónica Exceptions' Are Wrong." *TILEC Discussion Paper* No.2011-009 (2011).

Geradin, Damien. "Uber and the Rule of Law: Should Spontaneous Liberalization Be Applauded or Criticized?" *Competition Policy International* (2015).

Gerber, David J. *Law and Competition in the Twentieth Century Europe. Protecting Prometheus*. Oxford, 2003.

Geroski, Paul A. and Alexis Jacquemin. "Dominant Firms and Their Alleged Decline." *International Journal of Industrial Organization* 2.1 (1984): 1-27.

Geroski, Paul A. "Thinking Creatively about Markets." *International Journal of Industrial Organization* 16.6 (1998): 677-695.

Geroski, Paul A. "The Growth of Firms in Theory and in Practice." *CEPR* Discussion Paper No.2092 (2002): 1-30.

Giberson, Michael. "List of State Anti-Price Gouging Laws" (November 3, 2012), https://knowledgeproblem.com/2012/11/03/list-of-price-gouging-laws/.

Gibrat, Robert. *Les inegalités économiques*. Paris: Recueil Sirey, 1931.

Giertz, Eric. "Understanding the Swedish Saga through an Historical Exposé" *in* Eric GiertzZ, Annika Rickne and Petri Rouvinen (eds.) *Small and Beautiful – The ICT Success of Finland and Sweden*. Verket för innovationssystem-VINNOVA (2015): 62-95.

Gifford, Daniel J. and E. Thomas Sullivan. "Can International Antitrust Be Saved for the Post-Boeing Merger World? A Proposal to Minimize International Conflict and to Rescue Antitrust from Misuse." *The Antitrust Bulletin* 45.1 (2000): 55-118.

Gilbert, Richard J. "Mobility Barriers and the Value of Incumbency" *in* Richard Schmalensee and Robert D. Willig (eds.) *Handbook of Industrial Organization*, Vol. 1, 1989: 475-535.

Gilbert, Richard J. "Looking for Mr. Schumpeter: Where Are We in the Competition Innovation Debate?" *in* Adam B. Jaffe et al. (eds.) *Innovation Policy and the Economy*, 2006: 159-215.

Glazer, Kenneth L. and Brian R. Henry. "Coercive *vs*. Incentivizing Conduct: A Way out of the Section 2 Impasse." *Antitrust* 18.1 (2003): 45-51.

Glynn, Sean and Alan Booth. *Modern Britain: An Economic and Social History*. Burns & Oates, 1996.

Golich, Vicki L. "From Competition to Collaboration: The Challenge of Commercial-Class Aircraft Manufacturing." *International Organization* 46.4 (1992): 899-934.

González Díaz, Francisco E. and Jorge Padilla. "The linkLine Judgment - A European Perspective." *GCP Magazine* (April 1, 2009).

Grant, Robert M. "Toward a Knowledge-Based Theory of the Firm." *Strategic Management Journal* 17.S2 (1996): 109-122.

Gray, Horace M. "The Passing of the Public Utility Concept." *The Journal of Land & Public Utility Economics* 16.1 (1940): 8-20.

Greene, Hilary and Dennis A. Yao. "The Influences of Strategic Management on Antitrust Discourse." *The Antitrust Bulletin* 59.4 (2014): 789-825.

Griset, Pascal. "L'Etat et les Télécommunications Internationales au Début du XXème Siécle en France: Un Monopole Stérile." *Histoire, économie et société* 6.2 (1987): 181-207.

Grossi, Luigi, Sven Heim and Michael Waterson. "A Vision of the European Energy Future? The Impact of the German Response to the Fukushima Earthquake." *ZEW - Centre for European Economic Research* Discussion *Paper* No. 14-051 (2014): 1-45.

Gual, Jordi, Martin Hellwig, Anne Perrot, Michele Polo, Patrick Rey, Klaus Schmidt and Rune Stenbacka. "An Economic Approach to Article 82. Report to the European Commission by the European Advisory Group on Competition Policy" (EAGCP), 2005.

Hadley, Arthur T. *Railroad Transportation: Its History and Its Laws.* GT Putnam's Sons, 1885.

Hall, Richard. "The Strategic Analysis of Intangible Resources." *Strategic Management Journal* 13.2 (1992): 135-144.

Hall, Richard. "A Framework Linking Intangible Resources and Capabilities to Sustainable Competitive Advantage." *Strategic Management Journal* 14.8 (1993): 607-618.

Hamilton, Neil W. and Anne M. Caulfield. "The Defense of Natural Monopoly in Sherman Act Monopolization Cases." *DePaul Law Review* 33.3 (1983): 465-493.

Harbord, David and Tom Hoehn. "Barriers to Entry and Exit in European Competition Policy." *International Review of Law and Economics* 14.4 (1994): 411-435.

Haskel, Michael A. "The Benign Time Assumption's Role in the Application of 2 of the Sherman Antitrust Act." *Quinnipiac Law Review* 24 (2005): 265-299.

Hawker, Norman W. and Thomas N. Edmonds. "Strategic Management Concepts for Antitrust: Cooperation, Stakeholders and Sustainability." *The Antitrust Bulletin* 59.4 (2014): 769-788.

Hay, George A. and Kathryn McMahon. "The Diverging Approach to Price Squeezes in the United States and Europe." *Journal of Competition Law and Economics* 8.2 (2012): 259-296.

Hayek, Friedrich A. *The Road to Serfdom: Text and Documents: The Definitive Edition.* Routledge, [1944] 2014.

Hayek, Friedrich A. "The Meaning of Competition." *Individualism and Economic Order*, University of Chicago Press, 1948: 92-106.

Hayek, Friedrich A. "Competition as a Discovery Procedure." *The Quarterly Journal of Austrian Economics* 5.3 [1968] (2002): 9-23.

Hayek, Friedrich A. *Law, Legislation and Liberty*, (Vol. 1) *Rules and Order*. Routledge, [1973] 1998.

Hayek, Friedrich A. *Law, Legislation and Liberty*, (Vol. 2) *The Mirage of Social Justice*. Routledge, [1976] 1998.

Hayek, Friedrich A. *Law, Legislation and Liberty*, (Vol. 3) *The Political Order of a Free People*, Routledge, [1979] 1998.

Hayek, Friedrich A. *The Constitution of Liberty*. The University of Chicago Press, [1978] 2011.

Hayek, Friedrich A. "The Pretence of Knowledge." *The American Economic Review* 79.6 (1989): 3-7.

Hazlett, Thomas W. "The Curious Evolution of Natural Monopoly Theory" *in* Robert W. Poole (Ed.) *Unnatural Monopolies: The Case for Deregulating Public Utilities* (1985).

Hazlett, Thomas W., David Teece and Leonard Waverman. "Walled Garden Rivalry: The Creation of Mobile Network Ecosystems." *George Mason Law & Economics Research Paper* No. 11-50 (2011).

Heath, Joseph. "An Adversarial Ethic for Business: Or When Sun-Tzu Met the Stakeholder." *Journal of Business Ethics* 72.4 (2007): 359-374.

Heimler, Alberto. "Below-Cost Pricing and Loyalty-Inducing Discounts: Are They Restrictive and, If So, When?" *Competition Policy International* 1.2 (2005): 149-172.

Helfat, Constance E. "Know-How and Asset Complementarity and Dynamic Capability Accumulation: The Case of R&D." *Strategic Management Journal* (1997): 339-360.

Herman, Douglas A., Shawn W. Ulrick and Seth B. Sacher. "Dominance Thresholds: A Cautionary Note." *The Antitrust Bulletin* 59.4 (2014): 855-893.

Herrera Anchústegui, Ignacio. *Buyer Power in EU Competition Law*. Concurrences, 2017.

Hewitt, Gary. "Background Note" *in* OECD, *Loyalty and Fidelity Discounts and Rebates, Roundtable on Competition Policy*. DAFFE/COMP(2002)21: 19-48.

Hicks, John R. "Annual Survey of Economic Theory: The Theory of Monopoly." *Econometrica* 3.1 (1935): 1-20.

Hovenkamp, Herbert. *Enterprise and American Law, 1836-1937*. Cambridge, Massachusetts: Harvard University Press, 1991.

Hovenkamp, Herbert. *The Antitrust Enterprise. Principle and Execution*. Harvard University Press, 2005.

Huber, Peter William, Michael K. Kellogg and John Throne. *Federal Telecommunications Law*. Aspen Publishers Online, 1999.

Hughes, Alan. "Competition Policy and the Competitive Process: Europe in the 1990s." *Metroeconomica* 43.12 (1992): 1-46.

Hultink, Erik J., et al. "Launch Decisions and New Product Success: An Empirical Comparison of Consumer and Industrial Products." *Journal of Product Innovation Management* 17.1 (2000): 5-23.

Hunt, Shelby D. and Dennis B. Arnett. "Competition as an Evolutionary Process and Antitrust Policy." *Journal of Public Policy & Marketing* 20.1 (2001): 15-26.

Huurdeman, Anton A. *The Worldwide History of Telecommunications*. John Wiley & Sons, 2003.

Ibáñez Colomo, Pablo. "Exclusionary Discrimination under Article 102 TFEU." *Common Market Law Review* 51.1 (2014): 141-163.

Ibáñez Colomo, Pablo. "EU Competition Law in the Regulated Network Industries" *in* Jonathan Galloway (ed.) *Intersections of Antitrust: Policy and Regulation*. Oxford University Press, 2016.

Ibáñez Colomo, Pablo. "The Law on Abuses of Dominance and the System of Judicial Remedies." *Yearbook of European Law* 32.1 (2013): 389-431.

Italianer, Alexander. "Prepared Remarks on: Level-Playing Field and Innovation in Technology Markets." *Conference on Antitrust in Technology* (January 28, 2013).

Itami, Hiroyuki and Thomas W. Roehl. *Mobilizing Invisible Assets*. Harvard University Press, [1991] 2009.

Jacobson, Robert. "Unobservable Effects and Business Performance." *Marketing Science* 9.1 (1990): 74-85.

Jakopin, Nejc M. and Andreas Klein. "First-Mover and Incumbency Advantages in Mobile Telecommunications." *Journal of Business Research* 65.3 (2012): 362-370.

Jamison, Mark A. "A Further Look at Proper Cost Tests for Natural Monopoly." *University of Florida, Public Utility Research Center* (1997): 1-13.

Joliet, René. *Monopolization and Abuse of Dominant Position: A Comparative Study of American and European Approaches to the Control of Economic Power*. Collection scientifique de la Faculté de Droit de l'Université de Liège [1970] 1975.

Jones, Eliot. "Is Competition in Industry Ruinous?" *The Quarterly Journal of Economics* 34.3 (1920): 473-519.

Jorgenson, Dale. "Information Technology and the U.S. Economy." *The American Economic Review* 91.1 (2001): 1-32.

Joskow, Paul L. "Regulation of Natural Monopolies" *in* A. Mitchell Polinsky and Steven Shavell (eds.) *Handbook of Law and Economics*, Vol. 2, 2007: 1229-1348.

Kadar, Massimiliano. "European Union Competition Law in the Digital Era." *Zeitschrift für Wettbewerbsrecht* 4 (2015): 342.

Kamasak, Rifat. "The Contribution of Tangible and Intangible Resources, and Capabilities to a Firm's Profitability and Market Performance." *European Journal of Management and Business Economics* 26.2 (2017): 252-275.

Kaplow, Louis and Carl Shapiro. "Antitrust" *in* A. Mitchell Polinsky and Steven Shavell (eds.) *Handbook of Law and Economics*, Vol. 2, 2007: 1073-1225.

Kaplow, Louis. "Market Definition, Market Power." *International Journal of Industrial Organization* 43 (2015): 148-161.

Kaplow, Louis. "On the Relevance of Market Power." *Harvard Law Review* 130.5 (2017): 1303-1407.

Kellezi, Pranvera. "Abuse Below the Threshold of Dominance" in M.O. Mackendrot, B.C. Gallego and S. Enchelmaier, S. (eds.) *Abuse of Dominant Position: New Interpretation, New Enforcement Mechanisms?* Springer, 2008.

Keynes, John. M. "The General Theory of Employment." *The Quarterly Journal of Economics* 51.2 (1937): 209-223.

Kipnis, Jason. "Beating the System: Abuses of the Standards Adoption Process." *IEEE Communications Magazine* 38.7 (2000): 102-105.

Kirzner, Israel M. *Competition and Entrepreneurship*. The University of Chicago Press, 1973.

Kirzner, Israel M. *Perception, Opportunity, and Profit: Studies in the Theory of Entrepreneurship*. Chicago: University of Chicago Press, 1979.

Kirzner, Israel M. *How Markets Work: Disequilibrium, Entrepreneurship and Discovery*. London, Institute of Economic Affairs, 1997.

Kirzner, Israel M. "Hayek, the Nobel, and the Revival of Austrian Economics." *The Review of Austrian Economics* 28.3 (2015): 225-236.

Klein, Benjamin, Robert G. Crawford and Armen A Alchian, "Vertical Integration, Appropriable Rents, and the Competitive Contracting Process." *Journal of Law and Economics* 21.2 (1978): 297-326.

Klepper, Steven and Kenneth L. Simons. "Dominance by Birthright: Entry of Prior Radio Producers and Competitive Ramifications in the US Television Receiver Industry." *Strategic Management Journal* 21.10-11 (2000): 997-1016.

Klepper, Steven. "Firm Survival and the Evolution of Oligopoly." *RAND Journal of Economics* (2002): 37-61.

Knight, Frank H. *Risk, Uncertainty and Profit*. New York: Augustus M. Kelly, [1921] 1964.

Knight, Frank H. "The Meaning of Freedom." *Ethics* 52.1 (1941): 86-109.

Knight, Frank H. *The Ethics of Competition and Other Essays*. New York: Harper Bros, 1935.

Knight, Shawn. "Technology Before Its Time: 9 Products That Were Too Early to Market," *Techspot* [Blog] (October 11, 2013), http://www.techspot.com/article/723-tech-ahead-of-its-time/.

Kobayashi, Bruce H. "Spilled Ink or Economic Progress? The Supreme Court's Decision in *Illinois Tool Works v. Independent Ink*." *The Antitrust Bulletin* 53.1 (2008): 5-33.

Kobayashi, Bruce H. and Joshua D. Wright. "Federalism, Substantive Preemption, and Limits on Antitrust: An Application to Patent Holdup." *Journal of Competition Law and Economics* 5.3 (2009): 469-516.

Kobayashi, Bruce H. and Joshua D. Wright. "The Limits of Antitrust and Patent Holdup: A Reply to Cary et al." *Antitrust Law Journal* 78.2 (2012): 505-526.

Kogut, Bruce and Udo Zander. "Knowledge of the Firm, Combinative Capabilities, and the Replication of Technology." *Organization Science* 3.3 (1992): 383-397.

Kokkoris, Ioannis. *A Gap in the Enforcement of Article 82*. British Institute of International and Comparative Law, 2009.

Kolko, Gabriel. *Railroads and Regulations, 1877-1916*. Princeton University Press, [1965] 2015.

Korah, Valentine. "The Interface Between Intellectual Property and Antitrust: The European Experience." *Antitrust Law Journal* 69.3 (2002): 801-839.

Kovacic, William E. "The Intellectual DNA of Modern US Competition Law for Dominant Firm Conduct: The Chicago/Harvard Double Helix." *Columbia Business Law Review* (2007): 1-80.

Krattenmaker, Thomas G. and Steven C. Salop. "Anticompetitive Exclusion: Raising Rivals' Costs to Achieve Power over Price." *The Yale Law Journal* 96.2 (1986): 209-293.

Krattenmaker, Thomas G., Robert H. Lande and Steven C. Salop. "Monopoly Power and Market Power in Antitrust Law." *Georgetown Law Journal* 76.2 (1987): 241-270.

Kronenberger, Vincent. "A Model of the Transformation Process of Statutory Monopolies in European Community Law: From Practice to Theory." *European Business Organization Law Review* 2.2 (2001): 301-338.

Laffont, Jean-Jacques and Jean Tirole. *Competition in Telecommunications*. MIT Press, 2001.

Lahaye, Laura. "Mercantilism." *The Concise Encyclopedia of Economics*. Library of Economics and Liberty, 2008, http://www.econlib.org/library/Enc/Mercantilism.html.

Lamadrid de Pablo, Alfonso. "Competition Law as Fairness." *Journal of European Competition Law & Practice* 8.3 (2017): 147-148.

Lande, Robert H. "Resurrecting Incipiency: From *Von's Grocery* to Consumer Choice." *Antitrust Law Journal* 68.3 (2001): 875-898.

Lande, Robert H. "A Traditional and Textualist Analysis of the Goals of Antitrust: Efficiency, Preventing Theft from Consumers, and Consumer Choice." *Fordham Law Review* 81 (2012): 2349-2403.

Landes, William M. and Richard A. Posner. *The Economic Structure of Intellectual Property Law*. Harvard University Press, 2009.

Langlois, Richard N. "Antitrust: Where Did It Come from and What Did It Mean?" *University of Connecticut. Department of Economics Working Paper Series* 2016-07 (September 2016): 1-54.

Larouche, Pierre. *Competition Law and Regulation in European Telecommunications*. Hart Publishing, 2000.

Larouche, Pierre. "Europe and Investment in Infrastructure, with Emphasis on Electronic Communications" *in* G. Arts, W. Dicke and L. Hancher (eds.) *New Perspectives on Investment in Infrastructures*. WRR Studies, Amsterdam: Amsterdam University Press, 2008, 241-270.

Larouche, Pierre and Maarten Pieter Schinkel. "Continental Drift in the Treatment of Dominant Firms: Article 102 TFEU in Contrast to § 2 Sherman Act." *TILEC Discussion Paper No. 2013-020* (2013): 1-33.

Larouche, Pierre and Florian Schuett. "Repeated Interaction in Standard Setting." *TILEC Discussion Paper* No. 2016-010, *CentER Discussion Paper* No. 2016-021 (2016): 1-37.

Lehman Brothers Collection. *Contemporary Business Archives. Commercial Solvents Corp*. Harvard Business School, https://www.library.hbs.edu/hc/lehman/.

Letwin, William. *Law and Economic Policy in America: The Evolution of the Sherman Antitrust Act*. University of Chicago Press, 1981.

Lianos, Ioannis. "Categorical Thinking in Competition Law" *in* Ariel Ezrachi (ed.) *Article 82 EC: Reflections on Its Recent Evolution*. Hart Publishing, 2009.

Lieberman, Marvin B. "The Learning Curve and Pricing in the Chemical Processing Industries." *The RAND Journal of Economics* 15.2 (1984): 213-228.

Lieberman, Marvin B. and David B. Montgomery. "First-Mover Advantages." *Strategic Management Journal* 9(S1) (1988): 41-58.

Lieberman, Marvin B. and David B. Montgomery. "First-Mover (Dis)Advantages: Retrospective and Link with the Resource-Based View." *Strategic Management Journal* 19 (1998): 1111-1125.

Lieberman, Marvin B. and David B. Montgomery. "Conundra and Progress: Research on Entry Order and Performance." *Long Range Planning* 46 (2013): 312-324.

Liebowitz, Stan J. and Stephen E. Margolis. "The Fable of the Keys." *The Journal of Law and Economics* 33.1 (1990): 1-25.

Liebowitz, Stan J. and Stephen E. Margolis. "Path Dependence, Lock-in, and History." *Journal of Law, Economics, & Organization,* 11.1 (1995): 205-226.

Liebowitz, Stan J. and Stephen E. Margolis. "Should Technology Choice Be a Concern of Antitrust Policy?" *Harvard Journal of Law and Technology* 9.2 (1996): 283-318.

Liebowitz, Stan J. and Stephen E. Margolis. "Network Effects and the Microsoft Case" *in* Jerome Ellig (ed.) *Dynamic Competition and Public Policy: Technology, Innovation, and Antitrust Issues*. Cambridge University Press, 2001.

Liebowitz, Stan J. and Stephen E. Margolis. *Winners, Losers & Microsoft; Competition and Antitrust in High Technology*. Independent Institute, 2001.

Liebowitz, Stan J. and Stephen E. Margolis. *The Economics of QWERTY: History, Theory, and Policy*. NYU Press, 2002.

Liebowitz, Stan J. and Stephen E. Margolis. "The Troubled Path of the Lock-in Movement." *Journal of Competition Law and Economics* 9.1 (2012): 125-152.

Liffen, John. "Telegraphy and Telephones." *Industrial Archaeology Review* 35.1 (2013): 22-39.

Lippman, Steven A. and Richard P. Rumelt. "Uncertain Imitability: An Analysis of Interfirm Differences in Efficiency under Competition." *The Bell Journal of Economics* (1982): 418-438.

Littlechild, Stephen C. "Misleading Calculations of the Social Costs of Monopoly Power." *The Economic Journal* 91.362 (1981): 348-363.

Lockett, Andy and Steve Thompsonn. "The Resource-Based View and Economics." *Journal of Management* 27.6 (2001): 723-754.

Loeb, G. Hamilton. "The Communications Act Policy toward Competition: A Failure to Communicate." *Duke Law Journal* 1 (1978): 1-56.

Lopatka, John E. and William H. Page. "Posner's Program for the Antitrust Division: A Twenty-Five Year Perspective." *SMU Law Review* 48 (1994): 1713-1747.

Lopatka, John E. "Stephen Breyer and Modern Antitrust: A Snug Fit." *The Antitrust Bulletin* 40.1 (1995): 1-97.

Loy, Clement T. and Les Irwig. "Accuracy of Diagnostic Tests Read with and without Clinical Information: A Systematic Review." *Journal of the American Medical Association*, 292.13 (2004): 1602-1609.

Lyons, Bruce. "Inequality and Competition Policy." *CPI* (October 2017):1-6.

Ma, Hao. "Competitive Advantage: What's Luck Got to Do with It?" *Management Decision* 40.6 (2002): 525-536.

Machlup, Fritz, *The Political Economy of Monopoly - Business Labor and Government Policies*. Baltimore: The Johns Hopkins Press, [1952] 1967.

Machovec, Frank. *Perfect Competition and the Transformation of Economics*. Routledge, 2002.

Maier-Rigaud, Frank and Dovile Vaigauskaite. "Prokent/Tomra, a Textbook Case? Abuse of Dominance under Perfect Information." *Competition Policy Newsletter* 2 (2006): 19-24.

Makholm, Jeff D. *The Political Economy of Pipelines: A Century of Comparative Institutional Development*. University of Chicago Press, 2012.

Malerba, Franco, et al. "Competition and Industrial Policies in a 'History Friendly' Model of the Evolution of the Computer Industry." *International Journal of Industrial Organization* 19.5 (2001): 635-664.

Malthus, Thomas R. "An Inquiry into the Nature and Progress of Rent, and the Principles by which It Is Regulated." *Project Gutenberg eBook* #4336, [1815] 2013.

Mancke, Richard B. "Causes of Interfirm Profitability Differences: A New Interpretation of the Evidence." *The Quarterly Journal of Economics* 88.2 (1974): 182-193.

Mariniello, Mario, Damien Neven and Jorge Padilla. "Antitrust, Regulatory Capture and Economic Integration." *Bruegel Policy Contribution*, 2015/11.

Markham, Jesse Jr. "Lessons for Competition Law from the Economic Crisis: The Prospect for Antitrust Responses to the 'Too-Big-to-Fail' Phenomenon." *Fordham Journal of Corporate and Financial Law* 16.2 (2011): 261-322.

Markovits, Richard S. *Economics and the Interpretation and Application of U.S. and E.U. Antitrust Law: Volume I Basic Concepts and Economics-Based Legal Analyses of Oligopolistic and Predatory Conduct.* SpringerLink: Bücher. Springer Berlin Heidelberg, 2014.

Marshall, Alfred. 1890. "'Some Aspects of Competition.' The Address of the President of Section F- Economic Science and Statistics--of the British Association, at the Sixtieth Meeting, Held at Leeds, in September, 1890." *Journal of the Royal Statistical Society* 53.4 (1890): 612-643.

Martiningui, Ana and Richard Youngs (eds.). *Challenges for European Foreign Policy in 2012. What Kind of Geo-economic Europe?* Fride, 2011.

Marty, Frédéric. "As-Efficient Competitor Test in Exclusionary Prices Strategies: Does Post-Danmark Really Pave the Way Towards a More Economic Approach?" *GREDEG Working Papers Series* No. 2013-26.

Massie, Robert K. *Peter the Great: His Life and World*. Random House, 2012.

Mcardle, Megan. *The Up Side of Down: Why Failing Well Is the Key to Success*. Penguin, 2015.

McConnell, C.R. *Elements of Economic Analysis*. New York: McGraw-Hill, 1960.

McCraw, Thomas K. *Prophets of Regulation.* Harvard University Press, 1984.

McMahon, Kathryn. "The Regulation of a Margin Squeeze in the European Union and the Intersection of Competition Law and Sector-Specific Regulation 10.2 (2014): 167-204.

Meese, Alan J. "Monopolization, Exclusion, and the Theory of the Firm." *Minnesota Law Review* 89 (2004): 743-847.

Meese, Alan J. "Property, Aspen, and Refusals to Deal." *Antitrust Law Journal* 73.1 (2005): 81-114.

Megginson, William L. and Jeffry M. Netter. "From State to Market: A Survey of Empirical Studies on Privatization." *Journal of Economic Literature* 39.2 (2001): 321-389.

Melamed, Douglas. "Response. Antitrust Law Is Not That Complicated." *Harvard Law Review Forum* 130 (2017): 163-172.

Menger, Carl. *Principles of Economics*. Ludwig von Mises Institute, [1871] 2007.

Merrill, Thomas W. "Property and the Right to Exclude." *Nebraska Law Review* 77.4 (1998): 730-755.

Merrill, Thomas W. "Property and the Right to Exclude II." *Brigham-Kanner Property Rights Conference Journal* 3 (2014): 1-25.

Metcalfe, John Stanley. *Evolutionary Economics and Creative Destruction*. Vol. 1. Psychology Press, 1998.

Metcalfe, John Stanley and Ronald Ramlogan. "Competition and the Regulation of Economic Development." *The Quarterly Review of Economics and Finance* 45.2-3 (2005): 215-235.

Michalisin, Michael D., Douglas M. Kline and Robert D. Smith. "Intangible Strategic Assets and Firm Performance: A Multi-industry Study of the Resource-Based View." *Journal of Business Strategies* 17.2 (2000): 93-117.

Mill, John S. *Principles of Political Economy*. Econlib, [1848] 2009.

Millward, Robert. *Private and Public Enterprise in Europe: Energy, Telecommunications and Transport, 1830-1990*. Cambridge University Press, 2005.

Millward, Robert. "Business and the State" *in* Geoffrey G. Jones and Jonathan Zeitlin (eds.) *The Oxford Handbook of Business History* (2008): 529-557.

Min, Sungwook, Manohar U. Kalwani and William T. Robinson. "Market Pioneer and Early Follower Survival Risks: A Contingency Analysis of Really New Versus Incrementally New Product-Markets." *Journal of Marketing* 70 (2006): 15-33.

Monteiro, Guilherme Fowler A. and Nicolai Foss. "Resources and Market Definition: Rethinking the 'Hypothetical Monopolist' from a Resource-Based Perspective." *Managerial and Decision Economics* 39.3 (2018): 346-353.

Montgomery, David, Robert A. Baron and Mary K. Weisskopf. "Potential Effects of Proposed Price Gouging Legislation on the Cost and Severity of Gasoline Supply Interruptions." *Journal of Competition Law and Economics* 3.3 (2007): 357-397.

Monti, Giorgio. "Article 81 EC and public policy." *Common Market Law Review*, 39.5 (2002): 1057-1099.

Morgan, Mary S. "Competing Notions of 'Competition' in Late-Nineteenth Century American Economics." *Economic History Working Papers* 1.92 (1992): 1-49.

Mosca, Manuela. "On the Origins of the Concept of Natural Monopoly: Economies of Scale and Competition." *The European Journal of the History of Economic Thought* 15.2 (2008): 317-353.

Motta, Massimo. *Competition Policy: Theory and Practice*. Cambridge University Press, 2004.

Motta, Massimo and Alexandre de Streel. "Excessive Pricing in Competition Law: Never Say Never?" *in* Konkurrensverket (ed.) *The Pros and Cons of High Prices*, 2007: 14-46.

Mueller, Dennis C. "First-Mover Advantages and Path Dependence." *International Journal of Industrial Organization* 15.6 (1997): 827-850.

Mueller, Milton. "Universal Service in Telephone History: A Reconstruction." *Telecommunications Policy* 17.5 (1993): 352-369.

Mueller, Milton. "Universal Service and the Telecommunications Act: Myth Made law." *Communications of the ACM* 40.3 (1997): 39-47.

Musso, Pierre. "Aux origines de 'l'autonomie' des Télécommunications Françaises, la Loi de 1923." *Réseaux* 12.66 (1994): 99-117.

Nau, Henry. *International Politics and International Technology*. Johns Hopkins University Press, 1974.

Nelson, James R. "The Role of Competition in the Regulated Industries." *The Antitrust Bulletin* 11.1 (1966): 393-428.

Nelson, Richard R. and Sidney G. Winter. "Forces Generating and Limiting Concentration under Schumpeterian Competition." *The Bell Journal of Economics* 9.2 (1978): 524-548.

Nelson, Richard R. and Sidney G. Winter. *An Evolutionary Theory of Economic Change*. The Belknap Press of Harvard University Press, 1982.

Notz, William. "Monopolies in the Ancient Orient." *Bibliotecha Sacra* IV (1917): 254-283.

O'Donoghue, Robert and Jorge Padilla. *The Law and Economics of Article 82 EC*. Hart Publishing, 2006.

O'Donoghue, Robert and Jorge Padilla. *The Law and Economics of Article 102 TFEU*. Hart Publishing, 2013.

Oberholzer-Gee, Felix and Dennis A. Yao. "Antitrust-What Role for Strategic Management Expertise." *Boston University Law Review* 90 (2010): 1457-1477.

Ohlhausen, Hon Maureen K. "The Elusive Role of Competition in the Standard-Setting Antitrust Debate." *Stanford Technology Law Review* 20.93 (2017): 93-142.

Ormosi, Peter, Anna Rita Bennato, Steve Davies and Franco Mariuzzo. "Feasibility Study on the Microeconomic Impact of Enforcement of Competition Policies on Innovation." *Luxembourg: Publications Office of the European Union*, 2017, http://ec.europa.eu/competition/publications/reports/kd0417860enn.pdf.

Ortega Y Gasset, José. *The Revolt of the Masses*. New York: W.W. Norton, 1932.

Ortega Y Gasset, José. "Meditación de la Técnica." *Ensimismamiento y Alteración. Meditación de la Técnica y Otros Ensayos*. Alianza Editorial, [1933] 2014.

Ortiz Blanco, Luis. *Market Power in EU Antitrust Law*. Bloomsbury Publishing, 2011.

Pacheco de Almeida, Gonçalo, and Peter B. Zemsky. "Some Like It Free: Innovators' Strategic Use of Disclosure to Slow Down Competition." *Strategic Management Journal* 33.7 (2012): 773-793.

Paulis, Emil. "Article 82 EC and Exploitative Conduct" *in* Claus-Dieter Ehlermann and Isabela Atanasiu (eds.) *European Competition Law Annual 2003: What Is an Abuse of a Dominant Position?* Bloomsbury Publishing, 2006: 515-524.

Pelkmans, Jacques. “Making EU Network Markets Competitive.” *Oxford Review of Economic Policy* 17.3 (2001): 432-456.

Penrose, Edith T. *The Theory of the Growth of the Firm*. Oxford University Press [1959] 2009.

Peteraf, Margaret A. “The Cornerstones of Competitive Advantage: A Resource-Based View.” *Strategic Management Journal* 14.3 (1993): 179-191.

Petit, Nicolas. *Oligopoles, Collusion Tacite et Droit Communautaire de la Concurrence*. Bruylant, Bruxelles, 2008.

Petit, Nicolas. “The Future of the Court of Justice in EU Competition Law - New Role and Responsibilities” *in* Court of Justice of the EU (ed.) *The Court of Justice and the Construction of Europe: Analyses and Perspectives on Sixty Years of Case-Law*. Nomos Verlagsgesellschaft, 2013.

Petit, Nicolas. “Price Squeezes with Positive Margins in EU Competition Law: Economic and Legal Anatomy of a Zombie.” *Revue du Droit des Industries de Réseau* 2 (2014): 123-128.

Petit, Nicolas. “‘Financial Fair Play’ or ‘Oligopoleague’ of Football Clubs?: A Preliminary Review under European Union Competition Law.” *SSRN* (June 16, 2014).

Petit, Nicolas. “Intel, Leveraging Rebates and the Goals of Article 102 TFEU.” *European Competition Journal* 11.1 (2015): 26-68.

Petit, Nicolas, “La rationalisation au long cours de la restriction de concurrence par « objet » dans la jurisprudence de la Cour de justice de l’Union européenne.” *Actualité Juridique Contrats d’affaires* October (2015): 422-429.

Petit, Nicolas. “Theories of Self-Preferencing under Article 102 TFEU: A Reply to Bo Vesterdorf.” *SSRN* (2015): 1-18.

Petit, Nicolas. “Re-Pricing Through Disruption in Oligopolies with Tacit Collusion: A Framework for Abuse of Collective Dominance” *in OECD Hearing on Oligopoly Markets*, DAF/COMP/WD (2015) 52.

Petit, Nicolas. “Rebates and Article 102 TFEU: The European Commission’s Duty to Apply the Guidance Paper.” *Competition Law & Policy Debate* 2.1 (2016): 4-12.

Petit, Nicolas. “Chinese State Capitalism and Western Antitrust Policy.” *Concurrences* 4 (2016): 69-79.

Petit, Nicolas. “The Antitrust and Intellectual Property Intersection in European Union Law” *in* Roger D. Blair and Daniel Sokol (eds.) *Handbook of Antitrust, Intellectual Property and High Tech*. Cambridge University, 2017.

Pitelis, Christos N. and David J. Teece. “Cross-Border Market Co-creation, Dynamic Capabilities and the Entrepreneurial Theory of the Multinational Enterprise.” *Industrial and Corporate Change* 19.4 (2010): 1247-1270.

Plaiss, Adam. “From Natural Monopoly to Public Utility: Technological Determinism and the Political Economy of Infrastructure in Progressive-Era America.” *Technology and Culture* 57.4 (2016): 806-830.

Podolny, Joel M. and Damon J. Phillips. “The Dynamics of Organizational Status.” *Industrial and Corporate Change* 5.2 (1996): 453-471.

Poillot-Peruzzetto, Sylvaine. “Nouvel apport concernant les entreprises gérant un service d’intérêt économique général.” *Contrats Concurrence Consommation* 6 (2002): 98.

Porter, Michael E. *Competitive Strategy: Techniques for Analyzing Industries and Competition.* New York: Free Press, [1980] 2004.

Porter, Michael E. "Strategic Interaction: Some Lessons from Industry Histories for Theory and Antitrust Policy" *in* Steven C. Salop (ed.) *Strategy, Predation, and Antitrust Analysis.* Federal Trade Commission, 1981: 449-506.

Porter, Michael E. "The Contributions of Industrial Organization to Strategic Management." *Academy of Management Review* 6.4 (1981): 609-620.

Porter, Michael E. *Competitive Advantage: Creating and Sustaining Superior Performance.* New York: Free Press, 1985.

Posner, Richard A. "Natural Monopoly and Its Regulation." *Stanford Law Review* 21.3 (1968): 548-643.

Posner, Richard A. "Natural Monopoly and Its Regulation: A Reply." *Stanford Law Review* 22.3 (1970): 540-546.

Posner, Richard A. "Oligopoly and the Antitrust Laws: A Suggested Approach." *Stanford Law Review* 21 (1968): 1562-1606.

Posner, Richard A. *Antitrust Law.* University of Chicago Press, 2009.

Posner, Richard A. *Economic Analysis of Law.* Aspen Publishers, 2011.

Primeaux Jr, Walter J. "Some Problems with Natural Monopoly." *Antitrust Bulletin* 24 (1979): 63-85.

Qian, Lihong, Rajshree Agarwal and Glenn Hoetker. "Configuration of Value Chain Activities: The Effect of Pre-entry Capabilities, Transaction Hazards, and Industry evolution on Decisions to Internalize." *Organization Science* 23.5 (2012): 1330-1349.

Rand, Ayn. "Antitrust: The Rule of Unreason." *The Objectivist Newsletter* 1.2 (1962).

Rasmusen, Eric B., J. Mark Ramseyer and John S. Wiley Jr. "Naked Exclusion." *The American Economic Review* 81.5 (1991): 1137-1145.

Rato, Miguel and Nicolas Petit. "Abuse of Dominance in Technology-Enabled Markets: Established Standards Reconsidered?" *European Competition Journal* 9.1 (2013): 1-65.

Rawls, John. "Constitutional Liberty and the Concept of Justice" *in* Samuel Freeman (ed.) *Collected Papers.* Harvard University Press (1999): 73-95.

Ray, Gautam, Jay B. Barney and Waleed A. Muhanna. "Capabilities, Business Processes, and Competitive Advantage: Choosing the Dependent Variable in Empirical Tests of the Resource-Based View." *Strategic Management Journal* 25.1 (2004): 23-37.

Raymon, Neil. "Price Ceilings, Product Quality and Consumer Welfare." *Journal of Economics*, 46.4 (1986): 369-395.

Reader, David. "At a Crossroads in EU Merger Control: Can a Rethink on Foreign Takeovers Address the Imbalances of Globalisation?" *European Competition and Regulatory Law Review* 1.2 (2017): 127-138.

Reed, Richard and Robert J. Defillippi. "Causal Ambiguity, Barriers to Imitation, and Sustainable Competitive Advantage." *Academy of Management Review* 15.1 (1990): 88-102.

Reid, Gavin C. "The Theory of Natural Monopoly by William Sharkey." *The Economic Journal* 93.372 (1983): 929-931.

Reinganum, Jennifer F. “Uncertain Innovation and the Persistence of Monopoly.” *The American Economic Review* 73:4 (1983): 741-748.

Ridyard, Derek. “Compulsory Access under EC Competition Law - A New Doctrine of ‘Convenient Facilities’ and the Case for Price Regulation.” *European Competition Law Review* 25 (2004): 669-673.

Riegg, Ryan M. “Opportunism, Uncertainty, and Relational Contracting - Antitrust Rules in the Film Industry.” *UCLA Law*, Working Paper (2008).

Ritter, Cyril. “Refusal to Deal and Essential Facilities: Does Intellectual Property Require Special Deference Compared to Tangible Property.” *World Competition* 28.3 (2005): 281-298.

Roberts, Peter W. and Grahame R. Dowling. “Corporate Reputation and Sustained Superior Financial Performance.” *Strategic Management Journal* 23.12 (2002), 1077-1093.

Robinson, William T. and Sungwook Min. “Is the First to Market the First to Fail? Empirical Evidence for Industrial Goods Businesses.” *Journal of Marketing Research* 39.1 (2002): 120-128.

Röller, Lars-Hendrik. “Proper Quadratic Cost Functions with an Application to the Bell System.” *The Review of Economics and Statistics* (1990): 202-210.

Röller, Lars-Hendrik. “Exploitative Abuses.” ESMT, *Business Brief No. BB-107-002* (2007): 3-15.

Romer, Paul M. “Endogenous Technological Change.” *Journal of Political Economy* 98.5, Part 2 (1990): S71-S102.

Rosenberg, Nathan. “Uncertainty and Technological Change” *in* Nathan Rosenberg (ed.) *Studies on Science and the Innovation Process: Selected Works of Nathan Rosenberg*. World Scientific Publishing Co. Pte. Ltd (2009): 153-172.

Rossi, Lucia Serena. “A New Revision of the EU Treaties after Lisbon?” *in* Lucia S. Rossi and Federico Casolari (eds.) *The EU after Lisbon*. Springer International Publishing, 2014.

Rothbard, Murray N. *Power & Market: Government and the Economy*. Ludwig von Mises Institute, [1970] 2006.

Rothbard, Murray N. *An Austrian Perspective on the History of Economic Thought, vol. 1, Economic Thought Before Adam Smith*. Ludwig von Mises Institute, 1995.

Rousseva, Ekaterina and Mel Marquis. “Hell Freezes Over: A Climate Change for assessing Exclusionary Conduct under Article 102 TFEU.” *Journal of European Competition Law & Practice* 4 (2012): 32-50.

Rubin, Janice E. “‘Price Gouging,’ the Antitrust Laws, and Vertical Integration in the Petroleum Industry: How They Are Related.” *Congressional Research Service Report* RS22262 (May 28, 2008).

Rumelt, Richard P. “How Much Does Industry Matter?” *Strategic Management Journal* 12.3 (1991): 167-185.

Rumelt, Richard P., Dan Schendel and David J. Teece. “Strategic Management and Economics.” *Strategic Management Journal* 12 (1991): 5-29.

Rummel, Per. “Rebate Schemes under Article 102 TFEU: *Post Danmark II*.” *Common Market Law Review* 53.4 (2016): 1121-1131.

Salinger, Michael. "Remarks at the FTC Workshop on Section 5." (October 17, 2008), https://www.ftc.gov/sites/default/files/documents/public_events/section-5-ftc-act-competition-statute/transcript.pdf.

Sally, Razeen. "Ordoliberalism and the Social Market: Classical Political Economy from Germany." *New Political Economy* 1.2 (1996): 233-257.

Salop, Steven C. "Symposium on Mergers and Antitrust." *The Journal of Economic Perspectives* 1.2 (1987): 3-12.

Samuelson, Paul A. *Foundations of Economic Analysis*. Atheneum, [1948] 1964.

Sánchez Cantos, Pedro. "A Subadditivity Test for the Cost Function of the Principal European Railways." *Transport Reviews* 20.3 (2000): 275-290.

Sanderson, Margaret and Ralph A. Winter. "Profits Versus Rents in Antitrust Analysis: An Application to the Canadian Waste Services Merger." *Antitrust Law Journal* 70.2 (2002): 485-511, 511.

Sappington, David E.M. and J. Gregory Sidak. "Competition Law for State-Owned Enterprises." *Antitrust Law Journal* 71.2 (2003): 479-523.

Scherer, Frederic M. *Industrial Market Structure and Economic Performance*. Houghton Mifflin, 1980.

Schmalensee, Richard. "Product Differentiation Advantages of Pioneering Brands." *The American Economic Review* 72.3 (1982): 349-365.

Schmalensee, Richard. "Standards for Dominant Firm Conduct: What Can Economics Contribute?" *Working Paper* (Sloan School of Management) 1723-85 (1985): 1-50.

Schumpeter, Joseph A. *The Theory of Economic Development*. Routledge, [1911] 2017.

Schumpeter, Joseph A. *Business Cycles: A Theoretical, Historical and Statistical Analysis of the Capitalist Process*. New York, Toronto and London: McGraw-Hill Book Company, 1939.

Schumpeter, Joseph A. *Capitalism, Socialism and Democracy*. Routledge, [1943] 2003.

Schumpeter, Joseph A. *History of Economic Analysis*. Routledge, [1954] 2006.

Scitovsky, Tibor. "The Benefits of Asymmetric Markets." *The Journal of Economic Perspectives* 4.1 (1990): 135-148.

Scott, Anthony and Peter Pearse. "Natural Resources in a High-Tech Economy: Scarcity Versus Resourcefulness." *Resources Policy* 18.3 (1992): 154-166.

Sewel, William H. "Three Temporalities: Toward a Sociology of the Event." *The Historic Turn in the Human Sciences* (1990): 1-30.

Shapiro, Carl. "Setting Compatibility Standards: Cooperation or Collusion?" *in* Rochelle C. Dreyfuss, Diane L. Zimmerman, and Harry First (eds.) *Expanding the Bounds of Intellectual Property*. Oxford University Press, 2001.

Sharkey, William W. *The Theory of Natural Monopoly*. New York: Cambridge University Press, 1982.

Shelanski, Howard A. "The Case for Rebalancing Antitrust and Regulation." *Michigan Law Review* 109.5 (2011): 683-732.

Shenfield, John H. and Irwin M Stelzer. *The Antitrust Laws: A Primer*. American Enterprise Institute, 2001.

Shenoy, Sudha R. "The Sources of Monopoly." *New Individualist Review* 4 (1966): 41-44.

Shin, Richard T. and John S. Ying. "Unnatural Monopolies in Local Telephone." *The RAND Journal of Economics* 23.2 (1992): 171-183.

Sidak, J. Gregory and David J. Teece. "Dynamic Competition in Antitrust Law." *Journal of Competition Law and Economics* 5.4 (2009): 581-631.

Simpson, Claire. "Dominant Firms and Selective Discounting in the EU: When Is 'Meeting Competition' a Defence?" *European Competition Journal* 12.1 (2016): 1-27.

Skalamera, Morena. "Italy's Path to Gas Liberalisation: Corporate Power, Monopoly Distortions and the Russia Factor." *Contemporary Italian Politics* 7.2 (2015): 161-184.

Smiley, Robert H. and S. Abraham Ravid. "The Importance of Being First: Learning Price and Strategy." *The Quarterly Journal of Economics* 98.2(1983): 353-362.

Smith, Adam. *An Inquiry into the Nature and Causes of the Wealth of Nations*. Econlib [1776] 2009.

Snyder, Jeremy. "What's the Matter with Price Gouging?" *Business Ethics Quarterly* 19.2 (2009): 275-293.

Sokol, D. Daniel. "Limiting Anticompetitive Government Interventions that Benefit Special Interests." *George Mason Law Review* 17 (2009): 119-190.

Solow, Robert M. "Technical Change and the Aggregate Production Function." *The Review of Economics and Statistics* 39.3 (1957): 312-320.

Spender, J.-C. "Making Knowledge the Basis of a Dynamic Theory of the Firm." *Strategic Management Journal* 17.S2 (1996): 45-62.

Spulber, Daniel F. "Competition Policy and the Incentive to Innovate: The Dynamic Effects of *Microsoft* v. *Commission*." *Yale Journal on Regulation* 25.2 (2008): 247-301.

Srikanth, Kannan and Mihaela Stan. "Taking Time to Do It Right: The Impact of Time-Compressing Experience Accumulation on Organizational Quality Outcomes" *in* Proceedings of the 35th DRUID Celebration Conference 2013 in Barcelona (2013): 1-31.

Srivastava, Rajendra K., Tasadduq A. Shervani and Liam Fahey. "Market-Based Assets and Shareholder Value: A Framework for Analysis." *The Journal of Marketing* (1998): 2-18.

Stein, Paul D., et al. "Pulmonary Embolism as a Cause of Death in Patients Who Died with Cancer." *The American Journal of Medicine* 119.2 (2006): 163-165.

Stigler, George J. *The Organization of Industry*, University of Chicago Press, 1968.

Stigler, George J. "The Economists and the Problem of Monopoly." *University of Chicago Law Occasional Paper* No. 19 (1983): 3-22.

Stucke, Maurice E. and Ariel Ezrachi. "Artificial Intelligence & Collusion: When Computers Inhibit Competition." *Oxford Legal Studies Research Paper No. 18/2015; University of Tennessee Legal Studies Research Paper No. 267,* April 8, 2015.

Stumpers, F.L. "The History, Development, and Future of Telecommunications in Europe." *IEEE Communications Magazine* 22.5 (1984): 84-95.

Suarez, Fernando and Gianvito Lanzolla. "The Half-Truth of First-Mover Advantage" *Harvard Business Review* (April 2005).

Suarez, Fernando and Gianvito Lanzolla. "The Role of Environmental Dynamics in Building a First Mover Advantage Theory." *Academy of Management Review* 32.2 (2007): 377-392.

Subiotto, Romano, David R. Little and Romi Lepetska. "The Application of Article 102 TFEU by the European Commission and the European Courts." *Journal of European Competition Law & Practice* 3.2 (2012): 175-181.

Summer, William G. *Earth-Hunger and Other Essays*. Transaction Publishers, [1888] 1980.

Sutton, John. "Gibrat's Legacy." *Journal of Economic Literature* 35 (1997): 40-59.

Swanson, Daniel G. and William J. Baumol. "Reasonable and Nondiscriminatory (Rand) Royalties, Standards Selection, and Control of Market Power." *Antitrust Law Journal* 73.1 (2005): 1-58.

Sydow, Jörg, Georg Schreyögg and Jochen Koch. "Organizational Path Dependence: Opening the Black Box." *Academy of Management Review* 34.4 (2009): 689-709.

Thomas Lewis, Charlton and Charles Short. *A Latin Dictionary*. Oxford: Clarendon Press (1879).

Tadelis, Steven. "Reputation and Feedback Systems in Online Platform Markets." *Annual Review of Economics* 8 (2016): 321-340.

Taleb, Nassim Nicholas. *The Black Swan: The Impact of the Highly Improbable*. Random House, 2010.

Taleb, Nassim Nicholas. *Antifragile: Things that Gain from Disorder*. Random House Incorporated, 2012.

Taleb, Nassim Nicholas. *Skin in the Game: Hidden Asymmetries in Daily Life*. Allen Lande, 2018.

Taylor, Simon. "The Challenge of Competitive Neutrality in Public Procurement and Competition Policy: The UK Health Sector as Case Study." *Competition Policy International* 7 (2011): 2-8.

Teece, David J., Gary Pisano and Amy Shuen. "Dynamic Capabilities and Strategic Management." *Strategic Management Journal* 18.7 (1997): 509-533.

Teece, David J. and Mary Coleman. "The Meaning of Monopoly: Antitrust Analysis in High-Technology Industries." *Antitrust Bulletin* 43 (1998): 801-858.

Teece, David J. "Capturing Value from Knowledge Assets: The New Economy, Markets for Know-How, and Intangible Assets." *California Management Review* 40.3 (1998): 55-79.

Teece, David J. "Strategies for Managing Knowledge Assets: The Role of Firm Structure and Industrial Context." *Long Range Planning* 33.1 (2000): 35-54.

Tellis, Gerard J. and Peter N. Golder. "First to Market, First to Fail? Real Causes of Enduring Market Leadership." *MIT Sloan Management Review* 37.2 (1996): 65-75.

Temple Lang, John. "Defining Legitimate Competition: Companies' Duties to Supply Competitors and Access to Essential Facilities." *Fordham International Law Journal* 18.2 (1994): 437-524.

Temple Lang, John. "Commonly Accepted Errors and Misunderstandings in European Competition Law–Abuse of Dominance, and Patent Licensing." *19th St.Gallen International Competition Law Forum ICF* (2012).

Teruel Carrizosa, Mercedes. *Firm Growth, Persistence and Multiplicity of Equilibria: An Analysis of Spanish Manufacturing and Service Industries*. PhD Thesis, 2006.

Thierer, Adam D. "Unnatural Monopoly: Critical Moments in the Development of the Bell System Monopoly." *Cato Journal* 14.2 (1994): 267-285.

Thomas, Ashley Anne. *Balancing Power through the Market: Government Intervention in Cross-Border Mergers & Acquisitions*. Georgetown University, PhD Thesis, 2009.

Tirole, Jean. *The Theory of Industrial Organization*. MIT Press, 1988.

Tirole, Jean. "Market Failures and Public Policy," https://bfi.uchicago.edu/news/feature-story/regulation-and-market-power.

Tor, Avishalom. "Unilateral, Anticompetitive Acquisitions of Dominance or Monopoly Power." *Antitrust Law Journal* 76.3 (2010): 847-872.

Tóth, András. "CJEU Judgment in *Post Danmark II*: Role of Economic Evidence in Competition Cases." *European Networks Law & Regulation Quarterly* 3 (2015): 266-273.

Tullock, Gordon. "The Welfare Costs of Tariffs, Monopolies, and Theft." *Western Economic Journal* 5.3 (1967): 224-232.

US Department of State. "Oil Embargo Against the U.S. and Israel in 1973". *Office of the Historian*, https://history.state.gov/milestones/1969-1976/oil-embargo.

Ulbrich, Holley H. "Natural Monopoly in Principles Textbooks: A Pedagogical Note." *The Journal of Economic Education* 22.2 (1991): 179-182.

Van der Vijver, Tjarda. "Article 102 TFEU: How to Claim the Application of Objective Justifications in the Case of *prima facie* Dominance Abuses?" *Journal of European Competition Law & Practice* 4.2 (2013): 121-133.

Vanberg, Viktor J. *The Freiburg School: Walter Eucken and Ordoliberalism*. No. 04/11. Freiburg discussion papers on constitutional economics (2004).

Venit, James S. "EEC Patent Licensing Revisited: The Commission's Patent License Regulation." *The Antitrust Bulletin* 30.2 (1985): 457-526.

Venit, James S. "Cooperation, Initiative and Regulation—A Cross Cultural Inquiry" *in* Claus-Dieter Ehlermann and Mel Marquis (eds.) *European Competition Law Annual 2007: A Reformed Approach to Article 82 EC*. Bloomsbury Publishing, 2008.

Venit, James S. "Making Sense of *Post Danmark I* and *II*: Keeping the Hell Fires Well Stoked and Burning." *Journal of European Competition Law & Practice* 7.3 (2016): 165-179.

Vergne, Jean-Philippe and Rodolphe Durand. "The Path of Most Persistence: An Evolutionary Perspective on Path Dependence and Dynamic Capabilities." *Organization Studies* 32.3 (2011): 365-382.

Vermeulen, Freek and Harry Barkema. "Pace, Rhythm, and Scope: Process Dependence in Building a Profitable Multinational Corporation." *Strategic Management Journal* 23.7 (2002): 637-653.

Vermeulen, Freek. "Slow and Steady Wins the Growth Race." *Harvard Business Review* (February 2009).

Vickers, John. "How Does the Prohibition of Abuse of Dominance Fit with the Rest of Competition Policy?" *in* Claus-Dieter Ehlermann and Isabela Atanasiu (eds.)

European Competition Law Annual 2003: What Is an Abuse of a Dominant Position? Bloomsbury Publishing, 2006.

Viner, Jacob. "Power Versus Plenty as Objectives of Foreign Policy in the Seventeenth and Eighteenth Centuries." *World Politics* 1.1 (1948): 1-29.

Volmar, E. Keith. "Clinical History and Clinical Correlation" *in* E. Raouf Nakhleh (ed.) *Error Reduction and Prevention in Surgical Pathology*. New York: Springer, 2015: 85-101.

Von Mises, Ludwig. *Human Action. A Treatise on Economics*. Ludwig Von Mises Institute, [1949] 1998.

Von Mises, Ludwig. "Comments about the Mathematical Treatment of Economic Problems." *Journal of Libertarian Studies* 1.2 (1977): 97-100.

Vromen, Jack J. *"Economic Evolution." An Enquire into the Foundations of New Institutional Economics*. New York: Routledge, 1995.

Walker, Francis. "The Causes of Trusts and Some Remedies for Them." *American Economic Association Quarterly* 11.1 (1910): 290-320.

Wallace, Joel M. "'*Rambus v. FTC*' in the Context of Standard-Setting Organizations, Antitrust, and the Patent Hold-up Problem." *Berkeley Technology Law Journal* 24.1 (2009): 661-693.

Waller, Spencer Weber. "The Language of Law and the Language of Business." *Case Western Law Review* 52.1 (2001): 283-338.

Walras, Léon. *Elements of Pure Economics, or The Theory of Social Wealth*. Routledge, [1874] 2003.

Wang, Dingding Tina. "When Antitrust Met WTO: Why US Courts Should Consider US-China WTO Disputes in Deciding Antitrust Cases Involving Chinese Exports." *Columbia Law Review* (2012): 1096-1142.

Weber, Max. *Politics as a Vocation*. New York: Oxford University Press, [1921] 1946.

Wenar, Leif. *Blood Oil: Tyrants, Violence, and the Rules That Run the World*. Oxford University Press, 2015.

Wernerfelt, Birger. "A Resource-Based View of the Firm." *Strategic Management Journal* 5.2 (1984): 171-180.

Whalley, Jason and Peter Curwen. "Incumbency and Market Share within European Mobile Telecommunication Networks." *Telecommunications Policy* 36.3 (2012): 222-236.

Whish, Richard, and David Bailey. *Competition Law*. Oxford University Press, USA, 2015.

Williamson, Oliver E. "Dominant Firms and the Monopoly Problem: Market Failure Considerations." *Harvard Law Review* 85.8 (1972): 1512-1531.

Williamson, Oliver E. "Antitrust Enforcement and the Modern Corporation" *in* Victor R. Fuchs (ed.) *Economic Research: Retrospect and Prospect, Volume 3, Policy Issues and Research Opportunities in Industrial Organization*. NBER, 1972: 16-33.

Williamson, Oliver E. *Market and Hierarchies: Analysis and Antitrust Implications*. New York, Free Press: 1975.

Williamson, Oliver E. "Economies as an Antitrust Defense Revisited." *University of Pennsylvania Law Review* 125.4 (1977): 699-736.

Williamson, Oliver E. "Transaction-Cost Economics: The Governance of Contractual Relations." *The Journal of Law and Economics* 22.2 (1979): 233-261.

Williamson, Oliver E. *The Economic Institutions of Capitalism. Firms, Markets Relational Contracting*. New York: The Free Press, 1985.

Wils, Wouter P.J. "The Judgment of the EU General Court in Intel and the So-Called 'More Economic Approach' to Abuse of Dominance." *World Competition: Law and Economics Review* 37.4 (2014): 405-434.

Winerman, Marc and William E. Kovacic. "Learned Hand, Alcoa, and the Reluctant Application of the Sherman Act." *Antitrust Law Journal* 79.1 (2013): 295-348.

Woodcock, Ramsi A. "Inconsistency in Antitrust." *University of Miami Law Review* 68.1 (2013): 105-188.

Worcester, Dean A. Jr. "Why 'Dominant Firms' Decline." *Journal of Political Economy*, 65.4 (1957): 338-346.

Wright, Joshua D. "Antitrust Law and Competition for Distribution." *Yale Journal on Regulation* 23.2 (2006): 169-208.

Wright, Joshua D. and Douglas H. Ginsburg. "Whither Symmetry? Antitrust Analysis of Intellectual Property Rights at the FTC and DOJ." *George Mason University Law and Economics Research Paper Series* 13-71 (2013): 1-23.

Wübbeke, Jost, et al. "Made in China 2025: The Making of a High-Tech Superpower and Consequences for Industrial Countries." *Mercator Institute for China Studies* 2 (2016).

Yao, Dennis A. *Prepared Remarks Before the Illinois State Bar Association and Chicago Bar Association*. December 2, 1992.

Yergin, Daniel. *The Prize: The Epic Quest for Oil, Money & Power*. Simon and Schuster, 2011.

Zingales, Luigi. "Towards a Political Theory of the Firm." *Journal of Economic Perspectives* 31.3 (2017): 113-130.

Zu Knyphausen-Aufseß, Dodo, Christian Krys and Lars Schweizer. "Attacker's Advantages in a Homogeneous Market: The Case of GSM." *International Journal on Media Management* 4.4 (2002): 212-224.

Zwolinski, Matt. "The Ethics of Price Gouging." *Business Ethics Quarterly* 18.3 (2008): 347-378.

Other References

Baker and Mckenzie. Response to DG Competition's Article 82 Consultation, ec.europa.eu/competition/antitrust/art82/076.pdf.

Bayot, Jennifer. "Intel Accused of Antitrust Violations." *The New York Times* (June 29, 2005).

Consultation on the Green Paper on the Liberalisation of Telecommunication Infrastructure and Cable Television Networks. COM(95) 158 final, 3 May 1995.

ICN, Unilateral Conduct Working Group. "Report on the Objectives of Unilateral Conduct Laws, Assessment of Dominance/Substantial Market Power, and State-Created Monopolies." *6th Annual Conference of the International Competition Network (ICN) – Moscow* (2007): 1-99.

IRG, *EU Review of Communications Regulation – Independent Regulators Group (IRG) Common Position on Commission Working Documents* (April 27, 2000).

Malik, Om. "Intel's Revenge." *Forbes* (January 14, 1999).

OECD, *Application of Competition Policy to the Electricity Sector*, OECD/GD(97)132.

OECD, *Competition Issues in Liner Shipping*, DAF/COMP/WP2(2015)3.

OECD, *Competition Policy, Industrial Policy and National Champions*, DAF/COMP/GF(2009)9.

OECD, *Competitive Neutrality: Maintaining a Level Playing Field Between Public and Private Business*, 2012.

OECD, *Excessive Prices*. DAF/COMP(2011)18.

OECD, Executive Summary of the Roundtable on Fidelity Rebates held at the 125th meeting of the Competition Committee of the OECD, DAF/COMP/M(2016)1/ANN4/FINAL/en/pdf.

OECD, *Roundtable on Competition Policy, Industrial Policy and National Champions*, DAF/COMP/GF(2009)9.

OECD, *State Owned Enterprises and the Principle of Competitive Neutrality*, DAF/COMP(2009)37 289.

Politico, "Spanish league wants EU to referee Neymar transfer saga" (August 3, 2017), https://www.politico.eu/article/neymar-antitrust-complaint-la-liga-psg-transfer/.

Post Danmark. "Comments to DG Competition discussion paper on the application of Article 82 of the Treaty to exclusionary abuses," http://ec.europa.eu/competition/antitrust/art82/032.pdf.

The Economist, "The Rise of State Capitalism." (January 21, 2012).

Treaster, Joseph B. "Hurricane Charley: The Economics; With Storm Gone, Floridians Are Hit With Price Gouging." *New York Times* (August 18, 2004).

UNCTAD, United Nations Conference on Trade and Development, *World Investment Report 2017*, UNCTAD/WIR/2017, http://unctad.org/en/PublicationsLibrary/wir2017_en.pdf.

White House, A White Paper on The Economic Consequences of Gasoline "Price Gouging" Legislation (June 20, 2007), https://georgewbush-whitehouse.archives.gov/cea/text/Price_Gouging_WP_062007.html.

Yoshida, Junko. "Lurking Behind Every M&A Is China." *EE Times* (December 13, 2016).

Table of Cases, Opinions and Decisions

Case Law of the EU Courts

CJEU, Joined Cases C-56/60 and C-58/60, *Consten and Grundig v. Commission*, ECLI:EU:C:1966:41, **162**

CJEU, Case C-78/70, *Deutsche Grammophon and METRO*, ECLI:EU:C:1971:59, **162**

CJEU, Case C-6/72, *Europemballage Corporation and Continental Can Company v. Commission*, ECLI:EU:C:1973:22, **17, 248, 249, 276, 279**

CJEU, Joined Cases 6 and 7/73, *Istituto Chemioterapico Italiano SpA and Commercial Solvents v. Commission*, ECLI:EU:C:1974:18, **48, 157**

CJEU, Joined Cases, 40/73, 48/73, 50/73, 54/73-56/73, 111/73, 113/73 and 114/73, *Suiker Unie and Others v. Commission*, EU:C:1975:174, **2, 149**

CJEU, Case C-127/73, *BRT v. SABAM*, ECLI:EU:C:1974:25, **144**

CJEU, Case C-155/73, *Giuseppe Sacchi*, ECLI:EU:C:1974:40, **44, 142**

CJEU, Case C-27/76, *United Brands v. Commission*, ECLI:EU:C:1978:22, **7, 155, 156, 158, 241**

CJEU, Case C-85/76, *Hoffmann-La Roche v. Commission*, ECLI:EU:C:1979:36, **7, 11, 12, 180, 181, 189, 279**

CJEU, Case C-13/77, *SA GB-INNO-BM* v. *ATAB*, ECLI:EU:C:1977:185, **37, 46**

CJEU, Case C-77/77, *British Petroleum v. Commission*, ECLI:EU:C:1978:141, **237**

CJEU, Joined Cases C-100, 101, 102, 103/80, *Musique Diffusion Française v. Commission*, ECLI:EU:C:1983:158, **113**

CJEU, Joined Cases C-188 to 190/80, *France, Italy and United Kingdom v. Commission*, ECLI:EU:C:1982:134, **60**

CJEU, Case C-322/81, *Michelin v. Commission*, ECLI:EU:C:1983:313, **7, 110, 155, 180, 249, 278, 283**

CJEU, Case C-193/83, *Windsurfing v. Commission*, ECLI:EU:C:1986:75, **238**

CJEU, Case C-311/84, *SA Centre belge d'études de marché - Télémarketing (CBEM) v. SA Compagnie luxembourgeoise de télédiffusion (CLT) and SA Information publicité Benelux (IPB)*, ECLI:EU:C:1985:394, **44, 45, 48, 164**

CJEU, Case C-62/86, *AKZO v. Commission* ECLI:EU:C:1991:286, **62, 101, 108, 155, 196, 218**

CJEU, Case C-53/87, *CICRA and Others v. Renault*, ECLI:EU:C:1988:472, **164**

CJEU, Case C-238/87, *Volvo v. Veng*, ECLI:EU:C:1988:477, **164**

CJEU, Case C-18/88, *RTT/GB-Inno-BM*, ECLI:EU:C:1991:474, **46**

CJEU, Case C-202/88, *France v. Commission* ECLI:EU:C:1991:120, **65, 93**

CJEU, Case C-41/90, *Höfner and Elser v. Macrotron*, ECLI:EU:C:1991:161, **44**

CJEU, Joined cases C-48/90 and 66/90, *Netherlands and PTT Nederland v. Commission*, ECLI:EU:C:1992:63, **49**

CJEU, Case C-179/90, *Merci convenzionali porto di Genova SpA v. Siderurgica Gabrielli SpA*, ECLI:EU:C:1991:464, **45**

CJEU, Case C-323/90, *Commission v. Portugal*, ECLI:EU:C:1992:119, **146**

CJEU, Joined Cases C-241/91 P and C-242/91 P, *Radio Telefis Eireann (RTE) and Independent Television Publications Ltd (ITP) v. Commission*, ECLI:EU:C:1995:98, **107, 145, 164, 165**

CJEU, Case C-320/91, *Régie des Postes v. Corbeau*, ECLI:EU:C:1993:198, **44, 46**

CJEU, Case C-36/92 P, *Samenwerkende Elektriciteits-Produktiebedrijven (SEP) NV v. Commission*, ECLI:EU:C:1994:205, **146**

CJEU, Case C-387/92, *Banco Exterior de España v. Ayuntamiento de Valencia*, ECLI:EU:C:1994:100, **47**

CJEU, Case C-39/94, *SFEI and others*, ECLI:EU:C:1996:285, **47**

CJEU, Joined Cases C-68/94 and C-30/95, *France and Société Commerciale des Potasses et de l'Azote (SCPA) and Entreprise Minière et Chimique (EMC), v. Commission*, ECLI:EU:C:1998:148, **12**

CJEU, Case C-241/94, *France v. Commission*, ECLI:EU:C:1996:353, **47**

CJEU, Case C-333/94 P, *Tetra Pak International v. Commission*, ECLI:EU:C:1996:436, **102**

CJEU, Case C-242/95, *GT-Link A/S and De Danske Statsbaner (DSB)*, ECLI:EU:C:1997:376, **47**

CJEU, Joined Cases C-359/95P and C-379/95P *Commission and France v. Ladbroke Racing*, ECLI:EU:C:1997:531, **45**

CJEU, Case C-266/96, *Corsica Ferries France v. Gruppo Antichi Ormeggiatori del Porto di Genova and Others*, ECLI:EU:C:1998:306, **44**

CJEU, Joined Cases C-395/96 P and C-396/96 P, *Compagnie Maritime Belge Transports SA, Compagnie Maritime Belge SA and Dafra-Lines A/S v. Commission*, ECLI:EU:C:2000:132, **11, 50, 249**

CJEU, Case C-7/97, *Oscar Bronner GmbH & Co. KG* v. *Mediaprint Zeitungs- und Zeitschriftenverlag GmbH & Co. KG and Others*, ECLI:EU:C:1998:569, **104, 114, 164, 165, 167, 169, 170, 178**

CJEU, Case C-367/98, *Commission v. Portuguese Republic*, ECLI:EU:C:2002:326, **61**

CJEU, Case C-163/99, *Portugal v. Commission*, ECLI:EU:C:2001:189, **61, 143, 155**

CJEU, Joined Cases C-280/99 P, C-281/99 P and C-282/99 P, *Moccia Irme SpA, Ferriera Lamifer SpA and Ferriera Acciaieria Casilina SpA v. Commission*, ECLI:EU:C:2001:348, **8**

CJEU, Case C-462/99, *Connect Austria*, ECLI:EU:C:2003:297, **65, 95**

CJEU, Case C-481/01 P(R), *NDC Health v. Commission*, ECLI:EU:C:2002:223, **97**

CJEU, Case C-198/01, *Consorzio Industrie Fiammiferi (CIF) and Autorità Garante della Concorrenza e del Mercato*, ECLI:EU:C:2003:430, **77**

CJEU, Case C-418/01, *IMS Health GmbH & Co. OHG v. NDC Health GmbH & Co. KG*, ECLI:EU:C:2004:257, **17, 107, 164, 166**

CJEU, Case C-12/03, *Tetra Laval v. Commission*, ECLI:EU:C:2005:87, **12**

CJEU, Case C-327/03, *ISIS Multimedia and Firma 02*, ECLI:EU:C:2005:622, **65, 66, 95**

CJEU, Case C-544/03, *Mobistar and Belgacom Mobile*, ECLI:EU:C:2005:518, **85**

CJEU, Case C-552/03 P, *Unilever Bestfoods (formerly Van den Bergh Foods Ltd.) v. Commission*, ECLI:EU:C:2006:607, **218**

CJEU, Case 95/04 P, *British Airways v. Commission* ECLI:EU:C:2007:166, **180**

CJEU, Case C-238/05, *Asnef-Equifax, Servicios de Información sobre Solvencia y Crédito, SL, Administración del Estado v. Asociación de Usuarios de Servicios Bancarios (Ausbanc)*, ECLI:EU:C:2006:734, **278**

CJEU, Case 511/06 P, *Archer Daniels Midland Co. v. Commission*, ECLI:EU:C:2009:433, **114**

CJEU, Joined Cases, C-501/06 P, C-513/06 P and C-519/06 P, *GlaxoSmithKline Services Unlimited v. Commission*, ECLI:EU:C:2009:610, **8, 11**

CJEU, Case C-202/07 P, *France Télécom v. Commission*, EU:C:2009:214, **7**

CJEU, Case T-336/07, *Telefónica SA v. Commission*, EU:T:2012:172, **94, 145, 194**

CJEU, Case C-8/08, *T-Mobile Netherlands*, EU:C:2009:343, **8**

CJEU, Case C-280/08 P, Deutsche *Telekom AG v. Commission*, ECLI:EU:C:2010:603, **8, 11, 85, 94, 97, 145**

CJEU, Case C-52/09, *Konkurrensverket v. TeliaSonera Sverige AB*, ECLI:EU:C:2011:83, **7, 8, 11, 18, 88, 98, 106, 107, 113, 250**

CJEU, Case T-286/09, *Intel*, ECLI:EU:T:2014:547, **2, 7, 64, 180, 184, 218, 241**

CJEU, Case C-209/10, *Post Danmark A/S v. Konkurrencerådet* (*Post Danmark I*), ECLI:EU:C:2012:172, **5, 11, 12, 16, 18, 36, 61, 62, 86, 112, 190, 195, 250, 283**

CJEU, Case C-457/10 P, *AstraZeneca v. Commission*, ECLI:EU:C:2012:770, **8, 10, 257**

CJEU, Case C-549/10 P, *Tomra Systems and Others v. Commission*, EU:C:2012:221, **64, 72, 180, 182, 183**

CJEU, Case C-597/11 P, *Evropaïki Dynamiki v. Commission*, ECLI:EU:C:2012:616, **189**

CJEU, Case C-6/12, *P Oy*, ECLI:EU:C:2013:525, **47**

CJEU, Case T-79/12, *Cisco Systems and Messagenet v. Commission*, ECLI: EU:T:2013:635, **247**

CJEU, Case C-553/12 P, *Commission v. DEI*, ECLI:EU:C:2014:2083, **66, 95**

CJEU, Case C-67/13 P, *Groupement des cartes bancaires (CB) v. Commission*, ECLI: EU:C:2014:2204, **278**

CJEU, Case 170/13, *Huawei Technologies Co. Ltd v. ZTE Corp. and ZTE Deutschland GmbH*, ECLI:EU:C:2015:477, **7, 238**

CJEU, Case C-286/13 P, *Dole Food Company, Inc and Dole Fresh Fruit Europe v. Commission*, ECLI:EU:C:2015:184, **8**

CJEU, Case C-23/14, *Post Danmark v. Konkurrencerådet* (*Post Danmark II*), ECLI: EU:C:2015:651, **7, 63, 64, 72, 73, 147, 190**

CJEU, Case C-413/14 P, *Intel v. Commission*, ECLI:EU:C:2017:632, **18, 149, 181, 184, 241**
CJEU, Case C-123/16 P, *Orange Polska v. Commission*, ECLI:EU:C:2018:590, **113**
GC, Case T-65/89, *BPB Industries and British Gypsum*, ECLI:EU:T:1993:31, **180**
GC, Case T-69/89, *Radio Telefis Eireann v. Commission (Magill)*, ECLI:EU:T:1991:39, **164**
GC, Case T-39/90, *NV Samenwerkende Elektriciteits-Produktiebedrijven v. Commission*, ECLI:EU:T:1991:71, **146**
GC, Joined Case T-24/93 and T-25/93, T-26/93 and 28/93, *Compagnie Maritime Belge and Others v. Commission*, ECLI:EU:T:1996:139, **72, 79**
GC, Case T-229/94, *Deutsche Bahn*, ECLI:EU:T:1997:155, **190**
GC, Case T-111/96, *ITT Promedia v. Commission*, ECLI:EU:T:1998:183, **7, 195**
GC, Case T-228/97, *Irish Sugar plc v. Commission*, ECLI:EU:T:1999:246, **1, 2, 8, 10, 51**
GC, Joined Cases T-191/98 and T-212/98 to T-214/98, *Atlantic Container Line and Others v. Commission*, ECLI:EU:T:2003:245, **274**
GC, Case T-175/99, *UPS Europe SA v. Commission*, ECLI:EU:T:2002:78, **52**
GC, Case T-219/99, *British Airways v. Commission*, ECLI:EU:T:2003:343, **180, 247**
GC, Case T-342/99, *Airtours v. Commission*, ECLI:EU:T:2002:146, **12**
GC, Case T-168/01, *GlaxoSmithKline Services Unlimited v. Commission*, ECLI:EU:T:2006:265, **2**
GC, Case T-203/01, *Michelin v. Commission*, ECLI:EU:T:2003:250, **180**
GC, Case T-210/01, *General Electric v. Commission*, ECLI:EU:T:2005:456, **249**
GC, Case T-5/02, *Tetra Laval v. Commission*, ECLI:EU:T:2002:264, **12**
GC, Case T-271/03, *Deutsche Telekom v. Commission*, ECLI:EU:T:2008:101, **94, 96**
GC, Case T-328/03, *O2 (Germany) GmbH & Co OHG v. Commission*, ECLI:EU:T:2006:116, **99, 177**
GC, Case T-340/03, *France Télécom v.* Commission, ECLI:EU:T:2007:22, **7, 88, 111, 195**
GC, Case T-345/03, *Evropaïki Dynamiki v. Commission*, ECLI:EU:T:2008:67, **189**
GC, Case T-201/04, *Microsoft v. Commission*, ECLI:EU:T:2007:289, **2, 8, 107, 158, 164, 166, 167, 177, 179, 181, 186**
GC, Case T-87/05, *EDP v. Commission*, ECLI:EU:T:2005:333, **248**
GC, Case T-321/05, *AstraZeneca v. Commission*, ECLI:EU:T:2010:266, **238, 249, 257, 273, 279**
GC, Case T-155/06, *Tomra Systems ASA and Others v. Commission*, ECLI:EU:T:2010:370, **180, 182, 183, 218**
GC, Case T-232/06, *Evropaïki Dynamiki v. Commission*, ECLI:EU:T:2011:443, **95, 188**
GC, Case T-336/07, *Telefónica v. Commission*, ECLI:EU:T:2012:172, **94, 145**
GC, Case T-167/08, *Microsoft v. Commission*, ECLI:EU:T:2012:323, **114**
GC, Case T-286/09, *Intel* v. *Commission*, ECLI:EU:T:2014:547, **2, 7, 64, 180, 184, 218, 241**
GC, Case T-370/09, *GDF Suez SA v. Commission*, EU:T:2012:333, **85**
GC, Case T-432/10, *Vivendi*, ECLI:EU:T:2013:538, **115**
GC, Case T-201/11, *Si.Mobil*, ECLI:EU:T:2014:1096, **115**
GC, Case T-486/11, *Orange Polska v. Commission*, ECLI:EU:T:2015:1002, **106, 112, 113**
GC, Case T-472/13, *Lundbeck*, ECLI:EU:T:2016:449, **238**

GC, Case T-691/14, *Servier and others v. Commission*, ECLI:EU:T:2018:922, **239**
GC, Case T-851/14, *Slovak Telekom v. Commission*, ECLI:EU:T:2018:929, **5, 114, 115**

Opinions of the Advocate General

Opinion of AG Reischl in Case C-155/73, *Giuseppe Sacchi*, ECLI:EU:C:1974:22, **142**
Opinion of AG Reischl in Joined Cases C-188 to 190/80, *France, Italy and United Kingdom v. Commission*, ECLI:EU:C:1982:134, **60**
Opinion of AG Lenz in Case C-62/86, *AKZO v. Commission*, ECLI:EU:C:1989:154, **108**
Opinion of AG Tesauro in Case C-202/88, *France v. Commission*, ECLI:EU:C:1990:64, **55**
Opinion of AG Van Gerven in Joined Cases C-48 and 66/90, *Netherlands and PTT Nederland v. Commission*, ECLI:EU:C:1991:390, **49**
Opinion of AG Tesauro in Case C-364/92, *SAT Fluggesellschaft v. Eurocontrol*, ECLI: EU:C:1993:878, **142**
Opinion of AG Fennelly in Joined Cases C-395/96 P and C-396/96 P, *Compagnie Maritime Belge Transports SA, Compagnie Maritime Belge SA and Dafra-Lines A/S v. Commission*, ECLI:EU:C:1998:518, **11, 49, 50**
Opinion of AG Jacobs in Case C-7/97, *Oscar Bronner GmbH & Co. KG v. Mediaprint Zeitungs- und Zeitschriftenverlag GmbH & Co. KG and Others*, ECLI: EU:C:1998:264, **5, 105**
Opinion of AG Stix-Hackl in Joined Cases C-34/01 to C-38/01, *Enirisorse SpA v. Ministero delle Finanze*, ECLI:EU:C:2002:643, **80**
Opinion of AG Jacobs in Case C-198/01, *C.I.F. Consorzio Industrie Fiammiferi v. Autorità Garante della Concorrenza e del Mercato*, ECLI:EU:C:2003:58, **10**
Opinion of AG Poiares Maduro in Case C-109/03, *KPN Telecom BV v. Onafhankelijke Post en Telecommunicatie Autoriteit (OPTA)*, ECLI:EU:C:2004:437, **5, 105**
Opinion of AG Mazák in Case C-202/07 P, *France Télécom v. Commission*, ECLI: EU:C:2008:520, **103**
Opinion of AG Ruiz Jarabo Colomer in Case C-192/08, *TeliaSonera Finland Oyj*, ECLI:EU:C:2009:309, **10, 98, 116**
Opinion of AG Mazák in Case C-52/09, *TeliaSonera*, ECLI:EU:C:2010:483, **96, 106**
Opinion of AG Mengozzi in Case C-209/10, *Post Danmark A/S v. Konkurrencerådet*, ECLI:EU:C:2011:342, **70**
Opinion of AG Jääskinen in Case C-545/10, *Commission v. Czech Republic*, ECLI: EU:C:2012:791, **143**
Opinion of AG Jääskinen in Joined Cases C-105/12 to C-107/12, *De Staat der Nederlanden v. Essent NV and Essent Nederland BV* (C-105/12), *Eneco Holding NV* (C-106/12), *Delta NV* (C-107/12), ECLI:EU:C:2013:242, **143**
Opinion of AG Wathelet in Case C-553/12 P, *Commission v. DEI*, ECLI:EU:C:2013:807, **66**
Opinion of AG Wathelet in Case C-170/13, *Huawei Techs. Co. v. ZTE Corp.*, ECLI: EU:C:2015:477, **7, 238**
Opinion of AG Kokott in Case C-23/14, *Post Danmark II*, ECLI:EU:C:2015:343, **5, 63, 73, 86, 190**

Opinion of AG Wahl Opinion in Case C-177/16, *Biedrība 'Autortiesību un komunicēšanās konsultāciju aģentūra – Latvijas Autoru apvienība' v. Konkurences padome*, ECLI:EU:C:2017:286, **270, 279**

Decisions of the EU Commission

Commission Decision, Case COMP/IV/400, *Agreements between manufacturers of glass containers*, **144**
Commission Decision, Case COMP/IV/791, *Société Commerciale des Potasses et de l'Azote (SCPA) – Kali und Salz (formerly VDK)*, **144**
Commission Decision, Case COMP/IV/28.841, *ABG Oil Companies operating in the Netherlands*, **227, 236**
Commission Decision, Case COMP/IV/29.020, *Vitamins (Hoffmann-La Roche)*, **181**
Commission Decision, Case COMP/IV/29.395, *Windsurfing International*, **238**
Commission Decision, Case COMP/IV/29.491, *Bandengroothandel Frieschebrug BV/NV Nederlandsche Banden-Industrie Michelin*, **219**
Commission Decision, Case COMP/IV/29.839, *GVL*, **144**
Commission Decision, Case COMP/IV/30.178, *Napier Brown – British Sugar*, **51**
Commission Decision, Case COMP/IV/31.851, *Magill TV Guide/ITP, BBC and RTE*, **165**
Commission Decision, Case COMP/IV/32.009, *Elopak/Metal Box-Odin*, **176**
Commission Decision, Case COMP/IV/32031, *Auditel*, **146**
Commission Decision, Case COMP/IV/34.174, *Stena Sealink/B&I - Holyhead: Interim Measures*, **72**
Commission Decision, Case COMP/IV/34.621, 35.059/F-3, *Irish Sugar*, **51**
Commission Decision, Case COMP/IV/34.689, *Sea Containers/Stena Sealink*, **72**
Commission Decision, Case COMP/IV/34.801, *FAG Ð Flughafen Frankfurt/Main AG*, **175**
Commission Decision, Case COMP/35.141, *Deutsche Post I*, **51, 52, 70**
Commission Decision, Case COMP/IV/35.268, *ITT Promedia / Belgacom*, **273**
Commission Decision, Case COMP/IV/36.010, *Amministrazione Autonoma dei Monopoli di Stato*, **145**
Commission Decision, Case COMP/37.451, 37.578, 37.579, *Deutsche Telekom*, **87**
Commission Decision, Case COMP/37.507, *AstraZeneca*, **155, 187, 191**
Commission Decision, Case COMP/37.685, *GVG/FS Italian Railway*, **35, 71–73, 145**
Commission Decision, Case COMP/37.792, *Microsoft*, **158, 174**
Commission Decision, Case COMP/37.966, *Distrigaz*, **88**
Commission Decision, Case COMP/37.990, *Intel*, **158, 159, 183, 186, 189, 220**
Commission Decision, Case COMP/38.044, *NDC Health/IMS Health: Interim measures*, **157, 165**
Commission Decision, Case COMP/38.113, *Prokent/Tomra*, **182, 183, 186, 190**
Commission Decision, Case COMP/38.233, *Wanadoo Interactive*, **93, 98, 100, 102**
Commission Decision, Case COMP/38.369, *T-Mobile Deutschland/O2 Germany: Network Sharing Rahmenvertrag*, **177**
Commission Decision, Case COMP/38.636, *Rambus*, **3, 28, 263, 265, 267, 268**

Commission Decision, Case COMP/38.784, *Wanadoo España v. Telefónica*, **88, 98, 105, 110, 111, 145**
Commission Decision, Case COMP/39.226, *Lundbeck*, **238**
Commission Decision, Case COMP/39.315, *ENI*, **88**
Commission Decision, Case COMP/39.316, *Gaz de France*, **89**
Commission Decision, Case COMP/39.388, *German Electricity Wholesale Market*, **88**
Commission Decision, Case COMP/39.389, *German Electricity Balancing Market*, **88**
Commission Decision, Case COMP/39.401, *E.ON/GDF*, **111, 112**
Commission Decision, Case COMP/39.402, *RWE Gas Foreclosure*, **88**
Commission Decision, Case COMP/39.523, *Slovak Telekom*, **114, 115, 185**
Commission Decision, Case COMP/39.525, *Telekomunikacja Polska*, **88, 98–100, 107, 111, 117**
Commission Decision, Case COMP/39.740, *Google Search (Shopping)*, **64, 97, 118, 161, 167, 174, 175, 179, 185, 193, 215, 216**
Commission Decision, Case COMP/39.984, *Romanian Power Exchange/OPCOM*, **74**
Commission Decision, Case COMP/IV/M.877, *Boeing/McDonnell Douglas*, **42**
Commission Decision, Case COMP/M 3.440, *EDP/ENI/GDP*, **112**
Commission Decision, Case COMP/M.6570, *UPS/ TNT Express*, **6**
Commission Decision, Case COMP/SA N 161/04, *Portugal Custos ociosos em Portugal*, **92**
Commission Decision, Case COMP/SA 18.989, *Stranded costs compensations in Poland*, **92**
Commission Decision, Case COMP/SA N 691/2009, *Hungarian stranded cost compensation scheme*, **92**
Case COMP/39.816, *Upstream gas supplies in Central and Eastern Europe (Gazprom)*, **76**
Case COMP/40.394, *Aspen* (not yet decided), **241**

US Case Law

Munn v. Illinois, 94 U.S. 113 (1876).
Wabash, St. Louis & Pacific Railway Company v. Illinois, 118 U.S. 557 (1886), 135
Addyston Pipe and Steel Co. v. United States, 175 U.S. 211 (1899), **83**
United States v. American Tobacco Co., 221 U.S. 106 (1911), **251**
Standard Oil Co. v. United States, 221 U.S. 1 (1911), **38, 251, 257**
Standard Fashion Co. v. Magrane Houston Co., 258, U.S. 346 (1922), **246**
Schine Chain Theatres, Inc. v. United States, 334 U.S. 110 (1948), **245, 257, 281**
Lorain Journal v. United States, 342 U.S. 143, 154 (U.S. 1951), **251**
United States v. Singer Mfg. Co, 374 U.S. 174, 200 (U.S. 1963), **256**
Walker Process Equipment, Inc. v. Food Machinery & Chemical Corp., 382 U.S. 172 (1965), **254, 255**
United States v. Grinnell Corp., 384 U.S. 563 (1966), **227, 245, 250, 280**
United States v. United Shoe Mach. Corp., 391 U.S. 244 (1968), **280**
NCAA v. Board of Regents of Univ. of Okla, 468 U.S. 85, 109 (1984), **265**
Aspen Skiing Co. v. Aspen Highlands Skiing Corp., 472 U.S. 585 (1985), **240**

Eastman Kodak Co. v. Image Technical Services, Inc, 504 U.S. 451 (1992), **228**
Spectrum Sports, Inc. v. McQuillan, 506 U.S. 447 (1993), **6, 245**
Brooke Group Ltd. v. Brown & Williamson Tobacco Corp., 509 U.S. 209 (1993).
NYNEX Corp. v. Discon, Inc, 525 U.S. 128, 130 (1998), **264, 265**
Verizon Communications Inc. v. Law Offices of Curtis V. Trinko, LLP, 540 U.S. 398 (2004), **7, 29, 176, 241, 250, 252, 265, 270**
FTC v. Actavis, Inc., 133 S. Ct. 2223, 2227, 186 L. Ed. 2d 343 (2013), **255**
United States v. Aluminum Co. of America ("Alcoa"), 148 F.2d 416 (2d Cir. 1945), **1, 5, 173, 250, 252, 282**
American Cyanamid Company v. FTC, 363 F.2d 757 (6th Cir. 1966), **256**
Berkey Photo, Inc. v. Eastman Kodak Co., 603 F.2d 263 (2d Cir. 1979), **256, 265**
Omega Satellite Prods. Co. v. City of Indianapolis, 694 F.2d 119 (7th Cir. 1982), **151**
Barry Wright Corp. v. ITT Grinnell Corp., 724 F.2d 227 (1st Cir. 1983), **184**
Brunswick Corp. v. Riegel Textile Corp., 752 F.2d 261 (7th Cir. 1984), **256**
Exxon Corp. v. Berwick Bay Real Estates Partners, 748 F.2d 937 (5th Cir. 1984), **247**
In re Maxwell Commc'n Corp., 93 F.3d 1036 (2d Cir. 1996), **81**
Intergraph Corp. v. Intel Corp., 195 F.3d 1346 (Fed. Cir.1999), **257**
CSU, L.L.C. v. Xerox Corp. (In re Independent Serv. Orgs. Antitrust Litig.), 203 F.3d 1322 (Fed. Cir. 2000), **255**
United States v. Microsoft Corp., 253 F.3d 34 (D.C. Cir. 2001), **263, 279, 280**
Broadcom v. Qualcomm, 501 F.3d 297 (3d Cir. 2007), **267, 271, 273**
Rambus, Inc. v. F.T.C., 522 F.3d 456 (D.C. Cir. 2008), **262, 263, 269**
In re: Vitamin C Antitrust Litigation, 837 F.3d 175 (2d Cir. 2016), **80**
United States v. American Can Co, 230 F. 859 (D. Md. 1916), **246, 251**
Rambus, Inc. v. Infineon Techs. AG, 330 F.Supp.2d 679 (E.D. Va. 2004), **251, 269**

FTC

FTC, *In re. Dell Computer Corporation*, Docket No. C-3658, **260, 261, 269**
FTC, *In the Matter of Rambus*, Inc. Docket No. 9302, **262, 273**
FTC, *Biovail Corp.*, Docket No. C-4060, **258**
FTC, *Bristol-Myers Squibb Co.*, Docket No. C-4076, **258**

Other Decisions

OFCOM decision, Case CW/00760/03/04, *Investigation against BT about potential anti-competitive exclusionary behaviour*, **241**

Table of Legislation

EU Legislation

Treaty establishing the European Community (Nice consolidated version) *OJ* C 325, 24/12/2002, p. 0041-0041, **61**
Consolidated Version of the Treaty on the Functioning of the European Union - Article 102, May 9, 2008, *OJ* C 115, 2008, **245**
Directive 88/301/EEC of the European Commission of 16 May 1988 on "Competition in the Markets in Telecommunications Terminal Equipment," *OJ* L 131, 1988, p. 73, **65**
Directive 96/9/EC of the European Parliament and of the Council of 11 March 1996 on the legal protection of databases, *OJ* L 77, 1996, p. 20, **163**
Directive 96/19/EC of the European Commission of 13 March 1996 amending Directive 90/388/EEC with regard to the implementation of full competition in telecommunications markets, *OJ* L 074, 22/03/1996, p. 0013-0024, **110**
Directive 97/13/EC of the European Parliament and of the Council of 10 April 1997 on "A Common Framework for General Authorisations and Individual Licenses in the Field of Telecommunications Services," *OJ* L 117, 1997, p. 15, **66**
Directive 97/33/EC of the European Parliament and of the Council of 30 June 1997 on interconnection in Telecommunications with regard to ensuring universal service and interoperability through application of the principles of Open Network Provision (ONP) *OJ* L 199, 26/07/1997, p. 0032-0052, **110**
Regulation (EC) No. 2887/2000 of the European Parliament and of the Council of 18 December 2000 on unbundled access to the local loop, *OJ* L 336, 30.12.2000, p. 4-8, **93**
Directive 2001/14/EC of the European Parliament and of the Council of 26 February 2001 on the allocation of railway infrastructure capacity and the levying of charges for the use of railway infrastructure and safety certification, *OJ* L 75, 15.3.2001, p. 29-46, **142**

Council Regulation (EC) No. 139/2004 of 20 January 2004 on the control of concentrations between undertakings (the EC Merger Regulation), *OJ* L 24, 29.01.2004, p. 1-22, **276**

Directive 2006/112/EC of the European Council of 28 November 2006 on the common system of value added tax, *OJ* L 347, 11.12.2006, p. 1-118, **74**

Directive 2012/34/EU of the European Parliament and of the Council of 21 November 2012 establishing a single European railway area, *OJ* L 343, **143**

Directive 2014/24/EU of the European Parliament and of the Council of 26 February 2014 on public procurement and repealing Directive 2004/18/EC, *OJ* L 94, 28.3.2014, pp. 65-242, **37**

EU Commission's "Soft" Law

Guidelines on the application of EEC competition rules in the telecommunications sector (1991/C 233/02), *OJ* C 233, 6.9.1991, p. 2-26, **79**

Communication from the Commission - Methodology for Analysing State Aid Linked to Stranded Costs, *OJ* L 27, 30.1.1997, p. 20, **92**

Notice from the Commission on the application of the competition rules to the postal sector and on the assessment of certain State measures relating to postal services, *OJ* C 39, 06.02.1998, p. 2-18, **54**

Communication from the Commission - The results of the public consultation on the 1999 communications review and orientations for the new regulatory framework, COM des(2000) 239, 26 April 2000, **3** Communication from the Commission - Guidelines on the application of Article 81(3) of the Treaty, *OJ* C 101, 27.4.2004, p. 97-118, **8, 176**

Guidelines on the method of setting fines imposed pursuant to Article 23(2)(a) of Regulation No. 1/2003 *OJ* C 210, 1.9.2006, p. 2-5, **113**

Communication from the Commission - Guidance on the Commission's Enforcement Priorities in Applying Article 82 of the EC Treaty to abusive exclusionary conduct by dominant undertakings, *OJ* C/45/7, 24.2.2009, p. 7-20, **1**

Communication from the Commission to the European Parliament, the Council, the European Economic and Social Committee and the Committee of the Regions, Making the Internal Energy Market Work, COM/2012/0663 final, 15.11.2012, **84, 93**

Communication from the Commission - Guidelines on the application of Article 101 of the Treaty on the Functioning of the European Union to Technology Transfer Agreements, *OJ* C 89, 28.3.2014, p. 3-50, **176, 238**

US Legislation

The Sherman Antitrust Act of 1890 (Sherman Act, 26 Stat 209, 15 U.S.C. §§1-7), **1, 245**

Federal Trade Commission Act of 1914, Ch. 311, 38 Stat. 717 (1914), codified as amended at 15 U.S.C. §§41-58, **252**

Arkansas Code of 2010, §4-88, Consumer Protection, **231**

Idaho Code of 2011, §48, Monopolies and Trade Practices, **243**

North Carolina General Statute of 2011, §75, Monopolies, Trusts and Consumer Protection, **243**
H.R. 2070 – Federal Price Gouging Prevention Act of 2013, **241**
Ney York General Business Law of 2014, **242**
Arkansas Code of 2010, §4-88-303, **231**

US "Soft" Law

DOJ, "Competition and Monopoly: Single-Firm Conduct Under Section 2 of The Sherman Act" (2008, Report) (withdrawn without replacement on November 05, 2009), **190, 192, 280, 281**

Other Legislations

Japan Antimonopoly Act (AMA). Act on Prohibition of Private Monopolization and Maintenance of Fair Trade (Act No. 54 of April 14, 1947), **146**

Index

A

As efficient competitor (AEC)
  contestability, 73–74, 184
  Intel, 183
  natural monopoly, 147–149
  Post Danmark I, 63
  Post Danmark II, 63-64, 147
  rebates, 147, 183–185, 187, 191
  statutory monopoly, 192, 240

C

Competition for the market
  absence of, 85, 89–92, 97–99, 115
  adjacent markets, 98–104
  historical operator, 89–92, 115, 117
  investments, 92, 189
  public procurement, 188–189
  scalability, 272
  state resources, 89–92

D

Deception, 259–271

E

Equality of opportunity
  Article 106, 65–67
  Competitive process and, 95–98, 184–185
  Google Shopping, 97, 160–161, 192–195
  Historical operators, 93–98, 115, 118
  inequality, 66–68
  level playing field, 78, 118
Exploitative abuse
  excessive pricing, 277
  price gouging (regulation), 241–244

F

First-mover
  advantages, 28, 99, 103
  disadvantages, 100–102
  historical operators, 98–99
  pioneering, 100–101
Foreign statutory dominance, 76–81

G

Geoeconomics, 77–78
Google Shopping
  data accumulation, 216
  equality of opportunity, 97, 160–161, 192–195
  incumbency disadvantages, 192–197
  intangible resources, 215–218

H

Hayek, 12–14, 56, 177, 284
Historical operator
  former legal monopoly, 86–88, 90, 94, 98, 110, 112–114
  legacy, 83–119
  Post Danmark I, 87–115

Post Danmark II, 86

I

Incentives
- anticompetitive behavior, 116–117
- to invest (historical operator), 104–110, 114–115

Incumbency
- advantages, 184–190
- disadvantages, 192–197
- neutralization, 186, 188, 189
- public procurement, 188–189

Intangible resources
- adjacent markets, 98–104
- experience, 210–212
- inimitability, 203–206
- path dependence, 207–210
- reputation, 207–210
- time compression diseconomies, 204, 210–212
- time compression economies, 204, 207, 211

Intel
- endogenous change, 159–160
- more economic approach, 183

Intellectual property
- existence and exercise of, 162–163
- physical property, 163–168

Investments
- Article 101, 162, 176–177
- Asymmetry, 163–168
- deadweight loss, 169, 176, 253
- efforts, 155–168
- endogenous change, 159–160
- entry barrier, 160–161
- rival's investments, 156–158

L

Leveraging
- historical operators, 91, 111
- investments, 160
- statutory advantages, 36, 69–71

Luck
- accident, 31
- *British Petroleum*, 227, 236
- cheap exclusion, 234
- luck defense, 239–241
- lucky monopolist, 232–244
- opportunistic behavior, 232–235

N

Natural monopoly
- competition for the market, 151
- competitive process, 139–141
- more efficient, 150–151
- *Post Danmark II*, 147, 148
- railroads, 134–138
- telecommunications, 130–134

O

Objective justification
- investments, 165, 167, 177, 183, 193, 239
- luck, 239
- natural monopoly, 143
- statutory, 74–75

Origins
- are irrelevant
  - *Continental Can*, 17, 18
  - *Michelin I*, 219–220
  - *Frankfurt Airport*, 108
  - *Google Shopping*, 161
- are relevant
  - *KPN*, 105–107
  - *Post Danmark I*, 61–62, 64, 69–71, 76, 79
  - *Post Danmark II*, 63–64, 72, 73, 76
  - *Slovak Telekom*, 114–115

Ortega y Gasset, 172

P

Post Danmark I
- after *Post Danmark I*, 112–115
- *Google Shopping*, 194
- *obiter*, 86

R

Rambus, 261–270
Rebates
  Intel, 159–160
  non-contestable share, 73–74, 179–192
  Post Danmark II, 63, 72–74, 190
Recoupment
  OPCOM, 74–75
Refusal to supply, 71, 104–106, 109, 145, 166, 178, 179, 227, 239, 286
Road to dominance
  deadweight loss, 253, 256, 259, 271, 275, 282
  enforcement gap, 245, 247, 259, 274–281
  monopolization, 245, 247–274
  Rambus, 261–270
  Section 2 Sherman Act, 247–253

S

Schumpeter, 13, 18, 171, 226
Statutory
  advantages, 52, 58, 60, 68–71, 284, 285
  dominance, 30, 35–81
  facilitating entry, 61, 69, 71–73
  legal monopoly, 46, 49, 53, 61, 62, 75
  resources, 89–92

U

Uncertainty
  Article 101, 176
  competitive process, 168–172
  investments, 168–172
  nirvana fallacy, 171

INTERNATIONAL COMPETITION LAW SERIES

1. Ignacio De Leon, *Latin American Competition Law and Policy: A Policy in Search of Identity*, 2001 (ISBN 90-411-1542-0).
2. Wim Dejonghe & Wouter Van de Voorde (eds), *M & A in Belgium*, 2001 (ISBN 90-411-1594-3).
3. Yang-Ching Chao, Gee San, Changfa Lo & Jiming Ho (eds), *International and Comparative Competition Law and Policies*, 2001 (ISBN 90-411-1643-5).
4. Martin Mendelsohn & Stephen Rose, *Guide to the EC Block Exemption for Vertical Agreements*, 2002 (ISBN 90-411-9813-X).
5. Clifford A. Jones & Mitsuo Matsushita (eds), *Competition Policy in the Global Trading System: Perspectives from the EU, Japan and the USA*, 2002 (ISBN 90-411-1758-X).
6. Christian Koenig, Andreas Bartosch, Jens-Daniel Braun & Marion Romes (eds), *EC Competition and Telecommunications Law*. Second Edition, 2009 (ISBN 978-90-411-2564-4).
7. Jürgen Basedow (ed.), *Limits and Control of Competition with a View to International Harmonization*, 2002 (ISBN 90-411-1967-1).
8. Maureen Brunt, Economic Essays on Australian and New Zealand Competition Law, 2003 (ISBN 90-411-1991-4).
9. Ky P. Ewing, Jr., *Competition Rules for the 21st Century: Principles from America's Experience*, Second Edition, 2006 (ISBN 90-411-2477-2).
10. Joseph Wilson, *Globalization and the Limits of National Merger Control Laws*, 2003 (ISBN 90-411-1996-5).
11. Peter Verloop & Valérie Landes (eds), *Merger Control in Europe: EU, Member States and Accession States*, Fourth Edition, 2003 (ISBN 90-411-2056-4).
12. Themistoklis K. Giannakopoulos, *Safeguarding Companies' Rights in Competition and Anti-dumping/Anti-subsidies Proceedings*, Second Edition, 2011 (ISBN 978-90-411-3404-2).
13. Marjorie Holmes & Lesley Davey (eds), *A Practical Guide to National Competition Rules across Europe*, Second Edition, 2007 (ISBN 978-90- 411-2607-8).
14. Sigrid Stroux, *US and EU Oligopoly Control*, 2004 (ISBN 90-411-2296-6).
15. Tzong-Leh Hwang and Chiyuan Chen (eds), *The Future Development of Competition Framework*, 2004 (ISBN 90-411-2305-9).

16. Phedon Nicolaides, Mihalis Kekelekis and Maria Kleis, *State Aid Policy in the European Community: Principles and Practice,* Second Edition, 2008 (ISBN 978-90-411-2754-9).
17. Doris Hildebrand, *Economic Analyses of Vertical Agreements: A Self- Assessment*, 2005 (ISBN 90-411-2328-8).
18. Frauke Henning-Bodewig, *Unfair Competition Law: European Union and Member States*, 2005 (ISBN 90-411-2329-6).
19. Duarte Brito & Margarida Catalão-Lopes, *Mergers and Acquisitions: The Industrial Organization Perspective,* 2006 (ISBN 90-411-2451-9).
20. Nikos Th. Nikolinakos, *EU Competition Law and Regulation in the Converging Telecommunications, Media and IT Sectors*, 2006 (ISBN 90-411- 2469-1).
21. Mihalis Kekelekis, *The EC Merger Control Regulation: Rights of Defence. A Critical Analysis of DG COMP Practice and Community Courts' Jurisprudence*, 2006 (ISBN 90-411-2553-1).
22. Mark R. Joelson, *An International Antitrust Primer: A Guide to the Operation of United States, European Union and Other Key Competition Laws in the Global Economy*, Third Edition, 2006 (ISBN 90-411-2468-3).
23. Themistoklis K. Giannakopoulos, *A Concise Guide to the EU Anti-dumping/ Anti-subsidies Procedures*, 2006 (ISBN 90-411-2464-0).
24. George Cumming, Brad Spitz & Ruth Janal, *Civil Procedure Used for Enforcement of EC Competition Law by the English, French and German Civil Courts*, 2007 (ISBN 978-90-411-2471-5).
25. Jürgen Basedow (ed.), *Private Enforcement of EC Competition Law,* 2007 (ISBN 978-90-411-2613-9).
26. Jung Wook Cho, *Innovation and Competition in the Digital Network Economy: A Legal and Economic Assessment on Multi-tying Practices and Network Effects*, 2007 (ISBN 978-90-411-2574-3).
27. Akira Inoue, *Japanese Antitrust Law Manual: Law, Cases and Interpretation of the Japanese Antimonopoly Act*, 2007 (ISBN 978-90-411-2627-6).
28. René Barents, *Directory of EC Case Law on Competition,* 2007 (ISBN 978-90-411-2656-6).
29. Paul F. Nemitz (ed.), *The Effective Application of EU State Aid Procedures: The Role of National Law and Practice*, 2007 (ISBN 978-90-411-2657-3).
30. Jurian Langer, *Tying and Bundling as a Leveraging Concern under EC Competition Law,* 2007 (ISBN 978-90-411-2575-0).
31. Abel M. Mateus & Teresa Moreira (eds), *Competition Law and Economics – Advances in Competition Policy and Antitrust Enforcement*, 2007 (ISBN 978-90-411-2632-0).
32. Alberto Santa Maria, *Competition and State Aid: An Analysis of the EC Practice*, 2007 (ISBN 978-90-411-2617-7).
33. Barry J. Rodger (ed.), *Article 234 and Competition Law: An Analysis,* 2007 (ISBN 978-90-411-2605-4).

34. Alla Pozdnakova, *Liner Shipping and EU Competition Law*, 2008 (ISBN 978-90-411-2717-4).
35. Milena Stoyanova, *Competition Problems in Liberalized Telecommunications: Regulatory Solutions to Promote Effective Competition*, 2008 (ISBN 978-90-411-2736-5).
36. *EC State Aid Law/Le Droit des Aides d'Etat dans la CE. Liber Amicorum Francisco Santaolalla Gadea*, 2008 (ISBN 978-90-411-2774-7).
37. René Barents, *Directory of EU Case Law on State Aids*, Third Edition, 2019 (ISBN 978-94-035-1101-6).
38. Ignacio De Leon, *An Institutional Assessment of Antitrust Policy: The Latin American Experience*, 2009 (ISBN 978-90-411-2478-4).
39. Doris Hildebrand, *The Role of Economic Analysis in EU Competition Law: The European School*, Fourth Edition, 2016 (ISBN 978-90-411-6245-8).
40. Eugène Buttigieg, *Competition Law: Safeguarding the Consumer Interest. A Comparative Analysis of US Antitrust Law and EC Competition Law*, 2009 (ISBN 978-90-411-3119-5).
41. Ioannis Lianos & Ioannis Kokkoris (eds), *The Reform of EC Competition Law: New Challenges*, 2010 (ISBN 978-90-411-2692-4).
42. George Cumming & Mirjam Freudenthal, *Civil Procedure in EU Competition Cases before the English and Dutch Courts*, 2010 (ISBN 978-90-411-3192-8).
43. A.E. Rodriguez & Ashok Menon, *The Limits of Competition Policy: The Shortcomings of Antitrust in Developing and Reforming Economies*, 2010 (ISBN 978-90-411-3177-5).
44. Mika Oinonen, *Does EU Merger Control Discriminate against Small Market Companies? Diagnosing the Argument with Conclusions*, 2010 (ISBN 978-90-411-3261-1).
45. Eirik Østerud, *Identifying Exclusionary Abuses by Dominant Undertakings under EU Competition Law: The Spectrum of Tests*, 2010 (ISBN 978-90-411-3271-0).
46. Marco Botta, *Merger Control Regimes in Emerging Economies: A Case Study on Brazil and Argentina*, 2011 (ISBN 978-90-411-3402-8).
47. Jürgen Basedow & Wolfgang Wurmnest (eds), *Structure and Effects in EU Competition Law: Studies on Exclusionary Conduct and State Aid*, 2011 (ISBN 978-90-411-3174-4).
48. George Cumming (ed.), *Merger Decisions and the Rules of Procedure of the European Community Courts*, 2012 (ISBN 978-90-411-3671-8).
49. Eduardo Molan Gaban & Juliana Oliveira Domingues (eds), *Antitrust Law in Brazil: Fighting Cartels*, 2012 (ISBN 978-90-411-3670-1).
50. Giandonato Caggiano, Gabriella Muscolo & Marina Tavassi (eds), *Competition Law and Intellectual Property: A European Perspective*, 2012 (ISBN 978-90-411-3447-9).
51. Ben Van Rompuy, *Economic Efficiency: The Sole Concern of Modern Antitrust Policy? Non-efficiency Considerations under Article 101 TFEU*, 2012 (ISBN 978-90-411-3870-5).

52. Liyang Hou, *Competition Law and Regulation of the EU Electronic Communications Sector: A Comparative Legal Approach*, 2012 (ISBN 978-90-411-4047-0).
53. Barry Rodger, *Landmark Cases in Competition Law: Around the World in Fourteen Stories*, 2012 (ISBN 978-90-411-3843-9).
54. Andreas Scordamaglia-Tousis, *EU Cartel Enforcement: Reconciling Effective Public Enforcement with Fundamental Rights*, 2013 (ISBN 978-90-411-4758-5).
55. Bernardo Cortese (ed.), *EU Competition Law: Between Public and Private Enforcement*, 2014 (ISBN 978-90-411-4677-9).
56. Barry Rodger (ed.), *Competition Law: Comparative Private Enforcement and Collective Redress across the EU*, 2014 (ISBN 978-90-411-4559-8).
57. Nada Ina Pauer, *The Single Economic Entity Doctrine and Corporate Group Responsibility in European Antitrust Law*, 2014 (ISBN 978-90-411-5262-6).
58. Urška Petrovčič, *Competition Law and Standard Essential Patents: A Transatlantic Perspective*, 2014 (ISBN 978-90-411-4960-2).
59. David Telyas, *The Interface between Competition Law, Patents and Technical Standards*, 2014 (ISBN 978-90-411-5418-7).
60. Katerina Maniadaki, *EU Competition Law, Regulation and the Internet: The Case of Net Neutrality*, 2014 (ISBN 978-90-411-4140-8).
61. Horacio Vedia Jerez, *Competition Law Enforcement and Compliance across the World: A Comparative Review*, 2015 (ISBN 978-90-411-5815-4).
62. Kadir Ba, *The Substantive Appraisal of Joint Ventures under the EU Merger Control Regime*, 2015 (ISBN 978-90-411-5816-1).
63. Alberto Santa Maria, *Competition and State Aid: An Analysis of the EU Practice*, Second Edition, 2015 (ISBN 978-90-411-5818-5).
64. Lúcio Tomé Feteira, *The Interplay between European and National Competition Law after Regulation 1/2003: "United (Should) We Stand?"*, 2016 (ISBN 978-90-411-5663-1).
65. Giovanni Pitruzzella & Gabriella Muscolo (eds), *Competition and Patent Law in the Pharmaceutical Sector: An International Perspective*, 2016 (ISBN 978-90-411-5927-4).
66. Małgorzata Cyndecka, *The Market Economy Investor Test in EU State Aid Law: Applicability and Application*, 2016 (ISBN 978-90-411-6102-4).
67. Damiano Canapa, *Trademarks and Brands in Merger Control: An Analysis of the European and Swiss Legal Orders*, 2016 (ISBN 978-90-411-6717-0).
68. Inge Graef, *EU Competition Law, Data Protection and Online Platforms: Data as Essential Facility*, 2016 (ISBN 978-90-411-8324-8).
69. Anders Jessen, *Exclusionary Abuse after the* Post Danmark I *Case: The Role of the Effects-Based Approach under Article 102 TFEU*, 2017 (ISBN 978-90-411-8996-7).
70. Baskaran Balasingham, *The EU Leniency Policy: Reconciling Effectiveness and Fairness*, 2017 (ISBN 978-90-411-8479-5).
71. Eugene Stuart & Iana Roginska-Green, *Sixty Years of EU State Aid Law and Policy: Analysis and Assessment*, 2018 (ISBN 978-90-411-8869-4).

72. Anna Renata Pisarkiewicz, *Margin Squeeze in the Electronic Communications Sector: Critical Analysis of the Decisional Practice and Case Law*, 2018 (ISBN 978-90-411-6246-5).
73. Ploykaew Porananond, *Competition Law in the ASEAN Countries: Regional Law and National Systems*, 2018 (ISBN 978-90-411-9102-1).
74. Corinne Ruechardt, *EU State Aid Control of Infrastructure Funding*, 2018 (ISBN 978-90-411-9099-4).
75. Amalia Athanasiadou, *Patent Settlements in the Pharmaceutical Industry under US Antitrust and EU Competition Law*, 2018 (ISBN 978-94-035-0113-0).
76. Miroslava Marinova, *Fidelity Rebates in Competition Law: Application of the 'As Efficient Competitor' Test*, 2018 (ISBN 978-94-035-0570-1).
77. Gabriella Muscolo & Marina Tavassi, *The Interplay Between Competition Law and Intellectual Property: An International Perspective*, 2019 (ISBN 978-90-411-8687-4).
78. Fevzi Toksoy, Bahadir Balki & Hanna Stakheyeva, *Merger Control in the EU and Turkey: A Comparative Guide*, 2019 (ISBN 978-94-035-0934-1).
79. Paulo Burnier da Silveira & William Evan Kovacic (eds), *Global Competition Enforcement: New Players, New Challenges*, 2019 (ISBN 978-94-035-0283-0).
80. Giovanna Massarotto, *Antitrust Settlements: How a Simple Agreement Can Drive the Economy*, 2019 (ISBN 978-94-035-1133-7).
81. Marc Veenbrink, *Criminal Law Principles and the Enforcement of EU and National Competition Law: A Silent Takeover?*, 2020 (ISBN 978-94-035-1434-5).
82. Ferdinand Wollenschläger, Wolfgang Wurmnest & Thomas M.J. Möllers (eds), *Private Enforcement of European Competition and State Aid Law: Current Challenges and the Way Forward*, 2020 (ISBN 978-94-035-0281-6).
83. Jorge Marcos Ramos, *Firm Dominance in EU Competition Law: The Competitive Process and the Origins of Market Power*, 2020 (ISBN 978-94-035-2030-8).

www.ingramcontent.com/pod-product-compliance
Ingram Content Group UK Ltd.
Pitfield, Milton Keynes, MK11 3LW, UK
UKHW020235290926
15470UKWH00002B/558

9 789403 520308